P9-DXC-796

GOOD NEWS
for
Modern Man

GOOD NEWS

for Modern Man

THE NEW TESTAMENT
in Today's English Version

AMERICAN BIBLE SOCIETY

NEW YORK

GOOD NEWS FOR MODERN MAN
The New Testament in Today's English

ENG. N. T. TEV 265P
ABS-1967-250,000-525,000-W-2

PREFACE

THE NEW TESTAMENT is the book about Jesus Christ. Its name means that it is the record of God's new covenant with his people. This covenant, or agreement, is the good news of God's promise to save those who believe in Jesus Christ as Lord and Savior. The New Testament does not merely inform; it demands decision and calls for commitment on the part of those who read this Good News.

The twenty-seven books which make up the New Testament were written by perhaps as many as twelve different authors over a period of some fifty years. Although the books differ in content, a constant theme runs through all of them and joins them into a unity— God's love for man revealed in the person of Jesus Christ.

The four Gospels tell the story of the life, teaching, deeds, death, and resurrection of Jesus. They are followed by the Acts of the Apostles, which traces the spread of the gospel for some thirty years, from Jerusalem to Rome, the capital of the Empire. The letters of Paul were all written to meet specific needs faced by early Christians. The eight books that follow, known as the General Letters, are varied: some of them are addressed in general terms to believers everywhere, while others are written to individual churches or persons.

The last book in the New Testament is different from all the others. Its teaching concerning the victory of the Kingdom of God and the lordship of Christ is conveyed by means of visions, images, and symbols, many of which are very difficult for the modern reader to understand. But its central message, which may also be taken as the theme of the whole New Testament, is clearly proclaimed: "The power to rule over the world belongs now to our Lord and his Messiah, and he will rule for ever and ever!" (Revelation 11.15).

THIS TRANSLATION OF THE NEW TESTAMENT has been prepared by the American Bible Society for people who speak English as their own mother tongue or as an acquired language. As a distinctly new translation, it does not conform to traditional vocabulary or style, but seeks to express the meaning of the Greek text in words and forms accepted as standard by people everywhere who employ English as a means of communication. *Today's English Version* of the New Testament attempts to follow, in this century, the example set by the authors of the New Testament books who, for the most part, wrote in the standard, or common, form of the Greek language used throughout the Roman Empire. As much as possible, words and forms of English not in current use have been avoided; but no rigid limit has been set to the vocabulary employed.

A *Word List* at the end of the volume explains technical terms and rarely used words, and identifies a number of places and persons mentioned in the New Testament, in order to enable the reader to understand the text better in its historical setting. Some of the more important variations in Greek manuscripts and ancient versions, and some of the passages in the text which may be translated in more than one way, are listed in *Other Readings and Renderings*. An *Index* is provided which locates, by page numbers, some of the more important subjects, persons, places, and events in the New Testament. Finally there are a few line *Maps* designed to help the reader visualize the geographic setting of the countries and places mentioned in the New Testament.

The text from which this translation was made is the Greek New Testament prepared by an international committee of New Testament scholars, sponsored by several members of the United Bible Societies, and published in 1966. Verses marked with [   ] are not in the oldest and best manuscripts of the New Testament.

The basic text was translated by Dr. Robert G. Bratcher; the line drawings were prepared by Mlle. Annie Vallotton.

CONTENTS

MATTHEW

The Birth Record of Jesus Christ
(Also Luke 3.23–38)

1 This is the birth record of Jesus Christ, who was a descendant of David, who was a descendant of Abraham.

2 Abraham was the father of Isaac; Isaac was the father of Jacob; Jacob was the father of Judah and his brothers. 3 Judah was the father of Perez and Zerah (their mother was Tamar); Perez was the father of Hezron; Hezron was the father of Ram; 4 Ram was the father of Amminadab; Amminadab was the father of Nahshon; Nahshon was the father of Salmon; 5 Salmon was the father of Boaz (Rahab was his mother); Boaz was the father of Obed (Ruth was his mother); Obed was the father of Jesse; 6 Jesse was the father of King David.

David was the father of Solomon (his mother had been Uriah's wife); 7 Solomon was the father of Rehoboam; Rehoboam was the father of Abijah; Abijah was the father of Asa; 8 Asa was the father of Jehoshaphat; Jehoshaphat was the father of Joram; Joram was the father of Uzziah; 9 Uzziah was the father of Jotham; Jotham was the father of Ahaz; Ahaz was the father of Hezekiah; 10 Hezekiah was the father of Manasseh; Manasseh was the father of Amon; Amon was the father of Josiah; 11 Josiah was the father of Jechoniah and his brothers, at the time when the people of Israel were carried away to Babylon.

12 After the people were carried away to Babylon: Jechoniah was the father of Shealtiel; Shealtiel was the father of Zerubbabel; 13 Zerubbabel was the father of Abiud; Abiud was the father of Eliakim; Eliakim was the father of Azor; 14 Azor was the father of Zadok; Zadok was the father of Achim; Achim was the father of Eliud; 15 Eliud was the father of Eleazar; Eleazar was the father of Matthan; Matthan was the father of Jacob; 16 Jacob was the father of Joseph, the husband of Mary, who was the mother of Jesus, called the Messiah.

17 So then, there were fourteen sets of fathers and sons from Abraham to David, and fourteen from David to the time when the people were carried away to Babylon, and fourteen from then to the birth of the Messiah.

1

The Birth of Jesus Christ
(Also Luke 2.1–7)

¹⁸ This was the way that Jesus Christ was born. His mother Mary was engaged to Joseph, but before they were married she found out that she was going to have a baby by the Holy Spirit. ¹⁹ Joseph, to whom she was engaged, was a man who always did what was right; but he did not want to disgrace Mary publicly, so he made plans to break the engagement secretly. ²⁰ While he was thinking about all this, an angel of the Lord appeared to him in a dream and said: "Joseph, descendant of David, do not be afraid to take Mary to be your wife. For it is by the Holy Spirit that she has conceived. ²¹ She will give birth to a son and you will name him Jesus—for he will save his people from their sins."

²² Now all this happened in order to make come true what the Lord had said through the prophet: ²³ "The virgin will become pregnant and give birth to a son, and he will be called Emmanuel" (which means, "God is with us").

²⁴ So when Joseph woke up he did what the angel of the Lord had told him to do and married Mary. ²⁵ But he had no sexual relations with her before she gave birth to her son. And Joseph named him Jesus.

Visitors from the East

2 Jesus was born in the town of Bethlehem, in the land of Judea, during the time when Herod was king. Soon afterwards some men who studied the stars came from the east to Jerusalem ² and asked: "Where is the baby born to be the king of the Jews? We saw his star when it came up in the east, and we have come to worship him." ³ When King Herod heard about this he was very upset, and so was everybody else in Jerusalem. ⁴ He called together all the chief priests and the teachers of the Law and asked them, "Where will the Messiah be born?" ⁵ "In the town of Bethlehem, in Judea," they answered. "This is what the prophet wrote:

⁶ 'You, Bethlehem, in the land of Judah,
　　Are not by any means the least among the
　　　rulers of Judah;
　　For from you will come a leader
　　Who will guide my people Israel.' "
⁷ So Herod called the visitors from the east to a secret

meeting and found out from them the exact time the star had appeared. ⁸ Then he sent them to Bethlehem with these instructions: "Go and make a careful search for the child, and when you find him let me know, so that I may go and worship him too." ⁹ With this they left, and on their way they saw the star — the same one they had seen in the east — and it went ahead of them until it came and stopped over the place where the child was. ¹⁰ How happy they were, what gladness they felt, when they saw the star! ¹¹ They went into the house and saw the child with his mother Mary. They knelt down and worshiped him; then they opened their bags and offered him presents: gold, frankincense, and myrrh.

¹² God warned them in a dream not to go back to Herod; so they went back home by another road.

The Escape to Egypt

¹³ After they had left, an angel of the Lord appeared in a dream to Joseph and said: "Get up, take the child and his mother and run away to Egypt, and stay there until I tell you to leave. Herod will be looking for the child to kill him." ¹⁴ So Joseph got up, took the child and his mother, and left during the night for Egypt, ¹⁵ where he stayed until Herod died.

This was done to make come true what the Lord had said through the prophet, "I called my Son out of Egypt."

The Killing of the Children

¹⁶ When Herod realized that the visitors from the east had tricked him, he was furious. He gave orders to kill all the boys in Bethlehem and its neighborhood who were two years old and younger — in accordance with what he had learned from the visitors about the time when the star had appeared.

¹⁷ In this way what the prophet Jeremiah had said came true:

¹⁸ "A sound is heard in Ramah,
The sound of bitter crying and weeping.
Rachel weeps for her children,
She weeps and will not be comforted,
Because they are all dead."

The Return from Egypt

¹⁹ After Herod had died, an angel of the Lord appeared in a dream to Joseph, in Egypt, ²⁰ and said: "Get up, take the child and his mother, and go back to the country of Israel, because those who tried to kill the child are dead." ²¹ So Joseph got up, took the child and his mother, and went back to the country of Israel. ²² When he heard that Archelaus had succeeded his father Herod as king of Judea, Joseph was afraid to settle there. He was given more instructions in a dream, and so went to the province of Galilee ²³ and made his home in a town named Nazareth. He did this to make come true what the prophets had said, "He will be called a Nazarene."

The Preaching of John the Baptist
(Also Mark 1.1–8; Luke 3.1–18; John 1.19–28)

3 At that time John the Baptist came and started preaching in the desert of Judea. ² "Turn away from your sins," he said, "for the Kingdom of heaven is near!" ³ John was the one that the prophet Isaiah was talking about when he said:

"Someone is shouting in the desert:
'Get the Lord's road ready for him,
Make a straight path for him to travel!' "

⁴ John's clothes were made of camel's hair; he wore a leather belt around his waist, and ate locusts and wild honey. ⁵ People came to him from Jerusalem, from the whole province of Judea, and from all the country around the Jordan river. ⁶ They confessed their sins and he baptized them in the Jordan.

⁷ When John saw many Pharisees and Sadducees coming to him to be baptized, he said to them: "You snakes — who told you that you could escape from God's wrath that is about to come? ⁸ Do the things that will show that you have turned from your sins. ⁹ And do not think you can excuse yourselves by saying, 'Abraham is our ancestor.' I tell you that God can take these rocks and make descendants for Abraham! ¹⁰ The ax is ready to cut the trees at the roots; every tree that does not bear good fruit will be cut down and thrown in the fire. ¹¹ I baptize you with water to show that you have repented; but the one who will come after me will baptize you with the Holy Spirit and fire. He is much greater than I am; I am not good enough even to carry his sandals. ¹² He has his winnowing-shovel with him, to thresh out all the grain; he will gather his wheat into his barn, but burn the chaff in a fire that never goes out!"

The Baptism of Jesus
(Also Mark 1.9–11; Luke 3.21–22)

¹³ At that time Jesus went from Galilee to the Jordan, and came to John to be baptized by him. ¹⁴ But John tried to make him change his mind. "I ought to be baptized by you," John said, "yet you come to me!" ¹⁵ But Jesus answered him, "Let it be this way for now. For in this way we shall do all that God requires." So John agreed.

¹⁶ As soon as Jesus was baptized, he came up out of the water. Then heaven was opened to him, and he saw the Spirit of God coming down like a dove and lighting on him. ¹⁷ And then a voice said from heaven, "This is my own dear Son, with whom I am well pleased."

The Temptation of Jesus
(Also Mark 1.12–13; Luke 4.1–13)

4 Then the Spirit led Jesus into the desert to be tempted by the Devil. ² After spending forty days and nights without food, Jesus was hungry. ³ The Devil came to him

and said, "If you are God's Son, order these stones to turn into bread." [4] Jesus answered, "The scripture says, 'Man cannot live on bread alone, but on every word that God speaks.' "

[5] Then the Devil took Jesus to the Holy City, set him on the highest point of the Temple, [6] and said to him, "If you are God's Son, throw yourself down to the ground; for the scripture says,

'God will give orders to his angels about you:
They will hold you up with their hands,
So that you will not even hurt your feet on the
stones.' "

[7] Jesus answered, "But the scripture also says, 'You must not put the Lord your God to the test.' "

[8] Then the Devil took Jesus to a very high mountain and showed him all the kingdoms of the world, in all their greatness. [9] "All this I will give you," the Devil said, "if you kneel down and worship me." [10] Then Jesus answered, "Go away, Satan! The scripture says, 'Worship the Lord your God and serve only him!' "

[11] So the Devil left him; and angels came and helped Jesus.

Jesus Begins His Work in Galilee
(Also Mark 1.14–15; Luke 4.14–15)

¹² When Jesus heard that John had been put in prison, he went away to Galilee. ¹³ He did not settle down in Nazareth, but went and lived in Capernaum, a town by Lake Galilee, in the territory of Zebulun and Naphtali. ¹⁴ This was done to make come true what the prophet Isaiah had said:

¹⁵ "Land of Zebulun, land of Naphtali,
In the direction of the sea, on the other side of Jordan,
Galilee of the Gentiles!
¹⁶ The people who live in darkness
Will see a great light!
On those who live in the dark land of death
The light will shine!"

¹⁷ From that time Jesus began to preach his message: "Turn away from your sins! The Kingdom of heaven is near!"

Jesus Calls Four Fishermen
(Also Mark 1.16–20; Luke 5.1–11)

¹⁸ As Jesus walked by Lake Galilee, he saw two brothers who were fishermen, Simon (called Peter) and his brother Andrew, catching fish in the lake with a net. ¹⁹ Jesus said to them, "Come with me and I will teach you to catch men." ²⁰ At once they left their nets and went with him.

²¹ He went on and saw two other brothers, James and John, the sons of Zebedee. They were in their boat with their father Zebedee, getting their nets ready. Jesus called them; ²² at once they left the boat and their father, and went with Jesus.

Jesus Teaches, Preaches, and Heals
(Also Luke 6.17–19)

²³ Jesus went all over Galilee, teaching in their synagogues, preaching the Good News of the Kingdom, and healing people from every kind of disease and sickness. ²⁴ The news about him spread through the whole country of Syria, so that people brought him all those who were sick with all kinds of diseases, and afflicted with all sorts

of troubles: people with demons, and epileptics, and paralytics — Jesus healed them all. ²⁵ Great crowds followed him from Galilee and the Ten Towns, from Jerusalem, Judea, and the land on the other side of the Jordan.

The Sermon on the Mount

5 Jesus saw the crowds and went up a hill, where he sat down. His disciples gathered around him, ² and he began to teach them:

True Happiness
(Also Luke 6.20–23)

> ³ "Happy are those who know they are spiritually poor:
> the Kingdom of heaven belongs to them!
> ⁴ "Happy are those who mourn:
> God will comfort them!
> ⁵ "Happy are the meek:
> they will receive what God has promised!
> ⁶ "Happy are those whose greatest desire is to do what God requires:
> God will satisfy them fully!
> ⁷ "Happy are those who show mercy to others:
> God will show mercy to them!
> ⁸ "Happy are the pure in heart:
> they will see God!
> ⁹ "Happy are those who work for peace among men:
> God will call them his sons!

¹⁰ "Happy are those who suffer persecution because they
do what God requires:
the Kingdom of heaven belongs to them!
¹¹ "Happy are you when men insult you and mistreat
you and tell all kinds of evil lies against you because you
are my followers. ¹² Rejoice and be glad, because a great
reward is kept for you in heaven. This is how men mistreated the prophets who lived before you."

Salt and Light
(Also Mark 9.50; Luke 14.34–35)

¹³ "You are like salt for all mankind. But if salt loses its
taste, there is no way to make it salty again. It has become worthless; so it is thrown away and people walk on it.
¹⁴ "You are like light for the whole world. A city built
on a hill cannot be hid. ¹⁵ Nobody lights a lamp to
put it under a bowl; instead he puts it on the lamp-stand,
where it gives light for everyone in the house. ¹⁶ In the
same way your light must shine before people, so that they
will see the good things you do and give praise to your
Father in heaven."

Teaching about the Law

¹⁷ "Do not think that I have come to do away with the
Law of Moses and the teaching of the prophets. I have
not come to do away with them, but to give them real
meaning. ¹⁸ Remember this! As long as heaven and earth
last, the least point or the smallest detail of the Law will
not be done away with — not until the end of all things.
¹⁹ Therefore, whoever disobeys even the smallest of the
commandments, and teaches others to do the same, will
be least in the Kingdom of heaven. On the other hand,
whoever obeys the Law, and teaches others to do the
same, will be great in the Kingdom of heaven. ²⁰ I tell
you, then, that you will be able to enter the Kingdom of
heaven only if you are more faithful than the teachers of
the Law and the Pharisees in doing what God requires."

Teaching about Anger

²¹ "You have heard that men were told in the past, 'Do
not murder; anyone who commits murder will be brought
before the judge.' ²² But now I tell you: whoever is angry

with his brother will be brought before the judge; whoever calls his brother 'You good-for-nothing!' will be brought before the Council; and whoever calls his brother a worthless fool will be in danger of going to the fire of hell. [23] So if you are about to offer your gift to God at the altar and there you remember that your brother has something against you, [24] leave your gift there in front of the altar and go at once to make peace with your brother; then come back and offer your gift to God.

[25] "If a man brings a lawsuit against you and takes you to court, be friendly with him while there is time, before you get to court; once you are there he will turn you over to the judge, who will hand you over to the police, and you will be put in jail. [26] There you will stay, I tell you, until you pay the last penny of your fine."

Teaching about Adultery

[27] "You have heard that it was said, 'Do not commit adultery.' [28] But now I tell you: anyone who looks at a woman and wants to possess her is guilty of committing adultery with her in his heart. [29] So if your right eye causes you to sin, take it out and throw it away! It is much better for you to lose a part of your body than to have your whole body thrown into hell. [30] If your right hand causes you to sin, cut it off and throw it away! It is much better for you to lose one of your limbs than to have your whole body go off to hell."

Teaching about Divorce
(*Also Matt. 19.9; Mark 10.11–12; Luke 16.18*)

[31] "It was also said, 'Anyone who divorces his wife must give her a written notice of divorce.' [32] But now I tell you: if a man divorces his wife, and she has not been unfaithful, then he is guilty of making her commit adultery if she marries again; and the man who marries her also commits adultery."

Teaching about Vows

[33] "You have also heard that men were told in the past, 'Do not break your promise, but do what you have sworn to do before the Lord.' [34] But now I tell you: do not use any vow when you make a promise; do not swear by heaven, because it is God's throne; [35] nor by earth, be-

cause it is the resting place for his feet; nor by Jerusalem, because it is the city of the great King. ⁶³ Do not even swear by your head, because you cannot make a single hair white or black. ³⁷ Just say 'Yes' or 'No' — anything else you have to say comes from the Evil One."

Teaching about Revenge
(*Also Luke 6.29–30*)

³⁸ "You have heard that it was said, 'An eye for an eye, and a tooth for a tooth.' ³⁹ But now I tell you: do not take revenge on someone who does you wrong. If anyone slaps you on the right cheek, let him slap your left cheek too. ⁴⁰ And if someone takes you to court to sue you for your shirt, let him have your coat as well. ⁴¹ And if one of the occupation troops forces you to carry his pack one mile, carry it another mile. ⁴² When someone asks you for

something, give it to him; when someone wants to borrow something, lend it to him."

Love for Enemies
(*Also Luke 6.27–28, 32–36*)

⁴³ "You have heard that it was said, 'Love your friends, hate your enemies.' ⁴⁴ But now I tell you: love your enemies, and pray for those who mistreat you, ⁴⁵ so that you will become the sons of your Father in heaven. For he makes his sun to shine on bad and good people alike, and

gives rain to those who do right and those who do wrong. [46] Why should you expect God to reward you, if you love only the people who love you? Even the tax collectors do that! [47] And if you speak only to your friends, have you done anything out of the ordinary? Even the pagans do that! [48] You must be perfect — just as your Father in heaven is perfect."

Teaching about Charity

6 "Be careful not to perform your religious duties in public so that people will see what you do. If you do these things publicly you will not have any reward from your Father in heaven.

[2] "So when you give something to a needy person, do not make a big show of it, as the show-offs do in the synagogues and on the streets. They do it so that people will praise them. Remember this! They have already been paid in full. [3] But when you help a needy person, do it in such a way that even your closest friend will not know about it, [4] but it will be a private matter. And your Father, who sees what you do in private, will reward you."

Teaching about Prayer
(Also Luke 11.2–4)

[5] "And when you pray, do not be like the show-offs! They love to stand up and pray in the synagogues and on the street corners so that everybody will see them. Remember this! They have already been paid in full. [6] But when you pray, go to your room and close the door, and pray to your Father, who is unseen. And your Father, who sees what you do in private, will reward you.

[7] "In your prayers do not use a lot of words, as the pagans do, who think that God will hear them because of their long prayers. [8] Do not be like them; your Father already knows what you need before you ask him. [9] This is the way you should pray:

'Our Father in heaven:
May your name be kept holy,
[10] May your Kingdom come,
May your will be done on earth as it is in heaven.
[11] Give us today the food we need;
[12] Forgive us the wrongs that we have done,
As we forgive the wrongs that others have done us.

¹³ Do not bring us to hard testing, but keep us safe from the Evil One.'

¹⁴ For if you forgive others the wrongs they have done you, your Father in heaven will also forgive you. ¹⁵ But if you do not forgive the wrongs of others, then your Father in heaven will not forgive the wrongs you have done."

Teaching about Fasting

¹⁶ "And when you fast, do not put on a sad face like the show-offs do. They go around with a hungry look so that everybody will be sure to see that they are fasting. Remember this! They have already been paid in full. ¹⁷ When you go without food, wash your face and comb your hair, ¹⁸ so that others cannot know that you are fasting — only your Father, who is unseen, will know. And your Father, who sees what you do in private, will reward you."

Riches in Heaven
(Also Luke 12.33–34)

¹⁹ "Do not save riches here on earth, where moths and rust destroy, and robbers break in and steal. ²⁰ Instead,

save riches in heaven, where moths and rust cannot destroy, and robbers cannot break in and steal. ^{21} For your heart will always be where your riches are."

The Light of the Body
(Also Luke 11.34–36)

^{22} "The eyes are like a lamp for the body: if your eyes are clear, your whole body will be full of light; ^{23} but if your eyes are bad, your body will be in darkness. So if the light in you turns out to be darkness, how terribly dark it will be!"

God and Possessions
(Also Luke 16.13; 12.22–31)

^{24} "No one can be a slave to two masters: he will hate one and love the other; he will be loyal to one and despise the other. You cannot serve both God and money.

^{25} "This is why I tell you: do not be worried about the food and drink you need to stay alive, or about clothes for your body. After all, isn't life worth more than food? and isn't the body worth more than clothes? ^{26} Look at the birds flying around: they do not plant seeds, gather a harvest, and put it in barns; your Father in heaven takes care of them! Aren't you worth much more than birds? ^{27} Which one of you can live a few years more by worrying about it?

^{28} "And why worry about clothes? Look how the wild flowers grow: they do not work or make clothes for themselves. ^{29} But I tell you that not even Solomon, as rich as he was, had clothes as beautiful as one of these flowers. ^{30} It is God who clothes the wild grass — grass that is here today, gone tomorrow, burned up in the oven. Will he not be all the more sure to clothe you? How little is your faith! ^{31} So do not start worrying: 'Where will my food come from? or my drink? or my clothes?' ^{32}(These are the things the heathen are always after.) Your Father in heaven knows that you need all these things. ^{33} Instead, give first place to his Kingdom and to what he requires, and he will provide you with all these other things. ^{34} So do not worry about tomorrow; it will have enough worries of its own. There is no need to add to the troubles each day brings."

Judging Others
(Also Luke 6.37–38, 41–42)

7 "Do not judge others, so that God will not judge you — ² because God will judge you in the same way you judge others, and he will apply to you the same rules you apply to others. ³ Why, then, do you look at the speck in your brother's eye, and pay no attention to the log in your own eye? ⁴ How dare you say to your brother, 'Please, let me take that speck out of your eye,' when you have a log in your own eye? ⁵ You impostor! Take the log out of your own eye first, and then you will be able to see and take the speck out of your brother's eye.

⁶ "Do not give what is holy to dogs — they will only turn and attack you; do not throw your pearls in front of pigs — they will only trample them underfoot."

Ask, Seek, Knock
(Also Luke 11.9–13)

⁷ "Ask, and you will receive; seek, and you will find; knock, and the door will be opened to you. ⁸ For everyone who asks will receive, and he who seeks will find, and the door will be opened to him who knocks. ⁹ Would any one of you fathers give his son a stone, when he asks you for bread? ¹⁰ Or would you give him a snake, when he asks you for fish? ¹¹ As bad as you are, you know how to give good things to your children. How much more, then, your Father in heaven will give good things to those who ask him!

¹² "Do for others what you want them to do for you: this is the meaning of the Law of Moses and the teaching of the prophets."

The Narrow Gate
(Also Luke 13.24)

¹³ "Go in through the narrow gate, for the gate is wide and the road is easy that leads to hell, and there are many who travel it. ¹⁴ The gate is narrow and the way is hard that leads to life, and few people find it."

A Tree and Its Fruit
(Also Luke 6.43–44)

¹⁵ "Watch out for false prophets; they come to you looking like sheep on the outside, but they are really like wild

wolves on the inside. ¹⁶ You will know them by the way they act. Thorn bushes do not bear grapes, and briars do not bear figs. ¹⁷ A healthy tree bears good fruit, while a poor tree bears bad fruit. ¹⁸ A healthy tree cannot bear bad fruit, and a poor tree cannot bear good fruit. ¹⁹ Any tree that does not bear good fruit is cut down and thrown in the fire. ²⁰ So, then, you will know the false prophets by the way they act."

I Never Knew You
(Also Luke 13.25–27)

²¹ "Not every person who calls me 'Lord, Lord,' will enter into the Kingdom of heaven, but only those who do what my Father in heaven wants them to do. ²² When that Day comes, many will say to me, 'Lord, Lord! In your name we told God's message, by your name we drove out many demons and performed many miracles!' ²³ Then I will say to them, 'I never knew you. Away from me, you evildoers!' "

The Two House Builders
(Also Luke 6.47–49)

²⁴ "So then, everyone who hears these words of mine and obeys them will be like a wise man who built his house on the rock. ²⁵ The rain poured down, the rivers flooded over, and the winds blew hard against that house. But it did not fall, because it had been built on the rock. ²⁶ Everyone who hears these words of mine and does not obey them will be like a foolish man who built his house on the sand. ²⁷ The rain poured down, the rivers flooded over, the winds blew hard against that house, and it fell. What a terrible fall that was!"

The Authority of Jesus

²⁸ Jesus finished saying these things, and the crowds were amazed at the way he taught. ²⁹ He wasn't like their teachers of the Law; instead, he taught with authority.

Jesus Makes a Leper Clean
(Also Mark 1.40–45; Luke 5.12–16)

8 Jesus came down from the hill, and large crowds followed him. ² Then a leper came to him, knelt down before him, and said, "Sir, if you want to, you can make

me clean." ³ Jesus reached out and touched him. "I do want to," he answered. "Be clean!" At once he was clean from his leprosy. ⁴ Then Jesus said to him: "Listen! Don't tell anyone, but go straight to the priest and let him examine you; then offer the sacrifice that Moses ordered, to prove to everyone that you are now clean."

Jesus Heals a Roman Officer's Servant
(Also Luke 7.1–10)

⁵ When Jesus entered Capernaum, a Roman officer met him and begged for help: ⁶ "Sir, my servant is home sick in bed, unable to move, and suffering terribly." ⁷ "I will go and make him well," Jesus said. ⁸ "Oh no, sir," answered the officer. "I do not deserve to have you come into my house. Just give the order and my servant will get well. ⁹ I, too, am a man with superior officers over me, and I have soldiers under me; so I order this one, 'Go!' and he goes; and I order that one, 'Come!' and he comes; and I order my slave, 'Do this!' and he does it." ¹⁰ Jesus was surprised when he heard this, and said to the people who were following him: "I tell you, I have never seen such faith as this in anyone in Israel. ¹¹ Remember this! Many will come from the east and the west and sit down at the table in the Kingdom of heaven with Abraham, Isaac, and Jacob. ¹² But those who should be in the Kingdom will be thrown out into the darkness outside, where they will cry and gnash their teeth." ¹³ And Jesus said to the officer, "Go home, and what you believe will be done for you." And the officer's servant was healed that very hour.

Jesus Heals Many People
(Also Mark 1.29–34; Luke 4.38–41)

¹⁴ Jesus went to Peter's home, and there he saw Peter's mother-in-law sick in bed with a fever. ¹⁵ He touched her hand; the fever left her, and she got up and began to wait on him.

¹⁶ When evening came, people brought to Jesus many who had demons in them. Jesus drove out the evil spirits with a word and healed all who were sick. ¹⁷ He did this to make come true what the prophet Isaiah had said, "He himself took our illnesses and carried away our diseases."

The Would-Be Followers of Jesus
(Also Luke 9.57–62)

[18] Jesus noticed the crowd around him and gave orders to go to the other side of the lake. [19] A teacher of the Law came to him. "Teacher," he said, "I am ready to go with you wherever you go." [20] Jesus answered him, "Foxes have holes, and birds have nests, but the Son of Man has no place to lie down and rest." [21] Another man, who was a disciple, said, "Sir, first let me go and bury my father." [22] "Follow me," Jesus answered, "and let the dead bury their own dead."

Jesus Calms a Storm
(Also Mark 4.35–41; Luke 8.22–25)

[23] Jesus got into the boat, and his disciples went with him. [24] Suddenly a fierce storm hit the lake, so that the waves covered the boat. But Jesus was asleep. [25] The disciples went to him and woke him up. "Save us, Lord!" they said. "We are about to die!" [26] "Why are you so frightened?" Jesus answered. "How little faith you have!" Then he got up and gave a command to the winds and to the waves, and there was a great calm. [27] Everyone was amazed. "What kind of man is this?" they said. "Even the winds and the waves obey him!"

Jesus Heals Two Men with Demons
(Also Mark 5.1–20; Luke 8.26–39)

[28] Jesus came to the territory of the Gadarenes, on the other side of the lake, and was met by two men who came out of the burial caves. These men had demons in them and were very fierce, so dangerous that no one dared travel on that road. [29] At once they screamed, "What do you want with us, Son of God? Have you come to punish us before the right time?" [30] Not far away a large herd of pigs was feeding. [31] The demons begged Jesus, "If you are going to drive us out, send us into that herd of pigs." [32] "Go," Jesus told them; so they left and went off into the pigs. The whole herd rushed down the side of the cliff into the lake and were drowned.

[33] The men who had been taking care of the pigs ran away and went to the town, where they told the whole story, and what had happened to the men with the demons. [34] So everybody from that town went out to meet Jesus;

and when they saw him they begged him to leave their territory.

Jesus Heals a Paralyzed Man
(Also Mark 2.1–12; Luke 5.17–26)

9 Jesus got into the boat, went back across the lake, and came to his own town. ² Some people brought him a paralyzed man, lying on a bed. Jesus saw how much faith they had, and said to the paralyzed man, "Courage, my son! Your sins are forgiven." ³ Then some teachers of the Law said to themselves, "This man is talking against God!" ⁴ Jesus knew what they were thinking and said: "Why are you thinking such evil things? ⁵ Is it easier to say, 'Your sins are forgiven,' or to say, 'Get up and walk'? ⁶ I will prove to you, then, that the Son of Man has authority on earth to forgive sins." So he said to the paralyzed man, "Get up, pick up your bed, and go home!" ⁷ The man got up and went home. ⁸ When the people saw it, they were afraid, and praised God for giving such authority as this to men.

Jesus Calls Matthew
(Also Mark 2.13–17; Luke 5.27–32)

⁹ Jesus left that place, and as he walked along he saw a tax collector, named Matthew, sitting in his office. He said to him, "Follow me." And Matthew got up and followed him.

¹⁰ While Jesus was having dinner at his house, many tax collectors and outcasts came and joined him and his disciples at the table. ¹¹ Some Pharisees saw this and said to his disciples, "Why does your teacher eat with tax collectors and outcasts?" ¹² Jesus heard them and answered: "People who are well do not need a doctor, but only those who are sick. ¹³ Go and find out what this scripture means, 'I do not want animal sacrifices, but kindness.' For I have not come to call the respectable people, but the outcasts."

The Question about Fasting
(Also Mark 2.18–22; Luke 5.33–39)

¹⁴ Then the followers of John the Baptist came to Jesus, asking, "Why is it that we and the Pharisees fast often, but your disciples don't fast at all?" ¹⁵ Jesus answered: "Do you expect the guests at a wedding party to be sad as

long as the bridegroom is with them? Of course not! But the time will come when the bridegroom will be taken away from them, and then they will go without food.

¹⁶ "No one patches up an old coat with a piece of new cloth; for such a patch tears off from the coat, making an even bigger hole. ¹⁷ Nor does anyone pour new wine into used wineskins. If he does, the skins will burst, and then the wine pours out and the skins will be ruined. Instead, new wine is poured into fresh wineskins, and both will keep in good condition."

The Official's Daughter and the Woman who Touched Jesus' Cloak
(Also Mark 5.21–43; Luke 8.40–56)

¹⁸ While Jesus was saying this to them, a Jewish official came to him, knelt down before him, and said, "My daughter has just died; but come and place your hand on her and she will live." ¹⁹ So Jesus got up and followed him, and his disciples went with him.

²⁰ A certain woman, who had had severe bleeding for twelve years, came up behind Jesus and touched the edge of his cloak. ²¹ She said to herself, "If only I touch his cloak I will get well." ²² Jesus turned around and saw her, and said, "Courage, my daughter! Your faith has made

you well." At that very moment the woman became well.

²³ So Jesus went into the official's house. When he saw the musicians for the funeral, and the people all stirred up, ²⁴ he said, "Get out, everybody! The little girl is not dead — she is just sleeping!" They all started making fun of him. ²⁵ As soon as the people had been put out, Jesus went into the girl's room and took hold of her hand, and she got up. ²⁶ The news about this spread all over that part of the country.

Jesus Heals Two Blind Men

²⁷ Jesus left that place, and as he walked along two blind men started following him. "Have mercy on us, Son of David!" they shouted. ²⁸ When Jesus had gone indoors, the two blind men came to him and he asked them, "Do you believe that I can do this?" "Yes, sir!" they answered. ²⁹ Then Jesus touched their eyes and said, "May it happen, then, just as you believe!" — ³⁰ and their sight was restored. Jesus spoke harshly to them, "Don't tell this to anyone!" ³¹ But they left and spread the news about Jesus all over that part of the country.

Jesus Heals a Dumb Man

³² As the men were leaving, some people brought to Jesus a man who could not talk because he had a demon. ³³ As soon as the demon was driven out, the man started talking. Everybody was amazed. "We never saw the like in Israel!" they exclaimed. ³⁴ But the Pharisees said, "It is the chief of the demons who gives him the power to drive them out."

Jesus Has Pity for the People

³⁵ So Jesus went around visiting all the towns and villages. He taught in their synagogues, preached the Good News of the Kingdom, and healed people from every kind of disease and sickness. ³⁶ As he saw the crowds, his heart was filled with pity for them, because they were worried and helpless, like sheep without a shepherd. ³⁷ So he said to his disciples, "There is a great harvest, but few workers to gather it in. ³⁸ Pray to the owner of the harvest that he will send out more workers to gather in his harvest."

The Twelve Apostles
(Also Mark 3.13–19; Luke 6.12–16)

10 Jesus called his twelve disciples together and gave them authority to drive out the evil spirits and to heal every disease and every sickness. ² These are the names of the twelve apostles: first, Simon (called Peter) and his brother Andrew; James and his brother John, the sons of Zebedee; ³ Philip and Bartholomew; Thomas and Matthew, the tax collector; James, the son of Alphaeus, and Thaddaeus; ⁴ Simon, the patriot, and Judas Iscariot, who betrayed Jesus.

The Mission of the Twelve
(Also Mark 6.7–13; Luke 9.1–6)

⁵ Jesus sent these twelve men out with the following instructions: "Do not go to any Gentile territory or any Samaritan towns. ⁶ Go, instead, to the lost sheep of the people of Israel. ⁷ Go and preach, 'The Kingdom of heaven is near!' ⁸ Heal the sick, raise the dead, make the lepers clean, drive out demons. You have received without paying, so give without being paid. ⁹ Do not carry any gold, silver, or copper money in your pockets; ¹⁰ do not carry a beggar's bag for the trip, or an extra shirt, or shoes, or a walking stick. A worker should be given what he needs.

¹¹ "When you come to a town or village, go in and look for someone who is willing to welcome you, and stay with him until you leave that place. ¹² When you go into a house say, 'Peace be with you.' ¹³ If the people in that house welcome you, let your greeting of peace remain; but if they do not welcome you, then take back your greeting. ¹⁴ And if some home or town will not welcome you or listen to you, then leave that place and shake the dust off your feet. ¹⁵ Remember this! On the Judgment Day God will show more mercy to the people of Sodom and Gomorrah than to the people of that town!"

Coming Persecutions
(Also Mark 13.9–13; Luke 12.12–17)

¹⁶ "Listen! I am sending you just like sheep to a pack of wolves. You must be as cautious as snakes and as gentle as doves. ¹⁷ Watch out, for there will be men who

will arrest you and take you to court, and they will whip you in their synagogues. [18] You will be brought to trial before rulers and kings for my sake, to tell the Good News to them and to the Gentiles. [19] When they bring you to trial, do not worry about what you are going to say or how you will say it; when the time comes, you will be given what you will say. [20] For the words you speak will not be yours; they will come from the Spirit of your Father speaking in you.

[21] "Men will hand over their own brothers to be put to death, and fathers will do the same to their children; children will turn against their parents and have them put to death. [22] Everyone will hate you, because of me. But the person who holds out to the end will be saved. [23] And when they persecute you in one town, run away to another one. I tell you, you will not finish your work in all the towns of Israel before the Son of Man comes.

[24] "No pupil is greater than his teacher; no slave is greater than his master. [25] So a pupil should be satisfied to become like his teacher, and a slave like his master. If the head of the family is called Beelzebul, the members of the family will be called by even worse names!"

Whom to Fear
(*Also Luke 12.2–7*)

[26] "Do not be afraid of men, then. Whatever is covered up will be uncovered, and every secret will be made known. [27] What I am telling you in the dark you must repeat in broad daylight, and what you have heard in private you must tell from the housetops. [28] Do not be afraid of those who kill the body but cannot kill the soul; rather be afraid of God, who can destroy both body and soul in hell. [29] You can buy two sparrows for a penny; yet not a single one of them falls to the ground without your Father's consent. [30] As for you, even the hairs of your head have all been counted. [31] So do not be afraid: you are worth much more than sparrows!"

Confessing and Denying Christ
(*Also Luke 12.8–9*)

[32] "Whoever declares publicly that he belongs to me, I will do the same for him before my Father in heaven.

[33] But whoever denies publicly that he belongs to me, then I will deny him before my Father in heaven."

Not Peace, but a Sword
(Also Luke 12.51–53; 14.26–27)

[34] "Do not think that I have come to bring peace to the world; no, I did not come to bring peace, but a sword. [35] I came to set sons against their fathers, daughters against their mothers, daughters-in-law against their mothers-in-law; [36] a man's worst enemies will be the members of his own family.

[37] "Whoever loves his father or mother more than me is not worthy of me; whoever loves his son or daughter more than me is not worthy of me. [38] Whoever does not take up his cross and follow in my steps is not worthy of me. [39] Whoever tries to gain his own life will lose it; whoever loses his life for my sake will gain it."

Rewards
(Also Mark 9.41)

[40] "Whoever welcomes you, welcomes me; and whoever welcomes me, welcomes the one who sent me. [41] Whoever welcomes God's messenger because he is God's messenger will share in his reward; and whoever welcomes a truly good man, because he is that, will share in his reward. [42] And remember this! Whoever gives even a drink of cold water to one of the least of these my followers, because he is my follower, will certainly receive his reward."

The Messengers from John the Baptist
(*Also Luke 7.18-35*)

11 When Jesus finished giving these instructions to his twelve disciples, he left that place and went on to teach and preach in the towns near there.

² When John the Baptist heard in prison about Christ's works, he sent some of his disciples to him. ³ "Tell us," they asked Jesus, "are you the one John said was going to come, or should we expect someone else?" ⁴ Jesus answered: "Go back and tell John what you are hearing and seeing: ⁵ the blind can see, the lame can walk, the lepers are made clean, the deaf hear, the dead are raised to life, and the Good News is preached to the poor. ⁶ How happy is he who has no doubts about me!"

⁷ While John's disciples were going back, Jesus spoke about John to the crowds. "When you went out to John in the desert, what did you expect to see? A blade of grass bending in the wind? ⁸ What did you go out to see? A man dressed up in fancy clothes? People who dress like that live in palaces! ⁹ Tell me, what did you expect to see? A prophet? Yes, I tell you — you saw much more than a prophet. ¹⁰ For John is the one of whom the scripture says: 'Here is my messenger, says God; I will send him ahead of you to open the way for you.' ¹¹ Remember this! John the Baptist is greater than any man who has ever lived. But he who is least in the Kingdom of heaven is greater than he. ¹² From the time John preached his message until this very day the Kingdom of heaven has suffered violent attacks, and violent men try to seize it. ¹³ All the prophets and the Law of Moses, until the time of John, spoke about the Kingdom; ¹⁴ and if you are willing to believe their message, John is Elijah, whose coming was predicted. ¹⁵ Listen, then, if you have ears!

¹⁶ "Now, to what can I compare the people of this day? They are like children sitting in the market place. One group shouts to the other, ¹⁷ 'We played wedding music for you, but you would not dance! We sang funeral songs, but you would not cry!' ¹⁸ John came, and he fasted and drank no wine, and everyone said, 'He is a madman!' ¹⁹ The Son of Man came, and he ate and drank, and everyone said, 'Look at this man! He is a glutton and wine-drinker, and is a friend of tax collectors and out-

casts!' God's wisdom, however, is shown to be true by its results."

The Unbelieving Towns
(*Also Luke 10.13–15*)

[20] Then Jesus began to reproach the towns where he had performed most of his miracles, because the people had not turned from their sins. [21] "How terrible it will be for you, Chorazin! How terrible for you too, Bethsaida! For if the miracles which were performed in you had been performed in Tyre and Sidon, long ago the people there would have put on sackcloth, and sprinkled ashes on themselves to show they had turned from their sins! [22] Remember, then, that on the Judgment Day God will show more mercy to the people of Tyre and Sidon than to you! [23] And as for you, Capernaum! You wanted to lift yourself up to heaven? You will be thrown down to hell! For if the miracles which were performed in you had been performed in Sodom, it would still be in existence today! [24] Remember, then, that on the Judgment Day God will show more mercy to Sodom than to you!"

Come to Me and Rest
(*Also Luke 10.21–22*)

[25] At that time Jesus said: "O Father, Lord of heaven

and earth! I thank you because you have shown to the unlearned what you have hidden from the wise and learned. [26] Yes, Father, this was done by your own choice and pleasure.

[27] "My Father has given me all things. No one knows the Son except the Father, and no one knows the Father except the Son, and those to whom the Son wants to reveal him.

[28] "Come to me, all of you who are tired from carrying your heavy loads, and I will give you rest. [29] Take my yoke and put it on you, and learn from me, for I am gentle and humble in spirit; and you will find rest. [30] The yoke I will give you is easy, and the load I will put on you is light."

The Question about the Sabbath
(Also Mark 2.23–28; Luke 6.1–5)

12 Not long afterward Jesus was walking through the wheat fields on a Sabbath day. His disciples were hungry, so they began to pick heads of wheat and eat the grain. [2] When the Pharisees saw this, they said to Jesus, "Look, it is against our Law for your disciples to do this on the Sabbath!" [3] Jesus answered: "Have you never read what David did that time when he and his men were hungry? [4] He went into the house of God, and he and his men ate the bread offered to God, even though it was against the Law for them to eat that bread — only the priests were allowed to eat it. [5] Or have you not read in the Law of Moses that every Sabbath the priests in the Temple actually break the Sabbath law, yet they are not guilty? [6] There is something here, I tell you, greater than the Temple. [7] If you really knew what this scripture means, 'I do not want animal sacrifices, but kindness,' you would not condemn people who are not guilty. [8] For the Son of Man is Lord of the Sabbath."

The Man with a Crippled Hand
(Also Mark 3.1–6; Luke 6.6–11)

[9] Jesus left that place and went to one of their synagogues. [10] A man was there who had a crippled hand. There were some men present who wanted to accuse Jesus of wrongdoing; so they asked him, "Is it against our Law to cure on the Sabbath?" [11] Jesus answered: "What

if one of you has a sheep and it falls into a deep hole on the Sabbath? Will you not take hold of it and lift it out? [12] And a man is worth much more than a sheep! So, then, our Law does allow us to help someone on the Sabbath." [13] Then he said to the man, "Stretch out your hand." He stretched it out, and it became well again, just like the other one. [14] The Pharisees left and made plans against Jesus to kill him.

God's Chosen Servant

[15] When Jesus heard about it, he went away from that place; and many people followed him. He healed all the sick, [16] and gave them orders not to tell others about him, [17] to make come true what the prophet Isaiah had said:

> [18] "Here is my servant, says God, whom I have chosen,
> The one I love, with whom I am well pleased.
> I will put my Spirit on him,
> And he will announce my judgment to all people.
> [19] But he will not argue or shout,
> Nor will he make loud speeches in the streets;
> [20] He will not break off a bent reed,
> Nor will he put out a flickering lamp.
> He will persist until he causes justice to triumph;
> [21] And all people will put their hope in him."

Jesus and Beelzebul
(Also Mark 3.20–30; Luke 11.14–23)

[22] Then some people brought to Jesus a man who was blind and could not talk because he had a demon. Jesus healed the man, so that he was able to talk and see. [23] The crowds were all amazed. "Could he be the Son of David?" they asked. [24] When the Pharisees heard this they replied, "He drives out demons only because their ruler Beelzebul gives him power to do so." [25] Jesus knew what they were thinking and said to them: "Any country that divides itself into groups that fight each other will not last very long. And any town or family that divides itself into groups that fight each other will fall apart. [26] So if one group is fighting another in Satan's kingdom, this means that it is already divided into groups and will soon fall apart! [27] You

say that I drive out demons because Beelzebul gives me the power to do so. Well, then, who gives your followers the power to drive them out? Your own followers prove that you are completely wrong! ²⁸ No, it is God's Spirit who gives me the power to drive out demons, which proves that the Kingdom of God has already come upon you.

²⁹ "No one can break into a strong man's house and take away his belongings unless he ties up the strong man first; then he can plunder his house.

³⁰ "Anyone who is not for me is really against me; anyone who does not help me gather is really scattering. ³¹ For this reason I tell you: men can be forgiven any sin and any evil thing they say; but whoever says evil things against the Holy Spirit will not be forgiven. ³² Anyone who says something against the Son of Man will be forgiven; but whoever says something against the Holy Spirit will not be forgiven — now or ever."

A Tree and Its Fruit
(Also Luke 6.43–45)

³³ "To have good fruit you must have a healthy tree; if you have a poor tree you will have bad fruit. For a tree is known by the kind of fruit it bears. ³⁴ You snakes — how can you say good things when you are evil? For the mouth speaks what the heart is full of. ³⁵ A good man brings good things out of his treasure of good things; a bad man brings bad things out of his treasure of bad things.

³⁶ "And I tell you this: on the Judgment Day everyone will have to give account of every useless word he has ever spoken. ³⁷ For your words will be used to judge you, either to declare you innocent or to declare you guilty."

The Demand for a Miracle
(Also Mark 8.11–12; Luke 11.29–32)

³⁸ Then some teachers of the Law and some Pharisees spoke up. "Teacher," they said, "we want to see you perform a miracle." ³⁹ "How evil and godless are the people of this day!" Jesus exclaimed. "You ask me for a miracle? No! The only miracle you will be given is the miracle of the prophet Jonah. ⁴⁰ In the same way that Jonah spent three days and nights in the belly of the big fish, so will the Son of Man spend three days and nights in the depths of the earth. ⁴¹ On the Judgment Day the people of

Nineveh will stand up and accuse you, because they turned from their sins when they heard Jonah preach; and there is something here, I tell you, greater than Jonah! 42 On the Judgment Day the Queen from the South will stand up and accuse you, because she traveled halfway around the world to listen to Solomon's wise teaching; and there is something here, I tell you, greater than Solomon!"

The Return of the Evil Spirit
(Also Luke 11.24–26)

43 "When an evil spirit goes out of a man, it travels over dry country looking for a place to rest. If it can't find one, 44 it says to itself, 'I will go back to my house which I left.' So it goes back and finds it empty, clean, and all fixed up. 45 Then it goes out and brings along seven other spirits even worse than itself, and they come and live there. So that man is in worse shape, when it is all over, than he was at the beginning. This is the way it will happen to the evil people of this day."

Jesus' Mother and Brothers
(Also Mark 3.31–35; Luke 8.19–21)

46 Jesus was still talking to the people when his mother and brothers arrived. They stood outside, asking to speak with him. 47 So one of the people there said to him, "Look, your mother and brothers are standing outside, and they want to speak with you." 48 Jesus answered, "Who is my mother? Who are my brothers?" 49 Then he pointed to his disciples and said: "Look! Here are my mother and my brothers! 50 For the person who does what my Father in heaven wants him to do is my brother, my sister, my mother."

The Parable of the Sower
(Also Mark 4.1–9; Luke 8.4–8)

13 That same day Jesus left the house and went to the lakeside, where he sat down to teach. 2 The crowd that gathered around him was so large that he got into a boat and sat in it, while the crowd stood on the shore. 3 He used parables to tell them many things.

"There was a man who went out to sow. 4 As he scattered the seed in the field, some of it fell along the path, and the birds came and ate it up. 5 Some of it fell on rocky ground, where there was little soil. The seeds soon sprouted, because the soil wasn't deep. ⁶ When the sun came up it burned the young plants, and because the roots had not grown deep enough the plants soon dried up. ⁷ Some of the seed fell among thorns, which grew up and choked the plants. ⁸ But some seeds fell in good soil, and bore grain: some had one hundred grains, others sixty, and others thirty." ⁹ And Jesus said, "Listen, then, if you have ears!"

The Purpose of the Parables
(Also Mark 4.10–12; Luke 8.9–10)

¹⁰ Then the disciples came to Jesus and asked him, "Why do you use parables when you talk to them?" ¹¹ "The knowledge of the secrets of the Kingdom of heaven has been given to you," Jesus answered, "but not to them. ¹² For the man who has something will be given more, so that he will have more than enough; but the man who has nothing will have taken away from him even the little he has. ¹³ This is the reason that I use parables to talk to them: it is because they look, but do not see, and they listen, but do not hear or understand. ¹⁴ So the prophecy of Isaiah comes true in their case:

'You will listen and listen, but not understand;
You will look and look, but not see.
¹⁵ Because this people's mind is dull;
They have stopped up their ears,
And they have closed their eyes.
Otherwise, their eyes might see,
Their ears might hear,
Their minds might understand
And they might turn to me, says God,
And I would heal them.'

¹⁶ As for you, how fortunate you are! Your eyes see and your ears hear. ¹⁷ Remember this! Many prophets and many of God's people wanted very much to see what you see, but they could not, and to hear what you hear, but they did not."

Jesus Explains the Parable of the Sower
(Also Mark 4.13–20; Luke 8.11–15)

¹⁸ "Listen, then, and learn what the parable of the sower means. ¹⁹ Those who hear the message about the King-

dom but do not understand it are like the seed that fell along the path. The Evil One comes and snatches away what was sown in them. ²⁰ The seed that fell on rocky ground stands for those who receive the message gladly as soon as they hear it. ²¹ But it does not sink deep in them, and they don't last long. So when trouble or persecution comes because of the message, they give up at once. ²² The seed that fell among thorns stands for those who hear the message, but the worries about this life and the love for riches choke the message, and they don't bear fruit. ²³ And the seed sown in the good soil stands for those who hear the message and understand it: they bear fruit, some as much as one hundred, others sixty, and others thirty."

The Parable of the Weeds

²⁴ Jesus told them another parable: "The Kingdom of heaven is like a man who sowed good seed in his field. ²⁵ One night, when everyone was asleep, an enemy came and sowed weeds among the wheat, and went away. ²⁶ When the plants grew and the heads of grain began to form, then the weeds showed up. ²⁷ The man's servants came to him and said, 'Sir, it was good seed you sowed in your field; where did the weeds come from?' ²⁸ 'It was some enemy who did this,' he answered. 'Do you want us to go and pull up the weeds?' they asked him. ²⁹ 'No,' he answered, 'because as you gather the weeds you might pull up some of the wheat along with them. ³⁰ Let the wheat and the weeds both grow together until harvest, and then I will tell the harvest workers: Pull up the weeds first and tie them in bundles to throw in the fire; then gather in the wheat and put it in my barn.' "

The Parable of the Mustard Seed
(Also Mark 4.30–32; Luke 13.18–19)

³¹ Jesus told them another parable: "The Kingdom of heaven is like a mustard seed, the smallest of all seeds; ³² a man takes it and sows it in his field, and when it grows up it is the biggest of all plants. It becomes a tree, so that the birds come and make their nests in its branches."

The Parable of the Yeast
(Also Luke 13.20–21)

33 Jesus told them another parable: "The Kingdom of heaven is like yeast. A woman takes it and mixes it with a bushel of flour, until the whole batch of dough rises."

Jesus' Use of Parables
(Also Mark 4.33–34)

34 Jesus used parables to tell all these things to the crowds; he would not say a thing to them without using a parable. 35 He did this to make come true what the prophet had said:

"I will use parables when I speak to them,
I will tell them things unknown since the creation of the world."

Jesus Explains the Parable of the Weeds

36 Then Jesus left the crowd and went indoors. His disciples came to him and said, "Tell us what the parable of the weeds in the field means." 37 Jesus answered: "The man who sowed the good seed is the Son of Man; 38 the field is the world; the good seed is the people who belong to the Kingdom; the weeds are the people who belong to the Evil One; 39 and the enemy who sowed the weeds is the Devil himself. The harvest is the end of the age, and the harvest workers are angels. 40 Just as the weeds are gathered up and burned in the fire, so it will be at the end of the age: 41 the Son of Man will send out his angels and they will gather up out of his Kingdom all who cause people to sin, and all other evildoers, 42 and throw them into the fiery furnace, where they will cry and gnash their teeth. 43 Then God's people will shine like the sun in their Father's Kingdom. Listen, then, if you have ears!"

The Parable of the Hidden Treasure

44 "The Kingdom of heaven is like a treasure hidden in a field. A man happens to find it, so he covers it up again. He is so happy that he goes and sells everything he has, and then goes back and buys the field."

The Parable of the Pearl

45 "Also, the Kingdom of heaven is like a buyer looking for fine pearls. 46 When he finds one that is unusually

fine, he goes and sells everything he has, and buys the pearl."

The Parable of the Net

⁴⁷ "Also, the Kingdom of heaven is like a net thrown out in the lake, which catches all kinds of fish. ⁴⁸ When it is full, the fishermen pull it to shore and sit down to divide the fish: the good ones go into their buckets, the worthless ones are thrown away. ⁴⁹ It will be like this at the end of the age: the angels will go out and gather up the evil people from among the good, ⁵⁰ and throw them into the fiery furnace. There they will cry and gnash their teeth."

New and Old Truths

⁵¹ "Do you understand these things?" Jesus asked them. "Yes," they answered. ⁵² So he replied, "This means, then, that every teacher of the Law who becomes a disciple in the Kingdom of heaven is like a homeowner who takes new and old things out of his storage room."

Jesus Rejected at Nazareth
(Also Mark 6.1–6; Luke 4.16–30)

⁵³ When Jesus finished telling these parables, he left that place ⁵⁴ and went back to his home town. He taught in their synagogue, and those who heard him were amazed. "Where did he get such wisdom?" they asked. "And what about his miracles? ⁵⁵ Isn't he the carpenter's son? Isn't Mary his mother, and aren't James, Joseph, Simon, and Judas his brothers? ⁵⁶ Aren't all his sisters living here? Where did he get all this?" ⁵⁷ And so they rejected him. Jesus said to them: "A prophet is respected everywhere except in his home town and by his own family." ⁵⁸ He did not perform many miracles there because they did not have faith.

The Death of John the Baptist
(Also Mark 6.14–29; Luke 9.7–9)

14 It was at that time that Herod, the ruler of Galilee, heard about Jesus. ² "He is really John the Baptist who has come back to life," he told his officials. "That is why these powers are at work in him."

³ For Herod had ordered John's arrest, and had him

tied up and put in prison. He did this because of Herodias, his brother Philip's wife. ⁴ John the Baptist kept telling Herod, "It isn't right for you to marry her!" ⁵ Herod wanted to kill him, but he was afraid of the Jewish people, because they considered John to be a prophet.

⁶ On Herod's birthday the daughter of Herodias danced in front of the whole group. Herod was so pleased ⁷ that he promised her: "I swear that I will give you anything you ask for!" ⁸ At her mother's suggestion she asked him, "Give me right here the head of John the Baptist on a plate!" ⁹ The king was sad, but because of the promise he had made in front of all his guests he gave orders that her wish be granted. ¹⁰ So he had John beheaded in prison. ¹¹ The head was brought in on a plate and given to the girl, who took it to her mother. ¹² John's disciples came, got his body, and buried it; then they went and told Jesus.

Jesus Feeds the Five Thousand
(Also Mark 6.30–44; Luke 9.10–17; John 6.1–14)

¹³ When Jesus heard the news, he left that place in a boat and went to a lonely place by himself. The people heard about it, left their towns, and followed him by land. ¹⁴ Jesus got out of the boat, and when he saw the large

crowd his heart was filled with pity for them, and he healed their sick.

15 That evening his disciples came to him and said, "It is already very late, and this is a lonely place. Send the people away and let them go to the villages and buy food for themselves." 16 "They don't have to leave," answered Jesus. "You yourselves give them something to eat." 17 "All we have here are five loaves and two fish," they replied. 18 "Bring them here to me," Jesus said. 19 He ordered the people to sit down on the grass; then he took the five loaves and the two fish, looked up to heaven, and gave thanks to God. He broke the loaves and gave them to the disciples, and the disciples gave them to the people. 20 Everyone ate and had enough. Then the disciples took up twelve baskets full of what was left over. 21 The number of men who ate was about five thousand, not counting the women and children.

Jesus Walks on the Water
(*Also Mark 6.45–52; John 6.15–21*)

22 Then Jesus made the disciples get into the boat and go ahead of him to the other side of the lake, while he sent the people away. 23 After sending the people away, he went up a hill by himself to pray. When evening came, Jesus was there alone; 24 by this time the boat was far out in the lake, tossed about by the waves, for the wind was blowing against it. 25 Between three and six o'clock in the morning Jesus came to them, walking on the water. 26 When the disciples saw him walking on the water they were terrified. "It's a ghost!" they said, and screamed with fear. 27 Jesus spoke to them at once. "Courage!" he said. "It is I. Don't be afraid!" 28 Then Peter spoke up. "Lord," he said, "if it is really you, order me to come out on the water to you." 29 "Come!" answered Jesus. So Peter got out of the boat and started walking on the water to Jesus. 30 When he noticed the wind, however, he was afraid, and started to sink down in the water. "Save me, Lord!" he cried. 31 At once Jesus reached out and grabbed him and said, "How little faith you have! Why did you doubt?" 32 They both got back into the boat, and the wind died down. 33 The disciples in the boat worshiped Jesus. "Truly you are the Son of God!" they exclaimed.

Jesus Heals the Sick in Gennesaret
(Also Mark 6.53–56)

34 They crossed the lake and came to land at Gennesaret, 35 where the people recognized Jesus. So they sent for the sick people in all the surrounding country and brought them to Jesus. 36 They begged him to let the sick at least touch the edge of his cloak; and all who touched it were made well.

The Teaching of the Ancestors
(Also Mark 7.1–13)

15 Then some Pharisees and teachers of the Law came to Jesus from Jerusalem and asked him: 2 "Why is it that your disciples disobey the teaching handed down by our ancestors? They don't wash their hands in the proper way before they eat!" 3 Jesus answered: "And why do you disobey God's command and follow your own teaching? 4 For God said, 'Honor your father and mother,' and 'Anyone who says bad things about his father or mother must be put to death.' 5 But you teach that if a person has something he could use to help his father or mother, but says, 'This belongs to God,' 6 he does not need to honor his father. This is how you disregard God's word to follow your own teaching. 7 You hypocrites! How right Isaiah was when he prophesied about you!

8 'These people, says God, honor me with
        their words,
   But their heart is really far away from me.
9 It is no use for them to worship me,
   Because they teach man-made command-
        ments as though they were God's rules!' "

The Things that Make a Person Unclean
(Also Mark 7.14–23)

10 Then Jesus called the crowd to him and said to them: "Listen, and understand! 11 It is not what goes into a person's mouth that makes him unclean; rather, what comes out of it makes him unclean."

12 Then the disciples came to him and said, "Do you know that the Pharisees had their feelings hurt by what you said?" 13 "Every plant which my Father in heaven did not plant will be pulled up," answered Jesus. 14 "Don't

worry about them! They are blind leaders; and when one blind man leads another, both fall in the ditch." ¹⁵ Peter spoke up, "Tell us what this parable means." ¹⁶ Jesus said to them: "You are still no more intelligent than the others. ¹⁷ Don't you understand? Anything that goes into a person's mouth goes into his stomach and then on out of the body. ¹⁸ But the things that come out of the mouth come from the heart; such things make a man unclean. ¹⁹ For from his heart come the evil ideas which lead him to kill, commit adultery, and do other immoral things; to rob, lie, and slander others. ²⁰ These are the things that make a man unclean. But to eat without washing your hands as they say you should — this does not make a man unclean."

A Woman's Faith
(Also Mark 7.24–30)

²¹ Jesus left that place and went off to the territory near the cities of Tyre and Sidon. ²² A Canaanite woman who lived in that region came to him. "Son of David, sir!" she cried. "Have mercy on me! My daughter has a demon and is in a terrible condition." ²³ But Jesus did not say a word to her. His disciples came to him and begged him, "Send her away! She is following us and making all this noise!" ²⁴ Then Jesus replied, "I have been sent only to the lost sheep of the people of Israel." ²⁵ At this the woman came and fell at his feet. "Help me, sir!" she said.

[26] Jesus answered, "It isn't right to take the children's food and throw it to the dogs." [27] "That is true sir," she answered; "but even the dogs eat the leftovers that fall from their masters' table." [28] So Jesus answered her: "You are a woman of great faith! What you want will be done for you." And at that very moment her daughter was healed.

Jesus Heals Many People

[29] Jesus left that place and went along by Lake Galilee. He climbed a hill and sat down. [30] Large crowds came to him, bringing with them the lame, the blind, the crippled,

the dumb, and many other sick people, whom they placed at Jesus' feet; and he healed them. [31] The people were amazed as they saw the dumb speaking, the crippled whole, the lame walking, and the blind seeing; and they praised the God of Israel.

Jesus Feeds the Four Thousand
(Also Mark 8.1–10)

[32] Jesus called his disciples to him and said: "I feel sorry for these people, because they have been with me for three days and now have nothing to eat. I don't want to send them away without feeding them, because they might faint on their way home." [33] The disciples asked him, "Where will we find enough food in this desert to feed this crowd?" [34] "How much bread do you have?" Jesus asked. "Seven loaves," they answered, "and a few small fish." [35] So Jesus ordered the crowd to sit down on

the ground. ³⁶ Then he took the seven loaves and the fish, gave thanks to God, broke them and gave them to the disciples, and the disciples gave them to the people. ³⁷ They all ate and had enough. The disciples took up seven baskets full of pieces left over. ³⁸ The number of men who ate was four thousand, not counting the women and children.

³⁹ Then Jesus sent the people away, got into a boat, and went to the territory of Magadan.

The Demand for a Miracle
(Also Mark 8.11–13; Luke 12.54–56)

16 Some Pharisees and Sadducees came to Jesus. They wanted to trap him, so they asked him to perform a miracle for them, to show God's approval. ² But Jesus answered: "When the sun is setting you say, 'We are going to have fine weather, because the sky is red.' ³ And early in the morning you say, 'It is going to rain, because the sky is red and dark.' You can predict the weather by looking at the sky; but you cannot interpret the signs concerning these times! ⁴ How evil and godless are the people of this day!" Jesus added. "You ask me for a miracle? No! The only miracle you will be given is the miracle of Jonah." So he left them and went away.

The Yeast of the Pharisees and Sadducees
(Also Mark 8.14–21)

⁵ When the disciples crossed over to the other side of the lake, they forgot to take any bread. ⁶ Jesus said to them, "Look out, and be on your guard against the yeast of the Pharisees and Sadducees." ⁷ They started discussing among themselves: "He says this because we didn't bring any bread." ⁸ Jesus knew what they were saying, so he asked them: "Why are you discussing among yourselves about not having any bread? How little faith you have! ⁹ Don't you understand yet? Don't you remember when I broke the five loaves for the five thousand men? How many baskets did you fill? ¹⁰ And what about the seven loaves for the four thousand men? How many baskets did you fill? ¹¹ How is it that you don't understand that I was not talking to you about bread? Guard yourselves from the yeast of the Pharisees and Sadducees!" ¹² Then the disciples understood that he was not telling them to guard

themselves from the yeast used in bread, but from the teaching of the Pharisees and Sadducees.

Peter's Declaration about Jesus
(Also Mark 8.27–30; Luke 9.18–21)

¹³ Jesus went to the territory near the town of Caesarea Philippi, where he asked his disciples, "Who do men say the Son of Man is?" ¹⁴ "Some say John the Baptist," they answered. "Others say Elijah, while others say Jeremiah or some other prophet." ¹⁵ "What about you?" he asked them. "Who do you say I am?" ¹⁶ Simon Peter answered, "You are the Messiah, the Son of the living God." ¹⁷ "Simon, son of John, you are happy indeed!" answered Jesus. "For this truth did not come to you from any human being, but it was given to you directly by my Father in heaven. ¹⁸ And so I tell you: you are a rock, Peter, and on this rock I will build my church. Not even death will ever be able to overcome it. ¹⁹ I will give you the keys of the Kingdom of heaven: what you prohibit on earth will be prohibited in heaven; what you permit on earth will be permitted in heaven." ²⁰ Then Jesus ordered his disciples that they were not to tell anyone that he was the Messiah.

Jesus Speaks about His Suffering and Death
(Also Mark 8.31—9.1; Luke 9.22–27)

²¹ From that time on Jesus began to say plainly to his disciples: "I must go to Jerusalem and suffer much from the elders, the chief priests, and the teachers of the Law. I will be put to death, and on the third day I will be raised to life." ²² Peter took him aside and began to rebuke him. "God forbid it, Lord!" he said. "This must never happen to you!" ²³ Jesus turned around and said to Peter: "Get away from me, Satan! You are an obstacle in my way, for these thoughts of yours are men's thoughts, not God's!"

²⁴ Then Jesus said to his disciples: "If anyone wants to come with me, he must forget himself, carry his cross, and follow me. ²⁵ For the man who wants to save his own life will lose it; but the man who loses his life for my sake will find it. ²⁶ Will a man gain anything if he wins the whole world but loses his life? Of course not! There is nothing a man can give to regain his life. ²⁷ For the Son of Man is about to come in the glory of his Father with his angels,

and then he will repay everyone according to his deeds. [28] Remember this! There are some here who will not die until they have seen the Son of Man come as King."

The Transfiguration
(Also Mark 9.2–13; Luke 9.28–36)

17 Six days later Jesus took with him Peter, and the brothers James and John, and led them up a high mountain by themselves. [2] As they looked on, a change came over him: his face became as bright as the sun, and his clothes as white as light. [3] Then the three disciples saw Moses and Elijah talking with Jesus. [4] So Peter spoke up and said to Jesus, "Lord, it is a good thing that we are here; if you wish, I will make three tents here, one for you, one for Moses, and one for Elijah." [5] While he was talking, a shining cloud came over them and a voice said from the cloud: "This is my own dear Son, with whom I am well pleased — listen to him!" [6] When the disciples heard the voice they were so terrified that they threw

themselves face down to the ground. [7] Jesus came to them and touched them. "Get up," he said. "Don't be afraid!" [8] So they looked up and saw no one else except Jesus.

[9] As they came down the mountain Jesus ordered them: "Don't tell anyone about this vision you have seen until the Son of Man has been raised from death." [10] Then the disciples asked Jesus, "Why do the teachers of the Law say that Elijah has to come first?" [11] "Elijah does indeed come first," answered Jesus, "and he will get everything ready. [12] But I tell you this:

Elijah has already come and people did not recognize him, but treated him just as they pleased. In the same way the Son of Man will also be mistreated by them." [13] Then the disciples understood that he was talking to them about John the Baptist.

Jesus Heals a Boy with a Demon
(Also Mark 9.14–29; Luke 9.37–43a)

[14] When they returned to the crowd, a man came to Jesus, knelt before him, [15] and said: "Sir, have mercy on my son! He is epileptic and has such terrible fits that he often falls in the fire or in the water. [16] I brought him to your disciples, but they could not heal him." [17] Jesus answered: "How unbelieving and wrong you people are! How long must I stay with you? How long do I have to put up with you? Bring the boy here to me!" [18] Jesus commanded the demon and it went out, so that the boy was healed at that very moment.

[19] Then the disciples came to Jesus in private and asked him, "Why couldn't we drive the demon out?" [20] "It was because you do not have enough faith," answered Jesus. "Remember this! If you have faith as big as a mustard seed, you can say to this hill, 'Go from here to there!' and it will go. You could do anything! [21 But only prayer and fasting can drive this kind out; nothing else can.]"

Jesus Speaks again about His Death
(Also Mark 9.30–32; Luke 9.43b–45)

[22] When the disciples all came together in Galilee, Jesus said to them: "The Son of Man is about to be handed over to men [23] who will kill him; but on the third day he will be raised to life." The disciples became very sad.

Payment of the Temple Tax

[24] When Jesus and his disciples came to Capernaum, the collectors of the Temple tax came to Peter and asked, "Does your teacher pay the Temple tax?" [25] "Of course," Peter answered. When Peter went into the house, Jesus spoke up first: "Simon, what is your opinion? Who pays duties or taxes to the kings of this world? The citizens of the country or the foreigners?" [26] "The foreigners," answered Peter. "Well, then," replied Jesus, "that means that the citizens don't have to pay. [27] But we don't want to offend these people. So go to the lake and drop in a line; pull up the first fish you hook, and in its mouth you

will find a coin worth enough for my Temple tax and yours; take it and pay them our taxes."

Who Is the Greatest?
(*Also Mark 9.33–37; Luke 9.46–48*)

18 At that moment the disciples came to Jesus, asking, "Who is the greatest in the Kingdom of heaven?" [2] Jesus called a child, had him stand in front of them, [3] and said: "Remember this! Unless you change and become like children, you will never enter the Kingdom of heaven. [4] The greatest in the Kingdom of heaven is the one who humbles himself and becomes like this child. [5] And the person who welcomes in my name one such child as this, welcomes me."

Temptations to Sin
(*Also Mark 9.42–48; Luke 17.1–2*)

[6] "As for these little ones who believe in me — it would be better for a man to have a large millstone tied around his neck and be drowned in the deep sea, than for him to cause one of them to turn away from me. [7] How terrible for the world that there are things that make people turn away! Such things will always happen — but how terrible for the one who causes them!

[8] "If your hand or your foot makes you turn away, cut it off and throw it away! It is better for you to enter life without a hand or foot than to keep both hands and feet and be thrown into the eternal fire. [9] And if your eye makes you turn away, take it out and throw it away! It is better for you to enter life with only one eye than to keep both eyes and be thrown into the fire of hell."

The Parable of the Lost Sheep
(*Also Luke 15.3–7*)

[10] "See that you don't despise any of these little ones. Their angels in heaven, I tell you, are always in the presence of my Father in heaven. [[11] For the Son of Man came to save the lost.]

[12] "What do you think? What will a man do who has one hundred sheep and one of them gets lost? He will leave the other ninety-nine grazing on the hillside and go to look for the lost sheep. [13] When he finds it, I tell you, he feels far happier over this one sheep than over the

ninety-nine that did not get lost. ¹⁴ In just the same way your Father in heaven does not want any of these little ones to be lost."

A Brother Who Sins

¹⁵ "If your brother sins against you, go to him and show him his fault. But do it privately, just between yourselves. If he listens to you, you have won your brother back. ¹⁶ But if he will not listen to you, take one or two other persons with you, so that 'every accusation may be upheld by the testimony of two or three witnesses,' as the scripture says. ¹⁷ But if he will not listen to them, then tell the whole thing to the church. And then, if he will not listen to the church, treat him as though he were a foreigner or a tax collector."

Prohibiting and Permitting

¹⁸ "And so I tell all of you: what you prohibit on earth will be prohibited in heaven; what you permit on earth will be permitted in heaven.

¹⁹ "And I tell you more: whenever two of you on earth agree about anything you pray for, it will be done for you by my Father in heaven. ²⁰ For where two or three come together in my name, I am there with them."

The Parable of the Unforgiving Servant

²¹ Then Peter came to Jesus and asked, "Lord, how many times can my brother sin against me and I have to forgive him? Seven times?" ²² "No, not seven times," answered Jesus, "but seventy times seven. ²³ Because the Kingdom of heaven is like a king who decided to check on his servants' accounts. ²⁴ He had just begun to do so when one of them was brought in who owed him millions of dollars. ²⁵ He did not have enough to pay his debt, so his master ordered him to be sold as a slave, with his wife and his children and all that he had, in order to pay the debt. ²⁶ The servant fell on his knees before his master.

'Be patient with me,' he begged, 'and I will pay you everything!' ²⁷ The master felt sorry for him, so he forgave him the debt and let him go.

²⁸ "The man went out and met one of his fellow servants who owed him a few dollars. He grabbed him and started choking him. 'Pay back what you owe me!' he said. ²⁹ His

fellow servant fell down and begged him, 'Be patient with me and I will pay you back!' ³⁰ But he would not; instead, he had him thrown into jail until he should pay the debt. ³¹ When the other servants saw what had happened, they were very upset, and went to their master and told him everything. ³² So the master called the servant in. 'You worthless slave!' he said. 'I forgave you the whole amount you owed me, just because you asked me to. ³³ You should

have had mercy on your fellow servant, just as I had mercy on you.' ³⁴ The master was very angry, and he sent the servant to jail to be punished until he should pay back the whole amount." ³⁵ And Jesus concluded, "That is how my Father in heaven will treat you if you do not forgive your brother, every one of you, from your heart."

Jesus Teaches about Divorce
(Also Mark 10.1–12)

19 When Jesus finished saying these things, he left Galilee and went back to the territory of Judea, on the other side of the Jordan river. ² Large crowds followed him, and he healed them there.

³ Some Pharisees came to him and tried to trap him by asking, "Does our Law allow a man to divorce his wife for any and every reason?" ⁴ Jesus answered: "Haven't you read this scripture? 'In the beginning the Creator made them male and female, ⁵ and said, "For this reason a man will leave his father and mother and unite with his wife, and the two will become one." ' ⁶ So they are no longer two, but one. Man must not separate, then, what God has joined together." ⁷ The Pharisees asked him, "Why, then,

did Moses give the commandment for a man to give his wife a divorce notice and send her away?" 8 Jesus answered: "Moses gave you permission to divorce your wives because you are so hard to teach. But it was not this way at the time of creation. 9 I tell you, then, that any man who divorces his wife, and she has not been unfaithful, commits adultery if he marries some other woman."

10 His disciples said to him, "If this is the way it is between a man and his wife, it is better not to marry." 11 Jesus answered: "This teaching does not apply to everyone, but only to those to whom God has given it. 12 For there are different reasons why men cannot marry: some, because they were born that way; others, because men made them that way; and others do not marry because of the Kingdom of heaven. Let him who can do it accept this teaching."

Jesus Blesses Little Children
(Also Mark 10.13–16; Luke 18.15–17)

13 Some people brought children to Jesus for him to place his hands on them and pray, but the disciples scolded those people. 14 Jesus said, "Let the children come to me, and do not stop them, because the Kingdom of heaven belongs to such as these." 15 He placed his hands on them and left.

The Rich Young Man
(Also Mark 10.17–31; Luke 18.18–30)

16 Once a man came to Jesus. "Teacher," he asked, "what good thing must I do to receive eternal life?" 17 "Why do you ask me concerning what is good?" answered Jesus. "There is only One who is good. Keep the commandments if you want to enter life." 18 "What commandments?" he asked. Jesus answered: "Do not murder; do not commit adultery; do not steal; do not lie; 19 honor your father and mother; and love your neighbor as yourself." 20 "I have obeyed all these commandments," the young man replied. "What else do I need to do?" 21 Jesus said to him, "If you want to be perfect, go and sell all you have and give the money to the poor, and you will have riches in heaven; then come and follow me." 22 When the young man heard this he went away sad, because he was very rich.

23 Jesus then said to his disciples: "It will be very hard, I tell you, for a rich man to enter the Kingdom of heaven. 24 I tell you something else: it is much harder for a rich man to enter the Kingdom of God than for a camel to go through the eye of a needle." 25 When the disciples heard this they were completely amazed. "Who can be saved, then?" they asked. 26 Jesus looked straight at them and answered, "This is impossible for men; but for God everything is possible."

27 Then Peter spoke up. "Look," he said, "we have left everything and followed you. What will we have?" 28 Jesus said to them: "I tell you this: when the Son of Man sits on his glorious throne in the New Age, then you twelve followers of mine will also sit on thrones, to judge the twelve tribes of Israel. 29 And every one who has left houses or brothers or sisters or father or mother or children or fields for my sake, will receive a hundred times more, and will be given eternal life. 30 But many who now are first will be last, and many who now are last will be first."

The Workers in the Vineyard

20 "The Kingdom of heaven is like the owner of a vineyard who went out early in the morning to hire some men to work in his vineyard. 2 He agreed to pay them the regular wage, a silver coin a day, and sent them

to work in his vineyard. ³ He went out again to the market place at nine o'clock and saw some men standing there doing nothing, ⁴ so he told them, 'You also go to work in the vineyard, and I will pay you a fair wage.' ⁵ So they went. Then at twelve o'clock and again at three o'clock he did the same thing. ⁶ It was nearly five o'clock when he went to the market place and saw some other men still standing there. 'Why are you wasting the whole day here doing nothing?' he asked them. ⁷ 'It is because no one hired us,' they answered. 'Well, then, you also go to work in the vineyard,' he told them.

⁸ "When evening came, the owner told his foreman, 'Call the workers and pay them their wages, starting with those who were hired last, and ending with those who were hired first.' ⁹ The men who had begun to work at five o'clock were paid a silver coin each. ¹⁰ So when the men who were the first to be hired came to be paid, they thought they would get more — but they too were given a silver coin each. ¹¹ They took their money and started grumbling against the employer. ¹² 'These men who were hired last worked only one hour,' they said, 'while we put up with a whole day's work in the hot sun — yet you paid them the same as you paid us!' ¹³ 'Listen, friend,' the owner answered one of them. 'I have not cheated you. After all, you agreed to do a day's work for a silver coin. ¹⁴ Now, take your pay and go home. I want to give this man who was hired last as much as I have given you. ¹⁵ Don't I have the right to do as I wish with my own money? Or are you jealous simply because I am generous?' " ¹⁶ And Jesus added, "So those who are last will be first, and those who are first will be last."

Jesus Speaks a Third Time about His Death
(Also Mark 10.32–34; Luke 18.31–34)

¹⁷ As Jesus was going up to Jerusalem he took the twelve disciples aside and spoke to them privately, as they walked along. ¹⁸ "Listen," he told them, "we are going up to Jerusalem, where the Son of Man will be handed over to the chief priests and the teachers of the Law. They will condemn him to death ¹⁹ and then hand him over to the Gentiles, who will make fun of him, whip him, and nail him to the cross; and on the third day he will be raised to life."

A Mother's Request
(Also Mark 10.35–45)

20 Then the mother of Zebedee's sons came to Jesus with her sons, bowed before him, and asked him for a favor. 21 "What do you want?" Jesus asked her. She answered, "Promise that these two sons of mine will sit at your right and your left when you are King." 22 "You don't know what you are asking for," Jesus answered them. "Can you drink the cup that I am about to drink?" "We can," they answered. 23 "You will indeed drink from my cup," Jesus told them, "but I do not have the right to choose who will sit at my right and my left. These places belong to those for whom my Father has prepared them."

24 When the other ten disciples heard about this they became angry with the two brothers. 25 So Jesus called them all together to him and said: "You know that the rulers of the people have power over them, and the leaders rule over them. 26 This, however, is not the way it shall be among you. If one of you wants to be great, he must be the servant of the rest; 27 and if one of you wants to be first, he must be your slave — 28 like the Son of Man, who did not come to be served, but to serve and to give his life to redeem many people."

Jesus Heals Two Blind Men
(Also Mark 10.46–52; Luke 18.35–43)

29 As they were leaving Jericho a large crowd followed Jesus. 30 Two blind men who were sitting by the road heard that Jesus was passing by, so they began to shout, "Son of David! Have mercy on us, sir!" 31 The crowd scolded them and told them to be quiet. But they shouted even more loudly, "Son of David! Have mercy on us, sir!" 32 Jesus stopped and called them. "What do you want me to do for you?" he asked them. 33 "Sir," they answered, "we want you to open our eyes!" 34 Jesus had pity on them and touched their eyes; at once they were able to see, and followed him.

The Triumphant Entry into Jerusalem
(Also Mark 11.1–11; Luke 19.28–40; John 12.12–19)

21 As they approached Jerusalem, they came to Beth-phage, at the Mount of Olives. There Jesus sent two of the disciples on ahead 2 with these instructions:

"Go to the village there ahead of you, and at once you will find a donkey tied up and her colt with her. Untie them and bring them to me. ³ And if anyone says anything, tell him, 'The Master needs them'; and he will let them go at once."

⁴ This happened to make come true what the prophet had said:

⁵ "Tell the city of Zion:
Now your king is coming to you,
He is gentle and rides on a donkey,
He rides on a colt, the foal of a donkey."

⁶ So the disciples went ahead and did what Jesus had told them to do: ⁷ they brought the donkey and the colt, threw their cloaks over them, and Jesus got on. ⁸ A great crowd of people spread their cloaks on the road, while others cut branches from the trees and spread them on the road. ⁹ The crowds walking in front of Jesus and the

crowds walking behind began to shout, "Praise to David's Son! God bless him who comes in the name of the Lord! Praise be to God!"

¹⁰ When Jesus entered Jerusalem the whole city was thrown in an uproar. "Who is he?" the people asked.

[11] "This is the prophet Jesus, from Nazareth of Galilee," the crowds answered.

Jesus Goes to the Temple
(Also Mark 11.15–19; Luke 19.45–48; John 2.13–22)

[12] Jesus went into the Temple and drove out all those who bought and sold in the Temple; he overturned the tables of the money-changers and the stools of those who sold pigeons, [13] and said to them: "It is written in the Scriptures that God said, 'My house will be called a house of prayer.' But you are making it a hideout for thieves!"

[14] The blind and the crippled came to him in the Temple and he healed them. [15] The chief priests and the teachers of the Law became angry when they saw the wonderful things he was doing, and the children shouting and crying in the Temple, "Praise to David's Son!" [16] So they said to Jesus, "Do you hear what they are saying?" "Indeed I do," answered Jesus. "Haven't you ever read the scripture that says, 'You have trained children and babies to offer perfect praise'?" [17] Jesus left them and went out of the city to Bethany, where he spent the night.

Jesus Curses the Fig Tree
(Also Mark 11.12–14, 20–24)

[18] On his way back to the city, the next morning, Jesus was hungry. [19] He saw a fig tree by the side of the road and went to it, but found nothing on it except leaves. So he said to the tree, "You will never again bear fruit!" At once the fig tree dried up. [20] The disciples saw this and were astounded. "How did the fig tree dry up so quickly?" they asked. [21] "Remember this!" Jesus answered. "If you believe, and do not doubt, you will be able to do what I have done to this fig tree; not only this, you will even be able to say to this hill, 'Get up and throw yourself in the sea,' and it will. [22] If you believe, you will receive whatever you ask for in prayer."

The Question about Jesus' Authority
(Also Mark 11.27–33; Luke 20.1–8)

[23] Jesus came back to the Temple; and as he taught, the chief priests and the Jewish elders came to him and asked, "What right do you have to do these things? Who gave you this right?" [24] Jesus answered them: "I will ask you

just one question, and if you give me an answer I will tell you what right I have to do these things. 25 Where did John's right to baptize come from: from God or from man?" They started to argue among themselves: "What shall we say? If we answer, 'From God,' he will say to us, 'Why, then, did you not believe John?' 26 But if we say, 'From man,' we are afraid of what the people might do, because they are all convinced that John was a prophet." 27 So they answered Jesus, "We do not know." And he said to them, "Neither will I tell you, then, by what right I do these things."

The Parable of the Two Sons

28 "Now, what do you think? There was a man who had two sons. He went to the older one and said, 'Son, go work in the vineyard today.' 29 'I don't want to,' he answered, but later he changed his mind and went to the vineyard. 30 Then the father went to the other son and said the same thing. 'Yes, sir,' he answered, but he did not go. 31 Which one of the two did what his father wanted?" "The older one," they answered. "And I tell you this," Jesus said to them. "The tax collectors and the prostitutes are going into the Kingdom of God ahead of you. 32 For John the Baptist came to you showing you the right path to take, and you would not believe him; but the tax collectors and the prostitutes believed him. Even when you saw this you did not change your minds later on and believe him."

The Parable of the Tenants in the Vineyard
(Also Mark 12.1–12; Luke 20.9–19)

33 "Listen to another parable," Jesus said. "There was a landowner who planted a vineyard, put a fence around it, dug a hole for the winepress, and built a tower. Then he rented the vineyard to tenants and left home on a trip. 34 When the time came to harvest the grapes he sent his slaves to the tenants to receive his share. 35 The tenants grabbed his slaves, beat one, killed another, and stoned another. 36 Again the man sent other slaves, more than the first time, and the tenants treated them the same way. 37 Last of all he sent them his son. 'Surely they will respect my son,' he said. 38 But when the tenants saw the son they said to themselves, 'This is the owner's son. Come

on, let us kill him, and we will get his property!' ³⁹ So they grabbed him, threw him out of the vineyard, and killed him.

⁴⁰ "Now, when the owner of the vineyard comes, what will he do to those tenants?" Jesus asked. ⁴¹ "He will certainly kill those evil men," they answered, "and rent the vineyard out to other tenants, who will give him his share of the harvest at the right time." ⁴² Jesus said to them, "Haven't you ever read what the Scriptures say?

'The stone which the builders rejected as worthless
Turned out to be the most important stone.
This was done by the Lord,
How wonderful it is!'

⁴³ And so I tell you," added Jesus, "the Kingdom of God will be taken away from you and be given to a people who will produce the proper fruits. [⁴⁴ Whoever falls on this stone will be broken to pieces; and if the stone falls on someone it will crush him to dust.]"

⁴⁵ The chief priests and the Pharisees heard Jesus' parables and knew that he was talking about them, ⁴⁶ so they tried to arrest him. But they were afraid of the crowds, who considered Jesus to be a prophet.

The Parable of the Wedding Feast
(Also Luke 14.15–24)

22 Jesus again used parables in talking to the people. ² "The Kingdom of heaven is like a king who prepared a wedding feast for his son. ³ He sent his servants to tell the invited guests to come to the feast, but they did not want to come. ⁴ So he sent other servants with the message: 'Tell the guests, "My feast is ready now; my steers and prize calves have been butchered, and everything is ready. Come to the wedding feast!"' ⁵ But the invited guests paid no attention and went about their business: one went off to his farm, the other to his store, ⁶ while others grabbed the servants, beat them, and killed them. ⁷ The king was very angry, and sent his soldiers and killed those murderers, and burned down their city. ⁸ Then he called his servants. 'My wedding feast is ready,' he said, 'but the people I invited did not deserve it. ⁹ Now go to the main streets and invite to the feast as many people as you find.' ¹⁰ So the servants went out into the

streets and gathered all the people they could find, good and bad alike; and the wedding hall was filled with people.

11 "The king went in to look at the guests and he saw a man who was not wearing wedding clothes. 12 'Friend, how did you get in here without wedding clothes?' the king asked him. But the man said nothing. 13 Then the king told the servants, 'Tie him up hand and foot and throw him outside in the dark. There he will cry and gnash his teeth.' " 14 And Jesus concluded, "For many are invited, but few are chosen."

The Question about Paying Taxes
(Also Mark 12.13–17; Luke 20.20–26)

15 The Pharisees went off and made a plan to trap Jesus with questions. 16 Then they sent some of their disciples and some members of Herod's party to Jesus. "Teacher," they said, "we know that you are an honest man: you teach the truth about God's will for man, without worrying about what people think, because you pay no attention to what a man seems to be. 17 Tell us, then, what do you think? Is it against our Law to pay taxes to the Roman Emperor, or not?" 18 Jesus was aware of their evil plan, however, and so he said: "You impostors! Why are you trying to trap me? 19 Show me the coin to pay the tax!" They brought him the coin, 20 and he asked them, "Whose face and name are these?" 21 "The Emperor's," they answered. So Jesus said to them, "Well, then, pay to the Emperor what belongs to him, and pay to God what belongs to God." 22 When they heard this, they were filled with wonder; and they left him and went away.

The Question about Rising from Death
(Also Mark 12.18–27; Luke 20.27–40)

23 That same day some Sadducees came to Jesus. (They are the ones who say that people will not rise from death.) 24 "Teacher," they said, "Moses taught: 'If a man who has no children dies, his brother must marry the widow so they can have children for the dead man.' 25 Now, there were seven brothers who used to live here. The oldest got married, and died without having children, so he left his widow to his brother. 26 The same thing happened to the second brother, to the third, and finally to all seven.

[27] Last of all, the woman died. [28] Now, on the day when the dead are raised to life, whose wife will she be? All of them had married her!"

[29] Jesus answered them: "How wrong you are! It is because you don't know the Scriptures or God's power. [30] For when the dead are raised to life they will be like the angels in heaven, and men and women will not marry. [31] Now, about the dead being raised: haven't you ever read what God has told you? For he said, [32] 'I am the God of Abraham, the God of Isaac, and the God of Jacob.' This means that he is the God of the living, not of the dead." [33] When the crowds heard this they were amazed at his teaching.

The Great Commandment
(Also Mark 12.28–34; Luke 10.25–28)

[34] When the Pharisees heard that Jesus had silenced the Sadducees, they came together, [35] and one of them, a teacher of the Law, tried to trap him with a question. [36] "Teacher," he asked, "which is the greatest commandment in the Law?" [37] Jesus answered, " 'You must love the Lord your God with all your heart, and with all your soul, and with all your mind.' [38] This is the greatest and the most important commandment. [39] The second most important commandment is like it: 'You must love your neighbor as yourself.' [40] The whole Law of Moses and the teachings of the prophets depend on these two commandments."

The Question about the Messiah
(Also Mark 12.35–37; Luke 20.41–44)

[41] When the Pharisees gathered together, Jesus asked them: [42] "What do you think about the Messiah? Whose descendant is he?" "He is David's descendant," they answered. [43] "Why, then," Jesus asked, "did the Spirit inspire David to call him 'Lord'? For David said,

[44] 'The Lord said to my Lord:
Sit here at my right side,
Until I put your enemies under your feet.'

[45] If, then, David called him 'Lord,' how can the Messiah be David's descendant?" [46] No one was able to answer Jesus a single word, and from that day on no one dared ask him any more questions.

Jesus Warns against the Teachers of the Law and the Pharisees
(Also Mark 12.38–39; Luke 11.43, 46; 20.45–46)

23 Then Jesus spoke to the crowds and to his disciples. 2 "The teachers of the Law and the Pharisees," he said, "are the authorized interpreters of Moses' Law. 3 So you must obey and follow everything they tell you to do; do not, however, imitate their actions, because they do not practice what they preach. 4 They fix up heavy loads and tie them on men's backs, yet they aren't willing even to lift a finger to help them carry those loads. 5 They do everything just so people will see them. See how big are the containers with scripture verses on their foreheads and arms, and notice how long are the hems of their cloaks! 6 They love the best places at feasts and the reserved seats in the synagogues; 7 they love to be greeted with respect in the market places and have people call them 'Teacher.' 8 You must not be called 'Teacher,' for you are all brothers of one another and have only one Teacher. 9 And you must not call anyone here on earth 'Father,' for you have only the one Father in heaven. 10 Nor should you be called 'Leader,' because your one and only leader is the Messiah. 11 The greatest one among you must be your servant. 12 And whoever makes himself great will be humbled, and whoever humbles himself will be made great."

Jesus Condemns Their Hypocrisy
(Also Mark 12.40; Luke 11.39–42, 44, 52; 20.47)

13 "How terrible for you, teachers of the Law and Pharisees! Impostors! You lock the door to the Kingdom of heaven in men's faces, but you yourselves will not go in, and neither will you let people in who are trying to go in!

[14 "How terrible for you, teachers of the Law and Pharisees! Impostors! You take advantage of widows and rob them of their homes, and then make a show of saying long prayers! Because of this your punishment will be all the worse!]

15 "How terrible for you, teachers of the Law and Pharisees! Impostors! You sail the seas and cross whole countries to win one convert; and when you succeed, you make him twice as deserving of going to hell as you yourselves are!

[16] "How terrible for you, blind guides! You teach, 'If a man swears by the Temple he isn't bound by his vow; but if he swears by the gold in the Temple, he is bound.' [17] Blind fools! Which is more important, the gold or the Temple which makes the gold holy? [18] You also teach, 'If a man swears by the altar he isn't bound by his vow; but if he swears by the gift on the altar, he is bound.' [19] How blind you are! Which is more important, the gift or the altar which makes the gift holy? [20] So then, when a man swears by the altar he is swearing by it and by all the gifts on it; [21] and when a man swears by the Temple he is swearing by it and by God, the one who lives there; [22] and when a man swears by heaven he is swearing by God's throne and by him who sits on it.

[23] "How terrible for you, teachers of the Law and Pharisees! Impostors! You give to God one tenth even of the seasoning herbs, such as mint, dill, and cummin, but you neglect to obey the really important teachings of the Law, such as justice and mercy and honesty. These you should practice, without neglecting the others. [24] Blind guides! You strain a fly out of your drink, but swallow a camel!

[25] "How terrible for you, teachers of the Law and Pharisees! Impostors! You clean the outside of your cup and plate, while the inside is full of things you have gotten by violence and selfishness. [26] Blind Pharisee! Clean what is inside the cup first, and then the outside will be clean too!

[27] "How terrible for you, teachers of the Law and Pharisees! Impostors! You are like whitewashed tombs, which look fine on the outside, but are full of dead men's bones and rotten stuff on the inside. [28] In the same way, on the outside you appear to everybody as good, but inside you are full of lies and sins."

Jesus Predicts Their Punishment
(Also Luke 11.47–51)

[29] "How terrible for you, teachers of the Law and Pharisees! Impostors! You make fine tombs for the prophets, and decorate the monuments of those who lived good lives, [30] and you say, 'If we had lived long ago in the time of our ancestors, we would not have done what they did and killed the prophets.' [31] So you actually admit that you are the descendants of those who murdered the proph-

ets! ³² Go on, then, and finish up what your ancestors started! ³³ Snakes, and sons of snakes! How do you expect to escape from being condemned to hell? ³⁴ And so I tell you: I will send you prophets and wise men and teachers; you will kill some of them, nail others to the cross, and whip others in your synagogues, and chase them from town to town. ³⁵ As a result, the punishment for the murder of all innocent men will fall on you, from the murder of innocent Abel to the murder of Zechariah, Barachiah's son, whom you murdered between the Temple and the altar. ³⁶ I tell you indeed: the punishment for all these will fall upon the people of this day!"

Jesus' Love for Jerusalem
(Also Luke 13.34–35)

³⁷ "O Jerusalem, Jerusalem! You kill the prophets and stone the messengers God has sent you! How many times have I wanted to put my arms around all your people, just as a hen gathers her chicks under her wings, but you would not let me! ³⁸ Now your home will be completely forsaken. ³⁹ From now on you will never see me again, I tell you, until you say, 'God bless him who comes in the name of the Lord.' "

Jesus Speaks of the Destruction of the Temple
(Also Mark 13.1–2; Luke 21.5–6)

24 Jesus left and was going away from the Temple when his disciples came to him to show him the Temple's buildings. ² "Yes," he said, "you may well look at all these. I tell you this: not a single stone here will be left in its place; every one of them will be thrown down."

Troubles and Persecutions
(Also Mark 13.3–13; Luke 21.7–19)

³ As Jesus sat on the Mount of Olives, the disciples came to him in private. "Tell us when all this will be," they asked, "and what will happen to show that it is the time for your coming and the end of the age."

⁴ Jesus answered: "Watch out, and do not let anyone fool you. ⁵ Because many men will come in my name, saying, 'I am the Messiah!' and fool many people. ⁶ You are going to hear the noise of battles close by and the

news of battles far away; but, listen, do not be troubled. Such things must happen, but they do not mean that the end has come. ⁷ One country will fight another country, one kingdom will attack another kingdom. There will be famines and earthquakes everywhere. ⁸ All these things are like the first pains of childbirth.

⁹ "Then men will arrest you and hand you over to be punished, and you will be put to death. All mankind will hate you because of me. ¹⁰ Many will give up their faith at that time; they will betray each other and hate each other. ¹¹ Then many false prophets will appear and fool many people. ¹² Such will be the spread of evil that many people's love will grow cold. ¹³ But the person who holds out to the end will be saved. ¹⁴ And this Good News about the Kingdom will be preached through all the world, for a witness to all mankind — and then will come the end."

The Awful Horror
(Also Mark 13.14–23; Luke 21.20–24)

¹⁵ "You will see 'The Awful Horror,' of which the prophet Daniel spoke, standing in the holy place." (Note to the reader: understand what this means!) ¹⁶ "Then those who are in Judea must run away to the hills. ¹⁷ The man who is on the roof of his house must not take the time to go down and get his belongings from the house. ¹⁸ The man who is in the field must not go back to get his cloak. ¹⁹ How terrible it will be in those days for women who are pregnant, and for mothers who have little babies! ²⁰ Pray to God that you will not have to run away during the winter or on a Sabbath! ²¹ For the trouble at that time will be far more terrible than any there has ever been, from the beginning of the world to this very day. Nor will there ever be anything like it. ²² But God has already reduced the number of days; had he not done so, nobody would survive. For the sake of his chosen people, however, God will reduce the days.

²³ "Then, if anyone says to you, 'Look, here is the Messiah!' or 'There he is!' — do not believe him. ²⁴ For false Messiahs and false prophets will appear; they will perform great signs and wonders for the purpose of deceiving God's chosen people, if possible. ²⁵ Listen! I have told you this ahead of time.

²⁶ "Or, if people should tell you, 'Look, he is out in the

desert!' — don't go there; or if they say, 'Look, he is hiding here!' — don't believe it. [27] For the Son of Man will come like the lightning which flashes across the whole sky from the east to the west.

[28] "Wherever there is a dead body the vultures will gather."

The Coming of the Son of Man
(Also Mark 13.24–27; Luke 21.25–28)

[29] "Soon after the trouble of those days the sun will grow dark, the moon will no longer shine, the stars will fall from heaven, and the powers in space will be driven from their course. [30] Then the sign of the Son of Man will appear in the sky; then all the tribes of earth will weep, and they will see the Son of Man coming on the clouds of heaven with power and great glory. [31] The great trumpet will sound, and he will send out his angels to the four corners of the earth, and they will gather his chosen people from one end of the world to the other."

The Lesson of the Fig Tree
(Also Mark 13.28–31; Luke 21.29–33)

[32] "Let the fig tree teach you a lesson. When its branches become green and tender, and it starts putting out leaves, you know that summer is near. [33] In the same way, when you see all these things, you will know that the time is near, ready to begin. [34] Remember this! All these things will happen before the people now living have all died. [35] Heaven and earth will pass away; my words will never pass away."

No One Knows the Day and Hour
(Also Mark 13.32–37; Luke 17.26–30, 34–36)

[36] "No one knows, however, when that day and hour will come — neither the angels in heaven, nor the Son; the Father alone knows. [37] The coming of the Son of Man will be like what happened in the time of Noah. [38] Just as in the days before the Flood, people ate and drank, men and women married, up to the very day Noah went into the ark; [39] yet they did not know what was happening until the Flood came and swept them all away. That is how it will be when the Son of Man comes. [40] At that time two men will be working in the field: one will be taken away, the other will be left behind. [41] Two

women will be at the mill grinding meal: one will be taken away, the other will be left behind. ⁴²Watch out, then, because you do not know what day your Lord will come. ⁴³Remember this: if the man of the house knew the time when the thief would come, he would stay awake and not let the thief break into his house. ⁴⁴For this reason, then, you also must be always ready, because the Son of Man will come at an hour when you are not expecting him."

The Faithful or the Unfaithful Servant
(Also Luke 12.41–48)

⁴⁵"Who, then, is the faithful and wise servant? He is the one whom his master has placed in charge of the other servants, to give them their food at the proper time. ⁴⁶How happy is that servant if his master finds him doing this when he comes home! ⁴⁷Indeed, I tell you, the master will put that servant in charge of all his property. ⁴⁸But if he is a bad servant, he will tell himself, 'My master will not come back for a long time,' ⁴⁹and he will begin to beat his fellow servants, and eat and drink with drunkards. ⁵⁰Then that servant's master will come back some day when he does not expect him and at a time he does not know; ⁵¹the master will cut him to pieces, and make him share the fate of the impostors. There he will cry and gnash his teeth."

The Parable of the Ten Girls

25 "On that day the Kingdom of heaven will be like ten girls who took their oil lamps and went out to

meet the bridegroom. ² Five of them were foolish, and
the other five were wise. ³ The foolish ones took their
lamps but did not take any extra oil with them, ⁴ while
the wise ones took containers full of oil with their lamps.
⁵ The bridegroom was late in coming, so the girls began
to nod and fall asleep.

⁶ "It was already midnight when the cry rang out, 'Here
is the bridegroom! Come and meet him!' ⁷ The ten girls
woke up and trimmed their lamps. ⁸ Then the foolish
ones said to the wise ones, 'Let us have some of your oil,
because our lamps are going out.' ⁹ 'No, indeed,' the wise
ones answered back, 'there is not enough for you and us.
Go to the store and buy some for yourselves.' ¹⁰ So the
foolish girls went off to buy some oil, and while they were
gone the bridegroom arrived. The five girls who were
ready went in with him to the wedding feast, and the door
was closed.

¹¹ "Later the other girls arrived. 'Sir, sir! Let us in!'
they cried. ¹² 'But I really don't know you,' the bridegroom
answered." ¹³ And Jesus concluded, "Watch out, then,
because you do not know the day or hour."

The Parable of the Three Servants
(Also Luke 19.11–27)

¹⁴ "It will be like a man who was about to leave home
on a trip: he called his servants and put them in charge
of his property. ¹⁵ He gave to each one according to his
ability: to one he gave five thousand dollars, to the other
two thousand dollars, and to the other one thousand dollars. Then he left on his trip. ¹⁶ The servant who had received five thousand dollars went at once and invested his
money and earned another five thousand dollars. ¹⁷ In the
same way the servant who received two thousand dollars
earned another two thousand dollars. ¹⁸ But the servant
who received one thousand dollars went off, dug a hole
in the ground, and hid his master's money.

¹⁹ "After a long time the master of those servants came
back and settled accounts with them. ²⁰ The servant who
had received five thousand dollars came in and handed
over the other five thousand dollars. 'You gave me five
thousand dollars, sir,' he said. 'Look! Here are another
five thousand dollars that I have earned.' ²¹ 'Well done,
good and faithful servant!' said his master. 'You have been

faithful in managing small amounts, so I will put you in charge of large amounts. Come on in, and share my happiness!' [22] Then the servant who had been given two thousand dollars came in and said, 'You gave me two thousand dollars, sir. Look! Here are another two thousand dollars that I have earned.' [23] 'Well done, good and faithful servant!' said his master. 'You have been faithful in managing small amounts, so I will put you in charge of large amounts. Come on in and share my happiness!' [24] Then the servant who had received one thousand dollars came in and said: 'Sir, I know you are a hard man: you reap harvests where you did not plant, and gather crops where you did not scatter seed. [25] I was afraid, so I went off and hid your money in the ground. Look! Here is what belongs to you.' [26] 'You bad and lazy servant!' his master said. 'You knew, did you, that I reap harvests where I did not plant, and gather crops where I did not scatter seed? [27] Well, then, you should have deposited my money in the bank, and I would have received it all back with interest when I returned. [28] Now, take the money away from him and give it to the one who has ten thousand dollars. [29] For to every one who has, even more will be given, and he will have more than enough; but the one who has nothing, even the little he has will be taken away from him. [30] As for this useless servant — throw him outside in the darkness; there he will cry and gnash his teeth.' "

The Final Judgment

[31] "When the Son of Man comes as King, and all the angels with him, he will sit on his royal throne, [32] and all the earth's people will be gathered before him. Then he will divide them into two groups, just as a shepherd separates the sheep from the goats: [33] he will put the sheep at his right and the goats at his left. [34] Then the King will say to the people on his right: 'You who are blessed by my Father: come! Come and receive the kingdom which has been prepared for you ever since the creation of the world. [35] I was hungry and you fed me, thirsty and you gave me drink; I was a stranger and you received me in your homes, [36] naked and you clothed me; I was sick and you took care of me, in prison and you visited me.' [37] The righteous will then answer him: 'When, Lord, did we

ever see you hungry and feed you, or thirsty and give you drink? [38] When did we ever see you a stranger and welcome you in our homes, or naked and clothe you? [39] When did we ever see you sick or in prison, and visit you?' [40] The King will answer back, 'I tell you, indeed, whenever you did this for one of the least important of these brothers of mine, you did it for me!'

[41] "Then he will say to those on his left: 'Away from me, you who are under God's curse! Away to the eternal fire which has been prepared for the Devil and his angels! [42] I was hungry but you would not feed me, thirsty but you would not give me drink; [43] I was a stranger but you would not welcome me in your homes, naked but you would not clothe me; I was sick and in prison but you would not take care of me.' [44] Then they will answer him: 'When, Lord, did we ever see you hungry, or thirsty, or a stranger, or naked, or sick, or in prison, and we would not help you?' [45] The King will answer them back, 'I tell you, indeed, whenever you refused to help one of these least important ones, you refused to help me.' [46] These, then, will be sent off to eternal punishment; the righteous will go to eternal life."

The Plot against Jesus
(Also Mark 14.1–2; Luke 22.1–2; John 11.45–53)

26 When Jesus had finished teaching all these things, he said to his disciples, [2] "In two days, as you know, it will be the Feast of Passover, and the Son of Man will be handed over to be nailed to the cross."

[3] Then the chief priests and the Jewish elders met together in the palace of Caiaphas, the High Priest, [4] and made plans to arrest Jesus secretly and put him to death. [5] "We must not do it during the feast," they said, "or the people will riot."

Jesus Anointed at Bethany
(Also Mark 14.3–9; John 12.1–8)

[6] While Jesus was at the house of Simon the leper, in Bethany, [7] a woman came to him with an alabaster jar filled with an expensive perfume, which she poured on Jesus' head as he was eating. [8] The disciples saw this and became angry. "Why all this waste?" they asked. [9] "This perfume could have been sold for a large amount and the money given to the poor!" [10] Jesus was aware of what they

were saying and said to them: "Why are you bothering this woman? It is a fine and beautiful thing that she has done for me. [11] You will always have poor people with you, but I will not be with you always. [12] What she did was to pour this perfume on my body to get me ready for burial. [13] Now, remember this! Wherever this gospel is preached, all over the world, what she has done will be told in memory of her."

Judas Agrees to Betray Jesus
(Also Mark 14.10–11; Luke 22.3–6)

[14] Then one of the twelve disciples — the one named Judas Iscariot — went to the chief priests [15] and said, "What will you give me if I hand Jesus over to you?" So they counted out thirty silver coins and gave them to him. [16] From then on Judas was looking for a good chance to betray Jesus.

Jesus Eats the Passover Meal with His Disciples
(Also Mark 14.12–21; Luke 22.7–14, 21–23; John 13.21–30)

[17] On the first day of the Feast of Unleavened Bread the disciples came to Jesus and asked him, "Where do you want us to get the Passover supper ready for you?" [18] "Go to a certain man in the city," he said to them, "and tell him: 'The Teacher says, My hour has come; my disciples and I will celebrate the Passover at your house.'" [19] The disciples did as Jesus had told them and prepared the Passover supper.

[20] When it was evening Jesus and the twelve disciples sat down to eat. [21] During the meal Jesus said, "I tell you, one of you will betray me." [22] The disciples were very upset and began to ask him, one after the other, "Surely you don't mean me, Lord?" [23] Jesus answered: "One who dips his bread in the dish with me will betray me. [24] The Son of Man will die as the Scriptures say he will, but how terrible for that man who will betray the Son of Man! It would have been better for that man if he had never been born!" [25] Judas, the traitor, spoke up. "Surely you don't mean me, Teacher?" he asked. Jesus answered, "So you say."

The Lord's Supper
(Also Mark 14.22–26; Luke 22.15–20; 1 Cor. 11.23–25)

[26] While they were eating, Jesus took the bread, gave

a prayer of thanks, broke it, and gave to his disciples. "Take and eat it," he said; "this is my body." ²⁷ Then he took the cup, gave thanks to God, and gave it to them. "Drink it, all of you," he said; ²⁸ "for this is my blood, which seals God's covenant, my blood poured out for many for the forgiveness of sins. ²⁹ I tell you, I will never again drink this wine until the day I drink the new wine with you in my Father's Kingdom." ³⁰ Then they sang a hymn and went out to the Mount of Olives.

Jesus Predicts Peter's Denial
(Also Mark 14.27–31; Luke 22.31–34; John 13.36–38)

³¹ Then Jesus said to them: "This very night all of you will run away and leave me, for the scripture says, 'God will kill the shepherd and the sheep of the flock will be scattered.' ³² But after I am raised to life I will go to Galilee ahead of you." ³³ Peter spoke up and said to Jesus, "I will never leave you, even though all the rest do!" ³⁴ "Remember this!" Jesus said to Peter. "Before the rooster crows tonight you will say three times that you do not know me." ³⁵ Peter answered, "I will never say I do not know you, even if I have to die with you!" And all the disciples said the same thing.

Jesus Prays in Gethsemane
(Also Mark 14.32–42; Luke 22.39–46)

³⁶ Then Jesus went with his disciples to a place called Gethsemane, and he said to them, "Sit here while I go over there and pray." ³⁷ He took with him Peter, and Zebedee's two sons. Grief and anguish came over him, ³⁸ and he said to them, "The sorrow in my heart is so great

that it almost crushes me. Stay here and watch with me."
[39] He went a little farther on, threw himself face down to the ground, and prayed, "My Father, if it is possible, take this cup away from me! But not what I want, but what you want."

[40] Then he returned to the three disciples and found them asleep; and he said to Peter: "How is it that you three were not able to watch with me for one hour? [41] Keep watch, and pray, so you will not fall into temptation. The spirit is willing, but the flesh is weak."

[42] Again a second time Jesus went away and prayed, "My Father, if this cup cannot be taken away unless I drink it, your will be done." [43] He returned once more and found the disciples asleep; they could not keep their eyes open.

[44] Again Jesus left them, went away, and prayed the third time, saying the same words. [45] Then he returned to the disciples and said: "Are you still sleeping and resting? Look! The hour has come for the Son of Man to be handed over to the power of sinful men. [46] Rise, let us go. Look, here is the man who is betraying me!"

The Arrest of Jesus
(Also Mark 14.43–50; Luke 22.47–53; John 18.3–12)

[47] He was still talking when Judas, one of the twelve disciples, arrived. With him was a large crowd carrying swords and clubs, sent by the chief priests and the Jewish elders. [48] The traitor had given the crowd a signal: "The man I kiss is the one you want. Arrest him!" [49] When Judas arrived he went straight to Jesus and said, "Peace be with you, Teacher," and kissed him. [50] Jesus answered, "Be quick about it, friend!" Then they came up, arrested Jesus, and held him tight. [51] One of those who were with Jesus drew his sword and struck at the High Priest's slave, cutting off his ear. [52] Then Jesus said to him: "Put your sword back in its place, for all who take the sword will die by the sword. [53] Don't you know that I could call on my Father for help and at once he would send me more than twelve armies of angels? [54] But in that case, how could the Scriptures come true that say it must happen in this way?"

[55] Then Jesus spoke to the crowd: "Did you have to come with swords and clubs to capture me, as though

I were an outlaw? Every day I sat down and taught in the Temple, and you did not arrest me. [56] But all this has happened to make come true what the prophets wrote in the Scriptures."

Then all the disciples left him and ran away.

Jesus before the Council
(Also Mark 14.53–65; Luke 22.54–55, 63–71; John 18.13–14, 19–24)

[57] Those who had arrested Jesus took him to the house of Caiaphas, the High Priest, where the teachers of the Law and the elders had gathered together. [58] Peter followed him from a distance, as far as the courtyard of the High Priest's house. He went into the courtyard and sat down with the guards, to see how it would all come out. [59] The chief priests and the whole Council tried to find some false evidence against Jesus, to put him to death; [60] but they could not find any, even though many came up and told lies about him. Finally two men stepped forward [61] and said, "This man said, 'I am able to tear down God's Temple and three days later build it back up.' "

[62] The High Priest stood up and said to Jesus, "Have you no answer to give to this accusation against you?" [63] But Jesus kept quiet. Again the High Priest spoke to him: "In the name of the living God, I now put you on oath: tell us if you are the Messiah, the Son of God." [64] Jesus answered him: "So you say. But I tell all of you: from this time on you will see the Son of Man sitting at the right side of the Almighty, and coming on the clouds of heaven!" [65] At this the High Priest tore his clothes and said: "Blasphemy! We don't need any more witnesses! Right here you have heard his wicked words! [66] What do you think?" They answered, "He is guilty, and must die."

[67] Then they spat in his face and beat him; and those who slapped him [68] said, "Prophesy for us, Messiah! Tell us who hit you!"

Peter Denies Jesus
(Also Mark 14.66–72; Luke 22.56–62; John 18.15–18, 25–27)

[69] Peter was sitting outside in the courtyard, when one of the High Priest's servant girls came to him and said, "You, too, were with Jesus of Galilee." [70] But he denied it in front of them all. "I don't know what you are talking about," he answered, [71] and went on out to the en-

trance of the courtyard. Another servant girl saw him and said to the men there, "He was with Jesus of Nazareth." [72] Again Peter denied it, and answered, "I swear that I don't know that man!" [73] After a little while the men standing there came to Peter. "Of course you are one of them," they said. "After all, the way you speak gives you away!" [74] Then Peter made a vow: "May God punish me if I am not telling the truth! I do not know that man!" Just then a rooster crowed, [75] and Peter remembered what Jesus had told him, "Before the rooster crows, you will say three times that you do not know me." He went out and wept bitterly.

Jesus Taken to Pilate
(Also Mark 15.1; Luke 23.1–2; John 18.28–32)

27 Early in the morning all the chief priests and the Jewish elders made their plan against Jesus to put him to death. [2] They put him in chains, took him, and handed him over to Pilate, the Governor.

The Death of Judas
(Also Acts 1.18–19)

[3] When Judas, the traitor, saw that Jesus had been condemned, he repented and took back the thirty silver coins to the chief priests and the elders. [4] "I have sinned by betraying an innocent man to death!" he said. "What do we care about that?" they answered. "That is your business!" [5] Judas threw the money into the sanctuary and left them; then he went off and hanged himself.

[6] The chief priests picked up the money and said, "This is blood money, and it is against our Law to put it in the Temple treasury." [7] After reaching an agreement about it, they used the money to buy Potter's Field, as a cemetery for foreigners. [8] That is why that field is called "Field of Blood" to this very day.

[9] Then what the prophet Jeremiah had said came true: "They took the thirty silver coins (the amount the people of Israel had agreed to pay for him), [10] and used them to buy the potter's field, as the Lord commanded me."

Pilate Questions Jesus
(Also Mark 15.2–5; Luke 23.3–5; John 18.33–38)

[11] Jesus stood before the Governor, who questioned him. "Are you the king of the Jews?" he asked. "So you say,"

answered Jesus. [12] He said nothing, however, to the accusations of the chief priests and elders. [13] So Pilate said to him, "Don't you hear all these things they accuse you of?" [14] But Jesus refused to answer a single word, so that the Governor was greatly surprised.

Jesus Sentenced to Death
(Also Mark 15.6–15; Luke 23.13–25; John 18.39—19.16)

[15] At every Passover Feast the Governor was in the habit of setting free any prisoner the crowd asked for. [16] At that time there was a well-known prisoner named Jesus Barabbas. [17] So when the crowd gathered, Pilate asked them, "Which one do you want me to set free for you, Jesus Barabbas or Jesus called the Christ?" [18] He knew very well that they had handed Jesus over to him because they were jealous.

[19] While Pilate was sitting in the judgment hall, his wife sent him a message: "Have nothing to do with that innocent man, because in a dream last night I suffered much on account of him."

[20] The chief priests and the elders persuaded the crowds to ask Pilate to set Barabbas free and have Jesus put to death. [21] But the Governor asked them, "Which one of these two do you want me to set free for you?" "Barabbas!" they answered. [22] "What, then, shall I do with Jesus called the Christ?" Pilate asked them. "Nail him to the cross!" they all answered. [23] But Pilate asked, "What crime has he committed?" Then they started shouting at the top of their voices, "Nail him to the cross!" [24] When Pilate saw it was no use to go on, but that a riot might break out, he took some water, washed his hands in front of the crowd, and said, "I am not responsible for the death of this man! This is your doing!" [25] The whole crowd answered back, "Let the punishment for his death fall on us and on our children!" [26] Then Pilate set Barabbas free for them; he had Jesus whipped and handed him over to be nailed to the cross.

The Soldiers Make Fun of Jesus
(Also Mark 15.16–20; John 19.2–3)

[27] Then Pilate's soldiers took Jesus into the Governor's palace, and the whole company gathered around him. [28] They stripped off his clothes and put a scarlet robe on

him. [29] Then they made a crown out of thorny branches and put it on his head, and put a stick in his right hand; then they knelt before him and made fun of him. "Long live the King of the Jews!" they said. [30] They spat on him, and took the stick and hit him over the head. [31] When they finished making fun of him, they took the robe off and put his own clothes back on him, and then led him out to nail him to the cross.

Jesus Nailed to the Cross
(Also Mark 15.21–32; Luke 23.26–43; John 19.17–27)

[32] As they were going out they met a man from Cyrene named Simon, and they forced him to carry Jesus' cross. [33] They came to a place called Golgotha, which means "The Place of the Skull." [34] There they offered him wine to drink, mixed with gall; after tasting it, however, he would not drink it.

[35] They nailed him to the cross, and then divided his clothes among them by throwing dice. [36] After that they sat there and watched him. [37] Above his head they put the written notice of the accusation against him: "This is Jesus, the King of the Jews." [38] Then they nailed two bandits to crosses with Jesus, one on his right and the other on his left.

[39] People passing by shook their heads and threw insults at Jesus: [40] "You were going to tear down the Temple and build it up in three days! Save yourself, if you are God's Son! Come on down from the cross!" [41] In the same way the chief priests and the teachers of the Law and the elders made fun of him: [42] "He saved others but he cannot save himself! Isn't he the King of Israel? If he will come down off the cross now, we will believe in him! [43] He trusts in God and says he is God's Son. Well, then, let us see if God wants to save him now!" [44] Even the bandits who had been crucified with him insulted him in the same way.

The Death of Jesus
(Also Mark 15.33–41; Luke 23.44–49; John 19.28–30)

[45] At noon the whole country was covered with darkness, which lasted for three hours. [46] At about three o'clock Jesus cried out with a loud shout, *Eli, Eli, lema sabachthani?* which means, "My God, my God, why did

you abandon me?" [47] Some of the people standing there heard him and said, "He is calling for Elijah!" [48] One of them ran up at once, took a sponge, soaked it in wine, put it on the end of a stick, and tried to make him drink it. [49] But the others said, "Wait, let us see if Elijah is coming to save him!" [50] Jesus again gave a loud cry, and breathed his last.

[51] Then the curtain hanging in the Temple was torn in two, from top to bottom. The earth shook, the rocks split apart, [52] the graves broke open, and many of God's people who had died were raised to life. [53] They left the graves; and after Jesus rose from death they went into the Holy City, where many people saw them.

[54] When the army officer and the soldiers with him who were watching Jesus saw the earthquake and everything else that happened, they were terrified and said, "He really was the Son of God!" [55] There were many women there, looking on from a distance, who had followed Jesus from Galilee and helped him. [56] Among them were Mary Magdalene, Mary the mother of James and Joseph, and the mother of Zebedee's sons.

The Burial of Jesus
(Also Mark 15.42–47; Luke 23.50–56; John 19.38–42)

[57] When it was evening, a rich man from Arimathea arrived; his name was Joseph, and he also was a disciple

of Jesus. [58] He went into the presence of Pilate and asked for the body of Jesus. Pilate gave orders for the body to be given to Joseph. [59] So Joseph took it, wrapped it in a new linen sheet, [60] and placed it in his own grave, which he had just recently dug out of the rock. Then he rolled

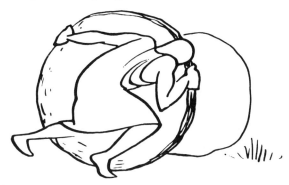

a large stone across the entrance to the grave and went away. [61] Mary Magdalene and the other Mary were sitting there, facing the grave.

The Guard at the Grave

[62] On the next day — that is, the day following Friday — the chief priests and the Pharisees met with Pilate [63] and said: "Sir, we remember that while that liar was still alive he said, 'I will be raised to life after three days.' [64] Give orders, then, for the grave to be safely guarded until the third day, so that his disciples will not be able to go and steal him, and then tell the people, 'He was raised from death.' This last lie would be even worse than the first one." [65] "Take a guard," Pilate told them; "go and guard the grave as best you can." [66] So they left, and made the grave secure by putting a seal on the stone and leaving the guard on watch.

The Resurrection
(Also Mark 16.1–10; Luke 24.1–12; John 20.1–10)

28 After the Sabbath, as Sunday morning was dawning, Mary Magdalene and the other Mary went to look at the grave. [2] Suddenly there was a strong earthquake; an angel of the Lord came down from heaven,

rolled the stone away, and sat on it. ³ His appearance was like lightning and his clothes were white as snow. ⁴ The guards were so afraid that they trembled and became like dead men.

⁵ The angel spoke to the women. "You must not be afraid," he said. "I know you are looking for Jesus who was nailed to the cross. ⁶ He is not here; he has risen, just as he said. Come here and see the place where he lay. ⁷ Quickly, now, go and tell his disciples: 'He has been raised from death, and now he is going to Galilee ahead of you; there you will see him!' Remember what I have

told you." ⁸ So they left the grave in a hurry, afraid and yet filled with joy, and ran to tell his disciples.

⁹ Suddenly Jesus met them and said, "Peace be with you." They came up to him, took hold of his feet, and worshiped him. ¹⁰ "Do not be afraid," Jesus said to them. "Go and tell my brothers to go to Galilee, and there they will see me."

The Report of the Guard

¹¹ While the women went on their way, some of the soldiers guarding the grave went back to the city and told the chief priests everything that had happened. ¹² The chief priests met with the elders and made their plan; they gave a large sum of money to the soldiers ¹³ and said: "You are to say that his disciples came during the night and stole his body while you were asleep. ¹⁴ And if the

Governor should hear of this, we will convince him and you will have nothing to worry about." ¹⁵ The guards took the money and did what they were told to do. To this very day that is the report spread around by the Jews.

Jesus Appears to His Disciples
(Also Mark 16.14–18; Luke 24.36–49; John 20.19–23; Acts 1.6–8)

¹⁶ The eleven disciples went to the hill in Galilee where Jesus had told them to go. ¹⁷ When they saw him they worshiped him, even though some of them doubted. ¹⁸ Jesus drew near and said to them: "I have been given all authority in heaven and on earth. ¹⁹ Go, then, to all peoples everywhere and make them my disciples: baptize them in the name of the Father and of the Son and of the Holy Spirit, ²⁰ and teach them to obey everything I have commanded you. And remember! I will be with you always, to the end of the age."

MARK

The Preaching of John the Baptist
(Also Matt. 3.1–12; Luke 3.1–18; John 1.19–28)

1 This is the Good News about Jesus Christ, the Son of God. 2 It began as the prophet Isaiah had written:

" 'Here is my messenger,' says God; 'I will
send him ahead of you to open the way
for you.'
3 Someone is shouting in the desert:
'Get the Lord's road ready for him,
Make a straight path for him to travel!' "

4 So John appeared in the desert, baptizing people and preaching his message. "Turn away from your sins and be baptized," he told the people, "and God will forgive your sins." 5 Everybody from the region of Judea and the city of Jerusalem went out to hear John. They confessed their sins and he baptized them in the Jordan river.

6 John wore clothes made of camel's hair, with a leather belt around his waist; he ate locusts and wild honey. 7 He announced to the people: "The man who will come after me is much greater than I am; I am not good enough even to bend down and untie his sandals. 8 I baptize you with water, but he will baptize you with the Holy Spirit."

The Baptism and Temptation of Jesus
(Also Matt. 3.13—4.11; Luke 3.21–22; 4.1–13)

9 Not long afterward Jesus came from Nazareth, in the region of Galilee, and John baptized him in the Jordan. 10 As soon as Jesus came up out of the water he saw heaven opening and the Spirit coming down on him like a dove. 11 And a voice came from heaven: "You are my own dear Son. I am well pleased with you."

12 At once the Spirit made him go into the desert. 13 He was there forty days, and Satan tempted him. Wild animals were there also, but angels came and helped him.

Jesus Calls Four Fishermen
(Also Matt. 4.12–22; Luke 4.14–15; 5.1–11)

14 After John had been put in prison, Jesus went to Galilee and preached the Good News from God. 15 "The

right time has come," he said, "and the Kingdom of God is near! Turn away from your sins and believe the Good News!"

¹⁶ As Jesus walked by Lake Galilee, he saw two fishermen, Simon and his brother Andrew, catching fish in the lake with a net. ¹⁷ Jesus said to them, "Come with me and I will teach you to catch men." ¹⁸ At once they left their nets and went with him.

¹⁹ He went a little farther on and saw two other brothers, James and John, the sons of Zebedee. They were in their boat getting their nets ready. ²⁰ As soon as Jesus saw them he called them; so they left their father Zebedee in the boat with the hired men and went with Jesus.

A Man with an Evil Spirit
(Also Luke 4.31–37)

²¹ They came to the town of Capernaum, and on the next Sabbath day Jesus went into the synagogue and began to teach. ²² The people who heard him were amazed at the way he taught. He wasn't like the teachers of the Law; instead, he taught with authority.

²³ Just then a man with an evil spirit in him came into the synagogue and screamed: ²⁴ "What do you want with us, Jesus of Nazareth? Are you here to destroy us? I know who you are: you are God's holy messenger!" ²⁵ Jesus commanded the spirit: "Be quiet, and come out of the man!" ²⁶ The evil spirit shook the man hard, gave a loud scream and came out of him. ²⁷ The people were all so amazed that they started saying to each other, "What is this? Some kind of new teaching? This man has authority

to give orders to the evil spirits, and they obey him!"
²⁸ And so the news about Jesus spread quickly everywhere
in the region of Galilee.

Jesus Heals Many People
(Also Matt. 8.14–17; Luke 4.38–41)

²⁹ They left the synagogue and went straight to the
home of Simon and Andrew; and James and John went
with them. ³⁰ Simon's mother-in-law was sick in bed with
a fever, and as soon as Jesus got there he was told about
her. ³¹ He went to her, took her by the hand and helped
her up. The fever left her and she began to wait on them.

³² When evening came, after the sun had set, people
brought to Jesus all the sick and those who had demons.
³³ All the people of the town gathered in front of the house.
³⁴ Jesus healed many who were sick with all kinds of diseases and drove out many demons. He would not let the
demons say anything, because they knew who he was.

Jesus Preaches in Galilee
(Also Luke 4.42–44)

³⁵ Very early the next morning, long before daylight,
Jesus got up and left the house. He went out of town to
a lonely place where he prayed. ³⁶ But Simon and his
companions went out searching for him; ³⁷ when they found
him they said, "Everyone is looking for you." ³⁸ But Jesus
answered: "We must go on to the other villages around
here. I have to preach in them also, because that is why I
came." ³⁹ So he traveled all over Galilee, preaching in the
synagogues and driving out demons.

Jesus Makes a Leper Clean
(Also Matt. 8.1–4; Luke 5.12–16)

⁴⁰ A leper came to Jesus, knelt down, and begged him for help. "If you want to," he said, "you can make me clean." ⁴¹Jesus was filled with pity and reached out and touched him. "I do want to," he answered. "Be clean!" ⁴² At once the leprosy left the man and he was clean. ⁴³ Then Jesus spoke harshly with him and sent him away at once. ⁴⁴ "Listen," he said, "don't tell this to anyone. But go straight to the priest and let him examine you; then offer the sacrifice that Moses ordered, to prove to everyone that you are now clean." ⁴⁵ But the man went away and began to spread the news everywhere. Indeed, he talked so much that Jesus could not go into a town publicly. Instead he stayed out in lonely places, and people came to him from everywhere.

Jesus Heals a Paralyzed Man
(Also Matt. 9.1–8; Luke 5.17–26)

2 A few days later Jesus came back to Capernaum, and the news spread that he was at home. ² So many people came together that there wasn't any room left, not even out in front of the door. Jesus was preaching the message to them ³ when some people came, bringing him a paralyzed man — four of them were carrying him. ⁴ Because of the crowd, however, they could not get him to Jesus. So they made a hole in the roof right above the place where Jesus was. When they had made an opening, they let the man down, lying on his mat. ⁵ Jesus saw how much faith they had, and said to the paralyzed man, "My son, your sins are forgiven." ⁶ Some teachers of the Law who were sitting there thought to themselves: ⁷ "How does he dare to talk against God like this? No man can forgive sins; only God can!" ⁸ At once Jesus knew their secret thoughts, so he said to them: "Why do you think such things? ⁹ Is it easier to say to this paralyzed man, 'Your sins are forgiven,' or to say, 'Get up, pick up your mat, and walk'? ¹⁰ I will prove to you, then, that the Son of Man has authority on earth to forgive sins." So he said to the paralyzed man, ¹¹ "I tell you, get up, pick up your mat, and go home!" ¹² While they all watched, the man got up, picked up his mat and hurried away. They were

all completely amazed and praised God, saying, "We have never seen anything like this!"

Jesus Calls Levi
(Also Matt. 9.9–13; Luke 5.27–32)

13 Jesus went back again to the shore of Lake Galilee. A crowd came to him and he started teaching them. 14 As he walked along he saw a tax collector, Levi the son of Alphaeus, sitting in his office. Jesus said to him, "Follow me." Levi got up and followed him.

15 Later on Jesus was having a meal in Levi's house. There were many tax collectors and outcasts who were following Jesus, and some of them joined him and his disciples at the table. 16 Some teachers of the Law, who were Pharisees, saw that Jesus was eating with these outcasts and tax collectors; so they asked his disciples, "Why does he eat with tax collectors and outcasts?" 17Jesus heard them and answered: "People who are well do not need a doctor, but only those who are sick. I have not come to call the respectable people, but the outcasts."

The Question about Fasting
(Also Matt. 9.14–17; Luke 5.33–39)

18 On one occasion the followers of John the Baptist and the Pharisees were fasting. Some people came to Jesus and asked him, "Why is it that the disciples of John the Baptist and the disciples of the Pharisees fast, but yours do not?" 19 Jesus answered: "Do you expect the guests at a wedding party to go without food? Of course not! As long as the bridegroom is with them they will not do that. 20 But the time will come when the bridegroom will be taken away from them; when that day comes then they will go without food.

21 "No one uses a piece of new cloth to patch up an old coat. If he does, the new patch will tear off some of the old cloth, making an even bigger hole. 22 Nor does anyone pour new wine into used wineskins. If he does, the wine will burst the skins, and both the wine and the skins will be ruined. No! Fresh skins for new wine!"

The Question about the Sabbath
(Also Matt. 12.1–8; Luke 6.1–5)

23 Jesus was walking through some wheat fields on a Sabbath day. As his disciples walked along with him, they began to pick the heads of wheat. 24 So the Pharisees said

to Jesus, "Look, it is against our Law for your disciples to do this on the Sabbath!" ²⁵ Jesus answered: "Have you never read what David did that time when he needed something to eat? He and his men were hungry, ²⁶ so he went into the house of God and ate the bread offered to God. This happened when Abiathar was the High Priest. According to our Law only the priests may eat this bread — but David ate it, and even gave it to his men." ²⁷ And Jesus said, "The Sabbath was made for the good of man; man was not made for the Sabbath. ²⁸ So the Son of Man is Lord even of the Sabbath."

The Man with a Crippled Hand
(*Also Matt. 12.9–14; Luke 6.6–11*)

3 Then Jesus went back to the synagogue, where there was a man who had a crippled hand. ² Some people were there who wanted to accuse Jesus of doing wrong; so they watched him very closely, to see whether he would cure anyone on the Sabbath. ³ Jesus said to the man with the crippled hand, "Come up here to the front." ⁴ Then he asked the people: "What does our Law allow us to do on the Sabbath? To help, or to harm? To save a man's life, or to destroy it?" But they did not say a thing. ⁵ Jesus was angry as he looked around at them, but at the same time he felt sorry for them, because they were so stubborn and wrong. Then he said to the man, "Stretch out your hand." He stretched it out and it became well again. ⁶ So the Pharisees left the meeting house and met at once with some members of Herod's party; and they made plans against Jesus to kill him.

A Crowd by the Lake

⁷ Jesus and his disciples went away to Lake Galilee, and a large crowd followed him. They came from Galilee, from Judea, ⁸ from Jerusalem, from the territory of Idumea, from the territory on the other side of the Jordan, and from the neighborhood of the cities of Tyre and Sidon. This large crowd came to Jesus because they heard of the things he was doing. ⁹ The crowd was so large that Jesus told his disciples to get a boat ready for him, so the people would not crush him. ¹⁰ He had healed many people, and all the sick kept pushing their way to him in order to touch him. ¹¹ And whenever the people

who had evil spirits in them saw him they would fall down before him and scream, "You are the Son of God!" [12] Jesus gave a stern command to the evil spirits not to tell who he was.

Jesus Chooses the Twelve Apostles
(Also Matt. 10.1–4; Luke 6.12–16)

[13] Then Jesus went up a hill and called to himself the men he wanted. They came to him [14] and he chose twelve, whom he named apostles. "I have chosen you to stay with me," he told them; "I will also send you out to preach, [15] and you will have authority to drive out demons." [16] These are the twelve he chose: Simon (Jesus gave him the name Peter); [17] James and his brother John, the sons of Zebedee (Jesus gave them the name Boanerges, which means "Men of Thunder"); [18] Andrew, Philip, Bartholomew, Matthew, Thomas, James the son of Alphaeus, Thaddaeus, Simon the patriot, [19] and Judas Iscariot, who became the traitor.

Jesus and Beelzebul
(*Also Matt. 12.22–32; Luke 11.14–23; 12.10*)

²⁰ Then Jesus went home. Again such a large crowd gathered that Jesus and his disciples had no time to eat. ²¹ When his family heard about this they set out to get him, because people were saying, "He's gone mad!"

²² Some teachers of the Law who had come from Jerusalem were saying, "He has Beelzebul in him!" Others said, "It is the chief of the demons who gives him the power to drive them out." ²³ So Jesus called the people to him and told them some parables: "How can Satan drive out Satan? ²⁴ If a country divides itself into groups that fight each other, that country will fall apart. ²⁵ If a family divides itself into groups that fight each other, that family will fall apart. ²⁶ So if Satan's kingdom divides into groups, it cannot last, but will fall apart and come to an end.

²⁷ "No one can break into a strong man's house and take away his belongings unless he ties up the strong man first; then he can plunder his house.

²⁸ "Remember this! Men can be forgiven all their sins and all the evil things they say, no matter how often they say them. ²⁹ But the person who says evil things against the Holy Spirit can never be forgiven, for he has committed an eternal sin." ³⁰ (Jesus said this because some had said, "He has an evil spirit in him.")

Jesus' Mother and Brothers
(*Also Matt. 12.46–50; Luke 8.19–21*)

³¹ Then Jesus' mother and brothers arrived. They stood outside the house and sent in a message, asking for him. ³² A crowd was sitting around Jesus, and they told him, "Look, your mother and brothers are outside, and they want you." ³³ Jesus answered, "Who is my mother? Who are my brothers?" ³⁴ He looked over the people sitting around him and said, "Look! Here are my mother and my brothers! ³⁵ For the person who does what God wants him to do is my brother, my sister, my mother."

The Parable of the Sower
(*Also Matt. 13.1–9; Luke 8.4–8*)

4 Again Jesus began to teach by Lake Galilee. The crowd that gathered around him was so large that he got into a boat and sat in it. The boat was out in the water,

while the crowd stood on the shore, at the water's edge. ² He used parables to teach them many things, and in his teaching said to them: ³ "Listen! There was a man who went out to sow. ⁴ As he scattered the seed in the field,

some of it fell along the path, and the birds came and ate it up. ⁵ Some of it fell on rocky ground, where there was little soil. The seeds soon sprouted, because the soil wasn't deep. ⁶ Then when the sun came up it burned the young plants, and because the roots had not grown deep enough the plants soon dried up. ⁷ Some of the seed fell among thorns, which grew up and choked the plants, and they didn't bear grain. ⁸ But some seeds fell in good soil, and the plants sprouted, grew, and bore grain: some had thirty grains, others sixty, and others one hundred." ⁹ And Jesus said, "Listen, then, if you have ears to hear with!"

The Purpose of the Parables
(Also Matt. 13.10–17; Luke 8.9–10)

¹⁰ When Jesus was alone, some of those who had heard him came to him with the twelve disciples and asked him to explain the parables. ¹¹ "You have been given the secret of the Kingdom of God," Jesus answered; "but the others, who are on the outside, hear all things by means of parables, ¹² so that,

'They may look and look, yet not see,
They may listen and listen, yet not under-
    stand,
For if they did, they might turn to God
And he would forgive them.' "

Jesus Explains the Parable of the Sower
(Also Matt. 13.18–23; Luke 8.11–15)

13 Then Jesus asked them: "Don't you understand this parable? How, then, will you ever understand any parable? 14 The sower sows God's message. 15 Sometimes the message falls along the path; these people hear it, but as soon as they hear it Satan comes and takes away the message sown in them. 16 Other people are like the seeds that fall on rocky ground. As soon as they hear the message they receive it gladly. 17 But it does not sink deep into them, and they don't last long. So when trouble or persecution comes because of the message, they give up at once. 18 Other people are like the seeds sown among the thorns. These are the ones who hear the message, 19 but the worries about this life, the love for riches, and all other kinds of desires crowd in and choke the message, and they don't bear fruit. 20 But other people are like the seeds sown in good soil. They hear the message, accept it, and bear fruit: some thirty, some sixty, and some one hundred."

A Lamp under a Bowl
(Also Luke 8.16–18)

21 And Jesus continued: "Does anyone ever bring in a lamp and put it under a bowl or under the bed? Doesn't he put it on the lamp-stand? 22 Whatever is hidden away will be brought out into the open, and whatever is covered up will be uncovered. 23 Listen, then, if you have ears to hear with!"

24 He also said to them: "Pay attention to what you hear! The same rules you use to judge others will be used by God to judge you — and with even greater severity. 25 The man who has something will be given more; the man who has nothing will have taken away from him even the little he has."

The Parable of the Growing Seed

²⁶ Jesus went on to say: "The Kingdom of God is like a man who scatters seed in his field. ²⁷ He sleeps at night, is up and about during the day, and all the while the seeds are sprouting and growing. Yet he does not know how it happens. ²⁸ The soil itself makes the plants grow and bear fruit: first the tender stalk appears, then the head, and finally the head full of grain. ²⁹ When the grain is ripe the man starts working with his sickle, for harvest time has come."

The Parable of the Mustard Seed
(Also Matt. 13.31–32, 34; Luke 13.18–19)

³⁰ "What shall we say the Kingdom of God is like?" asked Jesus. "What parable shall we use to explain it? ³¹ It is like a mustard seed, the smallest seed in the world. A man takes it and plants it in the ground; ³² after a while it grows up and becomes the biggest of all plants. It puts out such large branches that the birds come and make their nests in its shade."

³³ Jesus preached his message to the people, using many other parables like these; he told them as much as they could understand. ³⁴ He would not speak to them without using parables; but when he was alone with his disciples he would explain everything to them.

Jesus Calms a Storm
(Also Matt. 8.23–27; Luke 8.22–25)

³⁵ On the evening of that same day Jesus said to his disciples, "Let us go across to the other side of the lake." ³⁶ So they left the crowd; the disciples got into the boat that Jesus was already in, and took him with them. Other boats were there too. ³⁷ A very strong wind blew up and the waves began to spill over into the boat, so that it was about to fill with water. ³⁸ Jesus was in the back of the boat, sleeping with his head on a pillow. The disciples woke him up and said, "Teacher, don't you care that we are about to die?" ³⁹ Jesus got up and commanded the wind: "Be quiet!" and said to the waves, "Be still!" The wind died down, and there was a great calm. ⁴⁰ Then Jesus said to

them, "Why are you frightened? Are you still without faith?" [41] But they were terribly afraid, and began to say to each other, "Who is this man? Even the wind and the waves obey him!"

Jesus Heals a Man with Evil Spirits
(Also Matt. 8.28–34; Luke 8.26–39)

5 So they came to the other side of Lake Galilee, to the territory of the Gerasenes. [2] As soon as Jesus got out of the boat he was met by a man who came out of the burial caves. [3] This man had an evil spirit in him and lived among the graves. Nobody could keep him tied with chains any more; [4] many times his feet and hands had been tied, but every time he broke the chains, and smashed the irons on his feet. He was too strong for anyone to

stop him! ⁵ Day and night he wandered among the graves and through the hills, screaming and cutting himself with stones.

⁶ He was some distance away when he saw Jesus; so he ran, fell on his knees before him, ⁷ and screamed in a loud voice, "Jesus, Son of the Most High God! What do you want with me? For God's sake, I beg you, don't punish me!" ⁸ (He said this because Jesus was saying to him, "Evil spirit, come out of this man!") ⁹ So Jesus asked him, "What is your name?" The man answered, "My name is 'Mob' — there are so many of us!" ¹⁰ And he kept begging Jesus not to send the evil spirits out of that territory.

¹¹ A large herd of pigs was near by, feeding on the hillside. ¹² The spirits begged Jesus, "Send us to the pigs, and let us go into them." ¹³ So he let them. The evil spirits went out of the man and went into the pigs. The whole herd — about two thousand pigs in all — rushed down the side of the cliff into the lake and were drowned.

¹⁴ The men who had been taking care of the pigs ran away and spread the news in the town and among the farms. The people went out to see what had happened. ¹⁵ They came to Jesus and saw the man who used to have the mob of demons in him; he was sitting there, clothed and in his right mind — and they were all afraid. ¹⁶ Those who had seen it told the people what had happened to the man with the demons, and about the pigs. ¹⁷ So they began to ask Jesus to leave their territory.

¹⁸ As Jesus was getting into the boat, the man who had had the demons begged him, "Let me go with you!" ¹⁹ But Jesus would not let him. Instead he told him, "Go back home to your family and tell them how much the Lord has done for you, and how kind he has been to you!" ²⁰ So the man left and went all through the Ten Towns telling what Jesus had done for him; and all who heard it were filled with wonder.

Jairus' Daughter and the Woman
who Touched Jesus' Cloak
(Also Matt. 9.18–26; Luke 8.40–56)

²¹ Jesus went back across to the other side of the lake. There at the lakeside a large crowd gathered around him. ²² Jairus, an official of the local synagogue, came up, and when he saw Jesus he threw himself down at his feet

23 and begged him as hard as he could: "My little daughter is very sick. Please come and place your hands on her, so that she will get well and live!" 24 Then Jesus started off with him. So many people were going along with him that they were crowding him from every side.

25 There was a woman who had suffered terribly from severe bleeding for twelve years, 26 even though she had been treated by many doctors. She had spent all her money, but instead of getting better she got worse all the time. 27 She had heard about Jesus, so she came in the crowd behind him. 28 "If I touch just his clothes," she said to herself, "I shall get well." 29 She touched his cloak and her bleeding stopped at once; and she had the feeling inside herself that she was cured of her trouble. 30 At once Jesus felt that power had gone out of him. So he turned around in the crowd and said, "Who touched my clothes?" 31 His disciples answered, "You see that the people are crowding you; why do you ask who touched you?" 32 But Jesus kept looking around to see who had done it. 33 The woman realized what had happened to her; so she came, trembling with fear, and fell at his feet and told him the whole truth. 34 Jesus said to her, "My daughter, your faith has made you well. Go in peace, and be healed from your trouble."

35 While Jesus was saying this, some messengers came from Jairus' house and told him, "Your daughter has died. Why should you bother the Teacher any longer?" 36 Jesus paid no attention to what they said, but told him, "Don't be afraid, only believe." 37 Then he did not let anyone go on with him except Peter and James and his brother John. 38 They arrived at the official's house, where Jesus saw the confusion and heard all the loud crying and wailing. 39 He went in and said to them, "Why all this confusion? Why are you crying? The child is not dead — she is only sleeping!" 40 They all started making fun of him, so he put them all out, took the child's father and mother, and his three disciples, and went into the room where the child was lying. 41 He took her by the hand and said to her, *Talitha koum,* which means, "Little girl! Get up, I tell you!" 42 She got up at once and started walking around. (She was twelve years old.) When this happened they were completely amazed! 43But Jesus gave them strict orders not to tell anyone, and said, "Give her something to eat."

Jesus Rejected at Nazareth
(Also Matt. 13.53–58; Luke 4.16–30)

6 Jesus left that place and went back to his home town, followed by his disciples. [2] On the Sabbath day he began to teach in the synagogue. Many people were there, and when they heard him they were all amazed. "Where did he get all this?" they asked. "What wisdom is this that has been given him? How does he perform miracles? [3] Isn't he the carpenter, the son of Mary, and the brother of James, Joses, Judas, and Simon? Aren't his sisters living here?" And so they rejected him. [4] Jesus said to them: "A prophet is respected everywhere except in his home town, and by his relatives and his family." [5] He wasn't able to perform any miracles there, except that he placed his hands on a few sick people and healed them. [6] He was greatly surprised, because they did not have faith.

Jesus Sends out the Twelve Disciples
(Also Matt. 10.5–15; Luke 9.1–6)

Then Jesus went to all the villages around there, teaching the people. [7] He called the twelve disciples together and sent them out two by two. He gave them authority over the evil spirits [8] and ordered them: "Don't take anything with you on the trip except a walking stick; no bread, no beggar's bag, no money in your pockets. [9] Wear sandals, but don't wear an extra shirt." [10] He also told them: "When you come to a town, stay with the people who receive you in their home until you leave that place. [11] If you come to a place where people do not welcome you or will not listen to you, leave it and shake the dust off your feet. This will be a warning to them!" [12] So they went out and preached that people should turn away from their sins. [13] They drove out many demons, and poured oil on many sick people and healed them.

The Death of John the Baptist
(Also Matt. 14.1–12; Luke 9.7–9)

[14] Now King Herod heard about all this, because Jesus' reputation had spread everywhere. Some people said, "John the Baptist has come back to life! That is why these powers are at work in him." [15] Others, however, said, "He is Elijah." Others said, "He is a prophet, like one of the prophets of long ago."

¹⁶ When Herod heard it he said, "He is John the Baptist! I had his head cut off, but he has come back to life!" ¹⁷ Herod himself had ordered John's arrest, and had him tied up and put in prison. Herod did this because of Herodias, whom he had married, even though she was the wife of his brother Philip. ¹⁸ John the Baptist kept telling Herod: "It isn't right for you to marry your brother's wife!" ¹⁹ So Herodias held a grudge against John and wanted to kill him, but she couldn't because of Herod. ²⁰ Herod was afraid of John because he knew that John was a good and holy man, and so he kept him safe. He liked to listen to him, even though he became greatly disturbed every time he heard him.

²¹ Finally Herodias got her chance. It was on Herod's birthday, when he gave a feast for all the top government officials, the military chiefs, and the leading citizens of Galilee. ²² The daughter of Herodias came in and danced, and pleased Herod and his guests. So the king said to the girl, "What would you like to have? I will give you anything you want." ²³ With many vows he said to her, "I promise that I will give you anything you ask for, even as much as half my kingdom!" ²⁴ So the girl went out and asked her mother, "What shall I ask for?" "The head of John the Baptist," she answered. ²⁵ The girl hurried back at once to the king and demanded, "I want you to give me right now the head of John the Baptist on a plate!" ²⁶ This made the king very sad; but he could not refuse her, because of the vows he had made in front of all his guests. ²⁷ So he sent off a guard at once with orders to bring John's head. The guard left, went to the prison and cut John's head off; ²⁸ then he brought it on a plate and gave it to the girl, who gave it to her mother. ²⁹ When John's disciples heard about this, they came and got his body and laid it in a grave.

Jesus Feeds the Five Thousand
(Also Matt. 14.13–21; Luke 9.10–17; John 6.1–14)

³⁰ The apostles returned and met with Jesus, and told him all they had done and taught. ³¹ There were so many people coming and going that Jesus and his disciples didn't even have time to eat. So he said to them, "Let us go off by ourselves to some place where we will be alone and you

can rest a while." ³² So they started out in the boat by themselves to a lonely place.

³³ Many people, however, saw them leave and knew at once who they were; so they left from all the towns and ran ahead by land and got to the place ahead of Jesus and his disciples. ³⁴ When Jesus got out of the boat, he saw this large crowd, and his heart was filled with pity for them, because they looked like sheep without a shepherd. So he began to teach them many things. ³⁵ When it was getting late, his disciples came to him and said, "It is already very late, and this is a lonely place. ³⁶ Send the people away, and let them go to the nearby farms and villages and buy themselves something to eat." ³⁷ "You yourselves give them something to eat," Jesus answered. They asked, "Do you want us to go and buy two hundred dollars' worth of bread and feed them?" ³⁸ So Jesus asked them, "How much bread do you have? Go and see." When they found out they told him, "Five loaves, and two fish also."

³⁹ Jesus then told his disciples to make all the people divide into groups and sit down on the green grass. ⁴⁰ So the people sat down in rows, in groups of a hundred and groups of fifty. ⁴¹ Then Jesus took the five loaves and the two fish, looked up to heaven, and gave thanks to God. He broke the loaves and gave them to his disciples to distribute to the people. He also divided the two fish among them all. ⁴² Everyone ate and had enough. ⁴³ Then the disciples took up twelve baskets full of what was left of the bread and of the fish. ⁴⁴ The number of men who ate the bread was five thousand.

Jesus Walks on the Water
(Also Matt. 14.22–33; John 6.15–21)

⁴⁵ At once Jesus made his disciples get into the boat and go ahead of him to Bethsaida, on the other side of the lake, while he sent the crowd away. ⁴⁶ After saying good-bye to the disciples, he went away to a hill to pray. ⁴⁷ When evening came the boat was in the middle of the lake, while Jesus was alone on land. ⁴⁸ He saw that his disciples were having trouble rowing the boat, because the wind was blowing against them; so sometime between three and six o'clock in the morning he came to them, walking on the water. He was going to pass them by. ⁴⁹ But they saw him walking on the water. "It's a ghost!" they

thought, and screamed. ⁵⁰ For when they all saw him they were afraid. Jesus spoke to them at once, "Courage!" he said. "It is I. Don't be afraid!" ⁵¹ Then he got into the boat with them, and the wind died down. The disciples were completely amazed and utterly confused. ⁵² They had not understood what the loaves of bread meant; their minds could not grasp it.

Jesus Heals the Sick in Gennesaret
(Also Matt. 14.34–36)

⁵³ They crossed the lake and came to land at Gennesaret, where they tied up the boat. ⁵⁴ As they left the boat, people recognized Jesus at once. ⁵⁵ So they ran throughout the whole region and brought the sick lying on their mats to him, wherever they heard he was. ⁵⁶ And everywhere Jesus went, to villages, towns, or farms, people would take their sick to the market places and beg him to let the sick at least touch the edge of his cloak; and all who touched it were made well.

The Teaching of the Ancestors
(Also Matt. 15.1–9)

7 The Pharisees and some teachers of the Law who had come from Jerusalem gathered around Jesus. ² They noticed that some of his disciples were eating their food

with "unclean" hands — that is, they had not washed them in the way the Pharisees said people should.

³ For the Pharisees, as well as the rest of the Jews, follow the teaching they received from their ancestors: they don't eat unless they wash their hands in the proper way, ⁴ nor do they eat anything that comes from the market unless they wash it first. And they follow many other rules which they have received, such as the proper way to wash cups, pots, copper bowls, and beds.

⁵ So the Pharisees and the teachers of the Law asked Jesus, "Why is it that your disciples do not follow the teaching handed down by our ancestors, but instead eat with unclean hands?" ⁶ Jesus answered them: "How right Isaiah was when he prophesied about you! You are hypocrites, just as he wrote:

'These people, says God, honor me with their
words,
But their heart is really far away from me.
⁷ It is no use for them to worship me,
Because they teach man-made commandments as though they were God's rules!' "

⁸ And Jesus said, "You put aside the commandment of God and obey the teachings of men."

⁹ And Jesus continued: "You have a clever way of rejecting God's law in order to uphold your own teaching! ¹⁰ For Moses commanded, 'Honor your father and mother,' and, 'Anyone who says bad things about his father or mother must be put to death.' ¹¹ But you teach that if a person has something he could use to help his father or mother, but says, 'This is Corban' (which means, it belongs to God), ¹² he is excused from helping his father or mother. ¹³ In this way you disregard the word of God with the teaching you pass on to others. And there are many other things of this kind that you do."

The Things that Make a Person Unclean
(Also Matt. 15.10–20)

¹⁴ Then Jesus called the crowd to him once more and said to them: "Listen to me, all of you, and understand. ¹⁵ There is nothing that goes into a person from the outside which can make him unclean. Rather, it is what comes out of a person that makes him unclean. [¹⁶ Listen, then, if you have ears to hear with!]"

¹⁷ When he left the crowd and went into the house, his disciples asked him about this parable. ¹⁸ "You are no more intelligent than the others," Jesus said to them. "Don't you understand? Nothing that goes into a person from the outside can really make him unclean, ¹⁹ because it does not go into his heart but into his stomach and then goes on out of the body." (In saying this Jesus declared that all foods are fit to be eaten.) ²⁰And he went on to say: "It is what comes out of a person that makes him unclean. ²¹ For from the inside, from a man's heart, come the evil ideas which lead him to do immoral things, to rob, kill, ²² commit adultery, covet, and do all sorts of evil things; deceit, indecency, jealousy, slander, pride, and folly — ²³ all these evil things come from inside a man and make him unclean."

A Woman's Faith
(Also Matt. 15.21–28)

²⁴ Then Jesus left and went away to the territory near the city of Tyre. He went into a house, and did not want anyone to know he was there; but he could not stay hidden. ²⁵ A certain woman, whose daughter had an evil spirit in her, heard about Jesus and came to him at once and fell at his feet. ²⁶ The woman was a foreigner, born in Phoenicia of Syria. She begged Jesus to drive the demon out of her daughter. ²⁷ But Jesus answered, "Let us feed the children first; it isn't right to take the children's food and throw it to the dogs." ²⁸ "Sir," she answered, "even the dogs under the table eat the children's leftovers!" ²⁹ So Jesus said to her, "For such an answer you may go home; the demon has gone out of your daughter!" ³⁰ So she went back home and there found her child lying on the bed; the demon had indeed gone out of her.

Jesus Heals a Deaf and Dumb Man

³¹ Jesus then left the neighborhood of Tyre and went on through Sidon to Lake Galilee, going by way of the territory of the Ten Towns. ³² Some people brought him a man who was deaf and could hardly speak, and begged Jesus to place his hand on him. ³³ So Jesus took him off alone, away from the crowd, put his fingers in the man's ears, spat, and touched the man's tongue. ³⁴ Then Jesus looked up to heaven, gave a deep groan, and said to the man,

Ephphatha, which means, "Open up!" 35 At once the man's ears were opened, his tongue was set loose, and he began to talk without any trouble. 36 Then Jesus ordered them all not to speak of it to anyone; but the more he ordered them, the more they told it. 37 And all who heard were completely amazed. "How well he does everything!" they exclaimed. "He even makes the deaf to hear and the dumb to speak!"

Jesus Feeds the Four Thousand
(Also Matt. 15.32-39)

8 Not long afterward, another large crowd came together. When they had nothing left to eat, Jesus called the disciples to him and said: 2 "I feel sorry for these people, because they have been with me for three days and now have nothing to eat. 3 If I send them home without feeding them they will faint as they go, because some of them have come a long way." 4 His disciples asked him, "Where in this desert can anyone find enough food to feed all these people?" 5 "How much bread do you have?" Jesus asked. "Seven loaves," they answered.

6 He ordered the crowd to sit down on the ground. Then he took the seven loaves, gave thanks to God, broke them, and gave them to his disciples to distribute to the crowd; and the disciples did so. 7 They also had a few small fish. Jesus gave thanks for these and told the dis-

ciples to distribute them too. ⁸ Everybody ate and had
enough — there were about four thousand people. ⁹ Then
the disciples took up seven baskets full of pieces left over.
Jesus sent the people away, ¹⁰ and at once got into the boat
with his disciples and went to the district of Dalmanutha.

The Pharisees Ask for a Miracle
(Also Matt. 16.1–4)

¹¹ Some Pharisees came up and started to argue with
Jesus. They wanted to trap him, so they asked him to perform a miracle to show God's approval. ¹² Jesus gave a
deep groan and said: "Why do the people of this day ask
for a miracle? No, I tell you! No such proof will be given
this people!" ¹³ He left them, got back into the boat, and
started across to the other side of the lake.

The Yeast of the Pharisees and of Herod
(Also Matt. 16.5–12)

¹⁴ The disciples had forgotten to bring any extra bread,
and had only one loaf with them in the boat. ¹⁵ "Look
out," Jesus warned them, "and be on your guard against
the yeast of the Pharisees and the yeast of Herod." ¹⁶ They
started discussing among themselves: "He says this because we don't have any bread." ¹⁷ Jesus knew what they
were saying, so he asked them: "Why are you discussing
about not having any bread? Don't you know or understand yet? Are your minds so dull? ¹⁸ You have eyes —
can't you see? You have ears — can't you hear? Don't
you remember ¹⁹ when I broke the five loaves for the five
thousand people? How many baskets full of leftover pieces
did you take up?" "Twelve," they answered. ²⁰ "And when
I broke the seven loaves for the four thousand people,"
asked Jesus, "how many baskets full of leftover pieces did
you take up?" "Seven," they answered. ²¹ "And you still
don't understand?" he asked them.

Jesus Heals a Blind Man at Bethsaida

²² They came to Bethsaida, where some people brought
a blind man to Jesus and begged him to touch him.
²³ Jesus took the blind man by the hand and led him out
of the village. After spitting on the man's eyes, Jesus
placed his hands on him and asked him, "Can you see anything?" ²⁴ The man looked up and said, "I can see men,

but they look like trees walking around." ²⁵ Jesus again placed his hands on the man's eyes. This time the man looked hard, his eyesight came back, and he saw everything clearly. ²⁶ Jesus then sent him home with the order, "Don't go back into the village."

Peter's Declaration about Jesus
(Also Matt. 16.13–20; Luke 9.18–21)

²⁷ Then Jesus and his disciples went away to the villages of Caesarea Philippi. On the way he asked them, "Tell me, who do people say I am?" ²⁸ "Some say that you are John the Baptist," they answered; "others say that you are Elijah, while others say that you are one of the prophets." ²⁹ "What about you?" he asked them. "Who do you say I am?" Peter answered, "You are the Messiah." ³⁰ Then Jesus ordered them, "Do not tell anyone about me."

Jesus Speaks about His Suffering and Death
(Also Matt. 16.21–28; Luke 9.22–27)

³¹ Then Jesus began to teach his disciples: "The Son of Man must suffer much, and be rejected by the elders, the chief priests, and the teachers of the Law. He will be put to death, and after three days he will be raised to life." ³² He made this very clear to them. So Peter took him aside and began to rebuke him. ³³ But Jesus turned around, looked at his disciples, and rebuked Peter. "Get away from me, Satan," he said. "Your thoughts are men's thoughts, not God's!"

³⁴ Then Jesus called the crowd and his disciples to him. "If anyone wants to come with me," he told them, "he must forget himself, carry his cross, and follow me. ³⁵ For the man who wants to save his own life will lose it; but the man who loses his life for me and for the gospel will save

it. ³⁶ Does a man gain anything if he wins the whole world
but loses his life? Of course not! ³⁷ There is nothing a man
can give to regain his life. ³⁸ If, then, a man is ashamed
of me and of my teaching in this godless and wicked day,
then the Son of Man will be ashamed of him when he
comes in the glory of his Father with the holy angels."

9 And he went on to say: "Remember this! There are
some here who will not die until they have seen the
Kingdom of God come with power."

The Transfiguration
(Also Matt. 17.1–13; Luke 9.28–36)

² Six days later Jesus took Peter, James, and John with
him, and led them up a high mountain by themselves. As
they looked on, a change came over him, ³ and his clothes
became very shining and white; nobody in the world could
clean them as white. ⁴ Then the three disciples saw Elijah
and Moses, who were talking with Jesus. ⁵ Peter spoke up
and said to Jesus: "Teacher, it is a good thing that we are
here. We will make three tents, one for you, one for
Moses, and one for Elijah." ⁶ He and the others were so
frightened that he did not know what to say. ⁷ A cloud
appeared and covered them with its shadow, and a voice
came from the cloud: "This is my own dear Son — listen
to him!" ⁸ They took a quick look around but did not see
anybody else; only Jesus was with them.

⁹ As they came down the mountain Jesus ordered them:
"Don't tell anyone what you have seen, until the Son of
Man has been raised from death." ¹⁰ They obeyed his
order, but among themselves they started discussing the
matter: "What does this 'rising from death' mean?"
¹¹ And they asked Jesus: "Why do the teachers of the
Law say that Elijah has to come first?" ¹² His answer was:
"Elijah does indeed come first to get everything ready.
Yet why do the Scriptures say that the Son of Man will
suffer much and be rejected? ¹³ I tell you, however, that
Elijah has already come, and that people did to him all
they wanted to, just as the Scriptures say about him."

Jesus Heals a Boy with an Evil Spirit
(Also Matt. 17.14–21; Luke 9.37–43a)

¹⁴ When they joined the rest of the disciples, they saw
a large crowd there. Some teachers of the Law were ar-

guing with the disciples. ¹⁵ As soon as the people saw Jesus, they were greatly surprised and ran to him and greeted him. ¹⁶ Jesus asked his disciples, "What are you arguing with them about?" ¹⁷ A man in the crowd answered: "Teacher, I brought my son to you, because he has an evil spirit in him and cannot talk. ¹⁸ Whenever the spirit attacks him, it throws him to the ground, and he foams at the mouth, grits his teeth, and becomes stiff all over. I asked your disciples to drive the spirit out, but they could not." ¹⁹ Jesus said to them: "How unbelieving you people are! How long must I stay with you? How long do I have to put up with you? Bring the boy to me!" ²⁰ And they brought him to Jesus. As soon as the spirit saw Jesus, it threw the boy into a fit, so that he fell on the ground and rolled around, foaming at the mouth. ²¹ "How long has he been like this?" Jesus asked the father. "Ever since he was a child," he replied. ²² "Many times it has tried to kill him by throwing him in the fire and in the water. Have pity on us and help us, if you possibly can!" ²³ "Yes," said Jesus, "if *you* can! Everything is possible for the person who has faith." ²⁴ The father at once cried out, "I do have faith, but not enough. Help me!"

²⁵ Jesus noticed that the crowd was closing in on them, so he gave a command to the evil spirit. "Deaf and dumb spirit," he said, "I order you to come out of the boy and never go into him again!" ²⁶ With a scream the spirit threw the boy into a bad fit and came out. The boy looked like a corpse, so that everybody said, "He is dead!" ²⁷ But Jesus took the boy by the hand and helped him rise, and he stood up.

²⁸ After Jesus had gone indoors, his disciples asked him privately: "Why couldn't we drive the spirit out?" ²⁹ "Only prayer can drive this kind out," answered Jesus; "nothing else can."

Jesus Speaks again about His Death
(Also Matt. 17.22–23; Luke 9.43b–45)

³⁰ They left that place and went on through Galilee. Jesus did not want anyone to know where he was, ³¹ because he was teaching his disciples: "The Son of Man will be handed over to men who will kill him; three days later, however, he will be raised to life." ³² They did not under-

stand what this teaching meant, but they were afraid to ask him.

Who Is the Greatest?
(*Also Matt. 18.1–5; Luke 9.46–48*)

33 They came to Capernaum, and after going indoors Jesus asked his disciples: "What were you arguing about on the road?" 34 But they would not answer him, because on the road they had been arguing among themselves about who was the greatest. 35 Jesus sat down, called the twelve disciples and said to them: "Whoever wants to be first must place himself last of all and be the servant of all." 36 He took a child and made him stand in front of them. Then he put his arms around him and said to them, 37 "The person who in my name welcomes one of these children, welcomes me; and whoever welcomes me, welcomes not only me but also the one who sent me."

Who Is not against Us Is for Us
(*Also Luke 9.49–50*)

38 John said to him, "Teacher, we saw a man who was driving out demons in your name, and we told him to stop, because he doesn't belong to our group." 39 "Do not try to stop him," answered Jesus, "because no one who performs a miracle in my name will be able soon after to say bad things about me. 40 For whoever is not against us is for us. 41 Remember this! Anyone who gives you a drink of water because you belong to Christ will certainly receive his reward."

Temptations to Sin
(*Also Matt. 18.6–9; Luke 17.1–2*)

42 "As for these little ones who believe in me—it would be better for a man to have a large millstone tied around his neck and be thrown into the sea, than for him to cause one of them to turn away from me. 43 So if your hand makes you turn away, cut it off! It is better for you to enter life without a hand than to keep both hands and go off to hell, to the fire that never goes out. [44 There 'their worms never die, and the fire is never put out.'] 45 And if your foot makes you turn away, cut it off! It is better for you to enter life without a foot than to keep both feet and be thrown into hell. [46 There 'their worms never die, and

the fire is never put out.'] ⁴⁷ And if your eye makes you turn away, take it out! It is better for you to enter the Kingdom of God with only one eye, than to keep both eyes and be thrown into hell. ⁴⁸ There 'their worms never die, and the fire is never put out.'

⁴⁹ "For everyone will be salted with fire. ⁵⁰ Salt is good. But if it loses its saltness, how can you make it salty again? Have salt in yourselves, and be at peace with one another."

Jesus Teaches about Divorce
(Also Matt. 19.1–12; Luke 16.18)

10 Then Jesus left that place, went to the region of Judea, and crossed the Jordan river. Again crowds came flocking to him and he taught them, as he always did.

² Some Pharisees came to him and tried to trap him. "Tell us," they asked, "does our Law allow a man to divorce his wife?" ³ Jesus answered with a question: "What commandment did Moses give you?" ⁴ Their answer was, "Moses gave permission for a man to write a divorce notice and send his wife away." ⁵ Jesus said to them: "Moses wrote this commandment for you because you are so hard to teach. ⁶ But in the beginning, at the time of creation, it was said, 'God made them male and female. ⁷ And for this reason a man will leave his father and mother and unite with his wife, ⁸ and the two will become one.' So they are no longer two, but one. ⁹ Man must not separate, then, what God has joined together."

¹⁰ When they went back into the house, the disciples asked Jesus about this matter. ¹¹ He said to them: "The man who divorces his wife and marries another woman commits adultery against his wife; ¹² in the same way, the woman who divorces her husband and marries another man commits adultery."

Jesus Blesses Little Children
(Also Matt. 19.13–15; Luke 18.15–17)

¹³ Some people brought children to Jesus for him to touch them, but the disciples scolded those people. ¹⁴ When Jesus noticed it, he was angry and said to his disciples: "Let the children come to me! Do not stop them, because the Kingdom of God belongs to such as

these. ¹⁵ Remember this! Whoever does not receive the Kingdom of God like a child will never enter it." ¹⁶ Then he took the children in his arms, placed his hands on each of them, and blessed them.

The Rich Man
(Also Matt. 19.16–30; Luke 18.18–30)

¹⁷ As Jesus was starting again on his way, a man ran up, knelt before him, and asked him: "Good Teacher, what must I do to receive eternal life?" ¹⁸ "Why do you call me good?" Jesus asked him. "No one is good except God alone. ¹⁹ You know the commandments: 'Do not murder; do not commit adultery; do not steal; do not lie; do not cheat; honor your father and mother.'" ²⁰ "Teacher," the man said, "ever since I was young I have obeyed all these commandments." ²¹ With love Jesus looked straight at him and said: "You need only one thing. Go and sell all you have and give the money to the poor, and you will have riches in heaven; then come and follow me." ²² When the man heard this, gloom spread over his face and he went away sad, because he was very rich.

²³ Jesus looked around at his disciples and said to them, "How hard it will be for rich people to enter the Kingdom of God!" ²⁴ The disciples were shocked at these words, but Jesus went on to say: "My children, how hard it is to enter the Kingdom of God! ²⁵ It is much harder for a rich man to enter the Kingdom of God than for a camel to go through the eye of a needle." ²⁶ At this the disciples were completely amazed, and asked one another, "Who, then, can be saved?" ²⁷ Jesus looked straight at them and answered: "This is impossible for men, but not for God; everything is possible for God."

²⁸ Then Peter spoke up: "Look, we have left everything and followed you." ²⁹ "Yes," Jesus said to them, "and I tell you this: anyone who leaves home or brothers or sisters or mother or father or children or fields for me, and for the gospel, ³⁰ will receive much more in this present age. He will receive a hundred times more houses, brothers, sisters, mothers, children, and fields — and persecutions as well; and in the age to come he will receive eternal life. ³¹ But many who now are first will be last, and many who now are last will be first."

Jesus Speaks a Third Time about His Death
(Also Matt. 20.17–19; Luke 18.31–34)

32 They were now on the road going up to Jerusalem. Jesus was going ahead of the disciples, who were filled with alarm; the people who followed behind were afraid. Once again Jesus took the twelve disciples aside and spoke of the things that were going to happen to him. 33 "Look," Jesus told them, "we are going up to Jerusalem where the Son of Man will be handed over to the chief priests and the teachers of the Law. They will condemn him to death and then hand him over to the Gentiles. 34 These will make fun of him, spit on him, whip him, and kill him. And after three days he will be raised to life."

The Request of James and John
(Also Matt. 20.20–28)

35 Then James and John, the sons of Zebedee, came to Jesus. "Teacher," they said, "there is something we want you to do for us." 36 "What do you want me to do for you?" Jesus asked them. 37 They answered: "When you sit on your throne in the glorious Kingdom, we want you to let us sit with you, one at your right and one at your left." 38 Jesus said to them: "You don't know what you are asking for. Can you drink the cup that I must drink? Can you be baptized in the way I must be baptized?" 39 "We can," they answered. Jesus said to them: "You will indeed drink the cup I must drink and be baptized in the way I must be baptized. 40 But I do not have the right to choose who will sit at my right and my left. It is God who will give these places to those for whom he has prepared them."

41 When the other ten disciples heard about this they became angry with James and John. 42 So Jesus called them all together to him and said: "You know that the men who are considered rulers of the people have power over them, and the leaders rule over them. 43 This, however, is not the way it is among you. If one of you wants to be great, he must be the servant of the rest; 44 and if one of you wants to be first, he must be the slave of all. 45 For even the Son of Man did not come to be served; he came to serve and to give his life to redeem many people."

Jesus Heals Blind Bartimaeus
(Also Matt. 20.29–34; Luke 18.35–43)

46 They came to Jericho. As Jesus was leaving with his disciples and a large crowd, a blind man named Bartimaeus, the son of Timaeus, was sitting and begging by the road. 47 When he heard that it was Jesus of Nazareth, he

began to shout, "Jesus! Son of David! Have mercy on me!" 48 Many scolded him and told him to be quiet. But he shouted even more loudly, "Son of David, have mercy on me!" 49 Jesus stopped and said, "Call him." So they called the blind man. "Cheer up!" they said. "Get up, he is calling you." 50 He threw off his cloak, jumped up and came to Jesus. 51 "What do you want me to do for you?" Jesus asked him. "Teacher," the blind man answered, "I want to see again." 52 "Go," Jesus told him, "your faith has made you well." At once he was able to see, and followed Jesus on the road.

The Triumphant Entry into Jerusalem
(Also Matt. 21.1–11; Luke 19.28–40; John 12.12–19)

11 As they came near Jerusalem, at the towns of Bethphage and Bethany they came to the Mount of Olives. Jesus sent two of his disciples on ahead 2 with these instructions: "Go to the village there ahead of you. As

soon as you get there you will find a colt tied up that has never been ridden. Untie it and bring it here. ³ And if someone asks you, 'Why are you doing that?' tell him, 'The Master needs it and will send it back here at once.' " ⁴ So they went and found a colt out in the street, tied to the door of a house. As they were untying it, ⁵ some of the bystanders asked them, "What are you doing, untying that colt?" ⁶ They answered just as Jesus had told them, so the men let them go. ⁷ They brought the colt to Jesus, threw their cloaks over the animal, and Jesus got on. ⁸ Many people spread their cloaks on the road, while others cut branches in the fields and spread them on the road. ⁹ The people who were in front and those who followed behind began to shout, "Praise God! God bless him who comes in the name of the Lord! ¹⁰ God bless the coming kingdom of our father David! Praise be to God!"

¹¹ Jesus entered Jerusalem, went into the Temple, and looked around at everything. But since it was already late in the day, he went out to Bethany with the twelve disciples.

Jesus Curses the Fig Tree
(Also Matt. 21.18–19)

¹² The next day, as they were coming back from Bethany, Jesus was hungry. ¹³ He saw in the distance a fig tree covered with leaves, so he went to it to see if he could find any figs on it; but when he came to it he found only leaves, because it was not the right time for figs. ¹⁴ Jesus said to the fig tree: "No one shall ever eat figs from you again!" And his disciples heard him.

Jesus Goes to the Temple
(Also Matt. 21.12–17; Luke 19.45–48; John 2.13–22)

¹⁵ When they arrived in Jerusalem, Jesus went to the Temple and began to drive out all those who bought and sold in the Temple. He overturned the tables of the money-changers and the stools of those who sold pigeons, ¹⁶ and would not let anyone carry anything through the Temple courts. ¹⁷ He then taught the people, "It is written in the Scriptures that God said, 'My house will be called a house of prayer for all peoples.' But you have turned it into a hideout for thieves!"

¹⁸ The chief priests and the teachers of the Law heard

of this, so they began looking for some way to kill Jesus. They were afraid of him, because the whole crowd was amazed at his teaching.

¹⁹ When evening came, Jesus and his disciples left the city.

The Lesson from the Fig Tree
(*Also Matt. 21.20–22*)

²⁰ Early next morning, as they walked along the road, they saw the fig tree. It was dead all the way down to its roots. ²¹ Peter remembered what had happened and said to Jesus, "Look, Teacher, the fig tree you cursed has died!" ²² Jesus answered them: "Remember this! If you have faith in God, ²³ you can say to this hill, 'Get up and throw yourself in the sea.' If you do not doubt in your heart, but believe that what you say will happen, it will be done for you. ²⁴ For this reason I tell you: When you pray and ask for something, believe that you have received it,

and everything will be given you. ²⁵ And when you stand praying, forgive whatever you have against anyone, so that your Father in heaven will forgive your sins. [²⁶ If you do not forgive others, neither will your Father in heaven forgive your sins.]"

The Question about Jesus' Authority
(Also Matt. 21.23–27; Luke 20.1–8)

²⁷ So they came back to Jerusalem. As Jesus was walking in the Temple, the chief priests, the teachers of the Law, and the elders came to him ²⁸ and asked him: "What right do you have to do these things? Who gave you the right to do them?" ²⁹ Jesus answered them: "I will ask you just one question, and if you give me an answer I will tell you what right I have to do these things. ³⁰ Tell me, where did John's right to baptize come from: from God or from man?" ³¹ They started to argue among themselves: "What shall we say? If we answer, 'From God,' he will say, 'Why, then, did you not believe John?' ³² But if we say, 'From man . . .'" (They were afraid of the people, because everyone was convinced that John had been a prophet.) ³³ So their answer to Jesus was, "We don't know." And Jesus said to them, "Neither will I tell you, then, by what right I do these things."

The Parable of the Tenants in the Vineyard
(Also Matt. 21.33–46; Luke 20.9–19)

12 Then Jesus spoke to them in parables: "There was a man who planted a vineyard, put a fence around it, dug a hole for the winepress, and built a watch tower. Then he rented the vineyard to tenants and left home on a trip. ² When the time came for gathering the grapes, he sent a slave to the tenants to receive from them his share of the harvest. ³ The tenants grabbed the slave, beat him and sent him back without a thing. ⁴ Then the owner sent another slave; the tenants beat him over the head and treated him shamefully. ⁵ The owner sent another slave, and they killed him; and they treated many others the same way, beating some and killing others. ⁶ The only one left to send was the man's own dear son. Last of all, then, he sent his son to the tenants. 'I am sure they will respect my son,' he said. ⁷ But those tenants said to one another, 'This is the owner's son. Come on, let us

kill him, and the vineyard will be ours!' ⁸ So they took the son and killed him, and threw his body out of the vineyard.

⁹ "What, then, will the owner of the vineyard do?" asked Jesus. "He will come and kill those men and turn over the vineyard to other tenants. ¹⁰ Surely you have read this scripture?

'The stone which the builders rejected as worthless

Turned out to be the most important stone.

¹¹ This was done by the Lord,

How wonderful it is!' "

¹² The Jewish leaders tried to arrest Jesus, because they knew that he had told this parable against them. They were afraid of the crowd, however, so they left him and went away.

The Question about Paying Taxes
(Also Matt. 22.15–22; Luke 20.20–26)

¹³ Some Pharisees and some members of Herod's party were sent to Jesus to trap him with questions. ¹⁴ They came to him and said: "Teacher, we know that you are an honest man. You don't worry about what people think, because you pay no attention to what a man seems to be, but you teach the truth about God's will for man. Tell us, is it against our Law to pay taxes to the Roman Emperor? Should we pay them, or not?" ¹⁵ But Jesus saw through their trick and answered: "Why are you trying to trap me? Bring a silver coin, and let me see it." ¹⁶ They brought him one and he asked, "Whose face and name are these?" "The Emperor's," they answered. ¹⁷ So Jesus said, "Well, then, pay to the Emperor what belongs to him, and pay to God what belongs to God." And they were filled with wonder at him.

The Question about Rising from Death
(Also Matt. 22.23–33; Luke 20.27–40)

¹⁸ Some Sadducees came to Jesus. (They are the ones who say that people will not be raised from death.) ¹⁹ "Teacher," they said, "Moses wrote this law for us: 'If a man dies and leaves a wife, but no children, that man's brother must marry the widow so they can have children for the dead man.' ²⁰ Once there were seven brothers; the oldest got married, and died without having

children. ²¹ Then the next one married the widow, and he died without having children. The same thing happened to the third brother, ²² and then to the rest: all seven brothers married the woman and died without having children. Last of all, the woman died. ²³ Now, when all the dead are raised to life on the day of resurrection, whose wife will she be? All seven of them had married her!"

²⁴ Jesus answered them: "How wrong you are! And do you know why? It is because you don't know the Scriptures or God's power. ²⁵ For when the dead are raised to life they will be like the angels in heaven, and men and women will not marry. ²⁶ Now, about the dead being raised: haven't you ever read in the book of Moses the passage about the burning bush? For there it is written that God said to Moses, 'I am the God of Abraham, the God of Isaac, and the God of Jacob.' ²⁷ That means that he is the God of the living, not of the dead. You are completely wrong!"

The Great Commandment
(Also Matt. 22.34–40; Luke 10.25–28)

²⁸ A teacher of the Law was there who heard the discussion. He saw that Jesus had given the Sadducees a good answer, so he came to him with a question: "Which commandment is the most important of all?" ²⁹ "This is the most important one," said Jesus. " 'Hear, Israel! The Lord our God is the only Lord. ³⁰ You must love the Lord your God with all your heart, and with all your soul, and with all your mind, and with all your strength.' ³¹ The second most important commandment is this: 'You must love your neighbor as yourself.' There is no other commandment more important than these two." ³² The teacher of the Law said to Jesus: "Well done, Teacher! It is true, as you say, that only the Lord is God, and that there is no other god but he. ³³ And so man must love God with all his heart, and with all his mind, and with all his strength; and he must love his neighbor as himself. It is much better to obey these two commandments than to bring animals to be burned on the altar and offer other sacrifices to God." ³⁴ Jesus noticed how wise his answer was, and so he told him: "You are not far from the Kingdom of God." After this nobody dared to ask Jesus any more questions.

The Question about the Messiah
(*Also Matt. 22.41–46; Luke 20.41–44*)

35 As Jesus was teaching in the Temple he asked the question: "How can the teachers of the Law say that the Messiah will be the descendant of David? 36 The Holy Spirit inspired David to say:

'The Lord said to my Lord:

Sit here at my right side,

Until I put your enemies under your feet.'

37 David himself called him 'Lord': how, then, can the Messiah be David's descendant?"

Jesus Warns against the Teachers of the Law
(*Also Matt. 23.1–36; Luke 20.45–47*)

The large crowd heard Jesus gladly. 38 As he taught them he said: "Watch out for the teachers of the Law, who like to walk around in their long robes and be greeted with respect in the market place; 39 who choose the reserved seats in the synagogues and the best places at feasts. 40 They take advantage of widows and rob them of their homes, then make a show of saying long prayers! Their punishment will be all the worse!"

The Widow's Offering
(Also Luke 21.1–4)

⁴¹ As Jesus sat near the Temple treasury he watched the people as they dropped in their money. Many rich men dropped in much money; ⁴² then a poor widow came along and dropped in two little copper coins, worth about a penny. ⁴³ He called his disciples together and said to them: "I tell you that this poor widow put more in the offering box than all the others. ⁴⁴ For the others put in what they had to spare of their riches; but she, poor as she is, put in all she had — she gave all she had to live on."

Jesus Speaks of the Destruction of the Temple
(Also Matt. 24.1–2; Luke 21.5–6)

13 As Jesus was leaving the Temple, one of his disciples said, "Look, Teacher! What wonderful stones and buildings!" ² Jesus answered: "You see these great buildings? Not a single stone here will be left in its place; every one of them will be thrown down."

Troubles and Persecutions
(Also Matt. 24.3–14; Luke 21.7–19)

³ Jesus was sitting on the Mount of Olives, across from the Temple, when Peter, James, John, and Andrew came to him in private. ⁴ "Tell us when this will be," they said; "and tell us what is the sign that will show that it is the time for all these things to happen."

⁵ Jesus began to teach them: "Watch out, and don't let anyone fool you. ⁶ Many men will come in my name, saying, 'I am he!' and fool many people. ⁷ And don't be troubled when you hear the noise of battles close by and news of battles far away. Such things must happen, but they do not mean that the end has come. ⁸ One country will fight another country, one kingdom will attack another kingdom. There will be earthquakes everywhere, and there will be famines. These things are like the first pains of childbirth.

⁹ "You yourselves must watch out. For men will arrest you and take you to court. You will be beaten in the synagogues; you will stand before rulers and kings for my sake, to tell them the Good News. ¹⁰ The gospel must first be preached to all peoples. ¹¹ And when they arrest you and take you to court, do not worry ahead of

time about what you are going to say; when the time comes, say whatever is given to you then. For the words you speak will not be yours; they will come from the Holy Spirit. ¹² Men will hand over their own brothers to be put to death, and fathers will do the same to their children; children will turn against their parents and have them put to death. ¹³ Everyone will hate you because of me. But the person who holds out to the end will be saved."

The Awful Horror
(Also Matt. 24.15–28; Luke 21.20–24)

¹⁴ "You will see 'The Awful Horror' standing in the place where he should not be." (Note to the reader: understand what this means!) "Then those who are in Judea must run away to the hills. ¹⁵ The man who is on the roof of his house must not lose time by going down into the house to get anything to take with him. ¹⁶ The man who is in the field must not go back to the house for his cloak. ¹⁷ How terrible it will be in those days for women who are pregnant, and for mothers who have little babies! ¹⁸ Pray to God that these things will not happen in wintertime! ¹⁹ For the trouble of those days will be far worse than any the world has ever known, from the very beginning when God created the world until the present time. Nor will there ever again be anything like it. ²⁰ But the Lord has reduced the number of those days; if he had not, nobody would survive. For the sake of his chosen people, however, he has reduced those days.

²¹ "Then, if anyone says to you, 'Look, here is the Messiah!' or, 'Look, there he is!' — do not believe him. ²² For false Messiahs and false prophets will appear. They will perform signs and wonders for the purpose of deceiving God's chosen people, if possible. ²³ Be on your guard! I have told you everything ahead of time."

The Coming of the Son of Man
(Also Matt. 24.29–31; Luke 21.25–28)

²⁴ "In the days after that time of trouble the sun will grow dark, the moon will no longer shine, ²⁵ the stars will fall from heaven, and the powers in space will be driven from their course. ²⁶ Then the Son of Man will appear, coming in the clouds with great power and glory. ²⁷ He

will send out the angels to the four corners of the earth and gather God's chosen people from one end of the world to the other."

The Lesson of the Fig Tree
(Also Matt. 24.32–35; Luke 21.29–33)

²⁸ "Let the fig tree teach you a lesson. When its branches become green and tender, and it starts putting out leaves, you know that summer is near. ²⁹ In the same way, when you see these things happening, you will know that the time is near, ready to begin. ³⁰ Remember this! All these things will happen before the people now living have all died. ³¹ Heaven and earth will pass away; my words will never pass away."

No One Knows the Day or Hour
(Also Matt. 24.36–44)

³² "No one knows, however, when that day or hour will come — neither the angels in heaven, nor the Son; only the Father knows. ³³ Be on watch, be alert, for you do not know when the time will be. ³⁴ It will be like a man who goes away from home on a trip and leaves his servants in charge, each one with his own work to do; and he tells the doorkeeper to keep watch. ³⁵ Watch, then, because you do not know when the master of the house is coming — it might be in the evening, or at midnight, or before dawn, or at sunrise. ³⁶ If he comes suddenly, he must not find you asleep! ³⁷ What I say to you, then, I say to all: Watch!"

The Plot against Jesus
(Also Matt. 26.1–5; Luke 22.1–2; John 11.45–53)

14 It was now two days before the Feast of Passover and Unleavened Bread. The chief priests and teachers of the Law were looking for a way to arrest Jesus secretly and put him to death. ² "We must not do it during the feast," they said, "or the people might riot."

Jesus Anointed at Bethany
(Also Matt. 26.6–13; John 12.1–8)

³ Jesus was in the house of Simon the leper, in Bethany; while he was eating, a woman came in with an alabaster jar full of a very expensive perfume, made of

pure nard. She broke the jar and poured the perfume on Jesus' head. ⁴ Some of the people there became angry, and said to each other, "What was the use of wasting the perfume? ⁵ It could have been sold for more than three hundred dollars, and the money given to the poor!" And they criticized her harshly. ⁶ But Jesus said: "Leave her alone! Why are you bothering her? She has done a fine and beautiful thing for me. ⁷ You will always have poor people with you, and any time you want to you can help them. But I shall not be with you always. ⁸ She did what she could: she poured perfume on my body to prepare it for burial ahead of time. ⁹ Now, remember this! Wherever the gospel is preached, all over the world, what she has done will be told in memory of her."

Judas Agrees to Betray Jesus
(Also Matt. 26.14–16; Luke 22.3–6)

¹⁰ Then Judas Iscariot, one of the twelve disciples, went off to the chief priests in order to hand Jesus over to them. ¹¹ They were greatly pleased to hear what he had to say, and promised to give him money. So Judas started looking for a good chance to betray Jesus.

Jesus Eats the Passover Meal with His Disciples
(Also Matt. 26.17–25; Luke 22.7–14, 21–23; John 13.21–30)

¹² On the first day of the Feast of Unleavened Bread, the day the lambs for the Passover meal were killed, Jesus' disciples asked him: "Where do you want us to go and get your Passover supper ready?" ¹³ Then Jesus sent two of them out with these instructions: "Go into the city, and a man carrying a jar of water will meet you. ¹⁴ Follow him to the house he enters, and say to the owner of the house: 'The Teacher says, Where is my room where my disciples and I shall eat the Passover supper?' ¹⁵ Then he will show you a large upstairs room, fixed up and furnished, where you will get things ready for us." ¹⁶ The disciples left, went to the city, and found everything just as Jesus had told them; and they prepared the Passover supper.

¹⁷ When it was evening, Jesus came with the twelve disciples. ¹⁸ While they were at the table eating, Jesus said: "I tell you this: one of you will betray me — one who is eating with me." ¹⁹ The disciples were upset and

began to ask him, one after the other, "Surely you don't mean me, do you?" [20] Jesus answered: "It will be one of you twelve, one who dips his bread in the dish with me. [21] The Son of Man will die as the Scriptures say he will; but how terrible for that man who will betray the Son of Man! It would have been better for that man if he had never been born!"

The Lord's Supper
(Also Matt. 26.26–30; Luke 22.15–20; 1 Cor. 11.23–25)

[22] While they were eating, Jesus took the bread, gave a prayer of thanks, broke it, and gave it to his disciples. "Take it," he said, "this is my body." [23] Then he took the cup, gave thanks to God, and handed it to them; and they all drank from it. [24] Jesus said: "This is my blood which is poured out for many, my blood which seals God's covenant. [25] I tell you, I will never again drink this wine until the day I drink the new wine in the Kingdom of God." [26] Then they sang a hymn and went out to the Mount of Olives.

Jesus Predicts Peter's Denial
(Also Matt. 26.31–35; Luke 22.31–34; John 13.36–38)

[27] Jesus said to them: "All of you will run away and leave me, for the scripture says, 'God will kill the shepherd and the sheep will all be scattered.' [28] But after I am raised to life I will go to Galilee ahead of you." [29] Peter answered, "I will never leave you, even though all the

rest do!" ³⁰ "Remember this!" Jesus said to Peter. "Before the rooster crows two times tonight, you will say three times that you do not know me." ³¹ Peter answered even more strongly: "I will never say I do not know you, even if I have to die with you!" And all the disciples said the same thing.

Jesus Prays in Gethsemane
(Also Matt. 26.36–46; Luke 22.39–46)

³² They came to a place called Gethsemane, and Jesus said to his disciples, "Sit here while I pray." ³³ Then he took Peter, James, and John with him. Distress and anguish came over him, ³⁴ and he said to them: "The sorrow in my heart is so great that it almost crushes me. Stay here and watch." ³⁵ He went a little farther on, threw himself on the ground and prayed that, if possible, he might not have to go through the hour of suffering. ³⁶ "Father!" he prayed, "my Father! All things are possible for you. Take this cup away from me. But not what I want, but what you want."

³⁷ Then he returned and found the three disciples asleep, and said to Peter, "Simon, are you asleep? Weren't you able to stay awake for one hour?" ³⁸ And he said to them, "Keep watch, and pray, so you will not fall into temptation. The spirit is willing, but the flesh is weak."

³⁹ He went away once more and prayed, saying the same words. ⁴⁰ Then he came back to the disciples and found

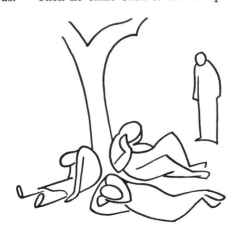

them asleep; they could not keep their eyes open. And they did not know what to say to him.

⁴¹ When he came back the third time, he said to them: "Are you still sleeping and resting? Enough! The hour has come! Look, the Son of Man is now handed over to the power of sinful men. ⁴² Rise, let us go. Look, here is the man who is betraying me!"

The Arrest of Jesus
(Also Matt. 26.47–56; Luke 22.47–53; John 18.3–12)

⁴³ He was still talking when Judas, one of the twelve disciples, arrived. A crowd carrying swords and clubs was with him, sent by the chief priests, the teachers of the Law, and the elders. ⁴⁴ The traitor had given the crowd a signal: "The man I kiss is the one you want. Arrest him and take him away under guard."

⁴⁵ As soon as Judas arrived he went up to Jesus and said, "Teacher!" and kissed him. ⁴⁶ So they arrested Jesus and held him tight. ⁴⁷ But one of those standing by drew his sword and struck at the High Priest's slave, cutting off his ear. ⁴⁸ Then Jesus spoke up and said to them: "Did you have to come with swords and clubs to capture me, as though I were an outlaw? ⁴⁹ Day after day I was with you teaching in the Temple, and you did not arrest me. But the Scriptures must come true." ⁵⁰ Then all the disciples left him and ran away.

⁵¹ A certain young man, dressed only in a linen cloth,

was following Jesus. They tried to arrest him, ⁵² but he ran away naked, leaving the linen cloth behind.

Jesus before the Council
(Also Matt. 26.57–68; Luke 22.54–55, 63–71; John 18.13–14, 19–24)

⁵³ Then they took Jesus to the High Priest's house, where all the chief priests, the elders, and the teachers of the Law were gathering. ⁵⁴ Peter followed far behind and went into the courtyard of the High Priest's house. There he sat down with the guards, keeping himself warm by the fire. ⁵⁵ The chief priests and the whole Council tried to find some evidence against Jesus, in order to put him to death, but they could not find any. ⁵⁶ Many witnesses told lies against Jesus, but their stories did not agree.

⁵⁷ Then some men stood up and told this lie against Jesus: ⁵⁸ "We heard him say, 'I will tear down this Temple which men made, and after three days I will build one that is not made by men.'" ⁵⁹ Not even they, however, could make their stories agree.

⁶⁰ The High Priest stood up in front of them all and questioned Jesus: "Have you no answer to the accusation they bring against you?" ⁶¹ But Jesus kept quiet and would not say a word. Again the High Priest questioned him: "Are you the Messiah, the Son of the Blessed God?" ⁶² "I am," answered Jesus, "and you will all see the Son of Man seated at the right side of the Almighty, and coming with the clouds of heaven!" ⁶³ The High Priest tore his robes and said, "We don't need any more witnesses! ⁶⁴ You heard his wicked words. What is your decision?" They all voted against him: he was guilty and should be put to death.

⁶⁵ Some of them began to spit on Jesus, and they blindfolded him and hit him. "Guess who hit you!" they said. And the guards took him and slapped him.

Peter Denies Jesus
(Also Matt. 26.69–75; Luke 22.56–62; John 18.15–18, 25–27)

⁶⁶ Peter was still down in the courtyard when one of the High Priest's servant girls came by. ⁶⁷ When she saw Peter warming himself, she looked straight at him and said, "You, too, were with Jesus of Nazareth." ⁶⁸ But he denied it. "I don't know . . . I don't understand what you are talking about," he answered, and went out into the passage-

way. Just then a rooster crowed. [69] The servant girl saw him there and began to repeat to the bystanders, "He is one of them!" [70] But Peter denied it again. A little while later the bystanders accused Peter again: "You can't deny

that you are one of them, because you, too, are from Galilee." [71] Then Peter made a vow: "May God punish me if I am not telling the truth! I do not know the man you are talking about!" [72] Just then a rooster crowed a second time, and Peter remembered how Jesus had said to him, "Before the rooster crows two times you will say three times that you do not know me." And he broke down and cried.

Jesus before Pilate
(Also Matt. 27.1–2, 11–14; Luke 23.1–5; John 18.28–38)

15 Early in the morning the chief priests met hurriedly with the elders, the teachers of the Law, and the whole Council, and made their plans. They put Jesus in chains, took him away and handed him over to Pilate. [2] Pilate questioned him: "Are you the king of the Jews?" Jesus answered: "So you say." [3] The chief priests accused Jesus of many things, [4] so Pilate questioned him again: "Aren't you going to answer? See how many things they accuse you of!" [5] Again Jesus refused to say a word, and Pilate was filled with surprise.

Jesus Sentenced to Death
(Also Matt. 27.15–26; Luke 23.13–25; John 18.39—19.16)

⁶ At every Passover Feast Pilate would set free any prisoner the people asked for. ⁷ At that time a man named Barabbas was in prison with the rebels who had committed murder in the riot. ⁸ When the crowd gathered and began to ask Pilate to do them the usual favor, ⁹ Pilate asked them: "Do you want me to set free for you the king of the Jews?" ¹⁰ He knew very well that the chief priests had handed Jesus over to him because they were jealous. ¹¹ But the chief priests stirred up the crowd to ask, instead, for Pilate to set Barabbas free for them. ¹² Pilate spoke again to the crowd: "What then, do you want me to do with the one you call the king of the Jews!" ¹³ They shouted back, "Nail him to the cross!" ¹⁴ "But what crime has he committed?" Pilate asked. They shouted all the louder, "Nail him to the cross!" ¹⁵ Pilate wanted to please the crowd, so he set Barabbas free for them. Then he had Jesus whipped and handed him over to be nailed to the cross.

The Soldiers Make Fun of Jesus
(Also Matt. 27.27–31; John 19.2–3)

¹⁶ The soldiers took Jesus inside the courtyard (that is, of the Governor's palace) and called together the rest of the company. ¹⁷ They put a purple robe on Jesus, made a crown out of thorny branches, and put it on his head. ¹⁸ Then they began to salute him: "Long live the King of the Jews!" ¹⁹ And they beat him over the head with a stick, spat on him, fell on their knees and bowed down to him. ²⁰ When they had finished making fun of him, they took off the purple robe and put his own clothes back on him. Then they led him out to nail him to the cross.

Jesus Nailed to the Cross
(Also Matt. 27.32–44; Luke 23.26–43; John 19.17–27)

²¹ On the way they met a man named Simon, who was coming into the city from the country, and they forced him to carry Jesus' cross. (This was Simon from Cyrene, the father of Alexander and Rufus.) ²² They brought Jesus to a place called Golgotha, which means "The Place of the Skull." ²³ There they tried to give him wine mixed with a drug called myrrh, but Jesus would not drink it. ²⁴ So they nailed him to the cross and divided his clothes among themselves, throwing dice to see who would get which piece of clothing. ²⁵ It was nine o'clock in the morning when they nailed him to the cross. ²⁶ The notice of the accusa-

tion against him was written, "The King of the Jews."
²⁷ They also nailed two bandits to crosses with Jesus, one
on his right and the other on his left. ²⁸ [In this way the
scripture came true which says: "He was included with
the criminals."]

²⁹ People passing by shook their heads and threw insults at Jesus: "Aha! You were going to tear down the
Temple and build it up in three days! ³⁰ Now come down
from the cross and save yourself!" ³¹ In the same way the
chief priests and the teachers of the Law made fun of
Jesus, saying to each other: "He saved others, but he
cannot save himself! ³² Let us see the Messiah, the king
of Israel, come down from the cross now, and we will
believe in him!" And the two who were crucified with
Jesus insulted him also.

The Death of Jesus
(Also Matt. 27.45–56; Luke 23.44–49; John 19.28–30)

³³ At noon the whole country was covered with darkness,
which lasted for three hours. ³⁴ At three o'clock Jesus
cried out with a loud shout, *Eloi, Eloi, lema sabachthani?*
which means, "My God, my God, why did you abandon
me?" ³⁵ Some of the people who were there heard him
and said, "Listen, he is calling for Elijah!" ³⁶ One of them
ran up with a sponge, soaked it in wine, and put it on the
end of a stick. Then he held it up to Jesus' lips and said,
"Wait! Let us see if Elijah is coming to bring him down
from the cross!" ³⁷ With a loud cry Jesus died.

³⁸ The curtain hanging in the Temple was torn in two,
from top to bottom. ³⁹ The army officer, who was standing
there in front of the cross, saw how Jesus had cried out
and died. "This man was really the Son of God!" he said.
⁴⁰ Some women were there, looking on from a distance.
Among them were Salome, Mary Magdalene, and Mary
the mother of the younger James and of Joses. ⁴¹ They
had followed Jesus while he was in Galilee and helped him.
Many other women were there also, who had come to
Jerusalem with him.

The Burial of Jesus
(Also Matt. 27.57–61; Luke 23.50–56; John 19.38–42)

⁴² It was getting on toward evening when Joseph of
Arimathea arrived. ⁴³ He was a respected member of the

Council, who looked for the coming of the Kingdom of God. It was Preparation day (that is, the day before the Sabbath); so Joseph went in bravely to the presence of Pilate and asked him for the body of Jesus. ⁴⁴ Pilate was surprised to hear that Jesus was already dead. He called the army officer and asked him if Jesus had been dead a long time. ⁴⁵ After hearing the officer's report, Pilate told Joseph he could have the body. ⁴⁶ Joseph bought a linen sheet, took the body down, wrapped it in the sheet and placed it in a grave which had been dug out of rock. Then he rolled a large stone across the entrance to the grave. ⁴⁷ Mary Magdalene and Mary the mother of Joses were watching, and saw where Jesus was laid.

The Resurrection
(*Also Matt. 28.1–8; Luke 24.1–12; John 20.1–10*)

16 After the Sabbath day was over, Mary Magdalene, Mary the mother of James, and Salome bought spices to go and anoint the body of Jesus. ² Very early on Sunday morning, at sunrise, they went to the grave. ³ On the way they said to one another, "Who will roll away the stone from the entrance to the grave for us?" ⁴ (It was a very large stone.) Then they looked up and saw that the stone had already been rolled back. ⁵ So they entered the grave, where they saw a young man, sitting at the right, who wore a white robe — and they were filled with alarm. ⁶ "Don't be alarmed," he said. "You are looking for Jesus

of Nazareth, who was nailed to the cross. But he is not
here — he has risen! Look, here is the place where they
laid him. ⁷Now go and give this message to his disciples,
including Peter: 'He is going to Galilee ahead of you;
there you will see him, just as he told you.'" ⁸So they
went out and ran from the grave, because fear and terror
were upon them. And they said nothing to anyone, because they were afraid.

AN OLD ENDING TO THE GOSPEL

Jesus Appears to Mary Magdalene
(Also Matt. 28.9–10; John 20.11–18)

[⁹ After Jesus rose from death, early on the first day of
the week, he appeared first to Mary Magdalene, from
whom he had driven out seven demons. ¹⁰ She went and
told it to his companions. They were mourning and crying;
¹¹ and when they heard her say that Jesus was alive and
that she had seen him, they did not believe her.

Jesus Appears to Two Disciples
(Also Luke 24.13–35)

¹² After this, Jesus appeared in a different manner to
two of them while they were on their way to the country.
¹³ They returned and told it to the others, but they would
not believe it.

Jesus Appears to the Eleven
(Also Matt. 28.16–20; Luke 24.36–49; John 20.19–23; Acts 1.6–8)

¹⁴ Last of all, Jesus appeared to the eleven disciples as
they were eating. He scolded them, because they did not
have faith and because they were too stubborn to believe
those who had seen him alive. ¹⁵ He said to them: "Go
to the whole world and preach the gospel to all mankind.
¹⁶ Whoever believes and is baptized will be saved; whoever
does not believe will be condemned. ¹⁷ Believers will be
given these signs of power: they will drive out demons in
my name; they will speak in strange tongues; ¹⁸ if they
pick up snakes or drink any poison, they will not be
harmed; they will place their hands on the sick, and they
will get well."

Jesus Is Taken up to Heaven
(Also Luke 24.50–53; Acts 1.9–11)

¹⁹ After the Lord Jesus had talked with them, he was taken up to heaven and sat at the right side of God. ²⁰ The disciples went and preached everywhere, and the Lord worked with them and proved that their preaching was true by giving them the signs of power.]

ANOTHER OLD ENDING

[⁹ The women went to Peter and his friends and gave them a brief account of all they had been told. ¹⁰ After this, Jesus himself sent out through his disciples, from the east to the west, the sacred and ever-living message of eternal salvation.]

LUKE

Introduction

1 Dear Theophilus:
Many have done their best to write a report of the things that have taken place among us. [2] They wrote what we have been told by those who saw these things from the beginning and proclaimed the message. [3] And so, your Excellency, because I have carefully studied all these matters from their beginning, I thought it good to write an orderly account for you. [4] I do this so that you will know the full truth of all those matters which you have been taught.

The Birth of John the Baptist Announced

[5] During the time when Herod was king of Judea, there was a priest named Zechariah, who belonged to the priestly order of Abiah. His wife's name was Elizabeth; she also belonged to a priestly family. [6] They both lived good lives in God's sight, and obeyed fully all the Lord's commandments and rules. [7] They had no children because Elizabeth could not have any, and she and Zechariah were both very old.

[8] One day Zechariah was doing his work as a priest before God, taking his turn in the daily service. [9] According to the custom followed by the priests, he was chosen by lot to burn the incense on the altar. So he went into the Temple of the Lord, [10] while the crowd of people outside prayed during the hour of burning the incense. [11] An

angel of the Lord appeared to him, standing at the right side of the altar where the incense was burned. [12] When Zechariah saw him he was troubled and felt afraid. [13] But the angel said to him: "Don't be afraid, Zechariah! God has heard your prayer, and your wife Elizabeth will bear you a son. You are to name him John. [14] How glad and happy you will be, and how happy many others will be when he is born! [15] For he will be a great man in the Lord's sight. He must not drink any wine or strong drink. From his very birth he will be filled with the Holy Spirit. [16] He will bring back many of the people of Israel to the Lord their God. [17] He will go as God's messenger, strong and mighty like the prophet Elijah. He will bring fathers and children together again; he will turn the disobedient people back to the way of thinking of the righteous; he will get the Lord's people ready for him."

[18] Zechariah said to the angel, "How shall I know if this is so? I am an old man and my wife also is old." [19] "I am Gabriel," the angel answered. "I stand in the presence of God, who sent me to speak to you and tell you this good news. [20] But you have not believed my message, which will come true at the right time. Because you have not believed you will be unable to speak; you will remain silent until the day my promise to you comes true."

[21] In the meantime the people were waiting for Zechariah, wondering why he was spending such a long time in the Temple. [22] When he came out he could not speak to them — and so they knew that he had seen a vision in the Temple. Unable to say a word, he made signs to them with his hands.

[23] When his period of service in the Temple was over, Zechariah went back home. [24] Some time later his wife Elizabeth became pregnant, and did not leave the house for five months. [25] "Now at last the Lord has helped me in this way," she said. "He has taken away my public disgrace!"

The Birth of Jesus Announced

[26] In the sixth month of Elizabeth's pregnancy God sent the angel Gabriel to a town in Galilee named Nazareth. [27] He had a message for a girl promised in marriage to a man named Joseph, who was a descendant of King David.

The girl's name was Mary. ²⁸ The angel came to her and said, "Peace be with you! The Lord is with you, and has greatly blessed you!" ²⁹ Mary was deeply troubled by the angel's message, and she wondered what his words meant. ³⁰ The angel said to her: "Don't be afraid, Mary, for God has been gracious to you. ³¹ You will become pregnant and give birth to a son, and you will name him Jesus. ³² He will be great and will be called the Son of the Most High God. The Lord God will make him a king, as his ancestor David was, ³³ and he will be the king of the descendants of Jacob for ever; his kingdom will never end!"

³⁴ Mary said to the angel, "I am a virgin. How, then, can this be?" ³⁵ The angel answered: "The Holy Spirit will come on you, and God's power will rest upon you. For this reason the holy child will be called the Son of God. ³⁶ Remember your relative Elizabeth. It is said that she cannot have children; but she herself is now six months pregnant, even though she is very old. ³⁷ For there is not a thing that God cannot do."

³⁸ "I am the Lord's servant," said Mary; "may it happen to me as you have said." And the angel left her.

Mary Visits Elizabeth

³⁹ Soon afterward Mary got ready and hurried off to the hill country, to a town in Judea. ⁴⁰ She went into Zechariah's house and greeted Elizabeth. ⁴¹ When Elizabeth heard Mary's greeting, the baby moved within her. Elizabeth was filled with the Holy Spirit, ⁴² and spoke in a loud voice: "Blessed are you among women! Blessed is the child you will bear! ⁴³ Why should this great thing happen to me, that my Lord's mother comes to visit me? ⁴⁴ For as soon as I heard your greeting, the baby within me jumped with gladness. ⁴⁵ How happy are you to believe that the Lord's message to you will come true!"

Mary's Song of Praise

⁴⁶ Mary said:
"My heart praises the Lord,
⁴⁷ My soul is glad because of God my Savior.
⁴⁸ For he has remembered me, his lowly servant!

And from now on all people will call me
blessed,

⁴⁹ Because of the great things the Mighty God
has done for me.

His name is holy;

⁵⁰ He shows mercy to all who fear him,
From one generation to another.

⁵¹ He stretched out his mighty arm
And scattered the proud people with all their
plans.

⁵² He brought down mighty kings from their
thrones,
And lifted up the lowly.

⁵³ He filled the hungry with good things,
And sent the rich away with empty hands.

⁵⁴ He kept the promise he made to our ancestors;
He came to the help of his servant Israel,

⁵⁵ And remembered to show mercy to Abraham
And to all his descendants for ever!"

⁵⁶ Mary stayed about three months with Elizabeth, and
then went back home.

The Birth of John the Baptist

⁵⁷ The time came for Elizabeth to have her baby, and
she gave birth to a son. ⁵⁸ Her neighbors and relatives
heard how wonderfully good the Lord had been to her,
and they all rejoiced with her.

⁵⁹ When the baby was a week old they came to circumcise him; they were going to name him Zechariah, his
father's name. ⁶⁰ But his mother said, "No! His name will
be John." ⁶¹ They said to her, "But you don't have a single
relative with that name!" ⁶² Then they made signs to his
father, asking him what name he would like the boy to
have. ⁶³ Zechariah asked for a writing pad and wrote, "His
name is John." How surprised they all were! ⁶⁴ At that
moment Zechariah was able to speak again, and he started
praising God. ⁶⁵ The neighbors were all filled with fear,
and the news about these things spread through all the hill
country of Judea. ⁶⁶ All who heard of it thought about it
and asked, "What is this child going to be?" For it was
plain that the Lord's power was with him.

Zechariah's Prophecy

⁶⁷ His father Zechariah was filled with the Holy Spirit,
and he prophesied:

⁶⁸ "Let us praise the Lord, the God of Israel!
For he came to the help of his people and set
them free.

⁶⁹ He raised up a mighty Savior for us,
One who is a descendant of his servant David.

⁷⁰ This is what he said long ago by means of his
holy prophets:

⁷¹ He promised to save us from our enemies,
And from the power of all those who hate us.

⁷² He said he would show mercy to our ancestors,
And remember his sacred covenant.

⁷³⁻⁷⁴ He made a solemn promise to our ancestor
Abraham,
And vowed that he would rescue us from our
enemies,
And allow us to serve him without fear,

⁷⁵ To be holy and righteous before him,
All the days of our life.

⁷⁶ You, my child, will be called a prophet of the
Most High God;
You will go ahead of the Lord
To prepare his road for him,

⁷⁷ To tell his people that they will be saved,
By having their sins forgiven.

⁷⁸ For our God is merciful and tender;
He will cause the bright dawn of salvation to
rise on us,

⁷⁹ And shine from heaven on all those who live
in the dark shadow of death,
To guide our steps into the path of peace."

⁸⁰ The child grew and developed in body and spirit; he
lived in the desert until the day when he would appear
publicly to the people of Israel.

The Birth of Jesus
(Also Matt. 1.18–25)

2 At that time Emperor Augustus sent out an order for
all the citizens of the Empire to register themselves
for the census. ² When this first census took place, Quiri-

nius was the governor of Syria. ³ Everyone, then, went to register himself, each to his own town.

⁴ Joseph went from the town of Nazareth, in Galilee, to Judea, to the town named Bethlehem, where King David was born. Joseph went there because he himself was a descendant of David. ⁵ He went to register himself with

Mary, who was promised in marriage to him. She was pregnant, ⁶ and while they were in Bethlehem, the time came for her to have her baby. ⁷ She gave birth to her first son, wrapped him in cloths and laid him in a manger — there was no room for them to stay in the inn.

The Shepherds and the Angels

⁸ There were some shepherds in that part of the country who were spending the night in the fields, taking care of their flocks. ⁹ An angel of the Lord appeared to them, and the glory of the Lord shone over them. They were terribly afraid, ¹⁰ but the angel said to them: "Don't be afraid! For I am here with goods news for you, which will bring great joy to all the people. ¹¹ This very night in David's town your Savior was born — Christ the Lord! ¹² This is what will prove it to you: you will find a baby wrapped in cloths and lying in a manger."

¹³ Suddenly a great army of heaven's angels appeared with the angel, singing praises to God:

¹⁴ "Glory to God in the highest heaven!
    And peace on earth to men with whom he is
      pleased!"

¹⁵ When the angels went away from them back into heaven, the shepherds said to one another, "Let us go to Bethlehem and see this thing that has happened, that the Lord has told us." ¹⁶ So they hurried off and found Mary and Joseph, and saw the baby lying in the manger. ¹⁷ When the shepherds saw him they told them what the angel had said about this child. ¹⁸ All who heard it were filled with wonder at what the shepherds told them. ¹⁹ Mary remembered all these things, and thought deeply about them. ²⁰ The shepherds went back, singing praises to God for all they had heard and seen; it had been just as the angel had told them.

Jesus Is Named

²¹ A week later, when the time came for the baby to be circumcised, he was named Jesus — the name which the angel had given him before he had been conceived.

Jesus Is Presented in the Temple

²² The time came for Joseph and Mary to do what the Law of Moses commanded and perform the ceremony of purification. So they took the child to Jerusalem to present him to the Lord. ²³ This is what is written in the law of the Lord: "Every first-born male shall be dedicated to

the Lord." ²⁴ They also went to offer a sacrifice as required by the law of the Lord: "A pair of doves or two young pigeons."

²⁵ Now there was a man living in Jerusalem whose name was Simeon. He was a good and God-fearing man, and was waiting for Israel to be saved. The Holy Spirit was with him, ²⁶ and he had been assured by the Holy Spirit that he would not die before he had seen the Lord's promised Messiah. ²⁷ Led by the Spirit, Simeon went into the Temple. When the parents brought the child Jesus into the Temple to do for him what the Law required, ²⁸ Simeon took the child in his arms, and gave thanks to God:

> ²⁹ "Now, Lord, you have kept your promise,
> And you may let your servant go in peace.
> ³⁰ For with my own eyes I have seen your salvation,
> ³¹ Which you have made ready in the presence of all peoples:
> ³² A light to reveal your way to the Gentiles,
> And to give glory to your people Israel."

³³ The child's father and mother were amazed at the things Simeon said about him. ³⁴ Simeon blessed them and said to Mary, his mother: "This child is chosen by God for the destruction and the salvation of many in Israel; he will be a sign from God which many people will speak against, ³⁵ and so reveal their secret thoughts. And sorrow, like a sharp sword, will break your own heart."

³⁶ There was a prophetess named Anna, daughter of Phanuel, of the tribe of Asher. She was an old woman who had been married for seven years, ³⁷ and then had been a widow for eighty-four years. She never left the Temple; day and night she worshiped God, fasting and praying. ³⁸ That very same hour she arrived and gave thanks to God, and spoke about the child to all who were waiting for God to redeem Jerusalem.

The Return to Nazareth

³⁹ When they finished doing all that was required by the law of the Lord, they returned to Galilee, to their home town of Nazareth. ⁴⁰ And the child grew and became strong; he was full of wisdom, and God's blessings were with him.

The Boy Jesus in the Temple

⁴¹ Every year Jesus' parents went to Jerusalem for the Feast of Passover. ⁴² When Jesus was twelve years old, they went to the feast as usual. ⁴³ When the days of the feast were over, they started back home, but the boy Jesus stayed in Jerusalem. His parents did not know this; ⁴⁴ they thought that he was with the group, so they traveled a whole day, and then started looking for him among their relatives and friends. ⁴⁵ They did not find him, so they went back to Jerusalem looking for him. ⁴⁶ On the third day they found him in the Temple, sitting with the Jewish teachers, listening to them and asking questions. ⁴⁷ All

who heard him were amazed at his intelligent answers. ⁴⁸ His parents were amazed when they saw him, and his mother said to him, "Son, why did you do this to us? Your father and I have been terribly worried trying to find you." ⁴⁹ He answered them, "Why did you have to look for me? Didn't you know that I had to be in my Father's house?" ⁵⁰ But they did not understand what he said to them.

⁵¹ So Jesus went back with them to Nazareth, where he was obedient to them. His mother treasured all these things in her heart. ⁵² And Jesus grew up, both in body and in wisdom, gaining favor with God and men. *people*

The Preaching of John the Baptist
(*Also Matt. 3.1–12; Mark 1.1–8; John 1.19–28*)

3 It was the fifteenth year of the rule of Emperor Tiberius; Pontius Pilate was governor of Judea, Herod was ruler of Galilee, and his brother Philip ruler of the territory of Iturea and Trachonitis; Lysanias was ruler of Abilene, ² and Annas and Caiaphas were high priests. It was at this time that the word of God came to John, the son of Zechariah, in the desert. ³ So John went throughout the whole territory of the Jordan river. "Turn away from your sins and be baptized," he preached, "and God will forgive your sins." ⁴ As the prophet Isaiah had written in his book:

"Someone is shouting in the desert:
'Get the Lord's road ready for him,
Make a straight path for him to travel!
⁵ All low places must be filled up,
All hills and mountains leveled off;
The winding roads must be made straight,
The rough paths made smooth;
⁶ And all mankind will see God's salvation!' "

⁷ Crowds of people came out to John to be baptized by him. "You snakes!" he said to them. "Who told you that you could escape from God's wrath that is about to come? ⁸ Do the things that will show that you have turned from your sins. And don't start saying among yourselves, 'Abraham is our ancestor.' I tell you that God can take these rocks and make descendants for Abraham! ⁹ The ax is ready to cut the trees down at the roots; every tree that does not bear good fruit will be cut down and thrown in the fire."

¹⁰ The people asked him, "What are we to do, then?" ¹¹ He answered, "Whoever has two shirts must give one to the man who has none, and whoever has food must share it." ¹² Some tax collectors came to be baptized, and they asked him, "Teacher, what are we to do?" ¹³ "Don't collect more than is legal," he told them. ¹⁴ Some soldiers also asked him, "What about us? What are we to do?" He said to them, "Don't take money from anyone by force or by false charges; be content with your pay."

¹⁵ People's hopes began to rise; and they began to wonder about John, thinking that perhaps he might be the Messiah. ¹⁶ So John said to all of them: "I baptize you with water, but one who is much greater than I is coming.

I am not good enough even to untie his sandals. He will baptize you with the Holy Spirit and fire. ¹⁷ He has his winnowing-shovel with him, to thresh out all the grain and gather the wheat into his barn; but he will burn the chaff in a fire that never goes out!"

¹⁸ In many different ways John urged the people as he preached the Good News to them. ¹⁹ But John spoke against Governor Herod, because he had married Herodias, his brother's wife, and had done many other evil things. ²⁰ Then Herod did an even worse thing by putting John in prison.

The Baptism of Jesus
(Also Matt. 3.13–17; Mark 1.9–11)

²¹ After all the people had been baptized, Jesus also was baptized. While he was praying, heaven was opened, ²² and the Holy Spirit came down upon him in bodily form, like a dove. And a voice came from heaven: "You are my own dear Son. I am well pleased with you."

The Genealogy of Jesus
(Also Matt. 1.1–17)

²³ When Jesus began his work he was about thirty years old; he was the son, so people thought, of Joseph, who was the son of Heli, ²⁴ the son of Matthat, the son of Levi, the son of Melchi, the son of Jannai, the son of Joseph, ²⁵ the son of Mattathias, the son of Amos, the son of Nahum, the son of Esli, the son of Naggai, ²⁶ the son of Maath, the son of Mattathias, the son of Semein, the son of Josech, the son of Joda, ²⁷ the son of Joanan, the son of Rhesa, the son of Zerubbabel, the son of Shealtiel, the son of Neri, ²⁸ the son of Melchi, the son of Addi, the son of Cosam, the son of Elmadam, the son of Er, ²⁹ the son of Joshua, the son of Eliezer, the son of Jorim, the son of Matthat, the son of Levi, ³⁰ the son of Simeon, the son of Judah, the son of Joseph, the son of Jonam, the son of Eliakim, ³¹ the son of Melea, the son of Menna, the son of Mattatha, the son of Nathan, the son of David, ³² the son of Jesse, the son of Obed, the son of Boaz, the son of Salmon, the son of Nahshon, ³³ the son of Amminadab, the son of Admin, the son of Arni, the son of Hezron, the son of Perez, the son of Judah, ³⁴ the son of Jacob, the son of Isaac, the son of Abraham, the son of Terah, the son of Nahor,

³⁵ the son of Serug, the son of Reu, the son of Peleg, the son of Eber, the son of Shelah, ³⁶ the son of Cainan, the son of Arphaxad, the son of Shem, the son of Noah, the son of Lamech, ³⁷ the son of Methuselah, the son of Enoch, the son of Jared, the son of Mahalaleel, the son of Cainan, ³⁸ the son of Enos, the son of Seth, the son of Adam, the son of God.

The Temptation of Jesus
(Also Matt. 4.1–11; Mark 1.12–13)

4 Jesus returned from the Jordan full of the Holy Spirit, and was led by the Spirit into the desert, ² where he was tempted by the Devil for forty days. He ate nothing all that time, so that he was hungry when it was over.

³ The Devil said to him, "If you are God's Son, order this stone to turn into bread." ⁴ Jesus answered, "The scripture says, 'Man cannot live on bread alone.' "

⁵ Then the Devil took him up and showed him in a second all the kingdoms of the world. ⁶ "I will give you all this power, and all this wealth," the Devil told him. "It was all handed over to me and I can give it to anyone I choose. ⁷ All this will be yours, then, if you kneel down before me." ⁸ Jesus answered, "The scripture says, 'Worship the Lord your God and serve only him!' "

⁹ Then the Devil took him to Jerusalem and set him on the highest point of the Temple, and said to him, "If you are God's Son, throw yourself down from here. ¹⁰ For the scripture says, 'God will order his angels to take good care of you.' ¹¹ It also says, 'They will hold you up with their hands so that you will not even hurt your feet on the stones.' " ¹² Jesus answered him, "The scripture says, 'You must not put the Lord your God to the test.' " ¹³ When the Devil finished tempting Jesus in every way, he left him for a while.

Jesus Begins His Work in Galilee
(Also Matt. 4.12–17; Mark 1.14–15)

¹⁴ Then Jesus returned to Galilee, and the power of the Holy Spirit was with him. The news about him spread throughout all that territory. ¹⁵ He taught in their synagogues and was praised by all.

Jesus Rejected at Nazareth
(Also Matt. 13.53–58; Mark 6.1–6)

[16] Then Jesus went to Nazareth, where he had been brought up, and on the Sabbath day he went as usual to the synagogue. He stood up to read the Scriptures, [17] and was handed the book of the prophet Isaiah. He unrolled the scroll and found the place where it is written:

[18] "The Spirit of the Lord is upon me.

He has anointed me to preach the Good News to the poor,

He has sent me to proclaim liberty to the captives,

And recovery of sight to the blind,

To set free the oppressed,

[19] To announce the year when the Lord will save his people!"

[20] Jesus rolled up the scroll, gave it back to the attendant, and sat down. All the people in the synagogue had their eyes fixed on him. [21] He began speaking to them: "This passage of scripture has come true today, as you heard it being read." [22] They were all well impressed with him, and marveled at the beautiful words that he spoke. They said, "Isn't he the son of Joseph?" [23] He said to them: "I am sure that you will quote the proverb to me, 'Doctor, heal yourself.' You will also say to me, 'Do here in your own home town the same things we were told happened in Capernaum.' [24] I tell you this," Jesus added: "A prophet is never welcomed in his own home town. [25] Listen to me: it is true that there were many widows in Israel during the time of Elijah, when there was no rain for three and a half years and there was a great famine throughout the whole land. [26] Yet Elijah was not sent to a single one of them, but only to a widow of Zarephath, in the territory of Sidon. [27] And there were many lepers in Israel during the time of the prophet Elisha; yet not one of them was made clean, but only Naaman the Syrian." [28] All the people in the synagogue were filled with anger when they heard this. [29] They rose up, dragged Jesus out of town, and took him to the top of the hill on which their town was built, to throw him over the cliff. [30] But he walked through the middle of the crowd and went his way.

A Man with an Evil Spirit
(Also Mark 1.21–28)

[31] Then Jesus went to Capernaum, a town in Galilee, where he taught the people on the Sabbath. [32] They were all amazed at the way he taught, for his words had authority. [33] There was a man in the synagogue who had the spirit of an evil demon in him; he screamed out in a loud voice: [34] "Ah! What do you want with us, Jesus of Nazareth? Are you here to destroy us? I know who you are: you are God's holy messenger!" [35] Jesus commanded the spirit: "Be quiet, and come out of the man!" The demon threw the man down in front of them all, and went out of him without doing him any harm. [36] Everyone was amazed, and they said to one another: "What kind of word is this? With authority and power this man gives orders to the evil spirits, and they come out!" [37] And the report about Jesus spread everywhere in that region.

Jesus Heals Many People
(Also Matt. 8.14–17; Mark 1.29–34)

[38] Jesus left the synagogue and went to Simon's home. Simon's mother-in-law was sick with a high fever, and they spoke to Jesus about her. [39] He went and stood at her bedside, and gave a command to the fever. The fever left her and she got up at once and began to wait on them.

[40] After sunset, all who had friends who were sick with various diseases brought them to Jesus; he placed his hands on every one of them and healed them all. [41] Demons, also, went out from many people, screaming, "You are the Son of God!" Jesus commanded them and would not let them speak, because they knew that he was the Messiah.

Jesus Preaches in Judea
(Also Mark 1.35–39)

[42] At daybreak Jesus left the town and went off to a lonely place. The people started looking for him, and when they found him they tried to keep him from leaving. [43] But he said to them, "I must preach the Good News of the Kingdom of God in other towns also, for that is what God sent me to do." [44] So he preached in the synagogues of Judea.

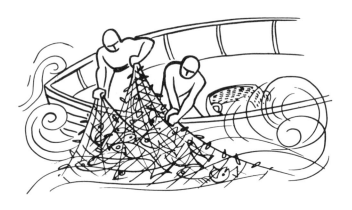

Jesus Calls the First Disciples
(Also Matt. 4.18–22; Mark 1.16–20)

5 One time Jesus was standing on the shore of Lake Gennesaret while the people pushed their way up to him to listen to the word of God. ² He saw two boats pulled up on the beach; the fishermen had left them and gone off to wash the nets. ³ Jesus got into one of the boats —it belonged to Simon—and asked him to push off a little from the shore. Jesus sat in the boat and taught the crowd.

⁴ When he finished speaking, he said to Simon, "Push the boat out further to the deep water, and you and your partners let your nets down for a catch." ⁵ "Master," Simon answered, "we worked hard all night long and caught nothing. But if you say so, I will let down the nets." ⁶ They let the nets down and caught such a large number of fish that the nets were about to break. ⁷ So they motioned to their partners in the other boat to come and help them. They came and filled both boats so full of fish that they were about to sink. ⁸ When Simon Peter saw what had happened, he fell on his knees before Jesus and said, "Go away from me, Lord, for I am a sinful man!" ⁹ He and all the others with him were amazed at the large number of fish they had caught. ¹⁰ The same was true of Simon's partners, James and John, the sons of Zebedee. Jesus said to Simon, "Don't be afraid; from now on you will be catching men." ¹¹ They pulled the boats on the beach, left everything and followed Jesus.

Jesus Makes a Leper Clean
(Also Matt. 8.1–4; Mark 1.40–45)

¹² Once Jesus was in a certain town where there was a man who was covered with leprosy. When he saw Jesus, he fell on his face before him and begged, "Sir, if you want to, you can make me clean!" ¹³ Jesus reached out and touched him. "I do want to," he said. "Be clean!" At once the leprosy left the man. ¹⁴ Jesus ordered him, "Don't tell this to anyone, but go straight to the priest and let him examine you; then offer the sacrifice, as Moses ordered, to prove to everyone that you are now clean." ¹⁵ But the news about Jesus spread all the more widely, and crowds of people came to hear him and be healed from their diseases. ¹⁶ But he would go away to lonely places, where he prayed.

Jesus Heals a Paralyzed Man
(Also Matt. 9.1–8; Mark 2.1–12)

¹⁷ One day when Jesus was teaching, some Pharisees and teachers of the Law were sitting there who had come from every town in Galilee and Judea, and from Jerusalem. The power of the Lord was present for Jesus to heal the sick. ¹⁸ Some men came carrying a paralyzed man on a bed, and they tried to take him into the house and lay him before Jesus. ¹⁹ Because of the crowd, however, they could find no way to take him in. So they carried him up on the roof, made an opening in the tiles, and let him down on his bed into the middle of the group in front of Jesus.

20 When Jesus saw how much faith they had, he said to the man, "Your sins are forgiven you, my friend." 21 The teachers of the Law and the Pharisees began to say to themselves: "Who is this man who speaks against God in this way? No man can forgive sins; God alone can!" 22 Jesus knew their thoughts and said to them: "Why do you think such things? 23 Is it easier to say, 'Your sins are forgiven you,' or to say, 'Get up and walk'? 24 I will prove to you, then, that the Son of Man has authority on earth to forgive sins." So he said to the paralyzed man, "I tell you, get up, pick up your bed, and go home!" 25 At once the man got up before them all, took the bed he had been lying on, and went home, praising God. 26 They were all completely amazed! Full of fear, they praised God, saying, "What marvelous things we have seen today!"

Jesus Calls Levi
(Also Matt. 9.9–13; Mark 2.13–17)

27 After this, Jesus went out and saw a tax collector named Levi, sitting in his office. Jesus said to him, "Follow me." 28 Levi got up, left everything and followed him.

29 Then Levi had a big feast in his house for Jesus, and there was a large number of tax collectors and other people sitting with them. 30 Some Pharisees and teachers of the Law who belonged to their group complained to Jesus' disciples. "Why do you eat and drink with tax collectors and outcasts?" they asked. 31 Jesus answered them: "People who are well do not need a doctor, but only those who are sick. 32 I have not come to call the respectable people to repent, but the outcasts."

The Question about Fasting
(Also Matt. 9.14–17; Mark 2.18–22)

33 Some people said to Jesus, "The disciples of John fast frequently and offer up prayers, and the disciples of the Pharisees do the same; but your disciples eat and drink." 34 Jesus answered: "Do you think you can make the guests at a wedding party go without food as long as the bridegroom is with them? Of course not! 35 But the time will come when the bridegroom will be taken away from them, and they will go without food in those days."

36 Jesus told them this parable also: "No one tears a piece off a new coat to patch up an old coat. If he does,

he will have torn the new coat, and the piece of new cloth will not match the old. ³⁷ Nor does anyone pour new wine into used wineskins. If he does, the new wine will burst the skins, the wine will pour out, and the skins will be ruined. ³⁸ No! New wine should be poured into fresh skins! ³⁹ And no one wants new wine after drinking old wine. 'The old is better,' he says."

The Question about the Sabbath
(Also Matt. 12.1–8; Mark 2.23–28)

6 Jesus was walking through some wheat fields on a Sabbath day. His disciples began to pick the heads of wheat, rub them in their hands, and eat the grain. ² Some Pharisees said, "Why are you doing what our Law says you cannot do on the Sabbath?" ³ Jesus answered them: "Haven't you read what David did when he and his men were hungry? ⁴ He went into the house of God, took the bread offered to God, ate it, and gave it also to his men. Yet it is against our Law for anyone to eat it except the priests." ⁵ And Jesus added, "The Son of Man is Lord of the Sabbath."

The Man with a Crippled Hand
(Also Matt. 12.9–14; Mark 3.1–6)

⁶ On another Sabbath Jesus went into a synagogue and taught. A man was there whose right hand was crippled. ⁷ Some teachers of the Law and Pharisees wanted some reason to accuse Jesus of doing wrong; so they watched him very closely to see if he would cure anyone on the Sabbath. ⁸ But Jesus knew their thoughts and said to the man with the crippled hand, "Stand up and come here to the front." The man got up and stood there. ⁹ Then Jesus said to them: "I ask you: What does our Law allow us to do on the Sabbath? To help or to harm? To save a man's life or destroy it?" ¹⁰ He looked around at them all, then said to the man, "Stretch out your hand." He did so, and his hand became well again. ¹¹ But they were filled with rage and began to discuss among themselves what they could do to Jesus.

Jesus Chooses the Twelve Apostles
(Also Matt. 10.1–4; Mark 3.13–19)

¹² At that time Jesus went up a hill to pray, and spent

the whole night there praying to God. ¹³ When day came he called his disciples to him and chose twelve of them, whom he named apostles: ¹⁴ Simon (whom he also named Peter) and his brother Andrew; James and John, Philip and Bartholomew, ¹⁵ Matthew and Thomas, James the son of Alphaeus and Simon (who was called the patriot), ¹⁶ Judas the son of James and Judas Iscariot, who became the traitor.

Jesus Teaches and Heals
(Also Matt. 4.23–25)

¹⁷ Coming down from the hill with them, Jesus stood on a level place with a large number of his disciples. A great crowd of people was there from all over Judea, and from Jerusalem, and from the coast cities of Tyre and Sidon; ¹⁸ they came to hear him and to be healed of their diseases. Those who were troubled by evil spirits also came and were healed. ¹⁹ All the people tried to touch him, for power was going out from him and healing them all.

Happiness and Sorrow
(Also Matt. 5.1–12)

²⁰ Jesus looked at his disciples and said:
"Happy are you poor:
    the Kingdom of God is yours!
²¹ "Happy are you who are hungry now:
    you will be filled!
"Happy are you who weep now:
    you will laugh!
²² "Happy are you when men hate you, and reject you, and insult you, and say that you are evil, because of the Son of Man! ²³ Be happy when that happens, and dance for joy, for a great reward is kept for you in heaven. For their ancestors did the very same things to the prophets.
²⁴ "But how terrible for you who are rich now:
    you have had your easy life!
²⁵ "How terrible for you who are full now:
    you will go hungry!
"How terrible for you who laugh now:
    you will mourn and weep!
²⁶ "How terrible when all men speak well of you; for their ancestors said the very same things to the false prophets."

Love for Enemies
(Also Matt. 5.38–48; 7.12a)

²⁷ "But I tell you who hear me: Love your enemies, do good to those who hate you, ²⁸ bless those who curse you, and pray for those who mistreat you. ²⁹ If anyone hits you on the cheek, let him hit the other one too; if someone takes your coat, let him have your shirt as well. ³⁰ Give to everyone who asks you for something, and when someone takes what is yours, do not ask for it back. ³¹ Do for others just what you want them to do for you.

³² "If you love only the people who love you, why should you expect a blessing? Even sinners love those who love them! ³³ And if you do good only to those who do good to you, why should you expect a blessing? Even sinners do that! ³⁴ And if you lend only to those from whom you hope to get it back, why should you expect a blessing? Even sinners lend to sinners, to get back the same amount! ³⁵ No! Love your enemies and do good to them; lend and expect nothing back. You will have a great

reward, and you will be sons of the Most High God. For he is good to the ungrateful and the wicked. ³⁶ Be merciful, just as your Father is merciful."

Judging Others
(Also Matt. 7.1–5)

³⁷ Do not judge others, and God will not judge you; do not condemn others, and God will not condemn you; forgive others, and God will forgive you. ³⁸ Give to others, and God will give to you: you will receive a full measure, a generous helping, poured into your hands — all that you

can hold. The measure you use for others is the one God will use for you."

39 And Jesus told them this parable: "One blind man cannot lead another one; if he does, both will fall into a ditch. 40 No pupil is greater than his teacher; but every pupil, when he has completed his training, will be like his teacher.

41 "Why do you look at the speck in your brother's eye, but pay no attention to the log in your own eye? 42 How can you say to your brother, 'Please, brother, let me take that speck out of your eye,' yet not even see the log in your own eye? You impostor! Take the log out of your own eye first, and then you will be able to see and take the speck out of your brother's eye."

A Tree and its Fruit
(Also Matt. 7.16–20; 12.33–35)

43 "A healthy tree does not bear bad fruit, nor does a poor tree bear good fruit. 44 Every tree is known by the fruit it bears; you do not pick figs from thorn bushes, or gather grapes from bramble bushes. 45 A good man brings good out of the treasure of good things in his heart; a bad man brings bad out of his treasure of bad things. For a man's mouth speaks what his heart is full of."

The Two House Builders
(Also Matt. 7.24–27)

46 "Why do you call me, 'Lord, Lord,' and don't do what I tell you? 47 Everyone who comes to me, and listens to my words, and obeys them — I will show you what he is like. 48 He is like a man who built a house: he dug deep and laid the foundation on the rock. The river flooded over and hit that house but it could not shake it, because the house had been well built. 49 But the one who hears my words and does not obey them is like a man who built a house on the ground without laying a foundation; when the flood hit that house it fell at once — what a terrible crash that was!"

Jesus Heals a Roman Officer's Servant
(Also Matt. 8.5–13)

7 When Jesus had finished saying all these things to the people, he went to Capernaum. 2 A Roman officer

there had a servant who was very dear to him; the man was sick and about to die. ³ When the officer heard about Jesus, he sent to him some Jewish elders to ask him to come and heal his servant. ⁴ They came to Jesus and begged him earnestly: "This man really deserves your help. ⁵ He loves our people and he himself built a synagogue for us." ⁶ So Jesus went with them. He was not far from the house when the officer sent friends to tell him: "Sir, don't trouble yourself. I do not deserve to have you come into my house, ⁷ neither do I consider myself worthy to come to you in person. Just give the order and my servant will get well. ⁸ I, too, am a man placed under the authority of superior officers, and I have soldiers under me. I order this one, 'Go!' and he goes; I order that one, 'Come!' and he comes; and I order my slave, 'Do this!' and he does it." ⁹ Jesus was surprised when he heard this; he turned around and said to the crowd following him, "I have never found such faith as this, I tell you, not even in Israel!" ¹⁰ The messengers went back to the officer's house and found his servant well.

Jesus Raises a Widow's Son

¹¹ Soon afterward Jesus went to a town named Nain; his disciples and a large crowd went with him. ¹² Just as he arrived at the gate of the town, a funeral procession was coming out. The dead man was the only son of a woman who was a widow, and a large crowd from the city was with her. ¹³ When the Lord saw her his heart was filled with pity for her and he said to her, "Don't cry." ¹⁴ Then he walked over and touched the coffin, and the men carrying it stopped. Jesus said, "Young man! Get up, I tell you!" ¹⁵ The dead man sat up and began to talk, and Jesus gave him back to his mother. ¹⁶ Everyone was filled with fear, and they praised God: "A great prophet has appeared among us!" and, "God has come to save his people!" ¹⁷ This news about Jesus went out through all of Judea and the surrounding territory.

The Messengers from John the Baptist
(Also Matt. 11.2–19)

¹⁸ John's disciples told him about all these things. John called two of them to him ¹⁹ and sent them to the Lord to ask him, "Are you the one John said was going to come,

or should we expect someone else?" ²⁰ When they came to Jesus they said, "John the Baptist sent us to ask, 'Are you the one he said was going to come, or should we expect someone else?' " ²¹ At that very time Jesus healed many people from their sicknesses, diseases, and evil spirits, and gave sight to many blind people. ²² He answered John's messengers: "Go back and tell John what you have seen and heard: the blind can see, the lame can walk, the lepers are made clean, the deaf can hear, the dead are raised to life, and the Good News is preached to the poor. ²³ How happy is he who has no doubts about me!"

²⁴ After John's messengers had left, Jesus began to speak about John to the crowds: "When you went out to John in the desert, what did you expect to see? A blade of grass bending in the wind? ²⁵ What did you go out to see? A man dressed up in fancy clothes? Really, those who dress like that and live in luxury are found in palaces! ²⁶ Tell me, what did you expect to see? A prophet? Yes, I tell you — you saw much more than a prophet. ²⁷ For John is the one of whom the scripture says, 'Here is my messenger, says God; I will send him ahead of you to open the way for you.' ²⁸ I tell you," Jesus added, "John is greater than any man ever born; but he who is least in the Kingdom of God is greater than he."

²⁹ All the people and the tax collectors heard him; they were the ones who had obeyed God's righteous demands and had been baptized by John. ³⁰ But the Pharisees and the teachers of the Law rejected God's purpose for themselves, and refused to be baptized by John.

³¹ "Now, to what can I compare the people of this day? What are they like? ³² They are like children sitting in the market place. One group shouts to the other, 'We played wedding music for you, but you would not dance! We sang funeral songs, but you would not cry!' ³³ John the Baptist came, and he fasted and drank no wine, and you said, 'He is a madman!' ³⁴ The Son of Man came, and he ate and drank, and you said, 'Look at this man! He is a glutton and wine-drinker, and is a friend of tax collectors and outcasts!' ³⁵ God's wisdom, however, is shown to be true by all who accept it."

Jesus at the Home of Simon the Pharisee

³⁶ A Pharisee invited Jesus to have dinner with him.

Jesus went to his house and sat down to eat. ³⁷ There was a woman in that town who lived a sinful life. She heard that Jesus was eating in the Pharisee's house, so she brought an alabaster jar full of perfume ³⁸ and stood behind Jesus, by his feet, crying and wetting his feet with her tears. Then she dried his feet with her hair, kissed them, and poured the perfume on them. ³⁹ When the Pharisee who had invited Jesus saw this, he said to himself, "If this man really were a prophet, he would know who this woman is who is touching him; he would know what kind of sinful life she leads!" ⁴⁰ Jesus spoke up and said to him, "Simon, I have something to tell you." "Yes, Teacher," he said, "tell me." ⁴¹ "There were two men who owed money to a moneylender," Jesus began; "one owed him five hundred dollars and the other one fifty dollars. ⁴² Neither one could pay him back, so he cancelled the debts of both. Which one, then, will love him more?" ⁴³ "I suppose," answered Simon, "that it would be the one who was forgiven more." "Your answer is correct," said Jesus. ⁴⁴ Then he turned to the woman and said to Simon: "Do you see this woman? I came into your home, and you gave me no water for my feet, but she has washed my feet with her tears and dried them with her hair. ⁴⁵ You

did not welcome me with a kiss, but she has not stopped kissing my feet since I came. ⁴⁶ You provided no oil for my head, but she has covered my feet with perfume. ⁴⁷ I tell you, then, the great love she has shown proves that her many sins have been forgiven. Whoever has been forgiven little, however, shows only a little love." ⁴⁸ Then Jesus said to the woman, "Your sins are forgiven." ⁴⁹ The others sitting at the table began to say to themselves, "Who is this, who even forgives sins?" ⁵⁰ But Jesus said to the woman, "Your faith has saved you; go in peace."

Women who Accompanied Jesus

8 Some time later Jesus made a trip through towns and villages, preaching the Good News about the Kingdom of God. The twelve disciples went with him, ² and so did some women who had been healed of evil spirits and diseases: Mary (who was called Magdalene), from whom seven demons had been driven out; ³ Joanna, the wife of Chuza who was an officer in Herod's court; Susanna, and many other women who helped Jesus and his disciples with their belongings.

The Parable of the Sower
(Also Matt. 13.1–9; Mark 4.1–9)

⁴ People kept coming to Jesus from one town after another; and when a great crowd gathered, Jesus told this parable:

⁵ "A man went out to sow his seed. As he scattered the seed in the field, some of it fell along the path, where it was stepped on, and the birds ate it. ⁶ Some of it fell on rocky ground, and when the plants sprouted they dried up, because the soil had no moisture. ⁷ Some of the seed fell among thorns which grew up with the plants and choked them. ⁸ And some seeds fell in good soil; the plants grew and bore grain, one hundred grains each." And Jesus added, "Listen, then, if you have ears to hear with!"

The Purpose of the Parables
(Also Matt. 13.10–17; Mark 4.10–12)

⁹ His disciples asked Jesus what this parable meant. ¹⁰ Jesus answered, "The knowledge of the secrets of the Kingdom of God has been given to you; but to the rest it comes by means of parables, so that they may look but not see, and listen but not understand."

Jesus Explains the Parable of the Sower
(Also Matt. 13.18–23; Mark 4.13–20)

[11] "This is what the parable means: the seed is the word of God. [12] The seed that fell along the path stands for those who hear; but the Devil comes and takes the message away from their hearts to keep them from believing and being saved. [13] The seed that fell on rocky ground stands for those who hear the message and receive it gladly. But it does not sink deep into them; they believe only for a while, and fall away when the time of temptation comes. [14] The seed that fell among thorns stands for those who hear; but the worries and riches and pleasures of this life crowd in and choke them, and their fruit never ripens. [15] The seed that fell in good soil stands for those who hear the message and retain it in a good and obedient heart, and persist until they bear fruit."

A Lamp under a Bowl
(Also Mark 4.21–25)

[16] "No one lights a lamp and covers it with a bowl or puts it under a bed. Instead, he puts it on the lamp-stand, so that people will see the light as they come in. [17] Whatever is hidden away will be brought out into the open, and whatever is covered up will be found and brought to light.

[18] "Be careful, then, how you listen; for whoever has something will be given more, but whoever has nothing will have taken away from him even the little he thinks he has."

Jesus' Mother and Brothers
(Also Matt. 12.46–50; Mark 3.31–35)

[19] Jesus' mother and brothers came to him, but were unable to join him because of the crowd. [20] Someone said to Jesus, "Your mother and brothers are standing outside and want to see you." [21] Jesus said to them all, "My mother and brothers are those who hear the word of God and obey it."

Jesus Calms a Storm
(Also Matt. 8.23–27; Mark 4.35–41)

[22] One day Jesus got into a boat with his disciples and said to them, "Let us go across to the other side of the lake." So they started out. [23] As they were sailing, Jesus

went to sleep. A strong wind blew down on the lake, and the boat began to fill with water, putting them all in great danger. ²⁴ The disciples came to Jesus and woke him up, saying, "Master, Master! We are about to die!" Jesus got up and gave a command to the wind and to the stormy water; they quieted down and there was a great calm. ²⁵ Then he said to the disciples, "Where is your faith?" But they were amazed and afraid, and said to one another: "Who is this man? He gives orders to the winds and waves, and they obey him!"

Jesus Heals a Man with Demons
(Also Matt. 8.28–34; Mark 5.1–20)

²⁶ They sailed on over to the territory of the Gergesenes, which is across the lake from Galilee. ²⁷ As Jesus stepped ashore, he was met by a man from the town who had demons in him. He had gone for a long time without clothes, and would not stay at home, but spent his time in the burial caves. ²⁸ When he saw Jesus he gave a loud cry, fell down before him and said in a loud voice: "Jesus, Son of the Most High God! What do you want with me? I beg you, don't punish me!" ²⁹ He said this because Jesus had ordered the evil spirit to go out of him. Many times it had seized him, and even though he was kept a prisoner, his hands and feet tied with chains, he would break the chains and be driven by the demon out into the desert. ³⁰ Jesus asked him, "What is your name?" "My name is 'Mob,' " he answered — because many demons had gone into him. ³¹ The demons begged Jesus not to send them into the abyss.

³² A large herd of pigs was near by, feeding on the hillside. The demons begged Jesus to let them go into the pigs — and he let them. ³³ So the demons went out of the man and into the pigs; the whole herd rushed down the side of the cliff into the lake and were drowned.

³⁴ The men who were taking care of the pigs saw what happened, so they ran off and spread the news in the town and among the farms. ³⁵ People went out to see what had happened. They came to Jesus and found the man from whom the demons had gone out sitting at the feet of Jesus, clothed, and in his right mind — and they were all afraid. ³⁶ Those who had seen it told the people how the man had been cured. ³⁷ Then the whole crowd from the territory

of the Gergesenes asked Jesus to go away, for they were all terribly afraid. So Jesus got into the boat and left. [38] The man from whom the demons had gone out begged Jesus, "Let me go with you." But Jesus sent him away, saying, [39] "Go back home and tell what God has done for you." The man went through the whole town telling what Jesus had done for him.

Jairus' Daughter and the Woman who Touched Jesus' Cloak
(Also Matt. 9.18–26; Mark 5.21–43)

[40] When Jesus returned to the other side of the lake the crowd welcomed him, for they had all been waiting for him. [41] Then a man named Jairus arrived, an official in the local synagogue. He threw himself down at Jesus' feet and begged him to go to his home, [42] for his only daughter, twelve years old, was dying.

As Jesus went along, the people were crowding him from every side. [43] A certain woman was there who had suffered from severe bleeding for twelve years; she had spent all she had on doctors, but no one had been able to cure her. [44] She came up in the crowd behind Jesus and touched the edge of his cloak, and her bleeding stopped at once. [45] Jesus asked, "Who touched me?" Everyone denied it, and Peter said, "Master, the people are all around you and crowding in on you." [46] But Jesus said, "Someone touched me, for I knew it when power went out of me." ⁴⁷ The woman saw that she had been found out, so she came, trembling, and threw herself at Jesus' feet. There, in front of everybody, she told him why she had touched him and how she had been healed at once. ⁴⁸ Jesus said to her, "My daughter, your faith has made you well. Go in peace."

⁴⁹ While Jesus was saying this, a messenger came from the official's house. "Your daughter has died," he told Jairus; "don't bother the Teacher any longer." ⁵⁰ But Jesus heard it and said to Jairus, "Don't be afraid; only believe, and she will be well." ⁵¹ When he arrived at the house he would not let anyone go in with him except Peter, John, and James, and the child's father and mother. ⁵² Everyone there was crying and mourning for the child. Jesus said, "Don't cry; the child is not dead — she is only sleeping!" ⁵³ They all made fun of him, because they knew that she was dead. ⁵⁴ But Jesus took her by the hand and called out, "Get up, child!" ⁵⁵ Her life returned and she got up at once; and Jesus ordered them to give her something to eat. ⁵⁶ Her parents were astounded, but Jesus commanded them not to tell anyone what had happened.

Jesus Sends out the Twelve Disciples
(Also Matt. 10.5–15; Mark 6.7–13)

9 Jesus called the twelve disciples together and gave them power and authority to drive out all demons and to cure diseases. ² Then he sent them out to preach the Kingdom of God and to heal the sick. ³ He said to them: "Take nothing with you for the trip: no walking stick, no beggar's bag, no food, no money, not even an extra shirt. ⁴ Wherever you are welcomed, stay in the same house until you leave that town; ⁵ wherever people don't welcome you, leave that town and shake the dust off your feet as a warning to them." ⁶ The disciples left and traveled through all the villages, preaching the Good News and healing people everywhere.

Herod's Confusion
(Also Matt. 14.1–12; Mark 6.14–29)

⁷ Herod, the ruler of Galilee, heard about all the things that were happening; he was very confused about it because some people said, "John the Baptist has come back to life!" ⁸ Others said that Elijah had appeared, while

others said that one of the prophets of long ago had come back to life. ⁹ Herod said, "I had John's head cut off; but who is this man I hear these things about?" And he kept trying to see Jesus.

Jesus Feeds the Five Thousand
(Also Matt. 14.13–21; Mark 6.30–44; John 6.1–14)

¹⁰ The apostles came back and told Jesus everything they had done. He took them with him and they went off by themselves to a town named Bethsaida. ¹¹ When the crowds heard about it they followed him. He welcomed them, spoke to them about the Kingdom of God, and healed those who needed it.

¹² When the sun had begun to set, the twelve disciples came to him and said, "Send the people away so they can go to the villages and farms around here and find food and lodging; for this is a lonely place." ¹³ But Jesus said to them, "You yourselves give them something to eat." They answered, "All we have is five loaves and two fish. Do you want us to go and buy food for this whole crowd?" ¹⁴ (There were about five thousand men there.) Jesus said to his disciples, "Make the people sit down in groups of about fifty each." ¹⁵ The disciples did so and made them all sit down. ¹⁶ Jesus took the five loaves and two fish, looked up to heaven, thanked God for them, broke them, and gave them to the disciples to distribute to the people. ¹⁷ They all ate and had enough; and the disciples took up twelve baskets of what the people left over.

Peter's Declaration about Jesus
(Also Matt. 16.13–19; Mark 8.27–29)

¹⁸ One time when Jesus was praying alone, the disciples came to him. "Who do the crowds say I am?" he asked them. ¹⁹ "Some say that you are John the Baptist," they answered. "Others say that you are Elijah, while others say that one of the prophets of long ago has come back to life." ²⁰ "What about you?" he asked them. "Who do you say I am?" Peter answered, "You are God's Messiah!"

Jesus Speaks about His Suffering and Death
(Also Matt. 16.20–28; Mark 8.30—9.1)

²¹ Then Jesus gave them strict orders not to tell this to anyone, ²² and added: "The Son of Man must suffer much,

and be rejected by the elders, the chief priests, and the teachers of the Law. He will be put to death, and be raised to life on the third day."

²³ And he said to all: "If anyone wants to come with me, he must forget himself, take up his cross every day, and follow me. ²⁴ For the person who wants to save his own life will lose it; but the one who loses his life for my sake will save it. ²⁵ Will a man gain anything if he wins the whole world but is himself lost or defeated? Of course not! ²⁶ If a man is ashamed of me and of my teaching, then the Son of Man will be ashamed of him when he comes in his glory and the glory of the Father and of the holy angels. ²⁷ Remember this! There are some here, I tell you, who will not die until they have seen the Kingdom of God."

The Transfiguration
(Also Matt. 17.1–8; Mark 9.2–8)

²⁸ About a week after he had said these things, Jesus took Peter, John, and James with him and went up a hill to pray. ²⁹ While he was praying, his face changed its appearance and his clothes became dazzling white. ³⁰ Suddenly two men were there talking with him. They were Moses and Elijah, ³¹ who appeared in heavenly glory and talked with Jesus about how he would soon fulfil God's purpose by dying in Jerusalem. ³² Peter and his companions were sound asleep, but they awoke and saw Jesus' glory and the two men who were standing with him. ³³ As the men were leaving Jesus, Peter said to him: "Master, it is a good thing that we are here. We will make three tents, one for you, one for Moses, and one for Elijah." (He really did not know what he was saying.) ³⁴ While he was still speaking, a cloud appeared and covered them with its shadow, and the disciples were afraid as the cloud came over them. ³⁵ A voice said from the cloud: "This is my Son, whom I have chosen — listen to him!" ³⁶ When the voice stopped, there was Jesus all alone. The disciples kept quiet about all this, and told no one at that time a single thing they had seen.

Jesus Heals a Boy with an Evil Spirit
(Also Matt. 17.14–18; Mark 9.14–27)

³⁷ The next day they went down from the hill, and a large crowd met Jesus. ³⁸ A man shouted from the crowd:

"Teacher! Look, I beg you, at my son — my only son!
39 A spirit attacks him with a sudden shout and throws him
into a fit, so that he foams at the mouth; it keeps on hurting him and will hardly let him go! 40 I begged your
disciples to drive it out, but they could not." 41 Jesus
answered: "How unbelieving and wrong you people are!
How long must I stay with you? How long do I have to
put up with you?" Then he said to the man, "Bring your
son here." 42 As the boy was coming, the demon knocked
him to the ground and threw him into a fit. Jesus gave
a command to the evil spirit, healed the boy, and gave him
back to his father. 43 All the people were amazed at the
mighty power of God.

Jesus Speaks again about His Death
(Also Matt. 17.22–23; Mark 9.30–32)

The people were still marveling at everything Jesus was
doing, when he said to his disciples: 44 "Don't forget what
I am about to tell you! The Son of Man is going to be
handed over to the power of men." 45 But they did not
know what this meant. It had been hidden from them so
that they could not understand it, and they were afraid
to ask him about the matter.

Who Is the Greatest?
(Also Matt. 18.1–5; Mark 9.33–37)

46 An argument came up among the disciples as to which

one of them was the greatest. ⁴⁷ Jesus knew what they were thinking, so he took a child, stood him by his side, ⁴⁸ and said to them: "The person who in my name welcomes this child, welcomes me; and whoever welcomes me, also welcomes the one who sent me. For he who is least among you all is the greatest."

Who Is not against You Is for You
(Also Mark 9.38–40)

⁴⁹ John spoke up. "Master," he said, "we saw a man driving out demons in your name, and we told him to stop, because he doesn't belong to our group." ⁵⁰ "Do not try to stop him," Jesus said to him and to the other disciples; "for whoever is not against you is for you."

A Samaritan Village Refuses to Receive Jesus

⁵¹ As the days drew near when Jesus would be taken up to heaven, he made up his mind and set out on his way to Jerusalem. ⁵² He sent messengers ahead of him, who left and went into a Samaritan village to get everything ready for him. ⁵³ But the people there would not receive him, because it was plain that he was going to Jerusalem. ⁵⁴ When the disciples James and John saw this they said, "Lord, do you want us to call fire down from heaven and destroy them?" ⁵⁵ Jesus turned and rebuked them; ⁵⁶ and they went on to another village.

The Would-Be Followers of Jesus
(Also Matt. 8.19–22)

⁵⁷ As they went on their way, a certain man said to Jesus, "I will follow you wherever you go." ⁵⁸ Jesus said to him, "Foxes have holes, and birds have nests, but the Son of Man has no place to lie down and rest." ⁵⁹ He said to another man, "Follow me." But he said, "Sir, first let me go and bury my father." ⁶⁰ Jesus answered, "Let the dead bury their own dead. You go and preach the Kingdom of God." ⁶¹ Another man said, "I will follow you, sir; but first let me go and say good-bye to my family." ⁶² Jesus said to him, "Anyone who starts to plow and then keeps looking back is of no use for the Kingdom of God."

Jesus Sends out the Seventy-two

10 After this the Lord chose another seventy-two men and sent them out, two by two, to go ahead of him to every town and place where he himself was about to go. ² He said to them: "There is a great harvest, but few workers to gather it in. Pray to the owner of the harvest that he will send out more workers to gather in his harvest. ³ Go! I am sending you like lambs among wolves. ⁴ Don't take a purse, or a beggar's bag, or shoes; don't stop to greet anyone on the road. ⁵ Whenever you go into a house, first say, 'Peace be with this house.' ⁶ If a peace-loving man lives there, let your greeting of peace remain on him; if not, take back your greeting of peace. ⁷ Stay in that same house, eating and drinking what they offer you; for a worker should be given his pay. Don't move around from one house to another. ⁸ Whenever you go into a town and are made welcome, eat what is set before you, ⁹ heal the sick in that town, and say to the people there, 'The Kingdom of God has come near you.' ¹⁰ But whenever you go into a town and are not welcomed there, go out in the streets and say, ¹¹ 'Even the dust from your town that sticks to our feet we wipe off against you; but remember this, the Kingdom of God has come near you!' ¹² I tell you that on the Judgment Day God will show more mercy to Sodom than to that town!"

The Unbelieving Towns
(Also Matt. 11.20–24)

¹³ "How terrible it will be for you, Chorazin! How terrible for you too, Bethsaida! For if the miracles which were performed in you had been performed in Tyre and Sidon, long ago the people there would have sat down, put on sackcloth, and sprinkled ashes on themselves to show that they had turned from their sins! ¹⁴ God will show more mercy on the Judgment Day to Tyre and Sidon than to you. ¹⁵ And as for you, Capernaum! You wanted to lift yourself up to heaven? You will be thrown down to hell!"

¹⁶ He said to his disciples: "Whoever listens to you, listens to me; whoever rejects you, rejects me; and whoever rejects me, rejects the one who sent me."

The Return of the Seventy-two

[17] The seventy-two men came back in great joy. "Lord," they said, "even the demons obeyed us when we commanded them in your name!" [18] Jesus answered them: "I saw Satan fall like lightning from heaven. [19] Listen! I have given you authority, so that you can walk on snakes and scorpions, and over all the power of the Enemy, and nothing will hurt you. [20] But don't be glad because the evil spirits obey you; rather be glad because your names are written in heaven."

Jesus Rejoices
(Also Matt. 11.25–27; 13.16–17)

[21] At that same time Jesus was filled with joy by the Holy Spirit, and said: "O Father, Lord of heaven and earth! I thank you because you have shown to the unlearned what you have hidden from the wise and learned. Yes, Father, this was done by your own choice and pleasure.

[22] "My Father has given me all things: no one knows who the Son is except the Father, and no one knows who the Father is except the Son and those to whom the Son wants to reveal him."

[23] Then Jesus turned to the disciples and said to them privately: "How happy are you, to see the things you see! [24] For many prophets and kings, I tell you, wanted to see what you see, but they could not, and to hear what you hear, but they did not."

The Parable of the Good Samaritan

[25] Then a certain teacher of the Law came up and tried to trap Jesus. "Teacher," he asked, "what must I do to receive eternal life?" [26] Jesus answered him, "What do the Scriptures say? How do you interpret them?" [27] The man answered: " 'You must love the Lord your God with all your heart, and with all your soul, and with all your strength, and with all your mind'; and, 'You must love your neighbor as yourself.' " [28] "Your answer is correct," replied Jesus; "do this and you will live."

[29] But the teacher of the Law wanted to put himself in the right, so he asked Jesus, "Who is my neighbor?" [30] Jesus answered: "A certain man was going down from

Jerusalem to Jericho, when robbers attacked him, stripped him and beat him up, leaving him half dead. [31] It so happened that a priest was going down that road; when he saw the man he walked on by, on the other side. [32] In the same way a Levite also came there, went over and looked at the man, and then walked on by, on the other side. [33] But a certain Samaritan who was traveling that way came upon him, and when he saw the man his heart was filled with pity. [34] He went over to him, poured oil and wine on his wounds and bandaged them; then he put the man on his own animal and took him to an inn, where he took care of him. [35] The next day he took out two silver coins and gave them to the innkeeper. 'Take care of him,' he told the innkeeper, 'and when I come back this way I will pay you back whatever you spend on him.' " [36] And Jesus concluded, "Which one of these three seems to you to have been a neighbor to the man attacked by the robbers?" [37] The teacher of the Law answered, "The one who was kind to him." Jesus replied, "You go, then, and do the same."

Jesus Visits Martha and Mary

[38] As Jesus and his disciples went on their way, he came to a certain village where a woman named Martha welcomed him in her home. [39] She had a sister named Mary, who sat down at the feet of the Lord and listened to his teaching. [40] Martha was upset over all the work she had to do; so she came and said, "Lord, don't you care that my sister has left me to do all the work by myself? Tell her to come and help me!" [41] The Lord answered her, "Martha, Martha! You are worried and troubled over so many things, [42] but just one is needed. Mary has chosen the right thing, and it will not be taken away from her."

Jesus' Teaching on Prayer
(Also Matt. 6.9–13; 7.7–11)

11 One time Jesus was praying in a certain place. When he finished, one of his disciples said to him, "Lord, teach us to pray, just as John taught his disciples." [2] Jesus said to them, "This is what you should pray:

'Father,
May your name be kept holy,
May your Kingdom come.
[3] Give us day by day the food we need.
[4] Forgive us our sins,
For we forgive everyone who has done us wrong.
And do not bring us to hard testing.' "

[5] And Jesus said to his disciples: "Suppose one of you should go to a friend's house at midnight and tell him, 'Friend, let me borrow three loaves of bread. [6] A friend of mine who is on a trip has just come to my house and I don't have a thing to offer him!' [7] And suppose your friend should answer from inside, 'Don't bother me! The door is already locked, my children and I are in bed, and I can't get up to give you anything.' [8] Well, what then? I tell you, even if he will not get up and give you the bread because he is your friend, yet he will get up and give you everything you need because you are not ashamed to keep on asking. [9] And so I say to you: Ask, and you will receive; seek, and you will find; knock, and the door will be opened to you. [10] For everyone who asks will receive, and he who seeks will find, and the door will be opened to him who knocks. [11] Would any one of you fathers give his son

a snake when he asks for fish? [12] Or would you give him a scorpion when he asks for an egg? [13] As bad as you are, you know how to give good things to your children. How much more, then, the Father in heaven will give the Holy Spirit to those who ask him!"

Jesus and Beelzebul
(Also Matt. 12.22–30; Mark 3.20–27)

[14] Jesus was driving out a demon that could not talk; when the demon went out, the man began to talk. The crowds were amazed, [15] but some of them said, "It is Beelzebul, the chief of the demons, who gives him the power to drive them out." [16] Others wanted to trap him, so they asked him to perform a miracle to show God's approval. [17] But Jesus knew their thoughts and said to them: "Any country that divides itself into groups that fight one another will not last very long; a family divided against itself falls apart. [18] So if Satan's kingdom has groups fighting each other, how can it last? You say that I drive out demons because Beelzebul gives me the power to do so. [19] If this is how I drive them out, how do your followers drive them out? Your own followers prove that you are completely wrong! [20] No, it is rather by means of God's power that I drive out demons, which proves that the Kingdom of God has already come to you.

[21] "When a strong man, with all his weapons ready, guards his own house, all his belongings are safe. [22] But when a stronger man attacks him and defeats him, he carries away all the weapons the owner was depending on and divides up what he stole.

[23] "Anyone who is not for me, is really against me; anyone who does not help me gather, is really scattering."

The Return of the Evil Spirit
(Also Matt. 12.43–45)

[24] "When an evil spirit goes out of a man, it travels over dry country looking for a place to rest; if it doesn't find one, it says to itself, 'I will go back to my house which I left.' [25] So it goes back and finds the house clean and all fixed up. [26] Then it goes out and brings seven other spirits even worse than itself, and they come and live there. So that man is in worse shape, when it is all over, than he was at the beginning."

True Happiness

27 When Jesus had said this, a woman spoke up from the crowd and said to him, "How happy is the woman who bore you and nursed you!" 28 But Jesus answered, "Rather, how happy are those who hear the word of God and obey it!"

The Demand for a Miracle
(Also Matt. 12.38–42)

29 As the people crowded around Jesus he went on to say: "How evil are the people of this day! They ask for a miracle as a sign of God's approval, but none will be given them except the miracle of Jonah. 30 In the same way that the prophet Jonah was a sign for the people of Nineveh, so the Son of Man will be a sign for the people of this day. 31 On the Judgment Day the Queen from the South will stand up and accuse the people of today, because she traveled halfway around the world to listen to Solomon's wise teaching; and there is something here, I tell you, greater than Solomon. 32 On the Judgment Day the people of Nineveh will stand up and accuse you, because they turned from their sins when they heard Jonah preach; and there is something here, I tell you, greater than Jonah!"

The Light of the Body
(Also Matt. 5.15; 6.22–23)

33 "No one lights a lamp and then hides it or puts it under a bowl; instead, he puts it on the lamp-stand, so that people may see the light as they come in. 34 Your eyes are like a lamp for the body: when your eyes are clear your whole body is full of light; but when your eyes are bad your whole body will be in darkness. 35 Be careful, then, that the light in you is not darkness. 36 If, then, your whole body is full of light, with no part of it in darkness, it will be bright all over, as when a lamp shines on you with its brightness."

Jesus Accuses the Pharisees and the Teachers of the Law
(Also Matt. 23.1–36; Mark 12.38–40)

37 When Jesus finished speaking, a Pharisee invited him

to eat with him; so he went in and sat down to eat. [38] The Pharisee was surprised when he noticed that Jesus had not washed before eating. [39] So the Lord said to him: "Now, then, you Pharisees clean the cup and plate on the outside, but inside you are full of violence and evil. [40] Fools! Did not God, who made the outside, also make the inside? [41] But give what is in your cups and plates to the poor, and everything will be clean for you.

[42] "How terrible for you, Pharisees! You give to God one tenth of the seasoning herbs, such as mint and rue and all the other herbs, but you neglect justice and the love for God. These you should practice, without neglecting the others.

[43] "How terrible for you, Pharisees! You love the reserved seats in the synagogues, and to be greeted with respect in the market places. [44] How terrible for you! You are like unmarked graves which people walk on without knowing it."

[45] One of the teachers of the Law said to him, "Teacher, when you say this you insult us too!" [46] Jesus answered: "How terrible for you, too, teachers of the Law!

You put loads on men's backs which are hard to carry, but you yourselves will not stretch out a finger to help them carry those loads. [47] How terrible for you! You make fine tombs for the prophets — the very prophets your ancestors murdered. [48] You yourselves admit, then, that you approve of what your ancestors did; for they murdered the prophets, and you build their tombs. [49] For this reason the Wisdom of God said: 'I will send them prophets and messengers; they will kill some of them and persecute others.' ⁵⁰ So the people of this time will be punished for the murder of all the prophets killed since the creation of the world, ⁵¹ from the murder of Abel to the murder of Zechariah, who was killed between the altar and the holy place. Yes, I tell you, the people of this time will be punished for them all!

⁵² "How terrible for you, teachers of the Law! You have kept the key that opens the door to the house of knowledge; you yourselves will not go in, and you stop those who are trying to go in!"

⁵³ When Jesus left that place the teachers of the Law and the Pharisees began to criticize him bitterly and ask him questions about many things, ⁵⁴ trying to lay traps for him and catch him in something wrong he might say.

A Warning against Hypocrisy
(Also Matt. 10.26–27)

12 As thousands of people crowded together, so that they were stepping on each other, Jesus said first to his disciples: "Be on guard against the yeast of the Pharisees — I mean their hypocrisy. ² Whatever is covered up will be uncovered, and every secret will be made known. ³ So then, whatever you have said in the dark will be heard in broad daylight, and whatever you have whispered in men's ears in a closed room will be shouted from the housetops."

Whom to Fear
(Also Matt. 10.28–31)

⁴ "I tell you, my friends, do not be afraid of those who kill the body but cannot afterward do anything worse. ⁵ I will show you whom to fear: fear God who, after killing, has the authority to throw into hell. Yes, I tell you, be afraid of him!

⁶ "Aren't five sparrows sold for two pennies? Yet not a single one of them is forgotten by God. ⁷ Even the hairs of your head have all been numbered. So do not be afraid: you are worth much more than many sparrows!"

Confessing and Denying Christ
(Also Matt. 10.32–33; 12.32; 10.19–20)

⁸ "I tell you: whoever declares publicly that he belongs to me, the Son of Man will do the same for him before the

angels of God; [9] but whoever denies publicly that he belongs to me, the Son of Man will also deny him before the angels of God.

[10] "Anyone who says a word against the Son of Man will be forgiven; but the one who says evil things against the Holy Spirit will not be forgiven.

[11] "When they bring you to be tried in the synagogues, or before governors or rulers, do not be worried about how you will defend yourself or what you will say. [12] For the Holy Spirit will teach you at that time what you should say."

The Parable of the Rich Fool

[13] A man in the crowd said to him, "Teacher, tell my brother to divide with me the property our father left us." [14] Jesus answered him, "Man, who gave me the right to judge, or to divide the property between you two?" [15] And he went on to say to them all: "Watch out, and guard yourselves from all kinds of greed; for a man's true life is not made up of the things he owns, no matter how rich he may be." [16] Then Jesus told them this parable: "A rich man had land which bore good crops. [17] He began to think to himself, 'I don't have a place to keep all my crops. What can I do? [18] This is what I will do,' he told himself; 'I will tear my barns down and build bigger ones, where I will store the grain and all my other goods. [19] Then I will say to myself: Lucky man! You have all the good things you need for many years. Take life easy, eat, drink, and enjoy yourself!' [20] But God said to him, 'You fool! This very night you will have to give up your life; then who will get all these things you have kept for yourself?' " [21] And Jesus concluded, "This is how it is with those who pile up riches for themselves but are not rich in God's sight."

Trust in God
(Also Matt. 6.25–34)

[22] Then Jesus said to the disciples: "This is why I tell you: Do not be worried about the food you need to stay alive, or about the clothes you need for your body. [23] For life is much more important than food, and body much more important than clothes. [24] Look at the crows: they don't plant seeds or gather a harvest; they don't have stor-

age rooms or barns; God feeds them! You are worth so much more than birds! ²⁵ Which one of you can live a few more years by worrying about it? ²⁶ If you can't manage even such a small thing, why worry about the other things? ²⁷ Look how the wild flowers grow: they don't work or make clothes for themselves. But I tell you that not even Solomon, as rich as he was, had clothes as beautiful as one of these flowers. ²⁸ It is God who clothes the wild grass — grass that is here today, gone tomorrow, burned up in the oven. Won't he be all the more sure to clothe you? How little is your faith! ²⁹ So don't be all upset, always looking for what you will eat and drink. ³⁰ (For the heathen of this world are always looking for all these things.) Your Father knows that you need these things. ³¹ Instead, put his Kingdom first in your life, and he will provide you with these things."

Riches in Heaven
(Also Matt. 6.19–21)

³² "Do not be afraid, little flock! For your Father is pleased to give you the Kingdom. ³³ Sell all your belongings and give the money to the poor. Provide for yourselves purses that don't wear out, and save your riches in heaven, where they will never decrease, for no thief can get to them, no moth can destroy them. ³⁴ For your heart will always be where your riches are."

Watchful Servants

³⁵ "Be ready for whatever comes, with your clothes fastened tight at the waist and your lamps lit, ³⁶ like serv-

ants who are waiting for their master to come back from a wedding feast. When he comes and knocks, they will open the door for him at once. [37] How happy are those servants whose master finds them awake and ready! I tell you, he will fasten his belt, have them sit down, and wait on them. [38] How happy are they if he finds them ready, even if he should come as late as midnight or even later! [39] And remember this! If the man of the house knew the time when the thief would come, he would not let the thief break into his house. [40] And you, too, be ready, because the Son of Man will come at an hour when you are not expecting him."

The Faithful or the Unfaithful Servant
(Also Matt. 24.45–51)

[41] Peter said, "Lord, are you telling this parable to us, or do you mean it for everybody?" [42] The Lord answered: "Who, then, is the faithful and wise servant? He is the one whom his master will put in charge, to run the household and give the other servants their share of the food at the proper time. [43] How happy is that servant if his master finds him doing this when he comes home! [44] Indeed, I tell you, the master will put that servant in charge of all his property. [45] But if that servant says to himself, 'My master is taking a long time to come back,' and begins to beat the other servants, both men and women, and eats and drinks and gets drunk, [46] then the master will come back some day when the servant does not expect him and at a time he does not know; the master will cut him to pieces, and make him share the fate of the disobedient.

[47] "The servant who knows what his master wants him to do, but does not get himself ready and do what his master wants, will be punished with a heavy whipping; [48] but the servant who does not know what his master wants, and does something for which he deserves a whipping, will be punished with a light whipping. The man to whom much is given, of him much is required; the man to whom more is given, of him much more is required."

Jesus the Cause of Division
(Also Matt. 10.34–36)

[49] "I came to set the earth on fire, and how I wish it were already kindled! [50] I have a baptism to receive, and

how distressed I am until it is over! ⁵¹ Do you suppose
that I came to bring peace to the world? Not peace, I tell
you, but division. ⁵² From now on a family of five will be
divided, three against two, two against three. ⁵³ Fathers
will be against their sons, and sons against their fathers;
mothers will be against their daughters, and daughters
against their mothers; mothers-in-law will be against their
daughters-in-law, and daughters-in-law against their mothers-in-law."

Understanding the Time
(Also Matt. 16.2–3)

⁵⁴ Jesus said also to the people: "When you see a cloud
coming up in the west, at once you say, 'It is going to
rain,' and it does. ⁵⁵ And when you feel the south wind
blowing, you say, 'It is going to get hot,' and it does.
⁵⁶ Impostors! You can look at the earth and the sky and
tell what it means; why, then, don't you know the meaning of this present time?"

Settle with Your Opponent
(Also Matt. 5.25–26)

⁵⁷ "And why do you not judge for yourselves the right
thing to do? ⁵⁸ If a man brings a lawsuit against you and
takes you to court, do your best to settle the matter with
him while you are on the way, so that he won't drag you
before the judge, and the judge hand you over to the police,
and the police put you in jail. ⁵⁹ You will not come out of
there, I tell you, until you pay the last penny of your fine."

Turn from Your Sins or Die

13 At that time some people were there who told Jesus
about the Galileans whom Pilate had killed while
they were offering sacrifices to God. ² Jesus answered them:
"Because these Galileans were killed in that way, do you
think it proves that they were worse sinners than all the
other Galileans? ³ No! I tell you that if you do not turn
from your sins, you will all die as they did. ⁴ What about
those eighteen in Siloam who were killed when the tower
fell on them? Do you suppose this proves that they were
worse than all the other people living in Jerusalem? ⁵ No!

I tell you that if you do not turn from your sins, you will all die as they did."

The Parable of the Unfruitful Fig Tree

⁶ Then Jesus told them this parable: "A man had a fig tree growing in his vineyard. He went looking for figs on it but found none. ⁷ So he said to his gardener, 'Look, for three years I have been coming here looking for figs on this fig tree and I haven't found any. Cut it down! Why should it go on using up the soil?' ⁸ But the gardener answered, 'Leave it alone, sir, just this one year; I will dig a trench around it and fill it up with fertilizer. ⁹ Then if the tree bears figs next year, so much the better; if not, then you will have it cut down.' "

Jesus Heals a Crippled Woman on the Sabbath

¹⁰ One Sabbath day Jesus was teaching in a synagogue. ¹¹ A woman was there who had an evil spirit in her that had kept her sick for eighteen years; she was bent over and could not straighten up at all. ¹² When Jesus saw her he called out to her, "Woman, you are free from your sickness!" ¹³ He placed his hands on her and at once she straightened herself up and praised God. ¹⁴ The official of the synagogue was angry that Jesus had healed on the Sabbath; so he spoke up and said to the people, "There are six days in which we should work; so come during those days and be healed, but not on the Sabbath!" ¹⁵ The Lord answered him by saying: "You impostors! Any one of you would untie his ox or his donkey from the stall and take it out to give it water on the Sabbath. ¹⁶ Now here is this

descendant of Abraham whom Satan has kept in bonds for eighteen years; should she not be freed from her bonds on the Sabbath?" [17] His answer made all his enemies ashamed of themselves, while all the people rejoiced over every wonderful thing that he did.

The Parable of the Mustard Seed
(Also Matt. 13.31–32; Mark 4.30–32)

[18] Jesus said: "What is the Kingdom of God like? What can I compare it with? [19] It is like a mustard seed, which a man took and planted in his field; the plant grew and became a tree, and the birds made their nests in its branches."

The Parable of the Yeast
(Also Matt. 13.33)

[20] Again Jesus asked: "What shall I compare the Kingdom of God with? [21] It is like the yeast which a woman takes and mixes in a bushel of flour, until the whole batch of dough rises."

The Narrow Door
(Also Matt. 7.13–14, 21–23)

[22] Jesus went through towns and villages, teaching and making his way toward Jerusalem. [23] Someone asked him, "Sir, will just a few people be saved?" Jesus answered them: [24] "Do your best to go in through the narrow door; for many people, I tell you, will try to go in but will not be able.

[25] "The master of the house will get up and close the door; then when you stand outside and begin to knock on the door and say, 'Open the door for us, sir!' he will answer you, 'I don't know where you come from!' [26] Then you will answer back, 'We ate and drank with you; you taught in our town!' [27] He will say again, 'I don't know where you come from. Get away from me, all you evildoers!' [28] What crying and gnashing of teeth there will be when you see Abraham, Isaac, and Jacob and all the prophets in the Kingdom of God, while you are kept outside! [29] People will come from the east and the west, from the north and the south, and sit at the table in the Kingdom of God. [30] Then those who are now last will be first, and those who are now first will be last."

Jesus' Love for Jerusalem
(Also Matt. 23.37–39)

³¹ At that same time some Pharisees came to Jesus and said to him, "You must get out of here and go somewhere else, for Herod wants to kill you." ³² Jesus answered them: "Go tell that fox: 'I am driving out demons and performing cures today and tomorrow, and on the third day I shall finish my work.' ³³ Yet I must be on my way today, tomorrow, and the next day; it is not right for a prophet to be killed anywhere except in Jerusalem.

³⁴ "O Jerusalem, Jerusalem! You kill the prophets, you stone the messengers God has sent you! How many times I wanted to put my arms around all your people, just as a hen gathers her chicks under her wings, but you would not let me! ³⁵ Now your home will be completely forsaken. You will not see me, I tell you, until the time comes when you say, 'God bless him who comes in the name of the Lord.' "

Jesus Heals a Sick Man

14 One Sabbath day Jesus went to eat a meal at the home of one of the leading Pharisees; and people were watching Jesus closely. ² A man whose legs and arms were swollen came to Jesus, ³ and Jesus spoke up and asked the teachers of the Law and the Pharisees, "Does our Law allow healing on the Sabbath, or not?" ⁴ But they would not say a thing. Jesus took the man, healed him and sent him away. ⁵ Then he said to them, "If any one of you had a son or an ox that happened to fall in a well on a Sabbath, would you not pull him out at once on the Sabbath itself?" ⁶ But they were not able to answer him about this.

Hospitality and Humility

⁷ Jesus noticed how some of the guests were choosing the best places, so he told this parable to all of them: ⁸ "When someone invites you to a wedding feast, do not sit down in the best place. For it could happen that someone more important than you had been invited, ⁹ and your host, who invited both of you, would come and say to you, 'Let him have this place.' Then you would be ashamed and have to sit in the lowest place. ¹⁰ Instead, when you are invited, go and sit in the lowest place, so that your host

will come to you and say, 'Come on up, my friend, to a better place.' This will bring you honor in the presence of all the other guests. [11] For everyone who makes himself great will be humbled, and whoever humbles himself will be made great."

[12] Then Jesus said to his host: "When you give a lunch or a dinner, do not invite your friends, or your brothers, or your relatives, or your rich neighbors — for they will invite you back and in this way you will be paid for what you did. [13] When you give a feast, invite the poor, the crippled, the lame, and the blind, [14] and you will be blessed; for they are not able to pay you back. You will be paid by God when the good people are raised from death."

The Parable of the Great Feast
(Also Matt. 22.1–10)

[15] One of the men sitting at the table heard this and said to Jesus, "How happy are those who will sit at the table in the Kingdom of God!" [16] Jesus said to him: "There was a man who was giving a great feast, to which he invited many people. [17] At the time for the feast he sent his servant to tell his guests, 'Come, everything is ready!' [18] But they all began, one after another, to make excuses. The first one told the servant, 'I bought a field, and have to go and look at it; please accept my apologies.' [19] Another one said, 'I bought five pairs of oxen and am on my way to try them out; please accept my apologies.' [20] Another one said, 'I have just gotten married, and for this reason I cannot come.' [21] The servant went back and told all this to his master. The master of the house was furious and said to his servant, 'Hurry out to the streets and alleys of the town, and bring back the poor, the crippled, the blind, and the lame.' [22] Soon the servant said, 'Your order has been carried out, sir, but there is room for more.' [23] So the master said to the servant, 'Go out to the country roads and lanes, and make people come in, so that my house will be full. [24] None of those men who were invited, I tell you all, will taste my dinner!' "

The Cost of Being a Disciple
(Also Matt. 10.37–38)

[25] Great crowds of people were going along with Jesus.

He turned and said to them: 26 "Whoever comes to me cannot be my disciple unless he hates his father and his mother, his wife and his children, his brothers and his sisters, and himself as well. 27 Whoever does not carry his own cross and come after me cannot be my disciple. 28 If one of you is planning to build a tower, he sits down first and figures out what it will cost, to see if he has enough money to finish the job. 29 If he doesn't, he will not be able to finish the tower after laying the foundation; and all who see what happened will make fun of him. 30 'This man began to build but can't finish the job!' they will say. 31 If a king goes out with ten thousand men to fight another king, who comes against him with twenty thousand men, he will sit down first and decide if he is strong enough to face that other king. 32 If he isn't, he will have to send messengers to meet the other king, while he is still a long way off, to ask for terms of peace. 33 In the same way," concluded Jesus, "none of you can be my disciple unless he gives up everything he has."

Worthless Salt
(Also Matt. 5.13; Mark 9.50)

34 "Salt is good, but if it loses its taste there is no way to make it good again. 35 It is no good for the soil or for the manure pile; it is thrown away. Listen, then, if you have ears!"

The Lost Sheep
(Also Matt. 18.12–14)

15 One time many tax collectors and outcasts came to listen to Jesus. 2 The Pharisees and the teachers of the Law started grumbling, "This man welcomes outcasts and even eats with them!" 3 So Jesus told them this parable: 4 "Suppose one of you has a hundred sheep and loses one of them — what does he do? He leaves the ninety-nine sheep in the pasture and goes looking for the lost sheep until he finds it. 5 When he finds it, he is so happy that he puts it on his shoulders, 6 carries it back home, and calls his friends and neighbors together. 'Rejoice with me,' he tells them, 'for I have found my lost sheep!' 7 In the same way, I tell you, there will be more joy in heaven over one sinner who repents than over ninety-nine respectable people who do not need to repent."

The Lost Coin

⁸ "Or suppose a woman who has ten silver coins loses one of them — what does she do? She lights a lamp, sweeps her house, and looks carefully everywhere until she finds it. ⁹ When she finds it, she calls her friends and neighbors together. 'Rejoice with me,' she tells them, 'for I have found the coin I lost!' ¹⁰ In the same way, I tell you, the angels of God rejoice over one sinner who repents."

The Lost Son

¹¹ Jesus went on to say: "There was a man who had two sons. ¹² The younger one said to his father, 'Father, give me now my share of the property.' So the father divided the property between his two sons. ¹³ After a few days the younger son sold his part of the property and left home

with the money. He went to a country far away, where he wasted his money in reckless living. ¹⁴ He spent everything he had. Then a severe famine spread over that country, and he was left without a thing. ¹⁵ So he went to work for one of the citizens of that country, who sent him out to his farm to take care of the pigs. ¹⁶ He wished he could fill himself with the bean pods the pigs ate, but no one gave him any. ¹⁷ At last he came to his senses and said: 'All my father's hired workers have more than they can eat, and here I am, about to starve! ¹⁸ I will get up and go to my father and say, "Father, I have sinned against God and against you. ¹⁹ I am no longer fit to be called your son; treat me as one of your hired workers." ' ²⁰ So he got up and started back to his father.

"He was still a long way from home when his father saw him; his heart was filled with pity and he ran, threw his arms around his son, and kissed him. ²¹ 'Father,' the son said, 'I have sinned against God and against you. I am no longer fit to be called your son.' ²² But the father called his servants: 'Hurry!' he said. 'Bring the best robe and put it on him. Put a ring on his finger and shoes on his feet. ²³ Then go get the prize calf and kill it, and let us celebrate with a feast! ²⁴ For this son of mine was dead,

but now he is alive; he was lost, but now he has been found.' And so the feasting began.

²⁵ "The older son, in the meantime, was out in the field. On his way back, when he came close to the house, he heard the music and dancing. ²⁶ He called one of the serv-

ants and asked him, 'What's going on?' ²⁷ 'Your brother came back home,' the servant answered, 'and your father killed the prize calf, because he got him back safe and sound.' ²⁸ The older brother was so angry that he would not go into the house; so his father came out and begged him to come in. ²⁹ 'Look,' he answered back to his father, 'all these years I have worked like a slave for you, and not once did I disobey an order of yours. What have you given me? Not even a goat for me to have a feast with my friends! ³⁰ But this son of yours wasted all your property on prostitutes, and when he comes back home you kill the prize calf for him!' ³¹ 'My son,' the father answered, 'you are always at home and everything I have is yours. ³² But we had to have a feast and be happy, for your brother was dead, but now he is alive; he was lost, but now he has been found.' "

The Shrewd Manager

16 Jesus said to his disciples: "There was a rich man who had a manager, and he was told that the manager was wasting his master's money. ² He called him in and said, 'What is this I hear about you? Turn in a complete account of your handling of my property, for you cannot be my manager any longer.' ³ 'My master is about to dismiss me from my job,' the man said to himself. 'What shall I do? I am not strong enough to dig ditches, and I am ashamed to beg. ⁴ Now I know what I will do! Then when my job is gone I shall have friends who will welcome me in their homes.' ⁵ So he called in all the people who were in debt to his master. To the first one he said, 'How much do you owe my master?' ⁶ 'One hundred barrels of olive oil,' he answered. 'Here is your account,' the manager told him; 'sit down and write fifty.' ⁷ To another one he said, 'And you — how much do you owe?' 'A thousand bushels of wheat,' he answered. 'Here is your account,' the manager told him; 'write eight hundred.' ⁸ The master of this dishonest manager praised him for doing such a shrewd thing; for the people of this world are much more shrewd in handling their affairs than the people who belong to the light."

⁹ And Jesus went on to say: "And so I tell you: make friends for yourselves with worldly wealth, so that when it gives out you will be welcomed in the eternal home.

[10] Whoever is faithful in small matters will be faithful in large ones; whoever is dishonest in small matters will be dishonest in large ones. [11] If, then, you have not been faithful in handling worldly wealth, how can you be trusted with true wealth? [12] And if you have not been faithful in what belongs to someone else, who will give you what belongs to you?

[13] "No servant can be the slave of two masters: he will hate one and love the other; he will be loyal to one and despise the other. You cannot serve both God and money."

Some Sayings of Jesus
(Also Matt. 11.12–13; 5.31–32; Mark 10.11–12)

[14] The Pharisees heard all this, and they made fun of Jesus, because they loved money. [15] Jesus said to them: "You are the ones who make yourselves look right in men's sight, but God knows your hearts. For what men think is of great value is worth nothing in God's sight.

[16] "The Law of Moses and the writings of the prophets were in effect up to the time of John the Baptist; since then the Good News about the Kingdom of God is being told, and everyone forces his way in. [17] But it is easier for heaven and earth to disappear than for the smallest detail of the Law to be done away with.

[18] "Any man who divorces his wife and marries another woman commits adultery; and the man who marries a divorced woman commits adultery."

The Rich Man and Lazarus

[19] "There was once a rich man who dressed in the most expensive clothes and lived in great luxury every day. [20] There was also a poor man, named Lazarus, full of sores, who used to be brought to the rich man's door, [21] hoping to fill himself with the bits of food that fell from the rich man's table. Even the dogs would come and lick his sores. [22] The poor man died and was carried by the angels to Abraham's side, at the feast in heaven; the rich man died and was buried. [23] He was in great pain in Hades; and he looked up and saw Abraham, far away, with Lazarus at his side. [24] So he called out, 'Father Abraham! Take pity on me, and send Lazarus to dip his finger in some water and cool off my tongue, for I am in great pain in

this fire!' ²⁵ But Abraham said: 'Remember, my son, that in your lifetime you were given all the good things, while Lazarus got all the bad things; but now he is enjoying it here, while you are in pain. ²⁶ Besides all that, there is a deep pit lying between us, so that those who want to cross over from here to you cannot do it, nor can anyone cross over to us from where you are.' ²⁷ The rich man said, 'Well, father, I beg you, send Lazarus to my father's house, ²⁸ where I have five brothers; let him go and warn them so that they, at least, will not come to this place of pain.' ²⁹ Abraham said, 'Your brothers have Moses and the prophets to warn them; let your brothers listen to what they say.' ³⁰ The rich man answered, 'That is not enough, father Abraham! But if someone were to rise from death and go to them, then they would turn from their sins.' ³¹ But Abraham said, 'If they will not listen to Moses and the prophets, they will not be convinced even if someone were to rise from death.' "

Sin
(Also Matt. 18.6–7, 21–22; Mark 9.42)

17 Jesus said to his disciples: "Things that make people fall into sin are bound to happen; but how terrible for the one who makes them happen! ² It would be better for him if a large millstone were tied around his neck and he were thrown into the sea, than for him to cause one of these little ones to sin. ³ Be on your guard!

"If your brother sins, rebuke him, and if he repents, forgive him. ⁴ If he sins against you seven times in one day, and each time he comes to you saying, 'I repent,' you must forgive him."

Faith

⁵ The apostles said to the Lord, "Make our faith greater." ⁶ The Lord answered: "If you had faith as big as a mustard seed, you could say to this mulberry tree, 'Pull yourself up by the roots and plant yourself in the sea!' and it would obey you."

A Servant's Duty

⁷ "Suppose one of you has a servant who is plowing or looking after the sheep. When he comes in from the field, do you say to him, 'Hurry along and eat your meal'?

[8] Of course not! Instead, you say to him, 'Get my supper ready, then put on your apron and wait on me while I eat and drink; after that you may eat and drink.' [9] The servant does not deserve thanks for obeying orders, does he? [10] It is the same with you; when you have done all you have been told to do, say, 'We are ordinary servants; we have only done our duty.' "

Jesus Makes Ten Lepers Clean

[11] As Jesus made his way to Jerusalem he went between Samaria and Galilee. [12] He was going into a certain village when he was met by ten lepers. They stood at a distance [13] and shouted, "Jesus! Master! Have pity on us!" [14] Jesus saw them and said to them, "Go and let the priests examine you." On the way they were made clean. [15] One of them, when he saw that he was healed, came back, praising God with a loud voice. [16] He threw himself to the ground at Jesus' feet, thanking him. The man was a Samaritan. [17] Jesus spoke up: "There were ten men made clean; where are the other nine? [18] Why is this foreigner the only one who came back to give thanks to God?" [19] And Jesus said to him, "Get up and go; your faith has made you well."

The Coming of the Kingdom
(Also Matt. 24.23–28, 37–41)

20 Some Pharisees asked Jesus when the Kingdom of God would come. His answer was: "The Kingdom of God does not come in such a way as to be seen. 21 No one will say, 'Look, here it is!' or, 'There it is!'; because the Kingdom of God is within you."

22 Then he said to the disciples: "The time will come when you will wish you could see one of the days of the Son of Man, but you will not see it. 23 There will be those who will say to you, 'Look, over there!' or, 'Look, over here!' But don't go out looking for it. 24 As the lightning flashes across the sky and lights it up from one side to the other, so will the Son of Man be in his day. 25 But first he must suffer much and be rejected by the people of this day. 26 As it was in the time of Noah, so shall it be in the days of the Son of Man. 27 Everybody kept on eating and drinking, men and women married, up to the very day Noah went into the ark and the Flood came and killed them all. 28 It will be as it was in the time of Lot. Everybody kept on eating and drinking, buying and selling, planting and building. 29 On the day Lot left Sodom, fire and sulphur rained down from heaven and killed them all. 30 That is how it will be on the day the Son of Man is revealed.

31 "The man who is on the roof of his house on that day must not go down into his house to get his belongings that are there; in the same way, the man who is out in the field must not go back to the house. 32 Remember Lot's wife! 33 Whoever tries to save his own life will lose it; whoever loses his life will save it. 34 On that night, I tell you, there will be two men sleeping in one bed: one will be taken away, the other left behind. 35 Two women will be grinding meal together: one will be taken away, the other left behind. [36 Two men will be in the field: one will be taken away, the other left behind.]" 37 The disciples asked him, "Where, Lord?" Jesus answered, "Where there is a dead body the vultures will gather."

The Parable of the Widow and the Judge

18 Then Jesus told them this parable, to teach them that they should always pray and never become discouraged. 2 "There was a judge in a certain town who

neither feared God nor respected men. ³ And there was a widow in that same town who kept coming to him and pleading for her rights: 'Help me against my opponent!' ⁴ For a long time the judge was not willing, but at last he said to himself, 'Even though I don't fear God or respect men, ⁵ yet because of all the trouble this widow is giving me I will see to it that she gets her rights; or else she will keep on coming and finally wear me out!' " ⁶ And the Lord continued: "Listen to what that corrupt judge said. ⁷ Now, will God not judge in favor of his own people who cry to him for help day and night? Will he be slow to help them? ⁸ I tell you, he will judge in their favor, and do it quickly. But will the Son of Man find faith on earth when he comes?"

The Parable of the Pharisee and the Tax Collector

⁹ Jesus also told this parable to people who were sure of their own goodness and despised everybody else. ¹⁰ "Two men went up to the Temple to pray; one was a Pharisee, the other a tax collector. ¹¹ The Pharisee stood apart by himself and prayed: 'I thank you, God, that I am not greedy, dishonest, or immoral, like everybody else; I thank you that I am not like that tax collector. ¹² I fast two days every week, and I give you one tenth of all my income.' ¹³ But the tax collector stood at a distance and would not even raise his face to heaven, but beat on his breast and said, 'O God, have pity on me, a sinner!' ¹⁴ I tell you," said Jesus, "this man, and not the other, was in the right with God when he went home. For everyone who makes himself great will be humbled, and everyone who humbles himself will be made great."

Jesus Blesses Little Children
(Also Matt. 19.13–15; Mark 10.13–16)

¹⁵ Some people brought their babies to Jesus to have him place his hands on them. But the disciples saw them and scolded them for doing so. ¹⁶ But Jesus called the children to him, and said: "Let the children come to me! Do not stop them, because the Kingdom of God belongs to such as these. ¹⁷ Remember this! Whoever does not receive the Kingdom of God like a child will never enter it."

The Rich Man
(*Also Matt. 19.16–30; Mark 10.17–31*)

18 A certain Jewish leader asked him: "Good Teacher, what must I do to receive eternal life?" 19 "Why do you call me good?" Jesus asked him. "No one is good except God alone. 20 You know the commandments: 'Do not commit adultery; do not murder; do not steal; do not lie; honor your father and mother.' " 21 The man replied, "Ever since I was young I have obeyed all these commandments." 22 When Jesus heard this, he said to him: "You still need to do one thing. Sell all you have and give the money to the poor, and you will have riches in heaven; then come and follow me." 23 But when the man heard this he became very sad, because he was very rich.

24 Jesus saw that he was sad and said: "How hard it is for rich people to enter the Kingdom of God! 25 It is much harder for a rich man to enter the Kingdom of God than for a camel to go through the eye of a needle." 26 The people who heard him asked, "Who, then, can be saved?" 27 Jesus answered, "What is impossible for men is possible for God."

28 Then Peter said, "Look! We have left our homes to follow you." 29 "Yes," Jesus said to them, "and I tell you this: anyone who leaves home or wife or brothers or parents or children for the sake of the Kingdom of God 30 will receive much more in the present age, and eternal life in the age to come."

Jesus Speaks a Third Time about His Death
(*Also Matt. 20.17–19; Mark 10.32–34*)

31 Jesus took the twelve disciples aside and said to them: "Listen! We are going to Jerusalem where everything the prophets wrote about the Son of Man will come true. 32 He will be handed over to the Gentiles, who will make fun of him, insult him, and spit on him. 33 They will whip him and kill him, but on the third day he will be raised to life." 34 The disciples did not understand any of these things; the meaning of the words was hidden from them, and they did not know what Jesus was talking about.

Jesus Heals a Blind Beggar
(*Also Matt. 20.29–34; Mark 10.46–52*)

35 Jesus was coming near Jericho, and a certain blind

man was sitting and begging by the road. ³⁶ When he heard the crowd passing by he asked, "What is this?" ³⁷ "Jesus of Nazareth is passing by," they told him. ³⁸ He cried out, "Jesus! Son of David! Have mercy on me!" ³⁹ The people in front scolded him and told him to be quiet. But he shouted even more loudly, "Son of David! Have mercy on me!" ⁴⁰ So Jesus stopped and ordered that the blind man be brought to him. When he came near, Jesus asked him, ⁴¹ "What do you want me to do for you?" "Sir," he answered, "I want to see again." ⁴² Then Jesus said to him, "See! Your faith has made you well." ⁴³ At once he was able to see, and he followed Jesus, giving thanks to God. When the crowd saw it, they all praised God.

Jesus and Zacchaeus

19 Jesus went on into Jericho and was passing through. ² There was a chief tax collector there, named Zacchaeus, who was rich. ³ He was trying to see who Jesus was, but he was a little man and could not see Jesus because of the crowd. ⁴ So he ran ahead of the crowd and climbed a sycamore tree to see Jesus, who would be going

that way. ⁵ When Jesus came to that place he looked up and said to Zacchaeus, "Hurry down, Zacchaeus, for I must stay in your house today." ⁶ Zacchaeus hurried down and welcomed him with great joy. ⁷ All the people who saw it started grumbling, "This man has gone as a guest to the home of a sinner!" ⁸ Zacchaeus stood up and said to the Lord, "Listen, sir! I will give half my belongings to the poor; and if I have cheated anyone, I will pay him back four times as much." ⁹ Jesus said to him, "Salvation has come to this house today; this man, also, is a descendant of Abraham. ¹⁰ For the Son of Man came to seek and to save the lost."

The Parable of the Gold Coins
(Also Matt. 25.14-30)

¹¹ Then Jesus told a parable to those who heard him say this. He was now almost at Jerusalem, and they supposed that the Kingdom of God was just about to appear. ¹² So he said: "There was a nobleman who went to a country far away to be made king and then come back home. ¹³ Before he left, he called his ten servants and gave them each a gold coin and told them, 'See what you can earn with this while I am gone.' ¹⁴ Now, his countrymen hated him, and so they sent messengers after him to say, 'We don't want this man to be our king.'

¹⁵ "The nobleman was made king and came back. At once he ordered his servants, to whom he had given the money, to appear before him in order to find out how much they had earned. ¹⁶ The first one came up and said, 'Sir, I have earned ten gold coins with the one you gave me.' ¹⁷ 'Well done,' he said; 'you are a good servant! Since you were faithful in small matters, I will put you in charge of ten cities.' ¹⁸ The second servant came and said, 'Sir, I have earned five gold coins with the one you gave me.' ¹⁹ To this one he said, 'You will be in charge of five cities.' ²⁰ Another servant came and said: 'Sir, here is your gold coin; I kept it hidden in a handkerchief. ²¹ I was afraid of you, because you are a hard man. You take what is not yours, and reap what you did not plant.' ²² He said to him: 'You bad servant! I will use your own words to condemn you! You know that I am a hard man, taking what is not mine and reaping what I have not planted. ²³ Well, then, why didn't you put my money in the bank? Then I would

have received it back with interest when I returned.'
24 Then he said to those who were standing there, 'Take the
gold coin away from him and give it to the servant who
has ten coins.' 25 They said to him, 'Sir, he already has
ten coins!' 26 'I tell you,' he replied, 'that to every one who
has, even more will be given; but the one who does not
have, even the little that he has will be taken away from
him. 27 Now, as for these enemies of mine who did not
want me to be their king: bring them here and kill them
before me!' "

The Triumphant Entry into Jerusalem
(Also Matt. 21.1–11; Mark 11.1–11; John 12.12–19)

28 Jesus said this and then went on to Jerusalem ahead
of them. 29 As he came near Bethphage and Bethany, at
the Mount of Olives, he sent two disciples ahead 30 with
these instructions: "Go to the village there ahead of you;
as you go in you will find a colt tied up that has never been
ridden. Untie it and bring it here. 31 If someone asks you,
'Why are you untying it?' tell him, 'The Master needs it.' "
32 They went on their way and found everything just as
Jesus had told them. 33 As they were untying the colt, its
owners said to them, "Why are you untying it?" 34 "The
Master needs it," they answered, 35 and took the colt to

Jesus. Then they threw their cloaks over the animal and
helped Jesus get on. [36] As he rode on, they spread their
cloaks on the road. [37] When he came near Jerusalem, at
the place where the road went down the Mount of Olives,
the large crowd of his disciples began to thank God and
praise him in loud voices for all the great things that they
had seen: [38] "God bless the king who comes in the name
of the Lord! Peace in heaven, and glory to God!"

³⁹ Then some of the Pharisees spoke up from the crowd to Jesus. "Teacher," they said, "command your disciples to be quiet!" ⁴⁰ Jesus answered, "If they keep quiet, I tell you, the stones themselves will shout."

Jesus Weeps over Jerusalem

⁴¹ He came closer to the city and when he saw it he wept over it, ⁴² saying: "If you only knew today what is needed for peace! But now you cannot see it! ⁴³ For the days will come upon you when your enemies will surround you with barricades, blockade you, and close in on you from every side. ⁴⁴ They will completely destroy you and the people within your walls; not a single stone will they leave in its place, because you did not recognize the time when God came to save you!"

Jesus Goes to the Temple
(Also Matt. 21.12–17; Mark 11.15–19; John 2.13–22)

⁴⁵ Jesus went into the Temple and began to drive out the merchants, ⁴⁶ saying to them: "It is written in the Scriptures that God said, 'My house will be called a house of prayer.' But you have turned it into a hideout for thieves!"

⁴⁷ Jesus taught in the Temple every day. The chief priests, the teachers of the Law, and the leaders of the people wanted to kill him, ⁴⁸ but they could not find how to do it, because all the people kept listening to him, not wanting to miss a single word.

The Question about Jesus' Authority
(Also Matt. 21.23–27; Mark 11.27–33)

20 One day, when Jesus was in the Temple teaching the people and preaching the Good News, the chief priests and the teachers of the Law, together with the elders, came ² and said to him, "Tell us, what right do you have to do these things? Who gave you the right to do them?" ³ Jesus answered them: "Now let me ask you a question. Tell me, ⁴ did John's right to baptize come from God or from man?" ⁵ They started to argue among themselves: "What shall we say? If we say, 'From God,' he will say, 'Why, then, did you not believe John?' ⁶ But if we say, 'From man,' this whole crowd here will stone us, because they are convinced that John was a prophet." ⁷ So

they answered, "We don't know where it came from."
8 And Jesus said to them, "Neither will I tell you, then, by
what right I do these things."

The Parable of the Tenants in the Vineyard
(Also Matt. 21.33–46; Mark 12.1–12)

9 Then Jesus told the people this parable: "A man
planted a vineyard, rented it out to tenants, and then left
home for a long time. 10 When the time came for harvest-
ing the grapes, he sent a slave to the tenants to receive
from them his share of the harvest. But the tenants beat
the slave and sent him back without a thing. 11 So he sent
another slave, but the tenants beat him also, treated him
shamefully, and sent him back without a thing. 12 Then he
sent a third slave; the tenants hurt him, too, and threw him
out. 13 Then the owner of the vineyard said, 'What shall
I do? I will send my own dear son; surely they will respect
him!' 14 But when the tenants saw him they said to one
another, 'This is the owner's son. Let us kill him, and the
vineyard will be ours!' 15 So they threw him out of the
vineyard and killed him.

"What, then, will the owner of the vineyard do to the
tenants?" Jesus asked. 16 "He will come and kill those men,
and turn over the vineyard to other tenants." When the
people heard this they said, "Surely not!" 17 Jesus looked
at them and asked, "What, then, does this scripture mean?

'The stone which the builders rejected as
   worthless
Turned out to be the most important stone.'

18 Everyone who falls on that stone will be cut to pieces;
and if the stone falls on someone, it will crush him to
dust."

The Question about Paying Taxes
(Also Matt. 22.15–22; Mark 12.13–17)

19 The teachers of the Law and the chief priests tried to
arrest Jesus on the spot, because they knew that he had
told this parable against them; but they were afraid of the
people. 20 So they watched for the right time. They bribed
some men to pretend they were sincere, and sent them to
trap Jesus with questions, so they could hand him over to
the authority and power of the Governor. 21 These spies
said to Jesus: "Teacher, we know that what you say and

teach is right. We know that you pay no attention to what a man seems to be, but teach the truth about God's will for man. 22 Tell us, is it against our Law for us to pay taxes to the Roman Emperor, or not?" 23 But Jesus saw through their trick and said to them, 24 "Show me a silver coin. Whose face and name are these on it?" 25 "The Emperor's," they answered. So Jesus said, "Well, then, pay to the Emperor what belongs to him, and pay to God what belongs to God." 26 They could not catch him in a thing there before the people, so they kept quiet, amazed at his answer.

The Question about Rising from Death
(Also Matt. 22.23–33; Mark 12.18–27)

27 Some Sadducees came to Jesus. (They are the ones who say that people will not rise from death.) They asked him: 28 "Teacher, Moses wrote this law for us: 'If a man dies and leaves a wife, but no children, that man's brother must marry the widow so they can have children for the dead man.' 29 Once there were seven brothers; the oldest got married, and died without having children. 30 Then the second one married the woman, 31 and then the third; the same thing happened to all seven — they died without having children. 32 Last of all, the woman died. 33 Now, on the day when the dead are raised to life, whose wife will she be? All seven of them had married her!"

34 Jesus answered them: "The men and women of this age marry, 35 but the men and women who are worthy to be raised from death and live in the age to come do not marry. 36 They are like angels and cannot die. They are the sons of God, because they have been raised from death. 37 And Moses clearly proves that the dead will be raised to life. In the passage about the burning bush he speaks of the Lord as 'the God of Abraham, the God of Isaac, and the God of Jacob.' 38 This means that he is the God of the living, not of the dead — for all are alive to him." 39 Some of the teachers of the Law spoke up, "A good answer, Teacher!" 40 For they did not dare ask Jesus any more questions.

The Question about the Messiah
(Also Matt. 22.41–46; Mark 12.35–37)

41 Jesus said to them: "How can it be said that the

Messiah will be the descendant of David? ⁴² Because David himself says in the book of Psalms:

'The Lord said to my Lord:

Sit here at my right side,

⁴³ Until I put your enemies

As a footstool under your feet.'

⁴⁴ David, then, called him 'Lord.' How can the Messiah be David's descendant?"

Jesus Warns against the Teachers of the Law
(Also Matt. 23.1–36; Mark 12.38–40)

⁴⁵ As the whole crowd listened to him, Jesus said to his disciples: ⁴⁶ "Watch out for the teachers of the Law, who like to walk around in their long robes, and love to be greeted with respect in the market place; who choose the reserved seats in the synagogues and the best places at feasts; ⁴⁷ who take advantage of widows and rob them of their homes, then make a show of saying long prayers! Their punishment will be all the worse!"

The Widow's Offering
(Also Mark 12.41–44)

21 Jesus looked around and saw rich men dropping their gifts in the Temple treasury, ² and he also saw a very poor widow dropping in two little copper coins. ³ And he said: "I tell you that this poor widow has really put in more than all the others. ⁴ For the others offered their gifts from what they had to spare of their riches; but she, poor as she is, gave all she had to live on."

Jesus Speaks of the Destruction of the Temple
(Also Matt. 24.1–2; Mark 13.1–2)

⁵ Some of them were talking about the Temple, how beautiful it looked with its fine stones and the gifts offered to God. Jesus said, ⁶ "All this you see — the time will come when not a single stone here will be left in its place; every one will be thrown down."

Troubles and Persecutions
(Also Matt. 24.3–14; Mark 13.3–13)

⁷ "Teacher," they asked, "when will this be? And what is the sign that will show that the time has come for it to happen?"

⁸ Jesus said: "Watch out; don't be fooled. For many men will come in my name saying, 'I am he!' and, 'The time has come!' But don't follow them. ⁹ Don't be afraid when you hear of wars and revolutions; such things must happen first, but they do not mean that the end is near." ¹⁰ He went on to say: "One country will fight another country, one kingdom will attack another kingdom; ¹¹ there will be terrible earthquakes, famines, and plagues everywhere; there will be awful things and great signs from the sky.

¹² "Before all these things take place, however, you will be arrested and persecuted; you will be handed over to trial in synagogues and be put in prison; you will be brought before kings and rulers for my sake. ¹³ This will be your chance to tell the Good News. ¹⁴ Make up your minds ahead of time not to worry about how you will defend yourselves; ¹⁵ for I will give you such words and wisdom that none of your enemies will be able to resist or deny what you say. ¹⁶ You will be handed over by your parents, your brothers, your relatives, and your friends; they will put some of you to death. ¹⁷ Everyone will hate you because of me. ¹⁸ But not a single hair from your heads will be lost. ¹⁹ Hold firm, for this is how you will save yourselves."

Jesus Speaks of the Destruction of Jerusalem
(Also Matt. 24.15–21; Mark 13.14–19)

²⁰ "When you see Jerusalem surrounded by armies, then you will know that soon she will be destroyed. ²¹ Then those who are in Judea must run away to the hills; those

who are in the city must leave, and those who are out in the country must not go into the city. ²² For these are 'The Days of Punishment,' to make come true all that the Scriptures say. ²³ How terrible it will be in those days for women who are pregnant, and for mothers with little babies! Terrible distress will come upon this land, and God's wrath will be against this people. ²⁴ They will be killed by the sword, and taken as prisoners to all countries, and the heathen will trample over Jerusalem until their time is up."

The Coming of the Son of Man
(Also Matt. 24.29–31; Mark 13.24–27)

²⁵ "There will be signs in the sun, the moon, and the stars. On earth, whole countries will be in despair, afraid of the roar of the sea and the raging tides. ²⁶ Men will faint from fear as they wait for what is coming over the whole earth; for the powers in space will be driven from their course. ²⁷ Then the Son of Man will appear, coming in a cloud with great power and glory. ²⁸ When these things begin to happen, stand up and raise your heads, for your salvation is near."

The Lesson of the Fig Tree
(Also Matt. 24.32–35; Mark 13.28–31)

²⁹ Then Jesus told them this parable: "Remember the fig tree and all the other trees. ³⁰ When you see their leaves beginning to appear you know that summer is near. ³¹ In the same way, when you see these things happening, you will know that the Kingdom of God is about to come.

³² "Remember this! All these things will take place before the people now living have all died. ³³ Heaven and earth will pass away; my words will never pass away."

The Need to Watch

³⁴ "Watch yourselves! Don't let yourselves become occupied with too much feasting and strong drink, and the worries of this life, or that Day may come on you suddenly. ³⁵ For it will come like a trap upon all men over the whole earth. ³⁶ Be on watch and pray always that you will have the strength to go safely through all these things that will happen, and to stand before the Son of Man."

³⁷ Jesus spent those days teaching in the Temple, and

when evening came he would go out and spend the night on the Mount of Olives. [38] All the people would go to the Temple early in the morning to listen to him.

The Plot against Jesus
(Also Matt. 26.1–5; Mark 14.1–2; John 11.45–53)

22 The time was near for the Feast of Unleavened Bread, which is called the Passover. [2] The chief priests and the teachers of the Law were trying to find some way of killing Jesus; for they were afraid of the people.

Judas Agrees to Betray Jesus
(Also Matt. 26.14–16; Mark 14.10–11)

[3] Then Satan went into Judas, called Iscariot, who was one of the twelve disciples. [4] So Judas went off and spoke with the chief priests and the officers of the Temple guard about how he could hand Jesus over to them. [5] They were pleased and offered to pay him money. [6] Judas agreed to it and started looking for a good chance to betray Jesus to them without the people knowing about it.

Jesus Prepares to Eat the Passover Meal
(Also Matt. 26.17–25; Mark 14.12–21; John 13.21–30)

[7] The day came during the Feast of Unleavened Bread when the lambs for the Passover meal had to be killed. [8] Jesus sent Peter and John with these instructions: "Go and get our Passover supper ready for us to eat." [9] "Where do you want us to get it ready?" they asked him. [10] He said: "Listen! As you go into the city a man carrying a jar of water will meet you. Follow him into the house that he enters, [11] and say to the owner of the house: 'The Teacher says to you, Where is the room where my disciples and I will eat the Passover supper?' [12] He will show you a large furnished room upstairs, where you will get everything ready." [13] They went off and found everything just as Jesus had told them, and prepared the Passover supper.

The Lord's Supper
(Also Matt. 26.26–30; Mark 14.22–26; 1 Cor. 11.23–25)

[14] When the hour came, Jesus took his place at the table with the apostles. [15] And he said to them: "I have wanted so much to eat this Passover meal with you before I suf-

fer! [16] For I tell you, I will never eat it until it is given its real meaning in the Kingdom of God." [17] Then Jesus took the cup, gave thanks to God, and said, "Take this and share it among yourselves; [18] for I tell you that I will not drink this wine from now on until the Kingdom of God comes." [19] Then he took the bread, gave thanks to God, broke it, and gave it to them, saying, "This is my body [which is given for you. Do this in memory of me." [20] In the same way he gave them the cup, after the supper, saying, "This cup is God's new covenant sealed with my blood which is poured out for you.]

[21] "But, look! The one who betrays me is here at the table with me! [22] For the Son of Man will die as God has decided it; but how terrible for that man who betrays him!" [23] Then they began to ask among themselves which one of them it could be who was going to do this.

The Argument about Greatness

[24] An argument came up among the disciples as to which one of them should be thought of as the greatest. [25] Jesus said to them: "The kings of this world have power over their people, and the rulers are called 'Friends of the People.' [26] But this is not the way it is with you; rather, the greatest one among you must be like the youngest, and the leader must be like the servant. [27] Who is greater, the one who sits down to eat or the one who serves him? The one who sits down, of course. But I am among you as one who serves.

[28] "You have stayed with me all through my trials; [29] and just as my Father has given me the right to rule, so I will make the same agreement with you. [30] You will eat and drink at my table in my Kingdom, and you will sit on thrones to judge the twelve tribes of Israel."

Jesus Predicts Peter's Denial
(Also Matt. 26.31–35; Mark 14.27–31; John 13.36–38)

[31] "Simon, Simon! Listen! Satan has received permission to test all of you, as a farmer separates the wheat from the chaff. [32] But I have prayed for you, Simon, that your faith will not fail. And when you turn back to me, you must strengthen your brothers." [33] Peter answered, "Lord, I am ready to go to prison with you and to die with you!" [34] "I tell you, Peter," Jesus answered, "the

rooster will not crow today until you have said three times that you do not know me."

Purse, Bag, and Sword

[35] Then Jesus said to them, "When I sent you out that time without purse, bag, or shoes, did you lack anything?" "Not a thing," they answered. [36] "But now," Jesus said, "whoever has a purse or a bag must take it; and whoever does not have a sword must sell his coat and buy one. [37] For I tell you this: the scripture that says, 'He was included with the criminals,' must come true about me. For that which was written about me is coming true." [38] The disciples said, "Look! Here are two swords, Lord!" "That is enough!" he answered.

Jesus Prays
(Also Matt. 26.36–46; Mark 14.32–42)

[39] Jesus left and went, as he usually did, to the Mount of Olives; and the disciples went with him. [40] When he came to the place he said to them, "Pray that you will not fall into temptation." [41] Then he went off from them, about the distance of a stone's throw, and knelt down and prayed. [42] "Father," he said, "if you will, take this cup away from me. Not my will, however, but your will be done." [[43] An angel from heaven appeared to him and strengthened him. [44] In great anguish he prayed even more fervently; his sweat was like drops of blood, falling to the ground.]

[45] Rising from his prayer, he went back to the disciples and found them asleep, so great was their grief. [46] And he said to them, "Why are you sleeping? Rise and pray that you will not fall into temptation."

The Arrest of Jesus
(Also Matt. 26.47–56; Mark 14.43–50; John 18.3–11)

⁴⁷ He was still speaking when a crowd arrived; Judas, one of the twelve disciples, was leading them, and he came up to Jesus to kiss him. ⁴⁸ But Jesus said, "Is it with a kiss, Judas, that you betray the Son of Man?" ⁴⁹ When the disciples who were with Jesus saw what was going to happen, they said, "Shall we strike with our swords, Lord?" ⁵⁰ And one of them struck the High Priest's slave and cut off his right ear. ⁵¹ But Jesus answered, "Enough of this!" He touched the man's ear and healed him.

⁵² Then Jesus said to the chief priests and the officers of the Temple guard and the elders who had come there to get him: "Did you have to come with swords and clubs, as though I were an outlaw? ⁵³ I was with you in the Temple every day, and you did not try to arrest me. But this hour belongs to you and to the power of darkness."

Peter Denies Jesus
(Also Matt. 26.57–58, 69–75; Mark 14.53–54, 66–72; John 18.12–18, 25–27)

⁵⁴ They arrested Jesus and took him away into the house of the High Priest; and Peter followed far behind. ⁵⁵ A fire had been lit in the center of the courtyard, and Peter joined those who were sitting around it. ⁵⁶ When one of the servant girls saw him sitting there at the fire, she looked straight at him and said, "This man too was with him!" ⁵⁷ But Peter denied it: "Woman, I don't even know him!" ⁵⁸ After a little while, a man noticed him and said, "You are one of them, too!" But Peter answered, "Man,

I am not!" ⁵⁹ And about an hour later another man insisted strongly: "There isn't any doubt that this man was with him, because he also is a Galilean!" ⁶⁰ But Peter answered, "Man, I don't know what you are talking about!" At once, while he was still speaking, a rooster crowed. ⁶¹ The Lord turned around and looked straight at Peter, and Peter remembered the Lord's words, how he had said, "Before the rooster crows today, you will say three times that you do not know me." ⁶² Peter went out and wept bitterly.

Jesus Mocked and Beaten
(Also Matt. 26.67–68; Mark 14.65)

⁶³ The men who were guarding Jesus made fun of him and beat him. ⁶⁴ They blindfolded him and asked him, "Who hit you? Guess!" ⁶⁵ And they said many other insulting things to him.

Jesus before the Council
(Also Matt. 26.59–66; Mark 14.55–64; John 18.19–24)

⁶⁶ When day came, the elders of the Jews, the chief priests, and the teachers of the Law met together, and Jesus was brought to their Council. ⁶⁷ "Tell us," they said, "are you the Messiah?" He answered: "If I tell you, you will not believe me, ⁶⁸ and if I ask you a question you will not answer me. ⁶⁹ But from now on the Son of Man will be seated at the right side of the Almighty God." ⁷⁰ They all said, "Are you, then, the Son of God?" He answered them, "You say that I am." ⁷¹ And they said, "We don't need any witnesses! We ourselves have heard his very own words!"

Jesus before Pilate
(Also Matt. 27.1–2, 11–14; Mark 15.1–5; John 18.28–38)

23 The whole group rose up and took Jesus before Pilate, ² where they began to accuse him: "We caught this man misleading our people, telling them not to pay taxes to the Emperor and claiming that he himself is Christ, a king." ³ Pilate asked him, "Are you the king of the Jews?" "You say it," answered Jesus. ⁴ Then Pilate said to the chief priests and the crowds, "I find no reason to condemn this man." ⁵ But they insisted even more strongly, "He is starting a riot among the people with his

teaching! He began in Galilee, went through all of Judea, and now has come here."

Jesus before Herod

6 When Pilate heard this he asked, "Is this man a Galilean?" 7 When he learned that Jesus was from the region ruled by Herod, he sent him to Herod, who was also in Jerusalem at that time. 8 Herod was very pleased when he saw Jesus, for he had heard about him and had been wanting to see him for a long time; he was hoping to see Jesus perform some miracle. 9 So Herod asked Jesus many questions, but Jesus did not answer a word. 10 The chief priests and the teachers of the Law stepped forward and made strong accusations against Jesus. 11 Herod and his soldiers made fun of Jesus and treated him with contempt. They put a fine robe on him and sent him back to Pilate. 12 On that very day Herod and Pilate became friends; they had been enemies before this.

Jesus Sentenced to Death
(Also Matt. 27.15–26; Mark 15.6–15; John 18.39—19.16)

13 Pilate called together the chief priests, the leaders, and the people, 14 and said to them: "You brought this man to me and said that he was misleading the people. Now, I have examined him here in your presence, and I have not found him guilty of any of the bad things you accuse him of. 15 Nor did Herod find him guilty, for he sent him back to us. There is nothing this man has done to deserve death. 16 I will have him whipped, then, and let him go." [17 At each Passover Feast Pilate had to set free one prisoner for them.] 18 The whole crowd cried out, "Kill him! Set Barabbas free for us!" 19 (Barabbas had been put in prison for a riot that had taken place in the city, and for murder.) 20 Pilate wanted to set Jesus free, so he called out to the crowd again. 21 But they shouted back, "To the cross with him! To the cross!" 22 Pilate said to them the third time: "But what crime has he committed? I cannot find anything he has done to deserve death! I will have him whipped and set him free." 23 But they kept on shouting at the top of their voices that Jesus should be nailed to the cross; and finally their shouting won. 24 So Pilate passed the sentence on Jesus that they were asking for. 25 He set free the man they wanted, the

one who had been put in prison for riot and murder, and turned Jesus over to them to do as they wished.

Jesus Nailed to the Cross
(Also Matt. 27.32–44; Mark 15.21–32; John 19.17–27)

²⁶ They took Jesus away. As they went, they met a man named Simon, from Cyrene, who was coming into the city from the country. They seized him, put the cross on him and made him carry it behind Jesus.

²⁷ A large crowd of people followed him; among them were some women who were weeping and wailing for him. ²⁸ Jesus turned to them and said: "Women of Jerusalem! Don't cry for me, but for yourselves and your children. ²⁹ For the days are coming when people will say, 'How lucky are the women who never had children, who never bore babies, who never nursed them!' ³⁰ That will be the time when people will say to the mountains, 'Fall on us!' and to the hills, 'Hide us!' ³¹ For if such things as these are done when the wood is green, what will it be like when it is dry?"

³² They took two others also, both of them criminals, to be put to death with Jesus. ³³ When they came to the place called "The Skull," they nailed Jesus to the cross there, and the two criminals, one on his right and one on his left. ³⁴ Jesus said, "Forgive them, Father! They don't know what they are doing." They divided his clothes among themselves by throwing dice. ³⁵ The people stood there watching, while the Jewish leaders made fun of him: "He saved others; let him save himself, if he is the Mes-

siah whom God has chosen!" ³⁶ The soldiers also made fun of him; they came up to him and offered him wine, ³⁷ and said, "Save yourself, if you are the king of the Jews!" ³⁸ These words were written above him: "This is the King of the Jews."

³⁹ One of the criminals hanging there threw insults at him: "Aren't you the Messiah? Save yourself and us!" ⁴⁰ The other one, however, rebuked him, saying: "Don't you fear God? Here we are all under the same sentence. ⁴¹ Ours, however, is only right, for we are getting what we deserve for what we did; but he has done no wrong." ⁴² And he said to Jesus, "Remember me, Jesus, when you come as King!" ⁴³ Jesus said to him, "I tell you this: today you will be in Paradise with me."

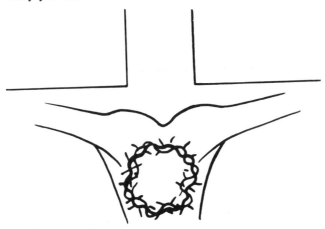

The Death of Jesus
(Also Matt. 27.45–56; Mark 15.33–41; John 19.28–30)

⁴⁴ It was about twelve o'clock when the sun stopped shining and darkness covered the whole country until three o'clock; ⁴⁵ and the curtain hanging in the Temple was torn in two. ⁴⁶ Jesus cried out in a loud voice, "Father! In your hands I place my spirit!" He said this and died. ⁴⁷ The army officer saw what had happened, and he praised God, saying, "Certainly he was a good man!" ⁴⁸ When the people who had gathered there to watch the spectacle saw what happened, they all went back home beating their breasts. ⁴⁹ All those who knew Jesus per-

sonally, including the women who had followed him from Galilee, stood off at a distance to see these things.

The Burial of Jesus
(Also Matt. 27.57–61; Mark 15.42–47; John 19.38–42)

⁵⁰⁻⁵¹ There was a man named Joseph, from the Jewish town of Arimathea. He was a good and honorable man, and waited for the coming of the Kingdom of God. Although a member of the Council, he had not agreed with their decision and action. ⁵² He went into the presence of Pilate and asked for the body of Jesus. ⁵³ Then he took the body down, wrapped it in a linen sheet, and placed it in a grave which had been dug out of the rock — a grave which had never been used. ⁵⁴ It was Friday, and the Sabbath was about to begin.

⁵⁵ The women who had followed Jesus from Galilee went with Joseph and saw the grave and how Jesus' body was laid in it. ⁵⁶ Then they went back home and prepared the spices and ointments for his body.

On the Sabbath they rested, as the Law commanded.

The Resurrection
(Also Matt. 28.1–10; Mark 16.1–8; John 20.1–10)

24 Very early on Sunday morning the women went to the grave carrying the spices they had prepared. ² They found the stone rolled away from the entrance to the grave, ³ so they went on in; but they did not find the body of the Lord Jesus. ⁴ They stood there uncertain about this, when suddenly two men in bright shining clothes stood by them. ⁵ Full of fear, the women bowed down to the ground, as the men said to them: "Why are you looking among the dead for one who is alive? ⁶ He is not here;

he has risen. Remember what he said to you while he was in Galilee: 7 'The Son of Man must be handed over to sinful men, be nailed to the cross and be raised to life on the third day.' " 8 Then the women remembered his words, 9 returned from the grave, and told all these things to the eleven disciples and all the rest. 10 The women were Mary Magdalene, Joanna, and Mary the mother of James; they and the other women with them told these things to the apostles. 11 But the apostles thought that what the women said was nonsense, and did not believe them. 12 But Peter got up and ran to the grave; he bent down and saw the grave cloths and nothing else. Then he went back home wondering at what had happened.

The Walk to Emmaus
(Also Mark 16.12–13)

13 On that same day two of them were going to a village named Emmaus, about seven miles from Jerusalem, 14 and they were talking to each other about all the things that had happened. 15 As they talked and discussed, Jesus himself drew near and walked along with them; 16 they saw him, but somehow did not recognize him. 17 Jesus said to them, "What are you talking about, back and forth, as you walk along?" And they stood still, with sad faces. 18 One of them, named Cleopas, asked him, "Are you the only man living in Jerusalem who does not know what has been happening there these last few days?" 19 "What things?" he asked. "The things that happened to Jesus of Nazareth," they answered. "This man was a prophet, and was considered by God and by all the people to be mighty in words and deeds. 20 Our chief priests and rulers handed him over to be sentenced to death, and they nailed him to the cross. 21 And we had hoped that he would be the one who was going to redeem Israel! Besides all that, this is now the third day since it happened. 22 Some of the women of our group surprised us; they went at dawn to the grave, 23 but could not find his body. They came back saying they had seen a vision of angels who told them that he is alive. 24 Some of our group went to the grave and found it exactly as the women had said, but they did not see him."

25 Then Jesus said to them: "How foolish you are, how slow you are to believe everything the prophets said!

26 Was it not necessary for the Messiah to suffer these things and enter his glory?" 27 And Jesus explained to them what was said about him in all the Scriptures, beginning with the books of Moses and the writings of all the prophets.

28 They came near the village to which they were going, and Jesus acted as if he were going farther; 29 but they held him back, saying, "Stay with us; the day is almost over and it is getting dark." So he went in to stay with them. 30 He sat at table with them, took the bread, and said the blessing; then he broke the bread and gave it to them. 31 Their eyes were opened and they recognized him; but he disappeared from their sight. 32 They said to each other, "Wasn't it like a fire burning in us when he talked to us on the road and explained the Scriptures to us?"

33 They got up at once and went back to Jerusalem, where they found the eleven disciples gathered together with the others 34 and saying, "The Lord is risen indeed! Simon has seen him!" 35 The two then explained to them what had happened on the road, and how they had recognized the Lord when he broke the bread.

Jesus Appears to His Disciples
(Also Matt. 28.16–20; Mark 16.14–18; John 20.19–23; Acts 1.6–8)

36 While they were telling them this, suddenly the Lord himself stood among them and said to them, "Peace be with you." 37 Full of fear and terror, they thought that they were seeing a ghost. 38 But he said to them: "Why are you troubled? Why are these doubts coming up in your minds? 39 Look at my hands and my feet and see that it is I, myself. Feel me, and you will see, for a ghost doesn't have flesh and bones, as you can see I have." 40 He said this and showed them his hands and his feet. 41 They still could not believe, they were so full of joy and wonder; so he asked them, "Do you have anything to eat here?" 42 They gave him a piece of cooked fish, 43 which he took and ate before them.

44 Then he said to them: "These are the very things I told you while I was still with you: everything written about me in the Law of Moses, the writings of the prophets, and the Psalms had to come true." 45 Then he opened their minds to understand the Scriptures, 46 and said to them: "This is what is written: that the Messiah must

suffer and be raised from death on the third day, ⁴⁷ and that in his name the message about repentance and the forgiveness of sins must be preached to all nations, beginning in Jerusalem. ⁴⁸ You are witnesses of these things. ⁴⁹ And I myself will send upon you what my Father has promised. But you must wait in the city until the power from above comes down upon you."

Jesus Is Taken up to Heaven
(Also Mark 16.19–20; Acts 1.9–11)

⁵⁰ Then he led them out of the city as far as Bethany, where he raised his hands and blessed them. ⁵¹ As he was blessing them, he departed from them and was taken up into heaven. ⁵² They worshiped him and went back into Jerusalem, filled with great joy, ⁵³ and spent all their time in the Temple giving thanks to God.

JOHN

The Word of Life

1 Before the world was created, the Word already existed; he was with God, and he was the same as God. ² From the very beginning, the Word was with God. ³ Through him God made all things; not one thing in all creation was made without him. ⁴ The Word had life in himself, and this life brought light to men. ⁵ The light shines in the darkness, and the darkness has never put it out.

⁶ God sent his messenger, a man named John, ⁷ who came to tell people about the light. He came to tell them, so that all should hear the message and believe. ⁸ He himself was not the light; he came to tell about the light. ⁹ This was the real light, the light that comes into the world and shines on all men.

¹⁰ The Word, then, was in the world. God made the world through him, yet the world did not know him. ¹¹ He came to his own country, but his own people did not receive him. ¹² Some, however, did receive him and believed in him; so he gave them the right to become God's children. ¹³ They did not become God's children by natural means, by being born as the children of a human father; God himself was their Father.

¹⁴ The Word became a human being and lived among us. We saw his glory, full of grace and truth. This was the glory which he received as the Father's only Son.

¹⁵ John told about him. He cried out, "This is the one I was talking about when I said, 'He comes after me, but he is greater than I am, because he existed before I was born.'"

¹⁶ Out of the fulness of his grace he has blessed us all, giving us one blessing after another. ¹⁷ God gave the Law through Moses; but grace and truth came through Jesus Christ. ¹⁸ No one has ever seen God. The only One, who is the same as God and is at the Father's side, he has made him known.

John the Baptist's Message
(Also Matt. 3.1–12; Mark 1.1–8; Luke 3.1–18)

¹⁹ This is what John said when the Jews in Jerusalem sent priests and Levites to ask him, "Who are you?"

²⁰ John did not refuse to answer, but declared openly and clearly, "I am not the Messiah." ²¹ "Who are you, then?" they asked. "Are you Elijah?" "No, I am not," John answered. "Are you the Prophet?" they asked. "No," he replied. ²² "Tell us who you are," they said. "We have to take an answer back to those who sent us. What do you say about yourself?" ²³ John answered, "This is what I am:

'The voice of one who shouts in the desert:
Make a straight path for the Lord to travel!' "
(This is what the prophet Isaiah had said.)

²⁴ The messengers had been sent by the Pharisees. ²⁵ They asked John, "If you are not the Messiah, nor Elijah, nor the Prophet, why do you baptize?" ²⁶ John answered: "I baptize with water; among you stands the one you do not know. ²⁷ He comes after me, but I am not good enough even to untie his sandals."

²⁸ All this happened in Bethany, on the other side of the Jordan river, where John was baptizing.

The Lamb of God

²⁹ The next day John saw Jesus coming to him and said: "Here is the Lamb of God who takes away the sin of the world! ³⁰ This is the one I was talking about when I said, 'A man comes after me, but he is greater than I am, because he existed before I was born.' ³¹ I did not know who he would be, but I came baptizing with water in order to make him known to Israel."

³² This is the testimony that John gave: "I saw the Spirit come down like a dove from heaven and stay on him. ³³ I still did not know him, but God, who sent me to baptize with water, said to me, 'You will see the Spirit come down and stay on a

man; he is the one who baptizes with the Holy Spirit.' ³⁴ I have seen it," said John, "and I tell you that he is the Son of God."

The First Disciples of Jesus

³⁵ The next day John was there again with two of his disciples, ³⁶ when he saw Jesus walking by. "Here is the Lamb of God!" he said. ³⁷ The two disciples heard him say this and went with Jesus. ³⁸ Jesus turned, saw them following him, and asked, "What are you looking for?" They answered, "Where do you live, Rabbi?" (This word, translated, means "Teacher.") ³⁹ "Come and see," he answered. So they went with him and saw where he lived, and spent the rest of that day with him. (It was about four o'clock in the afternoon.)

⁴⁰ One of the two who heard John, and went with Jesus, was Andrew, Simon Peter's brother. ⁴¹ At once Andrew found his brother Simon and told him, "We have found the Messiah." (This word means "Christ.") ⁴² Then he brought Simon to Jesus. Jesus looked at him and said, "You are Simon, the son of John. Your name will be Cephas." (This is the same as Peter, and means "Rock.")

Jesus Calls Philip and Nathanael

⁴³ The next day Jesus decided to go to Galilee. He found Philip and said to him, "Come with me!" ⁴⁴ (Philip was from Bethsaida, the town where Andrew and Peter lived.) ⁴⁵ So Philip found Nathanael and told him: "We have found the one of whom Moses wrote in the book of the Law, and of whom the prophets also wrote. He is Jesus, the son of Joseph, from Nazareth." ⁴⁶ "Can anything good come from Nazareth?" Nathanael asked. "Come and see," answered Philip.

⁴⁷ When Jesus saw Nathanael coming to him, he said about him, "Here is a real Israelite; there is nothing false in him!" ⁴⁸ Nathanael asked him, "How do you know me?" Jesus answered, "I saw you when you were under the fig tree, before Philip called you." ⁴⁹ "Teacher," answered Nathanael, "you are the Son of God! You are the King of Israel!" ⁵⁰ Jesus said, "Do you believe just because I told you I saw you when you were under the fig tree? You will see much greater things than this!" ⁵¹ And

he said to them, "I tell you the truth: you will see heaven open and God's angels going up and coming down on the Son of Man!"

The Wedding at Cana

2 Two days later there was a wedding in the town of Cana, in Galilee. Jesus' mother was there, ² and Jesus and his disciples had also been invited to the wedding. ³ When all the wine had been drunk, Jesus' mother said to him, "They are out of wine." ⁴ "You must not tell me what to do, woman," Jesus replied. "My time has not yet come." ⁵ Jesus' mother then told the servants, "Do whatever he tells you."

⁶ The Jews have religious rules about washing, and for this purpose six stone water jars were there, each one large enough to hold between twenty and thirty gallons. ⁷ Jesus said to the servants, "Fill these jars with water." They filled them to the brim, ⁸ and then he told them, "Now draw some water out and take it to the man in charge of the feast." They took it to him, ⁹ and he tasted the water, which had turned into wine. He did not know

where this wine had come from (but the servants who had drawn out the water knew); so he called the bridegroom [10] and said to him, "Everyone else serves the best wine first, and after the guests have drunk a lot he serves the ordinary wine. But you have kept the best wine until now!"

[11] Jesus performed this first of his mighty works in Cana of Galilee; there he revealed his glory, and his disciples believed in him.

[12] After this, Jesus and his mother, brothers, and disciples went to Capernaum, and stayed there a few days.

Jesus Goes to the Temple
(Also Matt. 21.12–13; Mark 11.15–17; Luke 19.45–46)

[13] It was almost time for the Jewish Feast of Passover, so Jesus went to Jerusalem. [14] In the Temple he found men selling cattle, sheep, and pigeons, and also the money-changers sitting at their tables. [15] He made a whip from cords and drove all the animals out of the Temple, both the sheep and the cattle; he overturned the tables of the money-changers and scattered their coins; [16] and he ordered the men who sold the pigeons, "Take them out of here! Do not make my Father's house a market place!" [17] His disciples remembered that the scripture says, "My devotion for your house, O God, burns in me like a fire."

[18] The Jews came back at him with a question, "What miracle can you perform to show us that you have the right to do this?" [19] Jesus answered, "Tear down this house of God and in three days I will build it again." [20] "You

are going to build it again in three days?" they asked him. "It has taken forty-six years to build this Temple!"

²¹ But the temple Jesus spoke of was his body. ²² When he was raised from death, therefore, his disciples remembered that he said this; and they believed the scripture and the words that Jesus had said.

Jesus Knows All Men

²³ While Jesus was in Jerusalem during the Passover Feast, many believed in him as they saw the mighty works he did. ²⁴ But Jesus did not trust himself to them, because he knew all men well. ²⁵ There was no need for anyone to tell him about men, for he well knew what goes on in their hearts.

Jesus and Nicodemus

3 There was a man named Nicodemus, a leader of the Jews, who belonged to the party of the Pharisees. ² One night he came to Jesus and said to him: "We know, Rabbi, that you are a teacher sent by God. No one could do the mighty works you are doing unless God were with him." ³ Jesus answered, "I tell you the truth: no one can see the Kingdom of God unless he is born again." ⁴ "How can a grown man be born again?" Nicodemus asked. "He certainly cannot enter his mother's womb and be born a second time!" ⁵ "I tell you the truth," replied Jesus, "that no one can enter the Kingdom of God unless he is born of water and the Spirit. ⁶ Flesh gives birth to flesh, and Spirit gives birth to spirit. ⁷ Do not be surprised because I tell you, 'You must all be born again.' ⁸ The wind blows wherever it wishes; you hear the sound it makes, but you do not know where it comes from or where it is going. It is the same way with everyone who is born of the Spirit." ⁹ "How can this be?" asked Nicodemus. ¹⁰ Jesus answered: "You are a great teacher of Israel, and you don't know this? ¹¹ I tell you the truth: we speak of what we know, and tell what we have seen — yet none of you is willing to accept our message. ¹² You do not believe me when I tell you about the things of this world; how will you ever believe me, then, when I tell you about the things of heaven? ¹³ And no one has ever gone up to heaven except the Son of Man, who came down from heaven."

¹⁴ As Moses lifted up the bronze snake on a pole in the

desert, in the same way the Son of Man must be lifted up, ¹⁵ so that everyone who believes in him may have eternal life. ¹⁶ For God loved the world so much that he gave his only Son, so that everyone who believes in him may not die but have eternal life. ¹⁷ For God did not send his Son into the world to be its Judge, but to be its Savior.

¹⁸ Whoever believes in the Son is not judged; whoever does not believe has already been judged, because he has not believed in God's only Son. ¹⁹ This is how the judgment works: the light has come into the world, but men love the darkness rather than the light, because they do evil things. ²⁰ And anyone who does evil things hates the light and will not come to the light, because he does not want his evil deeds to be shown up. ²¹ But whoever does what is true comes to the light, in order that the light may show that he did his works in obedience to God.

Jesus and John

²² After this, Jesus and his disciples went to the province of Judea. He spent some time with them there, and baptized. ²³ John also was baptizing in Aenon, not far from Salim, because there was plenty of water there. People were going to him and he was baptizing them. ²⁴ (John had not yet been put in prison.)

²⁵ Some of John's disciples began arguing with a Jew about the matter of religious washing. ²⁶ So they went to John and told him: "Teacher, you remember the man who was with you on the other side of the Jordan, the one you spoke about? Well, he is baptizing now, and everyone is going to him!" ²⁷ John answered: "No one can have anything unless God gives it to him. ²⁸ You yourselves are my witnesses that I said, 'I am not the Messiah, but I have been sent ahead of him.' ²⁹ The bridegroom is the one to whom the bride belongs; the bridegroom's friend stands by and listens, and he is glad when he hears the bridegroom's voice. This is how my own happiness is made complete. ³⁰ He must become more important, while I become less important."

He who Comes from Heaven

³¹ He who comes from above is greater than all; he who is from the earth belongs to the earth and speaks about earthly matters. He who comes from heaven is above all.

[32] He tells what he has seen and heard, but no one accepts his message. [33] Whoever accepts his message proves by this that God is true. [34] The one whom God has sent speaks God's words; for God gives him the fulness of his Spirit. [35] The Father loves his Son and has put everything in his power. [36] Whoever believes in the Son has eternal life; whoever disobeys the Son will never have life, but God's wrath will remain on him for ever.

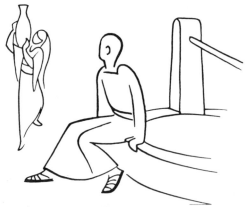

Jesus and the Woman of Samaria

4 The Pharisees heard that Jesus was winning and baptizing more disciples than John. [2] (Actually, Jesus himself did not baptize anyone; only his disciples did.) [3] When Jesus heard what was being said, he left Judea and went back to Galilee; [4] on his way there he had to go through Samaria.

[5] He came to a town in Samaria named Sychar, which was not far from the field that Jacob had given to his son Joseph. [6] Jacob's well was there, and Jesus, tired out by the trip, sat down by the well. It was about noon.

[7] A Samaritan woman came to draw some water, and Jesus said to her, "Give me a drink of water." [8] (His disciples had gone into town to buy food.) [9] The Samaritan woman answered, "You are a Jew and I am a Samaritan — how can you ask me for a drink?" (For Jews will not use the same dishes that Samaritans use.) [10] Jesus answered, "If you only knew what God gives, and who it is that is asking you for a drink, you would have asked

him and he would have given you living water." 11 "Sir,"
the woman said, "you don't have a bucket and the well is
deep. Where would you get living water? 12 Our ancestor
Jacob gave us this well; he, his sons, and his flocks all
drank from it. You don't claim to be greater than Jacob,
do you?" 13 Jesus answered: "Whoever drinks this water
will get thirsty again; 14 but whoever drinks the water that
I will give him will never be thirsty again. For the water
that I will give him will become in him a spring which
will provide him with living water, and give him eternal
life." 15 "Sir," the woman said, "give me this water! Then
I will never be thirsty again, nor will I have to come here
and draw water." 16 "Go call your husband," Jesus told
her, "and come back here." 17 "I don't have a husband,"
the woman said. Jesus replied: "You are right when you
say you don't have a husband. 18 You have been married
to five men, and the man you live with now is not really
your husband. You have told me the truth." 19 "I see you
are a prophet, sir," the woman said. 20 "My Samaritan
ancestors worshiped God on this mountain, but you Jews
say that Jerusalem is the place where we should worship
God." 21 Jesus said to her: "Believe me, woman, the time
will come when men will not worship the Father either on
this mountain or in Jerusalem. 22 You Samaritans do not
really know whom you worship; we Jews know whom we
worship, for salvation comes from the Jews. 23 But the
time is coming, and is already here, when the real worshipers will worship the Father in spirit and in truth.
These are the worshipers the Father wants to worship him.
24 God is Spirit, and those who worship him must worship
in spirit and in truth."

25 The woman said to him, "I know that the Messiah,
called Christ, will come. When he comes he will tell us
everything." 26 Jesus answered, "I am he, I who am talking with you."

27 At that moment Jesus' disciples returned; and they
were greatly surprised to find him talking with a woman.
But none of them said to her, "What do you want?" or
asked him, "Why are you talking with her?"

28 Then the woman left her water jar, went back to town,
and said to the people there, 29 "Come and see the man
who told me everything I have ever done. Could he be the
Messiah?" 30 So they left the town and went to Jesus.

³¹ In the meantime the disciples were begging Jesus, "Teacher, have something to eat!" ³² But he answered, "I have food to eat that you know nothing about." ³³ So the disciples started asking among themselves, "Could somebody have brought him food?" ³⁴ "My food," Jesus said to them, "is to obey the will of him who sent me and finish the work he gave me to do.

³⁵ "You have a saying, 'Four more months and then the harvest.' I tell you, take a good look at the fields: the crops are now ripe and ready to be harvested! ³⁶ The man who reaps the harvest is being paid and gathers the crops for eternal life; so that the man who plants and the man who reaps will be glad together. ³⁷ For the saying is true, 'One man plants, another man reaps.' ³⁸ I have sent you to reap a harvest in a field where you did not work; others worked there, and you profit from their work."

³⁹ Many of the Samaritans in that town believed in Jesus because the woman had said, "He told me everything I have ever done." ⁴⁰ So when the Samaritans came to him they begged him to stay with them; and Jesus stayed there two days.

⁴¹ Many more believed because of his message, ⁴² and they told the woman, "We believe now, not because of what you said, but because we ourselves have heard him, and we know that he is really the Savior of the world."

Jesus Heals an Official's Son

⁴³ After spending two days there, Jesus left and went to Galilee. ⁴⁴ For Jesus himself had said, "A prophet is not respected in his own country." ⁴⁵ When he arrived in Galilee the people there welcomed him, for they themselves had gone to the Passover Feast in Jerusalem and had seen everything that he had done during the feast.

⁴⁶ So Jesus went back to Cana of Galilee, where he had turned the water into wine. There was a government official there whose son in Capernaum was sick. ⁴⁷ When he heard that Jesus had come from Judea to Galilee, he went to him and asked him to go to Capernaum and heal his son, who was about to die. ⁴⁸ Jesus said to him, "None of you will ever believe unless you see great and wonderful works." ⁴⁹ "Sir," replied the official, "come with me before my child dies." ⁵⁰ Jesus said to him, "Go, your son will live!" The man believed Jesus' words and went. ⁵¹ On his

way home his servants met him with the news, "Your boy is going to live!" [52] He asked them what time it was when his son got better, and they said, "It was one o'clock yesterday afternoon when the fever left him." [53] The father remembered, then, that it was at that very hour when Jesus had told him, "Your son will live." So he and all his family believed.

[54] This was the second mighty work that Jesus did after coming from Judea to Galilee.

The Healing at the Pool

5 After this, there was a Jewish religious feast, and Jesus went to Jerusalem. [2] There is in Jerusalem, by the Sheep Gate, a pool with five porches; in the Hebrew language it is called Bethzatha. [3] A large crowd of sick people were lying on the porches — the blind, the lame, and the paralyzed. [They were waiting for the water to move; [4] for every now and then an angel of the Lord went down into the pool and stirred up the water. The first sick person to go down into the pool after the water was stirred up was healed from whatever disease he had.] [5] A man was there who had been sick for thirty-eight years. [6] Jesus saw him lying there, and he knew that the man had been sick for such a long time; so he said to him, "Do you want to get well?" [7] The sick man answered, "Sir, I don't have anyone here to put me in the pool when the water is stirred up; while I am trying to get in, somebody else gets there first." [8] Jesus said to him, "Get up, pick up your mat, and walk." [9] Immediately the man got well; he picked up his mat, and walked.

The day this happened was a Sabbath, [10] so the Jews told the man who had been healed, "This is a Sabbath, and it is against our Law for you to carry your mat." [11] He answered, "The man who made me well told me, 'Pick up your mat and walk.'" [12] They asked him, "Who is this man who told you to pick up your mat and walk?" [13] But the man who had been healed did not know who he was, for Jesus had left, because there was a crowd in that place.

[14] Afterward, Jesus found him in the Temple and said, "Look, you are well now. Quit your sins, or something worse may happen to you." [15] Then the man left and told the Jews that it was Jesus who had healed him. [16] For this

reason the Jews began to persecute Jesus, because he had done this healing on a Sabbath.

[17] So Jesus answered them, "My Father works always, and I too must work." [18] This saying made the Jews all the more determined to kill him; for not only had he broken the Sabbath law, but he had said that God was his own Father, and in this way had made himself equal with God.

The Authority of the Son

[19] So Jesus answered them: "I tell you the truth: the Son does nothing on his own; he does only what he sees his Father doing. What the Father does, the Son also does. [20] For the Father loves the Son and shows him all that he himself is doing. He will show him even greater things than this to do, and you will all be amazed. [21] For even as the Father raises the dead back to life, in the same way the Son gives life to those he wants to. [22] Nor does the Father himself judge anyone. He has given his Son the full right to judge, [23] so that all will honor the Son in the same way as they honor the Father. Whoever does not honor the Son does not honor the Father who sent him.

[24] "I tell you the truth: whoever hears my words, and believes in him who sent me, has eternal life. He will not be judged, but has already passed from death to life. [25] I tell you the truth: the time is coming — the time has already come — when the dead will hear the voice of the Son of God, and those who hear it will live. [26] Even as the Father is himself the source of life, in the same way he has made his Son to be the source of life. [27] And he has given the Son the right to judge, because he is the Son of Man. [28] Do not be surprised at this; for the time is coming when all the dead in the graves will hear his voice, [29] and they will come out of their graves: those who have done good will be raised and live, and those who have done evil will be raised and be condemned."

Witnesses to Jesus

[30] "I can do nothing on my own; I judge only as God tells me, so my judgment is right, because I am not trying to do what I want, but only what he who sent me wants.

[31] "If I testify on my own behalf, what I say is not to be accepted as real proof. [32] But there is someone else who

testifies on my behalf, and I know that what he says about me is true. [33] You sent your messengers to John, and he spoke on behalf of the truth. [34] It is not that I must have a man's witness; I say this only in order that you may be saved. [35] John was like a lamp, burning and shining, and you were willing for a while to enjoy his light. [36] But I have a witness on my behalf even greater than the witness that John gave: the works that I do, the works my Father gave me to do, these speak on my behalf and show that the Father has sent me. [37] And the Father, who sent me, also speaks on my behalf. You have never heard his voice, you have never seen his face; [38] so you do not have his words in you, because you will not believe in the one whom he sent. [39] You study the Scriptures because you think that in them you will find eternal life. And they themselves speak about me! [40] Yet you are not willing to come to me in order to have life.

[41] "I am not looking for praise from men. [42] But I know you; I know that you have no love for God in your hearts. [43] I have come with my Father's authority, but you have not received me; when someone comes with his own authority, you will receive him. [44] You like to have praise from one another, but you do not try to win praise from the only God; how, then, can you believe? [45] Do not think, however, that I will accuse you to my Father. Moses is the one who will accuse you — Moses, in whom you have hoped. [46] If you had really believed Moses, you would have believed me, for he wrote about me. [47] But since you do not believe what he wrote, how can you believe my words?"

Jesus Feeds the Five Thousand
(Also Matt. 14.13–21; Mark 6.30–44; Luke 9.10–17)

6 After this, Jesus went back across Lake Galilee (or, Lake Tiberias). [2] A great crowd followed him, because they had seen his mighty works in healing the sick. [3] Jesus went up a hill and sat down with his disciples. [4] The Passover Feast of the Jews was near. [5] Jesus looked around and saw that a large crowd was coming to him, so he said to Philip, "Where can we buy enough food to feed all these people?" [6] (He said this to try Philip out; actually he already knew what he would do.) [7] Philip answered, "For all these people to have even a little, it would take

more than two hundred dollars' worth of bread."
⁸ Another one of his disciples, Andrew, Simon Peter's
brother, said: ⁹ "There is a boy here who has five loaves of
barley bread and two fish. But what good are they for all
these people?" ¹⁰ "Make the people sit down," Jesus
told them. (There was a lot of grass there.) So all the
people sat down; there were about five thousand men.
¹¹ Jesus took the bread, gave thanks to God, and distributed it to the people sitting down. He did the same with
the fish, and they all had as much as they wanted. ¹² When
they were all full, he said to his disciples, "Pick up the
pieces left over; let us not waste a bit." ¹³ So they took
them all up, and filled twelve baskets with the pieces left
over from the five barley loaves which the people had eaten.

¹⁴ The people there, seeing this mighty work that Jesus
had done, said, "Surely this is the Prophet who was to
come to the world!" ¹⁵ Jesus knew that they were about
to come and get him and make him king by force; so he
went off again to the hills by himself.

Jesus Walks on the Water
(Also Matt. 14.22–33; Mark 6.45–52)

¹⁶ When evening came, his disciples went down to the
lake, ¹⁷ got into the boat, and went back across the lake
toward Capernaum. Night came on, and Jesus still had
not come to them. ¹⁸ By now a strong wind was blowing
and stirring up the water. ¹⁹ The disciples had rowed

about three or four miles when they saw Jesus walking on the water, coming near the boat, and they were terrified. [20] "Don't be afraid," Jesus told them, "it is I!" [21] They were willing to take him into the boat; and immediately the boat reached land at the place they were heading for.

The People Seek Jesus

[22] Next day the crowd which had stayed on the other side of the lake saw that only one boat was left there. They knew that Jesus had not gone in the boat with his disciples, but that they had left without him. [23] Other boats, from Tiberias, came to shore near the place where the crowd had eaten the bread, after the Lord had given thanks. [24] When the crowd saw that Jesus was not there, nor his disciples, they got into boats and went to Capernaum, looking for him.

Jesus the Bread of Life

[25] When the people found Jesus on the other side of the lake they said to him, "Teacher, when did you get here?" [26] Jesus answered: "I tell you the truth: you are looking for me because you ate the bread and had all you wanted, not because you saw my works of power. [27] Do not work for food that spoils; instead, work for the food that lasts for eternal life. This food the Son of Man will give you, because God, the Father, has put his mark of approval on him." [28] They asked him then, "What can we do in order to do God's works?" [29] Jesus answered, "This is the work God wants you to do: believe in the one he sent." [30] They replied: "What sign of power will you perform so that we may see it and believe you? What will you do? [31] Our ancestors ate manna in the desert, just as the scripture says: 'He gave them bread from heaven to eat.' " [32] "I tell you the truth," Jesus said. "What Moses gave you was not the bread from heaven; it is my Father who gives you the real bread from heaven. [33] For the bread that God gives is he who comes down from heaven and gives life to the world." [34] "Sir," they asked him, "give us this bread always." [35] "I am the bread of life," Jesus told them. "He who comes to me will never be hungry; he who believes in me will never be thirsty.

[36] "Now, I told you that you had seen me but would not believe. [37] Every one whom my Father gives me will come

to me. I will never turn away anyone who comes to me, [38] for I have come down from heaven to do the will of him who sent me, not my own will. [39] This is what he who sent me wants me to do: that I should not lose any of all those he has given me, but that I should raise them all to life on the last day. [40] For this is what my Father wants: that all who see the Son and believe in him should have eternal life; and I will raise them to life on the last day."

[41] The Jews started grumbling about him, because he said, "I am the bread that came down from heaven." [42] So they said: "This man is Jesus the son of Joseph, isn't he? We know his father and mother. How, then, does he now say he came down from heaven?" [43] Jesus answered: "Stop grumbling among yourselves. [44] No one can come to me unless the Father who sent me draws him to me; and I will raise him to life on the last day. [45] The prophets wrote, 'All men will be taught by God.' Everyone who hears the Father and learns from him comes to me. [46] This does not mean that anyone has seen the Father; he who is from God is the only one who has seen the Father.

[47] "I tell you the truth: he who believes has eternal life. [48] I am the bread of life. [49] Your ancestors ate the manna in the desert, but died. [50] But the bread which comes down from heaven is such that whoever eats it will not die. [51] I am the living bread which came down from heaven. If anyone eats this bread he will live for ever. And the bread which I will give him is my flesh, which I give so that the world may live."

[52] This started an angry argument among the Jews. "How can this man give us his flesh to eat?" they asked. [53] Jesus said to them: "I tell you the truth: if you do not eat the flesh of the Son of Man and drink his blood you will not have life in yourselves. [54] Whoever eats my flesh and drinks my blood has eternal life, and I will raise him to life on the last day. [55] For my flesh is the real food, my blood is the real drink. [56] Whoever eats my flesh and drinks my blood lives in me and I live in him. [57] The living Father sent me, and because of him I live also. In the same way, whoever eats me will live because of me. [58] This, then, is the bread that came down from heaven; it is not like the bread that your ancestors ate and then died. The one who eats this bread will live for ever." [59] Jesus said this as he taught in the synagogue in Capernaum.

The Words of Eternal Life

⁶⁰ Many of his disciples heard this and said, "This teaching is too hard. Who can listen to this?" ⁶¹ Without being told, Jesus knew that his disciples were grumbling about this; so he said to them: "Does this make you want to give up? ⁶² Suppose, then, that you should see the Son of Man go back up to the place where he was before? ⁶³ What gives life is the Spirit; the flesh is of no use at all. The words I have spoken to you are Spirit and life. ⁶⁴ Yet some of you do not believe." (For Jesus knew from the very beginning who were the ones that would not believe, and which one would betray him.) ⁶⁵ And he added, "This is the very reason I told you that no one can come to me unless the Father makes it possible for him to do so."

⁶⁶ Because of this, many of his followers turned back and would not go with him any more. ⁶⁷ So Jesus said to the twelve disciples, "And you — would you like to leave also?" ⁶⁸ Simon Peter answered him: "Lord, to whom

would we go? You have the words that give eternal life. ⁶⁹ And now we believe and know that you are the Holy One from God." ⁷⁰ Jesus answered them, "Did I not choose the twelve of you? Yet one of you is a devil!" ⁷¹ He was talking about Judas, the son of Simon Iscariot. For Judas, even though he was one of the twelve disciples, was going to betray him.

Jesus and His Brothers

7 After this, Jesus traveled in Galilee; he did not want to travel in Judea, because the Jews there were wanting to kill him. ² The Jewish Feast of Tabernacles was near, ³ so Jesus' brothers said to him: "Leave this place and go

to Judea, so that your disciples will see the works you are doing. ⁴ No one hides whàt he is doing if he wants to be well known. Since you are doing these things, let the whole world know about you!" ⁵ (Not even his brothers believed in him.) ⁶ Jesus said to them: "The right time for me has not yet come. Any time is right for you. ⁷ The world cannot hate you, but it hates me, because I keep telling it that its ways are bad. ⁸ You go on to the feast. I am not going to this feast, because the right time has not come for me." ⁹ He told them this, and stayed on in Galilee.

Jesus at the Feast of Tabernacles

¹⁰ After his brothers went to the feast, Jesus also went; however, he did not go openly, but went secretly. ¹¹ The Jews were looking for him at the feast. "Where is he?" they asked. ¹² There was much whispering about him in the crowd. "He is a good man," some people said. "No," others said, "he fools the people." ¹³ But no one talked about him openly, because they were afraid of the Jews.

¹⁴ The feast was nearly half over when Jesus went to the Temple and began teaching. ¹⁵ The Jews, greatly surprised, said, "How does this man know so much when he has never been to school?" ¹⁶ Jesus answered: "What I teach is not mine, but comes from God, who sent me. ¹⁷ Whoever is willing to do what God wants will know whether what I teach comes from God or whether I speak on my own authority. ¹⁸ A person who speaks on his own is trying to gain glory for himself. He who wants glory for the one who sent him, however, is honest and there is nothing false in him. ¹⁹ Moses gave you the Law, did he not? But not one of you obeys the Law. Why are you trying to kill me?" ²⁰ The crowd answered, "You have a demon in you! Who is trying to kill you?" ²¹ Jesus answered: "I did one great work and you were all surprised. ²² Because Moses ordered you to circumcise your sons (although it was not Moses but your ancestors who started it), you will circumcise a boy on the Sabbath. ²³ If a boy is circumcised on the Sabbath so that Moses' Law will not be broken, why are you angry with me because I made a man completely well on the Sabbath? ²⁴ Stop judging by external standards, but judge by true standards."

Is He the Messiah?

²⁵ Some of the people of Jerusalem said: "Isn't this the man they are trying to kill? ²⁶ Look! He is talking in public, and nobody says anything against him! Can it be that the leaders really know that he is the Messiah? ²⁷ But when the Messiah comes, no one will know where he is from. And we all know where this man comes from."

²⁸ As Jesus taught in the Temple he said in a loud voice: "Do you really know me, and know where I am from? But I have not come on my own. He who sent me, however, is true. You do not know him, ²⁹ but I know him, for I come from him and he sent me." ³⁰ Then they tried to arrest him, but no one laid a hand on him, because his hour had not yet come. ³¹ But many in the crowd believed in him, and said, "When the Messiah comes, will he do more mighty works than this man has done?"

Guards Are Sent to Arrest Jesus

³² The Pharisees heard the crowd whispering these things about him, so they and the chief priests sent some guards to arrest Jesus. ³³ Jesus said: "I shall be with you a little while longer, and then I shall go away to him who sent me. ³⁴ You will look for me, but you will not find me; for where I shall be you cannot go." ³⁵ The Jews said among themselves: "Where is he about to go so that we shall not find him? Will he go to the Greek cities where the Jews live and teach the Greeks? ³⁶ He says, 'You will look for me but you will not find me,' and, 'You cannot go where I shall be.' What does he mean?"

Streams of Living Water

³⁷ The last day of the feast was the most important. On that day Jesus stood up and said in a loud voice: "Whoever is thirsty should come to me and drink. ³⁸ As the scripture says, 'Whoever believes in me, streams of living water will pour out from his heart.'" ³⁹ (Jesus said this about the Spirit which those who believed in him were about to receive. At that time the Spirit had not yet been given, because Jesus had not been raised to glory.)

Division among the People

⁴⁰ Many of the people in the crowd heard him say this

and said, "This man is really the Prophet!" 41 Others said, "He is the Messiah!" But others said, "The Messiah will not come from Galilee! 42 The scripture says that the Messiah will be a descendant of David, and will be born in Bethlehem, the town where David lived." 43 So there was a division in the crowd because of him. 44 Some wanted to arrest him, but no one laid a hand on him.

The Unbelief of the Jewish Leaders

45 The guards went back to the chief priests and Pharisees, who asked them, "Why did you not bring him along?" 46 The guards answered, "Nobody has ever talked the way this man does!" 47 "Did he fool you, too?" the Pharisees asked them. 48 "Have you ever known one of our leaders or one Pharisee to believe in him? 49 This crowd does not know the Law of Moses, so they are under God's curse!" 50 Nicodemus was one of them; he was the one who had gone to see Jesus before. He said to them, 51 "According to our Law we cannot condemn a man before hearing him and finding out what he has done." 52 "Well," they answered, "are you also from Galilee? Study the Scriptures and you will learn that no prophet ever comes from Galilee."

The Woman Caught in Adultery

8 [Then everyone went home, but Jesus went to the Mount of Olives. 2 Early the next morning he went

back to the Temple. The whole crowd gathered around him, and he sat down and began to teach them. ³ The teachers of the Law and the Pharisees brought in a woman who had been caught committing adultery, and made her stand before them all. ⁴ "Teacher," they said to Jesus, "this woman was caught in the very act of committing adultery. ⁵ In our Law Moses gave a commandment that such a woman must be stoned to death. Now, what do you say?" ⁶ They said this to trap him, so they could accuse him. But Jesus bent over and wrote on the ground with his finger. ⁷ As they stood there asking questions,

Jesus straightened up and said to them, "Whichever one of you has committed no sin may throw the first stone at her." ⁸ Then he bent over again and wrote on the ground. ⁹ When they heard this they all left, one by one, the older ones first. Jesus was left alone, with the woman still standing there. ¹⁰ He straightened up and said to her, "Where are they, woman? Is there no one left to condemn you?"

11 "No one, sir," she answered. "Well, then," Jesus said, "I do not condemn you either. You may leave, but do not sin again."]

Jesus the Light of the World

12 Jesus spoke to them again: "I am the light of the world. Whoever follows me will have the light of life and will never walk in the darkness." 13 The Pharisees said to him, "Now you are testifying on your own behalf; what you say proves nothing." 14 "No," Jesus answered, "even if I do testify on my own behalf, what I say is true, because I know where I came from and where I am going. You do not know where I came from or where I am going. 15 You make judgments in a purely human way; I pass judgment on no one. 16 But if I were to pass judgment, my judging would be true, because I am not alone in this; the Father who sent me is with me. 17 It is written in your Law that when two witnesses agree, what they say is true. 18 I testify on my own behalf, and the Father who sent me also testifies on my behalf." 19 "Where is your father?" they asked him. "You know neither me nor my Father," Jesus answered. "If you knew me you would know my Father also."

20 Jesus said all this as he taught in the Temple, in the room where the offering boxes were placed. And no one arrested him, because his hour had not come.

You Cannot Go Where I Am Going

21 Jesus said to them again, "I will go away; you will look for me, but you will die in your sins. You cannot go where I am going." 22 So the Jews said, "He says, 'You cannot go where I am going.' Does this mean that he will kill himself?" 23 Jesus answered: "You come from here below, but I come from above. You come from this world, but I do not come from this world. 24 That is why I told you that you will die in your sins. And you will die in your sins if you do not believe that 'I Am Who I Am'." 25 "Who are you?" they asked him. Jesus answered: "What I have told you from the very beginning. 26 There are many things I have to say and judge about you. The one who sent me, however, is true, and I tell the world only what I have heard from him."

27 They did not understand that he was talking to them

about the Father. ²⁸ So Jesus said to them: "When you lift up the Son of Man you will know that 'I Am Who I Am'; then you will know that I do nothing on my own, but say only what the Father has taught me. ²⁹ And he who sent me is with me; he has not left me alone, because I always do what pleases him." ³⁰ Many who heard Jesus say these things believed in him.

Free Men and Slaves

³¹ So Jesus said to the Jews who believed in him, "If you obey my teaching you are really my disciples; ³² you will know the truth, and the truth will make you free." ³³ "We are the descendants of Abraham," they answered, "and we have never been anybody's slaves. What do you mean, then, by saying, 'You will be made free'?" ³⁴ Jesus said to them: "I tell you the truth: everyone who sins is a slave of sin. ³⁵ A slave does not belong to the family always; but a son belongs there for ever. ³⁶ If the Son makes you free, then you will be really free. ³⁷ I know you are Abraham's descendants. Yet you are trying to kill me, because you will not accept my teaching. ³⁸ I talk about what my Father has shown me, but you do what your father has told you."

³⁹ They answered him, "Our father is Abraham." "If you really were Abraham's children," Jesus replied, "you would do the same works that he did. ⁴⁰ But all I have ever done is to tell you the truth I heard from God. Yet you are trying to kill me. Abraham did nothing like this! ⁴¹ You are doing what your father did." "We are not bastards," they answered. "We have the one Father, God himself." ⁴² Jesus said to them: "If God really were your father, you would love me; for I came from God and now I am here. I did not come on my own, but he sent me. ⁴³ Why do you not understand what I say? It is because you cannot bear to listen to my message. ⁴⁴ You are the children of your father, the Devil, and you want to follow your father's desires. From the very beginning he was a murderer. He has never been on the side of truth, because there is no truth in him. When he tells a lie he is only doing what is natural to him, because he is a liar and the father of all lies. ⁴⁵ I tell the truth, and that is why you do not believe me. ⁴⁶ Which one of you can prove that I am guilty of sin? If I tell the truth, then why do you

not believe me? [47] He who comes from God listens to God's words. You, however, are not from God, and this is why you will not listen."

Jesus and Abraham

[48] The Jews replied to Jesus: "Were we not right in saying that you are a Samaritan and have a demon in you?" [49] "I have no demon," Jesus answered. "I honor my Father, but you dishonor me. [50] I am not seeking honor for myself. There is one who is seeking it and who judges in my favor. [51] I tell you the truth: whoever obeys my message will never die." [52] The Jews said to him: "Now we know for sure that you have a demon! Abraham died, and the prophets died, yet you say, 'Whoever obeys my message will never die.' [53] Our father Abraham died; you do not claim to be greater than Abraham, do you? And the prophets also died. Who do you think you are?" [54] Jesus answered: "If I were to honor myself, my own honor would be worth nothing. The one who honors me is my Father — the very one you say is your God. [55] You have never known him, but I know him. If I were to say that I do not know him, I would be a liar, like you. But I do know him, and I obey his word. [56] Your father Abraham rejoiced that he was to see my day; he saw it and was glad." [57] The Jews said to him, "You are not even fifty years old — and have you seen Abraham?" [58] "I tell you the truth," Jesus replied. "Before Abraham was born, 'I Am'." [59] They picked up stones to throw at him; but Jesus hid himself and left the Temple.

Jesus Heals a Man Born Blind

9 As Jesus walked along he saw a man who had been born blind. [2] His disciples asked him: "Teacher, whose sin was it that caused him to be born blind? His own or his parents' sin?" [3] Jesus answered: "His blindness has nothing to do with his sins or his parents' sins. He is blind so that God's power might be seen at work in him. [4] We must keep on doing the works of him who sent me, as long as it is day; the night is coming, when no one can work. [5] While I am in the world I am the light for the world." [6] After he said this, Jesus spat on the ground and made some mud with the spittle; he rubbed the mud on the man's eyes, [7] and told him, "Go wash your face in the

Pool of Siloam." (This name means "Sent.") So the man went, washed his face, and came back seeing.

8 His neighbors, then, and the people who had seen him begging before this, asked, "Isn't this the man who used to sit and beg?" 9 Some said, "He is the one," but others said, "No, he is not, he just looks like him." So the man himself said, "I am the man." 10 "How were your eyes opened?" they asked him. 11 He answered, "The man named Jesus made some mud, rubbed it on my eyes, and told me, 'Go to Siloam and wash your face.' So I went, and as soon as I washed I could see." 12 "Where is he?" they asked. "I do not know," he answered.

The Pharisees Investigate the Healing

13 Then they took the man who had been blind to the Pharisees. 14 The day that Jesus made the mud and opened the man's eyes was a Sabbath. 15 The Pharisees, then, asked the man again how he had received his sight. He told them, "He put some mud on my eyes, I washed my face, and now I can see." 16 Some of the Pharisees said, "The man who did this cannot be from God because he does not obey the Sabbath law." Others, however, said, "How could a man who is a sinner do such mighty works as these?" And there was a division among them.

17 So the Pharisees asked the man once more, "You say he opened your eyes — well, what do you say about him?" "He is a prophet," he answered. 18 The Jews, however, were not willing to believe that he had been blind and could now see, until they called the man's parents 19 and

asked them: "Is this your son? Do you say that he was born blind? Well, how is it that he can see now?" [20] His parents answered: "We know that he is our son, and we know that he was born blind. [21] But we do not know how it is that he is now able to see, nor do we know who opened his eyes. Ask him; he is old enough, and he can answer for himself!" [22] His parents said this because they were afraid of the Jews; for the Jews had already agreed that if anyone professed that Jesus was the Messiah he would be put out of the synagogue. [23] That is why his parents said, "He is old enough; ask him!"

[24] A second time they called back the man who had been born blind and said to him, "Promise before God that you will tell the truth! We know that this man is a sinner." [25] "I do not know if he is a sinner or not," the man replied. "One thing I do know: I was blind, and now I see." [26] "What did he do to you?" they asked. "How did he open your eyes?" [27] "I have already told you," he answered, "and you would not listen. Why do you want to hear it again? Maybe you, too, would like to be his disciples?" [28] They cursed him and said: "You are that fellow's disciple; we are Moses' disciples. [29] We know that God spoke to Moses; as for that fellow, we do not even know where he comes from!" [30] The man answered: "What a strange thing this is! You do not know where he comes from, but he opened my eyes! [31] We know that God does not listen to sinners; he does listen to people who respect him and do what he wants them to do. [32] Since the beginning of the world it has never been heard of that someone opened the eyes of a man born blind; [33] unless this man came from God, he would not be able to do a thing." [34] They answered back, "You were born and raised in sin — and you are trying to teach us?" And they threw him out of the synagogue.

Spiritual Blindness

[35] Jesus heard that they had thrown him out. He found him and said, "Do you believe in the Son of Man?" [36] The man answered, "Tell me who he is, sir, so I can believe in him!" [37] Jesus said to him, "You have already seen him, and he is the one who is talking with you now." [38] "I believe, Lord!" the man said, and knelt down before Jesus.

[39] Jesus said, "I came to this world to judge, so that the blind should see, and those who see should become blind." [40] Some Pharisees, who were there with him, heard him say this and asked him, "You don't mean that we are blind, too?" [41] Jesus answered, "If you were blind, then you would not be guilty; but since you say, 'We can see,' that means that you are still guilty."

The Parable of the Sheepfold

10 "I tell you the truth: the man who does not enter the sheepfold by the door, but climbs in some other way, is a thief and a robber. [2] The man who goes in by the door is the shepherd of the sheep. [3] The gatekeeper opens the gate for him; the sheep hear his voice as he calls his own sheep by name, and he leads them out. [4] When he has brought them out, he goes ahead of them, and the sheep follow him, because they know his voice. [5] They will

not follow someone else; instead, they will run away from him, because they do not know his voice."

[6] Jesus told them this parable, but they did not understand what he was telling them.

Jesus the Good Shepherd

[7] So Jesus said again: "I tell you the truth: I am the door for the sheep. [8] All others who came before me are thieves and robbers; but the sheep did not listen to them. [9] I am the door. Whoever comes in by me will be saved; he will come in and go out, and find pasture. [10] The thief comes only in order to steal, kill, and destroy. I have come in order that they might have life, life in all its fulness.

[11] "I am the good shepherd. The good shepherd is willing to die for the sheep. [12] The hired man, who is not a shepherd and does not own the sheep, leaves them and runs away when he sees a wolf coming; so the wolf

snatches the sheep and scatters them. [13] The hired man runs away because he is only a hired man and does not care for the sheep. [14-15] I am the good shepherd. As the Father knows me and I know the Father, in the same way I know my sheep and they know me. And I am willing to die for them. [16] There are other sheep that belong to me that are not in this sheepfold. I must bring them, too; they will listen to my voice, and they will become one flock with one shepherd.

[17] "The Father loves me because I am willing to give up my life, in order that I may receive it back again. [18] No one takes my life away from me. I give it up of my own free will. I have the right to give it, and I have the right to take it back. This is what my Father has commanded me to do."

[19] Again there was a division among the Jews because of these words. [20] Many of them were saying, "He has a demon! He is crazy! Why do you listen to him?" [21] But others were saying, "A man with a demon could not talk like this! How could a demon open the eyes of blind men?"

Jesus Rejected by the Jews

[22] The time came to celebrate the Feast of Dedication in Jerusalem; it was winter. [23] Jesus was walking in Solomon's Porch in the Temple, [24] when the Jews gathered around him and said, "How long are you going to keep us in suspense? Tell us the plain truth: are you the Messiah?" [25] Jesus answered: "I have already told you, but you would not believe me. The works I do by my Father's authority speak on my behalf; [26] but you will not believe because you are not my sheep. [27] My sheep listen to my voice; I know them, and they follow me. [28] I give them eternal life, and they shall never die; and no one can snatch them away from me. [29] What my Father has given me is greater than all, and no one can snatch them away from the Father's care. [30] The Father and I are one."

[31] Then the Jews once more picked up stones to throw at him. [32] Jesus said to them, "I have done many good works before you which the Father gave me to do; for which one of these do you want to stone me?" [33] The Jews answered back: "We do not want to stone you because of any good works, but because of the way in which

you insult God! You are only a man, but you are trying
to make yourself God!" ³⁴ Jesus answered: "It is written
in your own Law that God said, 'You are gods.' ³⁵ We
know that what the scripture says is true for ever; and God
called them gods, those people to whom his message
was given. ³⁶ As for me, the Father chose me and sent me
into the world. How, then, can you say that I insult God
because I said that I am the Son of God? ³⁷ Do not believe me, then, if I am not doing my Father's works.
³⁸ But if I do them, even though you do not believe me,
you should at least believe my works, in order that you
may know once and for all that the Father is in me, and
I am in the Father."

³⁹ Once more they tried to arrest him, but he slipped
out of their hands.

⁴⁰ Jesus went back again across the Jordan river to the
place where John had been baptizing, and stayed there.
⁴¹ Many people came to him. "John did no mighty
works," they said, "but everything he said about this man
was true." ⁴² And many people there believed in him.

The Death of Lazarus

11 A man named Lazarus, who lived in Bethany, became sick. Bethany was the town where Mary and
her sister Martha lived. ² (This Mary was the one who
poured the perfume on the Lord's feet and wiped them
with her hair; it was her brother Lazarus who was sick.)
³ The sisters sent Jesus a message, "Lord, your dear friend
is sick." ⁴ When Jesus heard it he said, "The final result
of this sickness will not be the death of Lazarus; this has
happened to bring glory to God, and will be the means by
which the Son of God will receive glory."

⁵ Jesus loved Martha and her sister, and Lazarus.
⁶ When he received the news that Lazarus was sick, he
stayed where he was for two more days. ⁷ Then he said
to the disciples, "Let us go back to Judea." ⁸ "Teacher,"
the disciples answered, "just a short time ago the Jews
wanted to stone you; and you plan to go back there?"
⁹ Jesus said: "A day has twelve hours, has it not? So if a
man walks in broad daylight he does not stumble, because
he sees the light of this world. ¹⁰ But if he walks during
the night he stumbles, because there is no light in him."
¹¹ Jesus said this, and then added. "Our friend Lazarus has

fallen asleep, but I will go wake him up." [12] The disciples answered, "If he is asleep, Lord, he will get well." [13] But Jesus meant that Lazarus had died; they thought he meant natural sleep. [14] So Jesus told them plainly, "Lazarus is dead; [15] but for your sake I am glad that I was not with him, so you will believe. Let us go to him." [16] Thomas (called the Twin) said to his fellow disciples, "Let us all go along with the Teacher, that we may die with him!"

Jesus the Resurrection and the Life

[17] When Jesus arrived, he found that Lazarus had been buried four days before. [18] Bethany was less than two miles from Jerusalem, [19] and many Jews had come to see Martha and Mary to comfort them about their brother's death.

[20] When Martha heard that Jesus was coming, she went out to meet him; but Mary stayed at home. [21] Martha said to Jesus, "If you had been here, Lord, my brother would not have died! [22] But I know that even now God will give you whatever you ask of him." [23] "Your brother will be raised to life," Jesus told her. [24] "I know," she replied, "that he will be raised to life on the last day." [25] Jesus said to her: "I am the resurrection and the life. Whoever believes in me will live, even though he dies; [26] and whoever lives and believes in me will never die. Do you believe this?" [27] "Yes, Lord!" she answered. "I do believe that you are the Messiah, the Son of God, who was to come into the world."

Jesus Weeps

[28] After Martha said this she went back and called her sister Mary privately. "The Teacher is here," she told her, "and is asking for you." [29] When Mary heard this she got up and hurried out to meet him. [30] (Jesus had not arrived in the village yet, but was still in the place where Martha had met him.) [31] The Jews who were in the house with Mary comforting her followed her when they saw her get up and hurry out. They thought that she was going to the grave, to weep there.

[32] When Mary arrived where Jesus was and saw him, she fell at his feet. "Lord," she said, "if you had been here, my brother would not have died!" [33] Jesus saw her weeping, and the Jews who had come with her weeping also;

his heart was touched, and he was deeply moved.
³⁴ "Where have you buried him?" he asked them.
"Come and see, Lord," they answered. ³⁵ Jesus wept.
³⁶ So the Jews said, "See how much he loved him!" ³⁷ But
some of them said, "He opened the blind man's eyes,
didn't he? Could he not have kept Lazarus from dying?"

Lazarus Brought to Life

³⁸ Deeply moved once more, Jesus went to the tomb,
which was a cave with a stone placed at the entrance.
³⁹ "Take the stone away!" Jesus ordered. Martha, the dead
man's sister, answered, "There will be a bad smell, Lord.
He has been buried four days!" ⁴⁰ Jesus said to her,
"Didn't I tell you that you would see God's glory if you
believed?" ⁴¹ They took the stone away. Jesus looked up
and said: "I thank you, Father, that you listen to me.
⁴² I know that you always listen to me, but I say this because of the people here, so they will believe that you
sent me." ⁴³ After he had said this he called out in a loud

voice, "Lazarus, come out!" ⁴⁴ The dead man came out,
his hands and feet wrapped in grave cloths, and a cloth
around his face. "Untie him," Jesus told them, "and let
him go."

The Plot against Jesus
(Also Matt. 26.1–5; Mark 14.1–2; Luke 22.1–2)

⁴⁵ Many of the Jews who had come to visit Mary saw

what Jesus did, and believed in him. ⁴⁶ But some of them returned to the Pharisees and told them what Jesus had done. ⁴⁷ So the Pharisees and the chief priests met with the Council and said: "What shall we do? All the mighty works this man is doing! ⁴⁸ If we let him go on in this way everyone will believe in him, and the Roman authorities will take action and destroy the Temple and our whole nation!" ⁴⁹ One of them, named Caiaphas, who was High Priest that year, said: "You do not know a thing! ⁵⁰ Don't you realize that it is better for you to have one man die for the people, instead of the whole nation being destroyed?" ⁵¹ (Actually, he did not say this of his own accord; rather, as he was High Priest that year, he was prophesying that Jesus was about to die for the Jewish people, ⁵² and not only for them, but also to bring together into one body all the scattered children of God.) ⁵³ So from that day on the Jewish authorities made plans to kill Jesus. ⁵⁴ Therefore Jesus did not travel openly in Judea, but left and went to a place near the desert, to a town named Ephraim, where he stayed with the disciples.

⁵⁵ The Jewish Feast of Passover was near, and many people went up from the country to Jerusalem, to perform the ceremony of purification before the feast. ⁵⁶ They were looking for Jesus, and as they gathered in the Temple they asked one another, "What do you think? Surely he will not come to the feast, will he?" ⁵⁷ The chief priests and the Pharisees had given orders that if anyone knew where Jesus was he must report it, so they could arrest him.

Jesus Anointed at Bethany
(Also Matt. 26.6–13; Mark 14.3–9)

12 Six days before the Passover, Jesus went to Bethany, where Lazarus lived, the man Jesus had raised from death. ² They had prepared a dinner for him there, and Martha helped serve it, while Lazarus sat at the table with Jesus. ³ Then Mary took a whole pint of a very expensive perfume made of nard, poured it on Jesus' feet, and wiped them with her hair. The sweet smell of the perfume filled the whole house. ⁴ One of Jesus' disciples, Judas Iscariot — the one who would betray him — said, ⁵ "Why wasn't this perfume sold for three hundred dollars and the money given to the poor?" ⁶ He said this, not because he cared

for the poor, but because he was a thief; he carried the money bag and would help himself from it. 7 But Jesus said: "Leave her alone! Let her keep what she has for the day of my burial. 8 You will always have poor people with you, but I will not be with you always."

The Plot against Lazarus

9 A large crowd of the Jews heard that Jesus was in Bethany, so they went there; they went, not only because of Jesus, but also to see Lazarus, whom Jesus had raised from death. 10 So the chief priests made plans to kill Lazarus too; 11 because on his account many Jews were leaving their leaders and believing in Jesus.

The Triumphant Entry into Jerusalem
(Also Matt. 21.1–11; Mark 11.1–11; Luke 19.28–40)

12 The next day the large crowd that had come to the Passover Feast heard that Jesus was coming to Jerusalem. 13 So they took branches from palm trees and went out to meet him, shouting: "Praise God! God bless him who comes in the name of the Lord! God bless the King of Israel!" 14 Jesus found a donkey and sat on it, just as the scripture says:

15 "Do not be afraid, city of Zion!
Now your King is coming to you,
Riding a young donkey."

16 His disciples did not understand this at the time; but when Jesus had been raised to glory they remembered that the scripture said this, and that they had done this for him.

17 The crowd that had been with Jesus when he called Lazarus out of the grave and raised him from death had reported what had happened. 18 That was why the crowd met him — because they heard that he had done this mighty work. 19 The Pharisees then said to each other, "You see, we are not succeeding at all! Look, the whole world is following him!"

Some Greeks Seek Jesus

20 Some Greeks were among those who went to Jerusalem to worship during the feast. 21 They came to Philip (he was from Bethsaida, in Galilee) and said, "Sir, we want to see Jesus." 22 Philip went and told Andrew,

and the two of them went and told Jesus. ²³ Jesus answered them: "The hour has now come for the Son of Man to be given great glory. ²⁴ I tell you the truth: a grain of wheat is no more than a single grain unless it is dropped into the ground and dies. If it does die, then it produces many grains. ²⁵ Whoever loves his own life will lose it; whoever hates his own life in this world will keep it for life eternal. ²⁶ Whoever wants to serve me must follow me, so that my servant will be with me where I am. My Father will honor him who serves me."

Jesus Speaks about His Death

²⁷ "Now my heart is troubled — and what shall I say? Shall I say, 'Father, do not let this hour come upon me'? But that is why I came, to go through this hour of suffering. ²⁸ O Father, bring glory to your name!" Then a voice spoke from heaven, "I have brought glory to it, and I will do so again."

²⁹ The crowd standing there heard the voice and said, "It thundered!" Others said, "An angel spoke to him!" ³⁰ But Jesus said to them: "It was not for my sake that this voice spoke, but for yours. ³¹ Now is the time for the world to be judged; now the ruler of this world will be overthrown. ³² When I am lifted up from the earth, I will draw all men to me." ³³ (In saying this he indicated the kind of death he was going to suffer.) ³⁴ The crowd answered back: "Our Law tells us that the Messiah will live for ever. How, then, can you say that the Son of Man must be lifted up? Who is this Son of Man?" ³⁵ Jesus answered: "The light will be among you a little longer. Live your lives while you have the light, so the darkness will not come upon you; because the one who lives in the dark does not know where he is going. ³⁶ Believe in the light, then, while you have it, so that you will be the people of the light."

The Unbelief of the Jews

After Jesus said this he went off and hid himself from them. ³⁷ Even though he had done all these mighty works before their very eyes they did not believe in him, ³⁸ so that what the prophet Isaiah had said might come true:

"Lord, who believed the message we told?
To whom did the Lord show his power?"

³⁹ For this reason they were not able to believe, because Isaiah also said:

⁴⁰ "God has blinded their eyes,
He has closed their minds,
So that their eyes would not see,
Their minds would not understand,
And they would not turn to me
For me to heal them."

⁴¹ Isaiah said this because he saw Jesus' glory, and spoke about him.

⁴² Even then, many Jewish leaders believed in Jesus; but because of the Pharisees they did not talk about it openly, so as not to be put out of the synagogue. ⁴³ They loved the approval of men rather than the approval of God.

Judgment by Jesus' Word

⁴⁴ Jesus spoke in a loud voice: "Whoever believes in me, believes not only in me but also in him who sent me. ⁴⁵ Whoever sees me, also sees him who sent me. ⁴⁶ I have come into the world as light, that everyone who believes in me should not remain in the darkness. ⁴⁷ Whoever hears my message and does not obey it, I will not judge him. I came, not to judge the world, but to save it. ⁴⁸ Whoever rejects me and does not accept my message, has one who will judge him. The word I have spoken will be his judge on the last day! ⁴⁹ Yes, because I have not spoken on my own, but the Father who sent me has commanded me what I must say and speak. ⁵⁰ And I know that his command brings eternal life. What I say, then, is what the Father has told me to say."

Jesus Washes His Disciples' Feet

13 It was now the day before the Feast of Passover. Jesus knew that his hour had come for him to leave this world and go to the Father. He had always loved those who were his own in the world, and he loved them to the very end.

² Jesus and his disciples were at supper. The Devil had already decided that Judas, the son of Simon Iscariot, would betray Jesus. ³ Jesus knew that the Father had given him complete power; he knew that he had come from God and was going to God. ⁴ So Jesus rose from the

table, took off his outer garment, and tied a towel around his waist. 5 Then he poured some water into a washbasin and began to wash the disciples' feet and dry them with the towel around his waist. 6 He came to Simon Peter, who said to him, "Are you going to wash my feet, Lord?" 7 Jesus answered him, "You do not know now what I am doing, but you will know later." 8 Peter declared, "You will never, at any time, wash my feet!" "If I do not wash your feet," Jesus answered, "you will no longer be my disciple." 9 Simon Peter answered, "Lord, do not wash only my feet, then! Wash my hands and head, too!" 10 Jesus said: "Whoever has taken a bath is completely clean and does not have to wash himself, except for his feet. All of you are clean — all except one." 11 (Jesus already knew who was going to betray him; that is why he said, "All of you, except one, are clean.")

12 After he had washed their feet, Jesus put his outer garment back on and returned to his place at the table. "Do you understand what I have just done to you?" he asked. 13 "You call me Teacher and Lord, and it is right that you do so, because I am. 14 I am your Lord and Teacher, and I have just washed your feet. You, then, should wash each other's feet. 15 I have set an example for you, so that you will do just what I have done for you. 16 I tell you the truth: no slave is greater than his master; no messenger is greater than the one who sent him. 17 Now you know this truth; how happy you will be if you put it into practice!

18 "I am not talking about all of you; I know those I have chosen. But the scripture must come true that says, 'The man who ate my food turned against me.' 19 I tell you this now before it happens, so that when it does happen you will believe that 'I Am Who I Am'. 20 I tell you the truth: whoever receives anyone I send, receives me also; and whoever receives me, receives him who sent me."

Jesus Predicts His Betrayal
(Also Matt. 26.20–25; Mark 14.17–21; Luke 22.21–23)

²¹ After Jesus said this, he was deeply troubled, and declared openly: "I tell you the truth: one of you is going to betray me." ²² The disciples looked at one another, completely puzzled about whom he meant. ²³ One of the

disciples, whom Jesus loved, was sitting next to Jesus. ²⁴ Simon Peter motioned to him and said, "Ask him who it is that he is talking about." ²⁵ So that disciple moved closer to Jesus' side and asked, "Who is it, Lord?" ²⁶ Jesus answered, "I will dip the bread in the sauce and give it to him; he is the man." So he took a piece of bread, dipped it, and gave it to Judas, the son of Simon Iscariot. ²⁷ As soon as Judas took the bread, Satan went into him. Jesus said to him, "Hurry and do what you must!" ²⁸ (None of those at the table understood what Jesus said to him. ²⁹ Since Judas was in charge of the money bag, some of the disciples thought that Jesus had told him to go to buy what they needed for the feast, or else that he had told him to give something to the poor.) ³⁰ Judas accepted the bread and went out at once. It was night.

The New Commandment

³¹ After Judas had left, Jesus said: "Now the Son of

Man's glory is revealed; now God's glory is revealed through him. [32] And if God's glory is revealed through him, then God himself will reveal the glory of the Son of Man, and he will do so at once. [33] My children, I shall not be with you very much longer. You will look for me; but I tell you now what I told the Jews, 'You cannot go where I am going.' [34] A new commandment I give you: love one another. As I have loved you, so you must love one another. [35] If you have love for one another, then all will know that you are my disciples."

Jesus Predicts Peter's Denial
(Also Matt. 26.31–35; Mark 14.27–31; Luke 22.31–34)

[36] "Where are you going, Lord?" Simon Peter asked him. "You cannot follow me now where I am going," answered Jesus; "but later you will follow me." [37] "Lord, why can't I follow you now?" asked Peter. "I am ready to die for you!" [38] Jesus answered: "Are you really ready to die for me? I tell you the truth: before the rooster crows you will say three times that you do not know me."

Jesus the Way to the Father

14 "Do not be worried and upset," Jesus told them. "Believe in God, and believe also in me. [2] There are many rooms in my Father's house, and I am going to prepare a place for you. I would not tell you this if it were not so. [3] And after I go and prepare a place for you, I will come back and take you to myself, so that you will be where I am. [4] You know how to get to the place where I am going." [5] Thomas said to him, "Lord, we do not know where you are going; how can we know the way to get there?" [6] Jesus answered him: "I am the way, I am the truth, I am the life; no one goes to the Father except by me. [7] Now that you have known me," he said to them, "you will know my Father also; and from now on you do know him, and you have seen him."

[8] Philip said to him, "Lord, show us the Father; that is all we need." [9] Jesus answered: "For a long time I have been with you all; yet you do not know me, Philip? Whoever has seen me has seen the Father. Why, then, do you say, 'Show us the Father'? [10] Do you not believe, Philip, that I am in the Father and the Father is in me? The words that I have spoken to you," Jesus said to his

disciples, "do not come from me. The Father, who remains in me, does his own works. [11] Believe me that I am in the Father and the Father is in me. If not, believe because of these works. [12] I tell you the truth: whoever believes in me will do the works I do — yes, he will do even greater ones, for I am going to the Father. [13] And I will do whatever you ask for in my name, so that the Father's glory will be shown through the Son. [14] If you ask me for anything in my name, I will do it."

The Promise of the Holy Spirit

[15] "If you love me, you will obey my commandments. [16] I will ask the Father, and he will give you another Helper, the Spirit of truth, to stay with you for ever. [17] The world cannot receive him, because it cannot see him or know him. But you know him, for he remains with you and lives in you.

[18] "I will not leave you alone; I will come back to you. [19] In a little while the world will see me no more, but you will see me; and because I live, you also will live. [20] When that day comes, you will know that I am in my Father, and that you are in me, just as I am in you.

[21] "Whoever accepts my commandments and obeys them, he is the one who loves me. My Father will love him who loves me; I too will love him and reveal myself to him." [22] Judas (not Judas Iscariot) said, "Lord, how can it be that you will reveal yourself to us and not to the world?" [23] Jesus answered him: "Whoever loves me will obey my message. My Father will love him, and my Father and I will come to him and live with him. [24] Whoever does not love me does not obey my words. The message you have heard is not mine, but comes from the Father, who sent me.

[25] "I have told you this while I am still with you. [26] The Helper, the Holy Spirit whom the Father will send in my name, will teach you everything, and make you remember all that I have told you.

[27] "Peace I leave with you; my own peace I give you. I do not give it to you as the world does. Do not be worried and upset; do not be afraid. [28] You heard me say to you, 'I am leaving, but I will come back to you.' If you loved me, you would be glad that I am going to the Father, because he is greater than I. [29] I have told you this now,

before it all happens, so that when it does happen you will believe. ³⁰ I cannot talk with you much longer, for the ruler of this world is coming. He has no power over me, ³¹ but the world must know that I love the Father; that is why I do everything as he commands me.

"Rise, let us go from this place."

Jesus the Real Vine

15 "I am the real vine, and my Father is the gardener. ² He breaks off every branch in me that does not bear fruit, and prunes every branch that does bear fruit, so that it will be clean and bear more fruit. ³ You have been made clean already by the message I have spoken to you. ⁴ Remain in union with me, and I will remain in union with you. Unless you remain in me you cannot bear fruit, just as a branch cannot bear fruit unless it remains in the vine.

⁵ "I am the vine, you are the branches. Whoever remains in me, and I in him, will bear much fruit; for you can do nothing without me. ⁶ Whoever does not remain in me is thrown out, like a branch, and dries up; such branches are gathered up and thrown into the fire, where they are burned. ⁷ If you remain in me, and my words remain in you, then you will ask for anything you wish, and you shall have it. ⁸ This is how my Father's glory is shown: by your bearing much fruit; and in this way you become my disciples. ⁹ I love you just as the Father loves me; remain in my love. ¹⁰ If you obey my commands, you will remain in my love, in the same way that I have obeyed my Father's commands and remain in his love.

¹¹ "I have told you this so that my joy may be in you, and that your joy may be complete. ¹² This is my commandment: love one another, just as I love you. ¹³ The greatest love a man can have for his friends is to give his life for them. ¹⁴ And you are my friends, if you do what I command. ¹⁵ I do not call you servants any longer, because a servant does not know what his master is doing. Instead, I call you friends, because I have told you everything I heard from my Father. ¹⁶ You did not choose me; I chose you, and appointed you to go and bear much fruit, the kind of fruit that endures. And the Father will give you whatever you ask of him in my name. ¹⁷ This, then, is what I command you: love one another."

The World's Hatred

¹⁸ "If the world hates you, you must remember that it has hated me first. ¹⁹ If you belonged to the world, then the world would love you as its own. But I chose you from this world, and you do not belong to it; this is why

the world hates you. ²⁰ Remember what I told you: 'No slave is greater than his master.' If they persecuted me, they will persecute you too; if they obeyed my message, they will obey yours too. ²¹ But they will do all this to you because you are mine; for they do not know him who sent me. ²² They would not have been guilty of sin if I had not come and spoken to them; as it is, they no longer have any excuse for their sin. ²³ Whoever hates me hates my Father also. ²⁴ They would not have been guilty of sin if I had not done the works among them that no one else ever did; as it is, they have seen what I did and they hate both me and my Father. ²⁵ This must be, however, so that what is written in their Law may come true, 'They hated me for no reason at all.'

²⁶ "The Helper will come — the Spirit of truth, who comes from the Father. I will send him from the Father, and he will speak about me. ²⁷ And you, too, will speak

about me, for you have been with me from the very beginning.

16 "I have told you this so that you will not fall away. 2 They will put you out of their synagogues. And the time will come when anyone who kills you will think that by doing this he is serving God. 3 They will do these things to you because they have not known either the Father or me. 4 But I have told you this, so that when the time comes for them to do these things, you will remember that I told you."

The Work of the Holy Spirit

"I did not tell you these things at the beginning, because I was with you. 5 But now I am going to him who sent me; but none of you asks me, 'Where are you going?' 6 And now that I have told you, sadness has filled your hearts. 7 But I tell you the truth: it is better for you that I go away, because if I do not go, the Helper will not come to you. But if I do go away, then I will send him to you. 8 And when he comes he will prove to the people of the world that they are wrong about sin, and about what is right, and about God's judgment. 9 They are wrong about sin, because they do not believe in me; 10 about what is right, because I am going to the Father and you will not see me any more; 11 about judgment, because the ruler of this world has already been judged.

12 "I have much more to tell you, but now it would be too much for you to bear. 13 But when the Spirit of truth comes, he will lead you into all the truth. He will not speak on his own, but he will tell you what he hears, and will speak of things to come. 14 He will give me glory, for he will take what I have to say and tell it to you. 15 All that my Father has is mine; that is why I said that the Spirit will take what I give him and tell it to you."

Sadness and Gladness

16 "In a little while you will not see me any more; and then a little while later you will see me." 17 Some of his disciples said to the others: "What does this mean? He tells us, 'In a little while you will not see me, and then a little while later you will see me'; and he also says, 'It is because I am going to the Father.' 18 What does this 'a little while' mean?" they asked. "We do not know what he

is talking about!" ¹⁹ Jesus knew that they wanted to ask him, so he said to them: "I said, 'In a little while you will not see me, and then a little while later you will see me.' Is this what you are asking about among yourselves? ²⁰ I tell you the truth: you will cry and weep, but the world will be glad; you will be sad, but your sadness will turn into gladness. ²¹ When a woman is about to give birth to a child she is sad, because her hour of suffering has come; but when the child is born she forgets her suffering, because she is happy that a baby has been born into the world. ²² That is the way it is with you: now you are sad, but I will see you again, and your hearts will be filled with gladness, the kind of gladness that no one can take away from you.

²³ "When that day comes you will not ask me for a thing. I tell you the truth: the Father will give you anything you ask of him in my name. ²⁴ Until now you have not asked for anything in my name; ask and you will receive, so that your happiness may be complete."

Victory over the World

²⁵ "I have told you these things by means of parables. But the time will come when I will use parables no more, but I will speak to you in plain words about the Father. ²⁶ When that day comes you will ask him in my name; and I do not say that I will ask him on your behalf, ²⁷ for the Father himself loves you. He loves you because you love me and have believed that I came from God. ²⁸ I did come from the Father and I came into the world; and now I am leaving the world and going to the Father."

²⁹ Then his disciples said to him: "Look, you are speaking very plainly now, without using parables. ³⁰ We know now that you know everything; you do not need someone to ask you questions. This makes us believe that you came from God." ³¹ Jesus answered them: "Do you believe now? ³² The time is coming, and is already here, when all of you will be scattered, each one to his own home, and I will be left all alone. But I am not really alone, because the Father is with me. ³³ I have told you this so that you will have peace through your union with me. The world will make you suffer. But be brave! I have defeated the world!"

Jesus Prays for His Disciples

17 After Jesus finished saying this, he looked up to heaven and said: "Father, the hour has come.

Give glory to your Son, that the Son may give glory to you. ² For you gave him authority over all men, so that he might give eternal life to all those you gave him. ³ And this is eternal life: for men to know you, the only true God, and to know Jesus Christ, whom you sent. ⁴ I showed your glory on earth; I finished the work you gave me to do. ⁵ O Father! Give me glory in your presence now, the same glory I had with you before the world was made.

⁶ "I have made you known to the men you gave me out of the world. They belonged to you, and you gave them to me. They have obeyed your word, ⁷ and now they know that everything you gave me comes from you. ⁸ For I gave them the message that you gave me, and they received it; they know that it is true that I came from you, and they believe that you sent me.

⁹ "I pray for them. I do not pray for the world, but for the men you gave me, because they belong to you. ¹⁰ All I have is yours, and all you have is mine; and my glory is shown through them. ¹¹ And now I am coming to you; I am no longer in the world, but they are in the world. O holy Father! Keep them safe by the power of your name, the name you gave me, so they may be one just as you and I are one. ¹² While I was with them I kept them safe by the power of your name, the name you gave me. I protected them, and not one of them was lost, except the man who was bound to be lost — that the scripture might

come true. [13] And now I am coming to you, and I say these things in the world so that they might have my joy in their hearts, in all its fulness. [14] I gave them your message and the world hated them, because they do not belong to the world, just as I do not belong to the world. [15] I do not ask you to take them out of the world, but I do ask you to keep them safe from the Evil One. [16] Just as I do not belong to the world, they do not belong to the world. [17] Make them your own, by means of the truth; your word is truth. [18] I sent them into the world just as you sent me into the world. [19] And for their sake I give myself to you, in order that they, too, may truly belong to you.

[20] "I do not pray only for them, but also for those who believe in me because of their mèssage. [21] I pray that they may all be one. O Father! May they be in us, just as you are in me and I am in you. May they be one, so that the world will believe that you sent me. [22] I gave them the same glory you gave me, so that they may be one, just as you and I are one: [23] I in them and you in me, so they may be completely one, in order that the world may know that you sent me and that you love them as you love me.

[24] "O Father! You have given them to me, and I want them to be with me where I am, so they may see my glory, the glory you gave me; for you loved me before the world was made. [25] O righteous Father! The world does not know you, but I know you, and these know that you sent me. [26] I made you known to them and I will continue to do so, in order that the love you have for me may be in them, and I may be in them."

The Arrest of Jesus
(Also Matt. 26.47–56; Mark 14.43–50; Luke 22.47–53)

18 After Jesus had said this prayer he left with his disciples and went across the brook Kidron. There was a garden in that place, and Jesus and his disciples went in. [2] Judas, the traitor, knew where it was, because many times Jesus had met there with his disciples. [3] So Judas went to the garden, taking with him a group of soldiers and some Temple guards sent by the chief priests and the Pharisees; they were armed and carried lanterns and torches. [4] Jesus knew everything that was going to happen to him; so he stepped forward and said to them, "Who is it

you are looking for?" ⁵ "Jesus of Nazareth," they answered. "I am he," he said.

Judas, the traitor, was standing there with them. ⁶ When Jesus said to them, "I am he," they moved back and fell to the ground. ⁷ Jesus asked them again, "Who is it you are

looking for?" "Jesus of Nazareth," they said. ⁸ "I have already told you that I am he," Jesus said. "If, then, you are looking for me, let these others go." ⁹ (He said this so that what he had said might come true: "Not a single one was lost, Father, of all those you gave me.") ¹⁰ Simon Peter had a sword; he drew it and struck the High Priest's slave, cutting off his right ear. The name of the slave was Malchus. ¹¹ Jesus said to Peter, "Put your sword back in its place! Do you think that I will not drink the cup of suffering my Father has given me?"

Jesus before Annas

¹² The group of soldiers with their commanding officer and the Jewish guards arrested Jesus, tied him up, ¹³ and took him first to Annas. He was the father-in-law of Caiaphas, who was High Priest that year. ¹⁴ It was Caiaphas who had advised the Jews that it was better that one man die for all the people.

Peter Denies Jesus
(Also Matt. 26.69–70; Mark 14.66–68; Luke 22.55–57)

¹⁵ Simon Peter and another disciple followed Jesus. That other disciple was well known to the High Priest, so he

went with Jesus into the courtyard of the High Priest's house. ¹⁶ Peter stayed outside by the gate. The other disciple, who was well known to the High Priest, went back out, spoke to the girl at the gate and brought Peter inside. ¹⁷ The girl at the gate said to Peter, "Aren't you one of the disciples of that man?" "No, I am not," answered Peter.

¹⁸ It was cold, so the servants and guards had built a charcoal fire and were standing around it, warming themselves. Peter went over and stood with them, warming himself.

The High Priest Questions Jesus
(Also Matt. 26.59–66; Mark 14.55–64; Luke 22.66–71)

¹⁹ The High Priest questioned Jesus about his disciples and about his teaching. ²⁰ Jesus answered: "I have always spoken publicly to everyone; all my teaching was done in the synagogues and in the Temple, where all the Jews come together. I have never said anything in secret. ²¹ Why, then, do you question me? Question the people who heard me. Ask them what I told them — they know what I said." ²² When Jesus said this, one of the guards there slapped him and said, "How dare you talk like this to the High Priest!" ²³ Jesus answered him: "If I have said something wrong, tell everyone here what it was. But if I am right in what I have said, why do you hit me?"

²⁴ So Annas sent him, still tied up, to Caiaphas the High Priest.

Peter Denies Jesus again
(Also Matt. 26.71–75; Mark 14.69–72; Luke 22.58–62)

²⁵ Peter was still standing there keeping himself warm. So the others said to him, "Aren't you one of the disciples of that man?" But Peter denied it. "No, I am not," he said. ²⁶ One of the High Priest's slaves, a relative of the man whose ear Peter had cut off, spoke up. "Didn't I see you with him in the garden?" he asked. ²⁷ Again Peter said "No" — and at once a rooster crowed.

Jesus before Pilate
(Also Matt. 27.1–2, 11–14; Mark 15.1–5; Luke 23.1–5)

²⁸ They took Jesus from Caiaphas' house to the Governor's palace. It was early in the morning. The Jews did

not go inside the palace because they wanted to keep them-selves ritually clean, in order to be able to eat the Passover meal. ²⁹ So Pilate went outside to meet them and said, "What do you accuse this man of?" ³⁰ Their answer was, "We would not have brought him to you if he had not committed a crime." ³¹ Pilate said to them, "You yourselves take him and try him according to your own law." The Jews replied, "We are not allowed to put any-one to death." ³² (This happened to make come true what Jesus had said when he indicated the kind of death he would die.) ³³ Pilate went back into the palace and called Jesus. "Are you the king of the Jews?" he asked him. ³⁴ Jesus answered, "Does this question come from you or have others told you about me?" ³⁵ Pilate replied: "Do you think I am a Jew? It was your own people and their chief priests who handed you over to me. What have you done?" ³⁶ Jesus said: "My kingdom does not belong to this world; if my kingdom belonged to this world, my fol-lowers would fight to keep me from being handed over to the Jews. No, my kingdom does not belong here!" ³⁷ So Piiate asked him, "Are you a king, then?" Jesus answered: "You say that I am a king. I was born and came into the world for this one purpose, to speak about the truth. Who-ever belongs to the truth listens to me." ³⁸ "And what is truth?" Pilate asked.

Jesus Sentenced to Death
(Also Matt. 27.15–31; Mark 15.6–20; Luke 23.13–25)

Then Pilate went back outside to the Jews and said to

them: "I cannot find any reason to condemn him. 39 But according to the custom you have, I always set free a prisoner for you during the Passover. Do you want me to set the king of the Jews free for you?" 40 They answered him with a shout, "No, not him! We want Barabbas!" (Barabbas was a bandit.)

19 Then Pilate took Jesus and had him whipped. 2 The soldiers made a crown of thorny branches and put it on his head; they put a purple robe on him, 3 and came to him and said, "Long live the King of the Jews!" And they went up and slapped him.

⁴ Pilate went back out once more and said to the crowd, "Look, I will bring him out here to you, to let you see that I cannot find any reason to condemn him." ⁵ So Jesus went outside, wearing the crown of thorns and the purple robe. Pilate said to them, "Look! Here is the man!" ⁶ When the chief priests and the guards saw him they shouted, "Nail him to the cross! Nail him to the cross!" Pilate said to them, "You take him, then, and nail him to the cross. I find no reason to condemn him." ⁷ The Jews answered back, "We have a law that says he ought to die, because he claimed to be the Son of God."

⁸ When Pilate heard them say this, he was even more afraid. ⁹ He went back into the palace and said to Jesus, "Where do you come from?" But Jesus gave him no answer. ¹⁰ Pilate said to him, "You will not speak to me? Remember, I have the authority to set you free, and also the authority to have you nailed to the cross." ¹¹ Jesus answered, "You have authority over me only because it was given to you by God. So the man who handed me over to you is guilty of a worse sin." ¹² When Pilate heard this he was all the more anxious to set him free. But the Jews shouted back, "If you set him free that means you are not the Emperor's friend! Anyone who claims to be a king is the Emperor's enemy!" ¹³ When Pilate heard these words, he took Jesus outside and sat down on the judge's seat in the place called "The Stone Pavement." (In Hebrew the name is "Gabbatha.")

¹⁴ It was then almost noon of the day before the Passover. Pilate said to the Jews, "Here is your king!" ¹⁵ They shouted back, "Kill him! Kill him! Nail him to the cross!" Pilate asked them, "Do you want me to nail your king to the cross?" The chief priests answered, "The only king we have is the Emperor!" ¹⁶ Then Pilate handed Jesus over to them to be nailed to the cross.

Jesus Nailed to the Cross
(Also Matt. 27.32–44; Mark 15.21–32; Luke 23.26–43)

So they took charge of Jesus. ¹⁷ He went out, carrying his own cross, and came to "The Place of the Skull," as it is called. (In Hebrew it is called "Golgotha.") ¹⁸ There they nailed him to the cross; they also nailed two other men to crosses, one on each side, with Jesus between them.

¹⁹ Pilate wrote a notice and had it put on the cross. "Jesus of Nazareth, the King of the Jews," is what he wrote. ²⁰ Many Jews read this, because the place where Jesus was nailed to the cross was not far from the city. The notice was written in Hebrew, Latin, and Greek. ²¹ The Jewish chief priests said to Pilate, "Do not write 'The King of the Jews,' but rather, 'This man said, I am the King of the Jews.'" ²² Pilate answered, "What I have written stays written."

²³ After the soldiers had nailed Jesus to the cross, they took his clothes and divided them into four parts, one part for each soldier. They also took the robe, which was made of one piece of woven cloth, without any seams in it. ²⁴ The soldiers said to each other, "Let us not tear it; let us throw dice to see who will get it." This happened to make the scripture come true:

"They divided my clothes among themselves,
They gambled for my robe."

So the soldiers did this.

²⁵ Standing close to Jesus' cross were his mother, his mother's sister, Mary the wife of Clopas, and Mary Magdalene. ²⁶ Jesus saw his mother and the disciple he loved standing there; so he said to his mother, "Woman, here is your son." ²⁷ Then he said to the disciple, "Here is your

mother." And from that time the disciple took her to live in his home.

The Death of Jesus
(Also Matt. 27.45–56; Mark 15.33–41; Luke 23.44–49)

28 Jesus knew that by now everything had been completed; and in order to make the scripture come true he said, "I am thirsty." 29 A bowl was there, full of cheap wine; they soaked a sponge in the wine, put it on a branch of hyssop, and lifted it up to his lips. 30 Jesus took the wine and said, "It is finished!" Then he bowed his head and died.

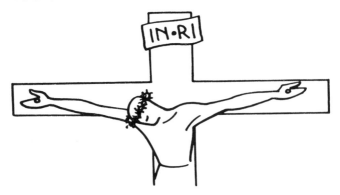

Jesus' Side Pierced

31 Then the Jews asked Pilate to allow them to break the legs of the men who had been put to death, and take them down from the crosses. They did this because it was Friday, and they did not want the bodies to stay on the crosses on the Sabbath day, since the coming Sabbath was especially holy. 32 So the soldiers went and broke the legs of the first man and then of the other man who had been put to death with Jesus. 33 But when they came to Jesus they saw that he was already dead, so they did not break his legs. 34 One of the soldiers, however, plunged his spear into Jesus' side, and at once blood and water poured out. 35 The one who saw this happen has spoken of it. We know that what he said is true, and he also knows that he speaks the truth, so that you also may believe. 36 This was done to make the scripture come true, "Not one of his

bones will be broken." ³⁷ And there is another scripture
that says, "People will look at him whom they pierced."

The Burial of Jesus
(Also Matt. 27.57–61; Mark 15.42–47; Luke 23.50–56)

³⁸ After this, Joseph, who was from the town of Arimathea, asked Pilate if he could take Jesus' body. (Joseph
was a follower of Jesus, but in secret, because he was
afraid of the Jews.) Pilate told him he could have the
body, so Joseph went and took it away. ³⁹ Nicodemus, who
at first had gone to see Jesus at night, went with Joseph,
taking with him about one hundred pounds of spices, a
mixture of myrrh and aloes. ⁴⁰ The two men took Jesus'
body and wrapped it in linen cloths with the spices; for
this is how the Jews prepare a body for burial. ⁴¹ There
was a garden in the place where Jesus had been put to
death, and in it there was a new tomb where no one had
ever been laid. ⁴² Since it was the day before the Jewish
Sabbath, and because the tomb was close by, they laid
Jesus there.

The Empty Tomb
(Also Matt. 28.1–8; Mark 16.1–8; Luke 24.1–12)

20 Early on Sunday morning, while it was still dark,
Mary Magdalene went to the tomb and saw that the
stone had been taken away from the entrance. ² She ran
and went to Simon Peter and the other disciple, whom

Jesus loved, and told them, "They have taken the Lord
from the tomb and we don't know where they have put
him!" ³ Then Peter and the other disciple left and went to
the tomb. ⁴ The two of them were running, but the other
disciple ran faster than Peter and reached the tomb first.
⁵ He bent over and saw the linen cloths, but he did not go
in. ⁶ Behind him came Simon Peter, and he went straight
into the tomb. He saw the linen cloths lying there ⁷ and the
cloth which had been around Jesus' head. It was not lying
with the linen cloths but was rolled up by itself. ⁸ Then the
other disciple, who had reached the tomb first, also went
in; he saw and believed. ⁹ (They still did not understand
the scripture which said that he must be raised from death.)
¹⁰ Then the disciples went back home.

Jesus Appears to Mary Magdalene
(Also Matt. 28.9–10; Mark 16.9–11)

¹¹ Mary stood crying outside the tomb. Still crying, she
bent over and looked in the tomb, ¹² and saw two angels
there, dressed in white, sitting where the body of Jesus had
been, one at the head, the other at the feet. ¹³ "Woman,
why are you crying?" they asked her. She answered,
"They have taken my Lord away, and I do not know
where they have put him!" ¹⁴ When she had said this, she
turned around and saw Jesus standing there; but she did
not know that it was Jesus. ¹⁵ "Woman, why are you crying?" Jesus asked her. "Who is it that you are looking
for?" She thought he was the gardener, so she said to him,
"If you took him away, sir, tell me where you have put
him, and I will go and get him." ¹⁶ Jesus said to her,
"Mary!" She turned toward him and said in Hebrew,
"Rabboni!" (This means "Teacher.") ¹⁷ "Do not hold
on to me," Jesus told her, "because I have not yet gone
back up to the Father. But go to my brothers and tell
them for me, 'I go back up to him who is my Father and
your Father, my God and your God.' " ¹⁸ So Mary Magdalene told the disciples that she had seen the Lord, and
that he had told her this.

Jesus Appears to His Disciples
(Also Matt. 28.16–20; Mark 16.14–18; Luke 24.36–49)

¹⁹ It was late that Sunday evening, and the disciples were
gathered together behind locked doors, because they were

afraid of the Jews. Then Jesus came and stood among them. "Peace be with you," he said. ²⁰ After saying this, he showed them his hands and his side. The disciples were filled with joy at seeing the Lord. ²¹ Then Jesus said to them again, "Peace be with you. As the Father sent me, so I send you." ²² He said this, and then he breathed on them and said, "Receive the Holy Spirit. ²³ If you forgive men's sins, then they are forgiven; if you do not forgive them, then they are not forgiven."

Jesus and Thomas

²⁴ One of the disciples, Thomas (called the Twin), was not with them when Jesus came. ²⁵ So the other disciples told him, "We saw the Lord!" Thomas said to them, "If I do not see the scars of the nails in his hands, and put my finger where the nails were, and my hand in his side, I will not believe."

²⁶ A week later the disciples were together indoors again, and Thomas was with them. The doors were locked, but Jesus came and stood among them and said, "Peace be with you." ²⁷ Then he said to Thomas, "Put your finger here, and look at my hands; then stretch out your hand and put it in my side. Stop your doubting and believe!" ²⁸ Thomas answered him, "My Lord and my God!" ²⁹ Jesus said to him, "Do you believe because you see me? How happy are those who believe without seeing me!"

The Purpose of this Book

³⁰ Jesus did many other mighty works in his disciples'

presence which are not written down in this book. ³¹ These have been written that you may believe that Jesus is the Messiah, the Son of God, and that through this faith you may have life in his name.

Jesus Appears to Seven Disciples

21 After this, Jesus showed himself once more to his disciples at Lake Tiberias. This is how he did it. ² Simon Peter, Thomas (called the Twin), Nathanael (the one from Cana in Galilee), the sons of Zebedee, and two other disciples of Jesus were all together. ³ Simon Peter said to the others, "I am going fishing." "We will come with you," they told him. So they went and got into the boat; but all that night they did not catch a thing. ⁴ As the sun was rising, Jesus stood at the water's edge, but the

disciples did not know that it was Jesus. [5] Then he said to them, "Young men, haven't you caught anything?" "Not a thing," they answered. [6] He said to them, "Throw your net out on the right side of the boat, and you will find some." So they threw the net out, and could not pull it back in, because they had caught so many fish. [7] The disciple whom Jesus loved said to Peter, "It is the Lord!" When Simon Peter heard that it was the Lord, he wrapped his outer garment around him (for he had taken his clothes off) and jumped into the water. [8] The rest of the disciples came to shore in the boat, pulling the net full of fish. They were not very far from land, about a hundred yards away. [9] When they stepped ashore they saw a charcoal fire there with fish and bread on it. [10] Then Jesus said to them, "Bring some of the fish you have just caught." [11] Simon Peter went aboard and dragged the net ashore, full of big fish, a hundred and fifty-three in all; even though there were so many, still the net did not tear. [12] Jesus said to them, "Come and eat." None of the disciples dared ask him, "Who are you?" because they knew it was the Lord. [13] So Jesus went over, took the bread, and gave it to them; he did the same with the fish.

[14] This, then, was the third time Jesus showed himself to the disciples after he was raised from death.

Jesus and Peter

[15] After they had eaten, Jesus said to Simon Peter, "Simon, son of John, do you love me more than these?" "Yes, Lord," he answered, "you know that I love you." Jesus said to him, "Take care of my lambs." [16] A second time Jesus said to him, "Simon, son of John, do you love me?" "Yes, Lord," he answered, "you know that I love you." Jesus said to him, "Take care of my sheep." [17] A third time Jesus said, "Simon, son of John, do you love me?" Peter became sad because Jesus asked him the third time, "Do you love me?" and said to him, "Lord, you know everything; you know that I love you!" Jesus said to him: "Take care of my sheep. [18] I tell you the truth: when you were young you used to fasten your belt and go anywhere you wanted to; but when you are old you will stretch out your hands and someone else will tie them and take you where you don't want to go." [19] (In saying this Jesus was indicating the way in which Peter would die

and bring glory to God.) Then Jesus said to him, "Follow
me!"

Jesus and the Other Disciple

²⁰ Peter turned around and saw behind him that other
disciple, whom Jesus loved — the one who had leaned
close to Jesus at the meal and asked, "Lord, who is going
to betray you?" ²¹ When Peter saw him, he said to Jesus,
"Lord, what about this man?" ²² Jesus answered him, "If
I want him to live on until I come, what is that to you?
Follow me!" ²³ So a report spread among the followers
of Jesus that this disciple would not die. But Jesus did
not say that he would not die; he said, "If I want him to
live on until I come, what is that to you?"

²⁴ He is the disciple who spoke of these things, the one
who also wrote them down; and we know that what he
said is true.

Conclusion

²⁵ Now, there are many other things that Jesus did. If
they were all written down one by one, I suppose that the
whole world could not hold the books that would be written.

THE ACTS OF THE APOSTLES

1 Dear Theophilus:

In my first book I wrote about all the things that Jesus did and taught, from the time he began his work [2] until the day he was taken up to heaven. Before he was taken up he gave instructions by the power of the Holy Spirit to the men he had chosen as his apostles. [3] For forty days after his death he showed himself to them many times, in ways that proved beyond doubt that he was alive; he was seen by them, and talked with them about the Kingdom of God. [4] And when they came together, he gave them this order: "Do not leave Jerusalem, but wait for the gift my Father promised, that I told you about. [5] For John baptized with water, but in a few days you will be baptized with the Holy Spirit."

Jesus Is Taken up to Heaven

[6] When the apostles met together with Jesus they asked him, "Lord, will you at this time give the Kingdom back to Israel?" [7] Jesus said to them: "The times and occasions are set by my Father's own authority, and it is not for you to know when they will be. [8] But you will be filled with power when the Holy Spirit comes on you, and you will be witnesses for me in Jerusalem, in all of Judea and Samaria, and to the ends of the earth." [9] After saying this, he was taken up into heaven as they watched him, and a cloud hid him from their sight.

[10] They still had their eyes fixed on the sky as he went away, when two men dressed in white suddenly stood beside them. [11] "Men of Galilee," they said, "why do you stand there looking up at the sky? This Jesus, who was taken up from you into heaven, will come back in the same way that you saw him go to heaven."

Judas' Successor

[12] Then the apostles went back to Jerusalem from the Mount of Olives, which is about half a mile away from the city. [13] They entered Jerusalem and went up to the room where they were staying: Peter, John, James and Andrew, Philip and Thomas, Bartholomew and Matthew, James the son of Alphaeus, Simon the patriot, and Judas the son of

James. [14] They all joined together in a group to pray frequently, together with the women, and Mary the mother of Jesus, and his brothers.

[15] A few days later there was a meeting of the believers, about one hundred and twenty in all, and Peter stood up to speak. [16] "My brothers," he said, "the scripture had to come true in which the Holy Spirit, speaking through David, predicted about Judas, who was the guide of the men who arrested Jesus. [17] Judas was a member of our group, for he had been chosen to have a part in our work."

[18] (With the money that Judas got for his evil act he bought a field, where he fell to his death; he burst open and all his insides spilled out. [19] All the people living in Jerusalem heard about it, and so in their own language they call that field Akeldama, which means "Field of Blood.")

[20] "For it is written in the book of Psalms,

'May his house become empty,
Let no one live in it.'

It is also written,

'May someone else take his place of service.'

[21-22] "So then, a man must join us as a witness to the resurrection of the Lord Jesus. He must be one of those who were in our group during the whole time that the Lord Jesus traveled about with us, beginning from the time John preached his baptism until the day Jesus was taken up from us into heaven." [23] So they proposed two men: Joseph, who was called Barsabbas (he was also called Justus), and Matthias. [24] Then they prayed: "Lord, you know the hearts of all men. And so, Lord, show us which one of these two you have chosen [25] to take this place of service as an apostle which Judas left to go to the place where he belongs." [26] After this they drew lots to choose between the two names. The name chosen was that of Matthias, and he was added to the group of the eleven apostles.

The Coming of the Holy Spirit

2 When the day of Pentecost arrived, all the believers were gathered together in one place. [2] Suddenly there was a noise from the sky which sounded like a strong wind blowing, and it filled the whole house where they were sitting. [3] Then they saw what looked like tongues of fire spreading out; and each person there was touched by a

tongue. ⁴ They were all filled with the Holy Spirit and began to talk in other languages, as the Spirit enabled them to speak.

⁵ There were Jews living in Jerusalem, religious men who had come from every country in the world. ⁶ When they heard this noise, a whole crowd gathered. They were all excited, because each one of them heard the believers talking in his own language. ⁷ In amazement and wonder they exclaimed: "These men who are talking like this — they are all Galileans! ⁸ How is it, then, that all of us hear them speaking in our own native language? ⁹ We are from Parthia, Media, and Elam; from Mesopotamia, Judea, and Cappadocia; from Pontus and Asia, ¹⁰ from Phrygia and Pamphylia, from Egypt and the regions of Libya near Cyrene; some of us are from Rome, ¹¹ both Jews and Gentiles converted to Judaism; and some of us are from Crete and Arabia — yet all of us hear them speaking in our own languages of the great things that God has done!" ¹² Amazed and confused they all kept asking each other, "What does this mean?" ¹³ But others made fun of the believers, saying, "These men are drunk!"

Peter's Message

¹⁴ Then Peter stood up with the other eleven apostles, and in a loud voice began to speak to the crowd: "Fellow

Jews, and all of you who live in Jerusalem, listen to me and pay attention to what I am about to say. ¹⁵ These men are not drunk, as you suppose; it is only nine o'clock in the morning. ¹⁶ Rather, this is what the prophet Joel spoke about:

¹⁷ 'This is what I will do in the last days, God says:

I will pour out my Spirit upon all men;
Your sons and your daughters will prophesy,
Your young men will see visions,
And your old men will dream dreams.
¹⁸ Yes, even on my slaves, both men and women,
I will pour out my Spirit in those days,
And they will prophesy.
¹⁹ I will perform miracles in the sky above,
And marvels on the earth below:
There will be blood and fire and thick smoke;
²⁰ The sun will become dark,
And the moon red as blood,
Before the great and glorious Day of the Lord arrives.
²¹ And then, whoever calls on the name of the Lord will be saved.'

²² "Listen to these words, men of Israel! Jesus of Nazareth was a man whose divine mission was clearly shown to you by the miracles, wonders, and signs which God did through him; you yourselves know this, for it took place here among you. ²³ God, in his own will and knowledge, had already decided that Jesus would be handed over to you; and you killed him, by letting sinful men nail him to the cross. ²⁴ But God raised him from the dead; he set him free from the pains of death, for it was impossible that death should hold him prisoner. ²⁵ For David said about him:

'I saw the Lord before me at all times,
For he is by my right side, so that I will not be troubled.
²⁶ Because of this my heart is glad and my words are full of joy;
And I, mortal though I am, will rest assured in hope,
²⁷ For you will not abandon my soul in the world of the dead,

You will not allow your devoted servant to
suffer decay.

²⁸ You have shown me the paths that lead to life,
And by your presence you will fill me with
joy.'

²⁹ "Brothers: I must speak to you quite plainly about
our patriarch David. He died and was buried, and his
grave is here with us to this very day. ³⁰ He was a prophet,
and he knew God's promise to him: God made a vow that
he would make one of David's descendants a king, just as
he was. ³¹ David saw what God was going to do, and so
he spoke about the resurrection of the Messiah when he
said:

'He was not abandoned in the world of the
dead,

His flesh did not decay.'

³² God has raised this very Jesus from the dead, and we
are all witnesses to this fact. ³³ He has been raised to the
right side of God and received from him the Holy Spirit,
as his Father had promised; and what you now see and
hear is his gift that he has poured out on us. ³⁴ For David
himself did not go up into heaven; rather he said:

'The Lord said to my Lord:

Sit here at my right side,

³⁵ Until I put your enemies

As a footstool under your feet.'

³⁶ "All the people of Israel, then, are to know for sure
that it is this Jesus, whom you nailed to the cross, that
God has made Lord and Messiah!"

³⁷ When the people heard this, they were deeply troubled, and said to Peter and the other apostles, "What shall
we do, brothers?" ³⁸ Peter said to them: "Turn away from
your sins, each one of you, and be baptized in the name
of Jesus Christ, so that your sins will be forgiven; and you
will receive God's gift, the Holy Spirit. ³⁹ For God's promise was made to you and your children, and to all who
are far away — all whom the Lord our God calls to himself."

⁴⁰ Peter made his appeal to them and with many other
words he urged them, saying, "Save yourselves from the
punishment coming to this wicked people!" ⁴¹ Many of
them believed his message and were baptized; about three
thousand people were added to the group that day. ⁴² They

spent their time in learning from the apostles, taking part in the fellowship, and sharing in the fellowship meals and the prayers.

Life among the Believers

⁴³ Many miracles and wonders were done through the apostles, which caused everyone to be filled with awe. ⁴⁴ All the believers continued together in close fellowship, and shared their belongings with one another. ⁴⁵ They would sell their property and possessions and distribute the money among all, according to what each one needed. ⁴⁶ Every day they continued to meet as a group in the Temple, and they had their meals together in their homes, eating the food with glad and humble hearts, ⁴⁷ praising God, and enjoying the good will of all the people. And every day the Lord added to their group those who were being saved.

The Lame Man Healed

3 One day Peter and John went to the Temple at three o'clock in the afternoon, the hour for prayers. ² There, at the "Beautiful Gate," as it was called, was a man who had been lame all his life. Every day he was carried to this gate to beg for money from the people who were going into the Temple. ³ When he saw Peter and John going in, he begged them to give him something. ⁴ They looked

straight at him and Peter said, "Look at us!" ⁵ So he looked at them, expecting to get something from them. ⁶ And Peter said to him, "I have no money at all, but I will give you what I have: in the name of Jesus Christ of Nazareth I order you to walk!" ⁷ Then he took him by his right hand and helped him up. At once the man's feet and ankles became strong; ⁸ he jumped up, stood on his feet and started walking around. Then he went into the Temple with them, walking and jumping and praising God. ⁹ The whole crowd saw him walking and praising God; ¹⁰ and when they recognized him as the beggar who sat at the Temple's "Beautiful Gate," they were all filled with surprise and amazement at what had happened to him.

Peter's Message in the Temple

¹¹ As the man held on to Peter and John, all the people were amazed and ran to them in "Solomon's Porch," as it was called. ¹² When Peter saw the people, he said to them: "Men of Israel, why are you surprised at this, and why do you stare at us? Do you think that it was by means of our own power or godliness that we made this man walk? ¹³ The God of Abraham, Isaac, and Jacob, the God of our ancestors, has given divine glory to his Servant Jesus. You handed him over to the authorities, and you rejected him in Pilate's presence, even after Pilate had decided to set him free. ¹⁴ He was holy and good, but you rejected him and instead you asked Pilate to do you the favor of turning loose a murderer. ¹⁵ And so you killed the Author of life. But God raised him from the dead — and we are witnesses to this. ¹⁶ It was the power of his name that gave strength to this lame man. What you see and know was done by faith in his name; it was faith in Jesus that made him well like this before you all.

¹⁷ "And now, my brothers, I know that what you and your leaders did to Jesus was done because of your ignorance. ¹⁸ God long ago announced by means of all the prophets that his Messiah had to suffer; and he made it come true in this way. ¹⁹ Repent, then, and turn to God, so that he will wipe away your sins, ²⁰ so that times of spiritual strength may come from the Lord's presence, and that he may send Jesus, who is the Messiah he has already chosen for you. ²¹ He must remain in heaven until the time comes for all things to be made new, as God an-

nounced by means of his holy prophets of long ago.
22 For Moses said: 'The Lord your God will send you a
prophet, just as he sent me, who will be of your own
people. You must listen to everything that he tells you.
23 Anyone who does not listen to what that prophet says
will be separated from God's people and destroyed.'
24 And the prophets, including Samuel and those who came
after him, all of them who had a message, also announced
these present days. 25 The promises of God through his
prophets are for you, and you share in the covenant which
God made with your ancestors. As he said to Abraham,
'Through your descendants I will bless all the people on
earth.' 26 And so God chose and sent his Servant to you
first, to bless you by making all of you turn away from
your wicked ways."

Peter and John before the Council

4 Peter and John were still speaking to the people when
the priests, the officer in charge of the Temple guards,
and the Sadducees came up to them. 2 They were an-
noyed because the two apostles were teaching the people
that Jesus had been raised from death, which proved that
the dead will be raised to life. 3 So they arrested them and
put them in jail until the next day, since it was already
late. 4 But many who heard the message believed; and the
number of men came to about five thousand.

5 The next day the Jewish leaders, the elders, and the
teachers of the Law gathered in Jerusalem. 6 They met
with the High Priest Annas, and Caiaphas, and John, and
Alexander, and the others who were members of the High
Priest's family. 7 They made the apostles stand before
them and asked them, "How did you do this? What power
do you have, or whose name did you use?" 8 Peter, full of
the Holy Spirit, answered them: "Leaders of the people
and elders: 9 if we are being questioned today about the
good deed done to the lame man and how he was made
well, 10 then you should all know, and all the people of
Israel should know, that this man stands here before you
completely well by the power of the name of Jesus Christ
of Nazareth — whom you crucified and God raised from
death. 11 Jesus is the one of whom the scripture says,

'The stone that you the builders despised
Turned out to be the most important stone.'

¹² Salvation is to be found through him alone; for there is no one else in all the world, whose name God has given to men, by whom we can be saved."

¹³ The members of the Council were amazed to see how bold Peter and John were, and to learn that they were ordinary men of no education. They realized then that they had been companions of Jesus. ¹⁴ But there was nothing that they could say, for they saw the man who had been made well standing there with Peter and John. ¹⁵ So they told them to leave the Council room, and started discussing among themselves. ¹⁶ "What shall we do with these men?" they asked. "Everyone living in Jerusalem knows that this extraordinary miracle has been performed by them, and we cannot deny it. ¹⁷ But to keep this matter from spreading any further among the people, let us warn them never again to speak to anyone in the name of Jesus." ¹⁸ So they called them back in and told them that under no condition were they to speak or to teach in the name of Jesus.

¹⁹ But Peter and John answered them: "You yourselves judge which is right in God's sight, to obey you or to obey God. ²⁰ For we cannot stop speaking of what we ourselves have seen and heard." ²¹ The Council warned them even more strongly, and then set them free. They could find no reason for punishing them, for the people were all praising God for what had happened. ²² The man on whom this miracle of healing had been performed was over forty years old.

The Believers Pray for Boldness

²³ As soon as they were set free, Peter and John returned to their group and told them what the chief priests and the elders had said. ²⁴ When they heard it, they all joined together in prayer to God: "Master and Creator of heaven, and earth, and sea, and all that is in them! ²⁵ By means of the Holy Spirit you spoke through our ancestor David, your servant, when he said:

'Why were the Gentiles furious,
Why did the peoples plot in vain?
²⁶ The kings of the earth prepared themselves,
And the rulers met together
Against the Lord and his Messiah.'

²⁷ For indeed Herod and Pontius Pilate met together in

this city with the Gentiles and the peoples of Israel against Jesus, your holy Servant, whom you made Messiah. [28] They gathered to do everything that you, by your power and will, had already decided would take place. [29] And now, Lord, take notice of the threats they made and allow us, your servants, to speak your message with all boldness. [30] Stretch out your hand to heal, and grant that wonders and miracles may be performed through the name of your holy Servant Jesus." [31] When they finished praying, the place where they were meeting was shaken. They were all filled with the Holy Spirit and began to speak God's message with boldness.

All Things Together

[32] The group of believers was one in mind and heart. No one said that any of his belongings was his own, but they all shared with one another everything they had. [33] With great power the apostles gave witness of the resurrection of the Lord Jesus, and God poured rich blessings on them all. [34] There was no one in the group who was in need. Those who owned fields or houses would sell them, bring the money received from the sale, [35] and turn it over to the apostles; and the money was distributed to each one according to his need.

[36] And so it was that Joseph, a Levite born in Cyprus, whom the apostles called Barnabas (which means "One who Encourages"), [37] sold a field he owned, brought the money, and turned it over to the apostles.

Ananias and Sapphira

5 But there was a man named Ananias, whose wife's name was Sapphira. He sold some property that belonged to them, [2] but kept part of the money for himself, as his wife knew, and turned the rest over to the apostles. [3] Peter said to him: "Ananias, why did you let Satan take control of your heart and make you lie to the Holy Spirit by keeping part of the money you received for the property? [4] Before you sold the property it belonged to you, and after you sold it the money was yours. Why, then, did you decide in your heart that you would do such a thing? You have not lied to men — you have lied to God!" [5] As soon as Ananias heard this he fell down dead; and all who heard about it were filled with fear. [6] The young men

came in, wrapped up his body, took him out, and buried him.

[7] About three hours later his wife came in, but she did not know what had happened. [8] Peter said to her, "Tell me, was this the full amount you and your husband received for your property?" "Yes," she answered, "the full amount." [9] So Peter said to her, "Why did you and your husband decide to put the Lord's Spirit to the test? The men who buried your husband are at the door right now, and they will carry you out too!" [10] At once she fell down at his feet and died. The young men came in and saw that she was dead, so they carried her out and buried her beside her husband. [11] The whole church and all the others who heard of this were filled with great fear.

Miracles and Wonders

[12] Many miracles and wonders were being performed among the people by the apostles. All the believers met together in a group in Solomon's Porch. [13] Nobody outside the group dared join them, even though the people spoke highly of them. [14] But more and more people were added to the group — a crowd of men and women who believed in the Lord. [15] As a result of what the apostles were doing, the sick people were carried out in the streets and placed on beds and mats so that, when Peter walked by, at least his shadow might pass over some of them. [16] And crowds of people came in from the towns around Jerusalem, bringing their sick and those who had evil spirits in them; and they were all healed.

The Apostles Persecuted

[17] Then the High Priest and all his companions, members of the local party of the Sadducees, became extremely jealous of the apostles; so they decided to take action. [18] They arrested the apostles and placed them in the public jail. [19] But that night an angel of the Lord opened the prison gates, led the apostles out, and said to them, [20] "Go and stand in the Temple, and tell the people all about this new life." [21] The apostles obeyed, and at dawn they entered the Temple and started teaching.

The High Priest and his companions called together all the Jewish elders for a full meeting of the Council; then they sent orders to the prison to have the apostles brought before them. ²² But when the officials arrived, they did not find the apostles in prison; so they returned to the Council and reported: ²³ "When we arrived at the jail we found it locked up tight and all the guards on watch at the gates; but when we opened the gates we did not find anyone inside!" ²⁴ When the officer in charge of the Temple guards and the chief priests heard this, they wondered what had happened to the apostles. ²⁵ Then a man came in who

said to them, "Listen! The men you put in prison are standing in the Temple teaching the people!" ²⁶ So the officer went off with his men and brought the apostles back. They did not use force, however, because they were afraid that the people might stone them.

²⁷ They brought the apostles in and made them stand before the Council, and the High Priest questioned them. ²⁸ "We gave you strict orders not to teach in the name of this man," he said; "but see what you have done! You have spread your teaching all over Jerusalem, and you want to make us responsible for his death!" ²⁹ Peter and the other apostles answered back: "We must obey God, not men. ³⁰ The God of our fathers raised Jesus from death, after you had killed him by nailing him to a cross. ³¹ And God raised him to his right side as Leader and Savior, to give to the people of Israel the opportunity to repent and have their sins forgiven. ³² We are witnesses to these things — we and the Holy Spirit, who is God's gift to those who obey him."

³³ When the members of the Council heard this they were so furious that they decided to have the apostles put to death. ³⁴ But one of them, a Pharisee named Gamaliel,

a teacher of the Law who was highly respected by all the people, stood up in the Council. He ordered the apostles to be taken out, 35 and then said to the Council: "Men of Israel, be careful what you are about to do to these men. 36 Some time ago Theudas appeared, claiming that he was somebody great; and about four hundred men joined him. But he was killed, all his followers were scattered, and his movement died out. 37 After this, Judas the Galilean appeared during the time of the census; he also drew a crowd after him, but he also was killed and all his followers were scattered. 38 And so in this case now, I tell you, do not take any action against these men. Leave them alone, for if this plan and work of theirs is a man-made thing, it will disappear; 39 but if it comes from God you cannot possibly defeat them. You could find yourselves fighting against God!" The Council followed Gamaliel's advice. 40 They called the apostles in, had them whipped, and ordered them never again to speak in the name of Jesus; and then they set them free. 41 The apostles left the Council, full of joy that God had considered them worthy to suffer disgrace for the name of Jesus. 42 And every day in the Temple and in people's homes they continued to teach and preach the Good News about Jesus the Messiah.

The Seven Helpers

6 Some time later, as the number of disciples kept growing, there was a quarrel between the Greek-speaking Jews and the native Jews. The Greek-speaking Jews said that their widows were being neglected in the daily distribution of funds. 2 So the twelve apostles called the whole group of disciples together and said: "It is not right for us to neglect the preaching of God's word in order to handle finances. 3 So then, brothers, choose seven men among you who are known to be full of the Holy Spirit and wisdom, and we will put them in charge of this matter. 4 We ourselves, then, will give our full time to prayers and the work of preaching." 5 The whole group was pleased with the apostles' proposal; so they chose Stephen, a man full of faith and the Holy Spirit, and Philip, Prochorus, Nicanor, Timon, Parmenas, and Nicolaus from Antioch, a Gentile who had been converted to Judaism. 6 The group presented them to the apostles, who prayed and placed their hands on them.

[7] And so the word of God continued to spread. The number of disciples in Jerusalem grew larger and larger, and a great number of priests accepted the faith.

The Arrest of Stephen

[8] Stephen, a man richly blessed by God and full of power, performed great miracles and wonders among the people. [9] But some men opposed him; they were members of the synagogue of the Free Men (as it was called), which had Jews from Cyrenia and Alexandria. They and other Jews from Cilicia and Asia started arguing with Stephen. [10] But the Spirit gave Stephen such wisdom that when he spoke they could not resist him. [11] So they paid some men to say, "We heard him speaking against Moses and against God!" [12] In this way they stirred up the people, the elders, and the teachers of the Law. They came to Stephen, seized him, and took him before the Council. [13] Then they brought in some men to tell lies about him. "This man," they said, "is always talking against our sacred Temple and the Law of Moses. [14] For we heard him say that this Jesus of Nazareth will tear down the Temple and change all the customs which have come down to us from Moses!" [15] All those sitting in the Council fixed their eyes on Stephen and saw that his face looked like the face of an angel.

Stephen's Speech

7 The High Priest asked Stephen, "Is this really so?" [2] And Stephen answered: "Brothers and fathers! Listen to me! The God of glory appeared to our ancestor Abraham while he was living in Mesopotamia, before he had gone to live in Haran, [3] and said to him, 'Leave your family and country and go to the land that I will show you.' [4] And so he left the land of Chaldea and went to live in Haran. After Abraham's father died, God made him move to this country, where you now live. [5] God did not then give Abraham any part of it as his own, not even a square foot of ground; but God promised that he would give it to him, and that it would belong to him and his descendants after him. At the time God made this promise Abraham had no children. [6] This is what God said to him: 'Your descendants will live in a foreign country, where they will be slaves and will be badly treated for four hun-

dred years. [7] But I will pass judgment on the people that they will serve,' God said, 'and afterward they will come out of that country and will worship me in this place.' [8] Then God gave to Abraham the ceremony of circumcision as a sign of the covenant. So Abraham circumcised Isaac a week after he was born; Isaac circumcised Jacob, and Jacob circumcised the twelve patriarchs.

[9] "The patriarchs were jealous of Joseph, and sold him as a slave in Egypt. But God was with him, [10] and brought him safely through all his troubles. When Joseph appeared before Pharaoh, the king of Egypt, God gave him a pleasing manner and wisdom. Pharaoh made Joseph governor over the country and the royal household. [11] Then there was a famine in all of Egypt and Canaan, which caused much suffering. Our ancestors could not find any food. [12] So when Jacob heard that there was grain in Egypt, he sent our ancestors on their first visit there. [13] On the second visit Joseph made himself known to his brothers, and Pharaoh came to know about Joseph's family. [14] So Joseph sent a message to his father Jacob, telling him and the whole family to come to Egypt; there were seventy-five people in all. [15] Then Jacob went down to Egypt, where he and our ancestors died. [16] Their bodies were moved to Shechem, where they were buried in the grave which Abraham had bought from the tribe of Hamor for a sum of money.

[17] "When the time drew near for God to keep the promise he had made to Abraham, the number of our people in Egypt had grown much larger. [18] At last a different king, who had not known Joseph, began to rule in Egypt. [19] He tricked our people and was cruel to our ancestors, forcing them to put their babies out of their homes, so that they would die. [20] It was at this time that Moses was born, a very beautiful child. He was brought up at home for three months, [21] and when he was put out of his home the daughter of Pharaoh adopted him and brought him up as her own son. [22] He was taught all the wisdom of the Egyptians, and became a great man in words and deeds.

[23] "When Moses was forty years old he decided to visit his fellow Israelites. [24] He saw one of them being mistreated by an Egyptian; so he went to his help and took revenge on the Egyptian by killing him. [25] (He thought that his own people would understand that God was going

to use him to set them free; but they did not understand.)
²⁶ The next day he saw two Israelites fighting, and he tried to make peace between them. 'Listen, men,' he said, 'you are brothers; why do you mistreat each other?' ²⁷ But the one who was mistreating the other pushed Moses aside. 'Who made you ruler and judge over us?' he asked. ²⁸ 'Do you want to kill me, just as you killed that Egyptian yesterday?' ²⁹ When Moses heard this he fled from Egypt and started living in the land of Midian. There he had two sons.

³⁰ "After forty years had passed, an angel appeared to Moses in the flames of a burning bush in the desert near Mount Sinai. ³¹ Moses was amazed by what he saw, and went near the bush to look at it closely. But he heard the Lord's voice: ³² 'I am the God of your ancestors, the God of Abraham and Isaac and Jacob.' Moses trembled with fear and dared not look. ³³ And the Lord said to him: 'Take your sandals off, for the place where you are standing is holy ground. ³⁴ I have looked and seen the cruel suffering of my people in Egypt. I have heard their groans, and I have come down to save them. Come now, I will send you to Egypt.'

³⁵ "This is the Moses who was rejected by the people of Israel. 'Who made you ruler and judge over us?' they asked. He is the one whom God sent as ruler and savior, with the help of the angel he saw in the burning bush. ³⁶ He led the people out of Egypt, performing miracles and wonders in Egypt and the Red Sea, and in the desert for forty years. ³⁷ He is the Moses who said to the people of Israel, 'God will send you a prophet, just as he sent me, who will be of your own people.' ³⁸ He is the one who was with the people of Israel assembled in the desert; he was there with our ancestors and with the angel who spoke to him on Mount Sinai; he received God's living messages to pass on to us.

³⁹ "But our ancestors refused to obey him; they pushed him aside and wished that they could go back to Egypt. ⁴⁰ So they said to Aaron: 'Make us some gods who will go in front of us. We do not know what has happened to that Moses who brought us out of Egypt.' ⁴¹ It was then that they made an idol in the shape of a calf and offered sacrifice to it, and had a feast in honor of what they themselves had made. ⁴² But God turned away from them, and gave

them over to worship the stars of heaven, as it is written in the book of the prophets:

> 'People of Israel! It was not to me
> That you slaughtered and sacrificed animals
> For forty years in the desert.

⁴³ It was the tent of the god Moloch that you carried,
> And the image of the star of your god Rephan;
> They were idols that you had made to worship.
> And so I will send you away beyond Babylon.'

⁴⁴ "Our ancestors had the tent of God's presence with them in the desert. It had been made as God had told Moses to make it, according to the pattern that Moses had been shown. ⁴⁵ Later on, our ancestors who received the tent from their fathers carried it with them when they went with Joshua and took over the land from the nations that God drove out before them. And it stayed there until the time of David. ⁴⁶ He won God's favor, and asked God to allow him to provide a house for the God of Jacob. ⁴⁷ But it was Solomon who built him a house.

⁴⁸ "But the Most High God does not live in houses built by men; as the prophet says:

> ⁴⁹ 'Heaven is my throne, says the Lord,
> And earth is my footstool.
> What kind of house would you build for me?
> Where is the place for me to rest?
> ⁵⁰ Did not I myself make all these things?'

⁵¹ "How stubborn you are! How heathen your hearts, how deaf you are to God's message! You are just like your ancestors: you too have always resisted the Holy Spirit! ⁵² Was there a single prophet that your ancestors did not persecute? They killed God's messengers, who long ago announced the coming of his righteous Servant. And now you have betrayed and murdered him. ⁵³ You are the ones who received God's law, that was handed down by angels — yet you have not obeyed it!"

The Stoning of Stephen

⁵⁴ As the members of the Council listened to Stephen they became furious and ground their teeth at him in

anger. ⁵⁵ But Stephen, full of the Holy Spirit, looked up to heaven and saw God's glory, and Jesus standing at the right side of God. ⁵⁶ "Look!" he said. "I see heaven opened and the Son of Man standing at the right side of God!" ⁵⁷ With a loud cry they stopped up their ears, and all rushed together at him at once. ⁵⁸ They threw him out of the city and stoned him. The witnesses left their cloaks in charge of a young man named Saul. ⁵⁹ They kept on stoning Stephen as he called on the Lord, "Lord Jesus, receive my spirit!" ⁶⁰ He knelt down and cried in a loud voice, "Lord! Do not remember this sin against them!" He said this and died.

8 And Saul approved of his murder.

Saul Persecutes the Church

That very day the church in Jerusalem began to suffer a cruel persecution. All the believers, except the apostles, were scattered throughout the provinces of Judea and Samaria. ² Some devout men buried Stephen, weeping for him with loud cries.

³ But Saul tried to destroy the church; going from house to house, he dragged the believers out, both men and women, and threw them into jail.

The Gospel Preached in Samaria

[4] The believers who were scattered went everywhere, preaching the message. [5] Philip went to the city of Samaria and preached the Messiah to the people there. [6] The crowds paid close attention to what Philip said. They all listened to him and saw the miracles that he performed. [7] Evil spirits came out with a loud cry from many people; many paralyzed and lame people were also healed. [8] And there was great joy in Samaria.

[9] In that city lived a man named Simon, who for some time had astounded the Samaritans with his magic. He claimed that he was someone great, [10] and everyone in the city, from all classes of society, paid close attention to him. "He is that power of God known as 'The Great Power,'" they said. [11] He had astounded them with his magic for such a long time that they paid close attention to him. [12] But when they believed Philip's message about the Good News of the Kingdom of God and the name of Jesus Christ, they were baptized, both men and women. [13] Simon himself also believed; and after being baptized he stayed close to Philip, and was astounded when he saw the great wonders and miracles that were being performed.

[14] The apostles in Jerusalem heard that the people of Samaria had received the word of God; so they sent Peter and John to them. [15] When they arrived, they prayed for the believers that they might receive the Holy Spirit. [16] For the Holy Spirit had not yet come down on any of them; they had only been baptized in the name of the Lord Jesus. [17] Then Peter and John placed their hands on them, and they received the Holy Spirit.

[18] Simon saw that the Spirit had been given to them when the apostles placed their hands on them. So he offered money to Peter and John, [19] and said, "Give this power to me too, so that anyone I place my hands on will receive the Holy Spirit." [20] But Peter answered him: "May you and your money go to hell, for thinking that you can buy God's gift with money! [21] You have no part or share in our work, because your heart is not right in God's sight. [22] Repent, then, from this evil plan of yours, and pray to the Lord that he will forgive you for thinking such a thing as this. [23] For I see that you are full of bitter envy, and are a prisoner of sin." [24] Simon said to Peter

and John, "Please pray to the Lord for me, so that none of these things you said might happen to me."

25 After they had given their testimony and spoken the Lord's message, Peter and John went back to Jerusalem. On their way they preached the Good News in many villages of Samaria.

Philip and the Ethiopian Official

26 An angel of the Lord spoke to Philip: "Get yourself ready and go south to the road that goes from Jerusalem to Gaza." (This road is no longer used.) 27-28 So Philip got ready and went. Now an Ethiopian eunuch was on his way home. This man was an important official in charge of the treasury of the Queen, or Candace, of Ethiopia. He had been to Jerusalem to worship God, and was going back in his carriage. As he rode along he was reading from the book of the prophet Isaiah. 29 The Holy Spirit said to Philip, "Go over and stay close to that carriage." 30 Philip ran over and heard him reading from the book of the prophet Isaiah; so he asked him, "Do you understand what you are reading?" 31 "How can I understand," the official replied, "unless someone explains it to me?" And he invited Philip to climb up and sit in the carriage with him. 32 The passage of scripture which he was reading was this:

"He was like a sheep that is taken to be
slaughtered,

He was like a lamb that makes no sound
when its wool is cut off.

He did not say a word.

33 He was humiliated, and justice was denied
him.

No one will be able to tell about his descendants,

For his life on earth has come to an end."

34 The official said to Philip, "Tell me, of whom is the prophet saying this? Of himself or of someone else?" 35 Philip began to speak; starting from this very passage of scripture, he told him the Good News about Jesus. 36 As they traveled down the road they came to a place where there was some water, and the official said, "Here is some water. What is to keep me from being baptized?" [37 Philip said to him, "You may be baptized if you believe

with all your heart." "I do," he answered; "I believe that Jesus Christ is the Son of God."] ³⁸ The official ordered the carriage to stop; and both of them, Philip and the official, went down into the water, and Philip baptized him. ³⁹ When they came up out of the water the Spirit of the Lord took Philip away. The official did not see him again, but continued on his way, full of joy. ⁴⁰ Philip found himself in Ashdod; and he went through all the towns preaching the Good News, until he arrived at Caesarea.

The Conversion of Saul
(Also Acts 22.6–16; 26.12–18)

9 In the meantime Saul kept up his violent threats of murder against the disciples of the Lord. He went to the High Priest ² and asked for letters of introduction to the Jewish synagogues in Damascus, so that if he should find any followers of the Way of the Lord there, he would be able to arrest them, both men and women, and take them back to Jerusalem.

³ On his way to Damascus, as he came near the city, a light from the sky suddenly flashed all around him. ⁴ He fell to the ground and heard a voice saying to him, "Saul, Saul! Why do you persecute me?" ⁵ "Who are you,

Lord?" he asked. "I am Jesus, whom you persecute," the voice said. [6] "But get up and go into the city, where you will be told what you must do." [7] Now the men who were traveling with Saul had stopped, not saying a word; they heard the voice but could not see anyone. [8] Saul got up from the ground and opened his eyes, but could not see a thing. So they took him by the hand and led him into Damascus. [9] For three days he was not able to see, and during that time he did not eat or drink anything.

[10] There was a disciple in Damascus named Ananias. He had a vision, in which the Lord said to him, "Ananias!" "Here I am, Lord," he answered. [11] The Lord said to him: "Get ready and go to Straight Street, and in the house of Judas ask for a man from Tarsus named Saul. He is praying, [12] and in a vision he saw a man named Ananias come in and place his hands on him so that he might see again." [13] Ananias answered: "Lord, many people have told me about this man, about all the terrible things he has done to your people in Jerusalem. [14] And he has come to Damascus with authority from the chief priests to arrest all who call on your name." [15] The Lord said to him: "Go, for I have chosen him to serve me, to make my name known to Gentiles and kings, and to the people of Israel. [16] And I myself will show him all that he must suffer for my sake."

[17] So Ananias went, entered the house and placed his hands on Saul. "Brother Saul," he said, "the Lord has sent me — Jesus himself, whom you saw on the road as you were coming here. He sent me so that you might see again and be filled with the Holy Spirit." [18] At once something like fish scales fell from Saul's eyes and he was able to see again. He stood up and was baptized; [19] and after he had eaten, his strength came back.

Saul Preaches in Damascus

Saul stayed for a few days with the disciples in Damascus. [20] He went straight to the synagogues and began to preach about Jesus. "He is the Son of God," he said. [21] All who heard him were amazed, and asked, "Isn't this the man who in Jerusalem was killing those who call on this name? And didn't he come here for the very purpose of arresting them and taking them back to the chief priests?"

²² But Saul's preaching became even more powerful, and his proofs that Jesus was the Messiah were so strong that the Jews who lived in Damascus could not answer him.

²³ After many days had gone by, the Jews gathered and made plans to kill Saul; ²⁴ but he was told of what they planned to do. Day and night they watched the city gates in order to kill him. ²⁵ But one night Saul's followers took him and let him down through an opening in the wall, lowering him in a basket.

Saul in Jerusalem

²⁶ Saul went to Jerusalem and tried to join the disciples. They would not believe, however, that he was a disciple, and they were all afraid of him. ²⁷ Then Barnabas came to his help and took him to the apostles. He explained to them how Saul had seen the Lord on the road, and that the Lord had spoken to him. He also told them how boldly Saul had preached in the name of Jesus in Damascus. ²⁸ And so Saul stayed with them and went all over Jerusalem, boldly preaching in the name of the Lord. ²⁹ He also talked and disputed with the Greek-speaking Jews, but they tried to kill him. ³⁰ When the brothers found out about this, they took Saul down to Caesarea and sent him away to Tarsus.

³¹ And so it was that the church throughout all of Judea and Galilee and Samaria had a time of peace. It was built up and grew in numbers through the help of the Holy Spirit, as it lived its life in reverence for the Lord.

Peter in Lydda and Joppa

³² Peter traveled everywhere, and one time he went to visit God's people who lived in Lydda. ³³ There he met a man named Aeneas, who was paralyzed and had not been able to get out of bed for eight years. ³⁴ "Aeneas," Peter said to him, "Jesus Christ makes you well. Get up and make your bed." At once Aeneas got up. ³⁵ All the people living in Lydda and Sharon saw him, and they turned to the Lord.

³⁶ In Joppa there was a woman named Tabitha, who was a believer. (Her name in Greek is Dorcas, meaning a deer.) She spent all her time doing good and helping the poor. ³⁷ At that time she got sick and died. Her body was washed and laid in a room upstairs. ³⁸ Joppa was not very

far from Lydda, and when the disciples in Joppa heard that Peter was in Lydda, they sent two men to him with the message, "Please hurry and come to us." ³⁹ So Peter got ready and went with them. When he arrived he was taken to the room upstairs. All the widows crowded around him, crying and showing him the shirts and coats that Dorcas had made while she was alive. ⁴⁰ Peter put them all out of the room, and knelt down and prayed; then he turned to the body and said, "Tabitha, get up!" She opened her eyes, and when she saw Peter she sat up. ⁴¹ Peter reached over and helped her get up. Then he called the believers and the widows, and presented her alive to them. ⁴² The news about this spread all over Joppa, and many people believed in the Lord. ⁴³ Peter stayed on in Joppa for many days with a leather-worker named Simon.

Peter and Cornelius

10 There was a man in Caesarea named Cornelius, a captain in the Roman army regiment called "The Italian Regiment." ² He was a religious man; he and his whole family worshiped God. He did much to help the Jewish poor people, and was constantly praying to God. ³ It was about three o'clock one afternoon when he had a vision, in which he clearly saw an angel of God come in and say to him, "Cornelius!" ⁴ He stared at the angel in fear and said, "What is it, sir?" The angel answered: "God has accepted your prayers and works of charity, and has remembered you. ⁵ And now send some men to Joppa to call for a certain man whose full name is Simon Peter. ⁶ He is a guest in the home of a leather-worker named Simon, who lives by the sea." ⁷ Then the angel who was speaking to him went away, and Cornelius called two of his house servants and a soldier, a religious man who was one of his personal attendants. ⁸ He told them what had happened and sent them off to Joppa.

⁹ The next day, as they were on their way and coming near Joppa, Peter went up on the roof of the house about noon in order to pray. ¹⁰ He became hungry, and wanted to eat; while the food was being prepared he had a vision. ¹¹ He saw heaven opened and something coming down that looked like a large sheet being lowered by its four corners to the earth. ¹² In it were all kinds of land ani-

mals, reptiles, and wild birds. ¹³ A voice said to him, "Get up, Peter; kill and eat!" ¹⁴ But Peter said, "Certainly not, Lord! I have never eaten anything considered defiled or unclean." ¹⁵ The voice spoke to him again: "Do not consider anything unclean that God has declared clean." ¹⁶ This happened three times; and then the thing was taken back up into heaven.

¹⁷ Peter wondered to himself about the meaning of this vision that he had seen. In the meantime the men sent by Cornelius had learned where Simon's house was, and were now standing in front of the gate. ¹⁸ They called out and asked, "Is there a guest here by the name of Simon Peter?" ¹⁹ Peter was still trying to understand what the vision meant when the Spirit said: "Listen! Three men are here looking for you. ²⁰ So get yourself ready and go down, and do not hesitate to go with them, for I have sent them." ²¹ So Peter went down and said to the men, "I am the man you are looking for. Why have you come?" ²² "Captain Cornelius sent us," they answered. "He is a good man who worships God and is highly respected by all the Jewish people. He was told by one of God's angels to invite you to his house, so he could hear what you have to say." ²³ Peter invited the men in and had them spend the night there.

The next day he got ready and went with them; and some of the brothers from Joppa went along with him. ²⁴ The following day he arrived in Caesarea, where Cornelius was waiting for him, together with relatives and close friends that he had invited. ²⁵ As Peter was about to go in, Cornelius met him, fell at his feet and bowed

down before him. ²⁶ But Peter made him rise. "Stand up," he said, "for I myself am only a man." ²⁷ Peter kept on talking to Cornelius as he went into the house, where he found many people gathered. ²⁸ He said to them: "You yourselves know very well that a Jew is not allowed by his religion to visit or associate with a Gentile. But God has shown me that I must not consider any man unclean or defiled. ²⁹ And so when you sent for me I came without any objection. I ask you, then, why did you send for me?"

³⁰ Cornelius said: "It was about this time three days ago that I was praying in my house at three o'clock in the afternoon. Suddenly a man dressed in shining clothes stood in front of me ³¹ and said: 'Cornelius! God has heard your prayer, and has remembered your works of charity. ³² Send someone to Joppa to call for a man whose full name is Simon Peter. He is a guest in the home of Simon the leather-worker, who lives by the sea.' ³³ And so I sent for you at once, and you have been good enough to come. Now we are all here in the presence of God, waiting to hear anything that the Lord has ordered you to say."

Peter's Speech

³⁴ Peter began to speak: "I now realize that it is true that God treats all men alike. ³⁵ Whoever fears him and does what is right is acceptable to him, no matter what race he belongs to. ³⁶ You know the message he sent to the people of Israel, proclaiming the Good News of peace through Jesus Christ, who is Lord of all men. ³⁷ You know of the great event that took place throughout all of Judea, beginning in Galilee, after the baptism that John preached. ³⁸ You know about Jesus of Nazareth, how God poured out on him the Holy Spirit and power. He went everywhere, doing good and healing all who were under the power of the Devil, for God was with him. ³⁹ We are witnesses of all that he did in the country of the Jews and in Jerusalem. They put him to death by nailing him to the cross. ⁴⁰ But God raised him from death on the third day, and caused him to appear. ⁴¹ He was not seen by all the people, but only by us who are the witnesses that God had already chosen. We ate and drank with him after God raised him from death. ⁴² And he commanded us to preach the gospel to the people, and to testify that he is the one whom God has appointed Judge of the living and

the dead. ⁴³ All the prophets spoke about him, saying that everyone who believes in him will have his sins forgiven through the power of his name."

The Gentiles Receive the Holy Spirit

⁴⁴ While Peter was still speaking, the Holy Spirit came down upon all those who were listening to the message. ⁴⁵ The Jewish believers who had come from Joppa with Peter were amazed that God had poured out his gift of the Holy Spirit upon the Gentiles also. ⁴⁶ For they heard them speaking with strange sounds and praising God's greatness. Peter spoke up: ⁴⁷ "These people have received the Holy Spirit, just as we also did. Can anyone, then, stop them from being baptized with water?" ⁴⁸ So he ordered them to be baptized in the name of Jesus Christ. Then they asked him to stay with them for a few days.

Peter's Report to the Church at Jerusalem

11 The apostles and the brothers throughout all of Judea heard that the Gentiles also had received the word of God. ² When Peter went up to Jerusalem, those who were in favor of circumcising Gentiles criticized him: ³ "You were a guest in the home of uncircumcised Gentiles, and you even ate with them!" ⁴ So Peter gave them a full account of what had happened, from the very beginning:

⁵ "I was praying in the city of Joppa, and I had a vision. I saw something coming down that looked like a large sheet being lowered by its four corners from heaven, and it stopped next to me. ⁶ I looked closely inside and saw four-footed animals, and beasts, and reptiles, and wild birds. ⁷ Then I heard a voice saying to me, 'Get up, Peter; kill and eat!' ⁸ But I said, 'Certainly not, Lord! No defiled or unclean food has ever entered my mouth.' ⁹ The voice spoke again from heaven, 'Do not consider anything unclean that God has declared clean.' ¹⁰ This happened three times, and finally the whole thing was drawn back up into heaven. ¹¹ At that very moment three men who had been sent to me from Caesarea arrived at the house where I was staying. ¹² The Spirit told me to go with them without hesitation. These six brothers also went with me to Caesarea, and we all went into the house of Cornelius. ¹³ He told us how he had seen an angel standing in his

house who said to him, 'Send someone to Joppa to call for
a man whose full name is Simon Peter. ¹⁴ He will speak
words to you by which you and all your family will be
saved.' ¹⁵ And when I began to speak, the Holy Spirit
came down on them just as on us at the beginning.
¹⁶ Then I remembered what the Lord had said: 'John baptized with water, but you will be baptized with the Holy
Spirit.' ¹⁷ It is clear that God gave those Gentiles the
same gift that he gave us when we believed in the Lord
Jesus Christ; who was I, then, to try to stop God!"
¹⁸ When they heard this, they stopped their criticism and
praised God, saying, "Then God has given to the Gentiles
also the opportunity to repent and live!"

The Church at Antioch

¹⁹ The believers were scattered by the persecution which
took place when Stephen was killed. Some of them went
as far as Phoenicia and Cyprus and Antioch, telling the
message to Jews only. ²⁰ But some of the believers, men
from Cyprus and Cyrene, went to Antioch and told the
message to Gentiles also, preaching to them the Good
News about the Lord Jesus. ²¹ The Lord's power was
with them, and a great number of people believed and
turned to the Lord.

²² The news about this reached the church in Jerusalem,
so they sent Barnabas to Antioch. ²³ When he arrived and
saw how God had blessed the people, he was glad and
urged them all to be faithful and true to the Lord with all
their hearts. ²⁴ Barnabas was a good man, full of the Holy
Spirit and faith. Many people were brought to the Lord.

²⁵ Then Barnabas went to Tarsus to look for Saul.
²⁶ When he found him, he brought him to Antioch. For
a whole year the two met with the people of the church
and taught a large group. It was at Antioch that the disciples were first called Christians.

²⁷ About that time some prophets went down from Jerusalem to Antioch. ²⁸ One of them, named Agabus, stood
up and by the power of the Spirit predicted that a great
famine was about to come over all the earth. (It came
when Claudius was Emperor.) ²⁹ The disciples decided
that each of them would send as much as he could to help
their brothers who lived in Judea. ³⁰ They did this, then,

and sent the money to the church elders by Barnabas and Saul.

More Persecution

12 About this time King Herod began to persecute some members of the church. ² He had James, the brother of John, put to death by the sword. ³ When he saw that this pleased the Jews, he went ahead and had Peter arrested. (This happened during the time of the Feast of Unleavened Bread.) ⁴ After his arrest Peter was put in jail, where he was handed over to be guarded by four groups of four soldiers each. Herod planned to bring him out to the Jewish people after Passover. ⁵ So Peter was kept in jail, but the people of the church were praying earnestly to God for him.

Peter Set Free from Prison

⁶ The night before Herod was going to bring him out to the people, Peter was sleeping between two guards. He

was tied with two chains, and there were guards on duty at the prison gate. ⁷ Suddenly an angel of the Lord stood there, and a light shone in the cell. The angel shook Peter by the shoulder, woke him up and said, "Hurry! Get up!" And at once the chains fell off his hands. ⁸ Then the angel said, "Tighten your belt and tie on your sandals." Peter did so, and the angel said, "Put your cloak around you and come with me." ⁹ Peter followed him out of the prison. He did not know, however, if what the angel was doing was real; he thought he was seeing a vision. ¹⁰ They passed by the first guard station, and then the second, and came at last to the iron gate that opens into the city. The gate opened for them by itself, and they went out. They walked down a street, and suddenly the angel left Peter.

¹¹ Then Peter realized what had happened to him, and said: "Now I know that it is really true! The Lord sent his angel, and he rescued me from Herod's power and from all the things the Jewish people expected to do."

¹² Aware of his situation, he went to the home of Mary, the mother of John Mark. Many people had gathered there and were praying. ¹³ Peter knocked at the outside door, and a servant girl named Rhoda came to answer it. ¹⁴ She recognized Peter's voice and was so happy that she ran back in without opening the door, and announced that Peter was standing outside. ¹⁵ "You are crazy!" they told her. But she insisted that it was true. So they answered, "It is his angel." ¹⁶ Meanwhile, Peter kept on knocking. They opened the door at last and when they saw him they were amazed. ¹⁷ He motioned with his hand for them to be quiet, and explained to them how the Lord had brought him out of prison. "Tell this to James and the rest of the brothers," he said; then he left and went somewhere else.

¹⁸ When morning came, there was a tremendous confusion among the guards: what had happened to Peter? ¹⁹ Herod gave orders to search for him, but they could not find him. So he had the guards questioned and ordered them to be put to death.

After this Herod went down from Judea and spent some time in Caesarea.

The Death of Herod

²⁰ Herod was very angry with the people of Tyre and Sidon; so they went in a group to see Herod. First they won Blastus over to their side; he was in charge of the palace. Then they went to Herod and asked him for peace, because their country got its food supplies from the king's country.

²¹ On a chosen day Herod put on his royal robes, sat on his throne, and made a speech to the people. ²² "It isn't

a man speaking, but a god!" they shouted. ²³ At once the angel of the Lord struck Herod down, because he did not give honor to God. He was eaten by worms and died.

²⁴ The word of God continued to spread and grow.

²⁵ Barnabas and Saul finished their mission and returned from Jerusalem, taking John Mark with them.

Barnabas and Saul Chosen and Sent

13 In the church at Antioch there were some prophets and teachers: Barnabas, Simeon (called the Black), Lucius (from Cyrene), Manaen (who had been brought up with Governor Herod), and Saul. ² While they were serving the Lord and fasting, the Holy Spirit said to them, "Set apart for me Barnabas and Saul, to do the work to which I have called them." ³ They fasted and prayed, placed their hands on them and sent them off.

In Cyprus

⁴ Barnabas and Saul, then, having been sent by the Holy Spirit, went down to Seleucia and sailed from there to the island of Cyprus. ⁵ When they arrived at Salamis, they preached the word of God in the Jewish synagogues. They had John Mark with them to help in the work.

⁶ They went all the way across the island to Paphos, where they met a certain magician named Bar-Jesus, a Jew who claimed to be a prophet. ⁷ He was a friend of the Governor of the island, Sergius Paulus, who was an intelligent man. The Governor called Barnabas and Saul before him because he wanted to hear the word of God. ⁸ But they were opposed by the magician Elymas (this is his name in Greek); he tried to turn the Governor away from the faith. ⁹ Then Saul — also known as Paul — was filled with the Holy Spirit; he looked straight at the magician ¹⁰ and said: "You son of the Devil! You are the enemy of everything that is good; you are full of all kinds of evil tricks, and you always keep trying to turn the Lord's truths into lies! ¹¹ The Lord's hand will come down on you now; you will be blind, and will not see the light of day for a time." At once Elymas felt a black mist cover his eyes, and he walked around trying to find someone to lead him by the hand. ¹² The Governor believed, when he

saw what had happened; he was greatly amazed at the teaching about the Lord.

In Antioch of Pisidia

¹³ Paul and his companions sailed from Paphos and came to Perga, in Pamphylia; but John Mark left them there and went back to Jerusalem. ¹⁴ They went on from Perga and came to Antioch of Pisidia; and on the Sabbath day they went into the synagogue and sat down. ¹⁵ After the reading from the Law of Moses and the writings of the prophets, the officials of the synagogue sent them a message: "Brothers: we want you to speak to the people if you have a message of encouragement for them." ¹⁶ Paul stood up, motioned with his hand and began to speak:

"Fellow Israelites and all Gentiles here who worship God: hear me! ¹⁷ The God of this people of Israel chose our ancestors, and made the people great during the time they lived as foreigners in the land of Egypt. God brought them out of Egypt by his great power, ¹⁸ and for forty years he endured them in the desert. ¹⁹ He destroyed seven nations in the land of Canaan and made his people the owners of the land ²⁰ for about four hundred and fifty years.

"After this he gave them judges, until the time of the prophet Samuel. ²¹ And when they asked for a king, God gave them Saul, the son of Kish, from the tribe of Benjamin, to be their king for forty years. ²² After removing him, God made David their king. This is what God said about him: 'I have found that David, the son of Jesse, is the kind of man I like, a man who will do all I want him to do.' ²³ It was Jesus, one of the descendants of David, that God made the Savior of the people of Israel, as he had promised. ²⁴ Before the coming of Jesus, John preached to all the people of Israel that they should turn from their sins and be baptized. ²⁵ And as John was about to finish his mission, he said to the people: 'Who do you think I am? I am not the one you are waiting for. But look! He is coming after me, and I am not good enough to take his sandals off his feet.'

²⁶ "My brothers, descendants of Abraham, and all Gentiles here who worship God: it is to us that this message of salvation has been sent! ²⁷ For the people who live in

Jerusalem, and their leaders, did not know that he is the Savior, nor did they understand the words of the prophets that are read every Sabbath day. Yet they made the prophets' words come true by condemning Jesus. [28] And even though they could find no reason to pass the death sentence on him, they asked Pilate to have him put to death. [29] And after they had done everything that the Scriptures say about him, they took him down from the cross and placed him in a grave. [30] But God raised him from the dead, [31] and for many days he was seen by those who had traveled with him from Galilee to Jerusalem. They are now witnesses for him to the people of Israel. [32-33] And we are here to bring the Good News to you: what God promised our ancestors he would do, he has now done for us, who are their descendants, by raising Jesus to life. As it is written in the second Psalm:

'You are my Son,
Today I have become your Father.'

[34] And this is what God said about raising him from the dead, never again to return to decay:

'I will give you the sacred and sure blessings
That I promised to David.'

[35] As indeed he says in another passage,

'You will not allow your devoted servant to
suffer decay.'

[36] For David served God's purposes in his own time; and then he died, and was buried beside his ancestors, and suffered decay. [37] But the one whom God raised from the dead did not suffer decay. [38-39] All of you, my brothers, are to know for sure that it is through Jesus that the message about forgiveness of sins is preached to you; you are to know that everyone who believes in him is set free from all the sins from which the Law of Moses could not set you free. [40] Take care, then, so that what the prophets said may not happen to you:

[41] 'Look, you scorners! Wonder and die!
For the work that I am doing in your own day
Is something that you will not believe,
Even when someone explains it to you!' "

[42] As Paul and Barnabas were leaving the synagogue, the people invited them to come back the next Sabbath and tell them more about these things. [43] After the people had left the meeting, Paul and Barnabas were fol-

lowed by many Jews and many Gentiles converted to Judaism. The apostles spoke to them and encouraged them to keep on living in the grace of God.

⁴⁴ The next Sabbath day nearly everyone in the town came to hear the word of the Lord. ⁴⁵ When the Jews saw the crowds, they were filled with jealousy; they spoke against what Paul was saying and insulted him. ⁴⁶ But Paul and Barnabas spoke out even more boldly: "It was necessary that the word of God should be spoken first to you. But since you reject it, and do not consider yourselves worthy of eternal life, we will leave you and go to the Gentiles. ⁴⁷ For this is the commandment that the Lord has given us:

'I have set you to be a light for the Gentiles,
To be the way of salvation for the whole
world.' "

⁴⁸ When the Gentiles heard this they rejoiced and praised the Lord's message; and those who had been chosen for eternal life became believers.

⁴⁹ The word of the Lord spread everywhere in that region. ⁵⁰ But the Jews stirred up the leading men of the city and the Gentile women of high society who worshiped God. They started a persecution against Paul and Barnabas, and threw them out of their region. ⁵¹ The apostles shook the dust off their feet against them and went on to

Iconium. ⁵² The disciples in Antioch were full of joy and the Holy Spirit.

In Iconium

14 The same thing happened in Iconium: Paul and Barnabas went to the Jewish synagogue and spoke in such a way that a great number of Jews and Gentiles became believers. ² But the Jews who would not believe stirred up the Gentiles and turned their feelings against the brothers. ³ The apostles stayed there for a long time. They spoke boldly about the Lord, who proved that their message about his grace was true by giving them the power to perform miracles and wonders. ⁴ The crowd in the city was divided: some were for the Jews, others for the apostles.

⁵ Then the Gentiles and the Jews, together with their leaders, decided to mistreat the apostles and stone them. ⁶ When the apostles learned about it they fled to Lystra and Derbe, cities in Lycaonia, and to the surrounding territory. ⁷ There they preached the Good News.

In Lystra and Derbe

⁸ There was a man sitting in Lystra whose feet were crippled; he had been lame from birth and had never been able to walk. ⁹ He listened to Paul's words. Paul saw that he believed and could be healed, so he looked straight at him ¹⁰ and said in a loud voice, "Stand up straight on your feet!" The man jumped up and started walking around. ¹¹ When the crowds saw what Paul had done, they started to shout in their own Lycaonian language, "The gods have become like men and have come down to us!" ¹² They gave Barnabas the name Zeus, and Paul the name Hermes, because he was the one who did the speaking. ¹³ The priest of the god Zeus, whose temple stood just outside the town, brought bulls and flowers to the gate. He and the crowds wanted to offer sacrifice to the apostles. ¹⁴When Barnabas and Paul heard what they were about to do, they tore their clothes and ran into the middle of the crowd, shouting: ¹⁵ "Why are you doing this, men? We are just men, human beings like you! We are here to announce the Good News, to turn you away from these worthless things to the living God, who made heaven, earth, sea, and all that is in them. ¹⁶ In the past

he allowed all peoples to go their own way. ¹⁷ But he has always given proof of himself by the good things he does: he gives you rain from heaven and crops at the right times; he gives you food and fills your hearts with happiness." ¹⁸ Even with these words the apostles could hardly keep the crowds from offering a sacrifice to them.

¹⁹ Some Jews came from Antioch of Pisidia and from Iconium; they won the crowds to their side, stoned Paul and dragged him out of town, thinking that he was dead. ²⁰ But when the believers gathered around him, he got up and went back into the town. The next day he and Barnabas went to Derbe.

The Return to Antioch in Syria

²¹ Paul and Barnabas preached the Good News in Derbe, and won many disciples. Then they went back to Lystra, then to Iconium, and then to Antioch of Pisidia. ²² They strengthened the believers and encouraged them to remain true to the faith. "We must pass through many troubles to enter the Kingdom of God," they taught. ²³ In each church they appointed elders for them; and with prayers and fasting they commended them to the Lord in whom they had put their trust.

²⁴ After going through the territory of Pisidia, they came to Pamphylia. ²⁵ They preached the message in Perga and then went down to Attalia, ²⁶ and from there they sailed back to Antioch, the place where they had been commended to the care of God's grace for the work they had now completed.

²⁷ When they arrived in Antioch they gathered the people of the church together and told them of all that God had done with them, and how he had opened the way for the Gentiles to believe. ²⁸ They stayed a long time there with the believers.

The Meeting at Jerusalem

15 Some men came from Judea to Antioch and started teaching the brothers: "You cannot be saved unless you are circumcised as the Law of Moses requires." ² Paul and Barnabas had a fierce argument and dispute with them about this; so it was decided that Paul and Barnabas and some of the others in Antioch should go to Jerusalem and see the apostles and elders about this matter.

³ They were sent on their way by the church, and as they went through Phoenicia and Samaria they reported how the Gentiles had turned to God; this news brought great joy to all the brothers. ⁴ When they arrived in Jerusalem, they were welcomed by the church, the apostles, and the elders, to whom they told all that God had done with them. ⁵ But some of the believers who belonged to the party of the Pharisees stood up and said, "They have to be circumcised and told to obey the Law of Moses."

⁶ The apostles and the elders met together to consider this question. ⁷ After a long debate Peter stood up and said: "My brothers, you know that a long time ago God chose me from among you to preach the message of Good News to the Gentiles, so that they could hear and believe. ⁸ And God, who knows the hearts of men, showed his approval of the Gentiles by giving the Holy Spirit to them, just as he had to us. ⁹ He made no difference between us and them; he forgave them their sins because they believed. ¹⁰ So then, why do you want to put God to the test now by laying a load on the backs of the believers which neither our ancestors nor we ourselves were able to carry? ¹¹ No! We believe and are saved by the grace of the Lord Jesus, just as they are."

¹² The whole group was silent as they heard Barnabas and Paul report all the wonders and miracles that God had done through them among the Gentiles. ¹³ When they finished speaking, James spoke up: "Listen to me, brothers! ¹⁴ Simon has just explained how God first

showed his care for the Gentiles by taking from among them a people to be all his own. ¹⁵ The words of the prophets agree completely with this. As the scripture says:

¹⁶ 'After this I will return, says the Lord,
 And I will raise David's fallen house;
 I will restore its ruins
 And build it up again.
¹⁷ And so all other people will seek the Lord,
 All the nations whom I have called to be my
 own.
¹⁸ So says the Lord, who made this known long
 ago.'

¹⁹ "It is my opinion," James went on, "that we should not trouble the Gentiles who are turning to God. ²⁰ Instead, we should write a letter telling them not to eat any food that is unclean because it has been offered to idols; to keep themselves from immorality; not to eat any animal that has been strangled, or any blood. ²¹ For the Law of Moses has been read for a very long time in the synagogues every Sabbath, and his words are preached in every town."

The Letter to the Gentile Believers

²² Then the apostles and the elders, together with the whole church, decided to choose some men from the group and send them to Antioch with Paul and Barnabas. They chose Judas, called Barsabbas, and Silas, two men who were highly respected by the brothers. ²³ They sent the following letter by them:

"The apostles and the elders, your brothers, send their greetings to all brothers of Gentile birth who live in Antioch and Syria and Cilicia. ²⁴ We have heard that some men of our group went out and troubled and upset you by what they said; they had not, however, received any instructions from us to do this. ²⁵ And so we have met together and have all agreed to choose some messengers and send them to you. They will go with our dear friends Barnabas and Paul, ²⁶ who have risked their lives in the service of our Lord Jesus Christ. ²⁷ We send you, then, Judas and Silas, who will tell you in person the same things we are writing. ²⁸ For the Holy Spirit and we have agreed not to put any other burden on you besides these necessary rules: ²⁹ Eat no food that has been offered to idols; eat no blood; eat no animal that has been strangled; and keep yourselves from immorality. You will do well if you keep yourselves from doing these things. Good-bye."

³⁰ The messengers were sent off and went to Antioch, where they gathered the whole group of believers and gave them the letter. ³¹ When the people read the letter, they were filled with joy by the message of encouragement. ³² Judas and Silas, who were themselves prophets, spoke a long time with the brothers, giving them courage and strength. ³³ After spending some time there, they were sent off in peace by the brothers, and went back to those who had sent them. [³⁴ But Silas decided to stay there.]

³⁵ Paul and Barnabas spent some time in Antioch. Together with many others, they taught and preached the word of the Lord.

Paul and Barnabas Separate

³⁶ Some time later Paul said to Barnabas, "Let us go back and visit the brothers in every city where we preached the word of the Lord, and find out how they are getting along." ³⁷ Barnabas wanted to take John Mark with them, ³⁸ but Paul did not think it was right to take him, because he had not stayed with them to the end of their mission, but had turned back and left them in Pamphylia. ³⁹ They had a sharp argument between them, and separated from each other. Barnabas took Mark and sailed off for Cyprus, ⁴⁰ while Paul chose Silas and left, commended by the brothers to the care of God's grace. ⁴¹ He went through Syria and Cilicia, strengthening the churches.

Timothy Goes with Paul and Silas

16 Paul traveled on to Derbe and Lystra. A believer named Timothy lived there; his mother, also a believer, was Jewish, but his father was Greek. ² All the brothers in Lystra and Iconium spoke well of Timothy. ³ Paul wanted to take Timothy along with him, so he circumcised him. He did so because all the Jews who lived in those places knew that Timothy's father was a Greek. ⁴ As they went through the towns they delivered to the believers the rules decided upon by the apostles and elders in Jerusalem, and told them to obey these rules. ⁵ So the churches were made stronger in the faith and grew in numbers every day.

In Troas: Paul's Vision

⁶ They traveled through the region of Phrygia and Galatia; the Holy Spirit did not let them preach the message in the province of Asia. ⁷ When they reached the border of Mysia, they tried to go into the province of Bithynia, but the Spirit of Jesus did not allow them. ⁸ So they traveled right on through Mysia and went down to Troas. ⁹ Paul had a vision that night in which he saw a man of Macedonia standing and begging him, "Come over to Macedonia and help us!" ¹⁰ As soon as Paul had this vision, we got ready to leave for Macedonia, for we decided that God had called us to preach the Good News to the people there.

In Philippi: the Conversion of Lydia

¹¹ We left by ship from Troas and sailed straight across to Samothrace, and the next day to Neapolis. ¹² From there we went inland to Philippi, a city of the first district of Macedonia; it is also a Roman colony. We spent several days in that city. ¹³ On the Sabbath day we went out of the city to the riverside, where we thought there would be a Jewish place for prayer. We sat down and talked to the women who gathered there. ¹⁴ One of those who heard us was Lydia, from Thyatira, who was a dealer in purple goods. She was a woman who worshiped God, and the Lord opened her mind to pay attention to what Paul was saying. ¹⁵ She and the people of her house were baptized. Then she invited us: "Come and stay in my house, if you have decided that I am a true believer in the Lord." And she persuaded us to go.

In Prison at Philippi

¹⁶ One day as we were going to the place of prayer, we were met by a slave girl who had an evil spirit in her that made her guess the future. She earned much money for her owners by telling fortunes. ¹⁷ She followed Paul and us, shouting, "These men are servants of the Most High God! They announce to you how you can be saved!" ¹⁸ She did this for many days, until Paul became so upset that he turned around and said to the spirit, "In the name of Jesus Christ I order you to come out of her!" The spirit went out of her that very moment. ¹⁹ When her

owners realized that their chance of making money was gone, they grabbed Paul and Silas and dragged them to the authorities in the public square. ²⁰ They brought them before the Roman officials and said: "These men are Jews, and they are causing trouble in our city. ²¹ They are teaching customs that are against our law; we are Romans and cannot follow those customs!" ²² The crowd joined the attack against them; the officials tore the clothes off Paul and Silas, and ordered them to be whipped. ²³ After a severe beating they were thrown into jail, and the jailer was ordered to lock them up tight. ²⁴ Upon receiving this order, the jailer threw them into the inner cell and fastened their feet between heavy blocks of wood.

²⁵ About midnight Paul and Silas were praying and singing hymns to God, and the other prisoners were listening to them. ²⁶ Suddenly there was a violent earthquake, which shook the prison to its foundations. At once all the doors opened, and the chains fell off all the prisoners. ²⁷ The jailer woke up, and when he saw the prison doors open he thought that all the prisoners had escaped; so he pulled out his sword and was about to kill himself. ²⁸ But Paul shouted at the top of his voice, "Don't harm yourself! We are all here!" ²⁹ The jailer called for a light, rushed in, and fell trembling at the feet of Paul and Silas. ³⁰ Then

he led them out and asked, "What must I do, sirs, to be saved?" [31] "Believe in the Lord Jesus," they said, "and you will be saved — you and your family." [32] And they preached the word of the Lord to him and to all the others in his house. [33] At that very hour of the night the jailer took them and washed off their wounds; and he and all his family were baptized at once. [34] He took Paul and Silas up into his house and gave them some food to eat. He and his family were filled with joy, because they now believed in God.

[35] The next morning the Roman authorities sent an order to the police officers: "Let those men go." [36] So the jailer told it to Paul: "The officials have sent an order for you and Silas to be released. You may leave, then, and go quietly away." [37] But Paul said to the police officers: "We were not found guilty of any crime, yet they whipped us in public — and we are Roman citizens! Then they threw us in prison. And now they want to send us away secretly? Not at all! The Roman officials themselves must come here and let us out." [38] The police officers reported these words to the Roman officials; and when they heard that Paul and Silas were Roman citizens, they were afraid. [39] So they went and apologized to them; then they led them out of the prison and asked them to leave the city. [40] Paul and Silas left the prison and went to Lydia's house. There they met the brothers, spoke words of encouragement to them, and left.

In Thessalonica

17 They traveled on through Amphipolis and Apollonia, and came to Thessalonica, where there was a Jewish synagogue. [2] According to his usual habit, Paul went to the synagogue. There during three Sabbath days he argued with the people from the Scriptures, [3] explaining them and proving from them that the Messiah had to suffer and be raised from death. "This Jesus whom I announce to you," Paul said, "is the Messiah." [4] Some of them were convinced and joined Paul and Silas; so did a large group of Greeks who worshiped God, and many of the leading women.

[5] But the Jews were jealous and gathered some of the worthless loafers from the streets and formed a mob.

They set the whole city in an uproar, and attacked the home of Jason, trying to find Paul and Silas and bring them out to the people. 6 But when they did not find them, they dragged Jason and some other brothers to the city authorities and shouted: "These men have caused trouble everywhere! Now they have come to our city, 7 and Jason has kept them in his house. They are all breaking the laws of the Emperor, saying that there is another king, by the name of Jesus." 8 With these words they threw the crowd and the city authorities in an uproar. 9 The authorities made Jason and the others pay the required amount of money to be released, and then let them go.

In Berea

10 As soon as night came, the brothers sent Paul and Silas to Berea. When they arrived, they went to the Jewish synagogue. 11 The people there were more open-minded than the people in Thessalonica. They listened to the message with great eagerness, and every day they studied the Scriptures to see if what Paul said was really true. 12 Many of them believed; and many Greek women of high society and many Greek men also believed. 13 But when the Jews in Thessalonica heard that Paul had preached the word of God in Berea also, they came there and started exciting and stirring up the mobs. 14 At once the brothers sent Paul away to the coast, but both Silas and Timothy stayed in Berea. 15 The men who were taking Paul went with him as far as Athens. Then they went back to Berea with instructions from Paul that Silas and Timothy join him as soon as possible.

In Athens

16 While Paul was waiting in Athens for Silas and Timothy, he was greatly upset when he noticed how full of idols the city was. 17 So he argued in the synagogue with the Jews and the Gentiles who worshiped God, and in the public square every day with the people who happened to come by. 18 Certain Epicurean and Stoic teachers also debated with him. Some said, "What is this ignorant show-off trying to say?" Others said, "He seems to be talking about foreign gods." They said this because Paul was preaching about Jesus and the resurrection. 19 So they

took Paul, brought him before the meeting of the Areopagus, and said: "We would like to know this new teaching that you are talking about. 20 Some of the things we hear you say sound strange to us, and we would like to know what they mean." 21 (For all the citizens of Athens and the foreigners who lived there liked to spend all their time telling and hearing the latest new thing.)

22 Paul stood up in front of the meeting of the Areopagus and said: "Men of Athens! I see that in every way you are very religious. 23 For as I walked through your city and looked at the places where you worship, I found also an altar on which is written, 'To an Unknown God.' That which you worship, then, even though you do not know it, is what I now proclaim to you. 24 God, who made the world and everything in it, is Lord of heaven and earth, and does not live in temples made by men. 25 Nor does he need anything that men can supply by working for him, since it is he himself who gives life and breath and everything else to all men. 26 From the one man he created all races of men, and made them live over the whole earth. He himself fixed beforehand the exact times and the limits of the places where they would live. 27 He did this so that they would look for him, and perhaps find him as they felt around for him. Yet God is actually not far from any one of us; 28 for

'In him we live and move and are.'

It is as some of your poets have also said,

'We too are his children.'

29 Since we are his children, we should not suppose that God's nature is anything like an image of gold or silver or stone, shaped by the art and skill of man. 30 God has overlooked the times when men did not know, but now he commands all men everywhere to turn away from their evil ways. 31 For he has fixed a day in which he will judge the whole world with justice, by means of a man he has chosen. He has given proof of this to everyone by raising that man from death!"

32 When they heard Paul speak about a raising from death, some of them made fun of him, but others said, "We want to hear you speak about this again." 33 And so Paul left the meeting. 34 Some men joined him and believed; among them was Dionysius, a member of the Areopagus, a woman named Damaris, and some others.

In Corinth

18 After this, Paul left Athens and went on to Corinth. ² There he met a Jew named Aquila, born in Pontus, who had just come from Italy with his wife Priscilla — because Emperor Claudius had ordered all the Jews to leave Rome. Paul went to see them, ³ and stayed

and worked with them, because he earned his living by making tents, just as they did. ⁴ He argued in the synagogue every Sabbath, trying to convince both Jews and Greeks.

⁵ When Silas and Timothy arrived from Macedonia, Paul gave his whole time to preaching the message, testifying to the Jews that Jesus is the Messiah. ⁶ When they opposed him and said evil things about him, he protested by shaking the dust from his clothes and saying to them: "If you are lost, you yourselves must take the blame for it! I am not responsible. From now on I will go to the Gentiles." ⁷ So he left them and went to live in the house of a Gentile named Titius Justus, who worshiped God; his house was next to the synagogue. ⁸ Crispus, the leader of the synagogue, believed in the Lord, he and all his family; and many other people in Corinth heard the message, believed, and were baptized.

⁹ One night Paul had a vision, in which the Lord said to him: "Do not be afraid, but keep on speaking and do

not give up, ¹⁰ for I am with you. No one will be able to harm you, because many in this city are my people." ¹¹ So Paul stayed there for a year and a half, teaching the people the word of God.

¹² When Gallio was made the Roman governor of Greece, the Jews got together, seized Paul and took him into court. ¹³ "This man," they said, "is trying to persuade people to worship God in a way that is against the law!" ¹⁴ Paul was about to speak when Gallio said to the Jews: "If this were a matter of some wrong or evil crime that has been committed, it would be reasonable for me to be patient with you Jews. ¹⁵ But since it is an argument about words and names and your own law, you yourselves must settle it. I will not be the judge of such things!" ¹⁶ And he drove them out of the court. ¹⁷ They all grabbed Sosthenes, the leader of the synagogue, and beat him in front of the court. But that did not bother Gallio a bit.

The Return to Antioch

¹⁸ Paul stayed on in Corinth with the brothers for many days, then left them and sailed off with Priscilla and Aquila for Syria. Before sailing he made a vow in Cenchreae and had his head shaved. ¹⁹ They arrived in Ephesus, where Paul left Priscilla and Aquila. He went into the synagogue and argued with the Jews. ²⁰ They asked him to stay with them a long time, but he would not consent. ²¹ Instead, he told them as he left, "If it is the will of God, I will come back to you." And so he sailed from Ephesus.

²² When he arrived at Caesarea he went to Jerusalem and greeted the church, and then went to Antioch. ²³ After spending some time there he left. He went through the region of Galatia and Phrygia, strengthening all the believers.

Apollos in Ephesus and Corinth

²⁴ A certain Jew named Apollos, born in Alexandria, came to Ephesus. He was an eloquent speaker and had a thorough knowledge of the Scriptures. ²⁵ He had been instructed in the Way of the Lord, and with great enthusiasm spoke and taught correctly the facts about Jesus. However, he knew only the baptism of John. ²⁶ He began

to speak boldly in the synagogue. When Priscilla and Aquila heard him, they took him home with them and explained to him more correctly the Way of God. 27 Apollos decided to go to Greece, so the believers in Ephesus helped him by writing to their brothers in Greece, urging them to welcome him there. When he arrived, he was a great help to those who through God's grace had become believers. 28 For with his strong arguments he defeated the Jews in public debates, proving from the Scriptures that Jesus is the Messiah.

Paul in Ephesus

19 While Apollos was in Corinth, Paul traveled through the interior of the province and arrived in Ephesus. There he found some disciples, 2 and asked them, "Did you receive the Holy Spirit when you believed?" "We have not even heard that there is a Holy Spirit," they answered. 3 "Well, then, what kind of baptism did you receive?" Paul asked. "The baptism of John," they answered. 4 Paul said: "The baptism of John was for those who turned from their sins; and he told the people of Israel that they should believe in the one who was coming after him — that is, in Jesus." 5 When they heard this, they were baptized in the name of the Lord Jesus. 6 Paul placed his hands on them, and the Holy Spirit came upon them; they talked with strange sounds and also spoke God's word. 7 They were about twelve men in all.

8 Paul went into the synagogue, and for three months spoke boldly with the people, arguing with them and trying to convince them about the Kingdom of God. 9 But some of them were stubborn and would not believe, and said evil things about the Way of the Lord before the whole group. So Paul left them and took the disciples with him; and every day he held discussions in the lecture hall of Tyrannus. 10 This went on for two years, so that all the people who lived in the province of Asia, both Jews and Gentiles, heard the word of the Lord.

The Sons of Sceva

11 God was performing unusual miracles through Paul. 12 Even handkerchiefs and aprons he had used were taken to the sick, and their diseases were driven away and the evil spirits would go out of them. 13 Some Jews who

traveled around and drove out evil spirits also tried to use the name of the Lord Jesus to do this. They said to the evil spirits, "I command you in the name of Jesus, whom Paul preaches." ¹⁴ It was the seven sons of a Jewish High Priest named Sceva who were doing so. ¹⁵ But the evil spirit said to them, "I know Jesus and I know about Paul; but you — who are you?" ¹⁶ The man who had the evil spirit in him attacked them with such violence that he defeated them. They all ran away from his house wounded and with their clothes torn off. ¹⁷ All the Jews and Gentiles who lived in Ephesus heard about this; they were all filled with fear, and the name of the Lord Jesus was given greater honor. ¹⁸ Many of the believers came, publicly admitting and revealing what they had done. ¹⁹ Many of those who had practiced magic brought their books together and burned them in the presence of everyone. They added up the price of the books and the total came to fifty thousand dollars. ²⁰ In this powerful way the word of the Lord kept spreading and growing stronger.

The Riot in Ephesus

²¹ After these things had happened, Paul made up his mind to travel through Macedonia and Greece and go on to Jerusalem. "After I go there," he said, "I must also see Rome." ²² So he sent Timothy and Erastus, two of his helpers, to Macedonia, while he spent more time in the province of Asia.

²³ It was at this time that there was serious trouble in Ephesus because of the Way of the Lord. ²⁴ A certain silversmith named Demetrius made silver models of the temple of the goddess Artemis, and his business brought a great deal of profit to the workers. ²⁵ So he called them all together, with others whose work was like theirs, and said to them: "Men, you know that our prosperity comes from this work. ²⁶ You can see and hear for yourselves what this fellow Paul is doing. He says that gods made by men are not gods at all, and has succeeded in convincing many people, both here in Ephesus and in nearly the whole province of Asia. ²⁷ There is the danger, then, that this business of ours will get a bad name. Not only that, there is also the danger that the temple of the great goddess Artemis will come to mean nothing, and that her

greatness will be destroyed — the goddess worshiped by everyone in Asia and in all the world!"

²⁸ As the crowd heard these words they became furious, and started shouting: "Great is Artemis of Ephesus!" ²⁹ The uproar spread throughout the whole city. The mob grabbed Gaius and Aristarchus, two Macedonians who were traveling with Paul, and rushed with them to the theater. ³⁰ Paul himself wanted to go before the crowd, but the believers would not let him. ³¹ Some of the provincial authorities, who were his friends, also sent him a message begging him not to show himself in the theater. ³² Meanwhile, the whole meeting was in an uproar: some people were shouting one thing, others were shouting something else, for most of them did not even know why they had come together. ³³ Some of the people concluded that Alexander was responsible, since the Jews made him go up to the front. Then Alexander motioned with his hand and tried to make a speech of defense before the people. ³⁴ But when they recognized that he was a Jew, they all shouted together the same thing for two hours: "Great is Artemis of Ephesus!"

³⁵ At last the city clerk was able to calm the crowd. "Men of Ephesus!" he said. "Everyone knows that the city of Ephesus is the keeper of the temple of the great Artemis and of the sacred stone that fell down from heaven. ³⁶ Nobody can deny these things. So then, you must calm down and not do anything reckless. ³⁷ You have brought these men here, even though they have not robbed temples or said evil things about our goddess. ³⁸ If Demetrius and his workers have an accusation against someone, there are the regular days for court and there are the authorities; they can accuse each other there. ³⁹ But if there is something more that you want, it will have to be settled in the legal meeting of citizens. ⁴⁰ For there is the danger that we will be accused of a riot in what has happened today. There is no excuse for all this uproar, and we would not be able to give a good reason for it." ⁴¹ After saying this, he dismissed the meeting.

To Macedonia and Greece

20 After the uproar died down, Paul called together the believers, and with words of encouragement said good-bye to them. Then he left and went on to Mace-

donia. ² He went through those regions and encouraged the people with many messages. Then he came to Greece, ³ where he stayed three months. He was getting ready to go to Syria when he discovered that the Jews were plotting against him; so he decided to go back through Macedonia. ⁴ Sopater, the son of Pyrrhus, from Berea, went with him; so did Aristarchus and Secundus, from Thessalonica; Gaius, from Derbe; Timothy; and Tychicus and Trophimus, from the province of Asia. ⁵ They went ahead and waited for us in Troas. ⁶ We sailed from Philippi after the Feast of Unleavened Bread, and five days later joined them in Troas, where we spent a week.

Paul's Last Visit in Troas

⁷ On Saturday evening we gathered together for the fellowship meal. Paul spoke to the people, and kept on speaking until midnight, since he was going to leave the next day. ⁸ There were many lamps in the upstairs room where we were meeting. ⁹ A young man named Eutychus was sitting in the window; and as Paul kept on talking, Eutychus got sleepier and sleepier, until he finally went sound asleep and fell from the third story to the ground. They

picked him up, and he was dead. ¹⁰ But Paul went down and threw himself on him and hugged him. "Don't worry," he said, "he is still alive!" ¹¹ Then he went back upstairs, broke bread, and ate. After talking with them for a long time until sunrise, Paul left. ¹² They took the young man home alive, and were greatly comforted.

From Troas to Miletus

¹³ We went on ahead to the ship and sailed off to Assos, where we were going to take Paul aboard. He had told us to do this, because he was going there by land. ¹⁴ When he met us in Assos, we took him aboard and went on to Mitylene. ¹⁵ We sailed from there and arrived off Chios the next day. A day later we came to Samos, and the following day we reached Miletus. ¹⁶ Paul had decided to sail on by Ephesus, so as not to lose any time in the province of Asia. He was in a hurry to arrive in Jerusalem, if at all possible, by the day of Pentecost.

Paul's Farewell Speech to the Elders of Ephesus

¹⁷ Paul sent a message from Miletus to Ephesus, asking the elders of the church to meet him. ¹⁸ When they came he said to them: "You know how I spent the whole time I was with you, from the first day I arrived in the province of Asia. ¹⁹ With all humility and tears I did my work as the Lord's servant, through the hard times that came to me because of the plots of the Jews. ²⁰ You know that I did not hold back anything that would be of help to you as I preached and taught you in public and in your homes. ²¹ To Jews and Gentiles alike I gave solemn warning that they should turn from their sins to God, and believe in our Lord Jesus. ²² And now, in obedience to the Holy Spirit, I am going to Jerusalem, not knowing what will happen to me there. ²³ I only know that in every city the Holy Spirit has warned me that prison and troubles wait for me. ²⁴ But I reckon my own life to be worth nothing to me, in order that I may complete my mission and finish the work that the Lord Jesus gave me to do, which is to declare the Good News of the grace of God.

²⁵ "I have gone about among all of you, preaching the Kingdom of God. And now I know that none of you will ever see me again. ²⁶ So I solemnly declare to you this very day: if any of you should be lost, I am not respon-

sible. ²⁷ For I have not held back from announcing to you the whole purpose of God. ²⁸ Keep watch over yourselves and over all the flock which the Holy Spirit has placed in your charge. Be shepherds of the church of God, which he made his own through the death of his own Son. ²⁹ For I know that after I leave, fierce wolves will come among you, and they will not spare the flock. ³⁰ And the time will come when some men from your own group will tell lies to lead the believers away after them. ³¹ Watch, then, and remember that with many tears, day and night, I taught every one of you for three years.

³² "And now I place you in the care of God and the message of his grace. He is able to build you up and give you the blessings he keeps for all his people. ³³ I have not coveted anyone's silver or gold or clothing. ³⁴ You yourselves know that with these hands of mine I have worked and provided everything that my companions and I have needed. ³⁵ I have shown you in all things that by working hard in this way we must help the weak, remembering the words that the Lord Jesus himself said, 'There is more happiness in giving than in receiving.'"

³⁶ When Paul finished, he knelt down with them all and prayed. ³⁷ They were all crying as they hugged him and kissed him good-bye. ³⁸ They were especially sad at the words he had said that they would never see him again. And so they went with him to the ship.

Paul Goes to Jerusalem

21 We said good-bye to them and left. After sailing straight across, we came to Cos; the next day we reached Rhodes, and from there we went on to Patara.

² There we found a ship that was going to Phoenicia; so we went aboard and sailed away. ³ We came to where we could see Cyprus, and sailed south of it on to Syria. We went ashore at Tyre, where the ship was going to unload its cargo. ⁴ We found some believers there, and stayed with them a week. By the power of the Spirit they told Paul not to go to Jerusalem. ⁵ But when our time with them was over, we left and went on our way. All of them, with their wives and children, went with us out of the city. We all knelt down on the beach and prayed. ⁶ Then we said good-bye to one another, and we went on board the ship while they went back home.

⁷ We continued our voyage, sailing from Tyre to Ptolemais, where we greeted the brothers and stayed with them for a day. ⁸ On the following day we left and arrived in Caesarea. There we went to the house of the evangelist Philip, and stayed with him. He was one of the seven men who had been chosen in Jerusalem. ⁹ He had four unmarried daughters who preached God's word. ¹⁰ We had been there for several days when a prophet named Agabus arrived from Judea. ¹¹ He came to us, took Paul's belt, tied up his own feet and hands with it, and said: "This is what the Holy Spirit says: The owner of this belt will be tied up in this way by the Jews in Jerusalem, and they will hand him over to the Gentiles." ¹² When we heard this, we and the people there begged Paul not to go to Jerusalem. ¹³ But he answered: "What are you doing, crying like this and breaking my heart? I am ready not only to be tied up in Jerusalem but even to die for the sake of the Lord Jesus." ¹⁴ We could not convince him. So we gave up and said, "May the Lord's will be done."

¹⁵ After spending some time there, we got our things ready and left for Jerusalem. ¹⁶ Some of the disciples from Caesarea also went with us, and took us to the house of the man we were going to stay with — Mnason, from Cyprus, who had been a believer since the early days.

Paul Visits James

¹⁷ When we arrived in Jerusalem the brothers welcomed us warmly. ¹⁸ The next day Paul went with us to see James; and all the church elders were present. ¹⁹ Paul greeted them and gave a complete report of everything that God had done among the Gentiles through his work.

[20] After hearing him, they all praised God. Then they said to Paul: "You can see how it is, brother. There are thousands of Jews who have become believers, and they are all very devoted to the Law. [21] They have been told about you that you have been teaching all the Jews who live in Gentile countries to abandon the Law of Moses, and have been telling them not to circumcise their children or follow the Jewish customs. [22] They are sure to hear that you have arrived. What should be done, then? [23] Do what we tell you. There are four men here who have taken a vow. [24] Go along with them and join them in the ceremony of purification and pay their expenses; then they will be able to shave their heads. In this way everybody will know that there is no truth in any of the things they have been told about you, but that you yourself live in accordance with the Law of Moses. [25] But as to the Gentiles who have become believers, we have sent them a letter telling them we decided that they must not eat any food that has been offered to idols, or any blood, or any animal that has been strangled, and that they must keep themselves from immorality." [26] Then Paul took the men and the next day performed the ceremony of purification with them. Then he went into the Temple and gave notice of how many days it would be until the end of the period of purification, when the sacrifice for each one of them would be offered.

Paul Arrested in the Temple

[27] When the seven days were about to come to an end, some Jews from the province of Asia saw Paul in the Temple. They stirred up the whole crowd and grabbed Paul. [28] "Men of Israel!" they shouted. "Help! This is the man who goes everywhere teaching everyone against the people of Israel, the Law of Moses, and this Temple. And now he has even brought some Gentiles into the Temple and defiled this holy place!" [29] (They said this because they had seen Trophimus from Ephesus with Paul in the city, and they thought that Paul had taken him into the Temple.) [30] Confusion spread through the whole city, and the people all ran together, grabbed Paul, and dragged him out of the Temple. At once the Temple doors were closed. [31] The mob was trying to kill Paul when a report was sent up to the commander of the Roman troops that all of Jerusalem was rioting. [32] At once the commander

took some officers and soldiers and rushed down to the crowd. When the people saw him with the soldiers, they stopped beating Paul. ³³ The commander went over to Paul, arrested him, and ordered him to be tied up with two chains. Then he asked, "Who is this man, and what has he done?" ³⁴ Some in the crowd shouted one thing, others something else. There was such confusion that the commander could not find out exactly what had happened; so he ordered his men to take Paul up into the fort. ³⁵ They got with him to the steps, and then the soldiers had to carry him because the mob was so wild. ³⁶ They were all coming after him and screaming, "Kill him!"

Paul Defends Himself

³⁷ As they were about to take Paul into the fort, he spoke to the commander: "May I say something to you?" "Do you speak Greek?" the commander asked. ³⁸ "Then you are not that Egyptian fellow who some time ago started a revolution and led four thousand armed terrorists out into the desert?" ³⁹ Paul answered: "I am a Jew, born in Tarsus of Cilicia, a citizen of an important city. Please, let me speak to the people." ⁴⁰ The commander gave him permission, so Paul stood on the steps and motioned with his hand to the people. When they were quiet, Paul spoke to them in Hebrew:

22 "Men, brothers and fathers, listen to me as I make my defense before you!" ² When they heard him speaking to them in Hebrew, they were even quieter; and Paul went on:

3 "I am a Jew, born in Tarsus of Cilicia, but brought up here in Jerusalem as a student of Gamaliel. I received strict instruction in the Law of our ancestors, and was just as dedicated to God as all of you here today are. 4 I persecuted to the death the people who followed this Way. I arrested men and women and threw them into prison. 5 The High Priest and the whole Council can prove that I am telling the truth. I received from them letters written to the Jewish brothers in Damascus, so I went there to arrest these people and bring them back in chains to Jerusalem to be punished."

Paul Tells of His Conversion
(Also Acts 9.1–19; 26.12–18)

6 "And as I was traveling and coming near Damascus, about midday a bright light suddenly flashed from the sky around me. 7 I fell to the ground and heard a voice saying to me, 'Saul, Saul! Why do you persecute me?' 8 'Who are you, Lord?' I asked. 'I am Jesus of Nazareth, whom you persecute,' he said to me. 9 The men with me saw the light but did not hear the voice of the one who was speaking to me. 10 I asked, 'What shall I do, Lord?' and the Lord said to me, 'Get up and go into Damascus, and there you will be told everything that God has determined for you to do.' 11 I was blind because of the bright light, and so my companions took me by the hand and led me into Damascus.

12 "There was a man named Ananias, a religious man who obeyed our Law and was highly respected by all the Jews living in Damascus. 13 He came to me, stood by me and said, 'Brother Saul, see again!' At that very moment I saw again and looked at him. 14 He said: 'The God of our ancestors has chosen you to know his will, to see his righteous Servant, and hear him speaking with his own voice. 15 For you will be a witness for him to tell all men what you have seen and heard. 16 And now, why wait any longer? Get up and be baptized and have your sins washed away by calling on his name.' "

Paul's Call to Preach to the Gentiles

17 "I went back to Jerusalem, and while I was praying in the Temple I had a vision, 18 in which I saw the Lord as he said to me, 'Hurry and leave Jerusalem quickly, be-

cause the people here will not accept your witness about me.' [19] 'Lord,' I answered, 'they know very well that I went to the synagogues and arrested and beat those who believe in you. [20] And when your witness Stephen was put to death, I myself was there, approving of his murder and taking care of the cloaks of his murderers.' [21] 'Go,' the Lord said to me, 'for I will send you far away to the Gentiles.' "

[22] The people listened to Paul until he said this; but then they started shouting at the top of their voices, "Away with him! Kill him! He's not fit to live!" [23] They were screaming and waving their clothes and throwing dust up in the air. [24] The Roman commander ordered his men to take Paul into the fort, and told them to whip him to find out why the Jews were screaming like this against him. [25] But when they had tied him up to be whipped, Paul said to the officer standing there, "Is it lawful for you to whip a Roman citizen who hasn't even been tried for any crime?" [26] When the officer heard this, he went to the commander and asked him, "What are you doing? That man is a Roman citizen!" [27] So the commander went to Paul and asked him, "Tell me, are you a Roman citizen?" "Yes," answered Paul. [28] The commander said, "I became one by paying a large amount of money." "But I am one by birth," Paul answered. [29] At once the men who were going to question Paul drew back from him; and the commander was afraid when he realized that Paul was a Roman citizen, and that he had put him in chains.

Paul before the Council

[30] The commander wanted to find out for sure what the Jews were accusing Paul of; so the next day he had Paul's chains taken off and ordered the chief priests and the whole Council to meet. Then he took Paul, and made him stand before them.

23 Paul looked straight at the Council and said, "My brothers! My conscience is perfectly clear about my whole life before God, to this very day." [2] The High Priest Ananias ordered those who were standing close to Paul to strike him on the mouth. [3] Paul said to him: "God will certainly strike you — you whitewashed wall! You sit there to judge me according to the Law, yet you break the Law by ordering them to strike me!" [4] The men

close to Paul said to him, "You are insulting God's High Priest!" 5 Paul answered: "I did not know, my brothers, that he was the High Priest. For the scripture says, 'You must not speak evil of the ruler of your people.' "

6 When Paul saw that some of the group were Sadducees and that others were Pharisees, he called out in the Council: "My brothers! I am a Pharisee, the son of Pharisees. I am on trial here because I hope that the dead will be raised to life!" 7 As soon as he said this, the Pharisees and Sadducees started to quarrel, and the group was divided. 8 (For the Sadducees say that people will not be raised from death, and that there are no angels or spirits—but the Pharisees believe in all three.) 9 So the shouting became louder, and some of the teachers of the Law who belonged to the party of the Pharisees stood up and protested strongly: "We cannot find a thing wrong with this man! Perhaps a spirit or an angel really did speak to him!"

10 The argument became so violent that the commander was afraid that Paul would be torn to pieces by them. So he ordered his soldiers to go down into the group and get Paul away from them, and take him into the fort.

11 The following night the Lord stood by Paul and said: "Courage! You have given your witness to me here in Jerusalem, and you must do the same in Rome also."

The Plot against Paul's Life

12 The next morning the Jews met together and made a plan. They took a vow that they would not eat or drink anything until they had killed Paul. 13 There were more than forty of them who planned this together. 14 Then they went to the chief priests and elders and said: "We have taken a solemn vow together not to eat a thing until we kill Paul. 15 Now then, you and the Council send word to the Roman commander to bring Paul down to you, pretending that you want to get more accurate information about him. But we will be ready to kill him before he ever gets here."

16 But the son of Paul's sister heard of the plot; so he went and entered the fort and told it to Paul. 17 Then Paul called one of the officers and said to him, "Take this young man to the commander; he has something to tell him." 18 The officer took him, led him to the commander

and said, "The prisoner Paul called me and asked me to bring this young man to you, for he has something to say to you." ¹⁹ The commander took him by the hand, led him off by himself and asked him, "What do you have to tell me?" ²⁰ He said: "The Jews have agreed to ask you tomorrow to take Paul down to the Council, pretending that the Council wants to get more accurate information about him. ²¹ But don't listen to them, because there are more than forty men who will be hiding and waiting for him. They have all taken a vow not to eat or drink until they kill him. They are now ready to do it, and are waiting for your decision." ²² The commander said, "Don't tell anyone that you have reported this to me." And he sent the young man away.

Paul Sent to Governor Felix

²³ Then the commander called two of his officers and said: "Get two hundred soldiers ready to go to Caesarea, together with seventy horsemen and two hundred spearmen, and be ready to leave by nine o'clock tonight. ²⁴ Provide some horses for Paul to ride, and get him safely through to Governor Felix." ²⁵ Then the commander wrote a letter that went like this:

²⁶ "Claudius Lysias to his Excellency, the Governor Felix: Greetings. ²⁷ The Jews seized this man and were about to kill him. I learned that he is a Roman citizen, so I went with my soldiers and rescued him. ²⁸ I wanted to know what they were accusing him of, so I took him down to their Council. ²⁹ I found out that he had not done a thing for which he deserved to die or be put in prison; the accusation against him had to do with questions about their own law. ³⁰ And when I was informed that the Jews are making a plot against him, I decided to send him to you. I told his accusers to make their charges against him before you."

³¹ The soldiers carried out their orders. They took Paul and brought him that night as far as Antipatris. ³² The next day the foot soldiers returned to the fort and left the horsemen to go on with him. ³³ They took him to Caesarea and delivered the letter to the Governor and turned Paul over to him. ³⁴ The Governor read the letter and asked Paul what province he was from. When he found out that he was from Cilicia, ³⁵ he said, "I will hear you

when your accusers arrive." Then he gave orders that Paul be kept under guard in Herod's palace.

Paul Accused by the Jews

24 After five days the High Priest Ananias went to Caesarea with some elders and a lawyer named Tertullus. They appeared before Governor Felix and made their charges against Paul. ² Tertullus was called and began to accuse Paul as follows:

"Your Excellency! Your wise leadership has brought us a long period of peace, and many necessary reforms are being made for the good of our country. ³ We welcome this everywhere at all times, and we are deeply grateful to you. ⁴ I do not want to take up too much of your time, however, so I beg you to be kind and listen to our brief account. ⁵ We found this man to be a dangerous nuisance; he starts riots among the Jews all over the world, and is a leader of the party of the Nazarenes. ⁶ He also tried to defile the Temple, and we arrested him. [We planned to judge him according to our own Law, ⁷ but the commander Lysias came in and with great violence took him from us. ⁸ Then Lysias gave orders that his accusers should come before you.] If you question this man, you yourself will be able to learn from him all the things that we are accusing him of." ⁹ The Jews also joined in the accusation and said that all this was true.

Paul's Defense before Felix

¹⁰ The Governor then motioned to Paul to speak, and Paul said:

"I know that you have been a judge over this nation for many years, and so I am happy to defend myself before you. ¹¹ As you can find out for yourself, it was no more than twelve days ago that I went up to Jerusalem to worship. ¹² The Jews did not find me arguing with anyone in the Temple, nor did they find me stirring up the people, either in their synagogues or anywhere else in the city. ¹³ Nor can they give you proof of the accusations they now bring against me. ¹⁴ I do admit this to you: I worship the God of our ancestors by following that Way which they say is false. But I also believe in all the things written in the Law of Moses and the books of the prophets. ¹⁵ I have the same hope in God that these themselves hold, that all men, both the good and the bad, will be raised from death. [16] And so I do my best always to have a clear conscience before God and men.

[17] "After being away from Jerusalem for several years, I went there to take some money to my own people and to offer sacrifices. [18] It was while I was doing this that they found me in the Temple, after I had completed the ceremony of purification. There was no crowd with me, and no disorder. [19] But some Jews from the province of Asia were there; they themselves ought to come before you and make their accusations, if they have anything against me. [20] Or let these men here tell what crime they found me guilty of when I stood before the Council — [21] except for the one thing I called out when I stood before them: 'I am being judged by you today for believing that the dead will be raised to life.' "

[22] Then Felix, who was well informed about the Way, brought the hearing to a close. "I will decide your case," he told them, "when the commander Lysias arrives." [23] He ordered the officer in charge of Paul to keep him under guard, but to give him some freedom and allow his friends to provide for his needs.

Paul before Felix and Drusilla

[24] After some days Felix came with his wife Drusilla, who was Jewish. He sent for Paul and listened to him as he talked about faith in Christ Jesus. [25] But as Paul went on discussing about goodness, self-control, and the coming Day of Judgment, Felix was afraid and said, "You may leave now. I will call you again when I get the chance." [26] At the same time he was hoping that Paul would give him some money; and for this reason he would call for him often and talk with him.

[27] After two years had passed, Porcius Festus took the place of Felix as Governor. Felix wanted to gain favor with the Jews, so he left Paul in prison.

Paul Appeals to the Emperor

25 Three days after Festus arrived in the province, he went from Caesarea to Jerusalem. [2] There the chief priests and the Jewish leaders brought their charges against Paul. They begged Festus [3] to do them the favor of having Paul come to Jerusalem, because they had made a plot

to kill him on the way. ⁴ Festus answered: "Paul is being kept a prisoner in Caesarea, and I myself will be going back there soon. ⁵ Let your leaders go to Caesarea with me and accuse the man, if he has done anything wrong."

⁶ Festus spent another eight or ten days with them, and then went to Caesarea. On the next day he sat down in the judgment court, and ordered Paul to be brought in. ⁷ When Paul arrived, the Jews who had come from Jerusalem stood around him and started making many serious charges against him, which they were not able to prove. ⁸ But Paul defended himself: "I have done nothing wrong against the Law of the Jews, or the Temple, or the Roman Emperor." ⁹ Festus wanted to gain favor with the Jews, so he asked Paul, "Would you want to go to Jerusalem and be tried on these charges before me there?" ¹⁰ Paul said: "I am standing before the Emperor's own judgment court, where I should be tried. I have done no wrong to the Jews, as you yourself well know. ¹¹ If I have broken the law and done something for which I deserve the death penalty, I do not ask to escape it. But if there is no truth in the charges they bring against me, no one can hand me over to them. I appeal to the Emperor." ¹² Then Festus, after conferring with his advisers, answered, "You have appealed to the Emperor, so to the Emperor you will go."

Paul before Agrippa and Bernice

¹³ Some time later King Agrippa and Bernice came to Caesarea to pay a visit of welcome to Festus. ¹⁴ After they had been there several days, Festus explained Paul's situation to the king: "There is a man here who was left a prisoner by Felix; ¹⁵ and when I went to Jerusalem, the Jewish chief priests and elders brought charges against him and asked me to condemn him. ¹⁶ But I told them that the Romans are not in the habit of handing over any man accused of a crime before he has met his accusers face to face, and has the chance of defending himself against the accusation. ¹⁷ When they all came here, then, I lost no time, but on the very next day I sat in the judgment court and ordered the man to be brought in. ¹⁸ His opponents stood up, but they did not accuse him of any of the evil crimes that I thought they would. ¹⁹ All they had were some arguments with him about their own religion and

about a certain dead man named Jesus; Paul claims that he is alive. [20] I was undecided about how I could get information on these matters, so I asked Paul if he would be willing to go to Jerusalem and be tried there on these charges. [21] But Paul appealed; he asked to be kept under guard and let the Emperor decide his case. So I gave orders for him to be kept under guard until I could send him to the Emperor." [22] Agrippa said to Festus, "I myself would like to hear this man." "You will hear him tomorrow," Festus answered.

[23] The next day Agrippa and Bernice came with much ceremony and honor, and entered the audience hall with the military chiefs and the leading men of the city. Festus gave the order and Paul was brought in. [24] Festus said: "King Agrippa, and all who are here with us: You see this man against whom all the Jewish people, both here and in Jerusalem, have brought complaints to me. They scream that he should not live any longer. [25] But I could not find that he had done anything for which he deserved the death sentence. And since he himself made an appeal to the Emperor, I have decided to send him. [26] But I do not have anything definite about him to write to the Emperor. So I have brought him here before you — and especially before you, King Agrippa! — so that, after investigating his case, I may have something to write. [27] For it seems unreasonable to me to send a prisoner without clearly indicating the charges against him."

Paul Defends Himself before Agrippa

26 Agrippa said to Paul, "You have permission to speak on your own behalf." Paul stretched out his hand and defended himself as follows:

[2] "King Agrippa! I consider myself fortunate that today I am to defend myself before you from all the things the Jews accuse me of. [3] This is especially true because you know so well all the Jewish customs and questions. I ask you, then, to listen to me with patience.

[4] "All the Jews know how I have lived ever since I was young. They know that from the beginning I have spent my whole life in my own country and in Jerusalem. [5] They have always known, if they are willing to testify, that from the very first I have lived as a member of the strictest party of our religion, the Pharisees. [6] And now I

stand here to be tried because I hope in the promise that God made to our ancestors — 7 the very promise that all twelve tribes of our people hope to receive, as they worship God day and night. And it is because of this hope, your Majesty, that I am being accused by the Jews! 8 Why do you Jews find it impossible to believe that God raises the dead?

9 "I myself thought that I should do everything I could against the name of Jesus of Nazareth. 10 That is what I did in Jerusalem. I received authority from the chief priests and put many of God's people in prison; and when they were sentenced to death, I also voted for it. 11 Many times I had them punished in all the synagogues, and tried to make them deny their faith. I was so furious with them that I even went to foreign cities to persecute them."

Paul Tells of His Conversion
(Also Acts 9.1–19; 22.6–16)

12 "It was for this purpose that I went to Damascus with the authority and orders from the chief priests. 13 It was on the road at midday, your Majesty, that I saw a light much brighter than the sun shining from the sky around me and the men traveling with me. 14 All of us fell to the ground, and I heard a voice say to me in the Hebrew language, 'Saul, Saul! Why are you persecuting me? You hurt yourself by hitting back, like an ox kicking against its owner's stick.' 15 'Who are you, Lord?' I asked. And the Lord said: 'I am Jesus, whom you persecute. 16 But get up and stand on your feet. I have appeared to you to appoint you as my servant; you are to tell others what you have seen of me today, and what I will show you in the future. 17 I will save you from the people of Israel and from the Gentiles, to whom I will send you. 18 You are to open their eyes and turn them from the darkness to the light, and from the power of Satan to God, so that through their faith in me they will have their sins forgiven and receive their place among God's chosen people.' "

Paul Tells of His Work

19 "And so, King Agrippa, I did not disobey the vision I had from heaven. 20 First in Damascus and in Jerusalem, and then in the whole country of Judea and among

the Gentiles, I preached that they must repent of their sins and turn to God, and do the things that would show they had repented. 21 It was for this reason that the Jews seized me while I was in the Temple, and tried to kill me. 22 But to this very day I have been helped by God, and so I stand here giving my witness to all, to the small and great alike. What I say is the very same thing the prophets and Moses said was going to happen: 23 that the Messiah must suffer and be the first one to rise from death, to announce the light of salvation to the Jews and to the Gentiles."

24 As Paul defended himself in this way, Festus shouted at him, "You are mad, Paul! Your great learning is driving you mad!" 25 Paul answered: "I am not mad, your Excellency! The words I speak are true and sober. 26 King Agrippa! I can speak to you with all boldness, because you know about these things. I am sure that you have taken notice of every one of them, for this thing has not happened hidden away in a corner. 27 King Agrippa, do you believe the prophets? I know that you do!" 28 Agrippa said to Paul, "In this short time you think you will make me a Christian?" 29 "Whether a short time or a long time," Paul answered, "my prayer to God is that you and all the rest of you who are listening to me today might become what I am — except, of course, for these chains!"

30 Then the king, the Governor, Bernice, and all the others got up, 31 and after leaving they said to each other, "This man has not done anything for which he should die or be put in prison." 32 And Agrippa said to Festus, "This man could have been released if he had not appealed to the Emperor."

Paul Sails for Rome

27 When it was decided that we should sail to Italy, they handed Paul and some other prisoners over to Julius, an officer in the Roman army regiment called "The Emperor's Regiment." 2 We went aboard a ship from Adramyttium, which was ready to leave for the seaports of the province of Asia, and sailed away. Aristarchus, a Macedonian from Thessalonica, was with us. 3 The next day we arrived at Sidon. Julius was kind to Paul and allowed him to go and see his friends, to be given what he needed. 4 We went on from there, and because the winds

were blowing against us we sailed on the sheltered side of the island of Cyprus. ⁵ We crossed over the sea off Cilicia and Pamphylia, and came to Myra, in Lycia. ⁶ There the officer found a ship from Alexandria that was going to sail for Italy, so he put us aboard.

⁷ We sailed slowly for several days, and with great difficulty finally arrived off the town of Cnidus. The wind would not let us go any farther in that direction, so we sailed down the sheltered side of the island of Crete, passing by Cape Salmone. ⁸ We kept close to the coast, and with great difficulty came to a place called Safe Harbors, not far from the town of Lasea.

⁹ We spent a long time there, until it became dangerous to continue the voyage, because by now the day of Atonement was already past. So Paul gave them this advice: ¹⁰ "Men, I see that our voyage from here on will be dangerous; there will be great damage to the cargo and to the ship, and loss of life as well." ¹¹ But the army officer was convinced by what the captain and the owner of the ship said, and not by what Paul said. ¹² The harbor was not a good one to spend the winter in; so most of the men were in favor of putting out to sea and trying to reach Phoenix, if possible. It is a harbor in Crete that faces southwest and northwest, and they could spend the winter there.

The Storm at Sea

¹³ A soft wind from the south began to blow, and the men thought that they could carry out their plan; so they pulled up the anchor and sailed as close as possible along the coast of Crete. ¹⁴ But soon a very strong wind — the one called "Northeaster" — blew down from the island. ¹⁵ It hit the ship, and since it was impossible to keep the ship headed into the wind, we gave up trying and let it be carried along by the wind. ¹⁶ We got some shelter when we passed to the south of the little island of Cauda. There, with some difficulty, we managed to make the ship's boat secure. ¹⁷ They pulled it aboard, and then fastened some ropes tight around the ship. They were afraid that they might run into the sandbanks off the coast of Libya; so they lowered the sail and let the ship be carried by the wind. ¹⁸ The violent storm continued, so on the next day they began to throw the ship's cargo overboard, ¹⁹ and on

the following day they threw the ship's equipment overboard with their own hands. [20] For many days we could not see the sun or the stars, and the wind kept on blowing very hard. We finally gave up all hope of being saved.

[21] After the men had gone a long time without food, Paul stood before them and said: "Men, you should have listened to me and not have sailed from Crete; then we would have avoided all this damage and loss. [22] But now I beg you, take courage! Not one of you will lose his life; only the ship will be lost. [23] For last night an angel of the God to whom I belong and whom I worship came to me [24] and said, 'Don't be afraid, Paul! You must stand before the Emperor; and God, in his goodness, has given you the lives of all those who are sailing with you.' [25] And so, men, take courage! For I trust in God that it will be just as I was told. [26] But we will be driven ashore on some island."

[27] It was the fourteenth night, and we were being driven by the storm on the Mediterranean. About midnight the sailors suspected that we were getting close to land. [28] So they dropped a line with a weight tied to it and found that the water was one hundred and twenty feet deep; a little later they did the same and found that it was ninety feet deep. [29] They were afraid that our ship would go on the rocks, so they lowered four anchors from the back of the ship and prayed for daylight. [30] The sailors tried to escape from the ship; they lowered the boat into the water and pretended that they were going to put out some anchors from the front of the ship. [31] But Paul said to the army officer and soldiers, "If these sailors don't stay on board, you cannot be saved." [32] So the soldiers cut the ropes that held the boat and let it go.

[33] Day was about to come, and Paul begged them all to eat some food: "You have been waiting for fourteen days now, and all this time you have not eaten a thing. [34] I beg you, then, eat some food; you need it in order to survive. Not even a hair of your heads will be lost." [35] After saying this, Paul took some bread, gave thanks to God before them all, broke it, and began to eat. [36] They took courage, and every one of them also ate some food. [37] There was a total of two hundred and seventy-six of us on board. [38] After everyone had eaten enough, they lightened the ship by throwing the wheat into the sea.

The Shipwreck

39 When day came, the sailors did not recognize the coast, but they noticed a bay with a beach and decided that, if possible, they would run the ship aground there. 40 So they cut off the anchors and left them in the water, and at the same time they untied the ropes that held the steering oars. Then they raised the sail at the front of the ship so that the wind would blow the ship forward, and headed for shore. 41 But the ship ran into a sandbank and went aground; the front part of the ship got stuck and could not move, while the back part was being broken to pieces by the violence of the waves.

42 The soldiers made a plan to kill all the prisoners, so that none of them would swim ashore and escape. 43 But the army officer wanted to save Paul, so he stopped them from doing this. Instead, he ordered all the men who could swim to jump overboard first and swim ashore; 44 the rest were to follow, holding on to the planks or to some broken pieces of the ship. And this was how we all got safely ashore.

In Malta

28 When we were safely ashore, we learned that the island was called Malta. 2 The natives there were very friendly to us. It had started raining and was cold, so they built a fire and made us all welcome. 3 Paul gathered up a bundle of sticks and was putting them on the fire when a snake came out, on account of the heat, and fastened itself to his hand. 4 The natives saw the snake hanging on Paul's hand and said to one another, "This man must be a murderer, but Fate will not let him live,

even though he escaped from the sea." [5] But Paul shook the snake off into the fire without being harmed at all. [6] They were waiting for him to swell up or suddenly fall down dead. But after waiting for a long time and not seeing anything unusual happening to him, they changed their minds and said, "He is a god!"

[7] Not far from that place were some fields that belonged to Publius, the chief of the island. He welcomed us kindly and for three days we were his guests. [8] Publius' father was in bed sick with fever and dysentery. Paul went into his room, prayed, placed his hands on him, and healed him. [9] When this happened, all the other sick people on the island came and were healed. [10] They gave us many gifts, and when we sailed they put on board what we needed for the voyage.

From Malta to Rome

[11] After three months we sailed away on a ship from Alexandria, called "The Twin Gods," which had spent the winter in the island. [12] We arrived in the city of Syracuse and stayed there for three days. [13] From there we sailed on and arrived in the city of Rhegium. The next day a wind began to blow from the south, and in two days we came to the town of Puteoli. [14] We found some believers there who asked us to stay with them a week. And so we came to Rome. [15] The brothers in Rome heard about us and came as far as Market of Appius and Three Inns to meet us. When Paul saw them, he thanked God and took courage.

In Rome

[16] When we arrived in Rome, Paul was allowed to live by himself with a soldier guarding him.

[17] After three days Paul called the local Jewish leaders to a meeting. When they gathered, he said to them: "My brothers! Even though I did nothing against our people or the customs that we received from our ancestors, I was made a prisoner in Jerusalem and handed over to the Romans. [18] They questioned me and wanted to release me, because they found that I had done nothing for which I deserved to die. [19] But when the Jews opposed this, I was forced to appeal to the Emperor, even though I had no accusation to make against my own people. [20] That is

why I asked to see you and talk with you; because I have this chain on me for the sake of him for whom the people of Israel hope." 21 They said to him: "We have not received any letters from Judea about you, nor have any of our brothers come from there with any news, or to say anything bad about you. 22 But we would like to hear your ideas, for we do know that everywhere people speak against this party that you belong to."

23 So they set a date with Paul, and a larger number of them came that day to where Paul was staying. From morning till night he explained and gave them his message about the Kingdom of God. He tried to convince them about Jesus by quoting from the Law of Moses and the writings of the prophets. 24 Some of them were convinced by his words, but others would not believe. 25 So they left, disagreeing among themselves, after Paul had said this one thing: "How well the Holy Spirit spoke through the prophet Isaiah to your ancestors! 26 For he said:

'Go and say to this people:
You will listen and listen, but not understand;
You will look and look, but not see.
27 Because this people's mind is dull;
They have stopped up their ears,
And they have closed their eyes.
Otherwise, their eyes might see,
Their ears might hear,
Their minds might understand,
And they might turn to me, says God,
And I would heal them.' "

28 And Paul added: "You are to know, then, that God's message of salvation has been sent to the Gentiles. They will listen!" [29 After Paul said this, the Jews left, arguing violently among themselves.]

30 For two years Paul lived there in a place he rented for himself, and welcomed all who came to see him. 31 He preached about the Kingdom of God and taught about the Lord Jesus Christ, speaking with all boldness and freedom.

PAUL'S LETTER TO THE ROMANS

1 From Paul, a servant of Christ Jesus, and an apostle chosen and called by God to preach his Good News.

[2] The Good News was promised long ago by God through his prophets, and written in the Holy Scriptures. [3] It is about his Son, our Lord Jesus Christ: as to his humanity, he was born a descendant of David; [4] as to his divine holiness, he was shown with great power to be the Son of God, by being raised from death. [5] Through him God gave me the privilege of being an apostle, for the sake of Christ, in order to lead people of all nations to believe and obey. [6] This also includes you who are in Rome, whom God has called to belong to Jesus Christ.

[7] And so I write to all of you in Rome whom God loves and has called to be his own people:

May God our Father and the Lord Jesus Christ give you grace and peace.

Prayer of Thanksgiving

[8] First, I thank my God, through Jesus Christ, for all of you; because the whole world is hearing of your faith. [9] God can prove that what I say is true — the God whom I serve with all my heart by preaching the Good News about his Son. God knows that I always remember you [10] every time I pray. I ask that God, in his good will, may at last make it possible for me to visit you now. [11] For I want very much to see you in order to share a spiritual blessing with you, to make you strong. [12] What I mean is that both you and I will be helped at the same time: you by my faith and I by your faith.

[13] You must remember this, my brothers: many times I have planned to visit you, but something has always kept me from doing so. I have wanted to win converts among you, too, as I have among other Gentiles. [14] For I have an obligation to all peoples, to the civilized and to the savage, to the educated and to the ignorant. [15] Therefore, I am eager to preach the Good News to you also who live in Rome.

The Power of the Gospel

¹⁶ For I have complete confidence in the gospel: it is God's power to save all who believe, first the Jews and also the Gentiles. ¹⁷ For the gospel reveals how God puts men right with himself: it is through faith alone, from beginning to end. As the scripture says, "He who is put right with God through faith shall live."

The Guilt of Mankind

¹⁸ God's wrath is revealed coming down from heaven upon all the sin and evil of men, whose evil ways prevent the truth from being known. ¹⁹ God punishes them, because what men can know about God is plain to them. God himself made it plain to them. ²⁰ Ever since God created the world, his invisible qualities, both his eternal power and his divine nature, have been clearly seen. Men can perceive them in the things that God has made. So they have no excuse at all! ²¹ They know God, but they do not give him the honor that belongs to him, nor do they thank him. Instead, their thoughts have become complete nonsense and their empty minds are filled with darkness. ²² They say they are wise, but they are fools; ²³ instead of worshiping the immortal God, they worship images made to look like mortal man or birds or animals or reptiles.

²⁴ Because men are such fools, God has given them over to do the filthy things their hearts desire, and they do shameful things with each other. ²⁵ They exchange the

truth about God for a lie; they worship and serve what God has created instead of the Creator himself, who is to be praised for ever! Amen.

[26] Because of what men do, God has given them over to shameful passions. Even the women pervert the natural use of their sex by unnatural acts. [27] In the same way the men give up natural sexual relations with women and burn with passion for each other. Men do shameful things with each other, and as a result they receive in themselves the punishment they deserve for their wrongdoing.

[28] Because men refuse to keep in mind the true knowledge about God, he has given them over to corrupted minds, so that they do the things that they should not. [29] They are filled with all kinds of wickedness, evil, greed, and vice; they are full of jealousy, murder, fighting, deceit, and malice. They gossip, [30] and speak evil of one another; they are hateful to God, insolent, proud, and boastful; they think of more ways to do evil; they disobey their parents; [31] they are immoral; they do not keep their promises, and they show no kindness or pity to others. [32] They know that God's law says that people who live in this way deserve death. Yet they continue to do these very things — and worse still, they approve of others who do them also.

God's Judgment

2 Do you, my friend, pass judgment on others? You have no excuse at all, whoever you are. For when you judge others, but do the same things that they do, you condemn yourself. [2] We know that God is right when he judges the people who do such things as these. [3] But you, my friend, do these very things yourself for which you pass judgment on others! Do you think you will escape God's judgment? [4] Or perhaps you despise his great kindness, and tolerance, and patience. Surely you know that God is kind because he is trying to lead you to repent! [5] But you have a hard and stubborn heart. Therefore, you are making your own punishment even greater on the Day when God's wrath and right judgments will be revealed. [6] For God will reward every person according to what he has done. [7] Some men keep on doing good, and seek glory, honor, and immortal life: to them God will give eternal life. [8] Other men are selfish and reject what is right, to follow what is wrong: on them God will pour his

wrath and anger. ⁹ There will be suffering and pain for all men who do what is evil, for the Jews first and also for the Gentiles. ¹⁰ But God will give glory, honor, and peace to all who do what is good, to the Jews first, and also to the Gentiles. ¹¹ For God treats all men alike.

¹² The Gentiles do not have the Law of Moses; they sin and are lost apart from the Law. The Jews have the Law; they sin and are judged by the Law. ¹³ For it is not by hearing the Law that men are put right with God, but by doing what the Law commands. ¹⁴ The Gentiles do not have the Law; but whenever of their own free will they do what the Law commands, they are a law to themselves, even though they do not have the Law. ¹⁵ Their conduct shows that what the Law commands is written in their hearts. Their consciences also show that this is true, since their thoughts sometimes accuse them and sometimes defend them. ¹⁶ This, according to the Good News I preach, is how it will be on that Day when God, through Jesus Christ, will judge all the secret thoughts in men's hearts.

The Jews and the Law

¹⁷ What about you? You call yourself a Jew; you depend on the Law and boast about God; ¹⁸ you know what God wants you to do, and you have learned from the Law to choose what is right; ¹⁹ you are sure that you are a guide for the blind, a light for those who are in darkness, ²⁰ an instructor for the foolish, and a teacher for the young. You are certain that in the Law you have the full content of knowledge and of truth. ²¹ You teach others — why don't you teach yourself? You preach, "Do not steal" — but do you yourself steal? ²² You say, "Do not commit adultery" — but do you commit adultery? You detest idols — but do you rob temples? ²³ You boast about having God's law — but do you bring shame on God by breaking his law? ²⁴ For the scripture says, "Because of you Jews, the Gentiles speak evil of God's name."

²⁵ If you obey the Law, your circumcision is of value; but if you disobey the Law, you might as well never have been circumcised. ²⁶ If the Gentile, who is not circumcised, obeys the commands of the Law, will not God regard him as though he were circumcised? ²⁷ And you Jews will be condemned by the Gentiles. For you break the Law, even

though you have it written down and are circumcised, while they obey the Law, even though they are not physically circumcised. ²⁸ After all, who is a real Jew, truly circumcised? Not the man who is a Jew on the outside, whose circumcision is a physical thing. ²⁹ Rather, the real Jew is the man who is a Jew on the inside, that is, whose heart has been circumcised, which is the work of God's Spirit, not of the written Law. This man receives his praise from God, not from men.

3 Do the Jews have any advantage over the Gentiles, then? Or is there any value in being circumcised? ² Much, indeed, in every way! In the first place, God trusted his message to the Jews. ³ What if some of them were not faithful? Does it mean that for this reason God will not be faithful? ⁴ Certainly not! God must be true, even though every man is a liar. As the scripture says:

> "You must be shown to be right when you
>   speak,
> You must win your case when you are being
>   tried."

⁵ But what if our doing wrong serves to show up more clearly God's doing right? What can we say? That God does wrong when he punishes us? (I speak here as men do.) ⁶ By no means! If God is not just, how can he judge the world?

⁷ But what if my untruth serves God's glory by making his truth stand out more clearly? Why should I still be condemned as a sinner? ⁸ Why not say, then, "Let us do evil that good may come"? Some people, indeed, have insulted me by accusing me of saying this very thing! They will be condemned, as they should be.

No Man Is Righteous

⁹ Well then, are we Jews in any better condition than the Gentiles? Not at all! I have already shown that Jews and Gentiles alike are all under the power of sin. ¹⁰ As the Scriptures say:

> "There is not a single man who is righteous,
> ¹¹ There is not one who understands,
>   Or who seeks for God.
> ¹² All men have turned away from God,
>   They have all gone wrong.
>   No one does what is good, not even one.

13 Their throat is like an open grave.
   Wicked lies roll off their tongues,
   And deadly words, like snake's poison, from
      their lips;
14 Their mouths are full of bitter curses.
15 They are quick to hurt and kill;
16 They leave ruin and misery wherever they go.
17 They have not known the path of peace,
18 Nor have they learned to fear God."

19 Now we know that everything in the Law applies to those who live under the Law, in order to stop all human excuses and bring the whole world under God's judgment. 20 For no man is put right in God's sight by doing what the Law requires; what the Law does is to make man know that he has sinned.

How God Puts Men Right

21 But now God's way of putting men right with himself has been revealed, and it has nothing to do with law. The Law and the prophets gave their witness to it: 22 God puts men right through their faith in Jesus Christ. God does this to all who believe in Christ, for there is no difference at all: 23 all men have sinned and are far away from God's saving presence. 24 But by the free gift of God's grace they are all put right with him through Christ Jesus, who sets them free. 25 God offered him so that by his death he should become the means by which men's sins are forgiven, through their faith in him. God offered Christ to show how he puts men right with himself. In the past, God was patient and overlooked men's sins; 26 but now in the present time he deals with men's sins, to prove that he puts men right with himself. In this way God shows that he himself is righteous and that he puts right everyone who believes in Jesus.

27 What, then, is there to boast about? Nothing! For what reason? Because a man obeys the Law? No, but because he believes. 28 For we conclude that a man is put right with God only through faith, and not by doing what the Law commands. 29 Or is God only the God of the Jews? Is he not the God of the Gentiles also? Of course he is. 30 God is one, and he will put the Jews right with himself on the basis of their faith, and the Gentiles right through their faith. 31 Does this mean that we do away

with the Law by this faith? No, not at all; instead, we uphold the Law.

The Example of Abraham

4 What shall we say, then, of Abraham, our racial ancestor? What did he find? ² If he was put right with God by the things he did, he would have something to boast about. But he cannot boast before God. ³ The scripture says, "Abraham believed God, and because of his faith God accepted him as righteous." ⁴ A man who works is paid; his wages are not regarded as a gift but as something that he has earned. ⁵ As for the man who does not work, however, but simply puts his faith in God, who declares the guilty to be innocent, it is his faith that God takes into account in order to put him right with himself. ⁶ This is what David meant when he spoke of the happiness of the man whom God accepts as righteous, apart from any works:

⁷ "How happy are those whose wrongs God has
    forgiven,
  Whose sins he has covered over!
⁸ How happy is the man whose sins the Lord
    will not keep account of!"

⁹ Does this happiness that David spoke of belong only to those who are circumcised? No. It belongs also to those who are not circumcised. For we have quoted the scripture, "Abraham believed God, and because of his faith God accepted him as righteous." ¹⁰ When did this take place? Was it before or after Abraham was circumcised? Before, not after. ¹¹ He was circumcised later, and his circumcision was a sign to prove that because of Abraham's faith God had accepted him as righteous before he had been circumcised. And so Abraham is the spiritual father of all who believe in God and are accepted as righteous by him, even though they are not circumcised. ¹² He is also the father of those who are circumcised, not just because they are circumcised, but because they live the same life of faith that our father Abraham lived before he was circumcised.

God's Promise Received through Faith

¹³ God promised Abraham and his descendants that the world would belong to him. This promise was made, not because Abraham obeyed the Law, but because he believed

and was accepted as righteous by God. [14] For if what God promises is to be given to those who obey the Law, then man's faith means nothing and God's promise is worthless. [15] The Law brings down God's wrath; but where there is no law, there is no disobeying of the law either.

[16] The promise was based on faith, then, in order that the promise should be guaranteed as God's free gift to all of Abraham's descendants — not just those who obey the Law, but also those who believe as Abraham did. For Abraham is the spiritual father of us all. [17] As the scripture says, "I have made you father of many nations." So the promise is good in the sight of God, in whom Abraham believed — the God who brings the dead to life and whose command brings into being what did not exist. [18] Abraham believed and hoped, when there was no hope, and so became "the father of many nations." Just as the scripture says, "Your descendants will be this many." [19] He was almost one hundred years old; but his faith did not weaken when he thought of his body, which was already practically dead, or of the fact that Sarah could not have children. [20] His faith did not leave him, and he did not doubt God's promise; his faith filled him with power, and he gave praise to God. [21] For he was absolutely sure that God would be able to do what he had promised. [22] That is why Abraham, through faith, "was accepted as righteous by God." [23] The words "he was accepted as righteous" were not written for him alone. [24] They were written also for us who are to be accepted as righteous, who believe in him who raised Jesus our Lord from death. [25] He was given over to die because of our sins, and was raised to life to put us right with God.

Right with God

5 Now that we have been put right with God through faith, we have peace with God through our Lord Jesus Christ. [2] He has brought us, by faith, into the grace of God in which we now stand. We rejoice, then, in the hope we have of sharing God's glory! [3] And we also rejoice in our troubles, for we know that trouble produces endurance, [4] endurance brings God's approval, and his approval creates hope. [5] This hope does not disappoint us, for God has poured out his love into our hearts by means of the Holy Spirit, who is God's gift to us.

⁶ For when we were still helpless, Christ died for the wicked, at the time that God chose. ⁷ It is a difficult thing for someone to die for a righteous person. It may be that someone might dare to die for a good person. ⁸ But God has shown us how much he loves us: it was while we were still sinners that Christ died for us! ⁹ By his death we are now put right with God; how much more, then, will we be saved by him from God's wrath. ¹⁰ We were God's enemies, but he made us his friends through the death of his Son. Now that we are God's friends, how much more will we be saved by Christ's life! ¹¹ But that is not all; we rejoice in God through our Lord Jesus Christ, who has now made us God's friends.

Adam and Christ

¹² Sin came into the world through one man, and his sin brought death with it. As a result, death spread to the whole human race, because all men sinned. ¹³ There was sin in the world before the Law was given; but since there was no law, no account was kept of sins. ¹⁴ But from the time of Adam to the time of Moses death ruled over all men, even over those who did not sin as Adam did by disobeying God's command.

Adam was a figure of the one who was to come. ¹⁵ But the two are not the same; for the free gift of God is not like Adam's sin. It is true that many men died because of the sin of that one man. But God's grace is much greater, and so is his free gift to so many men through the grace of the one man, Jesus Christ. ¹⁶ And there is a difference between God's gift and the sin of one man. After the one sin came the judgment of "Guilty"; but after so many sins comes the undeserved gift of "Not guilty!" ¹⁷ It is true that through the sin of one man death began to rule, because of that one man. But how much greater is the result of what was done by the one man, Jesus Christ! All who receive God's abundant grace and the free gift of his righteousness will rule in life through Christ.

¹⁸ So then, as the one sin condemned all men, in the same way the one righteous act sets all men free and gives them life. ¹⁹ And just as many men were made sinners as the result of the disobedience of one man, in the same way many will be put right with God as the result of the obedience of the one man.

²⁰ Law was introduced in order to increase wrongdoing; but where sin increased, God's grace increased much more. ²¹ So then, just as sin ruled by means of death, so also God's grace rules by means of righteousness, leading us to eternal life through Jesus Christ our Lord.

Dead to Sin but Alive in Christ

6 What shall we say, then? That we should continue to live in sin so that God's grace will increase? ² Certainly not! We have died to sin — how then can we go on living in it? ³ For surely you know this: when we were baptized into union with Christ Jesus, we were baptized into union with his death. ⁴ By our baptism, then, we were buried with him and shared his death, in order that, just as Christ was raised from death by the glorious power of the Father, so also we might live a new life.

⁵ For if we became one with him in dying as he did, in the same way we shall be one with him by being raised to life as he was. ⁶ For we know this: our old being has been put to death with Christ on his cross, in order that the power of the sinful self might be destroyed, so that we should no longer be the slaves of sin. ⁷ For when a person dies he is set free from the power of sin. ⁸ If we have died with Christ, we believe that we will also live with him. ⁹ For we know that Christ has been raised from death and will never die again — death has no more power over him. ¹⁰ The death he died was death to sin, once and for all; and the life he now lives is life to God. ¹¹ In the same way you are to think of yourselves as dead to sin but alive to God in union with Christ Jesus.

¹² Sin must no longer rule in your mortal bodies, so that you obey the desires of your natural self. ¹³ Nor must you surrender any part of yourselves to sin, to be used for wicked purposes. Instead, give yourselves to God, as men who have been brought from death to life, and surrender your whole being to him to be used for righteous purposes. ¹⁴ For sin must not rule over you; you do not live under law but under God's grace.

Slaves of Righteousness

¹⁵ What, then? Shall we sin, because we are not under law but under God's grace? By no means! ¹⁶ For surely you know this: when you surrender yourselves as slaves to obey someone, you are in fact the slaves of the master you obey — either of sin, which results in death, or of obedience, which results in being put right with God. ¹⁷ But thanks be to God! For at one time you were slaves to sin, but now you obey with all your heart the truths found in the teaching you received. ¹⁸ You were set free from sin and became the slaves of righteousness. ¹⁹ I use ordinary words because of the weakness of your natural selves. At one time you surrendered yourselves entirely as slaves to impurity and wickedness, for wicked purposes. In the same way you must now surrender yourselves entirely as slaves of righteousness, for holy purposes.

²⁰ When you were the slaves of sin, you were free from righteousness. ²¹ Well, what good did you receive from doing the things that you are ashamed of now? The result of those things is death! ²² But now you have been set

free from sin and are the slaves of God; as a result your life is fully dedicated to him, and at the last you will have eternal life. ²³ For sin pays its wage — death; but God's free gift is eternal life in union with Christ Jesus our Lord.

An Illustration from Marriage

7 Certainly you understand what I am about to say, my brothers, for all of you know about law: the law rules over a man only as long as he lives. ² A married woman, for example, is bound by the law to her husband as long as he lives; but if he dies, then she is free from the law that bound her to him. ³ So then, if she lives with another man while her husband is alive, she will be called an adulteress; but if her husband dies, she is legally a free woman, and does not commit adultery if she marries another man. ⁴ That is the way it is with you, too, my brothers. You also have died, as far as the Law is concerned, because you are part of the body of Christ; and now you belong to him who was raised from death in order that we might live useful lives for God. ⁵ For when we lived according to our human nature, the sinful desires stirred up by the Law were at work in our bodies, and produced death. ⁶ Now, however, we are free from the Law, because we died to that which once held us prisoners. No longer do we serve in the old way of a written law, but in the new way of the Spirit.

Law and Sin

⁷ What shall we say, then? That the Law itself is sinful? Of course not! But it was the Law that made me know what sin is. For I would not have known what it is to covet if the Law had not said, "Do not covet." ⁸ Sin found its chance to stir up all kinds of covetousness in me by working through the commandment. For sin is a dead thing apart from law. ⁹ I myself was once alive apart from law; but when the commandment came, sin sprang to life, ¹⁰ and I died. And the commandment which was meant to bring life, in my case brought death. ¹¹ For sin found its chance and deceived me by working through the commandment; by means of the commandment sin killed me.

¹² The Law itself is holy, and the commandment is holy, and right, and good. ¹³ Does this mean that what is good

brought about my death? By no means! It was sin that did it; by using what is good, sin brought death to me in order that its true nature as sin might be revealed. And so, by means of the commandment, sin becomes even more terribly sinful.

The Two Natures in Man

14 We know that the Law is spiritual; but I am mortal man, sold as a slave to sin. 15 I do not understand what I do; for I don't do what I would like to do, but instead I do what I hate. 16 When I do what I don't want to do, this shows that I agree that the Law is right. 17 So I am not really the one who does this thing; rather it is the sin that lives in me. 18 I know that good does not live in me — that is, in my human nature. For even though the desire to do good is in me, I am not able to do it. 19 I don't do the good I want to do; instead, I do the evil that I do not want to do. 20 If I do what I don't want to do, this means that no longer am I the one who does it; instead, it is the sin that lives in me.

21 So I find that this law is at work: when I want to do what is good, what is evil is the only choice I have. 22 My inner being delights in the law of God. 23 But I see a different law at work in my body — a law that fights against the law that my mind approves of. It makes me a prisoner to the law of sin which is at work in my body. 24 What an unhappy man I am! Who will rescue me from this body that is taking me to death? 25 Thanks be to God, through our Lord Jesus Christ!

This, then, is my condition: by myself I can serve God's law only with my mind, while my human nature serves the law of sin.

Life in the Spirit

8 There is no condemnation now for those who live in union with Christ Jesus. 2 For the law of the Spirit, which brings us life in union with Christ Jesus, has set me free from the law of sin and death. 3 What the Law could not do, because human nature was weak, God did. He condemned sin in human nature by sending his own Son, who came with a nature like man's sinful nature to do away with sin. 4 God did this so that the righteous demands of the Law might be fully satisfied in us who live

according to the Spirit, not according to human nature.
⁵ For those who live as their human nature tells them
to live, have their minds controlled by what human
nature wants. Those who live as the Spirit tells them to
live, have their minds controlled by what the Spirit wants.
⁶ To have your mind controlled by what human nature
wants will result in death; to have your mind controlled by
what the Spirit wants will result in life and peace. ⁷ And
so a man becomes an enemy of God when his mind is
controlled by what human nature wants; for he does not
obey God's law, and in fact he cannot obey it. ⁸ Those
who obey their human nature cannot please God.

⁹ But you do not live as your human nature tells you
to; you live as the Spirit tells you to — if, in fact, God's
Spirit lives in you. Whoever does not have the Spirit of
Christ does not belong to him. ¹⁰ But if Christ lives in
you, although your body is dead because of sin, yet the
Spirit is life for you because you have been put right
with God. ¹¹ If the Spirit of God, who raised Jesus from
death, lives in you, then he who raised Christ from death
will also give life to your mortal bodies by the presence of
his Spirit in you.

¹² So then, my brothers, we have an obligation, but not
to live as our human nature wants us to. ¹³ For if you live
according to your human nature, you are going to die;
but if, by the Spirit, you kill your sinful actions, you will
live. ¹⁴ Those who are led by God's Spirit are God's sons.
¹⁵ For the Spirit that God has given you does not make
you a slave and cause you to be afraid; instead, the Spirit
makes you God's sons, and by the Spirit's power we cry
to God, "Father! my Father!" ¹⁶ God's Spirit joins himself
to our spirits to declare that we are God's children.
¹⁷ Since we are his children, we will possess the blessings he
keeps for his people, and we will also possess with Christ
what God has kept for him; for if we share Christ's suffering, we will also share his glory.

The Future Glory

¹⁸ I consider that what we suffer at this present time
cannot be compared at all with the glory that is going to
be revealed to us. ¹⁹ All of creation waits with eager
longing for God to reveal his sons. ²⁰ For creation was
condemned to become worthless, not of its own will, but

because God willed it to be so. Yet there was this hope: [21] that creation itself would one day be set free from its slavery to decay, and share the glorious freedom of the children of God. [22] For we know that up to the present time all of creation groans with pain like the pain of childbirth. [23] But not just creation alone; we who have the Spirit as the first of God's gifts, we also groan within ourselves as we wait for God to make us his sons and set our whole being free. [24] For it was by hope that we were saved; but if we see what we hope for, then it is not really hope. For who hopes for something that he sees? [25] But if we hope for what we do not see, we wait for it with patience.

[26] In the same way the Spirit also comes to help us, weak that we are. For we do not know how we ought to pray; the Spirit himself pleads with God for us, in groans that words cannot express. [27] And God, who sees into the hearts of men, knows what the thought of the Spirit is; for the Spirit pleads with God on behalf of his people, and in accordance with his will.

[28] For we know that in all things God works for good with those who love him, those whom he has called according to his purpose. [29] For those whom God had already chosen he had also set apart to become like his Son, so that the Son should be the first among many brothers. [30] And so God called those whom he had set apart; not only did he call them, but he also put them right with himself; not only did he put them right with himself, but he also shared his glory with them.

God's Love in Christ Jesus

[31] Faced with all this, what can we say? If God is for us, who can be against us? [32] He did not even keep back his own Son, but offered him for us all! He gave us his Son — will he not also freely give us all things? [33] Who will accuse God's chosen people? God himself declares them not guilty! [34] Can anyone, then, condemn them? Christ Jesus is the one who died, or rather, who was raised to life and is at the right side of God. He pleads with God for us! [35] Who, then, can separate us from the love of Christ? Can trouble do it, or hardship, or persecution, or hunger, or poverty, or danger, or death? [36] As the scripture says,

"For your sake we are in danger of death the
   whole day long,
We are treated like sheep that are going to be
   slaughtered."

[37] No, in all these things we have complete victory through
him who loved us! [38] For I am certain that nothing can
separate us from his love: neither death nor life; neither
angels nor other heavenly rulers or powers; neither the
present nor the future; [39] neither the world above nor the
world below — there is nothing in all creation that will
ever be able to separate us from the love of God which
is ours through Christ Jesus our Lord.

God and His Chosen People

9 What I say is true; I belong to Christ and I do not lie.
   My conscience, ruled by the Holy Spirit, also assures
me that I am not lying. [2] How great is my sorrow, how
endless the pain in my heart for my people, my own flesh
and blood! [3] For their sake I could wish that I myself
were under God's curse and separated from Christ. [4] They
are God's chosen people; he made them his sons and
shared his glory with them; he made his covenants with
them and gave them the Law; they have the true worship;
they have received God's promises; [5] they are descended
from the patriarchs, and Christ, as a human being, belongs
to their race. May God, who rules over all, be praised
for ever! Amen.

[6] I am not saying that the promise of God has failed;

for not all the people of Israel are the chosen people of God. [7] Neither are all Abraham's descendants the children of God; for God said to Abraham, "Only the descendants of Isaac will be counted as yours." [8] This means that the children born in the natural way are not the children of God; instead, the children born as a result of God's promise are regarded as the true descendants. [9] For God's promise was made in these words: "At the right time I will come back and Sarah will have a son."

[10] And this is not all. For Rebecca's two sons had the same father, our ancestor Isaac. [11-12] But in order that the choice of one son might be completely the result of God's own purpose, God said to her, "The older will serve the younger." He said this before they were born, before they had done anything either good or bad; so God's choice was based on his call, and not on anything they did. [13] As the scripture says, "I loved Jacob, but I hated Esau."

[14] What shall we say, then? That God is unjust? Not at all. [15] For he said to Moses, "I will have mercy on whom I wish, I will take pity on whom I wish." [16] So then, it does not depend on what man wants or does, but only on God's mercy. [17] For the scripture says to Pharaoh, "I made you king for this very purpose, to use you to show my power, and to make my name known in all the world." [18] So then, God has mercy on whom he wishes, and he makes stubborn whom he wishes.

God's Wrath and Mercy

[19] One of you, then, will say to me, "If this is so, how can God find fault with a man? For who can resist God's will?" [20] But who are you, my friend, to talk back to God? A clay pot does not ask the man who made it, "Why did you make me like this?" [21] After all, the man who makes the pots has the right to use the clay as he wishes, and to make two pots from the same lump of clay, an expensive pot and a cheap one.

[22] And the same is true of what God has done. He wanted to show his wrath and to make his power known. So he was very patient in enduring those who were the objects of his wrath, who were ready to be destroyed. [23] And he wanted also to reveal his rich glory, which was poured out on us who are the objects of his mercy, those of us whom he has prepared to receive his glory. [24] For

we are the ones whom he called, not only from among the Jews but also from among the Gentiles. 25 For this is what he says in the book of Hosea:

> "The people who were not mine, I will call
> 'My People,'
> The nation that I did not love, I will call 'My
> Beloved.'
> 26 And in the very place where they were told,
> 'You are not my people,'
> There they will be called the sons of the liv-
> ing God."

27 And Isaiah exclaims about Israel: "Even if the people of Israel are as many as the grains of sand by the sea, yet only a few of them will be saved; 28 for the Lord will quickly settle his full account with all the world." 29 It is as Isaiah had said before, "If the Lord Almighty had not left us some descendants, we would have become like Sodom, we would have been like Gomorrah."

Israel and the Gospel

30 What shall we say, then? This: that the Gentiles, who were not trying to put themselves right with God, were put right with him through faith; 31 while the chosen people, who were seeking a law that would put them right with God, did not find it. 32 And why not? Because what they did was not based on faith but on works. They stumbled over the "stumbling stone" 33 that the scripture speaks of:

> "See, I put in Zion a stone that will make
> people stumble,
> A rock on which they will trip.
> But the one who believes in him will not be
> disappointed."

10 My brothers, how I wish with all my heart that my own people might be saved! How I pray to God for them! 2 For I can be a witness for them that they are deeply devoted to God. But their devotion is not based on true knowledge. 3 For they have not known the way in which God puts men right with himself, and have tried to set up their own way; and so they did not submit themselves to God's way of putting men right. 4 For Christ has brought the Law to an end, so that everyone who believes is put right with God.

Salvation Is for All

⁵ This is what Moses wrote about being put right with God by obeying the Law: "The man who does what the Law commands will live by it." ⁶ But this is what is said about being put right with God through faith: "Do not say to yourself, Who will go up into heaven?" (that is, to bring Christ down). ⁷ "Do not say either, Who will go down into the world below?" (that is, to bring Christ up from the dead). ⁸ This is what it says: "God's message is near you, on your lips and in your heart" — that is, the message of faith that we preach. ⁹ If you declare with your lips, "Jesus is Lord," and believe in your heart that God raised him from the dead, you will be saved. ¹⁰ For we believe in our hearts and are put right with God; we declare with our lips and are saved. ¹¹ For the scripture says, "Whoever believes in him will not be disappointed." ¹² This includes everyone, for there is no difference between Jews and Gentiles; God is the same Lord of all, and richly blesses all who call on him. ¹³ As the scripture says, "Everyone who calls on the name of the Lord will be saved."

¹⁴ But how can they call on him, if they have not believed? And how can they believe, if they have not heard the message? And how can they hear, if the message is not preached? ¹⁵ And how can the message be preached, if the messengers are not sent out? As the scripture says, "How wonderful is the coming of those who bring good news!" ¹⁶ But they have not all accepted the Good News. Isaiah himself said, "Lord, who believed our message?" ¹⁷ So then, faith comes from hearing the message, and the message comes through preaching Christ.

¹⁸ But I ask: Is it true that they did not hear the message? Of course they did — as the scripture says:

> "The sound of their voices went out over all
>   the earth,
> Their words reached the very ends of the
>   world."

¹⁹ Again I ask: Did the people of Israel not know? Moses himself is the first one to answer:

> "I will make you jealous of a people who are
>   not a real nation,

I will make you angry with a nation of foolish
people."

20 And Isaiah is bolder when he says:

"I was found by those who were not looking
for me,
I appeared to those who were not asking for
me."

21 But concerning Israel he says: "I held out my hands the
whole day long to a disobedient and rebellious people."

God's Mercy on Israel

11 I ask, then: Did God reject his own people? Certainly not! I myself am an Israelite, a descendant of
Abraham, a member of the tribe of Benjamin. 2 God has
not rejected his people, whom he chose from the beginning.
You know what the scripture says in the passage where
Elijah pleads with God against Israel: 3 "Lord, they have
killed your prophets and torn down your altars; I am the
only one left, and they are trying to kill me." 4 What answer
did God give him? "I have kept for myself seven thousand
men who have not worshiped the false god Baal." 5 It is the
same way now at this time: there is a small number of
those whom God has chosen, because of his mercy. 6 His
choice is based on his mercy, not on what they have done.
For if God's choice were based on what men do, then his
mercy would not be true mercy.

7 What then? The people of Israel did not find what
they were looking for. It was the small group that God
chose who found it; the rest grew deaf to God's call. 8 As
the scripture says, "God made them dull of heart and
mind; to this very day they cannot see with their eyes or
hear with their ears." 9 And David says:

"May they be caught and trapped at their
feasts,
May they fall, may they be punished!
10 May their eyes be closed so that they cannot
see;
And make them bend under their troubles at
all times."

11 I ask, then: When the Jews stumbled, did they fall to
their ruin? By no means! Because they sinned, salvation
has come to the Gentiles, to make the Jews jealous of them.
12 The sin of the Jews brought rich blessings to the world.

and their spiritual poverty brought rich blessings to the Gentiles. How much greater the blessings will be, then, when the complete number of Jews is included!

The Salvation of the Gentiles

¹³ I am speaking now to you Gentiles: as long as I am an apostle to the Gentiles I will take pride in my work. ¹⁴ Perhaps I can make the people of my own race jealous, and so be able to save some of them. ¹⁵ For when they were rejected, the world was made friends with God. What will it be, then, when they are accepted? It will be life for the dead!

¹⁶ If the first piece of bread is given to God, then the whole loaf is his also; and if the roots of a tree are offered to God, the branches are his also. ¹⁷ Some of the branches of the cultivated olive tree have been broken off, and the branch of a wild olive tree has been joined to it. You Gentiles are like that wild olive tree, and now you share the strength and rich life of the Jews. ¹⁸ Therefore you must not despise those who were broken off like branches.

How can you be proud? You are just a branch; you don't support the root — the root supports you.

¹⁹ But you will say, "Yes, but the branches were broken off to make room for me." ²⁰ This is true. They were broken off because they did not believe, while you remain in place because you believe. But do not have proud thoughts about it; instead, be afraid. ²¹ God did not spare the Jews, who are like natural branches; do you think he will spare you? ²² Here we see how kind and how severe

God is. He is severe toward those who have fallen, but kind to you — if you continue in his kindness; but if you do not, you too will be broken off. 23 And the Jews, if they abandon their unbelief, will be put back in the place where they were, for God is able to put them back again. 24 You Gentiles are like the branch of a wild olive tree that is broken off, and then, contrary to nature, is joined to the cultivated olive tree. The Jews are like this cultivated tree; and it will be much easier, then, for God to join these broken-off branches back to their own tree.

God's Mercy on All

25 There is a secret truth, my brothers, which I want you to know. It will keep you from thinking how wise you are. It is this: the stubbornness of the people of Israel is not permanent, but will last only until the complete number of Gentiles comes to God. 26 And this is how all Israel will be saved. As the scripture says:

"The Savior will come from Zion,
He will remove all wickedness from the
descendants of Jacob.
27 I will make this covenant with them,
When I take away their sins."

28 Because they reject the Good News, the Jews are God's enemies for the sake of you, the Gentiles. But because of God's choice, they are his friends for the sake of the patriarchs. 29 For God does not change his mind about whom he chooses and blesses. 30 As for you Gentiles, you disobeyed God in the past; but now you have received God's mercy because the Jews disobeyed. 31 In the same way, because of the mercy that you have received, the Jews now disobey God, in order that they also may now receive God's mercy. 32 For God has made all men prisoners of disobedience, that he might show mercy to them all.

Praise to God

33 How great are God's riches! How deep are his wisdom and knowledge! Who can explain his decisions? Who can understand his ways? 34 As the scripture says:

"Who knows the mind of the Lord?
Who is able to give him advice?
35 Who has ever given him anything,
To be paid back by him?"

[36] For all things were created by him, and all things exist through him and for him. To God be the glory for ever! Amen.

Life in God's Service

12 So then, my brothers, because of God's many mercies to us, I make this appeal to you: Offer yourselves as a living sacrifice to God, dedicated to his service and pleasing to him. This is the true worship that you should offer. [2] Do not conform outwardly to the standards of this world, but let God transform you inwardly by a complete change of your mind. Then you will be able to know the will of God — what is good, and is pleasing to him, and is perfect.

[3] For because of God's gracious gift to me, I say to all of you: Do not think of yourselves more highly than you should. Instead, be modest in your thinking, and each one of you judge himself according to the amount of faith that God has given him. [4] We have many parts in the one body, and all these parts have different functions. [5] In the same way, though we are many, we are one body in union with Christ and we are all joined to each other as different parts of one body. [6] So we are to use our different gifts in accordance with the grace that God has given us. If our gift is to preach God's message, we must do it according to the faith that we have. [7] If it is to serve, we must serve. If it is to teach, we must teach. [8] If it is to encourage others, we must do so. Whoever shares what he has with others, must do it generously; whoever has authority, must work hard; whoever shows kindness to others, must do it cheerfully.

[9] Love must be completely sincere. Hate what is evil, hold on to what is good. [10] Love one another warmly as brothers in Christ, and be eager to show respect for one another. [11] Work hard, and do not be lazy. Serve the Lord with a heart full of devotion. [12] Let your hope keep you joyful, be patient in your troubles, and pray at all times. [13] Share your belongings with your needy brothers, and open your homes to strangers.

[14] Ask God to bless those who persecute you; yes, ask him to bless, not to curse. [15] Rejoice with those who rejoice, weep with those who weep. [16] Show the same spirit

toward al! alike. Do not be proud, but accept humble duties. Do not think of yourselves as wise.

¹⁷ If someone does evil to you, do not pay him back with evil. Try to do what all men consider to be good. ¹⁸ Do everything possible, on your part, to live at peace with all men. ¹⁹ Never take revenge, my friends, but instead let

God's wrath do it. For the scripture says, "I will take revenge, I will pay back, says the Lord." ²⁰ Instead, as the scripture says: "If your enemy is hungry, feed him; if he is thirsty, give him to drink; for by doing this you will heap burning coals on his head." ²¹ Do not let evil defeat you; instead, conquer evil with good.

Duties toward the State Authorities

13 Everyone must obey the state authorities; for no authority exists without God's permission, and the existing authorities have been put there by God. ² Whoever opposes the existing authority opposes what God has ordered; and anyone who does so will bring judgment on himself. ³ For rulers are not to be feared by those who do good but by those who do evil. Would you like to be unafraid of the man in authority? Then do what is good, and he will praise you. ⁴ For he is God's servant working for your own good. But if you do evil, be afraid of him, for his power to punish is real. He is God's servant and carries out God's wrath on those who do evil. ⁵ For this reason you must obey the authorities — not just because of God's wrath, but also as a matter of conscience.

⁶ This is also the reason that you pay taxes; for the au-

thorities are working for God when they fulfil their duties.
⁷ Pay, then, what you owe them; pay them your personal
and property taxes, and show respect and honor for them
all.

Duties toward One Another

⁸ Be in debt to no one — the only debt you should have
is to love one another. Whoever loves his fellow man has
obeyed the Law. ⁹ The commandments, "Do not commit
adultery; do not murder; do not steal; do not covet" — all
these, and any others besides, are summed up in the one
command, "Love your neighbor as yourself." ¹⁰ Whoever
loves his neighbor will never do him wrong. To love, then,
is to obey the whole Law.

¹¹ You must do this, because you know what hour it is:
the time has come for you to wake up from your sleep.
For the moment when we will be saved is closer now than
it was when we first believed. ¹² The night is nearly over,
day is almost here. Let us stop doing the things that belong
to the dark. Let us take up the weapons for fighting in the
light. ¹³ Let us conduct ourselves properly, as people who
live in the light of day; no orgies or drunkenness, no immorality or indecency, no fighting or jealousy. ¹⁴ But take
up the weapons of the Lord Jesus Christ, and stop giving
attention to your sinful nature, to satisfy its desires.

Do Not Judge Your Brother

14 Accept among you the man who is weak in the
faith, but do not argue with him about his personal
opinions. ² One man's faith allows him to eat anything,
but the man who is weak in the faith eats only vegetables.
³ The man who will eat anything is not to despise the man
who doesn't; while the one who eats only vegetables is not
to pass judgment on the one who eats anything, for God
has accepted him. ⁴ Who are you to judge the servant of
someone else? It is his own Master who will decide whether
he succeeds or fails. And he will succeed, for the Lord is
able to make him succeed.

⁵ One man thinks that a certain day is more important
than the others, while another man thinks that all days are
the same. Each one should have his own mind firmly made
up. ⁶ He who thinks highly of a certain day does it in
honor of the Lord; he who eats anything does it in honor

of the Lord, for he gives thanks to God for the food. He who refuses to eat certain things does so in honor of the Lord, and he gives thanks to God. [7] For none of us lives for himself only, none of us dies for himself only; if we live, it is for the Lord that we live, [8] and if we die, it is for the Lord that we die. Whether we live or die, then, we belong to the Lord. [9] For Christ died and rose to life in order to be the Lord of the living and of the dead. [10] You, then — why do you pass judgment on your brother? And you — why do you despise your brother? All of us will stand before God, to be judged by him. [11] For the scripture says,

"As I live, says the Lord, everyone will kneel
    before me,
And everyone will declare that I am God."

[12] Every one of us, then, will have to give an account of himself to God.

Do Not Make Your Brother Fall

[13] So then, let us stop judging one another. Instead, this is what you should decide: not to do anything that would make your brother stumble, or fall into sin. [14] My union with the Lord Jesus makes me know for certain that nothing is unclean of itself; but if a man believes that something is unclean, then it becomes unclean for him. [15] If you hurt your brother because of something you eat, then you are no longer acting from love. Do not let the food that you eat ruin the man for whom Christ died! [16] Do not let what you regard as good acquire a bad name. [17] For God's Kingdom is not a matter of eating and drinking, but of the righteousness and peace and joy that the Holy Spirit gives. [18] And whoever serves Christ in this way wins God's pleasure and man's approval.

[19] So then, we must always aim at those things that bring peace, and that help strengthen one another. [20] Do not, because of food, destroy what God has done. All foods may be eaten, but it is wrong to eat anything that will cause someone else to fall into sin. [21] The right thing to do is to keep from eating meat, drinking wine, or doing anything else that will make your brother fall. [22] Keep what you believe about this matter, then, between yourself and God. Happy is the man who does not feel himself condemned when he does what he approves of! [23] But if he has doubts

about what he eats, God condemns him when he eats it, because his action is not based on faith. And anything that is not based on faith is sin.

Please Others, Not Yourselves

15 We who are strong in the faith ought to help the weak to carry their burdens. We should not please ourselves. ² Instead, each of us should please his brother for his own good, in order to build him up in the faith. ³ For Christ did not please himself. Instead, as the scripture says, "The insults spoken by those who insulted you have fallen on me." ⁴ For everything written in the Scriptures was written to teach us, in order that we might have hope through the patience and encouragement the Scriptures give us. ⁵ And may God, the source of patience and encouragement, enable you to have the same point of view among yourselves by following the example of Christ Jesus, ⁶ so that all of you together, with one voice, may praise the God and Father of our Lord Jesus Christ.

The Gospel to the Gentiles

⁷ Accept one another, then, for the glory of God, as Christ has accepted you. ⁸ For I tell you that Christ became a servant of the Jews to show that God is faithful, to make God's promises to the patriarchs come true, ⁹ and also to enable the Gentiles to praise God for his mercy. As the scripture says,

> "Therefore I will give thanks to you among the Gentiles,
> I will sing praises to your name."

¹⁰ Again it says,

> "Rejoice, Gentiles, with God's chosen people!"

[11] And again,

> "Praise the Lord, all Gentiles,
> Praise him greatly, all peoples!"

[12] And again, Isaiah says,

> "A descendant of Jesse will come;
> He will be raised to rule the Gentiles,
> And they will put their hope in him."

[13] May God, the source of hope, fill you with all joy and peace by means of your faith in him, so that your hope will continue to grow by the power of the Holy Spirit.

Paul's Reason for Writing So Boldly

[14] My brothers: I myself feel sure that you are full of goodness, that you are filled with all knowledge and are able to teach one another. [15] But in this letter I have been quite bold about certain subjects of which I have reminded you. I have been bold because of the privilege God has given me [16] of being a servant of Christ Jesus to work for the Gentiles. I serve as a priest in preaching the Good News from God, in order that the Gentiles may be an offering acceptable to God, dedicated to him by the Holy Spirit. [17] In union with Christ Jesus, then, I can be proud of my service for God. [18] I will be bold and speak only of what Christ has done through me to lead the Gentiles to obey God, by means of words and deeds, [19] by the power of signs and miracles, and by the power of the Spirit. And so, in traveling all the way from Jerusalem to Illyricum, I have proclaimed fully the Good News about Christ. [20] My ambition has always been to proclaim the Good News in places where Christ has not been heard of, so as not to build on the foundation laid by someone else. [21] As the scripture says,

> "Those who were not told about him will see,
> And those who have not heard will understand."

Paul's Plan to Visit Rome

[22] For this reason I have been prevented many times from coming to you. [23] But now that I have finished my work in these regions, and since I have been wanting for

so many years to come to see you, [24] I hope to do so now. I would like to see you on my way to Spain, and be helped by you to go there, after I have enjoyed visiting you for a while. [25] Right now, however, I am going to Jerusalem in the service of God's people there. [26] For the churches in Macedonia and Greece have freely decided to give an offering to help the poor among God's people in Jerusalem. [27] They themselves decided to do it. But, as a matter of fact, they have an obligation to help those poor; for the Jews shared their spiritual blessings with the Gentiles, and so the Gentiles ought to serve the Jews with their material blessings. [28] When I have finished this task, and have turned over to them the full amount of money that has been raised for them, I shall leave for Spain and visit you on my way there. [29] When I come to you, I know that I shall come with a full measure of the blessing of Christ.

[30] I urge you, brothers, by our Lord Jesus Christ and by the love that the Spirit gives: join me in praying fervently to God for me. [31] Pray that I may be kept safe from the unbelievers in Judea, and that my service in Jerusalem may be acceptable to God's people there. [32] And so I will come to you full of joy, if it is God's will, and enjoy a refreshing visit with you. [33] May God, our source of peace, be with all of you. Amen.

Personal Greetings

16 I recommend to you our sister Phoebe, who serves the church at Cenchreae. [2] Receive her in the Lord's name, as God's people should, and give her any help she may need from you; for she herself has been a good friend to many people and also to me.

[3] I send greetings to Prisca and Aquila, my fellow workers in the service of Christ Jesus, [4] who risked their lives for me. I am grateful to them — not only I, but all the Gentile churches as well. [5] Greetings also to the church that meets in their house.

Greetings to my dear friend Epaenetus, who was the first man in the province of Asia to believe in Christ. [6] Greetings to Mary, who has worked so hard for you. [7] Greetings to Andronicus and Junias, fellow Jews who were in prison with me; they are well known among the apostles, and they became Christians before I did.

⁸ My greetings to Ampliatus, my dear friend in the fellowship of the Lord. ⁹ Greetings to Urbanus, our fellow worker in Christ's service, and to Stachys, my dear friend. ¹⁰ Greetings to Apelles, whose loyalty to Christ has been proved. Greetings to those who belong to the family of Aristobulus. ¹¹ Greetings to Herodion, a fellow Jew, and to the Christian brothers in the family of Narcissus.

¹² My greetings to Tryphaena and Tryphosa, who work in the Lord's service, and to my dear friend Persis, who has done so much work for the Lord. ¹³ I send greetings to Rufus, that outstanding worker in the Lord's service, and to his mother, who has always treated me like a son. ¹⁴ My greetings to Asyncritus, Phlegon, Hermes, Patrobas, Hermas, and all the other Christian brothers with them. ¹⁵ Greetings to Philologus and Julia, to Nereus and his sister, to Olympas and to all of God's people who are with them.

¹⁶ Greet one another with a brotherly kiss. All the churches of Christ send you their greetings.

Final Instructions

¹⁷ I urge you, my brothers: watch out for those who cause divisions and upset people's faith, who go against the teaching which you have received; keep away from them. ¹⁸ For those who do such things are not serving Christ our Lord, but their own appetites. By their fine words and flattering speech they deceive the minds of innocent people. ¹⁹ Everyone has heard of your loyalty to the gospel, and for this reason I am happy about you. I want you to be wise about what is good, but innocent in what is evil. ²⁰ And God, our source of peace, will soon crush Satan under your feet.

The grace of our Lord Jesus be with you.

²¹ Timothy, my fellow worker, sends you his greetings; and so do Lucius, Jason, and Sosipater, fellow Jews.

²² I, Tertius, the writer of this letter, send you Christian greetings.

²³ My host Gaius, in whose house the church meets, sends you his greetings; Erastus, the city treasurer, and our brother Quartus, send you their greetings.

[²⁴ The grace of our Lord Jesus Christ be with you all. Amen.]

Concluding Prayer of Praise

²⁵ Let us give glory to God! He is able to make you stand firm in your faith, according to the Good News I preach, the message about Jesus Christ, and according to the revelation of the secret truth which was hidden for long ages in the past. ²⁶ Now, however, that truth has been brought out into the open through the writings of the prophets; and by the command of the eternal God it is made known to all nations, so that all may believe and obey.

²⁷ To the only God, who alone is all-wise, be the glory through Jesus Christ for ever! Amen.

PAUL'S FIRST LETTER TO THE CORINTHIANS

1 From Paul, who by the will of God was called to be an apostle of Christ Jesus, and from our brother Sosthenes —

² To the church of God which is in Corinth, to all who are called to be God's people, who belong to him in union with Christ Jesus, together with all people everywhere who call on the name of our Lord Jesus Christ, their Lord and ours:

³ May God our Father and the Lord Jesus Christ give you grace and peace.

Blessings in Christ

⁴ I always give thanks to my God for you, because of the grace he has given you through Christ Jesus. ⁵ For in union with Christ you have become rich in all things, including all speech and all knowledge. ⁶ The message about Christ has become so firmly fixed in you, ⁷ that you have not failed to receive a single blessing, as you wait for our Lord Jesus Christ to be revealed. ⁸ He will also keep you firm to the end, so that you will be found without fault in the Day of our Lord Jesus Christ. ⁹ God is to be trusted, the God who called you to have fellowship with his Son Jesus Christ, our Lord.

Divisions in the Church

¹⁰ I appeal to you, brothers, by the authority of our Lord Jesus Christ: agree, all of you, in what you say, so there will be no divisions among you; be completely united, with only one thought and one purpose. ¹¹ For some people from Chloe's family have told me quite plainly, my brothers, that there are quarrels among you. ¹² Let me put it this way: each one of you says something different. One says, "I am with Paul"; another, "I am with Apollos"; another, "I am with Peter"; and another, "I am with Christ." ¹³ Christ has been split up into groups! Was it Paul who died on the cross for you? Were you baptized as Paul's disciples?

¹⁴ I thank God that I did not baptize any of you except Crispus and Gaius. ¹⁵ No one can say, then, that you were baptized as my disciples. ¹⁶ (Oh yes, I also baptized Steph-

anas and his family; but I can't remember whether I baptized anyone else.) [17] Christ did not send me to baptize. He sent me to tell the Good News, and to tell it without using the language of men's wisdom, for that would rob Christ's death on the cross of all its power.

Christ the Power and the Wisdom of God

[18] For the message about Christ's death on the cross is nonsense to those who are being lost; but for us who are being saved, it is God's power. [19] For the scripture says,

> "I will destroy the wisdom of the wise,
> I will set aside the understanding of the scholars."

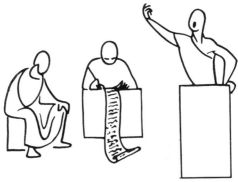

[20] So then, where does that leave the wise men? Or the scholars? Or the skillful debaters of this world? God has shown that this world's wisdom is foolishness!

[21] For God in his wisdom made it impossible for men to know him by means of their own wisdom. Instead, God decided to save those who believe, by means of the "foolish" message we preach. [22] Jews want miracles for proof, and Greeks look for wisdom. [23] As for us, we proclaim Christ on the cross, a message that is offensive to the Jews and nonsense to the Gentiles; [24] but for those whom God has called, both Jews and Gentiles, this message is Christ, who is the power of God and the wisdom of God. [25] For what seems to be God's foolishness is wiser than men's wisdom, and what seems to be God's weakness is stronger than men's strength.

[26] Now remember what you were, brothers, when God

called you. Few of you were wise, or powerful, or of high social status, from the human point of view. ²⁷ God purposely chose what the world considers nonsense in order to put wise men to shame, and what the world considers weak in order to put powerful men to shame. ²⁸ He chose what the world looks down on, and despises, and thinks is nothing, in order to destroy what the world thinks is important. ²⁹ This means that no single person can boast in God's presence. ³⁰ But God has brought you into union with Christ Jesus, and God has made Christ to be our wisdom; by him we are put right with God, we become God's own people, and are set free. ³¹ Therefore, as the scripture says, "Whoever wants to boast must boast of what the Lord has done."

The Message about Christ on the Cross

2 When I came to you, my brothers, to preach God's secret truth to you, I did not use long words and great learning. ² For I made up my mind to forget everything while I was with you except Jesus Christ, and especially

his death on the cross. ³ So when I came to you I was weak and trembled all over with fear, ⁴ and my speech and message were not delivered with skillful words of human wisdom, but with convincing proof of the power of

God's Spirit. [5] Your faith, then, does not rest on man's wisdom, but on God's power.

God's Wisdom

[6] Yet I do speak wisdom to those who are spiritually mature. But it is not the wisdom that belongs to this world, or to the powers that rule this world — powers which are losing their power. [7] The wisdom I speak is God's secret wisdom, hidden from men, which God had already chosen for our glory, even before the world was made. [8] None of the rulers of this world knew this wisdom. If they had known it, they would not have nailed the Lord of glory to the cross. [9] However, as the scripture says,

> "What no man ever saw or heard,
> What no man ever thought could happen,
> Is the very thing God prepared for those
> who love him."

[10] But it was to us that God made known his secret, by means of his Spirit. The Spirit searches everything, even the hidden depths of God's purposes. [11] As for a man, it is his own spirit within him that knows all about him; in the same way, only God's Spirit knows all about God. [12] We have not received this world's spirit; we have received the Spirit sent by God, that we may know all that God has given us.

[13] So then, we do not speak in words taught by human wisdom, but in words taught by the Spirit, as we explain spiritual truths to those who have the Spirit. [14] But the man who does not have the Spirit cannot receive the gifts that come from God's Spirit. He really does not understand them; they are nonsense to him, because their value can be judged only on a spiritual basis. [15] The man who has the Spirit is able to judge the value of everything, but no one is able to judge him. [16] As the scripture says,

> "Who knows the mind of the Lord?
> Who is able to give him advice?"

We, however, have the mind of Christ.

Servants of God

3 As a matter of fact, brothers, I could not talk to you as I talk to men who have the Spirit; I had to talk to you as men of this world, as children in the Christian

faith. ² I had to feed you milk, not solid food, because you were not ready for it. And even now you are not ready for it, ³ because you still live as men of this world. When there is jealousy among you, and you quarrel with one another, doesn't this prove that you are men of this world, living by this world's standards? ⁴ When one of you says, "I am with Paul," and another, "I am with Apollos" — aren't you acting like worldly men?

⁵ After all, who is Apollos? And who is Paul? We are simply God's servants, by whom you were led to believe. Each one of us does the work the Lord gave him to do:

⁶ I planted the seed, Apollos watered the plant, but it was God who made the plant grow. ⁷ The one who plants and the one who waters really do not matter. It is God who matters, for he makes the plant grow. ⁸ There is no difference between the man who plants and the man who waters; God will reward each one according to the work he has done. ⁹ For we are partners working together for God, and you are God's field.

You are also God's building. ¹⁰ Using the gift that God gave me, I did the work of an expert builder and laid the foundation, and another man is building upon it. But each one must be careful how he builds. ¹¹ For God has already placed Jesus Christ as the one and only foundation, and no other foundation can be laid. ¹² Some will use gold, or silver, or precious stones in building upon the foundation; others will use wood, or grass, or straw. ¹³ And the quality of each man's work will be seen when the Day of Christ exposes it. For that Day's fire will reveal every man's work: the fire will test it and show its real quality. [14] If what a man built on the foundation survives the fire, he will receive a reward. [15] But if any man's work is burnt up, then he will lose it; but he himself will be saved, as if he had escaped through the fire.

[16] Surely you know that you are God's temple, and that God's Spirit lives in you! [17] So if anyone destroys God's temple, God will destroy him. For God's temple is holy, and you yourselves are his temple.

[18] No one should fool himself. If anyone among you thinks that he is a wise man by this world's standards, he should become a fool, in order to be really wise. [19] For what this world considers to be wisdom is nonsense in God's sight. As the scripture says, "God traps the wise men in their cleverness"; [20] and another scripture says, "The Lord knows that the thoughts of the wise are worthless." [21] No one, then, should boast about what men can do. Actually everything belongs to you: [22] Paul, Apollos, and Peter; this world, life and death, the present and the future; all of these are yours, [23] and you belong to Christ, and Christ belongs to God.

Apostles of Christ

4 You should look on us as Christ's servants who have been put in charge of God's secret truths. [2] The one thing required of the man in charge is that he be faithful to his master. [3] Now, I am not at all concerned about being judged by you, or by any human standard; I don't even pass judgment on myself. [4] My conscience is clear, but that does not prove that I am really innocent. The Lord is the one who passes judgment on me. [5] So you should not pass judgment on anyone before the right time comes. Final judgment must wait until the Lord comes: he will bring to light the dark secrets and expose the hidden purposes of men's hearts. And then every man will receive from God the praise he deserves.

[6] For your sake, brothers, I have applied all this to Apollos and me. I have used us as an example, that you may learn what the saying means, "Observe the proper rules." None of you should be proud of one man and despise the other. [7] Who made you superior to the others?

Didn't God give you everything you have? Well, then, how can you brag, as if what you have were not a gift?

8 Already you have everything you need! Already you are rich! You have become kings, even though we are not! Well, I wish you really were kings, so that we could be kings together with you. 9 For it seems to me that God has given us apostles the very last place, like men condemned to die in public, as a spectacle for the whole world of angels and of men. 10 For Christ's sake we are fools; but you are wise in Christ! We are weak, but you are strong! We are despised, but you are honored! 11 To this very hour we go hungry and thirsty; we are clothed in rags; we are beaten; we wander from place to place; 12 we work hard to support ourselves. When we are cursed, we bless; when we are persecuted, we endure; 13 when we are insulted, we answer back with kind words. We are no more than this world's garbage; we are the scum of the earth to this very hour!

14 I write like this to you, not because I want to make you feel ashamed; I do it to instruct you as my own dear children. 15 For even if you have ten thousand teachers in your life in Christ, you have only one father. For in your life in Christ Jesus I have become your father, by bringing the Good News to you. 16 I beg you, then, follow my example. 17 For this purpose I am sending Timothy to you. He is my own dear and faithful son in the Lord. He will remind you of the principles which I follow in the new life in Christ Jesus, and which I teach in all the churches everywhere.

18 Some of you have become proud, thinking that I would not be coming to visit you. 19 If the Lord is willing, however, I will come to you soon, and then I will find out for myself what these proud ones can do, and not just what they can say! 20 For the Kingdom of God is not a matter of words, but of power. 21 Which do you prefer? Shall I come to you with a whip, or with a heart of love and gentleness?

Immorality in the Church

5 Now, it is actually being said that there is sexual immorality among you so terrible that not even the heathen would be guilty of it; for I am told that a man is living with his stepmother! 2 How then, can you be proud?

On the contrary, you should be filled with sadness, and the man who has done such a thing should be put out of your group! ³ As for me, even though I am far away from you in body, still I am there with you in spirit; and in the name of our Lord Jesus I have already passed judgment on the man who has done this terrible thing, as though I were there with you. ⁴ As you meet together, and I meet with you in my spirit, by the power of our Lord Jesus present with us, ⁵ you are to hand this man over to Satan for his body to be destroyed, so that his spirit may be saved in the Day of the Lord.

⁶ It is not right for you to be proud! You know the saying, "A little bit of yeast makes the whole batch of dough rise." ⁷ You must take out this old yeast of sin so that you will be entirely pure. Then you will be like a new batch of dough without any yeast, as indeed I know you actually are. For our Passover feast is ready, now that Christ, our Passover lamb, has been sacrificed. ⁸ Let us celebrate our feast, then, not with bread having the old yeast, the yeast of sin and immorality, but with the bread that has no yeast, the bread of purity and truth.

⁹ In the letter that I wrote you I told you not to associate with immoral people. ¹⁰ Now, I did not mean pagans who are immoral, or greedy, or lawbreakers, or who worship idols. To avoid them you would have to get out of the world completely! ¹¹ What I meant was that you should not associate with a man who calls himself a brother but is immoral, or greedy, or worships idols, or is a slanderer, or a drunkard, or a lawbreaker. Don't even sit down to eat with such a person.

¹²⁻¹³ After all, it is none of my business to judge outsiders. God will judge them. But should you not judge the members of your own fellowship? As the scripture says, "Take the evil man out of your group."

Lawsuits against Brothers

6 If one of you has a dispute with a brother, how dare he go before heathen judges, instead of letting God's people settle the matter? ² Don't you know that God's people will judge the world? Well, then, if you are to judge the world, aren't you capable of judging small matters? ³ Do you not know that we shall judge the angels? How much more, then, the things of this life! ⁴ If, then, such

matters come up, are you going to take them to be settled by people who have no standing in the church? [5] Shame on you! Surely there is at least one wise man in your fellowship who can settle a dispute between the brothers! [6] Instead, one brother goes to court against another, and lets unbelievers judge the case!

[7] The very fact that you have legal disputes among yourselves shows that you have failed completely. Would it not be better for you to be wronged? Would it not be better for you to be robbed? [8] Instead, you yourselves wrong one another, and rob one another, even your very brothers! [9] Surely you know that the wicked will not receive God's Kingdom. Do not fool yourselves: people who are immoral, or worship idols, or are adulterers, or homosexual perverts, [10] or who rob, or are greedy, or are drunkards, or who slander others, or are lawbreakers — none of these will receive God's Kingdom. [11] Some of you were like that. But you have been cleansed from sin; you have been dedicated to God; you have been put right with God through the name of the Lord Jesus Christ and by the Spirit of our God.

Use Your Bodies for God's Glory

[12] Someone will say, "I am allowed to do anything." Yes; but not everything is good for you. I could say, "I am allowed to do anything"; but I am not going to let anything make a slave of me. [13] Someone else will say, "Food is for the stomach, and the stomach is for food." Yes; but God will put an end to both. A man's body is not meant for immorality, but for the Lord; and the Lord is for the body. [14] God raised the Lord from death, and he will also raise us by his power.

[15] You know that your bodies are parts of the body of Christ. Shall I take a part of Christ's body and make it part of the body of a prostitute? Impossible! [16] Or perhaps you don't know that the man who joins his body to a prostitute becomes physically one with her? The scripture says quite plainly, "The two will become one body." [17] But he who joins himself to the Lord becomes spiritually one with him.

[18] Avoid immorality. Any other sin a man commits does not affect his body; but the man who commits immorality sins against his own body. [19] Don't you know that your

body is the temple of the Holy Spirit, who lives in you, the Spirit given you by God? You do not belong to yourselves but to God; [20] he bought you for a price. So use your bodies for God's glory.

Questions about Marriage

7 Now, to deal with the matters you wrote about.
A man does well not to marry. [2] But because there is so much immorality, every man should have his own wife, and every woman should have her own husband. [3] A man should fulfil his duty as a husband and a woman should fulfil her duty as a wife, and each should satisfy the other's needs. [4] The wife is not the master of her own body, but the husband is; in the same way the husband is not the master of his own body, but the wife is. [5] Do not deny yourselves to each other, unless you first agree to do so for a while, in order to spend your time in prayer; but then resume normal marital relations, so that your lack of self-control will not make you give in to Satan's temptation.

[6] I tell you this not as an order, but simply as a permission. [7] Actually I would prefer that all were as I am; but each one has the special gift that God has given him, one man this gift, another man that.

[8] Now, I say this to the unmarried and to the widows: it would be better for you to continue to live alone, as I do. [9] But if you cannot restrain your desires, go on and marry — it is better to marry than to burn with passion.

[10] For married people I have a command, not my own but the Lord's: a married woman must not leave her husband; [11] if she does, she must remain single or else be reconciled to her husband; and a husband must not divorce his wife.

[12] To the others I say (I, myself, not the Lord): if a Christian man has a wife who is an unbeliever and she agrees to go on living with him, he must not divorce her. [13] And if a Christian woman is married to a man who is an unbeliever, and he agrees to go on living with her, she must not divorce him. [14] For the unbelieving husband is made acceptable to God by being united to his wife, and the unbelieving wife is made acceptable to God by being united to her Christian husband. If this were not so, their children would be like pagan children; but as it is, they are acceptable to God. [15] However, if the one who is not

a believer wishes to leave the Christian partner, let him do so. In such cases the Christian partner, whether husband or wife, is free to choose; for God has called you to live in peace. [16] How can you be sure, Christian wife, that you will not save your husband? Or how can you be sure, Christian husband, that you will not save your wife?

Live as God Called You

[17] Each one should go on living according to the Lord's gift to him, and as he was when God called him. This is the rule I teach in all the churches. [18] If a circumcised man has accepted God's call, he should not try to remove the marks of circumcision; if an uncircumcised man has accepted God's call, he should not get circumcised. [19] Because being circumcised or not means nothing. What matters is to obey God's commandments. [20] Every man should remain as he was when he accepted God's call. [21] Were you a slave when God called you? Well, never mind; but if you do have a chance to become a free man, use it. [22] For a slave who has been called by the Lord is the Lord's free man; in the same way a free man who has been called by Christ is his slave. [23] God bought you for a price; so do not become men's slaves. [24] Brothers, each one should remain in fellowship with God as he was when he was called.

Questions about the Unmarried and the Widows

[25] Now, the matter about the unmarried: I do not have a command from the Lord, but I give my opinion as one who by the Lord's mercy is worthy of trust.

[26] Considering the present distress, I think it is better for a man to stay as he is. [27] Do you have a wife? Then don't try to get rid of her. Are you unmarried? Then don't look for a wife. [28] But if you do marry, you haven't committed a sin; and if an unmarried woman marries, she hasn't committed a sin. But I would rather spare you the everyday troubles that such people will have.

[29] This is what I mean, brothers: there is not much time left, and from now on married men should live as though they were not married; [30] those who weep, as though they were not sad; those who laugh, as though they were not happy; those who buy, as though they did not own what they bought; [31] those who deal in worldly goods, as though

they were not fully occupied with them. For this world, as it is now, will not last much longer.

³² I would like you to be free from worry. An unmarried man concerns himself with the Lord's work, because he is trying to please the Lord; ³³ but a married man concerns himself with worldly matters, because he wants to please his wife, ³⁴ and so he is pulled in two directions. An unmarried woman or a virgin concerns herself with the Lord's work, because she wants to be dedicated both in body and spirit; but a married woman concerns herself with worldly matters, because she wants to please her husband.

³⁵ I am saying this because I want to help you. I am not trying to put restrictions on you. Instead, I want you to do what is right and proper, and give yourselves completely to the Lord's service without any reservation.

³⁶ In the case of an engaged couple who have decided not to marry: if the man feels that he is not acting properly toward the girl; if his passions are too strong, and he feels that they ought to marry, then they should get married, as he wants to. There is no sin in this. ³⁷ But if a man, without being forced to do so, has firmly made up his mind not to marry; if he has his will under complete control, and has already decided in his own mind what to do — then he does well not to marry the girl. ³⁸ So the man who marries his girl does well, but the one who does not marry her will do even better.

³⁹ A married woman is not free as long as her husband lives; but if her husband dies, then she is free to be married to the man she wants; but it must be a Christian marriage. ⁴⁰ She will be happier, however, if she stays as she is. That is my opinion, and I think that I too have God's Spirit.

The Question about Food Offered to Idols

8 Now, the matter about food offered to idols.

It is true, of course, that "all of us have knowledge," as they say. Such knowledge, however, puffs a man up with pride; but love builds up. ² The person who thinks he knows something really doesn't know as he ought to know. ³ But the man who loves God is known by him.

⁴ So then, about eating the food offered to idols: we know that an idol stands for something that does not really

exist; we know that there is only the one God. ⁵ Even if there are so-called "gods," whether in heaven or on earth, and even though there are many of these "gods" and "lords," ⁶ yet there is for us only one God, the Father, who is the creator of all things, and for whom we live; and there is only one Lord, Jesus Christ, through whom all things were created, and through whom we live.

⁷ But not everyone knows this truth. Certain people are so used to idols that to this very day when they eat such food they still think of it as food that belongs to an idol; their conscience is weak and they feel they are defiled by the food. ⁸ Food, however, will not bring us any closer to God; we shall not lose anything if we do not eat, nor shall we gain anything if we do eat.

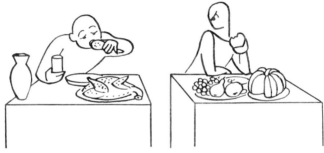

⁹ Be careful, however, and do not let your freedom of action make those who are weak in the faith fall into sin. ¹⁰ For if a man whose conscience is weak in this matter sees you, who have "knowledge," eating in the temple of an idol, will not this encourage him to eat food offered to idols? ¹¹ And so this weak man, your brother for whom Christ died, will perish because of your "knowledge"! ¹² And in this way you will be sinning against Christ by sinning against your brothers and wounding their weak conscience. ¹³ If food makes my brother sin, I myself will never eat meat again, so as not to make my brother fall into sin.

Rights and Duties of an Apostle

9 Am I not a free man? Am I not an apostle? Haven't I seen Jesus our Lord? And aren't you the result of my work for the Lord? ² Even if others do not accept me

as an apostle, surely you do! You yourselves, because of your life in the Lord, are proof of the fact that I am an apostle.

³ When people criticize me, this is how I defend myself: ⁴ Don't I have the right to be given food and drink for my work? ⁵ Don't I have the right to do what the other apostles do, and the Lord's brothers, and Peter, and take a Christian wife with me on my trips? ⁶ Or are Barnabas and I the only ones who have to work for our living? ⁷ Who ever heard of a soldier who paid his own expenses in the army? Or of a farmer who did not eat the grapes from his own vineyard? Or of a shepherd who did not use the milk from his own sheep?

⁸ I don't have to limit myself to these everyday examples, for the Law says the same thing. ⁹ We read in the Law of Moses, "Do not tie up the mouth of the ox when it treads out the grain." Now, is God concerned about oxen? ¹⁰ Or did he not really mean us when he said this? Of course this was written for us! The man who plows and the man who reaps should do their work in the hope of getting a share of the crop. ¹¹ We have sown spiritual seed among you. Is it too much if we reap material benefits from you? ¹² If others have the right to expect this from you, don't we have an even greater right?

But we haven't made use of this right. Instead, we have endured everything in order not to put any obstacle in the way of the Good News about Christ. ¹³ Surely you know that the men who work in the Temple get their food from the Temple, and that those who offer the sacrifices on the altar get a share of the sacrifices. ¹⁴ In the same way, the Lord has ordered that those who preach the gospel should get their living from it.

¹⁵ But I haven't made use of any of these rights, nor am I writing this now in order to claim such rights for myself. I would rather die first! Nobody is going to turn my rightful boast into empty words! ¹⁶ I have no right to boast just because I preach the gospel. After all, I am under orders to do so. And how terrible it would be for me if I did not preach the gospel! ¹⁷ If I did my work as a matter of free choice, then I could expect to be paid; but since I do it as a matter of duty, it means that I do it as a job given me to do. ¹⁸ What pay do I get, then? It is the privilege of preaching the Good News without charging

for it, without claiming my rights in my work for the gospel.

¹⁹ I am a free man, nobody's slave; but I make myself everybody's slave in order to win as many as possible. ²⁰ While working with the Jews, I live like a Jew in order to win them; and even though I myself am not subject to the Law of Moses, I live as though I were, when working with those who are, in order to win them. ²¹ In the same way, when with Gentiles I live like a Gentile, outside the Jewish Law, in order to win Gentiles. This does not mean that I don't obey God's law, for I am really under Christ's law. ²² Among the weak in faith I become weak like one of them, in order to win them. So I become all things to all men, that I may save some of them by any means possible.

²³ All this I do for the gospel's sake, in order to share in its blessings. ²⁴ Surely you know that in a race all the runners take part in it, but only one of them wins the prize.

Run, then, in such a way as to win the prize. ²⁵ Every athlete in training submits to strict discipline; he does so in order to be crowned with a wreath that will not last; but we do it for one that will last for ever. ²⁶ That is why I run straight for the finish line; that is why I am like a boxer, who does not waste his punches. ²⁷ I harden my body with blows and bring it under complete control, to keep from being rejected myself after having called others to the contest.

Warning against Idols

10 I want you to remember, brothers, what happened to our ancestors who followed Moses. They were all under the protection of the cloud, and all passed safely

through the Red Sea. ² In the cloud and in the sea they were all baptized as followers of Moses. ³ All ate the same spiritual bread, ⁴ and all drank the same spiritual drink; for they drank from that spiritual rock that went along with them; and that rock was Christ himself. ⁵ But even then God was not pleased with most of them, and so their dead bodies were scattered over the desert.

⁶ Now, all these things are examples for us, to warn us not to desire evil things, as they did, ⁷ nor to worship idols, as some of them did. As the scripture says, "The people sat down to eat and drink, and got up to dance." ⁸ We must not commit sexual immorality, as some of them did — and in one day twenty-three thousand of them fell dead. ⁹ We must not put the Lord to the test, as some of them did — and they were killed by the snakes. ¹⁰ You must not complain, as some of them did — and they were destroyed by the Angel of Death.

¹¹ All these things happened to them as examples for others, and they were written down as a warning for us. For we live at the time when the end is about to come.

¹² The one who thinks he is standing up better be careful that he does not fall. ¹³ Every temptation that has come your way is the kind that normally comes to people. For

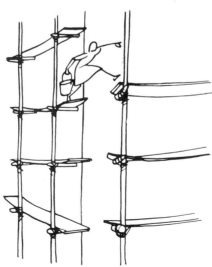

God keeps his promise, and he will not allow you to be tempted beyond your power to resist; but at the time you are tempted he will give you the strength to endure it, and so provide you with a way out.

14 So then, my dear friends, keep away from the worship of idols. 15 I speak to you as sensible people; judge for yourselves what I say. 16 The cup of blessing for which we give thanks to God: do we not share in the blood of Christ when we drink from this cup? And the bread we break: do we not share in the body of Christ when we eat this bread? 17 Because there is the one bread, all of us, though many, are one body; for we all share the same loaf.

18 Consider the Hebrew people: those who eat what is offered in sacrifice share in the altar's service to God. 19 What do I mean? That an idol or the food offered to it really amounts to anything? 20 No! What I am saying is that what is sacrificed on pagan altars is offered to demons, not to God. And I do not want you to be partners with demons. 21 You cannot drink from the Lord's cup and also from the cup of demons; you cannot eat at the Lord's table and also at the table of demons. 22 Or do we want to make the Lord jealous? Do you think that we are stronger than he?

23 "We are allowed to do anything," so they say. Yes, but not everything is good. "We are allowed to do anything" — but not everything is helpful. 24 No one should

be looking out for his own interests, but for the interests of others.

²⁵ You are free to eat anything sold in the meat market, without asking any questions because of conscience. ²⁶ For, as the scripture says, "The earth and everything in it belong to the Lord."

²⁷ If an unbeliever invites you to a meal and you decide to go, eat what is set before you without asking any questions because of conscience. ²⁸ But if someone tells you, "This is food that was offered to idols," then do not eat that food, for the sake of the one who told you so and for conscience' sake — ²⁹ that is, not your own conscience, but the other man's conscience.

"Well, then," someone asks, "why should my freedom to act be limited by another person's conscience? ³⁰ If I thank God for my food, why should anyone criticize me about food for which I give thanks?"

³¹ Well, whatever you do, whether you eat or drink, do it all for God's glory. ³² Live in such a way as to cause no trouble either to Jews, or Gentiles, or to the church of God. ³³ Just do as I do: I try to please everyone in all that I do, with no thought of my own good, but for the good of all, so they might be saved.

11 Imitate me, then, just as I imitate Christ.

Covering the Head in Worship

² I do praise you because you always remember me and follow the teachings that I have handed on to you. ³ But I want you to understand that Christ is supreme over every man, the husband is supreme over his wife, and God is supreme over Christ. ⁴ So a man who in public worship prays or speaks God's message with his head covered disgraces Christ. ⁵ And any woman who in public worship prays or speaks God's message with nothing on her head disgraces her husband; there is no difference between her and a woman whose head has been shaved. ⁶ If the woman does not cover her head, she might as well cut her hair. And since it is a shameful thing for a woman to shave her head or cut her hair, she should cover her head. ⁷ A man has no need to cover his head, because he reflects the image and glory of God. But woman reflects the glory of man; ⁸ for man was not created from woman, but woman from

man. ⁹ Nor was man created for woman's sake, but woman was created for man's sake. ¹⁰ On account of the angels, then, a woman should have a covering over her head to show that she is under her husband's authority. ¹¹ In our life in the Lord, however, woman is not independent of man, nor is man independent of woman. ¹² For as woman was made from man, in the same way man is born of woman; and all things come from God.

¹³ Judge for yourselves: is it proper for a woman to pray to God in public worship with nothing on her head? ¹⁴ Why, nature herself teaches you that long hair is a disgraceful thing for a man, ¹⁵ but is a woman's pride. Her long hair has been given her to serve as a covering. ¹⁶ But if anyone wants to argue about it, all I have to say is that neither we nor the churches of God have any other custom in worship.

The Lord's Supper

¹⁷ In the following instructions, however, I do not praise you; for your church meetings actually do more harm than good. ¹⁸ In the first place, I have been told that there are opposing groups in your church meetings; and this I believe is partly true. ¹⁹ (No doubt there must be divisions among you so that the ones who are in the right may be clearly seen.) ²⁰ When you meet together as a group, you do not come to eat the Lord's Supper. ²¹ For as you eat, each one goes ahead with his own meal, so that some are hungry while others get drunk. ²² Don't you have your own homes in which to eat and drink? Or would you rather despise the church of God and put to shame the people who are in need? What do you expect me to say to you about this? Should I praise you? Of course I do not praise you!

²³ For from the Lord I received the teaching that I passed on to you: that the Lord Jesus, on the night he was betrayed, took the bread, ²⁴ gave thanks to God, broke it, and said, "This is my body, which is for you. Do this in memory of me." ²⁵ In the same way, he took the cup after the supper and said, "This cup is God's new covenant, sealed with my blood. Whenever you drink it, do it in memory of me." ²⁶ For until the Lord comes, you proclaim his death whenever you eat this bread and drink from this cup.

²⁷ It follows, then, that if anyone eats the Lord's bread or drinks from his cup in an improper manner, he is guilty of sin against the Lord's body and blood. ²⁸ Everyone should examine himself, therefore, and with this attitude eat the bread and drink from the cup. ²⁹ For if he does not recognize the meaning of the Lord's body when he eats the bread and drinks from the cup, he brings judgment on himself as he eats and drinks. ³⁰ That is why many of you are sick and weak, and several have died. ³¹ If we would examine ourselves first, we would not come under God's judgment. ³² But we are judged and punished by the Lord, so that we shall not be condemned along with the world.

³³ So then, my brothers, when you gather together to eat the Lord's meal, wait for one another. ³⁴ And if anyone is hungry, he should eat at home, so that you will not come under God's judgment as you meet together. As for the other matters, I will settle them when I come.

Gifts from the Holy Spirit

12 Now, the matter about the gifts from the Holy Spirit.

I want you to know the truth about them, my brothers. ² You know that while you were still heathen you were controlled by dead idols, who always led you astray. ³ You must realize, then, that no one who is led by God's Spirit can say, "A curse on Jesus!", and no one can confess "Jesus is Lord," unless he is guided by the Holy Spirit.

⁴ There are different kinds of spiritual gifts, but the same Spirit gives them. ⁵ There are different ways of serving, but the same Lord is served. ⁶ There are different abilities to perform service, but the same God gives ability to everyone for all services. ⁷ Each one is given some proof of the Spirit's presence for the good of all. ⁸ The Spirit gives one man a message of wisdom, while to another man the same Spirit gives a message of knowledge. ⁹ One and the same Spirit gives faith to one man, while to another man he gives the power to heal. ¹⁰ The Spirit gives one man the power to work miracles; to another, the gift of speaking God's message; and to yet another, the ability to tell the difference between gifts that come from the Spirit and those that do not. To one man he gives the ability to speak with strange sounds; to

another, he gives the ability to explain what these sounds mean. ¹¹ But it is one and the same Spirit who does all this; he gives a different gift to each man, as he wishes.

One Body with Many Parts

¹² For Christ is like a single body, which has many parts; it is still one body, even though it is made up of different parts. ¹³ In the same way, all of us, Jews and Gentiles, slaves and free men, have been baptized into the one body by the same Spirit, and we have all been given the one Spirit to drink.

¹⁴ For the body itself is not made up of only one part, but of many parts. ¹⁵ If the foot were to say, "Because I am not a hand, I don't belong to the body," that would not make it stop being a part of the body. ¹⁶ And if the ear were to say, "Because I am not an eye, I don't belong to the body," that would not make it stop being a part of the body. ¹⁷ If the whole body were just an eye, how could it hear? And if it were only an ear, how could it smell? ¹⁸ As it is, however, God put every different part in the body just as he wished. ¹⁹ There would not be a body if it were all only one part! ²⁰ As it is, there are many parts, and one body.

²¹ So then, the eye cannot say to the hand, "I don't need you!" Nor can the head say to the feet, "Well, I don't need you!" ²² On the contrary; we cannot get along without the parts of the body that seem to be weaker, ²³ and those parts that we think aren't worth very much are the ones which we treat with greater care; while the parts of the body which don't look very nice receive special attention, ²⁴ which the more beautiful parts of our body do not need. God himself has put our bodies together in such a way as to give greater honor to those parts that lack it. ²⁵ And so there is no division in the body, but all its different parts have the same concern for one another. ²⁶ If one part of the body suffers, all the other parts suffer with it; if one part is praised, all the other parts share its happiness.

²⁷ All of you, then, are Christ's body, and each one is a part of it. ²⁸ In the church, then, God has put all in place: in the first place, apostles, in the second place, prophets, and in the third place, teachers; then those who perform miracles, followed by those who are given the power to heal, or to help others, or to direct them, or to speak with

strange sounds. ²⁹ They are not all apostles, or prophets, or teachers. Not all have the power to work miracles, ³⁰ or to heal diseases, or to speak with strange sounds, or to explain what these sounds mean. ³¹ Set your hearts, then, on the more important gifts.

Best of all, however, is the following way.

Love

13 I may be able to speak the languages of men and even of angels, but if I have not love, my speech is no more than a noisy gong or a clanging bell. ² I may have the gift of inspired preaching; I may have all knowledge and understand all secrets; I may have all the faith needed to move mountains — but if I have not love, I am nothing. ³ I may give away everything I have, and even give up my body to be burned — but if I have not love, it does me no good.

⁴ Love is patient and kind; love is not jealous, or conceited, or proud; ⁵ love is not ill-mannered, or selfish, or irritable; love does not keep a record of wrongs; ⁶ love is not happy with evil, but is happy with the truth. ⁷ Love never gives up: its faith, hope, and patience never fail.

⁸ Love is eternal. There are inspired messages, but they are temporary; there are gifts of speaking, but they will cease; there is knowledge, but it will pass. ⁹ For our gifts of knowledge and of inspired messages are only partial; ¹⁰ but when what is perfect comes, then what is partial will disappear.

¹¹ When I was a child, my speech, feelings, and thinking were all those of a child; now that I am a man, I have no more use for childish ways. ¹² What we see now is like

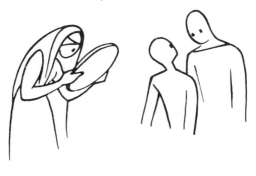

the dim image in a mirror; then we shall see face to face. What I know now is only partial; then it will be complete, as complete as God's knowledge of me.

¹³ Meanwhile these three remain: faith, hope, and love; and the greatest of these is love.

More about Gifts from the Spirit

14 It is love, then, that you should strive for. Set your hearts on spiritual gifts, especially the gift of speaking God's message. ² The one who speaks with strange sounds does not speak to men but to God, because no one understands him. He is speaking secret truths by the power of the Spirit. ³ But the one who speaks God's message speaks to men, and gives them help, encouragement, and comfort. ⁴ The man who speaks with strange sounds helps only himself, but the one who speaks God's message helps the whole church.

⁵ I would like for all of you to speak with strange sounds; but I would rather that all of you had the gift of speaking God's message. For the man who speaks God's message is of greater value than the one who speaks with strange sounds — unless there is someone present who can explain what he says, so that the whole church may be helped. ⁶ So when I come to you, brothers, what use will I be to you if I speak with strange sounds? Not a bit, unless I bring you some revelation from God, or some knowledge, or some inspired message or teaching.

⁷ Even such lifeless musical instruments as the flute and the harp — how will anyone know the tune that is being played unless the notes are sounded distinctly? ⁸ And if the man who plays the bugle does not sound a clear call, who will prepare for battle? ⁹ In the same way, how will anyone understand what you are talking about if your message by means of strange sounds is not clear? Your words will vanish in the air! ¹⁰ There are many different languages in the world, yet not a single one of them is without meaning. ¹¹ But if I do not know the language being spoken, the man who uses it will be a foreigner to me and I will be a foreigner to him. ¹² Since you are eager to have the gifts of the Spirit, above everything else you must try to make greater use of those which help build up the church.

¹³ The man who speaks with strange sounds, then, must

pray for the gift to explain what they mean. [14] For if I pray in this way, my spirit prays indeed, but my mind has no part in it. [15] What should I do, then? I will pray with my spirit, but I will pray also with my mind; I will sing with my spirit, but I will sing also with my mind. [16] When you give thanks to God in spirit only, how can an ordinary man taking part in the meeting say "Amen" to your prayer of thanksgiving? He has no way of knowing what you are saying. [17] Even if your prayer of thanks to God is quite good, the other man is not helped at all.

[18] I thank God that I speak with strange sounds much more than any of you. [19] But in church worship I would rather speak five words that can be understood, in order to teach others, than speak thousands of words with strange sounds.

[20] Do not be like children in your thinking, brothers; be children so far as evil is concerned, but be mature in your thinking. [21] In the Scriptures it is written:

"I will speak to this people, says the Lord:

I will speak through men of foreign languages,

And through the lips of foreigners.

But even then my people will not listen to me."

[22] So then, the gift of speaking with strange sounds is proof for unbelievers, not for believers, while the gift of speaking God's message is proof for believers, not for unbelievers.

[23] If, then, the whole church meets together and everyone starts speaking with strange sounds — if some ordinary people or unbelievers come in, won't they say that you are all crazy? [24] But if all speak God's message, when some unbeliever or ordinary person comes in he will be convinced of his sin by what he hears. He will be judged by all he hears, [25] his secret thoughts will be brought into the open, and he will bow down and worship God, confessing, "Truly God is here with you!"

Order in the Church

[26] What do I mean, my brothers? When you meet for worship, one man has a hymn, another a teaching, another a revelation from God, another a message with strange sounds, and still another the explanation of what it means. Everything must be of help to the church. [27] If someone is going to speak with strange sounds, two or three at the

most should speak, one after the other, and someone else must explain what is being said. ²⁸ If no person is there who can explain, then no one should speak out in the meeting, but only to himself and to God. ²⁹ Two or three who are given God's message should speak, while the others judge what they say. ³⁰ But if someone sitting in the meeting receives a message from God, the one who is speaking should stop. ³¹ All of you may speak God's message, one by one, so that all will learn and be encouraged. ³² The gift of speaking God's message should be under the speaker's control; ³³ for God has not called us to be disorderly, but peaceful.

As in all the churches of God's people, ³⁴ the women should keep quiet in the church meetings. They are not allowed to speak; as the Jewish Law says, they must not be in charge. ³⁵ If they want to find out about something, they should ask their husbands at home. It is a disgraceful thing for a woman to speak in a church meeting.

³⁶ Or could it be that the word of God came from you? Or are you the only ones to whom it came? ³⁷ If anyone supposes he is God's messenger or has a spiritual gift, he must realize that what I am writing you is the Lord's command. ³⁸ But if he does not pay attention to this, pay no attention to him.

³⁹ So then, my brothers, set your heart on speaking God's message, but do not forbid the speaking with strange sounds. ⁴⁰ Everything must be done in a proper and orderly way.

The Resurrection of Christ

15 And now I want to remind you, brothers, of the Good News which I preached to you, which you received, and on which your faith stands firm. ² That is the gospel, the message that I preached to you. You are saved by the gospel if you hold firmly to it — unless it was for nothing that you believed.

³ I passed on to you what I received, which is of the greatest importance: that Christ died for our sins, as written in the Scriptures; ⁴ that he was buried and raised to life on the third day, as written in the Scriptures; ⁵ that he appeared to Peter, and then to all twelve apostles. ⁶ Then he appeared to more than five hundred of his followers at once, most of whom are still alive, although

some have died. ⁷ Then he appeared to James, and then to all the apostles.

⁸ Last of all he appeared also to me — even though I am like one who was born in a most unusual way. ⁹ For I am the least of all the apostles — I do not even deserve to be called an apostle, because I persecuted God's church. ¹⁰ But by God's grace I am what I am, and the grace that he gave me was not without effect. On the contrary, I have worked harder than all the other apostles, although it was not really my own doing, but God's grace working with me. ¹¹ So then, whether it came from me or from them, this is what we all preach, this is what you believe.

Our Resurrection

¹² Now, since our message is that Christ has been raised from death, how can some of you say that the dead will not be raised to life? ¹³ If that is true, it means that Christ was not raised; ¹⁴ and if Christ has not been raised from death, then we have nothing to preach, and you have nothing to believe. ¹⁵ More than that, we are shown to be lying against God, because we said of him that he raised Christ from death — but he did not raise him, if it is true that the dead are not raised to life. ¹⁶ For if the dead are not raised, neither has Christ been raised. ¹⁷ And if Christ has not been raised, then your faith is a delusion and you are still lost in your sins. ¹⁸ It would also mean that the believers in Christ who have died are lost. ¹⁹ If our hope in Christ is good for this life only, and no more, then we deserve more pity than anyone else in all the world.

²⁰ But the truth is that Christ has been raised from death, as the guarantee that those who sleep in death will also be raised. ²¹ For just as death came by means of a man, in the same way the rising from death comes by means of a man. ²² For just as all men die because of their union to Adam, in the same way all will be raised to life because of their union to Christ. ²³ But each one in his proper order: Christ, the first of all; then those who belong to Christ, at the time of his coming. ²⁴ Then the end will come; Christ will overcome all spiritual rulers, authorities, and powers, and hand over the Kingdom to God the Father. ²⁵ For Christ must rule until God defeats all enemies and puts them under his feet. ²⁶ The last enemy to be defeated will be death. ²⁷ For the scripture says, "God put *all* things under his feet." It is clear, of course, that the words "all things" do not include God himself, who puts all things under Christ. ²⁸ But when all things have been placed under Christ's rule, then he himself, the Son, will place himself under God, who placed all under him; and God will rule completely over all.

²⁹ Now, what of those people who are baptized for the dead? What do they hope to accomplish? If it is true, as they claim, that the dead are not raised to life, why are they being baptized for the dead? ³⁰ And as for us — why would we run the risk of danger every hour? ³¹ Brothers, I face death every day! The pride I have in you in our life in Christ Jesus our Lord makes me declare this. ³² If, as it were, I have fought "wild beasts" here in Ephesus, simply from human motives, what have I gained? As the saying goes, "Let us eat and drink, for tomorrow we will die" — if the dead are not raised to life.

³³ Do not be fooled: "Bad companions ruin good character." ³⁴ Come back to your right senses and stop your sinful ways. I say this to your shame: some of you do not know God.

The Resurrection Body

³⁵ Someone will ask, "How can the dead be raised to life? What kind of body will they have?" ³⁶ You fool! When you plant a seed in the ground it does not sprout to life unless it dies. ³⁷ And what you plant in the ground is a bare seed, perhaps a grain of wheat, or of some other kind, not the full-bodied plant that will grow up. ³⁸ God

provides that seed with the body he wishes; he gives each seed its own proper body.

[39] And the flesh of living beings is not all the same kind of flesh: men have one kind of flesh, animals another, birds another, and fish another.

[40] And there are heavenly bodies and earthly bodies; there is a beauty that belongs to heavenly bodies, and another kind of beauty that belongs to earthly bodies. [41] The sun has its own beauty, the moon another beauty, and the stars a different beauty; and even among stars there are different kinds of beauty.

[42] This is how it will be when the dead are raised to life. When the body is buried it is mortal; when raised, it will be immortal. [43] When buried, it is ugly and weak; when raised, it will be beautiful and strong. [44] When buried, it is a physical body; when raised, it will be a spiritual body. There is, of course, a physical body, so there has to be a spiritual body. [45] For the scripture says: "The first man, Adam, was created a living being"; but the last Adam is the life-giving Spirit. [46] It is not the spiritual that comes first, but the physical, and then the spiritual. [47] The first Adam was made of the dust of the earth; the second Adam came from heaven. [48] Those who belong to the earth are like the one who was made of earth; those who are of heaven are like the one who came from heaven. [49] Just as we wear the likeness of the man made of earth, so we will wear the likeness of the Man from heaven.

[50] This is what I mean, brothers: what is made of flesh and blood cannot share in God's Kingdom, and what is mortal cannot possess immortality.

[51] Listen to this secret: we shall not all die, but in an instant we shall all be changed, [52] as quickly as the blinking of an eye, when the last trumpet sounds. For when it sounds, the dead will be raised immortal beings, and we shall all be changed. [53] For what is mortal must clothe itself with what is immortal; what will die must clothe itself with what cannot die. [54] So when what is mortal has been clothed with what is immortal, and when what will die has been clothed with what cannot die, then the scripture will come true: "Death is destroyed; victory is complete!"

[55] "Where, O Death, is your victory?
   Where, O Death, is your power to hurt?"

[56] Death gets its power to hurt from sin, and sin gets its power from the Law. [57] But thanks be to God who gives us the victory through our Lord Jesus Christ!

[58] So then, my dear brothers, stand firm and steady. Keep busy always in your work for the Lord, since you know that nothing you do in the Lord's service is ever without value.

The Offering for Fellow Believers

16 Now the matter about the money to be raised to help God's people in Judea: you must do what I told the churches in Galatia to do. [2] On the first day of every week each of you must put aside some money, in

proportion to what he has earned, and save it up, so there will be no need to collect money when I come. [3] After I come I shall send the men you have approved, with letters of introduction, to take your gift to Jerusalem. [4] If it seems worth while for me to go, then they will go along with me.

Paul's Plans

[5] I shall come to you after I have gone through Macedonia — for I am going through Macedonia. [6] I shall probably spend some time with you, perhaps the whole

winter, and then you can help me to continue my trip, wherever it is I shall go next. [7] For I do not want to see you just briefly in passing. I hope to spend quite a long time with you, if the Lord allows.

[8] But I plan to stay here in Ephesus until the day of Pentecost. [9] There is a real opportunity here for great and worth-while work, even though there are many opponents.

[10] If Timothy comes your way, however, be sure to make him feel welcome among you, for he is working for the Lord, just as I am. [11] No one is to look down on him, but you must help him continue his trip in peace, so that he will come back to me; for I am expecting him back with the brothers.

[12] Now, about brother Apollos: I have often encouraged him to visit you with the other brothers, but he is not completely convinced that he should go right now. When he gets the chance, however, he will go.

Final Words

[13] Be alert, stand firm in the faith, be brave, be strong. [14] Do all your work in love.

[15] You know about Stephanas and his family; they are the first Christian converts in Greece, and have given themselves to the service of God's people. I beg you, my brothers, [16] to follow the leadership of such people as these, and of anyone else who works and serves with them.

[17] I am happy over the coming of Stephanas, Fortunatus, and Achaicus; they have made up for your absence, [18] and have cheered me up, just as they cheered you up. Such men as these deserve notice.

[19] The churches in the province of Asia send you their greetings; Aquila and Priscilla and the church that meets in their house send warm Christian greetings. [20] All the brothers here send greetings.

Greet one another with a brotherly kiss.

[21] With my own hand I write this: *Greetings from Paul.*

[22] Whoever does not love the Lord — a curse on him! *Marana tha* — Our Lord, come!

[23] The grace of the Lord Jesus be with you.

[24] My love be with you all in Christ Jesus.

PAUL'S SECOND LETTER TO THE CORINTHIANS

1 From Paul, apostle of Christ Jesus by God's will, and from our brother Timothy —

To the church of God in Corinth, and to all God's people in all Greece:

² May God our Father and the Lord Jesus Christ give you grace and peace.

Paul Gives Thanks to God

³ Let us give thanks to the God and Father of our Lord Jesus Christ, the merciful Father, the God from whom all help comes! ⁴ He helps us in all our troubles, so that we are able to help those who have all kinds of troubles, using the same help that we ourselves have received from God. ⁵ Just as we have a share in Christ's many sufferings, so also through Christ we share in his great help. ⁶ If we suffer, it is for your help and salvation; if we are helped, then you too are helped and given the strength to endure with patience the same sufferings that we also endure. ⁷ So our hope in you is never shaken; we know that just as you share in our sufferings, you also share in the help we receive.

⁸ For we want to remind you, brothers, of the trouble we had in the province of Asia. The burdens laid upon us were so great and so heavy, that we gave up all hope of living. ⁹ We felt that the sentence of death had been passed against us. But this happened so that we should rely, not upon ourselves, but only on God, who raises the dead. ¹⁰ From such terrible dangers of death he saved us, and will save us; and we have placed our hope in him that

he will save us again, [11] as you help us by means of your prayers for us. So it will be that the many prayers for us will be answered, and God will bless us; and many will raise their voices to him in thanksgiving for us.

The Change in Paul's Plans

[12] This is the thing we are proud of: our conscience assures us that our lives in this world, and especially our relations with you, have been ruled by God-given frankness and sincerity, by the power of God's grace, and not by human wisdom. [13] For we write to you only what you can read and understand. And I hope you will come to understand completely [14] what you now understand only in part, that in the Day of the Lord Jesus you can be as proud of us as we shall be of you.

[15] I was so sure of all this that I made plans at first to visit you in order that you might be blessed twice. [16] For I planned to visit you on my way to Macedonia and again on my way back, to get help from you for my trip to Judea. [17] In planning this did I appear fickle? When I make my plans, do I make them from selfish motives, ready to say "Yes, yes" and "No, no" at the same time? [18] As God is true, my promise to you was not a "Yes" and a "No." [19] For Jesus Christ, the Son of God, who was preached among you by Silas, Timothy, and myself, is not one who is "Yes" and "No." On the contrary, he is God's "Yes"; [20] for it is he who is the "Yes" to all of God's promises. This is the reason that through Jesus Christ our "Amen" is said, to the glory of God. [21] For it is God himself who makes us sure, with you, of our life in Christ; it is God himself who has set us apart, [22] who placed his mark of ownership upon us, and who gave the Holy Spirit in our hearts as the guarantee of all that he has for us.

[23] I call upon God as my witness — he knows my heart! It was in order to spare you that I decided not to go to Corinth. [24] We are not trying to dictate to you what you must believe, for you stand firm in the faith. Instead, we are working with you for your own happiness.

2 So I made up my mind about this: I would not come to you again to make you sad. [2] For if I were to make you sad, who would be left to cheer me up? Only the very persons I had saddened! [3] That is why I wrote that letter to you — I did not want to come to you and be made sad

by the very people who should make me glad. For I am convinced that when I am happy, then you too are happy. [4] I wrote you with a greatly troubled and distressed heart, and with many tears, not to make you sad, but to make you realize how much I love you all.

Forgiveness for the Offender

[5] Now, if anyone has made somebody sad, he has not done it to me but to you; or to some of you, at least, since I do not want to be too hard on you. [6] It is enough for this person that he has been punished in this way by most of you. [7] Now, however, you should forgive him and encourage him, to keep him from becoming so sad as to give up completely. [8] Let him know, then, I beg you, that you really do love him. [9] For this is the reason I wrote you that letter: I wanted to find out how well you had stood the test, and whether you are always ready to obey my instructions. [10] When you forgive someone for what he has done, I forgive him too. For when I forgive — if, indeed, I have forgiven any wrong — I do it because of you, in Christ's presence, [11] in order to keep Satan from getting the upper hand over us; for we know what his plans are.

Paul's Anxiety in Troas

[12] When I arrived in Troas to preach the Good News about Christ, I found that the Lord had opened the way for the work there. [13] But I was deeply worried because I could not find our brother Titus. So I said good-bye to the people there, and went on to Macedonia.

Victory through Christ

[14] But thanks be to God! For in union with Christ we are always led by God as prisoners in Christ's victory procession. Like a sweet smell that spreads everywhere, God uses us to make Christ known to all men. [15] For we are like the sweet smell of the incense that Christ burns to God which goes out to those who are being saved and to those who are being lost. [16] For those who are being lost, it is a deadly stench that kills; for those who are being saved, it is a fragrance that brings life. Who, then, is capable for such a task? [17] We are not like so many others, who handle God's message as if it were cheap merchandise;

but because God has sent us, we speak with sincerity in his presence, as servants of Christ.

Servants of the New Covenant

3 Does this sound as if we were again boasting about ourselves? Could it be that, like some other people, we need letters of recommendation to you or from you? [2] You yourselves are the letter we have, written on our hearts, for everyone to know and read. [3] It is clear that Christ himself wrote this letter and sent it by us. It is written not with ink on stone tablets, but on human hearts, with the Spirit of the living God.

[4] We say this because we have confidence in God through Christ. [5] For there is nothing in us that allows us to claim that we are capable of doing this work. The capacity we have comes from God: [6] for it is he who made us capable of serving the new covenant, which consists not

of a written law, but of the Spirit. The written law brings death, but the Spirit gives life.

[7] The Law was carved in letters on stone tablets, and God's glory appeared when it was given. Even though it faded away, the brightness on Moses' face was so strong that the people of Israel could not keep their eyes fixed on him. If the Law, whose service was to bring death, came with such glory, [8] how much greater is the glory that belongs to the service of the Spirit! [9] The service by which men are condemned was glorious; how much more glorious is the service by which men are declared innocent! [10] We may say that, because of the far brighter glory now, the glory that was so bright in the past is gone. [11] For if

there was glory in that which lasted for a while, how much more glory is there in that which lasts for ever!

¹² Because we have this hope, we are very bold. ¹³ We are not like Moses, who had to put a veil over his face, so that the people of Israel might not see the brightness fade and disappear. ¹⁴ Their minds, indeed, were closed; and to this very day their minds are covered with the same veil, as they read the books of the old covenant. The veil is removed only when a man is joined to Christ. ¹⁵ Even today, whenever they read the Law of Moses, the veil still covers their minds. ¹⁶ But it is removed, as the scripture says: "Moses' veil was removed when he turned to the Lord." ¹⁷ Now, "the Lord" in this passage is the Spirit; and where the Spirit of the Lord is present, there is freedom. ¹⁸ All of us, then, reflect the glory of the Lord with uncovered faces; and that same glory, coming from the Lord who is the Spirit, transforms us into his very likeness, in an ever greater degree of glory.

Spiritual Treasure in Clay Pots

4 God, in his mercy, has given us this service, and so we do not become discouraged. ² We put aside all secret and shameful deeds; we do not act with deceit, nor do we falsify the word of God. In the full light of truth, we live in God's sight and try to commend ourselves to everyone's good conscience. ³ For if the gospel we preach is hidden, it is hidden only to those who are being lost. ⁴ They do not believe because their minds have been kept in the dark by the evil god of this world. He keeps them from seeing the light shining on them, the light that comes from the Good News about the glory of Christ, who is the exact likeness of God. ⁵ For it is not ourselves that we preach: we preach Jesus Christ as Lord, and ourselves as your servants for Jesus' sake. ⁶ The God who said, "Out of darkness the light shall shine!" is the same God who made his light shine in our hearts, to bring us the light of the knowledge of God's glory, shining in the face of Christ.

⁷ Yet we who have this spiritual treasure are like common clay pots, to show that the supreme power belongs to God, not to us. ⁸ We are often troubled, but not crushed; sometimes in doubt, but never in despair; ⁹ there are many enemies, but we are never without a friend; and though badly hurt at times, we are not destroyed. ¹⁰ At all

times we carry in our mortal bodies the death of Jesus, so that his life also may be seen in our bodies. [11] Throughout our lives we are always in danger of death for Jesus' sake, in order that his life may be seen in this mortal body of ours. [12] This means that death is at work in us; but life is at work in you.

[13] The scripture says, "I spoke because I believed." In the same spirit of faith, we also speak because we believe. [14] For we know that God, who raised the Lord Jesus to life, will also raise us up with Jesus and bring us, together with you, into his presence. [15] All this is for your sake; and as God's grace reaches more and more people, they will offer more prayers of thanksgiving, to the glory of God.

Living by Faith

[16] For this reason we never become discouraged. Even though our physical being is gradually decaying, yet our spiritual being is renewed day after day. [17] And this small and temporary trouble we suffer will bring us a tremendous and eternal glory, much greater than the trouble. [18] For we fix our attention, not on things that are seen, but on things that are unseen. What can be seen lasts only for a time; but what cannot be seen lasts for ever.

5 For we know that when this tent we live in — our body here on earth — is torn down, God will have a house in heaven for us to live in, a home he himself made, which will last for ever. [2] And now we sigh, so great is our desire to have our home which is in heaven put on over us; [3] for by being clothed with it we shall not be found without a body. [4] While we live in this earthly tent we groan with a feeling of oppression; it is not that we want to get rid of our earthly body, but that we want to have the heavenly one put on over us, so that what is mortal will be swallowed up by life. [5] God is the one who has prepared us for this change, and he gave us his Spirit as the guarantee of all that he has for us.

[6] So we are always full of courage. We know that as long as we are at home in this body we are away from the Lord's home. [7] For our life is a matter of faith, not of sight. [8] We are full of courage, and would much prefer to leave our home in this body and be at home with the Lord. [9] More than anything else, however, we want to

please him, whether in our home here or there. ¹⁰ For all of us must appear before Christ, to be judged by him, so that each one may receive what he deserves, according to what he has done, good or bad, in his bodily life.

Friendship with God through Christ

¹¹ We know what it means to fear the Lord, and so we try to persuade men. God knows us completely, and I hope that in your hearts you know me as well. ¹² We are not trying to recommend ourselves to you again; rather, we are trying to give you a good reason to be proud of us, so that you will be able to answer those who boast about a man's appearance, and not about his character. ¹³ Are we really insane? It is for God's sake. Or are we sane? It is for your sake. ¹⁴ For we are ruled by Christ's love for us, now that we recognize that one man died for all men, which means that all men take part in his death. ¹⁵ He died for all men so that those who live should no longer live for themselves, but only for him who died and was raised to life for their sake.

¹⁶ No longer, then, do we judge anyone by human standards. Even if at one time we judged Christ according to human standards, we no longer do so. ¹⁷ When anyone is joined to Christ he is a new being: the old is gone, the new has come. ¹⁸ All this is done by God, who through Christ changed us from enemies into his friends, and gave us the task of making others his friends also. ¹⁹ Our message is that God was making friends of all men through Christ. God did not keep an account of their sins against them, and he has given us the message of how he makes them his friends.

²⁰ Here we are, then, speaking for Christ, as though God himself were appealing to you through us: on Christ's behalf, we beg you, let God change you from enemies into friends! ²¹ Christ was without sin, but God made him share our sin in order that we, in union with him, might share the righteousness of God.

6 In our work together with God, then, we beg of you: you have received God's grace, and you must not let it be wasted. ² Hear what God says:

"I heard you in the hour of my favor,
I helped you in the day of salvation."

Listen! This is the hour to receive God's favor, today is

the day to be saved!

³ We do not want anyone to find fault with our work, so we try not to put obstacles in anyone's way. ⁴ Instead, in everything we do we show that we are God's servants, by enduring troubles, hardships, and difficulties with great patience. ⁵ We have been beaten, jailed, and mobbed; we have been overworked and have gone without sleep or food. ⁶ By our purity, knowledge, patience, and kindness we have shown ourselves to be God's servants; by the Holy Spirit, by our true love, ⁷ by our message of truth, and by the power of God. We have righteousness as our weapon, both to attack and to defend ourselves. ⁸ We are honored and disgraced; we are insulted and praised. We are treated as liars, yet we speak the truth; ⁹ as unknown, yet we are known by all; as though we were dead, but, as you see, we live on. Although punished, we are not killed; ¹⁰ although saddened, we are always glad; we seem poor, but we make many people rich; we seem to have nothing, yet we really possess everything.

¹¹ Dear friends in Corinth! We have spoken frankly to you, we have opened wide our hearts. ¹² We have not closed our hearts to you; it is you who have closed your hearts to us. ¹³ I speak now as though you were my children: show us the same feelings that we have for you. Open wide your hearts!

Warning against Pagan Influences

¹⁴ Do not try to work together as equals with unbe-

lievers, for it cannot be done. How can right and wrong be partners? How can light and darkness live together? 15 How can Christ and the Devil agree? What does a believer have in common with an unbeliever? 16 How can God's temple come to terms with pagan idols? For we are the temple of the living God! As God himself has said:

"I will make my home with them and live
among them,
I will be their God, and they shall be my
people."

17 And so the Lord says:

"You must leave them, and separate your-
selves from them.
Have nothing to do with what is unclean,
And I will accept you.
18 I will be your father,
And you shall be my sons and daughters,
Says the Lord Almighty."

7 All these promises are made to us, my dear friends! Let us, therefore, purify ourselves from everything that makes body or soul unclean, and let us seek to be completely holy, by living in the fear of God.

Paul's Joy

2 Make room for us in your hearts. We have done wrong to no one, we have ruined no one, nor tried to take advantage of anyone. 3 I do not say this to condemn you; for, as I have said before, you are so dear to us that we are together always, whether we live or die. 4 I am so sure of

you, I take such pride in you! In all our troubles I am still full of courage, I am running over with joy.

5 Even after we arrived in Macedonia we did not have any rest. There were troubles everywhere, quarrels with others, fears in our hearts. 6 But God, who encourages the downhearted, encouraged us with the coming of Titus. 7 It was not only his coming, but also his report of how you encouraged him. He told us how much you want to see me, how sorry you are, how ready you are to defend me; and so I am even happier now.

8 For even if that letter of mine made you sad, I am not sorry I wrote it. I could have been sorry about it when I saw that the letter made you sad for a while. 9 But now I am happy — not because I made you sad, but because your sadness made you change your ways. That sadness was used by God, and so we caused you no harm. 10 For the sadness that is used by God brings a change of heart that leads to salvation — and there is no regret in that! But worldly sadness causes death. 11 See what God did with this sadness of yours: how earnest it has made you, how eager to prove your innocence! Such indignation, such alarm, such feelings, such devotion, such readiness to punish wrongdoing! You have shown yourselves to be without fault in the whole matter.

12 So, even though I wrote that letter, I did it, not because of the one who did wrong, or the one who was wronged. Instead, I wrote it to make plain to you, in God's sight, how deep is your devotion to us. 13 This is why we were encouraged.

Not only were we encouraged; how happy Titus made us with his happiness over the way in which all of you helped to cheer him up. 14 I did boast of you to him, and you have not disappointed me. We have always spoken the truth to you. In the same way, the boast we made to Titus has proved true. 15 And so his love for you grows stronger, as he remembers how all of you were ready to obey, how you welcomed him with fear and trembling. 16 How happy I am that I can depend on you completely!

Christian Giving

8 We want you to know, brothers, what God's grace has done in the churches in Macedonia. 2 They have been severely tested by the troubles they went through; but

their joy was so great that they were extremely generous in their giving, even though they were very poor. ³ I assure you, they gave as much as they were able, and even more than that; of their own free will ⁴ they begged us and insisted on the privilege of having a part in helping God's people in Judea. ⁵ It was more than we could have hoped for! First they gave themselves to the Lord; and then, by God's will, they gave themselves to us as well. ⁶ So we urged Titus, who began this work, to continue it and help you complete this special service of love. ⁷ You are so rich in all you have: in faith, speech, and knowledge, in your eagerness to help, and in your love for us. And so we want you to be generous also in this service of love.

⁸ I am not laying down any rules. But by showing how eager others are to help, I am trying to find out how real your own love is. ⁹ For you know the grace of our Lord Jesus Christ: rich as he was, he made himself poor for your sake, in order to make you rich by means of his poverty.

¹⁰ This is my opinion on the matter: it is better for you to finish now what you began last year. You were the first, not only to act, but also to be willing to act. ¹¹ On with it, then, and finish the job! Be as eager to finish it as you were to plan it, and do it with what you have. ¹² For if you are eager to give, God will accept your gift on the basis of what you have to give, not on what you don't have.

¹³⁻¹⁴ I am not trying to relieve others by putting a burden on you; but since you have plenty at this time, it is only fair that you should help those who are in need. Then, when you are in need and they have plenty, they will help you. In this way both are treated equally. ¹⁵ As the scripture says,

> "The man who gathered much
> Did not have too much,
> And the man who gathered little
> Did not have too little."

¹⁶ How we thank God for making Titus as eager as we are to help you! ¹⁷ Not only did he welcome our request; he was so eager to help that of his own free will he decided to go to you. ¹⁸ With him we are sending the brother who is highly respected in all the churches for his work in preaching the gospel. ¹⁹ And besides that, he has been

chosen and appointed by the churches to travel with us as we carry out this service of love for the Lord's glory, and to show that we want to help.

20 We are being careful not to stir up any complaints about the way we handle this generous gift. 21 Our purpose is to do what is right, not only in the sight of the Lord, but also in the sight of men.

22 So we are sending our brother with them; we have tested him many times, and found him always very eager to help. And now that he has so much confidence in you, he is all the more eager to help. 23 As for Titus, he is my partner who works with me to help you; as for the other brothers who are going with him, they represent the churches and bring glory to Christ. 24 Show your love to them, that all the churches will be sure of it and know that we are right in boasting of you.

Help for Fellow Christians

9 There is really no need for me to write you about the help being sent to God's people in Judea. 2 I know that you are willing to help, and I have boasted of you to the people in Macedonia. "The brothers in Greece," I said, "have been ready to help since last year." Your eagerness has stirred up most of them. 3 Now I am sending these brothers, so that our boasting of you in this matter may not turn out to be empty words; but, just as I said, you will be ready with your help. 4 Or else, if the people from Macedonia should come with me and find out that you are not ready, how ashamed we would be — not to speak of your shame — for feeling so sure of you! 5 So I thought it necessary to urge these brothers to go to you ahead of me and get ready in advance the gift you promised to make. Then it will be ready when I arrive, and it will show that you give because you want to, not because you have to.

6 Remember this: the man who plants few seeds will have a small crop; the one who plants many seeds will have a large crop. 7 Each one should give, then, as he has decided, not with regret or out of a sense of duty; for God loves the one who gives gladly. 8 And God is able to give you more than you need, so that you will always have all you need for yourselves and more than enough for every good cause. 9 As the scripture says,

"He gives generously to the poor,
His kindness lasts for ever."

[10] And God, who supplies seed for the sower and bread to eat, will also supply you with all the seed you need and make it grow, to produce a rich harvest from your generosity. [11] He will always make you rich enough to be generous at all times, so that many will thank God for your gifts through us. [12] For this service you perform not only meets the needs of God's people, but also produces an outpouring of grateful thanks to God. [13] And because of the proof which this service of yours brings, many will give glory to God for your loyalty to the gospel of Christ, which you profess, and for your generosity in sharing with them and all others. [14] And so they will pray for you with great affection for you because of the extraordinary grace God has shown you. [15] Let us thank God for his priceless gift!

Paul Defends His Ministry

10 I, Paul, make a personal appeal to you — I who am said to be meek and mild when I am with you, but bold toward you when I am away from you. I beg of you, by the gentleness and kindness of Christ: [2] Do not force me to be bold with you when I come; for I am sure I can be bold with those who say that we act from worldly motives. [3] It is true that we live in the world; but we do not fight from worldly motives. [4] The weapons we use in our fight are not the world's weapons, but God's powerful weapons, with which to destroy strongholds. We destroy false arguments; [5] we pull down every proud obstacle that is raised against the knowledge of God; we take every thought captive and make it obey Christ. [6] And after you have proved your complete loyalty, we will be ready to punish any act of disloyalty.

[7] You are looking at things as they are on the outside. Is there someone there who reckons himself to be Christ's man? Well, let him think again about himself, for we are Christ's men just as much as he is. [8] For I am not ashamed, even if I have boasted somewhat too much of the authority that the Lord has given us — authority to build you up, that is, not to tear you down. [9] I do not want it to appear that I am trying to frighten you with my letters. [10] Someone will say, "Paul's letters are severe and

strong, but when he is with us in person he is weak, and his words are nothing!" ¹¹ Such a person must understand that there is no difference between what we write in our letters when we are away, and what we will do when we are there with you.

¹² Of course we would not dare classify ourselves or compare ourselves with some of those who rate themselves so highly. How stupid they are! They make up their own standards to measure themselves by, and judge themselves by their own standards! ¹³ As for us, however, our boasting will not go beyond certain limits; it will stay within the limits of the work which God has set for us, which includes our work among you. ¹⁴ And since you are within those

limits, we did not go beyond them when we came to you, bringing the Good News about Christ. ¹⁵ So we do not boast of the work that others have done beyond the limits God set for us. Instead, we hope that your faith may grow, and that we may be able to do a much greater work among you, always within the limits that God has set. ¹⁶ Then we can preach the Good News in other countries beyond you, and shall not have to boast of work already done in another man's field.

¹⁷ But as the scripture says, "Whoever wants to boast, must boast of what the Lord has done." ¹⁸ Because a man is really approved when the Lord thinks well of him, not when he thinks well of himself.

Paul and the False Apostles

11 I wish you would tolerate me, even when I am a bit foolish. Please do! ² I am jealous for you just as God is; for you are like a pure virgin whom I have promised in marriage to one man only, who is Christ. ³ I am afraid that your minds will be corrupted and that you will abandon your full and pure devotion to Christ — in the same way that Eve was deceived by the snake's clever lies. ⁴ For you gladly tolerate anyone who comes to you and preaches a different Jesus, not the one we preached; and you accept a spirit and a gospel completely different from the Spirit and the gospel you received from us!

⁵ I do not think that I am the least bit inferior to those very special "apostles" of yours! ⁶ Perhaps I am an amateur in speaking, but certainly not in knowledge; we have made this clear to you at all times and in all conditions.

⁷ I did not charge you a thing when I preached the Good News of God to you; I humbled myself in order to make you great. Was that wrong of me? ⁸ While I was working among you I was paid by other churches. I was robbing them, so to speak, to help you. ⁹ And during the time I was with you I did not bother you for help when I needed money; for the brothers who came from Macedonia brought me everything I needed. As in the past, so in the future: I will never be a burden to you! ¹⁰ By Christ's truth in me, I promise that this boast of mine will not be silenced anywhere in all of Greece. ¹¹ Why do I say this? Because I don't love you? God knows I do!

¹² I will go on doing what I am doing now, in order to keep those other "apostles" from having any reason for boasting and saying that they work in the same way that we do. ¹³ Those men are not true apostles — they are false apostles, who lie about their work and change themselves to look like real apostles of Christ. ¹⁴ Well, no wonder! Even Satan can change himself to look like an angel of light! ¹⁵ So it is no great thing if his servants change themselves to look like servants of right. In the end they will get exactly what they deserve for the things they do.

Paul's Sufferings as an Apostle

¹⁶ I repeat: no one should think that I am a fool. But if you do, at least accept me as a fool, just so I will have a little to boast of. ¹⁷ Of course what I am saying now is not what the Lord would have me say; in this matter of boasting I am really talking like a fool. ¹⁸ But since there are so many who boast for merely human reasons, I will do the same. ¹⁹ You yourselves are so wise, and so you gladly tolerate fools! ²⁰ You will tolerate anyone who orders you around, or takes advantage of you, or traps you, or looks down on you, or slaps you in the face. ²¹ I am ashamed to admit it: we were too timid to do that!

But if anyone dares to boast of something — I am talking like a fool — I will be just as daring. ²² Are they Hebrews? So am I. Are they Israelites? So am I. Are they Abraham's descendants? So am I. ²³ Are they Christ's servants? I sound like a madman — but I am a better servant than they are! I have worked much harder, I have been in prison more times, I have been whipped much more, and I have been near death more often. ²⁴ Five times I was given the thirty-nine lashes by the Jews; ²⁵ three times I was whipped by the Romans, and once I was stoned; I have been in three shipwrecks, and once I spent twenty-four hours in the water. ²⁶ In my many travels I have been in danger from floods and from robbers, in danger from fellow Jews and from Gentiles; there have been dangers in the cities, dangers in the wilds, dangers on the high seas, and dangers from false friends. ²⁷ There has been work and toil; often I have gone without sleep; I have been hungry and thirsty; I have often been without enough food, shelter, or clothing. ²⁸ And, not to mention other things, every day I am under the pressure of my concern for all the churches. ²⁹ When someone is weak, then I feel weak too; when someone falls into sin, I am filled with distress.

³⁰ If I must boast, I will boast of things that show how weak I am. ³¹ The God and Father of the Lord Jesus — blessed be his name for ever! — knows that I am not lying. ³² When I was in Damascus, the governor under King Aretas placed guards at the city gates to arrest me. ³³ But I was let down in a basket, through an opening in the wall, and escaped from him.

Paul's Visions and Revelations

12 I have to boast, even though it doesn't do any good. But I will now talk about visions and revelations given me by the Lord. ² I know a certain Christian man who fourteen years ago was snatched up to the highest heaven (I do not know whether this actually happened, or whether he had a vision — only God knows). ³ I repeat, I know that this man was snatched to Paradise (again, I do not know whether this actually happened, or whether it was a vision — only God knows), ⁴ and there he heard things which cannot be put into words, things that human lips may not speak. ⁵ So I will boast of this man — but I will not boast about myself, except the things that show how weak I am. ⁶ If I wanted to boast, I would not be a fool, because I would be telling the truth. But I will not boast, because I do not want anyone to have a higher opinion of me than he has from what he has seen me do and heard me say.

⁷ But to keep me from being puffed up with pride because of the wonderful things I saw, I was given a painful physical ailment, which acts as Satan's messenger to beat me and keep me from being proud. ⁸ Three times I prayed to the Lord about this, and asked him to take it away. ⁹ His answer was, "My grace is all you need; for my power is strongest when you are weak." I am most happy, then, to be proud of any weaknesses, in order to feel the protection of Christ's power over me. ¹⁰ I am content with weaknesses, insults, hardships, persecutions, and difficulties for Christ's sake. For when I am weak, then I am strong.

Paul's Concern for the Corinthians

[11] I am acting like a fool — but you have made me do it. You are the ones who ought to show your approval of me. For even if I am nothing, I am in no way inferior to those very special "apostles" of yours. [12] The things that prove that I am an apostle were done with all patience among you; there were signs and wonders and miracles. [13] How were you treated any worse than the other churches, except that I did not bother you for help? Please forgive me for being so unfair!

[14] This is now the third time that I am ready to come to visit you — and I will not make any demands on you. It is you I want, not your money. After all, children should not have to provide for their parents, but parents should provide for their children. [15] I will be glad to spend all I have, and myself as well, in order to help you. Will you love me less because I love you so much?

[16] You will agree, then, that I was not a burden to you. But, someone will say, I was tricky and trapped you with lies. [17] How? Did I take advantage of you through any of the messengers I sent? [18] I begged Titus to go, and I sent the other Christian brother with him. Would you say that Titus took advantage of you? Do not he and I act from the very same motives and behave in the same way?

[19] Perhaps you think that all along we have been trying to defend ourselves before you. No! We speak as Christ would have us speak, in the presence of God, and everything we do, dear friends, is done to help you. [20] I am afraid that when I get there I will find you different from what I would like you to be and you will find me different from what you would like me to be. I am afraid that I will find quarreling and jealousy, hot tempers and selfishness, insults and gossip, pride and disorder. [21] I am afraid that the next time I come my God will humiliate me in your presence, and I shall weep over many who sinned in the past and have not repented of the immoral things they have done, their sexual sins and lustful deeds.

Final Warnings and Greetings

13 This is now the third time that I am coming to visit you. "Any accusation must be upheld by the evidence of two or three witnesses" — as the scripture

says. ² I want to tell you who have sinned in the past, and all the others; I said it before, during my second visit to you, but I will say it again now that I am away: the next time I come nobody will escape punishment. ³ You will have all the proof you want that Christ speaks through me. When he deals with you he is not weak; instead he shows his power among you. ⁴ For even though it was in weakness that he was put to death on the cross, it is by God's power that he lives. In union with him we also are weak; but in our relations with you, we shall live with him by God's power.

⁵ Put yourselves to the test and judge yourselves, to find out whether you are living in faith. Surely you know that Christ Jesus is in you? — unless you have completely failed. ⁶ I trust you will know that we are not failures. ⁷ We pray to God that you will do no wrong — not in order to show that we are a success, but that you may do what is right, even though we may seem to be failures. ⁸ For we cannot do a thing against God's truth, but only for it. ⁹ We are glad when we are weak but you are strong. And so we also pray that you will become perfect. ¹⁰ That is why I write this while I am away from you; it is so that when I arrive I will not have to deal harshly with you in using the authority that the Lord gave me — authority to build you up, not to tear you down.

¹¹ And now, brothers, good-bye! Strive for perfection; listen to what I say; agree with one another, and live in peace. And the God of love and peace will be with you.

¹² Greet one another with a brotherly kiss.

All God's people send you their greetings.

¹³ The grace of the Lord Jesus Christ, the love of God, and the fellowship of the Holy Spirit be with you all.

PAUL'S LETTER TO THE GALATIANS

1 From Paul, whose call to be an apostle did not come from man or by means of man, but from Jesus Christ and God the Father, who raised him from death. ² All the brothers who are here join me in sending greetings to the churches of Galatia:

³ May God our Father and the Lord Jesus Christ give you grace and peace.

⁴ In order to set us free from this present evil age, Christ gave himself for our sins, in obedience to the will of our God and Father. ⁵ To God be the glory for ever and ever! Amen.

The One Gospel

⁶ I am surprised at you! In no time at all you are deserting the one who called you by the grace of Christ, and are going to another gospel. ⁷ Actually, there is no "other gospel," but I say it because there are some people who are upsetting you and trying to change the gospel of Christ. ⁸ But even if we, or an angel from heaven, should preach to you a gospel that is different from the one we preached to you, may he be condemned to hell! ⁹ We have said it before, and now I say it again: if anyone preaches to you a gospel that is different from the one you accepted, may he be condemned to hell!

¹⁰ Does this sound as if I am trying to win men's approval? No! I want God's approval! Am I trying to be popular with men? If I were still trying to do so, I would not be a servant of Christ.

How Paul Became an Apostle

¹¹ Let me tell you this, brothers: the gospel that I preach was not made by man. ¹² I did not receive it from any man, nor did anyone teach it to me. Instead, it was Jesus Christ himself who revealed it to me.

¹³ You have been told of the way I used to live when I was devoted to the Jewish religion, how I persecuted without mercy the church of God and did my best to destroy it. ¹⁴ I was ahead of most fellow Jews of my age

in my practice of the Jewish religion. I was much more devoted to the traditions of our ancestors.

15 But God, in his grace, chose me even before I was born, and called me to serve him. 16 And when he decided to reveal his Son to me, so that I might preach the Good News about him to the Gentiles, I did not go to any person for advice, 17 nor did I go to Jerusalem to see those who were apostles before me. Instead, I went at once to Arabia, and then I returned to Damascus. 18 It was three years later that I went to Jerusalem to get information from Peter, and I stayed with him for two weeks. 19 I did not see any other apostle except James, the Lord's brother.

20 What I write is true. I am not lying, so help me God!

21 Afterward I went to places in Syria and Cilicia. 22 All this time the members of the Christian churches in Judea did not know me personally. 23 They knew only what others said: "The man who used to persecute us is now preaching the faith that he once tried to destroy!" 24 And so they praised God because of me.

Paul and the Other Apostles

2 Fourteen years later I went back to Jerusalem with Barnabas; I also took Titus along with me. 2 I went because God revealed to me that I should go. In a private meeting with the leaders, I explained to them the gospel message that I preach to the Gentiles. I did not want my work in the past or in the present to go for nothing. 3 My companion Titus, even though he is Greek, was not forced to be circumcised, 4 although some men, who had pretended to be brothers and joined the group, wanted to circumcise him. These people had slipped in as spies, to find out about the freedom we have through our union with Christ Jesus. They wanted to make slaves of us. 5 We did not give in to them for a minute, in order to keep the truth of the gospel safe for you.

6 But those who seemed to be the leaders — I say this because it makes no difference to me what they were; for God does not judge by outward appearances — those leaders, I say, made no new suggestions to me. 7 On the contrary, they saw that God had given me the task of preaching the gospel to the Gentiles, just as he had given Peter the task of preaching the gospel to the Jews. 8 For by God's power I was made an apostle to the Gentiles, just

as Peter was made an apostle to the Jews. ⁹ James, Peter, and John, who seemed to be the leaders, recognized that God had given me this special task; so they shook hands with Barnabas and me. As partners we all agreed that we would work among the Gentiles and they among the Jews. ¹⁰ All they asked was that we should remember the needy in their group, the very thing I had worked hard to do.

Paul Rebukes Peter at Antioch

¹¹ When Peter came to Antioch, I opposed him in public, because he was clearly wrong. ¹² Before some men who had been sent by James arrived there, Peter had been eating with the Gentile brothers. But after these men arrived, he drew back and would not eat with them, because he was afraid of those who were in favor of circumcising the Gentiles. ¹³ The other Jewish brothers started acting like cowards, along with Peter; and even Barnabas was swept along by their cowardly action. ¹⁴ When I saw that they were not walking a straight path in line with the truth of the gospel, I said to Peter, in front of them all: "You are a Jew, yet you have been living like a Gentile, not like a Jew. How, then, can you try to force Gentiles to live like Jews?"

Jews and Gentiles Are Saved by Faith

¹⁵ Indeed, we are Jews by birth, and not Gentile sinners. ¹⁶ Yet we know that a man is put right with God only through faith in Jesus Christ, never by doing what the Law requires. We, too, have believed in Christ Jesus in order to be put right with God through our faith in Christ, and not by doing what the Law requires. For no man is put right with God by doing what the Law requires. ¹⁷ If, then, as we try to be put right with God by our union with Christ, it is found that we are sinners as much as the Gentiles are — does that mean that Christ has served the interests of sin? By no means! ¹⁸ If I start to build up again what I have torn down, it proves that I am breaking the Law. ¹⁹ So far as the Law is concerned, however, I am dead — killed by the Law itself — in order that I might live for God. I have been put to death with Christ on his cross, ²⁰ so that it is no longer I who live, but it is Christ who lives in me. This life that I live now, I live by faith in the Son of God, who loved me and gave his

life for me. 21 I do not reject the grace of God. If a man is put right with God through the Law, it means that Christ died for nothing!

Law or Faith

3 You foolish Galatians! Who put a spell on you? Right before your eyes you had a plain description of the death of Jesus Christ on the cross! 2 Tell me just this one thing: did you receive God's Spirit by doing what the Law requires, or by hearing and believing the gospel? 3 How can you be so foolish! You began by God's Spirit; do you now want to finish by your own power? 4 Did all your experience mean nothing at all? Surely it meant something! 5 When God gives you the Spirit and works miracles among you, does he do it because you do what the Law requires, or because you hear and believe the gospel?

6 It is just as the scripture says about Abraham: "He believed God, and because of his faith God accepted him as righteous." 7 You should realize, then, that the people who have faith are the real descendants of Abraham. 8 The scripture saw ahead of time that God would put the Gentiles right with himself through faith. Therefore the scripture preached the Good News to Abraham ahead of time: "Through you God will bless all the people on earth." 9 Abraham believed and was blessed; so all who believe are blessed as he was.

10 Those who depend on obeying the Law live under a curse. For the scripture says, "Whoever does not always obey everything that is written in the book of the Law is under the curse!" 11 Now, it is clear that no man is put right with God by means of the Law; because the scripture says, "He who is put right with God through faith shall live." 12 But the Law does not depend on faith. Instead, as the scripture says, "The man who does everything the Law requires will live by it."

13 But Christ, by becoming a curse for us, has set us free from the curse that the Law brings. As the scripture says, "Anyone who is hanged on a tree is under the curse." 14 Christ did so in order that the blessing God promised Abraham might be given to the Gentiles by means of Christ Jesus, that we, through faith, might receive the Spirit promised by God.

The Law and the Promise

¹⁵ Brothers, I am going to use an everyday example: when two men agree on a matter and sign a covenant, no one can break that covenant or add anything to it. ¹⁶ Now, God made his promises to Abraham and to his descendant. It does not say, "and to his descendants," meaning many people. It says, "and to your descendant," meaning one person only, who is Christ. ¹⁷ This is what I mean: God made a covenant and promised to keep it. The Law, which came four hundred and thirty years later, cannot break that covenant and cancel God's promise. ¹⁸ For if what God gives depends on the Law, then it no longer depends on his promise. However, God gave it to Abraham because he had promised it to him.

¹⁹ Why was the Law given, then? It was added in order to show what wrongdoing is, and was meant to last until the coming of Abraham's descendant, to whom the promise was made. The Law was handed down by angels, with a

man acting as a go-between. 20 But a go-between is not needed when there is only one person; and God is one.

The Purpose of the Law

21 Does this mean that the Law is against God's promises? No, not at all! For if a law had been given that could bring life to men, then man could be put right with God through law. 22 But the scripture has said that the whole world is under the power of sin, so that those who believe might receive the promised gift that is given on the basis of faith in Jesus Christ.

23 Before the time for faith came, however, the Law kept us all locked up as prisoners, until this coming faith should be revealed. 24 So the Law was in charge of us, to be our instructor until Christ came, so that we might be put right with God through faith. 25 Now that the time of faith is here, the instructor is no longer in charge of us.

26 For it is through faith that all of you are God's sons in union with Christ Jesus. 27 For you were baptized into union with Christ, and so have taken upon yourselves the qualities of Christ himself. 28 So there is no difference between Jews and Gentiles, between slaves and free men, between men and women: you are all one in union with Christ Jesus. 29 If you belong to Christ, then you are the descendants of Abraham, and will receive what God has promised.

4 But to continue: the son who will receive his father's property is treated just like a slave while he is young,

even though he really owns everything. ² While he is young, there are men who take care of him and manage his affairs until the time set by his father. ³ In the same way, we too were slaves of the ruling spirits of the universe, before we reached spiritual maturity. ⁴ But when the right time finally came, God sent his own Son. He came as the son of a human mother, and lived under the Jewish Law, ⁵ to set free those who were under the Law, so that we might become God's sons.

⁶ To show that you are his sons, God sent the Spirit of his Son into our hearts, the Spirit who cries, "Father, my Father." ⁷ So then, you are no longer a slave, but a son. And since you are his son, God will give you all he has for his sons.

Paul's Concern for the Galatians

⁸ In the past you did not know God, and so you were slaves of beings who are not gods. ⁹ But now that you know God — or, I should say, now that God knows you — how is it that you want to turn back to those weak and pitiful ruling spirits? Why do you want to become their slaves all over again? ¹⁰ You pay special attention to certain days, months, seasons, and years! ¹¹ I am afraid for you! Can it be that all my work for you has been for nothing?

¹² I beg you, my brothers, be like me. After all, I am like you. You have not done me any wrong. ¹³ You remember why I preached the gospel to you the first time; it was because I was sick. ¹⁴ But you did not despise or

reject me, even though my physical condition was a great trial to you. Instead, you received me as you would God's angel; you received me as you would Christ Jesus! [15] You were so happy! What has happened? I myself can say this about you: you would have taken out your own eyes, if you could, and given them to me! [16] Have I now become your enemy by telling you the truth?

[17] Those other people show a great interest in you, but their intentions are not good. All they want is to separate you from me, so that you will feel the same way toward them as they do toward you. [18] Now, it is good to have so great an interest for a good purpose — this is true always, and not only when I am with you. [19] My dear children! Once again, just like a mother in childbirth, I feel the same kind of pain for you, until Christ's nature is formed in you. [20] How I wish I were with you now, so that I could take a different attitude toward you. I am so worried about you!

The Example of Hagar and Sarah

[21] Let me ask those of you who want to be subject to the Law: do you not hear what the Law says? [22] It says that Abraham had two sons, one by a slave woman, the other by a free woman. [23] His son by the slave woman was born in the usual way, but his son by the free woman was born as a result of God's promise. [24] This can be taken as a figure: the two women are two covenants, one of which (Hagar, that is) comes from Mount Sinai, whose children are born slaves. [25] Hagar stands for Mount Sinai in Arabia, and she is a figure of the present city of Jerusalem, a slave along with all its people. [26] But the heavenly Jerusalem is free, and she is our mother. [27] For the scripture says:

> "Be happy, woman who never had children!
> Shout and cry with joy, you who never felt
>   the pains of childbirth!
> For the woman who was deserted will have
>   more children
> Than the woman living with the husband."

[28] Now, you, my brothers, are God's children as a result of his promise, just as Isaac was. [29] At that time the son who was born in the usual way persecuted the one who was born because of God's Spirit; and it is the same now.

[30] But what does the scripture say? It says, "Throw out the slave woman and her son; for the son of the slave woman will not share the father's property with the son of the free woman." [31] So then, my brothers, we are not the children of a slave woman, but of the free woman.

Preserve Your Freedom

5 Freedom is what we have — Christ has set us free! Stand, then, as free men, and do not allow yourselves to become slaves again.

[2] Listen! I, Paul, tell you this: if you allow yourselves to be circumcised, it means that Christ is of no use to you at all. [3] I want to emphasize this, and say again to any man who allows himself to be circumcised: he is obliged to obey the whole Law. [4] Those of you who try to be put right with God by obeying the Law have cut yourselves off from Christ. You are outside God's grace. [5] As for us, our hope is that God will put us right with him; and this is what we wait for, by the power of God's Spirit working through our faith. [6] For when we are in union with Christ Jesus, neither circumcision nor the lack of it makes any difference at all; what matters is faith that works through love.

[7] You were doing so well! Who made you stop obeying the truth? How did he persuade you? [8] It was not done by God, who calls you. [9] "It takes only a little yeast to raise the whole batch of dough," as they say. [10] But I still feel sure about you. Our union in the Lord makes me confident that you will not take a different view, and that the man who is upsetting you, whoever he may be, will be punished by God.

[11] But as for me, brothers, why am I still persecuted if I continue to preach that circumcision is necessary? If that were true, then my preaching about the cross of Christ would cause no trouble. [12] I wish that the people who are upsetting you would go all the way: let them go on and castrate themselves!

[13] As for you, my brothers, you were called to be free. But do not let this freedom become an excuse for letting your physical desires rule you. Instead, let love make you serve one another. [14] For the whole Law is summed up in one commandment: "Love your neighbor as yourself." [15] But if you act like animals, hurting and harming each

other, then watch out, or you will completely destroy one another.

The Spirit and Human Nature

16 This is what I say: let the Spirit direct your lives, and do not satisfy the desires of the human nature. 17 For what our human nature wants is opposed to what the Spirit wants, and what the Spirit wants is opposed to what human nature wants: the two are enemies, and this means that you cannot do what you want to do. 18 If the Spirit leads you, then you are not subject to the Law.

19 What human nature does is quite plain. It shows itself in immoral, filthy, and indecent actions; 20 in worship of idols and witchcraft. People become enemies, they fight, become jealous, angry, and ambitious. They separate into parties and groups; 21 they are envious, get drunk, have orgies, and do other things like these. I warn you now as I have before: those who do these things will not receive the Kingdom of God.

22 But the Spirit produces love, joy, peace, patience, kindness, goodness, faithfulness, 23 humility, and self-control. There is no law against such things as these. 24 And those who belong to Christ Jesus have put to death their human nature, with all its passions and desires. 25 The Spirit has given us life; he must also control our lives. 26 We must not be proud, or irritate one another, or be jealous of one another.

Bear One Another's Burdens

6 My brothers, if someone is caught in any kind of wrongdoing, those of you who are spiritual should set him right; but you must do it in a gentle way. And keep an eye on yourself, so that you will not be tempted.

too. [2] Help carry one another's burdens, and in this way you will obey the law of Christ. [3] If someone thinks he is something, when he really is nothing, he is only fooling himself. [4] Each one should judge his own conduct for himself. If it is good, then he can be proud of what he himself has done, without having to compare it with what someone else has done. [5] For everyone has to carry his own load.

[6] The man who is being taught the Christian message should share all the good things he has with his teacher.

[7] Do not deceive yourselves: no one makes a fool of God. A man will reap exactly what he plants. [8] If he plants in the field of his natural desires, from it he will gather the harvest of death; if he plants in the field of the Spirit, from the Spirit he will gather the harvest of eternal life. [9] So let us not become tired of doing good; for if we do not give up, the time will come when we will reap the harvest. [10] So then, as often as we have the chance we should do good to everyone, but especially to those who belong to our family in the faith.

Final Warning and Greeting

[11] See what big letters I make as I write to you now with my own hand! [12] Those who want to show off and brag about external matters are the ones who are trying to force you to be circumcised. They do it, however, only that they may not be persecuted for the cross of Christ. [13] Even those who practice circumcision do not obey the Law; they want you to be circumcised so they can boast that you submitted to this physical ceremony. [14] As for me, however, I will boast only of the cross of our Lord Jesus Christ; for by means of his cross the world is dead to me, and I am dead to the world. [15] It does not matter at all whether or not one is circumcised. What does matter is being a new creature. [16] As for those who follow this rule in their lives, may peace and mercy be with them — with them and with all God's people!

[17] To conclude: let no one give me any more trouble; for the scars I have on my body show that I am the slave of Jesus.

[18] May the grace of our Lord Jesus Christ be with you all, my brothers. Amen.

PAUL'S LETTER TO THE EPHESIANS

1 From Paul, who by God's will is an apostle of Christ
Jesus —
To God's people who live in Ephesus, those who are
faithful in their life in Christ Jesus:

2 May God our Father and the Lord Jesus Christ give
you grace and peace.

Spiritual Blessings in Christ

3 Let us give thanks to the God and Father of our Lord
Jesus Christ! For he has blessed us, in our union with
Christ, by giving us every spiritual gift in the heavenly
world. 4 Before the world was made, God had already
chosen us to be his in Christ, so that we would be holy and
without fault before him. Because of his love, 5 God had
already decided that through Jesus Christ he would bring
us to himself as his sons — this was his pleasure and
purpose. 6 Let us praise God for his glorious grace, for
the free gift he gave us in his dear Son!

7 For by the death of Christ we are set free, and our
sins are forgiven. How great is the grace of God, 8 which
he gave to us in such large measure! In all his wisdom
and insight 9 God did what he had purposed, and made
known to us the secret plan he had already decided to
complete by means of Christ. 10 God's plan, which he will
complete when the time is right, is to bring all creation
together, everything in heaven and on earth, with Christ
as head.

11 For all things are done according to God's plan and
decision; and God chose us to be his own people in union
with Christ because of his own purpose, based on what
he had decided from the very beginning. 12 Let us, then,
who were the first to hope in Christ, praise God's
glory!

13 And so it was with you also: when you heard the
true message, the Good News that brought you salvation,
you believed in Christ, and God put his stamp of ownership on you by giving you the Holy Spirit he had promised.
14 The Spirit is the guarantee that we shall receive what

God has promised his people, and assures us that God will give complete freedom to those who are his. Let us praise his glory!

Paul's Prayer

¹⁵ For this reason, ever since I heard of your faith in the Lord Jesus and your love for all God's people, ¹⁶ I have not stopped giving thanks to God for you. I remember you in my prayers, ¹⁷ and ask the God of our Lord Jesus Christ, the glorious Father, to give you the Spirit, who will make you wise and reveal God to you, so that you will know him. ¹⁸ I ask that your minds may be opened to see his light, so that you will know what is the hope to which he has called you, how rich are the wonderful blessings he promises his people, ¹⁹ and how very great is his power at work in us who believe. This power in us is the same as the mighty strength ²⁰ which he used when he raised Christ from death, and seated him at his right side in the heavenly world. ²¹ Christ rules there above all heavenly rulers, authorities, powers, and lords; he is above all titles of power in this world and in the next. ²² God put all things under Christ's feet, and gave him to the church as supreme Lord over all things. ²³ The church is Christ's body, the completion of him who himself completes all things everywhere.

From Death to Life

2 In the past you were spiritually dead because of your disobedience and sins. ² At that time you followed the world's evil way; you obeyed the ruler of the spiritual powers in space, the spirit who now controls the people who disobey God. ³ Actually all of us were like them, and lived according to our natural desires, and did whatever suited the wishes of our own bodies and minds. Like everyone else, we too were naturally bound to suffer God's wrath.

⁴ But God's mercy is so abundant, and his love for us is so great, ⁵ that while we were spiritually dead in our disobedience he brought us to life with Christ; it is by God's grace that you have been saved. ⁶ In our union with Christ Jesus he raised us up with him to rule with him in the heavenly world. ⁷ He did this to demonstrate for all time to come the abundant riches of his grace in the love he showed us in Christ Jesus. ⁸ For it is by God's grace that you have been saved, through faith. It is not your own doing, but God's gift. ⁹ There is nothing here to boast of, since it is not the result of your own efforts. ¹⁰ God is our Maker, and in our union with Christ Jesus he has created us for a life of good works, which he has already prepared for us to do.

One in Christ

¹¹ You Gentiles by birth — who are called the uncircumcised by the Jews, who call themselves the circumcised (which refers to what men themselves do on their bodies) — remember what you were in the past. ¹² At that time you were apart from Christ. You were foreigners, and did not belong to God's chosen people. You had no part in the covenants, which were based on God's promises to his people. You lived in this world without hope and without God! ¹³ But now, in union with Christ Jesus, you who used to be far away have been brought near by the death of Christ. ¹⁴ For Christ himself has brought us peace, by making the Jews and Gentiles one people. With his own body he broke down the wall that separated them and kept them enemies. ¹⁵ He abolished the Jewish Law, with its commandments and rules, in order to create out of the two races a single new people in union with himself, thus

making peace. [16] By his death on the cross Christ destroyed the hatred; by means of the cross he united both races into one single body and brought them back to God. [17] So Christ came and preached the Good News of peace to all — to you Gentiles, who were far away from God, and to the Jews, who were near to him. [18] It is through Christ that all of us, Jews and Gentiles, are able to come in the one Spirit into the presence of the Father.

[19] So then, you Gentiles are not foreigners or strangers any longer; you are now fellow-citizens with God's people, and members of the family of God! [20] You, too, are built upon the foundation laid by the apostles and prophets, the cornerstone being Christ Jesus himself. [21] He is the one who holds the whole building together and makes it grow into a sacred temple in the Lord. [22] In union with him you too are being built together with all the others into a house where God lives through his Spirit.

Paul's Work for the Gentiles

3 For this reason I, Paul, the prisoner of Christ Jesus for the sake of you Gentiles, pray to God. [2] Surely you have heard that God, in his grace, has given me this work to do for your good. [3] God revealed his secret plan and made it known to me. (I have written briefly about this, [4] and if you will read what I have written you can learn my understanding of the secret of Christ.) [5] In past times men were not told this secret, but God has revealed it now by the Spirit to his holy apostles and prophets. [6] The secret is this: by means of the gospel the Gentiles have a part with the Jews in God's blessings; they are members of the same body, and share in the promise that God made in Christ Jesus.

[7] I was made a servant of the gospel by God's special gift, which he gave me through the working of his power. [8] I am less than the least of all God's people; yet God gave me this privilege of taking to the Gentiles the Good News of the infinite riches of Christ, [9] and to make all men see how God's secret plan is to be put into effect. God, who is the Creator of all things, kept his secret hidden through all the past ages, [10] in order that at the present time, by means of the church, the angelic rulers and powers in the heavenly world might know God's wisdom, in all its different forms. [11] God did this according to his eternal

purpose, which he achieved through Christ Jesus our Lord. [12] In union with him, and through our faith in him, we have the freedom to enter into God's presence with all confidence. [13] I beg you, then, do not be discouraged because I am suffering for you; it is all for your benefit.

The Love of Christ

[14] For this reason, then, I fall on my knees before the Father, [15] from whom every family in heaven and on earth receives its true name. [16] I ask God, from the wealth of his glory, to give you power through his Spirit to be strong in your inner selves, [17] and that Christ will make his home in your hearts, through faith. I pray that you may have your roots and foundations in love, [18] and that you, together with all God's people, may have the power to understand how broad and long and high and deep is Christ's love. [19] Yes, may you come to know his love — although it can never be fully known — and so be completely filled with the perfect fulness of God.

[20] To him who is able to do so much more than we can ever ask for, or even think of, by means of the power working in us: [21] to God be the glory in the church and in Christ Jesus, for all time, for ever and ever! Amen.

The Unity of the Body

4 I urge you, then — I who am a prisoner because I serve the Lord: live a life that measures up to the standard God set when he called you. [2] Be humble, gentle, and patient always. Show your love by being helpful to one another. [3] Do your best to preserve the unity which the Spirit gives, by the peace that binds you together. [4] There is one body and one Spirit, just as there is one hope to which God has called you. [5] There is one Lord, one faith, one baptism; [6] there is one God and Father of all men, who is Lord of all, works through all, and is in all.

[7] Each one of us has been given a special gift, in proportion to what Christ has given. [8] As the scripture says,

"When he went up to the very heights

He took many captives with him;

He gave gifts to men."

[9] Now, what does "he went up" mean? It means that first

he came down — that is, down to the lower depths of the earth. [10] So he who came down is the same one who went up, above and beyond the heavens, to fill the whole universe with his presence. [11] It was he who "gave gifts to men"; he appointed some to be apostles, others to be prophets, others to be evangelists, others to be pastors and teachers. [12] He did this to prepare all God's people for the work of Christian service, to build up the body of Christ. [13] And so we shall all come together to that oneness in our faith and in our knowledge of the Son of God; we shall become mature men, reaching to the very height of Christ's full stature. [14] Then we shall no longer be children, carried by the waves, and blown about by every shifting wind of the teaching of deceitful men, who lead others to error by the tricks they invent. [15] Instead, by speaking the truth in a spirit of love, we must grow up in every way to Christ, who is the head. [16] Under his control all the different parts of the body fit together, and the whole body is held together by every joint with which it is provided. So when each separate part works as it should, the whole body grows and builds itself up through love.

The New Life in Christ

[17] In the Lord's name, then, I say this and insist on it: do not live any longer like the heathen, whose thoughts are worthless, [18] and whose minds are in the dark. They have no part in the life that God gives, because they are completely ignorant and stubborn. [19] They have lost all feeling of shame; they give themselves over to vice, and do all sorts of indecent things without restraint.

[20] That was not what you learned about Christ! [21] You certainly heard about him, and as his followers you were taught the truth which is in Jesus. [22] So get rid of your old self, which made you live as you used to — the old self which was being destroyed by its deceitful desires. [23] Your hearts and minds must be made completely new. [24] You must put on the new self, which is created in God's likeness, and reveals itself in the true life that is upright and holy.

[25] No more lying, then! Everyone must tell the truth to his brother, for we are all members together in the body of Christ. [26] If you become angry, do not let your anger

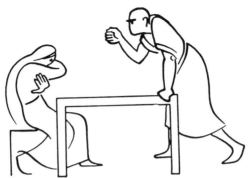

lead you into sin; and do not stay angry all day. ²⁷ Don't give the Devil a chance. ²⁸ The man who used to rob must stop robbing and start working, to earn an honest living for himself, and to be able to help the poor. ²⁹ Do not use harmful words in talking. Use only helpful words, the kind that build up and provide what is needed, so that what you say will do good to those who hear you. ³⁰ And do not make God's Holy Spirit sad; for the Spirit is God's mark of ownership on you, a guarantee that the Day will come when God will set you free. ³¹ Get rid of all bitterness, passion, and anger. No more shouting or insults! No more hateful feelings of any sort! ³² Instead, be kind and tender-hearted to one another, and forgive one another, as God has forgiven you in Christ.

Living in the Light

5 Since you are God's dear children, you must try to be like him. [2] Your life must be controlled by love, just as Christ loved us and gave his life for us, as a sweet-smelling offering and sacrifice which pleases God.

[3] Since you are God's people, it is not right that any questions of immorality, or indecency, or greed should even be mentioned among you. [4] Nor is it fitting for you to use obscene, foolish, or dirty words. Rather you should give thanks to God. [5] You may be sure of this: no man who is immoral, indecent, or greedy (for greediness is a form of idol worship) will ever receive a share in the Kingdom of Christ and of God.

[6] Do not let anyone deceive you with foolish words: it is because of these very things that God's wrath will come upon those who do not obey him. [7] So have nothing at all to do with such people. [8] You yourselves used to be in the darkness, but since you have become the Lord's people you are in the light. So you must live like people who belong to the light. [9] For it is the light that brings a rich harvest of every kind of goodness, righteousness, and truth. [10] Try to learn what pleases the Lord. [11] Have nothing to do with people who do worthless things that belong to the darkness. Instead, bring these out to the light. [12] (It is really too shameful even to talk about the things they do in secret.) [13] And when all things are brought out to the light, then their true nature is clearly revealed; [14] for anything that is clearly revealed becomes light. That is why it is said,

"Wake up, sleeper,
Rise from the dead!
And Christ will shine upon you."

[15] So pay close attention to how you live. Don't live like ignorant men, but like wise men. [16] Make good use of every opportunity you get, because these are bad days. [17] Don't be fools, then, but try to find out what the Lord wants you to do.

[18] Do not get drunk with wine, which will only ruin you; instead, be filled with the Spirit. [19] Speak to one another in the words of psalms, hymns, and sacred songs; sing hymns and psalms to the Lord, with praise in your

hearts. [20] Always give thanks for everything to God the Father, in the name of our Lord Jesus Christ.

Wives and Husbands

[21] Submit yourselves to one another, because of your reverence for Christ.

[22] Wives, submit yourselves to your husbands, as to the Lord. [23] For a husband has authority over his wife in the same way that Christ has authority over the church; and Christ is himself the Savior of the church, his body. [24] And so wives must submit themselves completely to their husbands, in the same way that the church submits itself to Christ.

[25] Husbands, love your wives in the same way that Christ loved the church and gave his life for it. [26] He did this to dedicate the church to God, by his word, after making it clean by the washing in water, [27] in order to present the church to himself, in all its beauty, pure and faultless, without spot or wrinkle, or any other imperfection. [28] Men ought to love their wives just as they love their own bodies. A man who loves his wife loves himself. [29] (No one ever hates his own body. Instead, he feeds it and takes care of it, just as Christ does the church; [30] for we are members of his body.) [31] As the scripture says, "For this reason, a man will leave his father and mother, and unite with his

wife, and the two will become one." [32] There is a great truth revealed in this scripture, and I understand it applies to Christ and the church. [33] But it also applies to you: every husband must love his wife as himself, and every wife must respect her husband.

Children and Parents

6 Children, it is your Christian duty to obey your parents, for this is the right thing to do. [2] "Honor your father and mother" is the first commandment that has a promise added: [3] "so that all may be well with you, and you may live a long time in the land."

[4] Parents, do not treat your children in such a way as to make them angry. Instead, raise them with Christian discipline and instruction.

Slaves and Masters

[5] Slaves, obey your human masters, with fear and trembling; and do it with a sincere heart, as though you were serving Christ. [6] Do this not only when they are watching you, to gain their approval; but with all your heart do what God wants, as slaves of Christ. [7] Do your work as slaves cheerfully, then, as though you served the Lord, and not merely men. [8] Remember that the Lord will reward every man, whether slave or free, for the good work he does.

[9] Masters, behave in the same way toward your slaves; and stop using threats. Remember that you and your slaves belong to the same Master in heaven, who treats everyone alike.

The Whole Armor of God

[10] Finally, build up your strength in union with the Lord, and by means of his mighty power. [11] Put on all the armor that God gives you, so that you will stand up against the Devil's evil tricks. [12] For we are not fighting against human beings, but against the wicked spiritual forces in the heavenly world, the rulers, authorities, and cosmic powers of this dark age. [13] So take up God's armor now! Then when the evil day comes, you will be able to resist the enemy's attacks, and after fighting to the end, you will still hold your ground.

[14] So stand ready: have truth for a belt tight around

your waist; put on righteousness for your breastplate, [15] and the readiness to announce the Good News of peace as shoes for your feet. [16] At all times carry faith as a

shield; with it you will be able to put out all the burning arrows shot by the Evil One. [17] And accept salvation for a helmet, and the word of God as the sword that the Spirit gives you. [18] Do all this in prayer, asking for God's help. Pray on every occasion, as the Spirit leads. For this reason keep alert and never give up; pray always for all God's people. [19] And pray also for me, that God will give me a message, when I am ready to speak, that I may speak boldly and make known the gospel's secret. [20] For the sake of this gospel I am an ambassador, though now I am in prison. Pray, therefore, that I may be bold in speaking of it, as I should.

Final Greetings

[21] Tychicus, our dear brother and faithful servant in the Lord's work, will give you all the news about me, so that you may know how I am getting along. [22] That is why I am sending him to you — to tell you how all of us are getting along, and so bring courage to your hearts.

[23] May God the Father and the Lord Jesus Christ give peace and love to all the brothers, with faith. [24] May God's grace be with all those who love our Lord Jesus Christ with undying love.

PAUL'S LETTER TO THE PHILIPPIANS

1 From Paul and Timothy, servants of Christ Jesus —
To all God's people living in Philippi who believe in
Christ Jesus, together with the church leaders and helpers:
² May God our Father and the Lord Jesus Christ give
you grace and peace.

Paul's Prayer for His Readers

³ I thank my God for you all every time I think of you;
⁴ and every time I pray for you, I pray with joy, ⁵ because
of the way in which you have helped me in the work of
the gospel, from the very first day until now. ⁶ And so I
am sure of this: that God, who began this good work in
you, will carry it on until it is finished in the Day of Christ
Jesus. ⁷ You are always in my heart! And so it is only
right for me to feel this way about you. For you have all
shared with me in this privilege that God has given me,
both now that I am in prison and also while I was free to
defend and firmly establish the gospel. ⁸ God knows that
I tell the truth when I say that my deep feeling for you
comes from the heart of Christ Jesus himself.

⁹ This is my prayer for you: I pray that your love will
keep on growing more and more, together with true knowledge and perfect judgment, ¹⁰ so that you will be able to
choose what is best. Then you will be free from all impurity and blame on the Day of Christ. ¹¹ Your lives will
be filled with the truly good qualities which Jesus Christ
alone can produce, for the glory and praise of God.

To Live is Christ

¹² I want you to know, my brothers, that the things that
have happened to me have really helped the progress of
the gospel. ¹³ As a result, the whole palace guard and all
the others here know that I am in prison because I am a
servant of Christ. ¹⁴ And my being in prison has given
most of the brothers more confidence in the Lord, so that
they grow bolder all the time in preaching the message
without fear.

¹⁵ Of course some of them preach Christ because they
are jealous and quarrelsome, but others preach him with

all good will. [16] These do so from love, for they know that God has given me the work of defending the gospel. [17] The others do not proclaim Christ sincerely, but from a spirit of selfish ambition; they think that they will make more trouble for me while I am in prison.

[18] It does not matter! I am happy about it — just so Christ is preached in every way possible, whether from wrong or right motives. And I will continue to be happy, [19] for I know that, because of your prayers and the help which comes from the Spirit of Jesus Christ, I shall be set free. [20] For my deep desire and hope is that I shall never fail my duty, but that at all times, and especially right now, I shall be full of courage, so that with my whole self I shall bring honor to Christ, whether I live or die. [21] For what is life? To me, it is Christ! Death, then, will bring something even better. [22] But if by living on I can do more worth-while work, then I am not sure which I should choose. [23] I am caught from both sides: I want very much to leave this life and be with Christ, which is a far better thing; [24] but it is much more important, for your sake, that I remain alive. [25] I am sure of this, and so I know that I will stay. I will stay on with you all, to add to your progress and joy in the faith. [26] So when I am with you again you will have even more reason to be proud of me, in your life in Christ Jesus.

[27] Now, the important thing is that your manner of life be as the gospel of Christ requires, so that, whether or not I am able to go to see you, I will hear that you stand firm with one common purpose, and fight together, with only one wish, for the faith of the gospel. [28] Don't be afraid of your enemies; always be courageous, and this will prove to them that they will lose, and that you will win — for it is God who gives you the victory! [29] For you have been given the privilege of serving Christ, not only by believing in him, but also by suffering for him. [30] Now you can take part with me in the fight. It is the same one you saw me fighting in the past and the same one I am still fighting, as you hear.

Christ's Humility and Greatness

2 Does your life in Christ make you strong? Does his love comfort you? Do you have fellowship with the Spirit? Do you feel kindness and compassion for one an-

other? ² I urge you, then, make me completely happy by having the same thoughts, sharing the same love, and being one in soul and mind. ³ Don't do anything from selfish ambition, or from a cheap desire to boast; but be humble toward each other, never thinking you are better than others. ⁴ And look out for each other's interests, not just for your own. ⁵ The attitude you should have is the one that Christ Jesus had:

⁶ He always had the very nature of God,
But he did not think that by force he should try to become equal with God.
⁷ Instead, of his own free will he gave it all up,
And took the nature of a servant.
He became like man, he appeared in human likeness;
⁸ He was humble and walked the path of obedience to death — his death on the cross.
⁹ For this reason God raised him to the highest place above,
And gave him the name that is greater than any other name,
¹⁰ So that, in honor of the name of Jesus,
All beings in heaven, and on the earth, and in the world below
Will fall on their knees,
¹¹ And all will openly proclaim that Jesus Christ is the Lord,
To the glory of God the Father.

Shining as Lights in the World

¹² So then, dear friends, as you always obeyed me when I was with you, it is even more important that you obey me now, while I am away from you. Keep on working, with fear and trembling, to complete your salvation, ¹³ for God is always at work in you to make you willing and able to obey his own purpose.

¹⁴ Do everything without complaining or arguing, ¹⁵ that you may be innocent and pure, as God's perfect children who live in a world of crooked and mean people. You must shine among them like stars lighting up the sky, ¹⁶ as you offer them the message of life. If you do so, I shall have reason to be proud of you on the Day of Christ; for it will show that all my effort and work have not been wasted.

17 Perhaps my life's blood is to be poured out like an offering on the sacrifice that your faith offers to God. If that is so, I am glad, and share my joy with you all. 18 In the same way, you too must be glad and share your joy with me.

Timothy and Epaphroditus

19 I trust in the Lord Jesus that I will be able to send Timothy to you soon, so that I may be encouraged by news of you. 20 He is the only one who shares my feelings, and who really cares about you. 21 Everyone else is concerned only about his own affairs, not about the cause of Jesus Christ. 22 And you yourselves know how he has proved his worth, how he and I, like father and son, have worked together for the sake of the gospel. 23 I hope to send him to you, then, as soon as I know how things are going to turn out for me; 24 and I trust in the Lord that I myself will be able to come to you soon.

25 I have thought it necessary to send you our brother Epaphroditus, who has worked and fought by my side, and who has served as your messenger in helping me. 26 He is anxious to see you all, and is very upset because you heard that he was sick. 27 Indeed he was sick, and almost died — but God had pity on him; and not only on him but on me, too, and spared me even greater sorrow. 28 I am all the more eager, therefore, to send him to you, so that you will be glad again when you see him, and my own sorrow will

disappear. 29 Receive him, then, with all joy, as a brother in the Lord. Show respect to all such men as he, 30 because he risked his life and nearly died, for the sake of the work of Christ, in order to give me the help that you yourselves could not give.

The True Righteousness

3 And in conclusion, my brothers, may the Lord give you much joy. It doesn't bother me to repeat what I have written before, and it will add to your safety. 2 Watch out for those who do evil things, those dogs, men who insist on cutting the body. 3 For we, not they, are the ones who have received the true circumcision, for we worship God by his Spirit, and rejoice in our life in Christ Jesus. We do not put any trust in external ceremonies. 4 I could, of course, put my trust in such things. If anyone thinks he can be safe in external ceremonies, I have even more reason to feel that way. 5 I was circumcised when I was a week old. I am an Israelite by birth, of the tribe of Benjamin, a pure-blooded Hebrew. So far as keeping the Jewish Law is concerned, I was a Pharisee, 6 and I was so zealous that I persecuted the church. So far as a man can be righteous by obeying the commands of the Law, I was without fault. 7 But all those things that I might count as profit I now reckon as loss, for Christ's sake. 8 Not only those things; I reckon everything as complete loss for the sake of what is so much more valuable, the knowledge of Christ Jesus my Lord. For his sake I have thrown everything away; I consider it all as mere garbage, so that I might gain Christ, 9 and be completely united with him. No longer do I have a righteousness of my own, the kind to be gained by obeying the Law. I now have the righteousness that is given through faith in Christ, the righteousness that comes from God, and is based on faith. 10 All I want is to know Christ and experience the power of his resurrection; to share in his sufferings and become like him in his death, 11 in the hope that I myself will be raised from death to life.

Running Toward the Goal

12 I do not claim that I have already succeeded in this, or have already become perfect. I keep going on to try

to possess it, for Christ Jesus has already possessed me.
¹³ Of course, brothers, I really do not think that I have
already reached it; the one thing I do, however, is to forget
what is behind me and do my best to reach what is ahead.

¹⁴ So I run straight toward the goal in order to win the
prize, which is God's call through Christ Jesus to the life
above.

¹⁵ All of us who are spiritually mature should have this
same attitude. If, however, some of you have a different
attitude, God will make this clear to you. ¹⁶ However that
may be, let us go forward according to the same rules we
have followed until now.

¹⁷ Keep on imitating me, brothers, all of you. We have
set the right example for you; so pay attention to those
who follow it. ¹⁸ I have told you this many times before,
and now I repeat it, with tears: there are many whose
lives make them enemies of Christ's death on the cross.
¹⁹ They are going to end up in hell, for their god is their
bodily desires, they are proud of what they should be
ashamed of, and they think only of things that belong to
this world. ²⁰ We, however, are citizens of heaven, and
we eagerly wait for our Savior to come from heaven, the
Lord Jesus Christ. ²¹ He will change our weak mortal
bodies and make them like his own glorious body, using
that power by which he is able to bring all things under
his rule.

Instructions

4 So, then, my brothers — and how dear you are to me, and how I miss you! how happy you make me, and how proud I am of you! — this, dear brothers, is how you should stand firm in your life in the Lord.

2 Euodia and Syntyche, please, I beg you, try to agree as sisters in the Lord. 3 And you too, my faithful partner, I want you to help these women; for they have worked hard with me to spread the gospel, together with Clement and all my other fellow workers, whose names are in God's book of the living.

4 May you always be joyful in your life in the Lord. I say it again: rejoice!

5 Show a gentle attitude toward all. The Lord is coming soon. 6 Don't worry about anything, but in all your prayers ask God for what you need, always asking him with a thankful heart. 7 And God's peace, which is far beyond human understanding, will keep your hearts and minds safe, in Christ Jesus.

8 In conclusion, my brothers, fill your minds with those things that are good and deserve praise: things that are true, noble, right, pure, lovely, and honorable. 9 Put into practice what you learned and received from me, both

from my words and from my deeds. And the God who gives us peace will be with you.

Thanks for the Gift

[10] How great is the joy I have in my life in the Lord! After so long a time, you once more had the chance of showing that you care for me. I don't mean that you had quit caring for me — you did not have a chance to show it. [11] And I am not saying this because I feel neglected; for I have learned to be satisfied with what I have. [12] I know what it is to be in need, and what it is to have more than enough. I have learned this secret, so that anywhere, at any time, I am content, whether I am full or hungry, whether I have too much or too little. [13] I have the strength to face all conditions by the power that Christ gives me.

[14] But it was very good of you to help me in my troubles. [15] You Philippians yourselves know very well that when I left Macedonia, in the early days of preaching the Good News, you were the only church to help me; you were the only ones who shared my profits and losses. [16] More than once, when I needed help in Thessalonica, you sent it to me. [17] It is not that I just want to receive gifts; rather, I want to see profit added to your account. [18] Here, then, is my receipt for everything you have given me — and it has been more than enough! I have all I need, now that Epaphroditus has brought me all your gifts. These are like a sweet-smelling offering to God, a sacrifice which is acceptable and pleasing to him. [19] And my God, with all his abundant wealth in Christ Jesus, will supply all your needs. [20] To our God and Father be the glory for ever and ever. Amen.

Final Greetings

[21] Greetings to all God's people who belong to Christ Jesus. The brothers here with me send you their greetings. [22] All God's people here send greetings, especially those who belong to the Emperor's palace.

[23] May the grace of the Lord Jesus Christ be with you all.

PAUL'S LETTER TO THE COLOSSIANS

1 From Paul, who by God's will is an apostle of Christ
Jesus, and from our brother Timothy—
² To God's people in Colossae, those who are our faithful brothers in Christ:
May God our Father give you grace and peace.

Prayer of Thanksgiving

³ We always give thanks to God, the Father of our
Lord Jesus Christ, when we pray for you. ⁴ For we have
heard of your faith in Christ Jesus, and of your love for
all God's people. ⁵ When the true message, the Good
News, first came to you, you heard of the hope it offers.
So your faith and love are based on what you hope for,
which is kept safe for you in heaven. ⁶ The gospel is
bringing blessings and spreading through the whole world,
just as it has among you ever since the day you first heard
of the grace of God and came to know it as it really is.
⁷ You learned this from Epaphras, our dear fellow servant, who is a faithful worker for Christ on our behalf.
⁸ He told us of the love that the Spirit has given you.

⁹ For this reason we always pray for you, ever since we
heard about you. We ask God to fill you with the knowledge of his will, with all the wisdom and understanding

that his Spirit gives. [10] Then you will be able to live as the Lord wants, and always do what pleases him. Your lives will be fruitful in all kinds of good works, and you will grow in your knowledge of God. [11] May you be made strong with all the strength which comes from his glorious might, that you may be able to endure everything with patience. [12] And give thanks, with joy, to the Father who has made you fit to have your share of what God has reserved for his people in the kingdom of light. [13] For he rescued us from the power of darkness and brought us safe into the kingdom of his dear Son, [14] by whom we are set free and our sins are forgiven.

The Person and Work of Christ

[15] Christ is the visible likeness of the invisible God. He is the first-born Son, superior to all created things. [16] For by him God created everything in heaven and on earth, the seen and the unseen things, including spiritual powers, lords, rulers, and authorities. God created the whole universe through him and for him. [17] He existed before all things, and in union with him all things have their proper place. [18] He is the head of his body, the church; he is the source of the body's life; he is the first-born Son who was raised from death, in order that he alone might have the first place in all things. [19] For it was by God's own decision that the Son has in himself the full nature of God. [20] Through the Son, then, God decided to bring the whole universe back to himself. God made peace through his Son's death on the cross, and so brought back to himself all things, both on earth and in heaven.

[21] At one time you were far away from God and made yourselves his enemies by the evil things you did and thought. [22] But now, by means of the physical death of his Son, God has made you his friends, in order to bring you, holy and pure and innocent, into his presence. [23] You must, of course, continue faithful on a firm and sure foundation, and not allow yourselves to be shaken from the hope you gained when you heard the gospel. It is of this gospel that I, Paul, became a servant — this gospel which has been preached to everybody in the world.

Paul's Ministry to the Church

[24] And now I am happy about my sufferings for you.

For by means of my physical sufferings I help complete what still remains of Christ's sufferings on behalf of his body, which is the church. [25] And I have been made a servant of the church by God, who gave me this task to perform for your good. It is the task of fully proclaiming his message, [26] which is the secret he hid through all past ages from all mankind, but has now revealed to his people. [27] For this is God's plan: to make known his secret to his people, this rich and glorious secret which he has for all peoples. And the secret is this: Christ is in you, which means that you will share the glory of God. [28] So we preach Christ to all men. We warn and teach everyone, with all possible wisdom, in order to bring each one into God's presence as a mature individual in union with Christ. [29] To get this done I toil and struggle, using the mighty strength that Christ supplies, which is at work in me.

2 Let me tell you how hard I have worked for you, and for the people in Laodicea, and for all those who do not know me personally. [2] I do so that their hearts may be filled with courage and that they may be drawn together in love and have the full wealth of assurance which true understanding brings. And so they will know God's secret, which is Christ himself. [3] He is the key that opens all the hidden treasures of God's wisdom and knowledge.

[4] I tell you, then: do not let anyone fool you with false arguments, no matter how good they seem to be. [5] For even though I am absent in body, yet I am with you in spirit, and I am glad as I see the resolute firmness with which you stand together in your faith in Christ.

Fulness of Life in Christ

[6] Since you have accepted Christ Jesus as Lord, live in union with him. [7] Keep your roots deep in him, build your lives on him, and become ever stronger in your faith, as you were taught. And be filled with thanksgiving.

[8] See to it, then, that no one makes a captive of you with the worthless deceit of human wisdom, which comes from the teachings handed down by men, and from the ruling spirits of the universe, and not from Christ. [9] For the full content of divine nature lives in Christ, in his humanity, [10] and you have been given full life in union with him. He is supreme over every spiritual ruler and authority.

¹¹ In union with him you were circumcised, not with the circumcision that is made by men, but with Christ's own circumcision, which consists of being freed from the power of this sinful body. ¹² For when you were baptized, you were buried with Christ, and in baptism you were also raised with Christ through your faith in the active power of God, who raised him from death. ¹³ You were at one time spiritually dead because of your sins, and because you were Gentiles outside the Law. But God has now brought you to life with Christ! God forgave us all our sins. ¹⁴ He cancelled the unfavorable record of our debts, with its binding rules, and did away with it completely by nailing

it to the cross. ¹⁵ And on that cross Christ freed himself from the power of the spiritual rulers and authorities; he made a public spectacle of them by leading them as captives in his victory procession.

¹⁶ So let no one make rules about what you eat or drink, or about the subject of holy days, or the new moon festival, or the sabbath. ¹⁷ All such things are only a shadow of things in the future; the reality is Christ. ¹⁸ Do not allow yourselves to be condemned by anyone who claims to be superior because of special visions, and insists on false humility and the worship of angels. Such a person is all puffed up, for no reason at all, by his human way of thinking, ¹⁹ and has stopped holding on to Christ, who is the head. Under Christ's control the whole body is nour-

ished and held together by its joints and ligaments, and grows as God wants it to grow.

Dying and Living with Christ

²⁰ You have died with Christ and are set free from the ruling spirits of the universe. Why, then, do you live as though you belonged to this world? Why do you obey such rules as ²¹ "Don't handle this," "Don't taste that," "Don't touch the other"? ²² All these things become useless, once they are used. These are only man-made rules and teachings. ²³ Of course they appear to have wisdom in their forced worship of angels, and false humility, and severe treatment of the body; but they have no real value in controlling physical passions.

3 You have been raised to life with Christ. Set your hearts, then, on the things that are in heaven, where Christ sits on his throne at the right side of God. ² Keep your minds fixed on things there, not on things here on earth. ³ For you have died, and your life is hidden with Christ in God. ⁴ Your real life is Christ, and when he appears, then you too will appear with him and share his glory!

The Old Life and the New

⁵ You must put to death, then, the earthly desires at work in you, such as immorality, indecency, lust, evil passions, and greed (for greediness is a form of idol worship). ⁶ Because of such things God's wrath will come upon those who do not obey him. ⁷ And you yourselves at one time used to live among such men, when your life was dominated by those desires.

⁸ But now you must get rid of all these things: anger, passion, and hateful feelings. No insults or obscene talk must ever come from your lips. ⁹ Do not lie to one another, for you have put off the old self with its habits, ¹⁰ and have put on the new self. This is the new man which God, its creator, is constantly renewing in his own image, to bring you to a full knowledge of himself. ¹¹ As a result, there are no Gentiles and Jews, circumcised and uncircumcised, barbarians, savages, slaves, or free men, but Christ is all, Christ is in all!

¹² You are the people of God; he loved you and chose

you for his own. Therefore, you must put on compassion, kindness, humility, gentleness, and patience. [13] Be helpful to one another, and forgive one another, whenever any of you has a complaint against someone else. You must forgive each other in the same way that the Lord has forgiven you. [14] And to all these add love, which binds all things together in perfect unity. [15] The peace that Christ gives is to be the judge in your hearts; for to this peace God has called you together in the one body. And be thankful. [16] Christ's message, in all its richness, must live in your hearts. Teach and instruct each other with all wisdom. Sing psalms, hymns, and sacred songs; sing to God, with thanksgiving in your hearts. [17] Everything you do or say, then, should be done in the name of the Lord Jesus, as you give thanks through him to God the Father.

Personal Relations in the New Life

[18] Wives, be obedient to your husbands, for that is what you should do as Christians.

[19] Husbands, love your wives, and do not be harsh with them.

[20] Children, it is your Christian duty to obey your parents always, for that is what pleases God.

[21] Parents, do not irritate your children, or they might become discouraged.

[22] Slaves, obey your human masters in all things, and do it not only when they are watching you, just to gain their approval, but do it with a sincere heart, because of your reverence for the Lord. [23] Whatever you do, work at it with all your heart, as though you were working for the Lord, and not for men. [24] Remember that the Lord will reward you; you will receive what he has kept for his people. For Christ is the real Master you serve. [25] And the wrongdoer, whoever he is, will be paid for the wrong things he does; for God treats everyone alike.

4 Masters, be right and fair in the way you treat your slaves. Remember that you too have a Master in heaven.

Instructions

[2] Be persistent in prayer, and keep alert as you pray, with thanks to God. [3] At the same time pray also for us,

that God will give us a good opportunity to preach his message, to tell the secret of Christ. For that is why I am now in prison. [4] Pray, then, that I may speak in such a way as to make it clear, as I should.

[5] Be wise in the way you act toward those who are not believers, making good use of every opportunity you have. [6] Your speech should always be pleasant and interesting, and you should know how to give the right answer to every person.

Final Greetings

[7] Our dear brother Tychicus, who is a faithful worker and fellow servant in the Lord's work, will give you all the news about me. [8] That is why I am sending him to you, to cheer you up by telling you how all of us are getting along. [9] With him goes Onesimus, the dear and faithful brother, who belongs to your group. They will tell you everything that is happening here.

[10] Aristarchus, who is in prison with me, sends you greetings, and so does Mark, the cousin of Barnabas. (You have already received instructions about him, to welcome him if he comes your way.) [11] Joshua, called Justus, also sends greetings. These three are the only Jewish converts who work with me for the Kingdom of God, and they have been a great help to me.

[12] Greetings from Epaphras, another member of your group, and a servant of Christ Jesus. He always prays fervently for you, asking God to make you stand firm, mature, and fully convinced, in complete obedience to his will. [13] I can personally testify to his hard work for you, and for the people in Laodicea and Hierapolis. [14] Luke, our dear doctor, and Demas send you their greetings.

[15] Give our best wishes to the brothers in Laodicea, and to Nympha and the church that meets in her house. [16] After you read this letter, make sure that it is read also in the church at Laodicea. At the same time, you are to read the letter Laodicea will send you. [17] And tell Archippus: "Be sure to finish the task you were given in the Lord's service."

[18] With my own hand I write this: *Greetings from Paul.* Do not forget my chains!

May God's grace be with you.

PAUL'S FIRST LETTER TO THE THESSALONIANS

1 From Paul, Silas, and Timothy—
To the people of the church in Thessalonica, who belong to God the Father and the Lord Jesus Christ:
May grace and peace be yours.

The Life and Faith of the Thessalonians

² We always thank God for you all, and always mention you in our prayers. ³ For we remember before our God and Father how you put your faith into practice, how your love made you work so hard, and how your hope in our Lord Jesus Christ is firm. ⁴ We know, brothers, that God loves you and has chosen you to be his own. ⁵ For we brought the Good News to you, not with words only, but also with power and the Holy Spirit, and with complete conviction of its truth. You know how we lived when we were with you; it was for your own good. ⁶ You imitated us and the Lord; and even though you suffered much, you received the message with the joy that comes from the Holy Spirit. ⁷ So you became an example to all believers in Macedonia and Greece. ⁸ For the message about the Lord went out from you not only to Macedonia and Greece, but the news of your faith in God has gone everywhere. There is nothing, then, that we need to say. ⁹ All those people speak of how you received us when we visited you, and how you turned away from idols to God, to serve the true and living God ¹⁰ and to wait for his Son to come from heaven — his Son Jesus, whom he raised from death, and who rescues us from God's wrath that is to come.

Paul's Work in Thessalonica

2 For you yourselves know, brothers, that our visit to you was not a failure. ² You know how we had already been mistreated and insulted in Philippi before we came to you in Thessalonica. Yet our God gave us courage to tell you the Good News that comes from him, even though there was much opposition. ³ For the appeal we make to you is not based on error or impure motives, nor do we try to trick anyone. ⁴ Instead, we always speak as God wants us to, because he approved us and entrusted the Good News to us. We do not try to please men, but to please God, who tests our motives. ⁵ For you know very well that we did not come to you with flattering talk, nor did we use words to cover up greed — God is our witness! ⁶ We did not try to get praise from anyone, either from you or from others, ⁷ even though we could have made demands on you as apostles of Christ. But we were gentle when we were with you, as gentle as a mother taking care of her children. ⁸ Because of our love for you we were ready to share with you not only the Good News from God but even our own lives. You were so dear to us! ⁹ Surely you remember, brothers, how we worked and toiled! We worked day and night so we would not be any trouble to you as we preached to you the Good News from God.

¹⁰ You are our witnesses, and so is God: our conduct toward you who believe was pure, and right, and without fault. ¹¹ You know that we treated each one of you just as a father treats his own children. ¹² We encouraged you, we comforted you, and we kept urging you to live the kind of life that pleases God, who calls you to share his own Kingdom and glory.

¹³ And for this other reason, also, we always give thanks to God. When we brought you God's message, you heard it and accepted it, not as man's message but as God's message, which indeed it is. For God is at work among you who believe. ¹⁴ You, my brothers, had the same things happen to you that happened to the churches of God in Judea, to the people there who belong to Christ Jesus. You suffered the same persecutions from your own countrymen that they suffered from the Jews, ¹⁵ who killed the Lord Jesus and the prophets, and persecuted us. How displeas-

ing they are to God! How hostile they are to all men!
[16] They even tried to stop us from preaching to the Gentiles the message that would bring them salvation. This is the last full measure of the sins they have always committed. And now God's wrath has at last fallen upon them!

Paul's Desire to Visit Them Again

[17] As for us, brothers, when we were separated from you for a little while — not in our thoughts, of course, but only in body — how we missed you and how hard we tried to see you again! [18] We wanted to go back to you. I, Paul, tried to go back more than once, but Satan would not let us. [19] After all, it is you — you, and no one else! — who are our hope, our joy, and our reason for boasting of our victory in the presence of our Lord Jesus when he comes. [20] Indeed, you are our pride and our joy!

3 Finally, we could not bear it any longer. So we decided to stay on alone in Athens [2] while we sent Timothy, our brother who works with us for God in preaching the Good News about Christ. We sent him to strengthen you and help your faith, [3] that none of you should turn back because of these persecutions. You yourselves know that such persecutions are part of God's will for us. [4] For while we were still with you, we told you ahead of time that we were going to be persecuted; and, as you well know, that is exactly what happened. [5] That is why I had to send Timothy. I could not bear it any longer, so I sent him to find out about your faith. Surely it could not be that the Devil had tempted you, and all our work had been for nothing!

[6] Now Timothy has come back to us from you, and he has brought the welcome news about your faith and love. He has told us that you always think well of us, and that you want to see us just as much as we want to see you. [7] So, in all our trouble and suffering we have been encouraged about you, brothers. It was your faith that encouraged us, [8] for now we really live if you stand firm in your life in the Lord. [9] For now we can give thanks to God for you. We thank him for the joy we have before our God because of you. [10] Day and night we ask him with all our heart to let us see you personally and supply what is needed in your faith.

[11] May our God and Father himself, and our Lord

Jesus, prepare the way for us to come to you! [12] May the Lord make your love for one another and for all people grow more and more and become as great as our love for you. [13] In this way he will make your hearts strong, and you will be perfect and holy in the presence of our God and Father when our Lord Jesus comes with all who belong to him.

A Life that Pleases God

4 Finally, brothers, you learned from us how you should live in order to please God. This is, of course, the way you have been living. And now we beg and urge you, in the name of the Lord Jesus, to do even more. [2] For you know the instructions we gave you, by the authority of the Lord Jesus. [3] This is God's will for you: he wants you to be holy and completely free from immorality. [4] Each of you men should know how to take a wife in a holy and honorable way, [5] not with a lustful desire, like the heathen who do not know God. [6] In this matter, then, no man

should do wrong to his brother or violate his rights. We have told you this before, we strongly warned you, that the Lord will punish those who do such wrongs. [7] God did not call us to live in immorality, but in holiness. [8] So then, whoever rejects this teaching is not rejecting man, but God, who gives you his Holy Spirit.

[9] There is no need to write you about love for your fellow believers. For you yourselves have been taught by God how you should love one another. [10] And you have

behaved in this way toward all the brothers in all of Macedonia. So we beg you, brothers, to do even more. ¹¹ Make it your aim to live a quiet life, to mind your own business, and earn your own living, just as we told you before. ¹² In this way you will win the respect of those who are not believers, and will not have to depend on anyone for what you need.

The Lord's Coming

¹³ Brothers, we want you to know the truth about those who have died, so that you will not be sad, as are those who have no hope. ¹⁴ We believe that Jesus died and rose again; so we believe that God will bring with Jesus those who have died believing in him.

¹⁵ For this is the Lord's teaching we tell you: we who are alive on the day the Lord comes will not go ahead of those who have died. ¹⁶ There will be the shout of command, the archangel's voice, the sound of God's trumpet, and the Lord himself will come down from heaven! Those who have died believing in Christ will be raised to life first; ¹⁷ then we who are living at that time will all be gathered up along with them in the clouds to meet the Lord in the air. And so we will always be with the Lord. ¹⁸ Therefore, cheer each other up with these words.

Be Ready for the Lord's Coming

5 There is no need to write you, brothers, about the times and occasions when these things will happen. ² For you yourselves know very well that the Day of the Lord will come like a thief comes at night. ³ When people say, "Everything is quiet and safe," then suddenly destruction will hit them! They will not escape — it will be like the pains that come upon a woman who is about to give birth. ⁴ But you, brothers, are not in the darkness, and the Day should not take you by surprise like a thief. ⁵ All of you are people who belong to the light, who belong to the day. We are not of the night or of the darkness. ⁶ So then, we should not be sleeping, like the others; we should be awake and sober. ⁷ It is at night when people sleep; it is at night when people get drunk. ⁸ But we belong to the day, and we should be sober. We must wear faith and love as a breastplate, and our hope of salvation as a helmet. ⁹ God did not choose us to suffer his wrath, but to possess salva-

tion through our Lord Jesus Christ, ¹⁰ who died for us in order that we might live together with him, whether we are alive or dead when he comes. ¹¹ For this reason encourage one another, and help one another, just as you are now doing.

Final Instructions and Greetings

¹² We beg you, brothers, to pay proper respect to those who work among you, those whom the Lord has chosen to guide and instruct you. ¹³ Treat them with the greatest respect and love, because of the work they do. Be at peace among yourselves.

¹⁴ We urge you brothers: warn the idle, encourage the timid, help the weak, be patient with all. ¹⁵ See that no one pays back wrong for wrong, but at all times make it your aim to do good to one another and to all people.

¹⁶ Be joyful always, ¹⁷ pray at all times, ¹⁸ be thankful in all circumstances. This is what God wants of you, in your life in Christ Jesus.

¹⁹ Do not restrain the Holy Spirit; ²⁰ do not despise in-

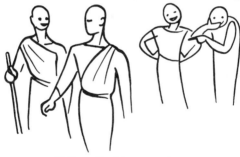

spired messages. ²¹ Put all things to the test: keep what is good, ²² and avoid every kind of evil.

²³ May the God who gives us peace make you completely his, and keep your whole being, spirit, soul, and body, free from all fault, at the coming of our Lord Jesus Christ. ²⁴ He who calls you will do it, for he is faithful!

²⁵ Pray also for us, brothers.

²⁶ Greet all the brothers with a brotherly kiss.

²⁷ I urge you, by the authority of the Lord, to read this letter to all the brothers.

²⁸ The grace of our Lord Jesus Christ be with you.

PAUL'S SECOND LETTER
TO THE THESSALONIANS

1 From Paul, Silas, and Timothy —
To the people of the church in Thessalonica, who belong to God our Father and the Lord Jesus Christ:
² May God the Father and the Lord Jesus Christ give you grace and peace.

The Judgment at Christ's Coming

³ We must thank God at all times for you, brothers! It is right for us to do so, because your faith is growing so much and the love each of you has for the others is becoming greater. ⁴ That is why we ourselves boast about you in the churches of God. We boast about the way you continue to endure and believe, through all the persecutions and sufferings you are experiencing.

⁵ Here is the proof of God's righteous judgment, for as a result of all this you will become worthy of his Kingdom, for which you are suffering. ⁶ For God will do what is right: he will bring suffering on those who make you suffer, ⁷ and he will give relief to you who suffer, and to us as well. He will do this when the Lord Jesus appears from heaven with his mighty angels, ⁸ with a flaming fire, to punish those who do not know God and those who do not obey the Good News about our Lord Jesus. ⁹ They will suffer the punishment of eternal destruction, separated from the presence of the Lord and from his glorious might, ¹⁰ when he comes on that Day to receive glory from all his people and honor from all who believe. You too will be among them, for you have believed the message that we told you.

¹¹ This is why we always pray for you. We ask our God to make you worthy of the life he called you to live. May he, by his power, fulfil all your desire for goodness and complete your work of faith. ¹² In this way the name of our Lord Jesus will receive glory from you, and you from him, by the grace of our God and the Lord Jesus Christ.

The Wicked One

2 Concerning the coming of our Lord Jesus Christ and our being gathered together to be with him: I beg you, brothers, [2] do not be so easily confused in your thinking or upset by the claim that the Day of the Lord has come. Perhaps this was said by someone prophesying, or by someone preaching. Or it may have been said that we wrote this in a letter. [3] Do not let anyone fool you in any way. For the Day will not come until the final Rebellion takes place and the Wicked One appears, who is destined to hell. [4] He will oppose everything which men worship and everything which men consider divine. He will put himself above them all, and even go in and sit down in God's temple and claim to be God!

[5] Don't you remember? I told you all this while I was with you. [6] Yet there is something that keeps this from happening now, and you know what it is. At the proper time, then, the Wicked One will appear. [7] The Mysterious Wickedness is already at work, but what is going to happen will not happen until the one who holds it back is taken out of the way. [8] Then the Wicked One will appear, and the Lord Jesus will kill him with the breath from his mouth and destroy him with his glorious appearing, when he comes. [9] The Wicked One will come with the power of Satan and perform all kinds of miracles and false signs and wonders, [10] and use every kind of wicked deceit on those who will perish. They will perish because they did not welcome and love the truth so as to be saved. [11] For this reason God sends the power of error to work in them so that they believe what is false. [12] The result is that all who have not believed the truth, but have taken pleasure in sin, will be condemned.

You Are Chosen for Salvation

[13] We must thank God at all times for you, brothers, you whom the Lord loves. For God chose you as the first to be saved by the Spirit's power to make you God's own people, and by your faith in the truth. [14] God called you to this through the Good News we preached to you; he called you to possess your share of the glory of our Lord Jesus Christ. [15] So then, brothers, stand firm and hold on

to those truths which we taught you, both in our preaching and in our letter.

[16] May our Lord Jesus Christ himself, and God our Father, who loved us and in his grace gave us eternal courage and a good hope, [17] fill your hearts with courage and make you strong to do and say all that is good.

Pray for Us

3 Finally, brothers, pray for us, that the Lord's message may continue to spread rapidly and receive glory, just as it did among you. [2] Pray also that God will rescue us from wicked and evil men. For not all people believe the message.

[3] But the Lord is faithful. He will make you strong and keep you safe from the Evil One. [4] And the Lord gives us confidence in you; we are sure that you are doing and will continue to do what we tell you.

[5] May the Lord lead your hearts to the love for God and to the endurance that is given by Christ.

The Obligation to Work

[6] In the name of the Lord Jesus Christ we command you, brothers: keep away from all brothers who are living a lazy life, who do not follow the instructions that we gave them. [7] You yourselves know very well that you should do just what we did. We were not lazy when we were with you. [8] We did not accept anyone's support without paying for it. Instead, we worked and toiled; day and night we kept working so as not to be an expense to any of you. [9] We did this, not because we do not have the right to demand our support; we did it to be an example for you to follow. [10] While we were with you we told you: "Whoever does not want to work is not allowed to eat."

[11] We say this because we hear that there are some people among you who live lazy lives, who do nothing except meddle in other people's business. [12] In the name of the Lord Jesus Christ we command these people and warn them: they must lead orderly lives and work to earn their own living.

[13] But you, brothers, must not get tired of doing good. [14] There may be someone there who will not obey the message we send you in this letter. If so, take note of him

and have nothing to do with him, so that he will be ashamed. ¹⁵ But do not treat him as an enemy; instead, warn him as a brother.

Final Words

¹⁶ May the Lord himself, who is our source of peace, give you peace at all times and in every way. The Lord be with you all.

¹⁷ With my own hand I write this: *Greetings from Paul.* This is the way I sign every letter; this is how I write.

¹⁸ May the grace of our Lord Jesus Christ be with you all.

PAUL'S FIRST LETTER TO TIMOTHY

1 From Paul, an apostle of Christ Jesus by order of God our Savior and Christ Jesus our hope —

² To Timothy, my true son in the faith:

May God the Father and Christ Jesus our Lord give you grace, mercy, and peace.

Warnings against False Teaching

³ I want you to stay in Ephesus, just as I urged you when I was on my way to Macedonia. Some people there are teaching false doctrines, and you must order them to stop. ⁴ Tell them to give up those legends and long lists of names of ancestors, for these only produce arguments; they do not serve God's plan, which is known by faith. ⁵ The purpose of this order is to arouse the love that comes from a pure heart, a clear conscience, and a genuine faith. ⁶ Some men have turned away from these and have lost their way in foolish discussions. ⁷ They want to be teachers of God's law, but they do not understand their own words or the matters about which they speak with so much confidence.

⁸ We know that the Law is good, if it is used as it should be used. ⁹ It must be remembered, of course, that laws are made, not for good people, but for lawbreakers and criminals, for the godless and sinful, for those who are not religious or spiritual, for men who kill their fathers or mothers, for murderers, ¹⁰ for the immoral, for sexual perverts, for kidnappers, for those who lie and give false testimony or do anything else contrary to the true teaching. ¹¹ That is the teaching found in the gospel that was entrusted to me to announce, the Good News from the glorious and blessed God.

Gratitude for God's Mercy

¹² I give thanks to Christ Jesus our Lord, who has given me strength for my work. I thank him for considering me worthy, and appointing me to serve him, ¹³ even though in the past I spoke evil of him, and persecuted and insulted him. But God was merciful to me, because I did not believe and so did not know what I was doing. ¹⁴ And our Lord poured out his abundant grace on me and gave me the faith and love which are ours in union with Christ

Jesus. [15] This is a true saying, to be completely accepted and believed: Christ Jesus came into the world to save sinners. I am the worst of them, [16] but it was for this very reason that God was merciful to me, in order that Christ Jesus might show his full patience in dealing with me, the worst of sinners, as an example for all those who would later believe in him and receive eternal life. [17] To the eternal King, immortal and invisible, the only God—to him be honor and glory for ever and ever! Amen.

[18] Timothy, my child, I entrust this command to you. It is according to the words of prophecy spoken long ago about you. Let those words be your weapons as you fight the good fight, [19] and keep your faith and clear conscience. Some men have not listened to their conscience, and have made a ruin of their faith. [20] Among them are Hymenaeus and Alexander, whom I have handed over to the power of Satan, so that they will be taught to stop speaking evil of God.

Church Worship

2 First of all, then, I urge that petitions and prayers, requests and thanksgivings be offered to God for all men; [2] for kings and all others who are in authority, that

we may live a quiet and peaceful life, in entire godliness and proper conduct. ³ This is good and it pleases God our Savior, ⁴ who wants all men to be saved and to come to know the truth. ⁵ For there is one God, and there is one who brings God and men together, the man Christ Jesus, ⁶ who gave himself to redeem all men. That was the proof, at the right time, that God wants all men to be saved, ⁷ and this is why I was sent as an apostle and teacher of the Gentiles, to proclaim the message of faith and truth. I am not lying, I am telling the truth!

⁸ I want men everywhere to pray, men who are dedicated to God and can lift up their hands in prayer without anger or argument.

⁹ I also want women to be modest and sensible about their clothes and to dress properly; not with fancy hair styles, or with gold ornaments or pearls or expensive dresses, ¹⁰ but with good deeds, as is proper for women who claim to be religious. ¹¹ Women should learn in silence and all humility. ¹² I do not allow women to teach or to have authority over men; they must keep quiet. ¹³ For Adam was created first, and then Eve. ¹⁴ And it was not Adam who was deceived; it was the woman who was deceived and broke God's law. ¹⁵ But a woman will be saved through having children, if she perseveres in faith and love and holiness, with modesty.

Leaders in the Church

3 This is a true saying: If a man is eager to be a church leader he desires an excellent work. ² A church leader must be a man without fault; he must have only one wife, be sober, self-controlled, and orderly; he must welcome strangers in his home; he must be able to teach; ³ he must not be a drunkard or a violent man, but gentle and peaceful; he must not love money; ⁴ he must be able to manage his own family well, and make his children obey him with all respect. ⁵ For if a man does not know how to manage his own family, how can he take care of the church of God? ⁶ He must not be a man who has been recently converted; else he will swell up with pride and be condemned, as the Devil was. ⁷ He should be a man who is respected by the people outside the church, so that he will not be disgraced and fall into the Devil's trap.

Helpers in the Church

8 Church helpers must also be of a good character and sincere; they must not drink too much wine or be greedy; 9 they should hold to the revealed truth of the faith with a clear conscience. 10 They should be tested first, and then, if they pass the test, they should serve. 11 Their wives also must be of good character, and not gossip; they must be sober and honest in everything. 12 A church helper must have only one wife, and be able to manage his children and family well. 13 Those who do a good work win for themselves a good standing and are able to speak boldly about the faith that is ours in union with Christ Jesus.

The Great Secret

14 As I write this letter to you, I hope to come and see you soon. 15 But if I delay, this letter will let you know how we should conduct ourselves in God's household, which is the church of the living God, the pillar and support of the truth. 16 No one can deny how great is the secret of our religion!

He appeared in human form,
Was shown to be right by the Spirit,
And was seen by angels.
He was preached among the nations,
Was believed in the world,
And was taken up to heaven.

False Teachers

4 The Spirit says clearly that some men will abandon the faith in later times; they will obey lying spirits and follow the teachings of demons. 2 These teachings come from the deceit of men who are liars, and whose consciences are dead, as if burnt with a hot iron. 3 Such men teach that it is wrong to marry, and to eat certain foods. But God created these foods to be eaten, after a prayer of thanks, by those who are believers and have come to know the truth. 4 Everything that God has created is good; nothing is to be rejected, but all is to be received with a prayer of thanks; 5 for the word of God and the prayer make it acceptable to God.

A Good Servant of Christ Jesus

⁶ If you give these instructions to the brothers you will be a good servant of Christ Jesus, as you feed yourself spiritually on the words of faith and of the true teaching which you have followed. ⁷ But keep away from those godless legends, which are not worth telling. Keep yourself in training for a godly life. ⁸ Physical exercise has some value in it, but spiritual exercise is valuable in every way, for it promises life both for now and for the future. ⁹ This is a true saying, to be completely accepted and believed. ¹⁰ That is why we struggle and work hard, for we have placed our hope on the living God who is Savior of all men, and especially of those who believe.

¹¹ Command and teach these things. ¹² Do not let anyone look down on you because you are young, but be an example for the believers, in your speech, your conduct, your love, faith, and purity. ¹³ Give your time and effort, until I come, to the public reading of the Scriptures, and to preaching and teaching. ¹⁴ Do not neglect the spiritual gift that is in you, which was given to you when the prophets spoke and the elders laid their hands on you. ¹⁵ Practice these things and give yourself to them, in order that your progress may be seen by all. ¹⁶ Watch yourself, and watch your teaching. Keep on doing these things, for if you do you will save both yourself and those who hear you.

Responsibilities toward Believers

5 Do not rebuke an older man, but appeal to him as if he were your father. Treat the younger men as your brothers, ² the older women as mothers, and the younger women as sisters, with all purity.

³ Show respect for widows who really are widows. ⁴ But if a widow has children or grandchildren, they should learn first to carry out their religious duties toward their own family and in this way repay their parents and grandparents, for that is what pleases God. ⁵ The woman who is a true widow, with no one to take care of her, has placed her hope in God and continues to pray and ask him for his help night and day. ⁶ But the widow who gives herself to pleasure has already died, even though she lives. ⁷ Give them this command, so that no one will reproach

them. 8 But if someone does not take care of his relatives, especially the members of his own family, he has denied the faith and is worse than an unbeliever.

9 Do not add any widow to the list of widows unless she is more than sixty years old. In addition, she must have been married only once, 10 and have a reputation for good deeds: a woman who brought up her children well, received strangers in her home, washed the feet of God's people, helped those in trouble, and gave herself to all kinds of good works.

11 But do not include the younger widows in the list; for when their desires make them want to marry, they turn away from Christ, 12 and so become guilty of breaking their first promise to him. 13 They also learn to waste their time in going around from house to house; but even worse, they learn to be gossips and busybodies, talking of things they should not. 14 So I would rather that the younger widows get married, have children, and take care of their homes, so as to give our enemies no chance of speaking evil of us. 15 For some widows have already turned away to follow Satan. 16 But if any woman who is a believer has widows in her family, she must take care of them, and not put the burden on the church, so that it may take care of the widows who are all alone.

17 The elders who do good work as leaders should be considered worthy of receiving double pay, especially those who work hard at preaching and teaching. 18 For the scripture says, "Do not tie up the mouth of the ox when it is treading out the grain," and, "The worker de-

serves his wages." ¹⁹ Do not listen to an accusation against an elder unless it is brought by two or three witnesses. ²⁰ Rebuke publicly all those who commit sins, so that the rest may be afraid.

²¹ In the presence of God, and of Christ Jesus, and of the holy angels, I solemnly call upon you to obey these instructions without showing any prejudice or favor to anyone in anything you do. ²² Be in no hurry to lay hands on anyone for the Lord's service. Take no part in the sins of others; keep yourself pure.

²³ Do not drink water only, but take a little wine to help your digestion, since you are sick so often.

²⁴ The sins of some men are plain to see, and their sins go ahead of them to judgment; but the sins of others are seen only later. ²⁵ In the same way good deeds are plainly seen, and even those that are not so plain cannot be hidden.

6 All who are slaves must consider their masters worthy of all respect, so that no one will speak evil of the name of God and of our teaching. ² Slaves belonging to masters who are believers must not despise them because they are their brothers. Instead, they are to serve them even better, because those who benefit from their work are believers whom they love.

False Teaching and True Riches

You must teach and preach these things. ³ Whoever teaches a different doctrine and does not agree with the true words of our Lord Jesus Christ and with the teaching of our religion ⁴ is swollen with pride and knows nothing. He has an unhealthy desire to argue and quarrel about words, and this brings on jealousy, dissension, insults, evil suspicions, ⁵ and constant arguments from men whose minds do not function and who no longer have the truth. They think that religion is a way to become rich.

⁶ Well, religion does make a man very rich, if he is satisfied with what he has. ⁷ What did we bring into the world? Nothing! What can we take out of the world? Nothing! ⁸ So then, if we have food and clothes, that should be enough for us. ⁹ But those who want to get rich fall into temptation and are caught in the trap of many foolish and harmful desires, which pull men down to ruin and destruction. ¹⁰ For the love of money is a source of all kinds of evil. Some have been so eager to have it that

they have wandered away from the faith and have broken their hearts with many sorrows.

Personal Instructions

[11] But you, man of God, avoid all these things. Strive for righteousness, godliness, faith, love, endurance, and gentleness. [12] Run your best in the race of faith, and win eternal life for yourself; for it was to this life that God called you when you made your good profession of faith before many witnesses. [13] Before God, who gives life to all things, and before Christ Jesus, who made the good profession before Pontius Pilate, I command you: [14] Obey the commandment and keep it pure and faultless, until the Day our Lord Jesus Christ will appear. [15] His appearing will be brought about at the right time by God, the blessed and only Ruler, the King of kings and the Lord of lords. [16] He alone is immortal; he lives in the light that no one can approach. No one has ever seen him, no one can ever see him. To him be honor and eternal might! Amen.

[17] Command those who are rich in the things of this life not to be proud, and to place their hope, not on such an uncertain thing as riches, but on God, who generously gives us everything for us to enjoy. [18] Command them to do good, to be rich in good works, to be generous and ready to share with others. [19] In this way they will store up for themselves a treasure which will be a solid foundation for the future. And then they will be able to win the life which is true life.

[20] Timothy, keep safe what has been turned over to your care. Avoid the godless talk and foolish arguments of "Knowledge," as some people wrongly call it. [21] For some have claimed to possess it, and as a result they have lost the way of faith.

God's grace be with you all.

PAUL'S SECOND LETTER TO TIMOTHY

1 From Paul, an apostle of Christ Jesus by God's will, sent to proclaim the promised life which we have in union with Christ Jesus —

2 To Timothy, my dear son:

May God the Father and Christ Jesus our Lord give you grace, mercy, and peace.

Thanksgiving and Encouragement

3 I give thanks to God, whom I serve with a clear conscience, as my ancestors did. I thank him as I remember you always in my prayers, night and day. 4 I remember your tears, and I want to see you very much, that I may be filled with joy. 5 I remember the sincere faith you have, the kind of faith that your grandmother Lois and your mother Eunice also had. I am sure that you have it also. 6 For this reason I remind you to keep alive the gift that God gave to you when I laid my hands on you. 7 For the Spirit that God has given us does not make us timid; instead, his Spirit fills us with power and love and self-control.

8 Do not be ashamed, then, of witnessing for our Lord; neither be ashamed of me, his prisoner. Instead, take your part in suffering for the Good News, as God gives you the strength for it. 9 He saved us and called us to be his own people, not because of what we have done, but because of his own purpose and grace. He gave this grace to us in Christ Jesus before the beginning of time, 10 but now it has been revealed to us through the appearing of our Savior, Christ Jesus. For Christ has ended the power of death, and through the Good News he has revealed immortal life.

11 God has appointed me to proclaim the Good News as an apostle and teacher, 12 and it is for this reason that I suffer these things. But I am still full of confidence, for I know whom I have trusted, and I am sure that he is able to keep safe until that Day what he has entrusted to me. 13 Hold to the true words that I taught you, as the example for you to follow, and stay in the faith and love that are ours in union with Christ Jesus. 14 Keep the good things that have been entrusted to you, through the power of the Holy Spirit who lives in us.

¹⁵ You know that everyone in the province of Asia deserted me, including Phygelus and Hermogenes. ¹⁶ May the Lord show mercy to the family of Onesiphorus, because he cheered me up many times. He was not ashamed that I am in prison, ¹⁷ but as soon as he arrived in Rome he started looking for me until he found me. ¹⁸ May the Lord grant him to receive mercy from the Lord on that Day! And you know very well how much he did for me in Ephesus.

A Loyal Soldier of Christ Jesus

2 As for you, my son, be strong through the grace that is ours in union with Christ Jesus. ² Take the words that you heard me preach in the presence of many witnesses, and give them into the keeping of men you can trust, men who will be able to teach others also.

³ Take your part in suffering, as a loyal soldier of Christ Jesus. ⁴ A soldier in active service wants to please his com-

manding officer, and so does not get mixed up in the affairs of civilian life. ⁵ An athlete who runs in a race cannot win the prize unless he obeys the rules. ⁶ The farmer who has done the hard work should have the first share of the harvest. ⁷ Think about what I am saying, for the Lord will enable you to understand all things.

⁸ Remember Jesus Christ, who was raised from death, who was a descendant of David, as told in the Good News I preach. ⁹ Because I preach the Good News I suffer, and I am even chained like a criminal. But the word of God is not in chains, ¹⁰ and for this reason I endure everything

for the sake of God's chosen people, in order that they too may obtain the salvation that is in Christ Jesus, together with eternal glory. [11] This is a true saying:

> "If we have died with him, we shall also
> live with him;

[12] If we continue to endure, we shall also rule
> with him;

> If we deny him, he also will deny us;

[13] If we are not faithful, he remains faithful,
> For he cannot be false to himself."

An Approved Worker

[14] Remind your people of this, and give them solemn warning in God's presence not to fight over words. It does no good, but only ruins the people who listen. [15] Do your best to win full approval in God's sight, as a worker who is not ashamed of his work, one who correctly teaches the message of God's truth. [16] Keep away from godless and foolish discussions, which only drive people farther away from God. [17] What they teach will be like an open sore that eats away the flesh. Two of these teachers are Hymenaeus and Philetus. [18] They have left the way of truth and are upsetting the faith of some believers by saying that our resurrection has already taken place. [19] But the solid foundation that God has laid cannot be shaken; and these words are written on it: "The Lord knows those who are his"; and, "Whoever says that he belongs to the Lord must turn away from wrongdoing."

[20] In a large house there are dishes and bowls of all kinds: some are made of silver and gold, others of wood and clay; some are for special occasions, others for ordinary use. [21] If anyone makes himself clean from all these evil things, he will be used for special purposes, for he is dedicated and useful to his Master, ready to be used for every good work. [22] Avoid the passions of youth, and strive for righteousness, faith, love, and peace, along with those who with a pure heart call for the Lord to help them. [23] But stay away from foolish and ignorant arguments; you know that they end up in quarrels. [24] The Lord's servant must not quarrel. He must be kind toward all, a good and patient teacher, [25] who is gentle as he corrects his opponents. It may be that God will give them the opportunity to repent and come to know the truth.

[26] And then they will return to their senses and escape from the trap of the Devil, who had caught them and made them obey his will.

The Last Days

3 Remember this! There will be difficult times in the last days. [2] For men will be selfish, greedy, boastful, and conceited; they will be insulting, disobedient to their parents, ungrateful, and irreligious; [3] they will be unkind, merciless, slanderers, violent, and fierce; they will hate the good; [4] they will be treacherous, reckless, and swollen with pride; they will love pleasure rather than God; [5] they will hold to the outward form of our religion, but reject its real power. Keep away from these men. [6] Some of them go into homes and get control over weak women who are weighed down by the guilt of their sins and driven by all kinds of desires, [7] women who are always trying to learn but who never can come to know the truth. [8] As Jannes and Jambres were opposed to Moses, so also these men are opposed to the truth — men whose minds do not function and who are failures in the faith. [9] But they will not go very far, because everyone will see how stupid they are, just as it happened to Jannes and Jambres.

Last Instructions

[10] But you have followed my teaching, my conduct, and my purpose in life; you have observed my faith, my patience, my love, my endurance, [11] my persecutions, and my sufferings. You know all the things that happened to me in Antioch, Iconium, and Lystra, the terrible persecutions I endured! But the Lord rescued me from them all. [12] All who want to live a godly life in union with Christ Jesus will be persecuted; [13] but evil men and impostors will keep on going from bad to worse, deceiving others and being deceived themselves. [14] But as for you, continue in the truths that you were taught and firmly believe. For you know who your teachers were, [15] and you know that ever since you were a child you have known the Holy Scriptures, which are able to give you the wisdom that leads to salvation through faith in Christ Jesus. [16] For all Scripture is inspired by God and is useful for teaching the truth, rebuking error, correcting faults, and giving instruc-

tion for right living, 17 so that the man who serves God may be fully qualified and equipped to do every kind of good work.

4 I solemnly call upon you in the presence of God and of Christ Jesus, who will judge all men, living and dead: because of his coming and of his Kingdom, I command you 2 to preach the message, to insist upon telling it, whether the time is right or not; to convince, reproach, and encourage, teaching with all patience. 3 For the time will come when men will not listen to true teaching, but will follow their own desires, and will collect for themselves more and more teachers who will tell them what they are itching to hear. 4 They will turn away from listening to the truth and give their attention to legends. 5 But you must keep control of yourself in all circumstances; endure suffering, do the work of a preacher of the Good News, and perform your whole duty as a servant of God.

6 As for me, the hour has come for me to be sacrificed; the time is here for me to leave this life. 7 I have done my best in the race, I have run the full distance, I have kept the faith. 8 And now the prize of victory is waiting for

me, the crown of righteousness which the Lord, the righteous Judge, will give me on that Day — and not only to me, but to all those who wait with love for him to appear.

Personal Words

⁹ Do your best to come to me soon. ¹⁰ For Demas fell in love with this present world and has deserted me; he has gone off to Thessalonica. Crescens went to Galatia, and Titus to Dalmatia. ¹¹ Only Luke is with me. Get Mark and bring him with you, for he can help me in the work. ¹² I sent Tychicus to Ephesus. ¹³ When you come, bring my coat that I left in Troas with Carpus; bring the books too, and especially the ones made of parchment.

¹⁴ Alexander the metalworker did me great harm; the Lord will reward him according to what he has done. ¹⁵ Be on your guard against him yourself, for he was violently opposed to our message.

¹⁶ No one stood by me the first time I defended myself; all deserted me. May God not count it against them! ¹⁷ But the Lord stayed with me and gave me strength, so that I was able to proclaim the full message for all the Gentiles to hear; and I was rescued from the lion's mouth. ¹⁸ And the Lord will rescue me from all evil, and take me safely into his heavenly Kingdom. To him be the glory for ever and ever! Amen.

Final Greetings

¹⁹ I send greetings to Prisca and Aquila, and to the family of Onesiphorus. ²⁰ Erastus stayed in Corinth, and I left Trophimus in Miletus, because he was sick. ²¹ Do your best to come before winter.

Eubulus, Pudens, Linus, and Claudia send their greetings, and so do all the other brothers.

²² The Lord be with your spirit.

God's grace be with you all.

PAUL'S LETTER TO TITUS

1 From Paul, a servant of God and an apostle of Jesus Christ.

I was chosen and sent to help the faith of God's chosen people and lead them to the truth taught by our religion, [2] which is based on the hope for eternal life. God, who does not lie, promised us this life before the beginning of time, [3] and at the right time he revealed it in his message. This was entrusted to me, and I proclaim it by order of God our Savior.

[4] I write to Titus, my true son in the faith that we share:

May God the Father and Christ Jesus our Savior give you grace and peace.

Titus' Work in Crete

[5] I left you in Crete for you to put in order the things that still needed doing, and to appoint church elders in every town. Remember my instructions: [6] an elder must be without fault; he must have only one wife, and his children must be believers and not have the reputation of being wild or disobedient. [7] For since he is in charge of God's work, the church leader should be without fault. He must not be arrogant or quick-tempered, or a drunkard, or violent, or greedy. [8] He must be hospitable and love what is good. He must be self-controlled, upright, holy, and disciplined. [9] He must hold firmly to the message, which can be trusted and which agrees with the doctrine. In this way he will be able to encourage others with the true teaching, and also show the error of those who are opposed to it.

[10] For there are many who rebel and deceive others with their nonsense, especially the converts from Judaism. [11] It is necessary to stop their talking, for they are upsetting whole families by teaching what they should not, for the shameful purpose of making money. [12] It was a Cretan himself, one of their own prophets, who said: "Cretans are always liars, and wicked beasts, and lazy gluttons." [13] And what he said is true. For this reason you must rebuke them sharply, that they might have a healthy faith, [14] and no longer hold on to Jewish legends and to human

commandments which come from men who have rejected the truth. ¹⁵ Everything is pure to those who are themselves pure; but nothing is pure to those who are defiled and unbelieving, for their minds and consciences have been defiled. ¹⁶ They claim that they know God, but their actions deny it. They are hateful and disobedient, not fit to do anything good.

Sound Doctrine

2 But you must teach what is required by sound doctrine. ² Tell the older men to be sober, sensible, and self-controlled; to be sound in their faith, love, and endurance. ³ In the same way tell the older women to behave as women who live a holy life should. They must not be slanderers, or slaves to wine. They must teach what is good ⁴ in order to train the younger women to love their husbands and children, ⁵ to be self-controlled and pure, and to be good housewives, who obey their husbands, so that no one will speak evil of the message from God.

⁶ In the same way urge the young men to be self-controlled. ⁷ You yourself, in all things, must be an example in good works. Be sincere and serious in your teaching. ⁸ Use sound words that cannot be criticized, so that your enemies may be put to shame by not having anything bad to say about us.

⁹ Slaves are to obey their masters and please them in all things. They must not talk back to them, ¹⁰ or steal from them. Instead, they must show that they are always good and faithful, so as to bring credit to the teaching about God our Savior in all they do.

¹¹ For God has revealed his grace for the salvation of all men. ¹² That grace instructs us to give up ungodly living and worldly passions, and to live self-controlled, upright, and godly lives in this world, ¹³ as we wait for the blessed Day we hope for, when the glory of our great God and Savior Jesus Christ will appear. ¹⁴ He gave himself for us, to rescue us from all wickedness and make us a pure people who belong to him alone and are eager to do good.

¹⁵ Teach these things, and use your full authority as you encourage and rebuke your hearers. Let none of them look down on you.

Christian Conduct

3 Remind your people to submit to rulers and authorities, to obey them, to be ready to do every good thing. [2] Tell them not to speak evil of anyone, but to be peaceful and friendly, and always show a gentle attitude toward all men. [3] For we ourselves were once foolish, disobedient, and wrong. We were slaves to passions and pleasures of all kinds. We spent our lives in malice and envy; others hated us and we hated them. [4] But when the kindness and love of God our Savior appeared, [5] he saved us. It was not because of any good works that we ourselves had done, but because of his own mercy that he saved us through the washing by which the Holy Spirit gives us new birth and new life. [6] For God abundantly poured out the Holy Spirit on us, through Jesus Christ our Savior, [7] that by his grace we might be put right with God and come into possession of the eternal life we hope for. [8] This is a true saying.

I want you to give special emphasis to these matters, so that those who believe in God may be concerned with giving their time to doing good works. These are good and useful for men. [9] But avoid stupid arguments, long lists of names of ancestors, quarrels, and fights about the Law. They are useless and worthless. [10] Give at least two warnings to the man who causes divisions, and then have nothing more to do with him. [11] For you know that such a person is corrupt, and his sins prove that he is wrong.

Final Instructions

[12] When I send Artemas or Tychicus to you, do your best to come to me in Nicopolis, for I have decided to spend the winter there. [13] Do your best to help Zenas the lawyer and Apollos to get started on their travels, and see to it that they have everything they need. [14] Have our people learn to give their time in doing good works, to provide for real needs; they should not live useless lives.

[15] All who are with me send you greetings. Give our greetings to our friends in the faith.

God's grace be with you all.

PAUL'S LETTER TO PHILEMON

¹ From Paul, a prisoner for the sake of Christ Jesus, and from our brother Timothy —

To our friend and fellow worker Philemon, ² and the church that meets in your house, and our sister Apphia, and our fellow soldier Archippus:

³ May God our Father and the Lord Jesus Christ give you grace and peace.

Philemon's Love and Faith

⁴ Every time I pray, brother Philemon, I mention you and give thanks to my God. ⁵ For I hear of your love for all God's people and the faith you have in the Lord Jesus. ⁶ My prayer is that our fellowship with you as believers will bring about a deeper understanding of every blessing which we have in our life in Christ. ⁷ Your love, dear brother, has brought me great joy and much encouragement! For you have cheered the hearts of all God's people.

A Request for Onesimus

⁸ For this reason I could be bold enough, as your brother in Christ, to order you to do what should be done. ⁹ But love compels me to make a request instead. I do this even though I am Paul, the ambassador of Christ Jesus and at present also a prisoner for his sake. ¹⁰ So I make a request to you on behalf of Onesimus, who is my own son in Christ; for while in prison I became his spiritual father. ¹¹ At one time he was of no use to you, but now he is useful both to you and to me.

¹² I am sending him back to you now, and with him goes my heart. ¹³ I would like to keep him here with me, while I am in prison for the gospel's sake, so that he could help me in your place. ¹⁴ However, I do not want to force you to help me; rather, I would like for you to do it of your own free will. So I will not do a thing unless you agree.

¹⁵ It may be that Onesimus was away from you for a short time so that you might have him back for all time. ¹⁶ For now he is not just a slave, but much more than a slave: he is a dear brother in Christ. How much he means

to me! And how much more he will mean to you, both as a slave and as a brother in the Lord!

17 So, if you think of me as your partner, welcome him back just as you would welcome me. 18 If he has done you any wrong, or owes you anything, charge it to my account. 19 Here, I will write this with my own hand: *I, Paul, will pay you back.* (I should not have to remind you, of course, that you owe your very life to me.) 20 So, my brother, please do me this favor, for the Lord's sake; cheer up my heart, as a brother in Christ!

21 I am sure, as I write this, that you will do what I ask — in fact I know that you will do even more. 22 At the same time, get a room ready for me, because I hope that God will answer the prayers of all of you and give me back to you.

Final Greetings

23 Epaphras, who is in prison with me for the sake of Christ Jesus, sends you his greetings, 24 and so do my fellow workers Mark, Aristarchus, Demas, and Luke.

25 May the grace of the Lord Jesus Christ be with you all.

THE LETTER TO THE HEBREWS

God's Word through His Son

1 In the past God spoke to our ancestors many times and in many ways through the prophets, 2 but in these last days he has spoken to us through his Son. He is the one through whom God created the universe, the one whom God has chosen to possess all things at the end. 3 He shines with the brightness of God's glory; he is the exact likeness of God's own being, and sustains the universe with his powerful word. After he had made men clean from their sins, he sat down in heaven at the right side of God, the Supreme Power.

The Son Greater than the Angels

4 The Son was made greater than the angels, just as the name that God gave him is greater than theirs. 5 For God never said to any of his angels,

> "You are my Son;
> Today I have become your Father."

Nor did God say to any angel,

> "I will be his Father,
> And he shall be my Son."

6 When God was about to send his first-born Son into the world, he also said,

> "All of God's angels must worship him."

7 This is what God said about the angels:

> "God makes his angels winds,
> And he makes his servants flames of fire."

8 About the Son, however, God said:

> "Your throne, O God, will last for ever and ever!
> With justice you rule over your kingdom.
> 9 You love the right and hate the wrong,
> That is why God, your God, chose you
> And gave you the joy of an honor far greater
> Than he gave to your companions."

10 He also said:

> "You, Lord, in the beginning created the earth,

And with your own hands you made the
　　heavens.

[11] They will all disappear, but you will remain.
　　They will all grow old like clothes;

[12] You will fold them up like a coat,
　　And they will be changed like clothes.
　　But you are the same, and you will never
　　　grow old."

[13] God never did say to any of his angels:
　　"Sit here at my right side,
　　Until I put your enemies
　　As a footstool under your feet."

[14] What are the angels, then? They are all spirits who serve
God and are sent by him to help those who are to receive
salvation.

The Great Salvation

2 That is why we must hold on all the more firmly to
the truths we have heard, so that we will not be carried
away. [2] The message given by the angels was shown to be
true, and anyone who did not follow it or obey it received
the punishment he deserved. [3] How, then, shall we escape
if we pay no attention to such a great salvation? The Lord
himself first announced this salvation, and those who heard
him proved to us that it is true. [4] At the same time God
added his witness to theirs by doing signs of power,
wonders, and many kinds of miracles. He also distributed
the gifts of the Holy Spirit according to his will.

The Leader to Salvation

[5] For God did not make the angels rulers over the world
he was about to create — the world of which we speak.
[6] Instead, as it is said somewhere in the Scriptures:

　　"What is man, O God, that you should think
　　　of him?
　　What is mere man, that you should care for
　　　him?

[7] You made him for a little while lower than the
　　angels,
　　You gave him the glory and honor that
　　　belong to a king,

[8] And made him ruler over all things."

It says that God made man "ruler over all things"; this

clearly includes everything. But we do not see man ruling over all things now. [9] But we do see Jesus! For a little while he was made lower than the angels, so that through God's grace he should die for all men. We see him crowned with glory and honor now because of the death he suffered. [10] It was only right for God — who creates and preserves all things — to make Jesus perfect through suffering, in order to bring many sons to share his glory. For Jesus is the one who leads them to salvation.

[11] He makes men pure from their sins, and both he and those who are made pure all have the same Father. That is why Jesus is not ashamed to call them his brothers. [12] As he says,

> "I will speak about you, O God, to my brothers,
> I will sing hymns to you before the whole gathering."

[13] He also says, "I will put my trust in God." And he also says, "Here I am with the children that God has given me."

[14] Since the children, as he calls them, are people of flesh and blood, Jesus himself became like them and shared their human nature. He did so that through his death he might destroy the Devil, who has the power over death, [15] and so set free those who were slaves all their lives because of their fear of death. [16] For it is clear that it is not the angels that he helps. Instead, as the scripture says, "He helps the descendants of Abraham." [17] This means that he had to become like his brothers in every way, in order to be their faithful and merciful high priest in his service to God, so that the people's sins would be forgiven. [18] And now he can help those who are tempted, because he himself was tempted and suffered.

Jesus Greater than Moses

3 My Christian brothers, who also have been called by God! Look at Jesus, whom God sent to be the High Priest of the faith we profess. [2] For he was faithful to God, who chose him to do this work, just as Moses was faithful in his work in God's whole house. [3] A man who builds a house receives more honor than the house itself. In the same way, Jesus is worthy of much more glory than Moses. [4] Every house, of course, is built by someone — and God is the one who has built all things. [5] And Moses

was faithful in God's whole house. He was a servant and spoke of the things that God would say in the future. [6] But Christ is faithful as the Son in charge of God's house. We are his house, if we keep our courage and our confidence in what we hope for.

A Rest for God's People

[7] For, as the Holy Spirit says:

"If you hear God's voice today,
[8] Do not be stubborn as you were when you rebelled against God,
As you were that day in the desert when you put him to the test.
[9] There your ancestors tempted and tried me, says God,
Even though they saw what I did for forty years.
[10] For that reason I was angry with those people,
And I said, 'They are always wrong in what they think,
They have never learned my ways.'
[11] I was angry and I made a vow:
'They shall never come in and rest with me!' "

[12] My brothers: be careful that no one among you has a heart so bad and unbelieving that he will turn away from the living God. [13] Instead, in order that none of you be deceived by sin and become stubborn, you must help one another every day, as long as the "today" in the scripture

applies to us. [14] For we are all partners with Christ, if we hold on firmly to the end the confidence we had at the beginning.

[15] This is what the scripture says:

"If you hear God's voice today,
Do not be stubborn as you were
When you rebelled against God."

[16] Who heard God's voice and rebelled against him? Actually it was all the people who were led out of Egypt by Moses. [17] With whom was God angry for forty years? He was angry with the people who sinned, who fell down dead in the desert. [18] When God made his vow, "They shall never come in and rest with me" — of whom was he speaking? He was speaking of those who rebelled. [19] We see, then, that they were not able to go in because they did not believe.

4 Now, God has left us the promise that we may go in and rest with him. Let us fear, then, so that none of you will be found to have failed to go in to that rest. [2] For we have heard the Good News, just as they did. They heard the message but it did them no good, because when they heard it they did not receive it with faith. [3] We who believe, then, do go in and rest with God. It is just as he said,

"I was angry and made a vow:
'They shall never come in and rest with me!' "

He said this even though his work was finished from the time he created the world. [4] For somewhere in the Scriptures this is said about the seventh day, "God rested on the seventh day from all his works." [5] This same matter is spoken of again: "They shall never come in and rest with me." [6] Those who first heard the Good News did not go in and rest with God because they did not believe. There are, then, others who are allowed to go in and rest with God. [7] That is shown by the fact that God sets another day which is called "Today." He speaks of it many years later by means of David, in the scripture already quoted,

"If you hear God's voice today,
Do not be stubborn."

[8] For if Joshua had led the people into God's rest, God would not have spoken later about another day. [9] As it is, however, there still remains for God's people a rest like

God's resting on the seventh day. [10] For anyone who goes in and rests with God will rest from his own works, just as God rested from his. [11] Let us, then, do our best to go in and rest with God. We must not, any of us, disobey as they did and fail to go in.

[12] For the word of God is alive and active. It is sharper than any double-edged sword. It cuts all the way through, to where soul and spirit meet, to where joints and marrow come together. It judges the desires and thoughts of men's hearts. [13] There is nothing that can be hid from God. Everything in all creation is exposed and lies open before his eyes; and it is to him that we must all give account of ourselves.

Jesus the Great High Priest

[14] Let us, then, hold firmly to the faith we profess. For we have a great high priest who has gone into the very presence of God — Jesus, the Son of God. [15] Our high priest is not one who cannot feel sympathy with our weaknesses. On the contrary, we have a high priest who was tempted in every way that we are, but did not sin. [16] Let us be brave, then, and come forward to God's throne, where there is grace. There we will receive mercy and find grace to help us just when we need it.

5 Every high priest is chosen from among the people and appointed to serve God on their behalf. He offers gifts and sacrifices for sins. [2] Since he himself is weak in many ways, he is able to be gentle with those who are ignorant and make mistakes. [3] And because he is himself weak, he must offer sacrifices not only for the sins of the people but also for his own sins. [4] No one chooses for himself the honor of being a high priest. It is only by God's call that a man is made a high priest — just as Aaron was called.

[5] In the same way, Christ did not take upon himself the honor of being a high priest. Instead, God said to him,

"You are my Son;

Today I have become your Father."

[6] He also said in another place,

"You will be a priest for ever,

In the priestly order of Melchizedek."

[7] In his life on earth Jesus made his prayers and requests with loud cries and tears to God, who could save him

from death. Because he was humble and devoted, God heard him. ⁸ But even though he was God's Son he learned to be obedient by means of his sufferings. ⁹ When he was made perfect, he became the source of eternal salvation for all those who obey him, ¹⁰ and God declared him to be high priest, in the priestly order of Melchizedek.

Warning against Falling Away

¹¹ There is much we have to say about this matter, but it is hard to explain to you, because you are so slow to understand. ¹² There has been enough time for you to be teachers — yet you still need someone to teach you the first lessons of God's message. Instead of eating solid food, you still have to drink milk. ¹³ Anyone who has to drink milk is still a child, without any experience in the matter of right and wrong. ¹⁴ Solid food, on the other hand, is for adults, who have trained and used their tastes to know the difference between good and evil.

6 Let us go forward, then, to mature teaching and leave behind us the beginning of the Christian message. We should not lay again the foundation of turning away from useless works and believing in God; ² of the teaching about baptisms and the laying on of hands; of the raising of the dead and the eternal judgment. ³ Let us go forward! And this is what we will do, if God allows.

⁴ For how can those who fall away be brought back to repent again? They were once in God's light. They tasted heaven's gift and received their share of the Holy Spirit. ⁵ They knew from experience that God's word is good, and they had felt the powers of the coming age. ⁶ And then

they fell away! It is impossible to bring them back to repent again, because they are nailing the Son of God to the cross once more and exposing him to public shame.

[7] God blesses the ground that drinks in the rain that often falls on it and grows plants that are useful to those for whom it is cultivated. [8] But if it grows thorns and weeds it is worth nothing; it is in danger of being cursed by God, and will be destroyed by fire.

[9] But even if we speak like this, dear friends, we feel sure about you. We know that you have the better blessings that belong to your salvation. [10] God is not unfair. He will not forget the work you did, nor the love you showed for him in the help you gave and still give your fellow Christians. [11] Our great desire is that each one of you keep up his eagerness to the end, so that the things you hope for will come true. [12] We do not want you to become lazy, but to be like those who believe and are patient, and so receive what God has promised.

God's Sure Promise

[13] When God made the promise to Abraham, he made a vow to do what he had promised. Since there was no one greater than himself, he used his own name when he made his vow. [14] He said, "I promise you that I will bless you and give you many descendants." [15] Abraham was patient, and so he received what God had promised. [16] When a man makes a vow he uses the name of someone greater than himself, and a vow settles all arguments between men. [17] God wanted to make it very clear to those who were to receive what he promised that he would never change his purpose; so he added his vow to the promise. [18] There are these two things, then, that cannot change and about which God cannot lie. So we who have found safety with him are greatly encouraged to hold firmly to the hope that is placed before us. [19] We have this hope as an anchor for our hearts. It is safe and sure, and goes through the curtain of the heavenly temple into the inner sanctuary. [20] Jesus has gone in there before us, on our behalf. He has become a high priest for ever, in the priestly order of Melchizedek.

The Priest Melchizedek

7 This Melchizedek was king of Salem and a priest of the Most High God. As Abraham was coming back

from the battle in which he killed the kings, Melchizedek met him and blessed him. ²Abraham gave him one tenth of everything he had. (The first meaning of Melchizedek's name is "King of Righteousness." And because he was king of Salem, his name also means "King of Peace.") ³ There is no record of Melchizedek's father or mother, or of any of his ancestors; no record of his birth or of his death. He is like the Son of God: he remains a priest for ever.

⁴ You see, then, how great he was! Abraham, the patriarch, gave him one tenth of all he got in the battle. ⁵ And those descendants of Levi who are priests are commanded by the Law to collect one tenth from the people of Israel — that is, they collect from their own countrymen, even though they too are descendants of Abraham. ⁶ Melchizedek was not descended from Levi, but he collected one tenth from Abraham and blessed him who received God's promises. ⁷ There is no doubt that the one who blesses is greater than the one who is blessed. ⁸ In the case of the priests, the tenth is collected by men who die; but as for Melchizedek, the tenth was collected by one who lives, as the scripture says. ⁹ And, so to speak, when Abraham paid the tenth, Levi (whose descendants collect the tenth) also paid it. ¹⁰ For Levi had not yet been born, but was, so to speak, in the body of his ancestor Abraham when Melchizedek met him.

¹¹ It was on the basis of the Levitical priesthood that the Law was given to the people of Israel. Now, if the work of the Levitical priests had been perfect, there would have been no need for a different kind of priest to appear, one who is in the priestly order of Melchizedek, not in Aaron's order. ¹² For when the priesthood is changed, there also has to be a change of the law. ¹³ And our Lord, of whom these things are said, belonged to a different tribe; and no member of his tribe ever served as a priest at the altar. ¹⁴ It is well known that he was born a member of the tribe of Judah; and Moses did not mention this tribe when he spoke of priests.

Another Priest, like Melchizedek

¹⁵ The matter becomes even plainer: a different priest has appeared, who is like Melchizedek. ¹⁶ He was not made a priest by human rules and regulations; he became

a priest through the power of a life which has no end.
[17] For the scripture says, "You will be a priest for ever, in the priestly order of Melchizedek." [18] The old rule, then, is set aside, because it was weak and useless. [19] For the Law of Moses could not make anything perfect. And now a better hope has been brought in, through which we come near to God.

[20] In addition, there is also God's vow. There was no such vow when the others were made priests. [21] But Jesus became a priest by means of a vow, when God said to him,

"The Lord has made a vow,

And will not change his mind:

'You will be a priest for ever.' "

[22] This difference, then, makes Jesus the guarantee also of a better covenant.

[23] There is another difference: those other priests were many because they died and could not continue their work. [24] But Jesus lives on for ever, and his work as priest does not pass on to someone else. [25] And so he is able, now and always, to save those who come to God through him, because he lives for ever to plead with God for them.

[26] Jesus, then, is the High Priest that meets our needs! He is holy; he has no fault or sin in him; he has been set apart from sinful men and raised above the heavens. [27] He is not like other high priests; he does not need to offer sacrifices every day, for his own sins first, and then for the sins of the people. He offered one sacrifice, once and for all, when he offered himself. [28] The Law of Moses appoints men who are imperfect to be high priests; but the word of God's vow, which came later than the Law, appoints the Son, who has been made perfect for ever.

Jesus Our High Priest

8 Here is the whole point of what we are saying: we have such a high priest as this, who sits at the right of the throne of the Divine Majesty in heaven. [2] He serves as high priest in the Most Holy Place, that is, in the real tent which was put up by the Lord, not by man.

[3] Every high priest is appointed to offer gifts and animal sacrifices to God; and so our high priest must also have something to offer. [4] If he were on earth, he would not be a priest at all, since there are priests who offer the gifts

according to the Jewish Law. ⁵ The work they do as priests is really only a copy and a shadow of what is in heaven. It is the same as it was with Moses. When he was about to put up the tent, God told him, "Be sure to make everything like the pattern you were shown on the mountain." ⁶ But, as it is, Jesus has been given priestly work which is much greater than theirs, just as the covenant which he arranged between God and men is a better one, because it is based on promises of better things.

⁷ If there had been nothing wrong with the first covenant, there would have been no need for a second one. ⁸ But God finds fault with his people when he says:

> "The days are coming, says the Lord,
> When I will draw up a new covenant with the people of Israel,
> And with the tribe of Judah.
> ⁹ It will not be like the covenant that I made with their ancestors
> On the day I took them by the hand to lead them out of the land of Egypt.
> They were not faithful to the covenant I made with them,
> And so I paid no attention to them, says the Lord.
> ¹⁰ Now, this is the covenant that I will draw up with the people of Israel
> After those days, says the Lord:
> I will put my laws in their minds,
> And I will write them on their hearts.
> I will be their God,
> And they shall be my people.
> ¹¹ None of them will have to teach his fellow-citizen,
> Nor will anyone have to tell his fellow-countryman,
> 'Know the Lord.'
> For they will all know me,
> From the least to the greatest of them.
> ¹² I will have mercy on their transgressions,
> And I will no longer remember their sins."

¹³ By speaking of a new covenant, God has made the first one old; and anything that is getting old and worn out will soon disappear.

Earthly and Heavenly Worship

9 The first covenant had rules for worship and a man-made place for worship as well. ² A tent was put up, the outside one, which was called the Holy Place. In it were the lamp, the table, and the bread offered to God. ³ Behind the second curtain was the tent called the Most Holy Place. ⁴ In it were the gold altar for the burning of incense, and the box of the covenant, all covered with gold. The box contained the gold jar with the manna in it, Aaron's rod that had sprouted leaves, and the two stone tablets with the words of the covenant written on them. ⁵ Above the box were the glorious creatures representing the Divine Presence, with their wings spread over the place where sins were forgiven. But this is not the time to explain everything in detail.

⁶ After these arrangements are made, the priests go into the outside tent every day to perform their duties; ⁷ but only the High Priest goes into the inside tent, and he does so only once a year. He takes blood with him which he offers to God on behalf of himself and for the sins which the people have committed without knowing they were sinning. ⁸ The Holy Spirit clearly teaches from all these arrangements that the way into the Most Holy Place has not yet been opened as long as the outside tent still stands. ⁹ This is a figure which refers to the present time. It means that the gifts and animal sacrifices offered to God cannot make the worshiper's heart perfect. ¹⁰ They have to do only with food, drink, and various cleansing ceremonies. These are all outward rules, which apply only until the time when God will reform all things.

¹¹ But Christ has already come as the High Priest of the good things that are already here. The tent in which he serves is greater and more perfect; it is not made by men, that is, it is not a part of this created world. ¹² When Christ went through the tent and entered once and for all into the Most Holy Place, he did not take the blood of goats and calves to offer as sacrifice; rather, he took his own blood and obtained eternal salvation for us. ¹³ The blood of goats and bulls and the ashes of the burnt calf are sprinkled on the people who are ritually unclean, and make them clean by taking away their ritual impurity. ¹⁴ Since this is true, how much more is accomplished by

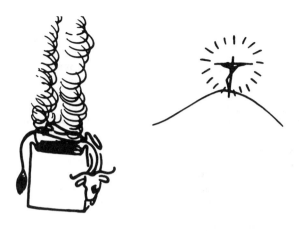

the blood of Christ! Through the eternal Spirit he offered himself as a perfect sacrifice to God. His blood will make our consciences clean from useless works, so that we may serve the living God.

¹⁵ For this reason Christ is the one who arranges a new covenant, so that those who have been called by God may receive the eternal blessings that God has promised. This can be done because there has been a death which sets men free from the wrongs they did while they were under the first covenant.

¹⁶ Where there is a will, it has to be proved that the man who made it has died. ¹⁷ For a will means nothing while the man who made it is alive; it goes into effect only after his death. ¹⁸ That is why even the first covenant was made good only with the use of blood. ¹⁹ First, Moses told the people all the commandments, as set forth in the Law. Then he took the blood of calves, together with water, and sprinkled both the book of the Law and all the people with hyssop and scarlet wool. ²⁰ He said, "This is the blood which seals the covenant that God has commanded you to obey." ²¹ In the same way, Moses also sprinkled the blood on the tent and over all the things used in worship. ²² Indeed, according to the Law, almost everything is made clean by blood; and sins are forgiven only if blood is poured out.

Christ's Sacrifice Takes Away Sins

²³ These things, which are copies of the heavenly

originals, had to be made clean in this way. But the heavenly things themselves require much better sacrifices. [24] For Christ did not go into a holy place made by men, a copy of the real one. He went into heaven itself, where he now appears on our behalf in the presence of God. [25] The Jewish High Priest goes into the Holy Place every year with the blood of an animal. But Christ did not go in to offer himself many times; [26] for then he would have had to suffer many times ever since the creation of the world. Instead, he has now appeared once and for all, when all ages of time are nearing the end, to remove sin through the sacrifice of himself. [27] Everyone must die once, and after that be judged by God. [28] In the same manner, Christ also was offered in sacrifice once to take away the sins of many. He will appear a second time, not to deal with sin, but to save those who are waiting for him.

10 The Jewish Law is not a full and faithful model of the real things. It is only a faint outline of the good things to come. The same sacrifices are offered for ever, year after year. How can the Law, then, by means of these sacrifices make perfect the people who come to God? [2] If the people worshiping God had been made really clean from their sins, they would not feel guilty of sin any more, and all sacrifices would stop. [3] As it is, however, the sacrifices serve to remind people of their sins, year after year. [4] For the blood of bulls and goats can never take sins away.

[5] For this reason, when Christ was about to come into the world, he said to God:

> "You do not want the sacrifice and offering
> 　of animals,
> But you have prepared a body for me.
> [6] You are not pleased with the offering of ani-
> 　mals burned whole on the altar,
> Or with sacrifices to take away sins.
> [7] Then I said, 'Here am I, O God,
> To do what you want me to —
> Just as it is written of me in the book of the
> 　Law.' "

[8] First he said: "You neither want nor are you pleased with sacrifices and offerings of animals, or with the offering of animals burned on the altar and the sacrifices to take

away sins." He said this even though all these sacrifices are offered according to the Law. ⁹ Then he said, "Here am I, O God, to do what you want me to do." So God does away with all the old sacrifices and puts the sacrifice of Christ in their place. ¹⁰ Because Jesus Christ did what God wanted him to do, we are all made clean from sin by the offering that he made of his own body, once and for all.

¹¹ Every Jewish priest stands and performs his services every day and offers the same sacrifices many times. But these sacrifices can never take away sins. ¹² Christ, however, offered one sacrifice for sins, an offering that is good for ever, and then sat down at the right side of God. ¹³ There he now waits until God puts his enemies as a footstool under his feet. ¹⁴ With one sacrifice, then, he has made perfect for ever those who are clean from sin.

¹⁵ For the Holy Spirit also gives us his witness. First he says:

¹⁶ "This is the covenant that I will make with them
  After those days, says the Lord:
  I will put my laws in their hearts,
  And I will write them on their minds."

¹⁷ And then he says, "I will not remember their sins and wicked deeds any longer." ¹⁸ So when these have been forgiven, an offering to take away sins is no longer needed.

Let Us Come Near to God

¹⁹ We have, then, brothers, complete freedom to go into the Most Holy Place by means of the death of Jesus. ²⁰ He opened for us a new way, a living way, through the curtain — that is, through his own body. ²¹ We have a great priest in charge of the house of God. ²² Let us come near to God, then, with a sincere heart and a sure faith, with hearts that have been made clean from a guilty conscience, and bodies washed with pure water. ²³ Let us hold on firmly to the hope we profess, because we can trust God to keep his promise. ²⁴ Let us be concerned with one another, to help one another to show love and to do good. ²⁵ Let us not give up the habit of meeting together, as some are doing. Instead, let us encourage one another, all the

more since you see that the Day of the Lord is coming near.

²⁶ For there is no longer any sacrifice that will take away sins if we purposely go on sinning after the truth has been made known to us. ²⁷ Instead, all that is left is to be afraid of what will happen: the Judgment and the fierce fire which will destroy those who oppose God! ²⁸ Anyone who disobeys the Law of Moses is put to death, without any mercy, when judged guilty from the evidence of two or three witnesses. ²⁹ What, then, of the man who despises the Son of God? who treats as a cheap thing the blood of God's covenant which made him pure? who insults the Spirit of grace? Just think how much worse is the punishment he will deserve! ³⁰ For we know who said, "I will take revenge, I will repay"; and who also said, "The Lord will judge his people." ³¹ It is a terrible thing to fall into the hands of the living God!

³² Remember how it was with you in the past. In those days, after God's light had shone on you, you suffered many things, yet were not defeated by the struggle. ³³ You were at times publicly insulted and mistreated, and at other times you were ready to join those who were being treated in this way. ³⁴ You shared the sufferings of prisoners, and when all your belongings were seized you endured your loss gladly, because you knew that you still had for yourselves something much better, which would last for ever. ³⁵ Do not lose your courage, then, for it brings with it a

great reward. ³⁶ You need to be patient, in order to do the will of God and receive what he promises. ³⁷ For, as the scripture says:

"Just a little while longer,
And he who is coming will come;
He will not delay.
³⁸ My righteous people, however, will believe
and live;
But if any of them turns back, I will not be
pleased with him."

³⁹ We are not people who turn back and are lost. Instead, we have faith and are saved.

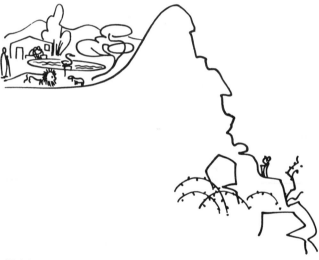

Faith

11 To have faith is to be sure of the things we hope for, to be certain of the things we cannot see. ² It was by their faith that the men of ancient times won God's approval.

³ It is by faith that we understand that the universe was created by God's word, so that what can be seen was made out of what cannot be seen.

⁴ It was faith that made Abel offer to God a better sacrifice than Cain's. Through his faith he won God's approval as a righteous man, for God himself approved

his gifts. By means of his faith Abel still speaks, even though he is dead.

5 It was faith that kept Enoch from dying. Instead, he was taken up to God, and nobody could find him, because God had taken him up. The scripture says that before Enoch was taken up he had pleased God. 6 No man can please God without faith. For he who comes to God must have faith that God exists and rewards those who seek him.

7 It was faith that made Noah hear God's warnings about things in the future that he could not see. He obeyed God, and built an ark in which he and his family were saved. In this way he condemned the world, and received from God the righteousness that comes by faith.

8 It was faith that made Abraham obey when God called him, and go out to a country which God had promised to give him. He left his own country without knowing where he was going. 9 By faith he lived in the country that God had promised him, as though he were a foreigner. He lived in tents with Isaac and Jacob, who had received the same promise from God. 10 For Abraham was waiting for the city which God has designed and built, the city with permanent foundations.

11 It was faith that made Abraham able to become a father even though he was too old and Sarah herself was unable to have children. He trusted God to keep his promise. 12 Though he was practically dead, from this one man there came as many descendants as there are stars in the sky, as many as the numberless grains of sand on the seashore.

13 It was in faith that all these persons died. They did not receive the things God had promised, but from a long way off they saw and welcomed them, and admitted openly that they were foreigners and refugees on earth. 14 Those who say such things make it clear that they are looking for a country of their own. 15 They did not think back to the country they had left; if they had, they would have had the chance to return. 16 Instead, it was a better country they longed for, the heavenly country. And so God is not ashamed to have them call him their God, for he has prepared a city for them.

17 It was faith that made Abraham offer his son Isaac as a sacrifice, when God put Abraham to the test. Abra-

ham was the one to whom God had made the promise, yet he was ready to offer his only son as a sacrifice. ¹⁸ God had said to him, "It is through Isaac that you will have descendants." ¹⁹ Abraham reckoned that God was able to raise Isaac back from death — and, so to speak, Abraham did receive Isaac back from death.

²⁰ It was faith that made Isaac promise blessings for the future to Jacob and Esau.

²¹ It was faith that made Jacob bless each of the sons of Joseph just before he died; he leaned on the top of his walking stick and worshiped God.

²² It was faith that made Joseph, when he was about to die, speak of the departure of the Israelites from Egypt, and leave instructions about what should be done with his body.

²³ It was faith that made the parents of Moses hide him for three months after he was born. They saw that he was a beautiful child, and they were not afraid to disobey the king's order.

²⁴ It was faith that made Moses, when he was grown, refuse to be called the son of Pharaoh's daughter. ²⁵ He preferred to suffer with God's people rather than to enjoy sin for a little while. ²⁶ He reckoned that to suffer scorn for the Messiah was worth far more than all the treasures of Egypt; because he kept his eyes on the future reward.

²⁷ It was faith that made Moses leave Egypt without being afraid of the king's anger; he would not turn back, as though he saw the invisible God. ²⁸ It was faith that made him establish the Passover and order the blood sprinkled on the doors, so the Angel of Death would not kill the first-born sons of the Israelites.

²⁹ It was faith that enabled the Israelites to cross the Red Sea as if on dry land; when the Egyptians tried to do it, the water swallowed them up.

³⁰ It was faith that made the walls of Jericho fall down, after the Israelites had marched around them for seven days. ³¹ It was faith that kept the harlot Rahab from being killed with those who disobeyed God, because she gave the spies a friendly welcome.

³² Should I go on? There isn't enough time for me to speak of Gideon, Barak, Samson, Jephthah, David, Samuel, and the prophets. ³³ Through faith they fought whole countries and won. They did what was right and received what God had promised. They shut the mouths of lions, ³⁴ put out fierce fires, escaped being killed by the sword. They were weak but became strong; they were mighty in battle and defeated the armies of foreigners. ³⁵ Through faith women received their dead raised back to life.

Others, refusing to accept freedom, died under torture in order to be raised to a better life. ³⁶ Some were mocked and whipped, and others were tied up and put in prison. ³⁷ They were stoned, they were sawn in two, they were killed with the sword. They went around clothed in skins of sheep or goats, poor, persecuted, and mistreated. ³⁸ The world was not good enough for them! They wandered like refugees in the deserts and hills, living in caves and holes in the ground.

³⁹ What a record these men have won by their faith! Yet they did not receive what God had promised, ⁴⁰ for God had decided on an even better plan for us. His purpose was that they would be made perfect only with us.

God Our Father

12 As for us, we have this large crowd of witnesses around us. Let us rid ourselves, then, of everything that gets in the way, and the sin which holds on to us so tightly, and let us run with determination the race that lies before us. ² Let us keep our eyes fixed on Jesus, on whom our faith depends from beginning to end. He did not give up because of the cross! On the contrary, because of the joy that was waiting for him, he thought nothing of the disgrace of dying on the cross, and is now seated at the right side of God's throne.

³ Think of what he went through, how he put up with so much hatred from sinful men! So do not let yourselves

become discouraged and give up. ⁴ For in your struggle against sin you have not yet had to fight to the point of being killed. ⁵ Have you forgotten the encouraging words which God speaks to you as his sons?

> "My son, pay attention when the Lord pun-
> ishes you,
> And do not be discouraged when he rebukes
> you.
> ⁶ For the Lord punishes everyone he loves,
> And whips everyone he accepts as a son."

⁷ Endure what you suffer as being a father's punishment; because your suffering shows that God is treating you as his sons. Was there ever a son who was not punished by his father? ⁸ If you are not punished as all his sons are, it means you are not true sons, but bastards. ⁹ In the case of our human fathers, they punished us and we respected them. How much more, then, should we submit to our spiritual Father and live! ¹⁰ Our human fathers punished us for a short time, as it seemed right to them. But God does it for our own good, so that we may share his holiness. ¹¹ When we are punished, it seems to us at the time something to make us sad, not glad. Later, however, those who have been disciplined by such punishment reap the peaceful reward of a righteous life.

Instructions and Warnings

¹² Lift up your limp hands, then, and strengthen your weak knees! ¹³ Keep walking on straight paths, so that the lame foot may not be disabled, but instead be healed.

¹⁴ Try to be at peace with all men, and try to live a holy life, for no one will see the Lord without it. ¹⁵ Be careful that no one turns back from the grace of God. Be careful that no one becomes like a bitter plant that grows up and troubles many with its poison. ¹⁶ Be careful that no one becomes immoral or unspiritual like Esau, who for a single meal sold his rights as the older son. ¹⁷ Afterward, you know, he wanted to receive his father's blessing; but he was turned back, because he could not find a way to change what he had done, even though he looked for it with tears.

¹⁸ You have not come, as the people of Israel came, to what you can feel, to Mount Sinai with its blazing fire, the

darkness and the gloom, the storm, 19 the noise of a trumpet, and the sound of a voice. When the people heard the voice they begged not to have to hear another word, 20 for they could not bear the order which said, "If even an animal touches the mountain it must be stoned to death." 21 The sight was so terrible that Moses said, "I am trembling and afraid!"

22 Instead, you have come to Mount Zion and to the city of the living God, the heavenly Jerusalem, with its thousands of angels. 23 You have come to the joyful gathering of God's oldest sons, whose names are written in heaven. You have come to God, who is the Judge of all men, and to the spirits of righteous men made perfect. 24 You have come to Jesus, who arranged the new covenant, and to the sprinkled blood that tells of much better things than Abel's blood.

25 Be careful, then, and do not refuse to hear him who speaks. Those who refused to hear him who gave the divine message on earth did not escape. How much less shall we escape, then, if we turn away from him who speaks from heaven! 26 His voice shook the earth at that time, but now he has promised, "I will once more shake not only the earth but heaven as well." 27 The words "once more" plainly show that the created things will be shaken and removed, so that the things that are not shaken will remain.

28 Let us be thankful, then, because we receive a kingdom that cannot be shaken. Let us be grateful and worship God in a way that will please him, with reverence and fear; 29 for our God is indeed a destroying fire.

How to Please God

13 Keep on loving one another as brothers in Christ. 2 Remember to welcome strangers in your homes. There were some who did it and welcomed angels without knowing it. 3 Remember those who are in prison, as though you were in prison with them. Remember those who are suffering, as though you were suffering as they are.

4 Marriage should be honored by all, and husbands and wives must be faithful to each other. God will judge those who are immoral and those who commit adultery.

5 Keep your lives free from the love of money, and be

satisfied with what you have. For God has said, "I will never leave you; I will never abandon you." 6 Let us be bold, then, and say,

"The Lord is my helper,
I will not be afraid!
What can man do to me?"

7 Remember your former leaders, who spoke God's message to you. Think back on how they lived and died, and imitate their faith. 8 Jesus Christ is the same yesterday, today, and for ever. 9 Do not let different and strange teachings lead you from the right way. It is good for our souls to be made strong by God's grace, not by obeying rules about foods; those who obey these rules have not been helped by them.

10 The priests who serve in the Jewish tent have no right to eat of the sacrifice on our altar. 11 The Jewish High Priest brings the blood of the animals into the Most Holy Place to offer it as a sacrifice for sins; but the bodies of the animals are burned outside the camp. 12 For this reason Jesus also died outside the city gate, in order to cleanse the

people from sin with his own blood. [13] Let us, then, go to him outside the camp and share his shame. [14] For there is no permanent city for us here on earth; we are looking for the city which is to come. [15] Let us, then, always offer praise to God as our sacrifice through Jesus; that is, let us always give thanks to his name with our voices. [16] Do not forget to do good and to help one another, for these are the sacrifices that please God.

[17] Obey your leaders and follow their orders. They watch over your souls without resting, since they must give an account of their service to God. If you obey them, they will do their work gladly; else they will do it with sadness, and that would not be of any help to you.

[18] Keep on praying for us. We are sure we have a clear conscience, for we want to do the right thing at all times. [19] And I beg you all the more to pray that God will send me back to you the sooner.

Prayer

[20] God has raised from the dead our Lord Jesus, who is the Great Shepherd of the sheep because of his death, by which the eternal covenant is sealed. [21] May the God of peace provide you with every good thing you need in order to do his will, and may he, through Jesus Christ, do in us what pleases him. And to Christ be the glory for ever and ever! Amen.

Final Words

[22] I beg you, my brothers, to listen patiently to this message of encouragement; for this letter I have written you is not very long. [23] I want you to know that our brother Timothy has been let out of prison. If he comes soon enough, I will have him with me when I see you.

[24] Give our greetings to all your leaders and to all God's people. The brothers from Italy send you their greetings.

[25] May God's grace be with you all.

THE LETTER FROM JAMES

1 From James, a servant of God and of the Lord Jesus Christ:

Greetings to all God's people, scattered over the whole world.

Faith and Wisdom

2 My brothers! Consider yourselves fortunate when all kinds of trials come your way, 3 for you know that when your faith succeeds in facing such trials, the result is the ability to endure. 4 But be sure that your endurance carries you all the way, without failing, so that you may be perfect and complete, lacking nothing. 5 But if any of you lacks wisdom, he should pray to God, who will give it to him; for God gives generously and graciously to all. 6 But you must believe when you pray, and not doubt at all; for whoever doubts is like a wave in the sea that is driven and blown about by the wind. 7 Any such person must not think that he will receive anything from the Lord, 8 for he is unsure and undecided in every step he takes.

Poverty and Riches

9 The poor brother must be proud when God lifts him up, 10 and the rich brother when God brings him down. For the rich will pass away like the bloom of a wild plant. 11 The sun rises with its blazing heat and burns the plant; its bloom falls off, and its beauty is destroyed. In the same way the rich man will be destroyed while busy conducting his affairs.

Testing and Tempting

12 Happy is the man who remains faithful under trials; for when he succeeds in passing the test he will be given life, the prize which God has promised to those who love him. 13 If a man is tempted by such testing, he must not say, "This temptation comes from God." For God cannot be tempted by evil, and he himself tempts no one. 14 But a person is tempted when he is drawn away and trapped by his own evil desire; 15 then his evil desire conceives and gives birth to sin; and sin, when it is full-grown, gives birth to death.

¹⁶ Do not be deceived, my dear brothers! ¹⁷ Every good gift and every perfect present comes from heaven; it comes down from God, the Creator of the heavenly lights. He does not change, nor does he cause darkness by turning. ¹⁸ By his own will he brought us into being through the word of truth, so that we should occupy first place among all his creatures.

Hearing and Doing

¹⁹ Remember this, my dear brothers! Everyone must be quick to listen, but slow to speak, and slow to become angry. ²⁰ For man's anger does not help to achieve God's righteous purposes. ²¹ Rid yourselves, then, of every filthy habit and all wicked conduct. Submit to God and accept the word that he plants in your hearts, which is able to save you.

²² Do not fool yourselves by just listening to his word. Instead, put it into practice. ²³ For whoever listens to the word but does not put it into practice is like a man who looks in a mirror and sees himself as he is. ²⁴ He takes a look at himself and then goes away, and at once forgets what he looks like. ²⁵ But the man who looks closely into the perfect law that sets men free, who keeps on paying attention to it, and does not simply listen and then forget it, but puts it into practice — that man will be blessed by God in what he does.

²⁶ Does anyone think he is a religious man? If he does not control his tongue his religion is worthless and he de-

ceives himself. ²⁷ This is what God the Father considers to be pure and genuine religion: to take care of orphans and widows in their suffering, and to keep oneself from being corrupted by the world.

Warning against Prejudice

2 My brothers! In your life as believers in our Lord Jesus Christ, the Lord of glory, you must never treat people in different ways because of their outward appearance. ² Suppose a rich man wearing a gold ring and fine clothes comes in to your meeting, and a poor man in ragged clothes also comes in. ³ If you show more respect to the well-dressed man and say to him, "Have this best seat here," but say to the poor man, "Stand, or sit down here on the floor by my seat," ⁴ then you are guilty of creating distinctions among yourselves and making judgments based on evil motives.

⁵ Listen, my dear brothers! God chose the poor people of this world to be rich in faith and to possess the Kingdom which he promised to those who love him. ⁶ But you dishonor the poor! Who oppresses you and drags you before the judges? The rich! ⁷ They are the ones who speak evil of that good name which God has given you.

⁸ You will be doing the right thing if you obey the law of the Kingdom, which is found in the scripture, "Love your neighbor as yourself." ⁹ But if you treat people according to their outward appearance, you are guilty of sin, and the Law condemns you as a lawbreaker. ¹⁰ For who-

ever breaks only one command of the Law is guilty of breaking them all. ¹¹ For the same one who said, "Do not commit adultery," also said, "Do not kill." Even if you do not commit adultery, you have become a lawbreaker if you kill. ¹² Speak and act as men who will be judged by the law that sets men free. ¹³ For God will not show mercy when he judges the man who has not been merciful; but mercy triumphs over judgment.

Faith and Actions

¹⁴ My brothers! What good is it for a man to say, "I have faith," if his actions do not prove it? Can that faith save him? ¹⁵ Suppose there are brothers or sisters who need clothes and don't have enough to eat. ¹⁶ What good is there in your saying to them, "God bless you! Keep warm and eat well!" — if you don't give them the necessities of life? ¹⁷ This is how it is with faith: if it is alone and has no actions with it, then it is dead.

¹⁸ But someone will say, "You have faith and I have actions." My answer is, "Show me how you can have faith without actions; I will show you my faith by my actions." ¹⁹ You believe that there is only one God? Good! The demons also believe — and tremble with fear. ²⁰ Foolish man! Do you want to be shown that faith without actions is useless? ²¹ How was our ancestor Abraham put right with God? It was through his actions, when he offered his son Isaac on the altar. ²² Can't you see? His faith and his actions worked together; his faith was made perfect through his actions. ²³ And the scripture came true that said, "Abraham believed God, and because of his faith God accepted him as righteous." And God called him "My friend Abraham." ²⁴ So you see that a man is put right with God by what he does, and not because of his faith alone.

²⁵ It was the same with the prostitute Rahab. She was put right with God because of her actions, by welcoming the Jewish messengers and helping them leave by a different road. ²⁶ For just as the body without the spirit is dead, so also faith without actions is dead.

The Tongue

3 My brothers! Not many of you should become teachers, for you know that we teachers will be judged with

greater strictness than others. ² All of us often make mistakes. The person who never makes a mistake in what he says is perfect, able also to control his whole being. ³ We put the bit into the mouths of horses to make them obey us,

and we are able to make them go where we want. ⁴ Or think of a ship: big as it is, and driven by such strong winds, it can be steered by a very small rudder, and goes wherever the pilot wants it to go. ⁵ This is how it is with the tongue: small as it is, it can boast about great things.

Just think how large a forest can be set on fire by a tiny flame! ⁶ And the tongue is like a fire. It is a world of wrong, occupying its place in our bodies and spreading evil through our whole being! It sets on fire the entire course of our existence with the fire that comes to it from hell itself. ⁷ Man is able to tame, and has tamed, all other creatures — wild animals and birds, reptiles and fish. ⁸ But no man has ever been able to tame the tongue. It is evil and uncontrollable, full of deadly poison! ⁹ We use it to give thanks to our Lord and Father, and also to curse our fellow men, created in the likeness of God! ¹⁰ Words of thanksgiving and cursing pour out from the same mouth. My brothers! This should not happen! ¹¹ No spring of water pours out sweet and bitter water from the same opening! ¹² A fig tree, my brothers, cannot bear olives; a vine cannot bear figs; nor can salty water produce fresh water.

The Wisdom from Above

¹³ Is there a wise and understanding man among you? He is to prove it by his good life, by his good deeds per-

formed with humility and wisdom. [14] But if in your heart you are jealous, bitter, and selfish, then you must not be proud and tell lies against the truth. [15] This kind of wisdom does not come down from heaven; it belongs to the world, it is unspiritual and demonic. [16] For where there is jealousy and selfishness, there is also disorder and every kind of evil. [17] But the wisdom from above is pure, first of all; it is also peaceful, gentle, and friendly; it is full of compassion and produces a harvest of good deeds; it is free from prejudice and hypocrisy. [18] And righteousness is the harvest that is produced from the seeds the peacemakers planted in peace.

Friendship with the World

4 Where do all the fights and quarrels among you come from? They come from your passions, which are constantly fighting within your bodies. [2] You want things, but you cannot have them, so you are ready to kill; you covet things, but you cannot get them, so you quarrel and fight. You do not have what you want because you do not ask God for it. [3] And when you ask you do not receive it, because your motives are bad; you ask for things to use for your own pleasures. [4] Unfaithful people! Don't you know that to be the world's friend means to be God's enemy? Whoever wants to be the world's friend makes himself God's enemy. [5] Do not think that the scripture means nothing that says, "The spirit that God placed in us is filled with fierce desires." [6] But the grace that God gives is even stronger. For the scripture says, "God resists the proud, but gives grace to the humble." [7] Submit yourselves, therefore, to God. Oppose the Devil, and he will flee from you. [8] Come near to God, and he will come near to you. Wash your hands, sinners! Cleanse your hearts, you hypocrites! [9] Be sorrowful, cry, and weep; exchange your laughter for crying, and your joy for gloom! [10] Humble yourselves before God, and he will lift you up.

Warning against Judging a Brother

[11] Do not speak against one another, my brothers. Whoever speaks against his brother, or judges him, speaks against the Law and judges it. If you judge the Law, then you are no longer a man who obeys the Law, but one who judges it. [12] God is the only lawgiver and judge. He alone

can both save and destroy. Who do you think you are, to judge your fellow man?

Warning against Boasting

¹³ Now listen to me, you who say, "Today or tomorrow we will travel to a certain city, where we will spend a year, and go into business and make much money." ¹⁴ You do not even know what your life tomorrow will be like! For you are like a thin fog, which appears for a moment and then disappears. ¹⁵ This, then, is what you should say: "If the Lord is willing, we will live and do this and that." ¹⁶ But now you are proud, and you boast; all such boasting is wrong. ¹⁷ So then, the man who does not do the good he knows he should do is guilty of sin.

Warning to the Rich

5 And now, you rich people, listen to me! Weep and wail over the miseries that are coming upon you! ² Your riches have rotted away, and your clothes have been eaten by moths. ³ Your gold and silver are covered with rust, and this rust will be a witness against you, and eat up your flesh like fire. You have piled up riches in these last days. ⁴ You have not paid the wages to the men who work in your fields. Hear their complaints! And the cries of those who gather in your crops have reached the ears of God, the Lord Almighty! ⁵ Your life here on earth has been full of luxury and pleasure. You have made yourselves fat for the day of slaughter. ⁶ You have condemned and murdered the innocent man, and he does not resist you.

Patience and Prayer

⁷ Be patient, then, my brothers, until the Lord comes. See how the farmer is patient as he waits for his land to produce precious crops. He waits patiently for the autumn and spring rains. ⁸ And you also must be patient! Keep your hopes high, for the day of the Lord's coming is near.

⁹ Do not complain against one another, brothers, so that God will not judge you. The Judge is near, ready to come in! ¹⁰ Brothers, remember the prophets who spoke in the name of the Lord. Take them as examples of patient endurance under suffering. ¹¹ We call them happy because they endured. You have heard of Job's patience, and you

know how the Lord provided for him in the end. For the Lord is full of mercy and compassion.

¹² Above all, my brothers, do not use an oath when you make a promise; do not swear by heaven, or by earth, or by anything else. Say only "Yes" when you mean yes, and "No" when you mean no, so that you will not come under God's judgment.

¹³ Is there any one of you who is in trouble? He should pray. Is any one happy? He should sing praises. ¹⁴ Is there any one of you who is sick? He should call the church elders, who will pray for him and pour oil on him in the name of the Lord. ¹⁵ This prayer, made in faith, will save the sick man: the Lord will restore him to health, and the sins he has committed will be forgiven. ¹⁶ Therefore, confess your sins to one another, and pray for one another, so that you will be healed. The prayer of a righteous man has a powerful effect. ¹⁷ Elijah was the same kind of person that we are. He prayed earnestly that there would be no rain, and no rain fell on the land for three and a half years. ¹⁸ Once again he prayed, and the sky poured out its rain and the earth produced its crops.

¹⁹ My brothers! If one of you wanders away from the truth, and another one brings him back again, ²⁰ remember this: whoever turns a sinner back from his wrong ways will save that sinner's soul from death, and cause a great number of sins to be forgiven.

THE FIRST LETTER FROM PETER

1 From Peter, apostle of Jesus Christ —
To God's chosen people who live as refugees scattered throughout the provinces of Pontus, Galatia, Cappadocia, Asia, and Bithynia. ² You were chosen as a result of God the Father's own purpose, to be made a holy people by his Spirit, and to obey Jesus Christ and be made clean by his blood.

May grace and peace be yours in full measure.

A Living Hope

³ Let us give thanks to the God and Father of our Lord Jesus Christ! Because of his great mercy, he gave us new life by raising Jesus Christ from the dead. This fills us with a living hope, ⁴ and so we look forward to possess the rich blessings that God keeps for his people. He keeps them for you in heaven, where they cannot decay or spoil or fade away. ⁵ They are for you, who through faith are kept safe by God's power, as you wait for the salvation which is ready to be revealed at the end of time.

⁶ Be glad about this, even though it may now be necessary for you to be sad for a while because of the many kinds of trials you suffer. ⁷ Their purpose is to prove that your faith is genuine. Even gold, which can be destroyed, is tested by fire; and so your faith, which is much more precious than gold, must also be tested, that it may endure. Then you will receive praise and glory and honor on the Day when Jesus Christ is revealed. ⁸ You love him, although you have not seen him; you believe in him, although you do not now see him; and so you rejoice with a great and glorious joy, which words cannot express, ⁹ because you are receiving the purpose of your faith, the salvation of your souls.

¹⁰ It was concerning this salvation that the prophets made careful search and investigation; and they prophesied about this gift that God would give you. ¹¹ They tried to find out when the time would be and how it would come; for the Spirit of Christ in them pointed to this time in predicting the sufferings that Christ would have to endure, and the glory that would follow. ¹² God revealed to these prophets that their work was not for their own benefit, but for yours,

as they spoke about the truths which you have now heard. The messengers of the Good News, who spoke by the power of the Holy Spirit sent from heaven, told you these truths. These are truths which even the angels would like to understand.

A Call to Holy Living

[13] Have your minds ready for action, then. Keep alert, and set your hope completely on the blessing which will be given you when Jesus Christ is revealed. [14] Be obedient to God, and do not allow your lives to be shaped by those desires that you had when you were still ignorant. [15] Instead, be holy in all that you do, just as God who called you is holy. [16] For the scripture says, "You must be holy, because I am holy."

[17] You call him Father, when you pray to God, who judges all men alike, according to what each one has done; you must, therefore, spend the rest of your lives here on earth in reverence for him. [18] For you know what was paid to set you free from the worthless manner of life you received from your ancestors. It was not something that loses its value, such as silver or gold; [19] you were set free by the costly sacrifice of Christ, who was like a lamb without defect or spot. [20] He had been chosen by God before the creation of the world, and was revealed in these last days for your sake. [21] Through him you believe in God, who raised him from death and gave him glory; and so your faith and hope are fixed on God.

[22] Now that you have purified yourselves by obeying the truth, and have a sincere love for your fellow believers, love one another earnestly with all your hearts. [23] For through the living and eternal word of God you have been born again as the children of a parent who is immortal, not mortal. [24] As the scripture says,

> "All men are like the wild grass,
> And all their glory is like its flower;
> The grass dies, and its flower falls off,

[25] But the word of the Lord remains for ever."
This is the word that the Good News brought to you.

The Living Stone and the Holy Nation

2 Rid yourselves, therefore, of all evil; no more lying, or hypocrisy, or jealously, or insulting language! [2] Be

like newborn babies, always thirsty for the pure spiritual milk, so that by drinking it you may grow up and be saved. ³ For, as the scripture says, "You have tasted the Lord's kindness."

⁴ Come to the Lord, the living stone rejected as worthless by men, but chosen as valuable by God. ⁵ Come as living stones, and let yourselves be used in building the spiritual temple, where you will serve as holy priests, to offer spiritual and acceptable sacrifices to God through Jesus Christ. ⁶ For the scripture says:

> "I chose a valuable stone
> Which I now place as the cornerstone in Zion;
> And whoever believes in him will never be disappointed."

⁷ This stone is of great value for you who believe; but for those who do not believe:

> "The stone which the builders rejected as worthless
> Turned out to be the most important stone."

⁸ And another scripture says,

> "This is the stone that will make men stumble,
> The rock that will make them fall."

They stumbled because they did not believe in the word; such was God's will for them.

⁹ But you are the chosen race, the King's priests, the holy nation, God's own people, chosen to proclaim the wonderful acts of God, who called you from the darkness into his own marvelous light. ¹⁰ At one time you were not God's people, but now you are his people; at one time you did not know God's mercy, but now you have received his mercy.

Slaves of God

¹¹ I appeal to you, my friends, as strangers and refugees in this world! Do not give in to bodily passions, which are always at war against the soul. ¹² Your conduct among the heathen should be so good that when they accuse you of being evildoers they will have to recognize your good deeds, and therefore praise God on the Day of his coming.

¹³ Submit yourselves, for the Lord's sake, to every human authority: to the Emperor, who is the supreme authority, ¹⁴ and to the governors, who have been sent by him

to punish the evildoers and praise those who do good.
¹⁵ For this is God's will: he wants you to silence the ignorant talk of foolish men by the good things you do.
¹⁶ Live as free men; do not use your freedom, however,
to cover up any evil, but live as God's slaves. ¹⁷ Respect
all men, love your fellow believers, fear God, and respect
the Emperor.

The Example of Christ's Suffering

¹⁸ You servants must submit yourselves to your masters
and show them complete respect, not only to those who
are kind and considerate, but also to those who are harsh.
¹⁹ God will bless you for this, if you endure the pain of
undeserved suffering because you are conscious of his will.
²⁰ For what credit is there in enduring the beatings you
deserve for having done wrong? But if you endure suffering even when you have done right, God will bless you
for it. ²¹ It was to this that God called you; because
Christ himself suffered for you and left you an example,
so that you would follow in his steps. ²² He committed no
sin; no one ever heard a lie come from his lips. ²³ When
he was cursed he did not answer back with a curse; when
he suffered he did not threaten, but placed his hopes in
God, the righteous Judge. ²⁴ Christ himself carried our
sins on his body to the cross, so that we might die to sin
and live for righteousness. By his wounds you have been
healed. ²⁵ You were like sheep that had lost their way;
but now you have been brought back to follow the Shepherd and Keeper of your souls.

Wives and Husbands

3 In the same way you wives must submit yourselves to
your husbands, so that if some of them do not believe
God's word, they will be won over to believe by your conduct. It will not be necessary for you to say a word, ² for
they will see how pure and reverent your conduct is. ³ You
should not use outward aids to make yourselves beautiful,
as in the way you fix your hair, or in the jewelry you put
on, or the dresses you wear. ⁴ Instead, your beauty should
consist of your true inner self, the ageless beauty of a
gentle and quiet spirit, which is of great value in God's
sight. ⁵ For in this way the devout women of the past,
who hoped in God, used to make themselves beautiful;

they submitted themselves to their husbands. ⁶ Sarah was like that; she obeyed Abraham and called him "My master." You are now her daughters if you do good and are not afraid of anything.

⁷ You husbands, also, in living with your wives you must recognize that they are the weaker sex and so you must treat them with respect; for they also will receive, together with you, God's gift of life. Do this so that nothing will interfere with your prayers.

Suffering for Doing Right

⁸ To conclude: you must all have the same thoughts and the same feelings; love one another as brothers, and be kind and humble with one another. ⁹ Do not pay back evil with evil, or cursing with cursing; instead pay back

with a blessing, for a blessing is what God promised to give you when he called you. ¹⁰ As the scripture says:
> "Whoever wants to enjoy life and have happy days
> Must no longer speak evil, and must stop telling lies.
> ¹¹ He must turn away from evil and do good,
> He must seek peace and pursue it.
> ¹² For the Lord keeps his eyes on the righteous
> And always listens to their prayers;
> But he turns against those who do evil."

¹³ Who will harm you if you are eager to do what is good? ¹⁴ But even if you should suffer for doing what is right, how happy you are! Do not be afraid of men, and do not worry. ¹⁵ But have reverence for Christ in your hearts, and make him your Lord. Be ready at all times to answer anyone who asks you to explain the hope you have in you. ¹⁶ But do it with gentleness and respect.

Keep your conscience clear, so that when you are insulted, those who speak evil of your good conduct as followers of Christ may be made ashamed of what they say. [17] For it is better to suffer for doing good, if this should be God's will, than for doing wrong. [18] For Christ himself died for you; once and for all he died for sins, a good man for bad men, in order to lead you to God. He was put to death physically, but made alive spiritually; [19] and in his spiritual existence he went and preached to the imprisoned spirits. [20] These were the spirits of those who had not obeyed God, when he waited patiently during the days that Noah was building the ark. The few people in the ark — eight in all — were saved by the water. [21] This water was a figure pointing to baptism, which now saves you, not by washing off bodily dirt, but by the promise made to God from a good conscience. Baptism saves you through the resurrection of Jesus Christ, [22] who has gone to heaven and is at the right side of God, ruling over all angels and heavenly authorities and powers.

Changed Lives

4 Since Christ suffered physically, you too must strengthen yourselves with the same way of thinking; for whoever suffers physically is no longer involved with sin. [2] From now on, then, you must live the rest of your earthly lives controlled by God's will, not by human passions. [3] For you have spent enough time in the past doing what the heathen like to do. Your lives were spent in indecency, lust, drunkenness, orgies, drinking parties, and the disgusting worship of idols. [4] And now the heathen are surprised when you do not join them in the same wild and reckless living, and so they insult you. [5] But they must give an account of themselves to God, who is ready to judge the living and the dead. [6] This is why the Good News was preached also to the dead, to those who had been judged in their physical existence as all men are judged; it was preached to them so that in their spiritual existence they may live as God lives.

Good Managers of God's Gifts

[7] The end of all things is near. You must be self-controlled and alert, to be able to pray. [8] Above everything, love one another earnestly, for love covers over many sins.

[9] Open your homes to each other, without complaining. [10] Each one, as a good manager of God's different gifts, must use for the good of others the special gift he has received from God. [11] Whoever preaches, must preach God's words; whoever serves, must serve with the strength that God gives him, so that in all things praise may be given to God through Jesus Christ, to whom belong the glory and the power for ever and ever! Amen.

Suffering as a Christian

[12] My dear friends, do not be surprised at the painful test you are suffering, as though something unusual were happening to you. [13] Rather be glad that you are sharing Christ's sufferings, so that you may be full of joy when his glory is revealed. [14] Happy are you if you are insulted because you are Christ's followers; for this means that the glorious Spirit, the Spirit of God, has come down on you. [15] None of you should suffer for being a murderer, or a thief, or a criminal, or for trying to manage other people's business. [16] But if you suffer because you are a Christian, don't be ashamed of it, but thank God that you bear Christ's name.

[17] The time has come for the Judgment to begin, and God's own people are the first to be judged. If it starts with us, how will it end with those who do not believe the Good News from God? [18] As the scripture says,

    "If it is difficult for good men to be saved,
    What will become of godless and sinful
       men?"

[19] So then, those who suffer because this is God's will for them, should by their good deeds trust themselves completely to their Creator, who always keeps his promise.

The Flock of God

5 I appeal to the church elders among you, I who am an elder myself. I am a witness of Christ's sufferings, and I will have a share of the glory which will be revealed. I appeal to you: [2] be shepherds of the flock God gave you, and look after it willingly, as God wants you to, and not unwillingly. Do your work, not for mere pay, but from a real desire to serve. [3] Do not try to rule over those who have been given into your care, but be examples to the flock. [4] And when the Chief Shepherd appears, you will

receive the glorious crown which will never lose its brightness.

⁵ In the same way, you younger men must submit yourselves to the older men. And all of you must put on the apron of humility, to serve one another; for the scripture says, "God resists the proud, but gives grace to the humble." ⁶ Humble yourselves, then, under God's mighty hand, so that he will lift you up in his own good time. ⁷ Throw all your worries on him, for he cares for you.

⁸ Be alert, be on watch! For your enemy, the Devil, roams around like a roaring lion, looking for someone to devour. ⁹ Be firm in your faith and resist him, for you know that your fellow believers in all the world are going through the same kind of sufferings. ¹⁰ But after you have suffered for a little while, the God of all grace, who calls you to share his eternal glory in union with Christ, will himself perfect you, and give you firmness, strength, and a sure foundation. ¹¹ To him be the power for ever! Amen.

Final Greetings

¹² I write you this brief letter with the help of Silvanus, whom I regard as a faithful brother. I want to encourage you and give my testimony that this is the true grace of God. Stand firm in it.

¹³ Your sister church in Babylon, also chosen by God, sends you greetings, and so does my son Mark. ¹⁴ Greet each other with the kiss of Christian love.

May peace be with all of you who belong to Christ.

THE SECOND LETTER FROM PETER

1 From Simon Peter, a servant and apostle of Jesus Christ —

To those who through the righteousness of our God and Savior Jesus Christ have been given a faith as precious as ours:

2 May grace and peace be yours in full measure, through your knowledge of God and of Jesus our Lord.

God's Call and Choice

3 His divine power has given us everything we need to live a godly life through our knowledge of the one who called us to share his own glory and goodness. 4 In this way he has given us precious and very great promises, in order that by receiving what he has promised you may escape from the destructive passion that exists in the world, and come to share the divine nature. 5 For this very reason, do your best to add goodness to your faith; and to your goodness add knowledge; 6 to your knowledge add self-control; to your self-control add endurance; to your endurance add godliness; 7 to your godliness add brotherly love; and to your brotherly love add love. 8 These are the qualities you need, and if you have them in abundance they will make you active and effective in your knowledge of our Lord Jesus Christ. 9 But whoever does not have them is so shortsighted that he cannot see, and has forgotten that his past sins have been washed away.

10 So then, my brothers, try even harder to make God's call and his choice of you a permanent experience; for if you do so you will never fall away. 11 In this way you will be given the full right to enter the eternal Kingdom of our Lord and Savior Jesus Christ.

12 For this reason I will always remind you of these matters, even though you already know them and have been firmly fixed in the truth you have received. 13 I think it only right for me to stir up your memory of these matters, as long as I am still alive. 14 For I know that I shall soon put off this mortal body, as our Lord Jesus Christ plainly told me. 15 I will do my best, then, to provide a way for you to remember these matters at all times after my death.

Eyewitnesses of Christ's Glory

¹⁶ For we have not depended on made-up legends in making known to you the mighty coming of our Lord Jesus Christ. With our own eyes we saw his greatness! ¹⁷ We were there when he was given honor and glory by God the Father, when the voice came to him from the Supreme Glory, saying, "This is my own dear Son, with whom I am well pleased!" ¹⁸ We ourselves heard this voice coming from heaven, when we were with him on the sacred mountain.

¹⁹ So we are even more confident of the message proclaimed by the prophets. You will do well to pay attention to it, for it is like a lamp shining in a dark place, until the Day dawns and the light of the morning star shines in your hearts. ²⁰ Above all else, however, remember this: no one can explain, by himself, a prophecy in the Scriptures. ²¹ For no prophetic message ever came just from the will of man, but men were carried along by the Holy Spirit as they spoke the message that came from God.

False Teachers

2 False prophets appeared in the past among the people, and in the same way false teachers will appear among you. They will bring in destructive, untrue doctrines, and deny the Master who saved them, and so bring upon themselves sudden destruction. ² Even so, many will follow their immoral ways; and, because of what they do, people will speak evil of the Way of truth. ³ In their greed these false teachers will make a profit out of telling you made-up stories. For a long time now their Judge has been ready, and their Destroyer has been wide awake!

⁴ For God did not spare the angels who sinned, but threw them into hell, where they are kept chained in darkness, waiting for the Day of Judgment. ⁵ God did not spare the ancient world, but brought the Flood on the world of wicked men; the only ones he saved were Noah, who preached righteousness, and seven other people. ⁶ God condemned the cities of Sodom and Gomorrah, destroying them with fire, and made an example of them for the wicked, of what will happen to them. ⁷ He rescued Lot, a good man, who was troubled by the immoral conduct of lawless men. ⁸ For that good man, living among them,

day after day saw and heard such things that his good heart was tormented by their evil deeds. ⁹ And so the Lord knows how to rescue godly men from their trials, and how to keep the wicked under punishment for the Day of Judgment, ¹⁰ especially those who follow their filthy bodily lusts and despise God's authority.

These false teachers are bold and arrogant, and show no respect for the glorious beings above; instead, they insult them. ¹¹ Even the angels, who are so much stronger and mightier than these false teachers, do not accuse them with insults in the presence of the Lord. ¹² But these men act by instinct, like wild animals born to be captured and killed; they insult things they do not understand. They will be destroyed like wild animals; ¹³ they will be paid with suffering for the suffering they caused. Pleasure for them is to do anything in broad daylight that will satisfy their bodily appetites; they are a shame and a disgrace as they join you in your meals, all the while enjoying their deceitful ways! ¹⁴ They want to look at nothing else but immoral women; their appetite for sin is never satisfied. They lead weak people into a trap. Their hearts are trained to be greedy. They are under God's curse! ¹⁵ They have left the straight path and have lost their way; they have followed the path taken by Balaam the son of Bosor, who loved the money he would get for doing wrong, ¹⁶ and was rebuked for his transgression. For a dumb ass spoke with a human voice and stopped the prophet's insane action.

¹⁷ These men are like dried-up springs, like clouds blown along by a storm; God has reserved a place for them in the deepest darkness. ¹⁸ They make proud and stupid statements, and use immoral bodily lusts to trap those who are just barely escaping from among people who live in error. ¹⁹ They promise them freedom, while they themselves are slaves of destructive habits—for a man is a slave of anything that has defeated him. ²⁰ For if men have escaped from the deadly forces of the world through their knowledge of our Lord and Savior Jesus Christ, and then are again caught by them and defeated, such men are in worse condition at the end than they were at the beginning. ²¹ It would have been much better for them never to have known the way of righteousness than to have known it and then to turn away from the sacred command that was

given them! ²² What happened to them shows that the proverb is true, "A dog goes back to what it has vomited," and, "A pig that has been washed goes back to roll in the mud."

The Promise of the Lord's Coming

3 My dear friends! This is now the second letter I have written you. In both letters I have tried to arouse pure thoughts in your minds by reminding you of these things. ² I want you to remember the words that were spoken long ago by the holy prophets, and the command from the Lord and Savior which was given you by your apostles. ³ First of all, you must understand that in the last days some men will appear whose lives are controlled by their own passions. They will make fun of you ⁴ and say: "He promised to come, didn't he? Where is he? Our fathers have already died, but everything is still the same as it was since the creation of the world!" ⁵ They purposely ignore this fact: long ago God spoke, and the heavens and earth were created. The earth was formed out of water, and by water, ⁶ and it was by water also, the water of the Flood, that the old world was destroyed. ⁷ But the heavens and earth that now exist are being preserved, by the same word of God, for destruction by fire. They are being kept for the day when wicked men will be judged and destroyed.

⁸ But do not forget this one thing, my dear friends! There is no difference in the Lord's sight between one day and a thousand years; to him the two are the same. ⁹ The Lord is not slow to do what he has promised, as some think. Instead, he is patient with you, because he does not want anyone to be destroyed, but wants all to turn away from their sins.

[10] But the Day of the Lord will come as a thief. On that Day the heavens will disappear with a shrill noise, the heavenly bodies will burn up and be destroyed, and the earth with everything in it will vanish. [11] Since all these things will be destroyed in this way, what kind of people should you be? Your lives should be holy and dedicated to God, [12] as you wait for the Day of God, and do your best to make it come soon — the Day when the heavens will burn up and be destroyed, and the heavenly bodies will be melted by the heat. [13] But God has promised new heavens and a new earth, where righteousness will be at home, and we wait for these.

[14] And so, my friends, as you wait for that Day, do your best to be pure and faultless in God's sight and to be at peace with him. [15] Look on our Lord's patience as the opportunity he gives you to be saved, just as our dear brother Paul wrote to you, using the wisdom God gave him. [16] This is what he writes in all his letters when he deals with this subject. There are some difficult things in his letters which ignorant and unstable people explain falsely, as they do with other passages of the Scriptures. Thus they bring on their own destruction.

[17] But you, my friends, already know this. Be on your guard, then, so that you will not be led away by the errors of lawless men and fall from your secure position. [18] But continue to grow in the grace and knowledge of our Lord and Savior Jesus Christ. To him be the glory, now and for ever! Amen.

THE FIRST LETTER OF JOHN

The Word of Life

1 We write to you about the Word of life, which has existed from the very beginning: we have heard it, and we have seen it with our eyes; yes, we have seen it, and our hands have touched it. ² When this life became visible, we saw it; so we speak of it and tell you about the eternal life which was with the Father and was made known to us. ³ What we have seen and heard we tell to you also, so that you will join with us in the fellowship that we have with the Father and with his Son Jesus Christ. ⁴ We write this in order that our joy may be complete.

God Is Light

⁵ Now this is the message that we have heard from his Son and announce to you: God is light and there is no darkness at all in him. ⁶ If, then, we say that we have fellowship with him, yet at the same time live in the darkness, we are lying both in our words and in our actions. ⁷ But if we live in the light — just as he is in the light — then we have fellowship with one another, and the blood of Jesus, his Son, makes us clean from every sin.

⁸ If we say that we have no sin, we deceive ourselves and there is no truth in us. ⁹ But if we confess our sins to God, we can trust him, for he does what is right — he will forgive us our sins and make us clean from all our wrongdoing. ¹⁰ If we say that we have not sinned, we make a liar out of God, and his word is not in us.

Christ Our Helper

2 I write you this, my children, so that you will not sin; but if anyone does sin, we have Jesus Christ, the righteous, who pleads for us with the Father. ² For Christ himself is the means by which our sins are forgiven, and not our sins only, but also the sins of all men.

³ If we obey God's commands, then we are sure that we know him. ⁴ If someone says, "I do know him," but does not obey his commands, such a person is a liar and there is no truth in him. ⁵ But he who obeys his word is

the one whose love for God has really been made perfect. This is how we can be sure that we live in God: ⁶ he who says that he lives in God should live just as Jesus Christ did.

The New Command

⁷ My dear friends, this command I write you is not new; it is the old command, the one you have had from the very beginning. The old command is the message you have already heard. ⁸ However, the command I write you is new, and its truth is seen in Christ and also in you. For the darkness is passing away, and the real light is already shining.

⁹ He who says that he is in the light, yet hates his brother, is in the darkness to this very hour. ¹⁰ He who loves his brother stays in the light, and so he has nothing in himself that will cause someone else to sin. ¹¹ But he who hates his brother is in the darkness; he walks in it, and he does not know where he is going, because the darkness has made him blind.

¹² I write to you, my children, because your sins are forgiven for the sake of Christ's name. ¹³ I write to you, fathers, because you know him who has existed from the beginning. I write to you, young men, because you have defeated the Evil One.

¹⁴ I write to you children, because you know the Father. I write to you, fathers, because you know him who has existed from the beginning. I write to you, young men, because you are strong; the word of God lives in you and you have defeated the Evil One.

¹⁵ Do not love the world or anything that belongs to the world. If you love the world, you do not have the love for

the Father in you. [16] Everything that belongs to the world
— what the sinful self desires, what people see and want,
and everything in this world that people are so proud of
— none of this comes from the Father; it all comes from
the world. [17] The world and everything in it that men
desire is passing away; but he who does what God wants
lives for ever.

The Enemy of Christ

[18] My children, the end is near! You were told that the
Enemy of Christ would come; and now many enemies of
Christ have already appeared, and so we know that the
end is near. [19] These people really did not belong to our
group, and that is why they left us; if they had belonged
to our group, they would have stayed with us. But they
left so that it might be clear that none of them really belonged to our group.

[20] But you have had the Holy Spirit poured out on you
by Christ, and so all of you know the truth. [21] I write you,
then, not because you do not know the truth; instead, it is
because you do know it, and also know that no lie ever
comes from the truth.

[22] Who, then, is the liar? It is he who says that Jesus is
not the Christ. This one is the Enemy of Christ — he
rejects both the Father and the Son. [23] For he who rejects
the Son also rejects the Father; he who accepts the Son
has the Father also.

[24] Be sure, then, to keep in your hearts the message you
heard from the beginning. If what you heard from the
beginning stays in your hearts, then you will always live
in union with the Son and the Father. [25] And this is what
Christ himself promised to give us — eternal life.

[26] I write you this about those who are trying to deceive
you. [27] But as for you, Christ has poured out his Spirit
on you. As long as his Spirit remains in you, you do not
need anyone to teach you. For the Spirit teaches you about
everything, and what he teaches is true, not false. Obey
the Spirit's teaching, then, and remain in Christ.

[28] Yes, my children, remain in him, so that we may be
full of courage when he appears and need not hide in
shame from him on the Day he comes. [29] You know that
Christ is righteous; you should know, then, that everyone
who does what is right is God's child.

Children of God

3 See how much the Father has loved us! His love is so great that we are called God's children — and so, in fact, we are. This is why the world does not know us: it has not known God. ² My dear friends, we are now God's children, but it is not yet clear what we shall become. But this we know: when Christ appears, we shall become like him, because we shall see him as he really is. ³ Everyone who has this hope in Christ keeps himself pure, just as Christ is pure.

⁴ Whoever sins is guilty of breaking God's law; for sin is a breaking of the law. ⁵ You know that Christ appeared in order to take away men's sins, and that there is no sin in him. ⁶ So everyone who lives in Christ does not continue to sin; but whoever continues to sin has never seen him, nor has he ever known him.

⁷ Let no one deceive you, children! Whoever does what is right is righteous, just as Christ is righteous. ⁸ Whoever continues to sin belongs to the Devil, for the Devil has sinned from the very beginning. The Son of God appeared for this very reason, to destroy the Devil's works.

⁹ Whoever is a child of God does not continue to sin, because God's very nature is in him; and because God is his Father, he is not able to continue to sin. ¹⁰ Here is the clear difference between God's children and the Devil's children: anyone who does not do what is right, or does not love his brother, is not God's child.

Love One Another

¹¹ For the message you heard from the very beginning is this: we must love one another. ¹² We must not be like Cain; he belonged to the Evil One, and murdered his own brother. Why did Cain murder him? Because the things he did were wrong, but the things his brother did were right.

¹³ So do not be surprised, my brothers, if the people of the world hate you. ¹⁴ We know that we have left death and come over into life; we know it because we love our brothers. Whoever does not love is still in death. ¹⁵ Whoever hates his brother is a murderer; and you know that a murderer does not have eternal life in him. ¹⁶ This is how we know what love is: Christ gave his life for us. We too,

then, ought to give our lives for our brothers! ¹⁷ If a man
is rich and sees his brother in need, yet closes his heart
against his brother, how can he claim that he has love for
God in his heart? ¹⁸ My children! Our love should not be
just words and talk; it must be true love, which shows
itself in action.

Courage before God

¹⁹ This, then, is how we will know that we belong to the
truth. This is how our hearts will feel sure in God's presence. ²⁰ For if our heart condemns us, we know that God
is greater than our heart, and he knows everything. ²¹ And
so, my dear friends, if our heart does not condemn us, we
have courage in God's presence. ²² We receive from him
whatever we ask, because we obey his commands and do
what pleases him. ²³ This is what he commands: that we
believe in the name of his Son Jesus Christ and love one
another, just as Christ commanded us. ²⁴ Whoever obeys
God's commands lives in God and God lives in him. And
this is how we know that God lives in us: we know it because of the Spirit he has given us.

The True and the False Spirit

4 My dear friends: do not believe all who claim to have
the Spirit, but test them to find out if the spirit they
have comes from God. For many false prophets have gone
out everywhere. ² This is how you will be able to know
whether it is God's Spirit: everyone who declares that
Jesus Christ became mortal man has the Spirit who comes
from God. ³ But anyone who denies this about Jesus does
not have the Spirit from God. This spirit is from the Enemy
of Christ; you heard that it would come, and now it is here
in the world already.

⁴ But you belong to God, my children, and have defeated the false prophets; for the Spirit who is in you is
more powerful than the spirit in those who belong to the
world. ⁵ They speak about matters of the world and the
world listens to them because they belong to the world.
⁶ But we belong to God. Whoever knows God listens to
us; whoever does not belong to God does not listen to us.
This is the way, then, that we can tell the difference between the Spirit of truth and the spirit of error.

God Is Love

[7] Dear friends! Let us love one another, for love comes from God. Whoever loves is a child of God and knows God. [8] Whoever does not love does not know God, because God is love. [9] This is how God showed his love for us: he sent his only Son into the world that we might have life through him. [10] This is what love is: it is not that we have loved God, but that he loved us and sent his Son to be the means by which our sins are forgiven.

[11] Dear friends, if this is how God loved us, then we should love one another. [12] No one has ever seen God; if we love one another, God lives in us and his love is made perfect within us.

[13] This is how we are sure that we live in God and he lives in us: he has given us his Spirit. [14] And we have seen and tell others that the Father sent his Son to be the Savior of the world. [15] Whoever declares that Jesus is the Son of God, God lives in him, and he lives in God. [16] And we ourselves know and believe the love which God has for us.

God is love, and whoever lives in love lives in God and God lives in him. [17] This is the purpose of love being made perfect in us: it is that we may be full of courage on Judgment Day, because our life in this world is the same as Christ's. [18] There is no fear in love; perfect love drives out all fear. So then, love has not been made per-

fect in the one who fears, because fear has to do with punishment.

[19] We love because God first loved us. [20] If someone
says, "I love God," yet hates his brother, he is a liar. For
he cannot love God, whom he has not seen, if he does not
love his brother, whom he has seen. [21] This, then, is the
command that Christ gave us: he who loves God must
love his brother also.

Our Victory over the World

5 Whoever believes that Jesus is the Messiah is a child of
God; and whoever loves a father loves also his child.
[2] This is how we know that we love God's children: it is
by loving God and obeying his commands. [3] For this is
what love for God means: it means that we obey his
commands. And his commands are not too hard for us,
[4] for every child of God is able to defeat the world. This
is how we win the victory over the world: with our faith.
[5] Who can defeat the world? Only he who believes that
Jesus is the Son of God.

The Witness about Jesus Christ

[6] Jesus Christ is the one who came; he came with the
water of his baptism and the blood of his death. He came
not only with the water, but with both the water and the
blood. And the Spirit himself testifies that this is true; for
the Spirit is truth. [7] There are three witnesses, [8] the Spirit,
the water, and the blood; and all three agree. [9] We believe
the witness that men give; the witness that God gives is
much stronger, and this is the witness that God has given
about his Son. [10] So whoever believes in the Son of God
has this witness in his heart; but whoever does not believe
God, has made a liar out of him, for he has not believed
what God has said as a witness about his Son. [11] This,
then, is the witness: God has given us eternal life, and
this life is ours in his Son. [12] Whoever has the Son has
this life; whoever does not have the Son of God does not
have life.

Eternal Life

[13] I write you this so that you may know that you have
eternal life — you who believe in the name of the Son of
God. [14] This is why we have courage in God's presence;

we are sure that he will hear us if we ask him for anything that is according to his will. ¹⁵ He hears us whenever we ask him; since we know this is true, we know also that he gives us what we ask from him.

¹⁶ If anyone sees his brother commit a sin that does not lead to death, he should pray to God, who will give him life. This applies to those whose sins do not lead to death. But there is sin which leads to death, and I do not say that you should pray to God about that. ¹⁷ All wrongdoing is sin, but there is sin which does not lead to death.

¹⁸ We know that no child of God keeps on sinning, for the Son of God keeps him safe, and the Evil One cannot harm him.

¹⁹ We know that we belong to God and that the whole world is under the rule of the Evil One.

²⁰ We know that the Son of God has come and has given us understanding, so that we know the true God. Our lives are in the true God—in his Son Jesus Christ. This is the true God, and this is eternal life.

²¹ My children, keep yourselves away from false gods!

THE SECOND LETTER OF JOHN

[1] From the Elder —
To the dear Lady and to her children, whom I truly love. I am not the only one, but all who know the truth love you, [2] because the truth remains in us and will be with us for ever.

[3] May God the Father and Jesus Christ, the Father's Son, give us grace, mercy, and peace; may they be ours in truth and love.

Truth and Love

[4] How happy I was to find that some of your children live in the truth, just as the Father commanded us. [5] And so I ask you, dear Lady: let us all love one another. This is no new command I write you; it is the command which we have had from the beginning. [6] This love I speak of means that we must live in obedience to God's commands. The command, as you have heard from the beginning, is this: you must all live in love.

[7] Many deceivers have gone out over the world, men who do not declare that Jesus Christ became mortal man. Such a person is a deceiver, he is the Enemy of Christ. [8] Watch yourselves, then, so that you will not lose what you have worked for, but will receive your reward in full.

[9] Anyone who does not stay with the teaching of Christ, but goes beyond it, does not have God. Whoever does stay with the teaching has both the Father and the Son. [10] If anyone comes to you, then, who does not bring this teaching, do not welcome him in your home; do not even say, "Peace be with you." [11] For anyone who wishes him peace becomes his partner in the evil things he does.

Final Words

[12] I have so much to tell you, but I would rather not do it with paper and ink; instead, I hope to visit you and talk with you personally, so that we shall be completely happy.

[13] The children of your dear Sister send you their greetings.

THE THIRD LETTER OF JOHN

[1] From the Elder —
To my dear Gaius, whom I truly love.

[2] My dear friend, I pray that everything may go well with you, and that you may be in good health — as I know you are well in spirit. [3] I was so happy when some brothers arrived and told how faithful you are to the truth — just as you always live in the truth. [4] Nothing makes me happier than to hear that my children live in the truth.

Gaius is Praised

[5] My dear friend, you are so faithful in the work you do for the brothers, even when they are strangers. [6] They have spoken of your love to the church here. Please help them to continue their trip in a way that will please God. [7] For they set out on their trip in the service of Christ without accepting any help from unbelievers. [8] We Christians, then, must help these men, so that we may share in their work for the truth.

Diotrephes and Demetrius

[9] I wrote a short letter to the church; but Diotrephes, who loves to be their leader, will not pay any attention to what I say. [10] When I come, then, I will bring up everything he has done: the terrible things he says about us and the lies he tells! But that is not enough for him; he will not receive the brothers when they come, and even stops those who want to receive them and tries to drive them out of the church!

[11] My dear friend, do not imitate what is bad, but imitate what is good. Whoever does good belongs to God; whoever does what is bad has not seen God.

[12] Everyone speaks well of Demetrius; truth itself speaks well of him. And we add our witness, and you know that what we say is true.

Final Greetings

[13] I have so much to tell you, but I do not want to do it

with pen and ink. ¹⁴ I hope to see you soon, and then we will talk personally.

¹⁵ Peace be with you.

All your friends send greetings. Greet all our friends personally.

THE LETTER FROM JUDE

[1] From Jude, a servant of Jesus Christ, and the brother of James —

To those who have been called by God, who live in the love of God the Father and the protection of Jesus Christ:

[2] May mercy, peace, and love be yours in full measure.

False Teachers

[3] My dear friends! I was doing my best to write to you about the salvation we share in common, when I felt the need of writing you now to encourage you to fight on for the faith which once and for all God has given to his people. [4] For some godless men, who have slipped in unnoticed among us, distort the message about the grace of God to excuse their immoral ways, and reject Jesus Christ, our only Master and Lord. Long ago the Scriptures predicted this condemnation that they have received.

[5] For even though you are fully aware of all this, I want to remind you of how the Lord saved the people of Israel from the land of Egypt, but afterward destroyed those who did not believe. [6] Remember the angels who did not stay within the limits of their proper authority, but abandoned their own dwelling-place: God has kept them in the darkness below, bound in eternal chains for that great Day on which they will be condemned. [7] Remember Sodom and Gomorrah, and the nearby towns, whose people acted as the angels did and committed sexual immorality and perversion: they suffer the punishment of eternal fire as a plain warning to all.

[8] In the same way also, these men have visions which make them sin against their own bodies; they despise God's authority; they insult the glorious beings above. [9] Not even the chief angel Michael has done this. In his quarrel with the Devil, when they argued about who would have the body of Moses, Michael did not dare condemn the Devil with insulting words, but said, "The Lord rebuke you!" [10] But these men insult things they do not understand; and those things that they know by instinct, like wild animals, are the very things that destroy them. [11] How terrible for them! They have followed the way that Cain took; they have given themselves over to error for the sake of money, as Balaam did; they have been de-

stroyed by rebelling like Korah rebelled. [12] They are like dirty spots in your fellowship meals, with their shameless carousing. They take care of themselves only. They are like clouds carried along by the wind and bringing no rain. They are like trees that bear no fruit, even in autumn, trees that have been pulled up by the roots and are completely dead. [13] They are like wild waves of the sea, with their shameful deeds showing up like foam. They are like wandering stars, for whom God has reserved a place for ever in the deepest darkness.

[14] It was Enoch, the seventh direct descendant from Adam, who long ago prophesied about them: "See! The Lord will come with many thousands of his holy angels, [15] to bring judgment on all, to condemn all godless sinners for all the godless deeds they have performed, and for all the terrible words those godless men have spoken against God!" [16] These men are always grumbling and blaming others; they follow their own evil desires; they brag about themselves, and flatter others in order to get their own way.

Warnings and Instructions

[17] But remember, my friends! Remember what you were told in the past by the apostles of our Lord Jesus Christ. [18] For they said to you, "When the last days come, men will appear who will make fun of you, men who follow their own evil desires." [19] These are the men who cause divisions, who are controlled only by natural desires, not by the Spirit. [20] But you, my friends, keep on building yourselves up in your most sacred faith. Pray in the power of the Holy Spirit, [21] and keep yourselves in the love of God, as you wait for our Lord Jesus Christ in his mercy to give you eternal life.

[22] Show mercy toward those who have doubts; [23] save them, by snatching them out of the fire. Show mercy also, mixed with fear, to others as well; but hate their very clothes, stained by their sinful lusts.

Prayer of Praise

[24] To him who is able to keep you from falling, and present you faultless and joyful before his glory — [25] to the only God our Savior, through Jesus Christ our Lord, be glory, majesty, might, and authority, from all ages past, and now, and for ever and ever! Amen.

THE REVELATION TO JOHN

1 In this book are written the things that Jesus Christ revealed. These things were given him by God, for him to show God's servants what must happen very soon. Christ made these things known to his servant John by sending his angel to him. ² John has told all that he has seen. This is his report concerning the message from God and the truth revealed by Jesus Christ. ³ Happy is the one who reads this book, and happy are those who listen to the words of this prophetic message and obey what is written in this book! For the time is near when all this will happen.

Greetings to the Seven Churches

⁴ From John to the seven churches in the province of Asia:

Grace and peace be yours from God, who is, who was, and who is to come, and from the seven spirits in front of his throne, ⁵ and from Jesus Christ, the faithful witness, the first-born Son who was raised from death, who is also the ruler of the kings of the earth.

He loves us, and by his death he has freed us from our sins ⁶ and made us a kingdom of priests to serve his God and Father. To Jesus Christ be the glory and power for ever and ever! Amen.

⁷ Look, he is coming with the clouds! Everyone will see him, including those who pierced him. All peoples of earth will mourn because of him. Certainly so! Amen.

⁸ "I am the Alpha and the Omega," says the Lord God Almighty, who is, who was, and who is to come.

A Vision of Christ

⁹ I am John, your brother, and in union with Jesus I share with you in suffering, and in his Kingdom, and in enduring. I was put on the island named Patmos because I had proclaimed God's word and the truth that Jesus revealed. ¹⁰ On the Lord's day the Spirit took control of me, and I heard a loud voice, that sounded like a trumpet, speaking behind me. ¹¹ It said: "Write down what you see, and send the book to these seven churches: in

Ephesus, Smyrna, Pergamum, Thyatira, Sardis, Philadelphia, and Laodicea."

12 I turned around to see who was talking to me. There I saw seven gold lamp-stands. 13 Among them stood a being who looked like a man, wearing a robe that reached to his feet, and a gold band around his chest. 14 His hair was white as wool, or as snow, and his eyes blazed like fire; 15 his feet shone like brass melted in the furnace and then polished, and his voice sounded like a mighty waterfall. 16 He held seven stars in his right hand, and a sharp two-edged sword came out of his mouth. His face was as bright as the midday sun. 17 When I saw him I fell down at his feet like a dead man. He placed his right hand on me and said: "Don't be afraid! I am the first and the last. 18 I am the living one! I was dead, but look, I am alive for ever and ever. I have authority over death and the world of the dead. 19 Write, then, the things you see, both the things that are now, and the things that will happen afterward. 20 Here is the secret meaning of the seven stars that you see in my right hand, and of the seven gold lamp-stands: the seven stars are the angels of the seven churches, and the seven lamp-stands are the seven churches."

The Message to Ephesus

2 "To the angel of the church in Ephesus write:
"This is the message from the one who holds the seven stars in his right hand, who walks among the seven gold lamp-stands. 2 I know what you have done; I know how hard you have worked and how patient you have been. I know that you cannot tolerate evil men, and that you have tested those who say they are apostles but are not, and have found out that they are liars. 3 You are patient, you have suffered troubles for my sake, and you have not given up. 4 But here is what I have against you: you do not love me now as you did at first. 5 Remember how far you have fallen! Turn from your sins and do what you did at first. If you don't turn from your sins, I will come to you and take your lamp-stand from its place. 6 But here is what you have in your favor: you hate what the Nicolaitans do, as much as I.

7 "If you have ears, then, listen to what the Spirit says to the churches!

"To those who have won the victory I will give the right to eat the fruit of the tree of life that grows in the Garden of God."

The Message to Smyrna

⁸ "To the angel of the church in Smyrna write:

"This is the message from the one who is the first and the last, who died and lived again. ⁹ I know your troubles; I know that you are poor — but really you are rich! I know the evil things said against you by those who claim to be Jews, but are not; they are a group that belongs to Satan! ¹⁰ Do not be afraid of anything you are about to suffer. Listen! The Devil will put you to the test by having some of you thrown into prison; your troubles will last ten days. Be faithful until death, and I will give you the crown of life.

¹¹ "If you have ears, then, listen to what the Spirit says to the churches!

"Those who win the victory will not be hurt by the second death."

The Message to Pergamum

¹² "To the angel of the church in Pergamum write:

"This is the message from the one who has the sharp two-edged sword. ¹³ I know where you live, there where Satan has his throne. You are true to me, and you did not abandon your faith in me even during the time when Antipas, a faithful witness for me, was killed there where Satan lives. ¹⁴ But here are a few things I have against you: there with you are some who follow the teaching of Balaam, who taught Balak how to cause the people of Israel to sin by eating food that had been offered to idols, and by committing immorality. [15] In the same way, you also have people among you who follow the teaching of the Nicolaitans. [16] Turn from your sins, then! If not, I will come to you soon and fight against those people with the sword that comes out of my mouth.

[17] "If you have ears, then, listen to what the Spirit says to the churches!

"To those who have won the victory I will give some of the hidden manna. I will also give each of them a white stone, on which a new name is written, which no one knows except the one who receives it."

The Message to Thyatira

[18] "To the angel of the church in Thyatira write:

"This is the message from the Son of God, whose eyes blaze like fire, whose feet shine like polished brass. [19] I know what you do. I know your love, your faithfulness, your service, and your patience. I know that you are doing more now than you did at first. [20] But here is what I have against you: you tolerate that woman Jezebel, who calls herself a messenger of God. She teaches and misleads my servants into committing immorality and eating food that has been offered to idols. [21] I have given her time to turn from her sins, but she does not wish to turn from her immorality. [22] Therefore I will throw her on a bed where she and those who committed adultery with her will suffer terribly. I will do this now, unless they repent from the wicked things they did with her. [23] I will also kill her children, and then all the churches will know that I am he who knows men's thoughts and wishes. I will repay each one of you according to what you have done.

[24] "But the rest of you in Thyatira have not followed this evil teaching; you have not learned what the others call 'the deep secrets of Satan.' I say to you that I will not put any other burden on you. [25] But you must hold firmly to what you have until I come. [26-28] To those who win the victory, who continue to do what I want until the very end, I will give the same authority which I received from my Father: I will give them authority over the nations, to rule

them with an iron rod and to break them to pieces like clay pots. I will also give them the morning star.

²⁹ "If you have ears, then, listen to what the Spirit says to the churches!"

The Message to Sardis

3 "To the angel of the church in Sardis write:

"This is the message from the one who has the seven spirits of God and the seven stars. I know what you are doing; I know that you have the reputation of being alive, even though you are dead! ² So wake up, and strengthen what you still have, before it dies completely. For I find that what you have done is not yet perfect in the sight of my God. ³ Remember, then, what you were taught and how you heard it; obey it, and turn from your sins. If you do not wake up, I will come upon you like a thief, and you will not even know the hour when I come. ⁴ But a few of you there in Sardis have kept your clothes clean. You will walk with me, clothed in white, for you are worthy to do so. ⁵ Those who win the victory will be clothed like this in white, and I will not remove their names from the book of the living. In the presence of my Father and of his angels I will declare openly that they belong to me.

⁶ "If you have ears, then, listen to what the Spirit says to the churches!"

The Message to Philadelphia

⁷ "To the angel of the church in Philadelphia write:

"This is the message from the one who is holy and true, who holds the key that belonged to David, who opens so that none can close, who closes so that none can open. ⁸ I know what you do; I know that you have a little power; you have followed my teaching and have been faithful to me. I have opened a door before you, which no one can close. ⁹ Listen! As for that group that belongs to Satan, those liars who claim that they are Jews, but are not, I will make them come before you and fall down and worship you. They will all know that I love you. ¹⁰ Because you have kept my order to be patient, I will also keep you safe from the time of trouble which is coming upon the whole world, to test all the people on earth. ¹¹ I am coming soon. Keep safe what you have, so that no one will rob you of your victory prize. ¹² I will make him who is victorious a pillar in the temple of my God, and he will never again leave it. I will write on him the name of my God, and the name of the city of my God, the new Jerusalem, which will come down out of heaven from my God. I will also write on him my new name.

¹³ "If you have ears, then, listen to what the Spirit says to the churches!"

The Message to Laodicea

¹⁴ "To the angel of the church in Laodicea write:

"This is the message from the Amen, the faithful and true witness, who is the origin of all that God has created. ¹⁵ I know what you have done; I know that you are neither cold nor hot. How I wish you were either one or the other! ¹⁶ But because you are barely warm, neither hot nor cold, I am about to spit you out of my mouth! ¹⁷ 'I am rich and well off,' you say, 'I have all I need.' But you do not know how miserable and pitiful you are! You are poor, naked, and blind. ¹⁸ I advise you, then, to buy gold from me, pure gold, in order to be rich. Buy also white clothing to dress yourself and cover up your shameful nakedness. Buy also some medicine to put on your eyes, so that you may see. ¹⁹ I reprove and punish all whom I love. Be in earnest, then, and turn from your sins. ²⁰ Listen!

I stand at the door and knock; if anyone hears my voice and opens the door, I will come into his house and eat with him, and he will eat with me. ²¹ To those who win the victory I will give the right to sit by me on my throne, just as I have been victorious, and now sit by my Father on his throne.

²² "If you have ears, then, listen to what the Spirit says to the churches!"

Worship in Heaven

4 At this point I had another vision, and saw an open door in heaven.

And the voice that sounded like a trumpet, which I had heard speaking to me before, said, "Come up here, and I will show you what must happen after this." ² At once the Spirit took control of me. There in heaven was a throne, with someone sitting on it. ³ His face gleamed like such precious stones as jasper and carnelian; all around the throne there was a rainbow the color of an emerald. ⁴ In a circle around the throne were twenty-four other thrones, on which were seated twenty-four elders dressed in white, and wearing gold crowns. ⁵ From the throne came flashes of lightning, and sounds, and peals of thunder. There were seven lighted torches burning before the throne; these are the seven spirits of God. ⁶ In front of the throne there was what looked like a sea of glass, clear as crystal.

Surrounding the throne, on each of its sides, were four living creatures covered with eyes in front and in back. ⁷ The first living creature looked like a lion; the second looked like a calf; the third had a face like a man's face; and the fourth looked like a flying eagle. ⁸ Each one of the four living creatures had six wings, and they were covered over with eyes, inside and out. They never stop their singing day or night:

"Holy, holy, holy, is the Lord God Almighty,
Who was, who is, and who is to come."

⁹ As often as the four living creatures sing songs of glory and honor and thanks to the one who sits on the throne, who lives for ever and ever, ¹⁰ the twenty-four elders fall down before the one who sits on the throne, and worship him who lives for ever and ever. They throw their crowns before the throne, and say:

¹¹ "Our Lord and God! You are worthy
To receive glory, and honor, and power.
For you created all things,
And by your will they were given existence
and life."

The Scroll and the Lamb

5 I saw a scroll in the right hand of the one who sat on the throne; it was covered with writing on both sides, and was sealed with seven seals. ² And I saw a mighty angel who proclaimed in a loud voice: "Who is worthy to break the seals and open the scroll?" ³ But no one was found in heaven, or on earth, or in the world below, who could open the scroll and look inside it. ⁴ I cried bitterly because no one had been found who was worthy to open the scroll or to look inside it. ⁵ Then one of the elders said to me: "Don't cry. Look! The Lion from Judah's tribe, the great descendant of David, has won the victory and can break the seven seals and open the scroll."

⁶ Then I saw a Lamb standing in the center of the throne, surrounded by the four living creatures and the elders. The Lamb appeared to have been killed. It had seven horns and seven eyes, which are the seven spirits of God which have been sent into all the world. ⁷ The Lamb went and took the scroll from the right hand of the one who sat on the throne. ⁸ As he did so, the four living creatures and the twenty-four elders fell down before the Lamb. Each had a harp, and gold bowls filled with incense, which are the prayers of God's people. ⁹ They sang a new song:

"You are worthy to take the scroll
And to break open its seals.
For you were killed, and by your death
You bought men for God,
From every tribe, and language, and people,
    and nation.
¹⁰ You have made them a kingdom of priests to
    serve our God;
And they shall rule on earth."

¹¹ Again I looked, and I heard angels, thousands and tens of thousands of them! They stood around the throne, the four living creatures, and the elders, ¹² and sang in a loud voice:

"The Lamb who was killed is worthy
To receive power, wealth, wisdom, and
    strength,
Honor, glory, and praise!"

¹³ And I heard every creature in heaven, on earth, and in

the world below, and every creature in the sea — all creatures in the whole universe — and they were singing:

"To him who sits on the throne, and to the
    Lamb,
Be praise and honor, glory and might,
For ever and ever!"

¹⁴ The four living creatures answered, "Amen!" And the elders fell down and worshiped.

The Seals

6 Then I saw the Lamb break open the first of the seven seals, and I heard one of the four living creatures say in a voice that sounded like thunder: "Come!" ² I looked, and there was a white horse. Its rider held a bow, and he was given a crown. He went out as a conqueror to conquer.

³ Then the Lamb broke open the second seal; and I heard the second living creature say: "Come!" ⁴ Another horse came out, a red one. Its rider was given the power to bring war on the earth, that men should kill each other; he was given a large sword.

⁵ Then the Lamb broke open the third seal; and I heard the third living creature say: "Come!" I looked, and there was a black horse. Its rider held a pair of scales in his hand. ⁶ I heard what sounded like a voice coming from among the four living creatures. It said: "A quart of wheat for a whole day's wages, and three quarts of barley for a whole day's wages. But do not damage the olive oil and the wine!"

[7] Then the Lamb broke open the fourth seal; and I heard the fourth living creature say: "Come!" [8] I looked, and there was a pale-colored horse. Its rider was named Death, and Hades followed close behind. They were given authority over a fourth of the earth, to kill with sword, with famine, with disease, and with the wild animals of earth.

[9] Then the Lamb broke open the fifth seal. I saw underneath the altar the souls of those who had been killed because they had proclaimed God's word and had been faithful in their witnessing. [10] They shouted in a loud voice: "Almighty Lord, holy and true! How long will it be until you will judge the people of earth and punish them for killing us?" [11] Each of them was given a white robe; and they were told to rest a little while longer, until the total number was reached of their fellow servants and brothers who were to be killed as they had been.

[12] And I saw the Lamb break open the sixth seal. There was a violent earthquake, and the sun became black, like coarse black cloth, and the moon turned completely red, like blood; [13] the stars fell out of the sky to earth, like unripe figs falling from the tree when a strong wind shakes it. [14] The sky disappeared, like a scroll being rolled up, and every mountain and island was moved from its place. [15] Then the kings of the earth, the rulers and the military chiefs, the rich and the mighty, and all other men, slave and free, hid themselves in caves and under rocks on the mountains. [16] They called out to the mountains and to the rocks: "Fall down on us and hide us from the eyes of the one who sits on the throne, and from the wrath of the Lamb! [17] For the great day of their wrath is here, and who can stand up against it?"

The 144,000 People of Israel

7 After this I saw four angels standing at the four corners of the earth, holding back the four winds of the earth, so that no wind should blow on the earth, or on the sea, or on any tree. [2] And I saw another angel coming up from the east with the seal of the living God. He called out in a loud voice to the four angels to whom God had given the power to damage the earth and the sea. [3] The

angel said: "Do not harm the earth, or the sea, or the trees, until we mark the servants of our God with a seal on their foreheads." 4 And I was told the number of those who were marked with God's seal on their foreheads: it was a hundred and forty-four thousand, from every tribe of the people of Israel. 5 There were twelve thousand from the tribe of Judah marked with the seal; twelve thousand from the tribe of Reuben; twelve thousand from the tribe of Gad; 6 twelve thousand from the tribe of Asher; twelve thousand from the tribe of Naphtali; twelve thousand from the tribe of Manasseh; 7 twelve thousand from the tribe of Simeon; twelve thousand from the tribe of Levi; twelve thousand from the tribe of Issachar; 8 twelve thousand from the tribe of Zebulun; twelve thousand from the tribe of Joseph; and twelve thousand from the tribe of Benjamin.

The Great Crowd

9 After this I looked, and there was a great crowd — no one could count all the people! They were from every nation, tribe, people, and language, and they stood in front of the throne and of the Lamb, dressed in white robes, and holding palm branches in their hands. 10 They called out in a loud voice: "Our salvation comes from our God, who sits on the throne, and from the Lamb!" 11 All the angels stood around the throne, the elders, and the four living creatures. Then they fell down on their faces before the throne and worshiped God, 12 saying: "Amen! Praise, and glory, and wisdom, and thanks, and honor, and power, and might, belong to our God for ever and ever! Amen!"

13 One of the elders asked me, "Who are those people dressed in white robes, and where do they come from?" 14 "I don't know, sir. You do," I answered. He said to me: "These are the people who have come safely through the great persecution. They washed their robes and made them white with the blood of the Lamb. 15 That is why they stand before God's throne and serve him day and night in his temple. He who sits on the throne will protect them with his presence. 16 Never again will they hunger or thirst; neither sun nor any scorching heat will burn them; 17 for the Lamb, who is in the center of the throne, will be their shepherd, and guide them to springs of living water; and God will wipe away every tear from their eyes."

The Seventh Seal

8 When the Lamb broke open the seventh seal, there was silence in heaven for about half an hour. ² Then I saw the seven angels who stand before God; they were given seven trumpets.

³ Another angel, who had a gold incense container, came and stood at the altar. He was given much incense to add to the prayers of all God's people and offer on the altar that stands before the throne. ⁴ The smoke of the burning incense went up with the prayers of God's people from the hands of the angel standing before God. ⁵ Then the angel took the incense container, filled it with fire from the altar, and threw it on the earth. There were peals of thunder, sounds, flashes of lightning, and an earthquake.

The Trumpets

⁶ Then the seven angels with the seven trumpets prepared to blow them.

⁷ The first angel blew his trumpet. Hail and fire, mixed with blood, came pouring down on the earth. A third of the earth was burned up, and a third of the trees were burned up, and every blade of green grass was burned up.

⁸ Then the second angel blew his trumpet. Something that looked like a large mountain burning with fire was thrown into the sea. A third of the sea was turned into blood, ⁹ and a third of all living creatures in the sea died, and a third of all ships were destroyed.

¹⁰ Then the third angel blew his trumpet. A large star, burning like a torch, dropped from the sky and fell on a third of the rivers, and on the springs of water. ¹¹ (The name of the star is Bitterness.) A third of the water turned bitter, and many men died from drinking the water, because it had turned bitter.

¹² Then the fourth angel blew his trumpet. A third of

the sun was struck, and a third of the moon, and a third of the stars, so that their light lost a third of its brightness; there was no light during a third of the day and during a third of the night also.

13 Then I looked, and I heard an eagle that was flying high in the air say in a loud voice: "Oh horror! horror!

How horrible it will be for all who live on earth when the sound comes from the trumpets that the other three angels must blow!"

9 Then the fifth angel blew his trumpet. I saw a star which had fallen from the sky to earth; it was given the key to the abyss. 2 The star opened the abyss, and smoke poured out of it, like the smoke from a large furnace; the sunlight and the air were made dark by the smoke from the abyss. 3 Locusts came down out of the smoke onto the earth, and they were given power like that of scorpions. 4 They were told not to harm the grass, or the trees, or any other plant; they could harm only the men who do not have the mark of God's seal on their foreheads. 5 The locusts were not allowed to kill these men, but only to torture them for five months. The pain caused by their torture is like the pain a man suffers when stung by a scorpion. 6 During the five months those men will seek death, but will not find it; they will want to die, but death will flee from them.

7 The locusts looked like horses ready for battle; on their heads they had what seemed to be gold crowns, and their faces were like men's faces. 8 Their hair was like women's hair, their teeth were like lions' teeth. 9 Their chests were covered with what looked like iron breastplates, and the

sound made by their wings was like the noise of many horse-drawn chariots rushing into battle. [10] They have tails and stings, like those of a scorpion, and it is with their tails that they have the power to hurt men for five months. [11] They have a king ruling over them, who is the angel in charge of the abyss. His name in Hebrew is Abbadon; in Greek the name is Apollyon (meaning "The Destroyer").

[12] The first horror is over; after this there are still two more horrors to come.

[13] Then the sixth angel blew his trumpet. I heard a voice coming from the corners of the gold altar standing before God. [14] The voice said to the sixth angel who had the trumpet: "Release the four angels who are bound at the great river Euphrates!" [15] The four angels were released; they had been prepared for this very hour of this very day of this very month and year, to kill a third of all mankind. [16] I was told the number of mounted troops: it was two hundred million. [17] And in my vision I saw the horses and their riders: they had breastplates red as fire, blue as sapphire, and yellow as sulphur. The horses' heads were like lions' heads, and from their mouths came out fire, smoke, and sulphur. [18] A third of mankind was killed by those three plagues: the fire, the smoke, and the sulphur coming out of the horses' mouths. [19] For the power of the horses is in their mouths, and also in their tails. Their tails are like snakes, with heads, and they use them to hurt people.

[20] The rest of mankind, all those who had not been killed by these plagues, did not turn away from what they themselves had made. They did not stop worshiping the demons and the idols of gold, silver, bronze, stone, and wood, which cannot see, or hear, or walk. [21] Nor did those men repent of their murders, their magic, their immorality, or their stealing.

The Angel and the Little Scroll

10 Then I saw another mighty angel coming down out of heaven. He was dressed in a cloud, with a rainbow around his head; his face was like the sun, and his legs were like columns of fire. [2] He had a small scroll open in his hand. He put his right foot on the sea, and his left foot on the land, [3] and called out in a loud voice that

sounded like the roar of lions. After he had called out, the seven thunders answered back with a roar. 4 As soon as they spoke, I was about to write. But I heard a voice speak from heaven: "Keep secret what the seven thunders said; do not write it down!"

5 Then the angel that I saw standing on the sea and on the land raised his right hand to heaven 6 and made a vow in the name of God, who lives for ever and ever, who created heaven and all things in it, the earth and all things in it, and the sea and all things in it. The angel said: "There will be no more delay! 7 But when the seventh angel blows his trumpet, then God will accomplish his secret plan, as he announced it to his servants, the prophets."

8 Then the voice that I had heard speaking from heaven spoke to me again, saying: "Go and take the open scroll which is in the hand of the angel standing on the sea and on the land." 9 I went to the angel and asked him to give me the little scroll. He said to me, "Take it and eat it; it will turn sour in your stomach, but in your mouth it will be sweet as honey." 10 I took the little scroll from his hand and ate it, and it tasted sweet as honey in my mouth. But after I had swallowed it, it turned sour in my stomach.

11 Then I was told, "Once again you must speak God's message about many peoples and nations, languages and kings."

The Two Witnesses

11 I was then given a measuring stick, like a rod, and told: "Get up and measure the temple of God and the altar, and count those who are worshiping in the

temple. ² But omit the outer courts of the temple. Do not measure them, for they have been given to the heathen, who will trample on the Holy City for forty-two months. ³ I will send my two witnesses, dressed in sackcloth; and they will proclaim God's message during those twelve hundred and sixty days."

⁴ The two witnesses are the two olive trees and the two lamps that stand before the Lord of the earth. ⁵ If anyone tries to harm them, fire comes out of their mouths and destroys their enemies; and in this way whoever shall try to harm them will be killed. ⁶ They have authority to shut up the sky so there will be no rain during the time they speak God's message. They have authority also over the springs of water, to turn them into blood; they have authority also to strike the earth with every kind of plague as often as they wish.

⁷ When they finish proclaiming their message, the beast that comes up out of the abyss will fight against them. He will defeat them and kill them, ⁸ and their bodies will lie on the street of the great city, where their Lord was nailed to the cross. The symbolic name of that city is Sodom, or Egypt. ⁹ People of all nationalities, from every tribe, language, and nation, will look at their bodies for three and a half days, and will not allow them to be buried. ¹⁰ The people of earth will be happy over the death of these two. They will celebrate, and send presents to one another, because those two prophets brought much suffering upon the people of earth. ¹¹ After three and a half days a life-giving breath came from God and entered them, and they stood up; all who saw them were terribly afraid. ¹² Then the two prophets heard a loud voice say to them from heaven: "Come up here!" As their enemies watched, they went up into heaven in a cloud. ¹³ At that very moment there was a violent earthquake; a tenth of the city was destroyed, and a total of seven thousand people were killed in the earthquake. The rest of the people were terrified and praised the greatness of the God of heaven.

¹⁴ The second horror is over; but look! The third horror will come soon.

The Seventh Trumpet

¹⁵ Then the seventh angel blew his trumpet, and there

were loud voices in heaven, saying, "The power to rule over the world belongs now to our Lord and his Messiah, and he will rule for ever and ever!" [16] Then the twenty-four elders who sit on their thrones before God fell down on their faces and worshiped God, [17] saying:

> "Lord God Almighty, the one who is and who
>   was!
> We thank you that you have used your
>   great power
> And have begun to rule!

[18] The heathen were filled with rage,
>   For it is the time for your wrath to come,
>   And for the dead to be judged;
>   The time to give the reward to your servants
>   the prophets,
>   And to all your people, great and small,
>   To all who fear you.
>   It is the time to destroy those who destroy the
>   earth!"

[19] God's temple in heaven was opened, and the ark holding the covenant was seen in his temple. Then there were flashes of lightning, sounds, peals of thunder, an earthquake, and heavy hail.

The Woman and the Dragon

12 Then a great sign appeared in heaven: there was a woman, whose dress was the sun and who had the moon under her feet, and a crown of twelve stars on her head. [2] She was soon to give birth, and the pains and suffering of childbirth made her cry out.

[3] Another sign appeared in heaven. There was a huge red dragon with seven heads and ten horns, and a crown on each of his heads. [4] With his tail he dragged a third of the stars out of the sky and threw them to earth. He stood in front of the woman who was about to give birth, in order to eat her child as soon as it was born. [5] Then the woman gave birth to a son, who will rule over all nations with an iron rod. But the child was snatched away and taken to God and his throne. [6] The woman fled to the desert; there God had prepared a place for her, where she will be taken care of for twelve hundred and sixty days.

[7] Then war broke out in heaven! Michael and his angels fought against the dragon, who fought back with his angels;

8 but the dragon was defeated, and he and his angels were not allowed to stay in heaven any longer. 9 The huge dragon was thrown out! He is that old serpent, named the Devil, or Satan, that deceived the whole world. He was thrown down to earth, and all his angels with him.

10 Then I heard a loud voice in heaven saying: "Now God's salvation has come! Now God has shown his power as King! Now his Messiah has shown his authority! For the accuser of our brothers, who stood before God accusing them day and night, has been thrown out of heaven. 11 Our brothers won the victory over him by the blood of the Lamb, and by the truth which they proclaimed; and they were willing to give up their lives and die. 12 And so rejoice, you heavens, and all you who live there! But how terrible for the earth and the sea! For the Devil has come down to you, and he is filled with rage, for he knows that he has only a little time left."

13 When the dragon realized that he had been thrown down to the earth, he began to pursue the woman who had given birth to the boy. 14 The woman was given the two wings of a large eagle in order to fly to her place in the desert, where she will be taken care of for three and a half years, safe from the serpent's attack. 15 Then the serpent made water pour out of his mouth like a river after the woman, so that the flood of water would carry her away. 16 But the earth helped the woman; it opened its mouth and swallowed the water that had come from the dragon's

mouth. ¹⁷ Then the dragon was furious with the woman, and went off to fight against the rest of her descendants, all those who obey God's commandments and are faithful to the truth revealed by Jesus. ¹⁸ And the dragon stood on the seashore.

The Two Beasts

13 Then I saw a beast coming up out of the sea. It had ten horns and seven heads, with a crown on each of its horns, and a wicked name written on its heads. ² The beast I saw looked like a leopard, with feet like a bear's feet, and a mouth like a lion's mouth. The dragon gave the beast his own power, his throne, and his vast authority. ³ One of the heads of the beast seemed to have been killed, but the fatal wound had healed. The whole earth was amazed and followed after the beast. ⁴ All people worshiped the dragon because he had given his authority to the beast. They worshiped the beast also, saying: "Who is like the beast? Who can fight against it?"

⁵ The beast was allowed to say terribly wicked things, and it was permitted to have authority for forty-two months. ⁶ It began to curse God, and God's name, and the place where he lives, including all those who live in heaven. ⁷ It was allowed to fight against God's people and to defeat them, and it was given authority over every tribe and people, every language and nation. ⁸ All people living on earth will worship it, that is, everyone whose name has not been written, before the world began, in the book of the living that belongs to the Lamb that was killed.

⁹ "Listen, then, if you have ears to hear with! ¹⁰ Whoever is meant to be captured, will surely be captured; whoever is meant to be killed by the sword, will surely be killed by the sword. This calls for endurance and faith on the part of God's people."

¹¹ Then I saw another beast coming up out of the earth. It had two horns like a lamb's horns, and it spoke like a dragon. ¹² It used the vast authority of the first beast in its presence. It forced the earth and all who live on it to worship the first beast, whose fatal wound had been healed. ¹³ This second beast performed great miracles; it made fire come down out of heaven to earth, in the presence of all men. ¹⁴ And it deceived all the people living on earth by means of the miracles which it was allowed to perform in

the presence of the first beast. The beast told all the people of the world to build an image in honor of the beast that had been wounded by the sword, and yet lived. [15] The second beast was allowed to breathe life into the image of the first beast, so that the image could talk and put to death all those who would not worship it. [16] The beast forced all men, small and great, rich and poor, slave and free, to have a mark placed on their right hands and on their foreheads. [17] No one could buy or sell unless he had this mark, that is, the beast's name or the number that stands for the name.

[18] This calls for wisdom. Whoever is intelligent can figure out the meaning of the number of the beast, because the number stands for a man's name. Its number is six hundred and sixty-six.

The Song of the Redeemed

14 Then I looked, and there was the Lamb standing on Mount Zion; with him were a hundred and forty-four thousand people who have his name and his Father's name written on their foreheads. [2] And I heard a voice from heaven that sounded like the roar of a mighty waterfall, like a loud peal of thunder. The voice I heard sounded like the music made by harpists playing their harps. [3] They stood facing the throne and the four living creatures and the elders, and they sang a new song which no one could learn except the one hundred and forty-four thousand people who have been redeemed from the earth. [4] They are the men who have kept themselves pure by not having relations with women; they are unmarried. They follow the Lamb wherever he goes; they have been redeemed from the rest of mankind and are the first ones to be offered to God and to the Lamb. [5] They have never been known to lie; they are without fault.

The Three Angels

[6] Then I saw another angel flying high in the air, with an eternal message of Good News to announce to the peoples of the earth, to every nation and tribe and language and people. [7] He said in a loud voice: "Fear God, and praise his greatness! For the time has come for him to judge mankind. Bow in worship, then, before God, who made heaven, earth, sea, and the springs of water!"

[8] A second angel followed the first one, saying: "She has fallen! The great Babylon has fallen! She gave her wine to all peoples, and made them drink it — the strong wine of her immoral lust!"

[9] A third angel followed the first two, saying in a loud voice: "Whoever worships the beast and its image, and receives the mark on his forehead or on his hand, [10] will himself drink God's wine, the wine of his anger, which he has poured at full strength into the cup of his wrath! All who do this will be tormented in fire and sulphur before the holy angels and the Lamb. [11] The smoke of the fire that torments them goes up for ever and ever. There is no relief, day or night, for those who worshiped the beast and its image, for anyone who received the mark of its name."

[12] This calls for endurance on the part of God's people, those who obey God's commandments and are faithful to Jesus.

[13] Then I heard a voice from heaven saying: "Write this: Happy are the dead who from now on die in the service of the Lord!" "Certainly so," answers the Spirit. "They will enjoy rest from their hard work; for they take with them the results of their service."

The Harvest of the Earth

[14] Then I looked, and there was a white cloud, and sitting on the cloud was a being who looked like a man, with a gold crown on his head and a sharp sickle in his hand. [15] Then another angel went out from the temple and cried out in a loud voice to the one who was sitting on the cloud: "Use your sickle and reap the harvest, because the

right time has come; the earth is ripe for the harvest!"
[16] Then the one who sat on the cloud swung his sickle on the earth, and the earth's harvest was reaped.

[17] Then I saw another angel come out of the temple in heaven, and he also had a sharp sickle.

[18] Then another angel, who is in charge of the fire, came from the altar. He shouted in a loud voice to the angel who had the sharp sickle: "Use your sickle, and cut the grapes from the vineyard of the earth, because the grapes are ripe!" [19] So the angel swung his sickle on the earth, cut the grapes from the vine, and threw them into the winepress of God's great anger. [20] The grapes were squeezed out in the winepress outside the city, and blood came out of the winepress in a flood two hundred miles long and about five feet deep.

The Angels with the Last Plagues

15 Then I saw another great and amazing sign in heaven: seven angels with seven plagues. These are the last plagues, for they are the final expression of God's wrath.

[2] Then I saw what looked like a sea of glass, mixed with fire; I also saw those who had won the victory over the beast and its image, and over the one whose name is given by a number. They were standing by the sea of glass, holding harps that God had given them. [3] They were singing the song of Moses, the servant of God, and the song of the Lamb:

"Lord, God Almighty,
How great and wonderful are your deeds!
King of all nations,
How right and true are your ways!
[4] Who will not fear you, Lord?
Who will refuse to declare your greatness?
For you alone are holy.
All the nations will come
And worship before you,
For your righteous deeds are seen by all."

[5] After this I saw the temple in heaven open, with the tent of God's presence in it. [6] The seven angels who had the seven last plagues came out of the temple; they were dressed in clean white linen, and had gold bands tied around their chests. [7] Then one of the four living crea-

tures gave the seven angels seven gold bowls full of the wrath of God, who lives for ever and ever. [8] The temple was filled with smoke from the glory and power of God, and no one could go into the temple until the end of the seven plagues brought by the seven angels.

The Bowls of God's Wrath

16 Then I heard a loud voice speaking from the temple to the seven angels: "Go and pour out the seven bowls of God's wrath on the earth!"

[2] The first angel went and poured out his bowl on the earth. Terrible and painful sores appeared on those who had the mark of the beast, and on those who had worshiped its image.

[3] Then the second angel poured out his bowl on the sea. The water became like the blood of a dead person, and every living creature in the sea died.

[4] Then the third angel poured out his bowl on the rivers and the springs of water, and they turned into blood. [5] I heard the angel in charge of the waters say: "You are righteous in these judgments you have made, O Holy One, who is and who was! [6] They poured out the blood of God's people and of the prophets, and so you have given them blood to drink. They are getting what they deserve!" [7] Then I heard a voice from the altar saying, "Lord, God Almighty! True and righteous indeed are your judgments!"

[8] Then the fourth angel poured out his bowl on the sun, and it was allowed to burn men with its fiery heat. [9] Men were burned by the fierce heat, and they cursed the name of God, who has authority over these plagues; but they would not turn from their sins and praise his greatness.

[10] Then the fifth angel poured out his bowl on the throne of the beast. Darkness fell over the beast's kingdom, and men bit their tongues because of their pain, [11] and they cursed the God of heaven for their pains and sores. But they did not turn from their evil ways.

[12] Then the sixth angel poured out his bowl on the great river Euphrates. The river dried up, to provide a way for the kings who come from the east. [13] Then I saw three unclean spirits, that looked like frogs, coming out of the mouth of the dragon, the mouth of the beast, and the mouth of the false prophet. [14] They are the spirits of demons that perform miracles. These three spirits go out

to the kings over the whole earth, to bring them together
for the war on the great day of Almighty God.

¹⁵ "Listen! I am coming like a thief! Happy is he who
stays awake and takes care of his clothing, so that he will
not walk around naked and be ashamed in public!"

¹⁶ Then the spirits brought the kings together in the place
that in Hebrew is called Armageddon.

¹⁷ Then the seventh angel poured out his bowl in the air.
A loud voice came from the throne in the temple, saying:
"It is done!" ¹⁸ There were flashes of lightning, sounds,
peals of thunder, and a terrible earthquake. There never
has been such an earthquake since the creation of man;
this was the worst earthquake of all! ¹⁹ The great city was
split into three parts, and the cities of all countries were
destroyed. God remembered great Babylon, and made her
drink the wine from his cup — the wine of his furious
wrath. ²⁰ All the islands disappeared, all the mountains
vanished. ²¹ Great stones of hail, each weighing as much
as a hundred pounds, fell from the sky on men. And men
cursed God because of the plague of hail, for it was such
a terrible plague.

The Great Prostitute

17 Then one of the seven angels who had the seven
bowls came to me and said: "Come, and I will
show you how the great prostitute is to be punished, that
great city that is built near many rivers. ² The kings of
the earth committed immorality with the great prostitute,
and the people of the world became drunk from drinking
the wine of her immorality."

³ The Spirit took control of me, and the angel carried
me to a desert. There I saw a woman sitting on a red
beast that had wicked names written all over it; the beast had
seven heads and ten horns. ⁴ The woman was dressed in
purple and scarlet, covered with gold ornaments, precious
stones, and pearls. In her hand she held a gold cup full of
obscene and filthy things, the result of her immorality.
⁵ On her forehead was written a name that has a secret
meaning: "The Great Babylon, mother of all prostitutes
and perverts of the world." ⁶ And I saw that the woman
was drunk with the blood of God's people, and the blood
of those who were killed because they had been loyal to
Jesus.

When I saw her I was completely amazed. 7 "Why are you amazed?" the angel asked me. "I will tell you the secret meaning of the woman and of the beast that carries her, the beast with seven heads and ten horns. 8 The beast you saw was once alive, but lives no longer; it is about to come up from the abyss and will go off to be destroyed. The people living on earth whose names have not been written, before the world began, in the book of the living, will all be amazed as they look at the beast. For it was once alive, but lives no longer, and it will reappear.

9 "This calls for wisdom and understanding. The seven heads are seven hills, the hills that the woman sits on. They are also seven kings: 10 five of them have fallen, one still rules, and the other one has not yet come; when he comes he must remain only a little while. 11 And the beast that was once alive, but lives no longer, is itself an eighth king who belongs to the first seven and goes off to be destroyed.

12 "The ten horns you saw are ten kings who have not yet begun to rule, but who will be given authority to rule as kings for one hour with the beast. 13 These ten all have the same purpose, and give their power and authority to the beast. 14 They will fight against the Lamb; but the Lamb, and his called, chosen, and faithful followers with him, will defeat them, for he is Lord of lords and King of kings."

15 The angel also said to me: "The waters you saw, on which the woman sits, are peoples and crowds and nations and languages. 16 The ten horns you saw, and the beast, will hate the prostitute; they will take away everything she has and leave her naked; they will eat her flesh and destroy her with fire. 17 For God placed in their hearts the desire to carry out his purpose, by acting with one accord and giving to the beast their power to rule, until God's words come true.

18 "The woman you saw is the great city that dominates the kings of the earth."

The Fall of Babylon

18 After this I saw another angel coming down out of heaven. He had great authority, and his splendor brightened the whole earth. 2 He cried out in a loud voice: "She has fallen! The great Babylon has fallen! She is now haunted by demons and unclean spirits; all kinds of filthy

and hateful birds live in her. [8] For she gave her wine to all peoples and made them drink it — the strong wine of her immoral lust. The kings of the earth committed immorality with her, and the businessmen of the world grew rich from her unrestrained lust."

[4] Then I heard another voice from heaven, saying:

"Come out, my people! Come out from her!
You must not take part in her sins,
You must not share her punishments!
[5] For her sins are piled up as high as heaven,
And God remembers her wicked ways.
[6] Treat her exactly as she has treated you,
Pay her back twice as much as she has done.
Fill her cup with a drink twice as strong
As the drink she prepared for you.
[7] Give her as much suffering and grief
As the glory and luxury she gave herself.
For she keeps telling herself:
'Here I sit, a queen!
I am no widow,
I will never know grief!'
[8] Because of this her plagues will all strike her
in one day:
Disease, grief, and famine;
She will be burned with fire.
For the Lord God, who judges her, is
mighty."

[9] The kings of the earth who shared her immorality and lust will cry and weep for the city when they see the smoke of her burning. [10] They stand a long way off, because they are afraid of her suffering, and say: "How terrible! How awful! This great and mighty city Babylon! In just one hour you have been punished!"

[11] The businessmen of the earth also cry and mourn for her, because no one buys their goods any longer; [12] no one buys their gold, silver, precious stones, and pearls; their goods of linen, purple cloth, silk, and scarlet; all kinds of rare woods, and all kinds of objects made of ivory and of expensive wood, of bronze, iron, and marble; [13] and cinnamon, spice, incense, myrrh, and frankincense; wine and oil, flour and wheat, cattle and sheep, horses and carriages, slaves and even men's souls. [14] The businessmen say to her: "All the good things you longed to own have dis-

appeared, and all your wealth and glamor are gone, and you will never find them again!" ¹⁵ The businessmen, who became rich from doing business in that city, will stand a long way off, because they are afraid of her suffering. They will cry and mourn, ¹⁶ and say: "How terrible! How awful for the great city! She used to dress herself in linen and purple and scarlet, and cover herself with gold ornaments, precious stones, and pearls! ¹⁷ And in one hour she has lost all this wealth!"

All the ship captains and passengers, the sailors and all others who earn their living on the sea, stood a long way off, ¹⁸ and cried out as they saw the smoke of her burning: "There never has been another city like the great city!" ¹⁹ They threw dust on their heads, they cried and mourned: "How terrible! How awful for the great city! She is the city where all who have ships sailing the seas became rich on her wealth! And in one hour she has lost everything!"

²⁰ Rejoice, because of her destruction, O heaven! Rejoice, God's people, and the apostles and prophets! For God has judged her for what she did to you!

²¹ Then a mighty angel picked up a stone the size of a large millstone and threw it into the sea, saying: "This is how the great city Babylon will be thrown down with violence, and will never be seen again. ²² The music of harpists and musicians, of players of the flute and the trumpet, will never be heard in you again! No workman in any trade will ever be found in you again; and the sound of the millstone will be heard no more! ²³ Never again will the light of a lamp be seen in you; no more will the voices of bride and groom be heard in you. Your businessmen were the most powerful in all the world, and with your false magic you deceived all the peoples of the world!"

²⁴ Babylon was punished because the blood of prophets

and of God's people was found in the city; yes, the blood of all those who have been killed on earth.

19 After this I heard what sounded like the loud voice of a great crowd of people in heaven, saying: "Praise God! Salvation, glory, and power belong to our God! ² True and righteous are his judgments! For he has condemned the great prostitute who was corrupting the earth with her immorality. God has punished her because she killed his servants." ³ Again they shouted: "Praise God! The smoke from the burning of the great city goes up for ever and ever!" ⁴ The twenty-four elders and the four living creatures fell down and worshiped God who was seated on the throne, and said: "Amen! Praise God!"

The Wedding Feast of the Lamb

⁵ Then there came from the throne the sound of a voice, saying: "Praise our God, all his servants, and all men, both great and small, who fear him!" ⁶ Then I heard what sounded like the voice of a great crowd, like the roar of a mighty waterfall, like loud peals of thunder. I heard them say: "Praise God! For the Lord, our Almighty God, is King! ⁷ Let us rejoice and be glad; let us praise his greatness! For the time has come for the wedding of the Lamb, and his bride has prepared herself for it. ⁸ She has been permitted to dress herself with clean shining linen." (The linen is the righteous deeds of God's people.)

⁹ Then the angel said to me: "Write this: Happy are those who have been invited to the wedding feast of the Lamb." And the angel added, "These are the true words of God." ¹⁰ I fell down at his feet to worship him, but he said to me: "Don't do it! I am a fellow servant of yours, and of your brothers, all those who hold to the truth that Jesus revealed. Worship God!"

For the truth that Jesus revealed is what inspires the prophets.

The Rider on the White Horse

¹¹ Then I saw heaven open, and there was a white horse. Its rider is called Faithful and True; it is with justice that he judges and fights his battles. ¹² His eyes were like a flame of fire, and he wore many crowns on his head. He had a name written on him, but no one except himself knows what it is. ¹³ The robe he wore was covered with

blood. The name by which he is called is "The Word of God." [14] The armies of heaven followed him, riding on white horses and dressed in clean white linen. [15] A sharp sword came out of his mouth, with which he will defeat the nations. He will rule over them with a rod of iron, and he will squeeze out the wine in the winepress of the furious wrath of the Almighty God. [16] On his robe and on his leg was written the name: "King of kings and Lord of lords."

[17] Then I saw an angel standing in the sun. He shouted in a loud voice to all the birds flying in mid-air: "Come, and gather together for God's great feast! [18] Come and eat the flesh of kings, generals, and soldiers, the flesh of horses and their riders, the flesh of all men, slave and free, great and small!"

[19] Then I saw the beast and the kings of the earth and their armies gathered to fight against the one who rides the horse, and against his army. [20] The beast was taken prisoner, together with the false prophet who had performed miracles in his presence. (It was by those miracles that he had deceived those who had the mark of the beast, and those who had worshiped the image of the beast.) The beast and the false prophet were both thrown alive into the lake of fire that burns with sulphur. [21] Their armies were killed by the sword that comes out of the mouth of the one who rides the horse; and all the birds ate all they could of their flesh.

The Thousand Years

20 Then I saw an angel coming down from heaven, holding in his hand the key of the abyss, and a heavy chain. ² He seized the dragon, that old serpent — that is, the Devil, or Satan — and tied him up for a thousand years. ³ The angel threw him into the abyss, locked it and sealed it, so that he could not deceive the nations any more until the thousand years were over. After that he must be set loose for a little while.

⁴ Then I saw thrones, and those who sat on them; they were given the power to judge. I also saw the souls of those who had been executed because they had proclaimed the truth that Jesus revealed and the word of God. They had not worshiped the beast or its image, nor had they received the mark of the beast on their foreheads or hands. They lived and ruled as kings with Christ for a thousand years. ⁵ (The rest of the dead did not come to life until the thousand years were over.) This is the first raising of the dead. ⁶ Happy and greatly blessed are those who have a part in this first raising of the dead. The second death has no power over them; they shall be priests of God and of Christ, and they will rule with him for a thousand years.

The Defeat of Satan

⁷ After the thousand years are over, Satan will be set loose from his prison, ⁸ and he will go out to deceive the nations scattered over all the world, that is, Gog and Magog. Satan will bring them all together for battle, as many as the grains of sand on the seashore. ⁹ They spread out over the earth and surrounded the camp of God's people and the city that he loves. But fire came down from heaven and destroyed them. ¹⁰ Then the Devil, who deceived them, was thrown into the lake of fire and sulphur, where the beast and the false prophet had already been thrown; and they will be tormented day and night, for ever and ever.

The Final Judgment

¹¹ Then I saw a large white throne and the one who sits on it. Earth and heaven fled from his presence, and were seen no more. ¹² And I saw the dead, great and small alike, standing before the throne. Books were opened, and then another book was opened, the book of the living. The

dead were judged according to what they had done, as was written in the books. ¹³ Then the sea gave up its dead. Death and the world of the dead also gave up the dead they held. And all were judged according to what they had done. ¹⁴ Then death and the world of the dead were thrown into the lake of fire. (This lake of fire is the second death.) ¹⁵ Whoever did not have his name written in the book of the living was thrown into the lake of fire.

The New Heaven and the New Earth

21 Then I saw a new heaven and a new earth. The first heaven and the first earth disappeared, and the sea vanished. ² And I saw the Holy City, the new Jerusalem, coming down out of heaven from God, prepared and ready, like a bride dressed to meet her husband. ³ I heard a loud voice speaking from the throne: "Now God's home is with men! He will live with them, and they shall be his people. God himself will be with them, and he will be their God. ⁴ He will wipe away all tears from their eyes. There will be no more death, no more grief, crying, or pain. The old things have disappeared."

⁵ Then the one who sits on the throne said, "And now I make all things new!" He also said to me, "Write this, because these words are true and can be trusted." ⁶ And he said: "It is done! I am the Alpha and the Omega, the beginning and the end. To anyone who is thirsty I will give a free drink of water from the spring of the water of life. ⁷ Whoever wins the victory will receive this from me: I will be his God, and he will be my son. ⁸ But the cowards, the traitors, and the perverts, the murderers and the immoral, those who practice magic and those who worship idols, and all liars — the place for them is the lake burning with fire and sulphur, which is the second death."

The New Jerusalem

⁹ One of the seven angels who had the seven bowls full of the seven last plagues came to me and said, "Come, and I will show you the Bride, the wife of the Lamb." ¹⁰ The Spirit took control of me, and the angel carried me to the top of a very high mountain. He showed me Jerusalem, the Holy City, coming down out of heaven from God, ¹¹ shin-

ing with the glory of God. The city shone like a precious stone, like a jasper, clear as crystal. ¹² It had a great, high wall, with twelve gates, and with twelve angels in charge of the gates. On the gates were written the names of the twelve tribes of the people of Israel. ¹³ There were three gates on each side: three on the east, three on the south, three on the north, and three on the west. ¹⁴ The city's wall was built on twelve stones, on which were written the names of the twelve apostles of the Lamb.

¹⁵ The angel who spoke to me had a gold measuring stick, to measure the city, its gates, and its wall. ¹⁶ The city was perfectly square, as long as it was wide. The angel measured the city with his measuring stick: it was fifteen hundred miles long, and was as wide and as high as it was long. ¹⁷ The angel also measured the wall, and it was two hundred and sixteen feet high, according to the normal unit of measure, which he was using. ¹⁸ The wall was made of jasper, and the city itself was made of pure gold, as clear as glass. ¹⁹ The foundation stones of the city wall were adorned with all kinds of precious stones. The first foundation stone was jasper, the second sapphire, the third agate, the fourth emerald, ²⁰ the fifth onyx, the sixth carnelian, the seventh yellow quartz, the eighth beryl, the ninth topaz, the tenth chalcedony, the eleventh turquoise, the twelfth amethyst. ²¹ The twelve gates are twelve pearls; each gate is made from a single pearl. The street of the city is of pure gold, transparent as glass.

²² I did not see a temple in the city, because its temple

is the Lord God, the Almighty, and the Lamb. 23 The city has no need of the sun or the moon to shine on it, for the glory of God shines on it, and the Lamb is its lamp. 24 The peoples of the world will walk by its light, and the kings of the earth will bring their wealth into it. 25 The gates of the city will stand open all day; they will never be closed, because there will be no night there. 26 The greatness and the wealth of the nations will be brought into the city. 27 But nothing that is defiled will enter the city, nor anyone who does shameful things or tells lies. Only those whose names are written in the Lamb's book of the living will enter the city.

22 The angel also showed me the river of the water of life, sparkling like crystal, which comes from the throne of God and of the Lamb, 2 and flows down the middle of the city's street. On each side of the river was the tree of life, which bears fruit twelve times a year, once every month; and its leaves are for the healing of the nations. 3 Nothing that is under God's curse will be found in the city.

The throne of God and of the Lamb will be in the city, and his servants will worship him. 4 They will see his face, and his name will be written on their foreheads. 5 There shall be no more night, and they will not need lamps or sunlight, for the Lord God will be their light, and they will rule as kings for ever and ever.

The Coming of Jesus

⁶ Then the angel said to me: "These words are true and can be trusted. And the Lord God, who gives his Spirit to the prophets, sent his angel to show his servants what must happen very soon."

⁷ "Listen!" says Jesus. "I am coming soon! Happy are those who obey the prophetic words in this book!"

⁸ I, John, have heard and seen all these things. And when I finished hearing and seeing them, I fell down at the feet of the angel who had shown me these things to worship him. ⁹ But he said to me: "Don't do it! I am a fellow servant of yours, and of your brothers the prophets, and of all those who obey the words in this book. Worship God!" ¹⁰ And he said to me: "Do not keep the prophetic words of this book a secret, for the time is near when all this will happen. ¹¹ Whoever is evil must go on doing evil, and whoever is filthy must go on being filthy; whoever is good must go on doing good, and whoever is holy must go on being holy."

¹² "Listen!" says Jesus. "I am coming soon! I will bring my rewards with me to give to each one according to what he has done. ¹³ I am the Alpha and the Omega, the first and the last, the beginning and the end."

¹⁴ Happy are those who wash their robes clean, and so have the right to eat the fruit from the tree of life, and to go through the gates into the city. ¹⁵ But outside the city are the perverts and those who practice magic, the immoral and the murderers, those who worship idols, and those who are liars, both in words and deeds.

¹⁶ "I, Jesus, have sent my angel to announce these things to you in the churches. I am the descendant from the family of David; I am the bright morning star."

¹⁷ The Spirit and the Bride say, "Come!"

Everyone who hears this must also say, "Come!"

Come, whoever is thirsty; accept the water of life as a gift, whoever wants it.

Conclusion

¹⁸ I, John, solemnly warn everyone who hears the prophetic words of this book: if anyone adds anything to them, God will add to his punishment the plagues described in this book. ¹⁹ And if anyone takes away anything from

the prophetic words of this book, God will take away from him his share of the fruit of the tree of life, and his share of the Holy City, which are described in this book.

[20] He who gives his testimony to all this, says, "Certainly so! I am coming soon!"

So be it. Come, Lord Jesus!

[21] May the grace of the Lord Jesus be with all.

WORD LIST

A

Aaron The brother of Moses, who was chosen by God to be the chief priest in Israel (Exodus 28.1—30.10).

Abyss A very deep hole in the earth where, according to ancient Jewish teaching, the evil spirits are imprisoned until their final punishment.

Achaia A Roman province covering what is now the southern half of Greece (the northern half of modern Greece was known as Macedonia). In this translation "Greece" is used for Achaia and also for *Hellas* (Acts 20.2), which was the native Greek name corresponding to the Roman name Achaia. The capital city of the province was Corinth; other cities in Achaia mentioned in the New Testament are Cenchreae, Athens, and Nicopolis.

Agate A semi-precious stone of varying colors.

Agrippa Herod Agrippa II, great-grandson of Herod the Great, was king of Chalcis, a small country north of Palestine, and ruler of nearby territories. Paul made his defense before him and his sister Bernice (Acts 25.13—26.32).

Alabaster A soft stone, of light creamy color, from which vases and jars were made.

Aloes A sweet-smelling substance, derived from a plant, which the Jews spread on the cloths they wrapped around a body to be buried.

Alpha The first letter of the Greek alphabet. The expression "I am the Alpha and the Omega" (Revelation 1.8; 21.6; 22.13) means "I am the first and the last."

Altar The place where sacrifices were offered to God.

Amen A Hebrew word which means "it is so" or "may it be so." It can also be translated "certainly," "truly," or "surely." In Revelation 3.14 it is used as a title for Christ.

Amethyst A semi-precious stone, usually purple or violet in color.

Ancestor Someone who lived in the past, from whom a person is descended.

Anoint To pour or rub oil on someone in order to honor him, or select him for some special work. The word is also used in a figurative sense. "The Anointed One" is the title of the one whom God chose and appointed to be Savior and Lord. Oil was also used by the Jews on a sick person to make him well; it was also used on a dead body to prepare it for burial.

Apostle One of the group of twelve men whom Jesus chose to be his followers and helpers. The word means "messenger," and is also used in the New Testament of Paul and of other Christian workers.

Areopagus A hill in Athens where the city council met. For this reason the council itself was called Areopagus, even after it no longer met on the hill.

Aretas King of the country of Nabatea, which was to the south and east of Palestine.

Ark (1) The vessel built by Noah in which he, his family, and the animals survived the Flood (Genesis 6.9—8.19). (2) The wooden chest, covered with gold, in which were kept the two stone tablets on which were written the ten commandments. Other sacred objects of the Jews were also kept in the ark, which was placed in the tabernacle (Exodus 25.10–22; Hebrews 9.4–5).

Armageddon The place mentioned in Revelation 16.16; it is not certain whether the name refers to an actual place ("the hill of Megiddo"), or is used as a symbol.

Artemis The Greek name of an ancient goddess of fertility, worshiped especially in Asia Minor.

Asia A Roman province in the western part of what was later known as Asia Minor, and is today part of the country of Turkey. Besides the seven cities of Asia listed in the book of Revelation (1.4, 11; 2.1—3.22), other cities in the province mentioned in the New Testament are Colossae, Hierapolis, and Miletus. The capital of the province was Ephesus.

Atonement, Day of The most important of the Jewish holy days, when the High Priest would offer sacrifice for the sins of the people of Israel (Leviticus 16.29–34). It was held on the 10th day of the month Tishri (around October 1).

Augustus One of the titles of Gaius Octavius, who was Roman Emperor from 27 B.C. to A.D. 14 (Luke 2.1).

B

Baal The name of the god worshiped by the ancient people of Canaan.

Babylon The capital city of the ancient land of Babylonia, east of Palestine, on the rivers Tigris and Euphrates. In the New Testament the name Babylon probably refers to the city of Rome.

Balaam A native of Pethor, near the Euphrates river, who was asked by Balak, king of Moab, to curse the people of Israel. Instead, Balaam obeyed God's command and blessed Israel (Numbers 22.1—24.25; Deuteronomy 23.3–6; Joshua 13.22).

Balak The king of Moab, a country on the southeast side of the Dead Sea. He led the people of Israel to worship idols (Numbers 22.1—24.25; Revelation 2.14).

Bastard A person born of parents who are not legally married.

Beelzebul The name given to the Devil as the chief of the evil spirits.

Bernice Sister of King Agrippa II (Acts 25.13—26.32).

Beryl A semi-precious stone, usually green or bluish-green in color.

Blasphemy An evil thing said against God.

Breastplate Part of a soldier's armor, made of leather or metal, which covered the breast, and sometimes the back, to protect him from the enemy's attack.

Briar A small plant with thorns on its stem and branches.

C

Caesar The title given to the Roman Emperor.

Carnelian A semi-precious stone, usually red in color.

Census The registration of citizens and their property, to determine how much tax they had to pay.

Chalcedony A semi-precious stone, usually milky or gray in color.

Christ Originally a title, the Greek equivalent of the Hebrew word "Messiah." It means "the anointed one." Jesus is called the Christ because he is the one whom God chose and sent as Savior and Lord.

Cinnamon The sweet-smelling inner bark of a tree, used as a spice on food.

Circumcise To cut off the foreskin of a Jewish baby boy as a sign of God's covenant with the people of Israel (Genesis 17.9–14).

Claudius Roman Emperor A.D. 41–54 (Acts 11.28; 18.2).

Convert A person who is converted, or turned, from one belief or faith to another.

Council The supreme religious court of the Jews, composed of seventy leaders of the Jewish people and presided over by the High Priest.

Covenant The agreement that God made with Abraham (Genesis 17.1–8), and later with the people of Israel (Deuteronomy 29.10–15).

Cummin A small garden plant, whose seeds are ground up and used for seasoning foods.

D

Dalmatia The southern half of the province of Illyricum.

Dedication, Feast of The Jewish feast, lasting eight days, which celebrated the restoration and rededication of the altar in the Temple by the Jewish patriot Judas Maccabeus, in 165 B.C. The feast began on the 25th day of the month Chislev (around December 10).

Defile To make dirty, or impure. Certain foods and practices were prohibited by the Jewish Law because they were thought to make a person spiritually or ceremonially unclean. In this condition such a person could not take part in the public worship until he had performed certain rituals which would remove the defilement.

Demon An evil spirit with the power to harm people, that was regarded as a messenger and servant of the Devil.

Descendant A person who is related by family line to someone who lived a long time before him.

Dill A small garden plant, whose seeds are ground up and used for seasoning foods.

Disciple A person who follows and learns from someone else. The word is used in the New Testament of the followers of John the Baptist and Paul; it is especially used of the followers of Jesus, particularly of the twelve apostles.

Dough Flour mixed with water to be baked into bread.

Dragon An imaginary beast, thought to be like a huge lizard. It is also called a serpent, and appears in the Bible as a figure of the Devil (Revelation 12.3—13.4; 20.2–3).

Drusilla Sister of King Agrippa II and wife of the Roman governor Felix (Acts 24.24).

E

Elders Three different groups in the New Testament are called elders: (1) in the Gospels, the elders are respected

Jewish religious leaders, some of whom were members of the supreme Council; (2) in Acts 11–21 and the Epistles, the elders are Christian church officers who had general responsibility for the work of the church; (3) in Revelation, the 24 elders are part of God's court in heaven, perhaps as representatives of God's people.

Elijah The Old Testament prophet who was expected to appear to announce the coming of the Messiah (Malachi 4.5–6; Matthew 17.9–13).

Emerald A very valuable stone, green in color.

Epicureans Those who followed the teaching of Epicurus (died 270 B.C.), who taught that happiness is the highest good in life.

Epileptic A person who suffers from a nervous disease which causes convulsions and fainting.

Eunuch A man who has been made physically incapable of having normal sexual relations.

F

Fast To go without food for a while as a religious duty.

Felix The Roman governor of Judea A.D. 52–60, before whom Paul defended himself (Acts 23.24—24.27).

Festus The Roman governor of Judea A.D. 60–62, before whom Paul defended himself and made his appeal to the Roman Emperor (Acts 25.1—26.32).

Foal The young of an animal of the horse family.

Frankincense A valuable incense, suitable for a gift.

G

Gabriel One of God's chief angels, who was sent to Zechariah, father of John the Baptist (Luke 1.11–20), and to Mary, mother of Jesus (Luke 1.26–38).

Galatia A Roman province in the eastern part of what was later known as Asia Minor, and is today part of the country of Turkey. The cities of Antioch of Pisidia, Iconium, Lystra, and Derbe were in the province of Galatia.

Gall A very bitter liquid made from a plant.

Gallio The Roman governor of Greece A.D. 51–52 (Acts 18.12–17).

Gamaliel One of the greatest Jewish teachers, a member of the supreme Council of the Jews (Acts 5.34–40), who had been Paul's teacher (Acts 22.3).

Generation The average period, about 30 years in length, from the time a man becomes an adult to the time his son becomes an adult.

Gennesaret Another name for Lake Galilee (Luke 5.1).

Gentile A person who is not a Jew.

Gomorrah A city near the Dead Sea which God destroyed by fire because of the great wickedness of its people (Genesis 19.24–28).

H

Hades The Greek name, in the New Testament, for the world of the dead; the same as Sheol in the Old Testament.

Hermes The name of a Greek god, who served as messenger of the gods.

Herod (1) Herod the Great (Matthew 2.1–22; Luke 1.5) was king of all the country of the Jews 37–4 B.C. He was responsible for the killing of the baby boys in Bethlehem soon after Jesus was born. (2) Herod (whose full name was Herod Antipas) was ruler of Galilee 4 B.C.–A.D. 39 (Matthew 14.1–10; Mark 6.14–27; Luke 3.1, 19–20; 9.7–9; 13.31; 23.6–12; Acts 4.27; 13.1). He was son of Herod the Great, and although called a king (Mark 6.14), he was not a king as his father had been. He was responsible for the death of John the Baptist. (3) Herod (whose full name was Herod Agrippa I) was ruler of all the land of the Jews, with the title of king, A.D. 41–44 (Acts 12.1–23). He was grandson of Herod the Great. He put the apostle James to death and arrested Peter.

Herodias The wife of Herod Antipas, ruler of Galilee. Before marrying Herod she had been the wife of his half-brother Philip (Matthew 14.3–12; Mark 6.17–28; Luke 3.19).

Herod's party A political party composed of Jews who favored one of the descendants of Herod the Great to rule over them instead of the Roman governor.

High Priest The priest who occupied the highest office in the Jewish priestly system and was president of the supreme Council of the Jews. Once a year (on the Day of Atonement) he would enter the holiest part of the Temple and offer sacrifice for himself and for the sins of the people of Israel.

Homosexual A man who has sexual relations with another man.

Hyssop A small bushy plant, used in ceremonies of sprinkling.

I

Illyricum A province on the coast of the Adriatic Sea, north of the province of Macedonia, in what is now Yugoslavia.

Incense Material which is burned in order to produce a pleasant smell.

Inn A house where travelers can buy food and lodging.

J

Jasper A semi-precious stone of varying colors. The jasper mentioned in the Bible was probably green.

Jesse The father of King David, one of the ancestors of Jesus (Matthew 1.5–6; Acts 13.22; Romans 15.12).

K

Kingdom of God, Kingdom of heaven The titles used to describe God's ruling over the world as king. There is no difference between the two titles, both of which refer primarily to God's possession and exercise of his power, not to a place or a time in history. This Kingdom is spoken of as being already present and also as coming in the future.

L

Law The name the Jews applied to the first five books of the Old Testament, also called the books of Moses. Sometimes the name is also used in a more general sense of the whole Old Testament.

Leper Someone suffering from a disease called leprosy. It is probable that in the Bible the word translated "leprosy" had a wider range of meaning than it does now, and was used as the name of several other skin diseases as well.

Levite A member of the priestly tribe of Levi, who had the duty of helping in the services in the Temple (Numbers 3.1–13).

Locust A grasshopper, a winged insect extremely harmful to plants; locusts fly in huge swarms and eat crops and other plants.

Lot The nephew of Abraham who escaped with his daughters from the city of Sodom when it was destroyed by God. Lot's wife, however, did not escape (Genesis 19.12–29; Luke 17.28–32; 2 Peter 2.6–8).

M

Macedonia A Roman province covering what is now the northern half of Greece. Its capital city was Thessalonica. Other cities in the province mentioned in the New Testament are Neapolis, Philippi, Amphipolis, Apollonia, and Berea.

Magdalene Mary Magdalene, a follower of Jesus, was one of those to whom Jesus appeared after he was raised from death (Mark 15.40–47; Luke 8.2; John 20.1–18). Her name indicates that she was born in Magdala, a town on the west side of Lake Galilee.

Manna The food of the Israelites during their travels in the wilderness. It was small, white, and flaky, and looked like small seeds (Exodus 16.14–21; Numbers 11.7–9).

Messiah The title (meaning "the anointed one") given to the promised Savior whose coming was promised by the Hebrew prophets; the same as "Christ."

Michael One of God's chief angels (Jude 9; Revelation 12.7).

Mint A small garden plant, whose leaves are used for seasoning foods.

Moloch One of the gods of the ancient people of Canaan.

Mustard A large plant which grows from a very small seed. The seeds may be ground into powder and used as spice on food.

Myrrh The hardened sap of a tree, with a pleasant smell, and suitable for a gift (Matthew 2.11; Revelation 18.13). It served also as a medicine (Mark 15.23), and was also used by the Jews in preparing bodies for burial (John 19.39).

N

Nard A plant from which an expensive perfume was made.

Nazarene Someone from the town of Nazareth. The name was used as a title for Jesus, and also as a name for the early Christians (Acts 24.5).

Nicolaitans A group referred to in Revelation 2.6 and 15, whose teachings and actions are condemned. They apparently practised idolatry and immorality, but nothing definite is known as to when, where, and by whom the group was started.

Nineveh The ancient capital of Assyria, on the east side of the river Tigris, where the prophet Jonah preached (Jonah 3.1–10; Luke 11.30, 32).

Noah The Old Testament patriarch who built an ark in which he, his family, and the animals were saved from the flood that God sent on the earth (Genesis 6.5—9.28).

O

Omega The last letter of the Greek alphabet. The expression "I am the Alpha and the Omega" (Revelation 1.8; 21.6; 22.13) means "I am the first and the last."

Onyx A semi-precious stone of varying colors.

Outcasts In the Gospels this name, which in many translations appears as "sinners," refers to those Jews who did not obey all the rules laid down by the religious leaders. The Pharisees were especially strict about foods that should not be eaten and about relationships with people who were not Jews. The leaders of the Jews despised these people and condemned Jesus for associating with them (Mark 2.15–17; Luke 7.34; 15.1–2).

P

Parable A story used by Jesus to teach spiritual lessons.

Paradise A name for heaven (Luke 23.43; 2 Corinthians 12.3).

Paralytic Someone who suffers from a disease that prevents him from moving part or all of his body.

Parchment The skin of an animal, usually a sheep or a goat, which was prepared to be written on.

Passover, Feast of The Jewish feast, on the 14th day of the month Nisan (around April 1), which celebrated the deliverance of the ancient Hebrews from their captivity in Egypt. The angel of death killed the first-born in the Egyptian homes but "passed over" the Hebrew homes (Exodus 12.23–27).

Patriarchs The famous ancestors of the Jewish race, such as Abraham, Isaac, and Jacob, with whom God made his covenants.

Pentecost, Day of The Jewish feast of wheat harvest, on the 6th day of the month Sivan (around May 20). The name Pentecost (meaning "fiftieth") comes from the fact that the feast was held 50 days after Passover.

Pervert One who commits unnatural sexual acts.

Pharaoh The title of the kings of ancient Egypt. Two different kings of Egypt are mentioned in the New Testament: the one who ruled during the time of Joseph, the son of Jacob (Acts 7.10–13; Genesis 40.1—50.26), and the one who ruled during the time of Moses (Acts 7.21; Romans 9.17; Hebrews 11.24; Exodus 1.8—14.31).

Pharisees A Jewish religious party. They were strict in obeying the Law of Moses and other regulations which had been added to it through the centuries.

Pilate Pontius Pilate was the Roman governor of Judea, Samaria, and Idumea, A.D. 26–36 (Mark 15.1–15; Luke 3.1; Acts 3.13; 1 Timothy 6.13).

Potter A man who makes pots and other vessels out of clay.

Preparation, Day of The sixth day of the week, on which the Jews made the required preparations to observe the Sabbath day.

Prophet A man who proclaims God's message to men. (1) The term usually refers to the Old Testament prophets (Matthew 5.12, 17; 13.17), such as Isaiah (Matthew 3.3), Jeremiah (Matthew 2.17), Jonah (Matthew 12.39), Daniel (Matthew 24.15), and Joel (Acts 2.16). (2) The term also refers to prophets in the Church (Acts 13.1; 1 Corinthians 12.28–29; Ephesians 4.11). (3) The term is applied also to John the Baptist (Matthew 11.9; 14.5; Luke 1.76), and to Jesus (Matthew 21.11, 46; Luke 7.16; 24.19; John 9.17). (4) "The Prophet" promised by Moses was expected to appear and announce the coming of the Messiah (Deuteronomy 18.15, 18; John 6.14; 7.40; Acts 3.22–23).

Prune To cut the branches off a fruit tree in order to make it bear more and better fruit.

Q

Quartz A semi-precious stone of varying colors, usually white.

R

Rabbi A Hebrew word which means "my teacher."

Rephan The name of an ancient god that was worshiped as the ruler of the planet Saturn.

Ritual An established form for conducting a religious service.

Rue A small garden plant whose leaves are used for seasoning foods.

S

Sabbath The seventh day of the Jewish week, the holy day on which no work was permitted.

Sadducees A small Jewish religious party, composed largely of priests. They based their beliefs exclusively on the first five books of the Old Testament, and so differed in several matters of belief and practice from the larger party of the Pharisees.

Samaritan A native of Samaria, the province between Judea and Galilee. There was much hatred between the Jews and the Samaritans, because of differences in politics, race, customs, and religion.

Sanctuary A building dedicated to the worship of God. Sometimes the word may refer to the central place of worship, and not to the whole building.

Sapphire A very valuable stone, usually blue in color.

Saul (1) The first king of Israel (1 Samuel 13—31, Acts 13.21); (2) the Hebrew name of the apostle Paul (Acts 7.58, 8.1, 3, 9.1–30, 11.25–30, 12.25, 13.1–9).

Scorpion A small creature, which has eight legs and a long tail with a poisonous sting. It can inflict a very painful, and sometimes fatal, wound.

Scriptures In the New Testament the word refers to the collected body of Jewish sacred writings, known to us as the Old Testament. Various names are used: the Law (or the Law of Moses) and the prophets (Matthew 5.17; 7.12; Luke 2.22; 24.44; Acts 13.15; 28.23); the Holy Scriptures (Romans 1.2; 2 Timothy 3.15); the old covenant (2 Corinthians 3.14). The singular "scripture" refers to a single passage of the Old Testament.

Serpent A name given to the dragon, which appears in the Bible as a figure of the Devil (Revelation 12.3–17; 20.2–3).

Sheepfold An enclosure where sheep were kept, usually at night, to protect them from wild animals and thieves.

Shepherd A man, or boy, who takes care of sheep.

Sickle A tool consisting of a curved metal blade and a wooden handle, used for cutting wheat and other crops.

Sodom A city near the Dead Sea which God destroyed by fire because of the great wickedness of its people (Genesis 19.24–28).

Solomon's Porch A covered court on the east side of the Temple in Jerusalem.

Son of David A title which the Jews used of the expected Messiah as the descendant and successor of King David.

Son of Man The title used by Jesus to refer to himself as the one chosen by God to be the Savior (Mark 10.45). As used by Jesus, this title emphasized both his present lowly condition (Mark 8.31, Luke 9.58) and his future glory (Matthew 25.31, Mark 8.38).

Spice One of several pleasant-smelling vegetable products which were used by the Jews in preparing bodies for burial.

Stoics Those who followed the teachings of the philosopher Zeno (died 265 B.C.), who taught that happiness is to be found in being free from pleasure and pain.

Sulphur A yellow substance which burns with great heat and produces an unpleasant smell.

Synagogue The place where Jews met every Sabbath day for their public worship; it was also used as a social center and as a school for Jewish children during week days.

T

Tabernacle A large tent-like construction, described in detail in Exodus 26, where God had his dwelling among his people.

Tabernacles, Feast of The Jewish feast, lasting eight days, which in New Testament times celebrated the time when the ancient Hebrews lived in tents during their travels through the wilderness. In Old Testament times it was also known as the Feast of Ingathering (Exodus 23.16; Leviticus 23.33–43). The feast began on the 15th day of the month Tishri (around October 6).

Teachers of the Law Men who taught and interpreted the teachings of the Old Testament, especially the first five books.

Tenant A man who raises crops on land owned by someone else, and turns over a large part of the harvest to the owner to pay for the use of his land.

Ten Towns A group of ten Gentile towns, most of which were to the east and southeast of Lake Galilee.

Tiberias Another name of Lake Galilee (John 6.1; 21.1).

The town of Tiberias (John 6.23) was on the west side of Lake Galilee.

Tiberius   Roman Emperor A.D. 14–37. It was in the 15th year of his rule (about A.D. 29) that John the Baptist began his work (Luke 3.1).

Topaz   A semi-precious stone, usually yellow in color.

Turquoise   A semi-precious stone, blue or bluish-green in color.

U

Unleavened Bread, Feast of   The Jewish feast, lasting seven days after Passover, which also celebrated the deliverance of the ancient Hebrews from Egypt. The name came from the practice of not using leaven (or yeast) in making bread during that week (Exodus 12.14–20). It was held from the 15th to the 22nd day of the month Nisan (around the first week of April).

V

Vow   A strong declaration, or promise, usually made while calling upon God to punish the speaker if the statement is not true or the promise is not kept.

W

Winnowing-shovel   A tool like a shovel, or large fork, used to separate the wheat from the chaff.

Wreath   Flowers or leaves arranged in a circle, to be placed on a person's head. In ancient times a wreath of leaves was the prize given to winners in athletic contests.

Y

Yeast   A substance, also called leaven, which is added to flour of wheat or barley to make it rise before being baked into bread.

Yoke   A heavy bar of wood which is fitted over the necks of two oxen in order for them to pull a plow or a cart. The word is used figuratively to describe the lessons that a teacher passes on to his pupils.

Z

Zeus   The name of the supreme god of the Greeks.

Zion   The name of a hill in the city of Jerusalem; the name is often used to mean Jerusalem itself.

OTHER READINGS AND RENDERINGS

THERE are many places in the New Testament where the various Greek manuscripts, and other textual sources, have different texts: these are called *variant readings,* and some of the more important ones are listed below. There are also many passages in the Greek New Testament which may be understood and translated in two or more different ways: these are called *alternative renderings,* and some of them are included in this list.

MATTHEW

5.22 is angry: *some mss. add* without cause

6.11 we need: *or* for today; *or* for tomorrow

11.12 has suffered violent attacks: *or* has been coming violently

12.31 any evil thing they say: *or* any evil thing they say against God

16.2b–3 *Some mss. omit the words in verse 2 after* But Jesus answered, *and all of verse 3.*

18.14 your Father: *some mss. read* my Father

18.15 *Some mss. omit* against you

21.3 The Master: *or* Their owner

24.33 the time is near, ready to begin: *or* he is near, ready to come

24.36 *Some mss. omit* nor the Son

24.51 cut him to pieces: *or* throw him out

26.50 Be quick about it, friend! *or* Why are you here, friend?

MARK

1.1 *Some mss. omit* the Son of God

1.4 John appeared . . . baptizing people and preaching: *some mss. read* John the Baptist appeared . . . preaching

1.41 pity: *some mss. read* anger

3.28 evil things they say: *or* evil things they say against God

5.36 paid no attention to: *or* overheard

6.22 The daughter of Herodias: *some mss. read* His daughter Herodias

6.48 pass them by: *or* join them

7.4 anything that comes from the market unless they wash it first: *or* anything after they come from the market unless they wash themselves first

11.3 The Master: *or* Its owner

13.29 the time is near, ready to begin: *or* he is near, ready to come

LUKE

6.10 said: *some mss. add* angrily

8.43 *Some mss. omit* she had spent all she had on doctors

9.54 destroy them: *some mss. add* as Elijah did

9.55 rebuked them: *some mss. add* and said, "You don't know what kind of Spirit you belong to; for the

593

Son of Man did not come to destroy men's lives but to save them."

10.21 by the Holy Spirit: *some mss. read* by the Spirit; *others read* in his spirit

12.46 cut him to pieces: *or* throw him out

17.21 within: *or* among

18.11 stood apart by himself and prayed: *some mss. read* stood up and said this prayer to himself

23.34 *Some mss. omit* Jesus said . . . they are doing."

24.12 *Some mss. omit this verse.*

24.36 *Some mss. omit* and said to them, "Peace be with you."

24.40 *Some mss. omit this verse.*

24.51 *Some mss. omit* and was taken up into heaven.

JOHN

1.3–4 The Word had life in himself: *or* What was made had life in union with the Word

1.18 The only One, who is the same as God, and: *some mss. read* The only Son, who

3.3 again: *or* from above

3.7 again: *or* from above

7.8 I am not going: *some mss. read* I am not yet going

7.52 no prophet ever comes: *one ms. reads* the Prophet will not come

8.1–11 *Some mss. omit this section; others place it after John 21.24; others place it after Luke 21.38; one ms. places it after John 7.36.*

8.25 What I have told you from the very beginning: *or* Why should I speak to you at all?

8.39 If you really were . . . you would do: *some mss. read* If you are . . . do

10.16 they will become: *some mss. read* there will be

10.29 What my Father has given me is greater: *some mss. read* My Father, who gave them to me, is greater

13.10 *Some mss. omit* except for his feet

14.1 Believe: *or* You believe

14.7 Now that you have known me . . . you will know: *some mss. read* If you had known me . . . you would know

16.23 The Father will give you anything you ask of him in my name: *some mss. read* if you ask the Father for anything, he will give it to you in my name

17.11 keep them safe by the power of your name, the name you gave me: *some mss. read* by the power of your name keep safe those you have given me

17.12 I kept them safe by the power of your name, the name you gave me: *some mss. read* by the power of your name I kept safe those you have given me

20.31 you may believe: *some mss. read* you may keep on believing

ACTS

3.22 just as he sent me: *or* like me

4.1 priests: *some mss. read* chief priests

7.37 just as he sent me: *or* like me

7.46 a house for the God: *some mss. read* a dwelling place for the house

8.26 This road is no longer used: *or* This is the desert road.

10.19 Three: *one ms. reads* Two; *other mss. read* Some

12.25 from: *some mss. read* to

13.18 endured: *some mss. read* took care of

16.12 a city of the first district of Macedonia: *some mss. read* the main city of the district of Macedonia; *or* the main city of that district in Macedonia

16.8 traveled right on through: *or* passed by

19.9 every day: *some mss. add* from 11:00 A.M. until 4:00 P.M.

19.21 Paul made up his mind: *or* Paul, led by the Spirit, decided

20.7 Saturday: *or* Sunday

20.28 God: *some mss. read* the Lord

20.28 the death of his own Son: *or* his own death

27.37 two hundred and seventy-six: *some mss. read* two hundred and seventy-five; *others read* seventy-six; *others read* about seventy-six

ROMANS

1.17 put right with God through faith shall live: *or* put right with God shall live through faith

5.1 we have peace: *some mss. read* let us have peace

5.2 we rejoice: *or* let us rejoice

5.3 we also rejoice: *or* let us also rejoice

8.2 me: *some mss. read* you

8.10 the Spirit is life for you: *or* your spirit is alive

8.28 in all things God works for good with those who love him: *some mss. read* all things work for good for those who love God

9.5 May God, who rules over all, be for ever praised: *or* And may he, who is God ruling over all, be for ever praised

12.16 accept humble duties: *or* make friends with the lowly

1 CORINTHIANS

2.1 secret truth: *some mss. read* testimony

2.13 to those who have the Spirit: *or* with words given by the Spirit

7.36–38 The man *and* the girl *in this passage may be* a father and his daughter, *instead of* an engaged couple who have decided not to marry

13.3 to be burned: *some mss. read* in order to boast

15.19 If our hope in Christ is good for this life only, and no more: *or* If all we have in this life is our hope in Christ

2 CORINTHIANS

1.12 frankness: *some mss. read* holiness

3.16 Moses' veil was removed when he turned: *or* The veil is removed when a man turns

5.19 God was making friends of all men through Christ: *or* God was in Christ making friends of all men

GALATIANS

3.11 put right with God through faith shall live: *or* put right with God shall live through faith

4.25 Hagar stands for Mount Sinai: *some mss. read* Sinai is a mountain

EPHESIANS

1.1 *Some mss. omit* in Ephesus

1.23 who himself completes all things everywhere: *or* who is himself completely filled with God's fulness

PHILIPPIANS

2.6 to become: *or* to remain

COLOSSIANS

2.15 Christ freed himself from the power of the spiritual rulers and authorities: *or* Christ stripped the spiritual rulers and authorities of their power

3.6 *Some mss. omit* upon those who do not obey him

1 THESSALONIANS

4.4 how to take a wife: *or* how to control his own body

1 TIMOTHY

2.15 she perseveres: *or* they persevere

3.2 have only one wife: *or* be married only once

3.12 have only one wife: *or* be married only once

2 TIMOTHY

1.12 what he has entrusted to me: *or* what I have entrusted to him

3.16 all Scripture is inspired . . . and is useful: *or* every Scripture inspired . . . is also useful

TITUS

1.6 have only one wife: *or* be married only once

HEBREWS

11.11 Abraham able to become a father even though he was too old and Sarah herself was unable to have children: *some mss. read* Sarah herself was able to conceive even though she was too old to have children

JAMES

4.5 The spirit that God placed in us is filled with fierce desires: *or* God yearns jealously over the spirit that he placed in us

2 PETER

3.10 vanish: *some mss. read* be found; *other mss. read* be burned up; *one ms. reads* be found destroyed

JUDE

5 the Lord: *some mss. read* God; *other mss. read* Jesus

REVELATION

12.18 And the dragon stood: *some mss. read* And I stood, *connecting this verse with what follows*

15.3 all nations: *some mss. read* the ages

22.21 all: *some mss. read* God's people; *others read* all of God's people

INDEX

MAPS

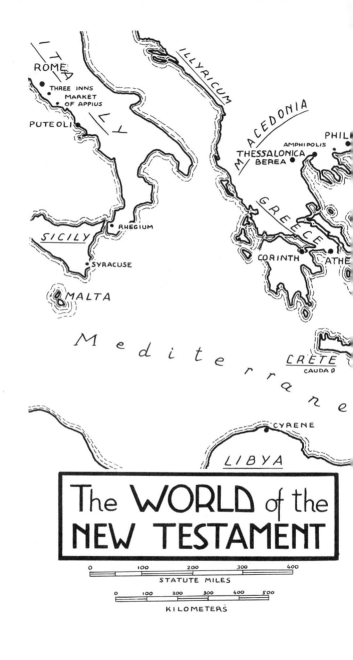

ITALY

ROME
THREE INNS
MARKET OF APPIUS
PUTEOLI

ILLYRICUM

MACEDONIA
AMPHIPOLIS
THESSALONICA
BEREA
PHIL

SICILY
RHEGIUM
SYRACUSE
MALTA

GREECE
CORINTH
ATHE

Mediterranean

CRETE
CAUDA

CYRENE
LIBYA

The WORLD of the NEW TESTAMENT

| 0 | 100 | 200 | 300 | 400 |
STATUTE MILES

| 0 | 100 | 200 | 300 | 400 | 500 |
KILOMETERS

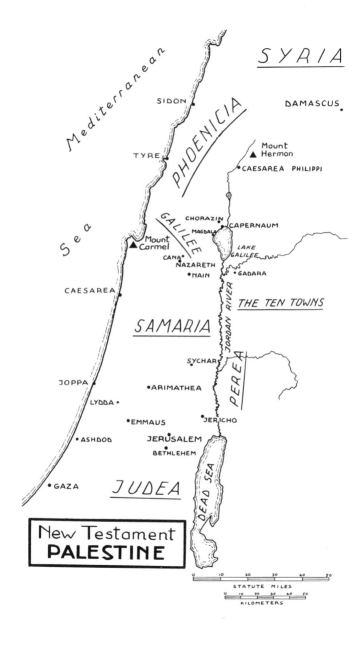

SYRIA

Mediterranean

SIDON

DAMASCUS

PHOENICIA

TYRE

Mount Hermon

CAESAREA PHILIPPI

Sea

GALILEE

CHORAZIN

MAGDALA

CAPERNAUM

Mount Carmel

LAKE GALILEE

CANA

NAZARETH

GADARA

NAIN

CAESAREA

THE TEN TOWNS

JORDAN RIVER

SAMARIA

SYCHAR

PEREA

JOPPA

ARIMATHEA

LYDDA

EMMAUS

JERICHO

ASHDOD

JERUSALEM

BETHLEHEM

DEAD SEA

GAZA

JUDEA

New Testament
PALESTINE

0   10   20   30   40   50
STATUTE MILES
0 10 20 30 40 50
KILOMETERS

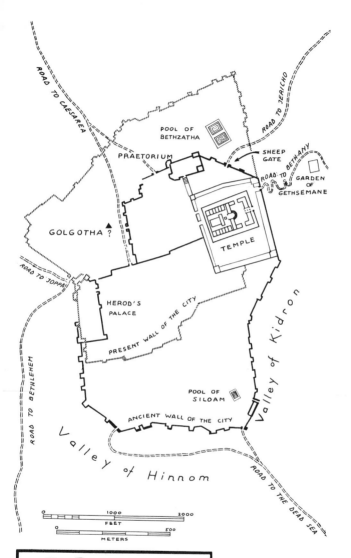

ROAD TO CAESAREA

ROAD TO JERICHO

POOL OF BETHZATHA

PRAETORIUM

SHEEP GATE

ROAD TO BETHANY

GARDEN OF GETHSEMANE

GOLGOTHA ?

TEMPLE

ROAD TO JOPPA

HEROD'S PALACE

PRESENT WALL OF THE CITY

Valley of Kidron

ROAD TO BETHLEHEM

POOL OF SILOAM

ANCIENT WALL OF THE CITY

Valley of Hinnom

ROAD TO THE DEAD SEA

0   1000   2000
FEET
0   500
METERS

JERUSALEM
and its surroundings